Contents

THE EMERGENCE OF HUMANKIND

BOOKS BY JOHN E. PFEIFFER

The Human Brain
The Changing Universe
From Galaxies to Man
The Thinking Machine
The Search for Early Man
The Cell
The Emergence of Man
The Emergence of Society
The Creative Explosion

FOURTH EDITION

THE EMERGENCE OF HUMANKIND

John E. Pfeiffer

 HARPER & ROW, PUBLISHERS, New York
Cambridge, Philadelphia, San Francisco,
London, Mexico City, São Paulo, Singapore, Sydney

1817

Sponsoring Editor: Alan McClare
Project Editor: Holly Detgen
Cover Design: Betty L. Sokol
Cover Photo: © Loren McIntyre, Woodfin Camp & Associates
Text Art: Danmark & Michaels
Photo Research: Mira Schachne
Production: Jeanie Berke
Compositor: Ruttle, Shaw & Wetherill, Inc.
Printer and Binder: R. R. Donnelly & Sons Company

This is a revised edition of *The Emergence of Man,* Third Edition

The Emergence of Humankind, Fourth Edition
Copyright © 1985 by Harper & Row, Publishers, Inc.

Library of Congress Cataloging in Publication Data

Pfeiffer, John E., 1915–
  The emergence of humankind.

  Rev. ed. of: The emergence of man. 3rd ed. ©1978.
  Bibliography: p.
  Includes index.
  1. Human evolution. 2. Man, Prehistoric. 3. Society,
Primitive. I. Pfeiffer, John E., 1915–   . Emergence
of man. II. Title.
GN281.P45 1985   573.2   84-15784
ISBN 0-06-045201-3

84 85 86 87 88 9 8 7 6 5 4 3 2 1

Illustrations

DIAGRAMS

MAPS

Preface

"How can your book be out of date—it all happened so long ago!" My friend was only half joking. It is not unreasonable to expect that by this time we would have arrived at a fairly solid notion of how the human species evolved, at least in broad outline. Unfortunately, we are almost as uncertain about what happened in times past as we are about what will happen in times to come (or, for that matter, about what is happening in the world right now).

The good news is that new evidence continues to accumulate, and investigators are somewhat readier than they were a few years ago to modify their theories accordingly. A consensus is developing on the age of the human species that turns out to be some 5 million years instead of two to three times older, as generally believed during the 1970s. It also seems to have been a humbler beginning, with regular big-game hunting, once considered a major factor in the emergence of the human family, a relatively recent development.

Human evolution has a sweep and rhythm of its own. Prospects hardly seemed bright for breeds of chimpanzee-like creatures that were moving along the edges of dense ancestral forests and adapting to a wide-open world of woodlands and grassy savannas. And for millions of years thereafter, nothing much happened, as far as we can tell from the fossil record. Then the rate of evolution started accelerating, still slowly at first, but faster and faster, with an extra burst beginning perhaps 40,000 or so years ago when modern-type people appeared.

Their story, which continues to unfold in our times, has guided the organization of this book. My main objective is to bring together in a single narrative section recent discoveries in archeology, geology, and other disciplines which relate more or less directly to the transition from ape to human—to the rise not only of a new species but of an entirely new kind of evolution that involved more than purely physical adaptations. The first eleven chapters present information about these changes, much of it gathered since the publication of my third edition in 1978. The focus is on inanimate evidence, fossil bones, and flint artifacts excavated at representative sites.

The second section of the book focuses on living research, on what we are learning about times past from studies of present-day primates, human and non-human. The behavior and anatomy of prosimians, or premonkeys, monkeys, and apes include clues to adaptations under way long before our ancestors arrived on the scene, and provide a broad perspective on our own developments, on our potentialities and limitations. At a still broader level, we try to see ourselves in the context of the evolution of mammals—indeed, of all social creatures.

The chapters in this section include recent observations of nonhuman primates in the wild, human hunter-gatherers still at large in the world's dwindling wildernesses as well as their city-dwelling brethren, whose behavior makes prehistory come alive. Also included are chapters on experimental archeology, the human infant, and the acquisition and evolution of language, the most human thing about human beings. The objective is always to learn more about our origins as a guide to what we may become.

EDITOR'S NOTE

The previous editions of this book were titled *The Emergence of Man*. However, because this book is obviously not just about "men" but about the physical and cultural development of both men and women, this fourth edition is titled *The Emergence of Humankind*.

JOHN E. PFEIFFER

Acknowledgments

We know a great deal more about atoms and cells, and about a variety of nonhuman species, than we do about ourselves—a situation reflected in the underdeveloped state of the social sciences as compared to the physical and biological sciences. The social sciences, however, are beginning to come into their own with anthropology, particularly archeological anthropology, at the forefront as far as sophisticated analysis is concerned.

More schools are providing fuller accounts of what happened in prehistory and at an earlier age, often in the eighth and ninth grades. High school and college students are exposed to information once offered only to graduate students. Above all, many barriers are being broken down, notably the barriers that separate academic departments and that have done so much to frustrate the study of human evolution and human behavior, the self-knowledge we need most. Findings about life in prehistoric times bear on problems in neurophysiology, psychology, psychiatry, animal behavior, and architecture—and research in these areas, in turn, bears on problems in archeology and anthropology in general.

In presenting material from such diverse sources, I have received help from many persons. I was fortunate to meet Sherwood Washburn of the University of California, Berkeley, early in the preparation of this book. He indicated the nature of the work ahead in its full complexity, advised me in the planning of research, field trips, and interviews, and kept me posted on progress in his own research and in the research of his students and other associates. Throughout the writing of this book Clark Howell, also of the University of California, has given most generously of his time, sharing his extensive knowledge and evaluating controversial points in a field where controversies are common and evaluation is exceedingly tricky. At Harvard, Hallam Movius contributed a great deal to the archeological chapters.

Above all, there is my debt to the late François Bordes of the University of Bordeaux. It is not only what I learned from him about excavating methods and the analysis of artifact assemblages of Neanderthal people, although that was considerable, but also what he conveyed simply by being himself—a feeling for the honesty, passion, and imagination that go into creative research. For the sheer flow of stimulating ideas, I owe much to Lewis Binford of the University of New Mexico, who launched the new archeology and continues to lead the way as his ideas evolve. When archeology becomes a science, when we know enough to come up routinely with disprovable hypotheses, a large part of the credit will go to Binford.

A number of investigators contributed to my archeological education by permitting me to dig with them, on the theory that first-hand experience is essential in writing about any area of research. I worked with Bordes at Combe Grenal in the Dordogne, André Leroi-Gourhan of the University of Paris at Arcy-sur-Cure in the Yonne Valley, and Cynthia Irwin-Williams of Eastern New Mexico University in the foothills of the Rockies. Mary Leakey and the late Louis Leakey of the Center for Prehistory and Archaeology in Nairobi, Kenya, served as my guides in the Olduvai Gorge.

Revil Mason and Phillip Tobias of the University of the Witwatersrand in Johannesburg, Ray Inskeep of Oxford University, and Ronald Singer of the University of Chicago showed me South African sites, including those of the earliest hominids and several Bushman art sites. Desmond Clark, another Berkeley investigator, led me through some formidable back country during a search for new sites in the Karonga district of northern Malawi; Lya Dams of the Royal Belgian Society of Anthropology, J. Gonzales Echegaray of the Centro de Investigacion y Museo de Altamira in Santillana del Mar, M. A. Garcia-Guinea of the Santander Museo de Prehistoria y Arqueologia, and Lawrence Straus of the University of New Mexico conducted me through art caves in France and Spain. My observations of nonhuman primates included several weeks spent in East Africa with Irven DeVore of Harvard University following baboon troops in Nairobi Park and the Amboseli Game Reserve.

Checking for accuracy and proper emphasis is a major task in a book like this, which draws on so many areas of research. I am reasonably sure that most errors have been found and corrected, since I made a point of checking with individuals whose work is described. I take full responsibility, however, for any errors that remain.

The following are among the investigators who provided me with information during interviews, or read chapters or sections of chapters: Emiliano de Aguirre, Museo Nacional de Ciencias Naturales, Madrid; Mary Ainsworth, University of Virginia; Owen Aldis, Behavioral Science Research Fund, Menlo Park, California; Christopher Alexander, University of California, Berkeley; Jeanne and Stuart Altmann, University of Chicago; Anthony Ambrose, St. Mary's

Hospital, London; Richard Andrew, University of Sussex, England; Robert Arambourou, University of Bordeaux; Christian and Claude Archambeau, Sarlat, France; Paul Bahn, University of Liverpool; Robert Bailey, Harvard University; Ofer Bar-Yosef, Hebrew University, Jerusalem; Alex Bavelas, University of British Columbia; Joseph Birdsell, University of California, Los Angeles; Ben Blount, University of Georgia; Noel Boaz, New York University; John Bowlby, Tavistock Clinic, London; Robert Braidwood, University of Chicago; Charles Brain, Transvaal Museum, Pretoria, South Africa; Harvey Bricker, Tulane University; Alison Brooks, George Washington University; Henry Bunn, University of California, Berkeley; Karl Butzer, University of Chicago; David Bygott, Cambridge University, England; Errett Callahan, Virginia Commonwealth University; Matt Cartmill, Duke University; Elizabeth Cashdan, University of Pittsburgh; Michael Chance, University of Birmingham, England; Dorothy Cheney, University of California, Los Angeles; James Chisholm, University of New Mexico; Tim Clutton-Brock, Cambridge University, England; Glen Cole, Field Museum of Natural History, Chicago; Desmond Collins, University of London; Yves Coppens, Musée de L'Homme, Paris; Shirley Coryndon, British Museum (Natural History), London; the late Don Crabtree, Idaho State University Museum.

Also Raymond Dart, University of the Witwatersrand, Johannesburg; Paulette Daubisse, Grotte Font-de-Gaume, Les Eyzies-de-Tayac, France; Lyle Davidson, Harvard University; Brigitte and Gilles Delluc, Perigeaux, France; Woodrow Denham, University of California, Berkeley; Ellen Dissanayake, New School for Social Research, New York; Patricia Draper, University of New Mexico; John Eisenberg, National Zoological Park, Smithsonian Institution; Richard Estes, Harvard University; Brian Fagen, University of California, Santa Barbara; Robert Fagen, University of Pennsylvania; William Farrand, University of Michigan; Kent Flannery, University of Michigan; Mary Foster, University of California, Berkeley; Roger Fouts, University of Oklahoma; Robin Fox, Rutgers University; David Frayer, University of Kansas; Leslie Freeman, University of Chicago; Gordon Gallup, State University of New York, Albany; Clive Gamble, University of Southampton, England; Allen and Beatrice Gardner, University of Nevada; the late Dorothy Garrod, Villebois, Lavalette, France; Norman Geschwind, Harvard Medical School; Eugene Giles, University of Illinois; Ian Glover, Institute of Archaeolgoy, London; Robert Good, Sloan-Kettering Institute, New York; Jane Goodall, Gombe Stream Research Center, Tanzania; Morris Goodman, Wayne State University; Richard Gould, Brown University; the late Ronald Hall, University of Bristol, England; Annette Hamilton, Macquarie University, Australia; Robert Harding, University of Pennsylvania; Jack Harlan, University of Illinois; Harry Harlow, University of Wisconsin; Henry Harpending, University of New Mexico; John Hartung, State University of New York, Brooklyn; Richard Hay, University of Illinois, Urbana; June Helm, University of Iowa; Gordon Hewes, University of Colorado; the late Eric Higgs, Cambridge University, England; Jane Hill, Wayne State University; Robert Hinde, Cambridge University, England; Charles Hockett, Cornell University; Ralph Holloway, Columbia University; Nancy Howell, University of Toronto; Sarah Hrdy, Harvard University; Corinne Hutt, University of Keele, England; Dell Hymes, University of Pennsylvania; Glynn Isaac, Harvard University; Junichiro Itani, University of Kyoto, Japan; Arthur Jelinek, University of Arizona; Helle Jensen, University of Aarhus, Denmark; Peter Jewell, University College, London; Donald Johanson, Institute of Human Origins, Berkeley; Clifford Jolly, New York University; Nicholas Blurton Jones, University of California, Santa Barbara; Rhys Jones, Australian National University, Canberra; Sheldon Judson, Princeton University; William Jungers, State University of New York, Stony Brook.

Also Richard Katz, Harvard University; Richard Kay, Duke University; Lawrence Keeley, University of Illinois; Charles Keller, University of Illinois; Suzanne Keller, Princeton University; Jack Kelso, University of Colorado; James Kennett, University of Rhode Island; William Kessen, Yale University; Richard Klein, University of Chicago; Linda Koebner, New York Zoological Society; Melvin Konner, Emery University; Ronald Lampert, Australian National University, Canberra; Jane Lancaster, University of Oklahoma; Ray Larick, State University of New York, Binghamton; Foss and Helen Leach, University of Otago, New Zealand; the late Louis Leakey and Mary and Richard Leakey, National Museums of Kenya, Nairobi; Richard Lee, University of Toronto; Marjorie LeMay, Harvard Medical School; the late Eric Lenneberg, Cornell Univesity College of Medicine; Arlette Leroi-Gourhan, Musée de L'Homme, Paris; Jerome Lettvin, Massachusetts Institute of Technology; William Longacre, University of Arizona; Michel Lorblanchet, Centre National de la Recherche Scientifique, Gramat, France; Owen Lovejoy, Kent State University; Henry de Lumley, Musée de L'Homme, Paris; Vincent Maglio, Rutgers University Medical School; Brian Maguire, University of the Witwatersrand, Johannesburg; Alan Mann, University of Pennsylvania; Peter Marler, Rockefeller University; Jacques Marsal, Grotte de Lascaux, Montignac, France; Robert Martin, University College, London; Ernst Mayr, Harvard University; Patrick McGinnis, Cambridge University, England; William McGrew, University of Stirling, Scotland; Paul McLean, National Institute of Mental Health; David McNeill, University of Chicago; Paul Mellars, Cambridge University, England; George Miller, Princeton University; Marvin Minsky, Massachusetts Institute of Technology; Donald Mitchell, State University of New York College, Buffalo; James Moore, Queens College, New York; John Mulvaney, Australian National University, Canberra.

Also John Napier, Royal Free Hospital, London; Walle Nauta, Massachusetts Institute of Technology; Mark Newcomer, Institute of Archaeology, London; Toshisada Nishida, University of Tokyo; the late Kenneth Oakley, British Museum (Natural History), London; James O'Connell, University of Utah; Donald Omark, University of Chicago; Armand Oppenheimer, Sharon, Connecticut; Bryan Patterson, Harvard University; Nadine Peacock, Harvard University; Jean Perrot, French Archaeological Mission, Jerusalem; Nicolas Peterson, Australian National University, Canberra; David Pilbeam, Harvard University; Richard Potts, Yale University; David Premack, University of Pennsylvania; Karl Pribram, Stanford University; Leonard Radinsky, University of Chicago; Yoel Rak, Tel-Aviv University, Israel; Colin Renfrew, Cambridge University, England; Vernon Reynolds, Oxford University, England; Jean-Philippe Rigaud, University of Bordeaux; Philip Rightmire, State University of New York, Binghamton; John

Robinson, University of Wisconsin; Thelma Rowell, University of California, Berkeley; James Sackett, University of California, Los Angeles; Vincent Sarich, University of California, Berkeley; George Schaller, New York Zoological Society; Kathy Schick, University of California, Berkeley; Margaret Schoeninger, Johns Hopkins University; Carmel Schrire, Rutgers University; Robert Seyfarth, University of California, Los Angeles; Paul Sherman, Cornell University; Pat Shipman, Johns Hopkins University; Richard Shweder, University of Chicago; Ann and Gale Sieveking, British Museum, London; George Silberbauer, Monash University, Australia; Joan Silk, University of California, Davis; Elwyn Simons, Duke University; the late George Gaylord Simpson, University of Arizona; Anne and Michael Simpson, Cambridge University, England; Barbara Smuts, Harvard University; Olga Soffer, University of Wisconsin; Ralph and Rose Solecki, Columbia University; Denise de Sonneville-Bordes, University of Bordeaux; Augustus Sordinas, Memphis State University; John Speth, University of Michigan; Axel Steensberg, University of Copenhagen, Denmark; Jack Stern, State University of New York, Stony Brook; the late Theodor Strehlow, University of Adelaide, Australia; Randall Susman, State University of New York, Stony Brook; Alan Swedlund, University of Massachusetts, Amherst.

Also James Tanner, Institute of Child Health, London; Nancy Tanner, University of California, Santa Cruz; Geza Teleki, George Washington University; David Thomas, American Museum of Natural History; Harold Thomas, Harvard University; Lionel Tiger, Rutgers University; Niko Tinbergen, Oxford University, England; Jacques Tixier, Centre National de la Recherche Scientifique, Meudon, France; Nicholas Toth, University of California, Berkeley; Erik Trinkaus, University of New Mexico; Robert Trivers, University of California, Santa Cruz; Jurgen Troels-Smith, National Museum of Copenhagen, Denmark; Peter Ucko, University of Southampton, England; Jean Vertut, Issy-sur-Moulineaux, France; Denis Vialou, Institut de Paleontologie Humaine, Paris; Paola Villa, University of Wyoming; the late John Waechter, Institute of Archaeology, London; Alan Walker, Johns Hopkins University; Samuel Wasser, University of Washington; the late Joseph Weiner, University of London; Robert Whallon, University of Michigan; Peter White, University of Sydney, Australia; Randall White, New York University; Tim White, University of California, Berkelely; Polly Wiessner, Langaa, Denmark; Edwin Wilmsen, Boston University; Alan Wilson, University of California, Berkeley; Edward Wilson, Harvard University; Bruce Winterhalder, University of North Carolina; Howard Winters, New York University; John Witthoft, University of Pennsylvania; Martin Wobst, University of Massachusetts, Amherst; Milford Wolpoff, University of Michigan; Richard Wrangham, University of Michigan; Henry Wright, University of Michigan; Richard Wright, University of Sydney, Australia; Vero Wynne-Edwards, University of Aberdeen, Scotland; John Yellen, George Washington University; John Young, University College, London; and Adrienne Zihlman, University of California, Santa Cruz.

Since I am a freelancer, this book would never have been completed without financial support. I received travel grants from the Wenner-Gren Foundation for Anthropological Research for work in England and France, and from the National

Institute of Mental Health for my first trip to Africa and the Olduvai Gorge. Special thanks are due to the Carnegie Corporation of New York for two "reflective year" grants which permitted me not only to revisit Africa and Europe but also to take time out for organizing notes and writing. A two-year grant from the Harry Frank Guggenheim Foundation made many things possible, including some of the research for this fourth edition.

For background research I drew heavily on the resources of libraries at the Marine Biological Laboratory in Woods Hole, Princeton University, Harvard University, the Wenner-Gren Foundation, the Musée de L'Homme in Paris, the Institute of Archaeology in London, and the British Museum (Natural History).

Alan McClare deserves very special thanks for overseeing the writing of the fourth edition. I appreciate his editorial help, his advice (almost always followed), and his patience in dealing with an author unversed in proper manuscript preparation. And I am grateful to Jennifer Jones and Lucy Zakarian for hours spent keeping track of illustrations, captions, and credits.

JEP

Illustration Credits

Courtesy of the Library Services Department, American Museum of Natural History; p. 161, François Bordes; p. 164, François Bordes; p. 165, Lewis Binford, University of New Mexico; p. 170, Courtesy of the Library Services Department, American Museum of Natural History; p. 176, Don E. Crabtree; p. 183, Zdenek Burian; p. 185, Zdenek Burian; p. 186, National Science Foundation; p. 187, Zdenek Burian; p. 189, Joe Ben Wheat; p. 195, Copyright Novosti Press Agency; p. 199, French Government Tourist Office; p. 200, Commissariat Général au Tourisme, photograph by C. Pécha; p. 202, Courtesy of the Library Services Department, American Museum of Natural History; p. 204, Jean Vertut; p. 206, Courtesy of the Library Services Department, American Museum of Natural History; p. 208, Jean Vertut; p. 209 (top), Jean Vertut; p. 209 (bottom), Courtesy of the Library Services Department, American Museum of Natural History; p. 210, Courtesy of the Library Services Department, American Museum of Natural History; p. 210, Courtesy of the Library Services Department, American Museum of Natural History; p. 211, Lawrence Straus; p. 213, French Government Tourist Office; p. 216, John Pfeiffer; p. 217, Jean Vertut; p. 222, Courtesy of the Library Services Department, American Museum of Natural History; p. 231, Nancy S. DeVore/Anthro-Photo; p. 232, Stuart A. Altmann and Jeanne Altmann; p. 233, Stuart A. Altmann and Jeanne Altmann; p. 234, Irven DeVore/Anthro-Photo; p. 236, Irven DeVore/Anthro-Photo; p. 237, Irven DeVore/Anthro-Photo; p. 239, Irven DeVore/Anthro-Photo; p. 241, Irven DeVore/Anthro-Photo; p. 242, Stuart A. Altmann and Jeanne Altmann; p. 250, Photograph by Baron Hugo van Lawick, © National Geographic Society; p. 252, Photograph by Baron Hugo van Lawick, © National Geographic Society; p. 255, © Linda Koebner; p. 263, H. F. Harlow, University of Wisconsin Primate Lab; p. 264, H. F. Harlow, University of Wisconsin Primate Lab; p. 264, H. F. Harlow, University of Wisconsin Primate Lab; p. 265, William A. Mason; p. 266, © Linda Koebner; p. 267, © Linda Koebner; p. 268, © Linda Koebner; p. 270, Richard Wright; p. 276, Stuart A. Altmann and Jeanne Altmann; p. 283, Richard A. Gould and Jeanne Altmann; p. 286, Richard A. Gould and Jeanne Altmann; p. 287, Richard A. Gould and Jeanne Altmann; p. 290, Richard A. Gould and Jeanne Altmann; p. 291, Richard A. Gould and Jeanne Altmann; p. 292, Richard A. Gould and Jeanne Altmann; p. 293, Richard A. Gould and Jeanne Altmann; p. 294, Richard A. Gould and Jeanne Altmann; p. 298, Richard A. Gould and Jeanne Altmann; p. 299, Richard A. Gould and Jeanne Altmann; p. 301 Richard A. Gould and Jeanne Altmann; p. 301, Richard A. Gould and Jeanne Altman; p. 302, Richard A. Gould and Jeanne Altmann; p. 303, Australian News and Information Bureau, photograph by Don Edwards; p. 304, Australian News and Information Bureau, photograph by M. Jensen; p. 309, Irven DeVore/Anthro-Photo; p. 310, Stan Washburn/Anthro-Photo; p. 311, Irven DeVore/Anthro-Photo; p. 318, Irven DeVore/Anthro-Photo; p. 329, Don E. Crabtree; p. 330, Don E. Crabtree; p. 339, Solebury School; p. 346, Tiffany Field, Mailman Center for Child Development, University of Miami; p. 348, J. A. Ambrose; p. 353, J. A. Ambrose; p. 363, Beatrice T. Gardner; p. 366, Allen Gardner and Beatrice Gardner, University of Nevada; p. 367, David Premack; p. 382, Stuart A. Altmann and Jeanne Altmann; p. 383, Nicholas G. Blurton Jones; p. 384, © Linda Koebner; p. 385, Nicholas G. Blurton Jones; p. 387, Corinne Hutt

Prologue: The Search for Human Origins

Parts of the past still endure in Africa in stretches of relic wilderness wide as inland seas. There is a hilltop in Kenya's Amboseli Game Reserve, for instance, where you look west across a savanna that extends bright and yellowish brown and bone-dry as far as the eye can see. This is usually an empty semidesert land with a few flat-topped fever trees and nothing abroad but dust devils, little whirlwinds which appear out of nowhere as brown spiral puffs and spin along for a distance and then vanish.

But a change takes place during certain dry-season days. The land becomes a great gathering place, and the Amboseli hilltop becomes an observation post. There is a massive coming together of species, as if to a sanctuary or an Ark. Streams of animals move toward a place not far from the foot of the hill, a large pool of stagnant green-gray water.

I remember watching the scene one glaring mid-July morning. A herd of zebras was already drinking at the edge of the pool while, not yet at the edge, wildebeests with curved horns and high shoulders moved slowly in a single file as if queuing up for their turn; and behind them more animals and still more stretched back until all I could make out were black specks in the far distance. Suddenly the zebras panicked, perhaps at a rustle in the low bushes nearby, and dashed from the pool. Then some of the wildebeests waded in, drank, and left; a herd of gazelles took their place and left after another brief panic; half a dozen ostriches, two troops of baboons, and a lone giraffe followed, and on and on all day till sunset.

This is the part of Africa that is dying, the wild and primeval part, the

Africa that once belonged to animals other than humans. This Africa produces a strange sort of double vision or double perspective, a sense of being in two worlds. One world, of course, is completely alien. The savanna and all that is going on there are so different from anything the observer has known that it might just as well be happening on another planet. One is a spectator, uninvolved, uncommitted, trying to take it in.

The other world, where an undercurrent of nostalgia stirs, is like a place known long ago and revisited. One responds to it for the same reason that one responds to all lonely places—whether during walks along beaches with no one in sight, camping out in a ravine in the desert, going off paved highways to dirt roads, on tracks into the interior, or going into trackless areas, heading for lakes and canyons with waterfalls and no roads leading to them. Something is lost by living too long away from such places. A feeling of belonging to the wilderness persists, and the feeling is strongest and most moving in Africa because that is the land of our ancestors.

They lived as animals among animals. They were once part of the great processions that approached water holes along ancient trails and waited their turn during times of thirst. They stepped aside unhurried and without looking up as wildebeests and zebras moved by, strode through herds of gazelles, and chased the baboons, their closest relatives in the crowd. They came to drink and bolted in panic when they heard sounds in the bushes. And sometimes near the edges of stagnant waters they became victims of lions and other predators.

Their way of life is not remote. Hominids, members of the human family, have spent millions of years foraging in wildernesses, and only a few thousand years living in cities. They have been wild animals for millions of years and domesticated animals, or rather partly domesticated animals, for only a fraction of that span. Far from having arrived, they are just beginning to find their way, their place in the scheme of things.

This is the point of the statement that we are the missing link between anthropoid apes and human beings. The assumption that we are already fully human is open to argument. It leads to questions which are difficult to answer—for example, the question of why we so frequently behave in a fashion which we ourselves consider inhuman. Such contradictions emphasize the need for a shift in viewpoint. The sense of urgency about things to come demands a harder and longer look at the way things were. We must look backward as well as forward.

In a time when the accent is more and more on what the future may bring, on visits to other planets and the problem of surviving and evolving on our own planet, research on the remote past is beginning to come into its own. Investigators are engaged in an expanding effort to look at the past more realistically, and a major part of that effort is the search for fresh evidence about human origins. Everything suggests that the events of prehistoric times are as important in understanding the species as the events of infancy and early childhood are in understanding the individual.

The marks of the past may endure for long periods. Imagine a prehistoric twilight with hunter-gatherers living and settling by a stream. They scoop a hollow place in the earth for a hearth, sharpen old flints and shape new ones, eat by the

Some prominent mammals

fire and come close for warmth, curling up at the edge of the fire to sleep. After a stay of a few days or a few weeks, they abandon camp as the seasons change. Leaves and branches fall and form new earth; winds blow in dust and sand and volcanic ash. The area is flooded, and a lake appears. Sediment drifts down through the waters and settles and accumulates on the bottom.

Then the lake dries up, and another cycle starts. Decades pass and centuries and millennia, and something endures. The original occupation floor may be preserved like a flower pressed between pages of a diary or a fossil imprint of a fern on rock. Discarded tools, charred bones, and the remains of fires that sputtered out long ago are traces of camps where people stayed awhile and disturbed the earth and then moved on. There are sites where living patterns have persisted for as long as 2 to 3 million years.

A worldwide search is under way for new sites which will reveal more about the ways of creatures in the first throes of becoming human. Every lead is followed up, every tale of fields and caves rich in ancient fossils (which usually turn out to be the bones of modern animals). Expeditions are searching in backcountry lakes in the 4000-mile African Rift Valley, on slopes rising from the flat plains of northern Thailand, among the foothills of the Rockies and Himalayas and Urals, along the Mediterranean coast, in the deserts of Australia, and in valleys gouged out of the plateaus of central Spain.

Expeditions are part adventure and part sheer drudgery. Work in the field often begins with the inspection of geological maps indicating where promising deposits lie, exposed or near the surface; ancient lake sediments or dunes or river banks may include the remains of prehistoric camps and campers. The next step may involve aerial photographs of the mapped terrain, pairs of photographs placed edge to edge and looked at through a stereo viewer so that trees, cliffs, gullies, hills, and other features appear sharp and in three dimensions, as if one were flying over the region on a clear day.

The latest advance in the technology of site searching involves remote-sensing eye-in-the-sky satellites. Equipped with television-type scanning devices, they view the world from heights of about 500 miles and take synchronized photographs in green, red, and infrared light every 25 seconds, each photograph covering an area of about 10,000 square miles (100 miles on a side). Some of the photographs, specifically the ones covering the Chaco Canyon National Monument region of New Mexico, are being studied in intensive detail for use in identifying places where people lived many thousands of years ago, extinct river beds and lakes, soils rich in organic matter and clays, hidden springs and other water sources, fine debris at the bottom of cliffs, stream and beach gravel, and wind-deposited sands which may contain ancient artifacts. In this way, the insights gained in the course of checking a region already well known archeologically can be used to examine features of satellite photographs of lesser known regions.

The real work starts after photography and other techniques have pinpointed a number of likely areas for detailed on-the-ground surveying. Since most unexplored regions are located far off the beaten track in country too rugged even for Land Rovers, surveying means getting out and walking. On a typical day you wake at sunrise, tramp through brush and brambles, bending low to avoid the thorns, half slide and half fall down the steep steps of ravines, follow the courses of dried-out stream beds, and then try to find your way back before nightfall. You may walk 15 miles or more in 8 hours, with about 40 minutes off to eat and rest, and that goes on day after day for as long as it takes to cover an area systematically.

Every search is a gamble, and many searches end with little or nothing to show for them. Under such conditions, when success comes, it is especially sweet. For example, an important site was discovered a number of years ago by Desmond Clark of the University of California in Berkeley just as he was on the verge of quitting. The setting is one of the wildest and most magnificent in Africa, near the southern end of Lake Tanganyika where the Kalambo River winds sluggishly through a high valley, moves faster as it nears the edge of a cliff, and plunges 700 feet into a dark tropical canyon. One morning Clark was walking back from the falls along the spillway gorge when, after nearly falling into a pit dug by natives to trap wild pigs, he happened to look down at a point where the river makes a sharp meander.

"I almost missed the place completely," he recalls. "The grass, which is normally about 8 feet high and thick as your finger, had been burned off, revealing a sheer erosion cut in the river bank, and you look at practically every sheer cut. This one was touch and go, but I did look. I hung on to a couple of roots, lowered myself over the edge, and found some nice tools dating back to the Middle Stone Age of Africa about 25,000 to 30,000 years ago. Then I dropped to the bottom, where still older tools, hand axes and cleavers, were sticking out from the bank as well as pieces of carbonized wood. I could hardly believe that it was the real thing.''

Clark came back three years later for a full-scale effort. Modern excavating techniques demand time and patience because thousands of tools, flakes, and other objects are uncovered bit by bit with trowels and brushes. Furthermore, one never knows how long a dig will take, how much time one will need to pass through layer after layer until reaching bedrock. It required nearly 12 months of digging over several seasons to do the job at Kalambo, and many excavations take a great deal longer.

The general practice is not to excavate a site completely, because of the peculiar nature of archeological evidence. In other sciences experiments can always be repeated and results checked. Astronomers can always make new observations of the sun and planets; biologists have an ample supply of organisms for continuing laboratory studies. Once an archeologist excavates a site, however, there can be no checking or retracing of steps. That particular arrangement of buried objects is unique. There is no other arrangement like it, and it can never be fully re-created again. Clues missed because of carelessness or ignorance are gone forever.

An appalling amount of information has been lost because of bad practices in the not very remote past. Profit-minded diggers have destroyed many fine sites simply to obtain a few beautifully worked flint or bone tools to sell to museums, tourists, or private collectors by using rush tactics to complete in a few hours excavations which should have been carried out for weeks. One notorious plunderer was caught in the act of trying to remove a section of the ceiling of a French rock shelter, a section containing a sculpted fish. The organized looting of archeological sites is an international scandal and will no doubt continue for a long time despite laws prescribing punishments for offenders. The laws are not always strictly enforced; government officials often look the other way and sometimes do nothing to prevent the purchase of looted material by museum directors and other collectors whose desire for objects of art keeps the looters in business.

Such problems aside, the routine demands of modern excavating are enough to tax the ingenuity and patience of legitimate workers. The earth contains evidence too small to be detected by the naked eye, evidence which earlier workers generally missed. In a technique known as flotation, used more than half a century ago by Danish investigators, dirt from excavated layers may be poured into a bucket with a window-screen bottom which is partly submerged in water. Most of the dirt passes through the screen, but low-density material floats to the top of the water in the bucket and is scooped off with a fine-mesh strainer. This material, which may include tiny fragments of small-game and fish bones as well as nuts and other plant remains, is an important source of clues to prehistoric diets.

Another increasingly useful technique is the analysis of fossil pollen, grains whose tough outer coatings have been preserved in such fine detail that grasses, shrubs, oak, holly, pine, juniper, palm, and dozens of other plants can be identified under the microscope. It is painstaking work. Each grain is examined at magnifications of 400 to more than 1500 times for size, shape, types, and distribution of spiny and rodlike extensions, and for a wide variety of surface features. Each grain has about 40 to 50 significant features which must be noted. Hundreds of grains may be analyzed daily, and a project may continue for weeks. The results provide invaluable aid in reconstructing past climates and environments.

The general stress is on increasingly intensive studies, studies designed to extract more and more information from archeological deposits. Certain mollusks which prehistoric people ate in quantity show shell growth patterns like tree rings. Since the rings tend to be formed at a regular rate and are about 20 times broader in summer than in winter, microscopic studies of excavated shells indicate when the mollusks were harvested and eaten and, of course, the season when the site was occupied. Experimental procedures are based on examinations of fish scales, teeth, microscopic stonelike remains of plants known as plant "opals," or phytoliths, and other items that may provide clues to prehistoric living.

Contemporary diggers, knowing of such research, generally leave one-half or more of a site undug for future workers who will come with more advanced techniques and greater knowledge. In exceptional situations, however, sites may be excavated completely and in a hurry—specifically, when they are scheduled to be destroyed for nonarcheological reasons, which is happening more and more frequently as construction crews build new homes and highways for expanding populations. Work was halted for five months during the building of new apartments on the French Riviera, when bulldozers exposed tools and other signs of a prehistoric camp. In this case, as in the case of Nile Valley sites flooded by the Aswan Dam in Egypt, the objective was to recover as much evidence as possible in a limited time.

Emotional involvement and bitter feuding, by no means unknown in the harder sciences, reach a strikingly high level among specialists in prehistory. "There is something about exploring the past that affects you," says one anthropologist who has been in the thick of several heated debates. "It seems that every time people find a human bone they go crazy on the spot." Investigators have been known to deal out and respond to criticism with a measure of deep resentment, as if being wrong were a slur on one's moral character rather than an inevitable result of learning.

The phenomenon is related to the nature of the discipline, the fragility of our theories, the sustained loneliness of searches which may or may not yield exciting finds, and the temptation to make the most—and perhaps a bit more—of what does turn up. Also, the fact that everyone makes mistakes and that sites once dug can never be fully reconstructed may instill a kind of defensiveness in the excavator, and that may have something to do with the extra sensitivity to criticism and the readiness to indulge in polemics. In a larger sense, there is the old and powerful tendency to see ourselves through distorting lenses, to romanticize our nature and our origins.

One myth—conceived a long time ago, perpetuated in numerous popular articles and textbooks (including earlier editions of this one), and presently in the process of being discarded—involves the notion of big-game hunting as the driving force in the transition from ape to human. It evokes an image of conquest and courage at the human dawn, a mammoth at bay, trapped in a pitfall, trumpeting its pain and rage, being put to death by men hurling rocks and spears. For one thing, this scenario amounts to a putdown of women. It implies that they were bit players in the human drama, concerned solely and unadventurously with having babies and gathering plant food, making only minor if any contributions to the advancement of the species. The distortion goes beyond sexism, however. It puts all our earliest ancestors on a pedestal, exaggerating their uniqueness and assuming that they were among the most dangerous and cleverest of predators from the beginning, which was hardly the case.

The current version of human origins is more balanced if rather less melodramatic. The hominids of 3 to 4 million years ago were small and probably hairy creatures, something more than apes but considerably less than human. They had shifted from an almost full-time existence in dense ancestral forests to a more varied life style in open woodlands and grassy savannas. Their brains were not large compared with ours, about the size of contemporary chimpanzee brains. But they seem to have been human in one significant respect—they walked upright. If their diets were anything like those of chimpanzees, their closest living relatives, they preferred a selection of ripe fruits above all else, although more often than not they had to make do with second- and third-best choices.

Early hominids, like most primates—including most human beings alive today—subsisted primarily on plant foods. They probably exploited natural abundances of grass shoots and seeds, nuts and berries as well as fruit, succulent leaves and other traditional forest fare. Also, they may now and then have gone after insects, snakes, lizards, and an occasional small mammal. Omnivores and opportunists, they were adapting to new conditions. The very variety of their diets demanded a wide knowledge about other wild species. Since different plants ripen at different times and places, it paid off to keep extensive areas under surveillance, to monitor the environment. Some plants are poisonous, and it must have taken long periods of trial and error and many mysterious deaths to learn the hard way which plants to avoid. The wilderness also nourished competitors, fellow primates and other animals in pursuit of the same foods, and predators on the prowl for fresh meat, hominid meat included. Survival depended on a knowledge of the behavior of competitors.

Change came slowly in the beginning. Although brain size is by no means an infallible criterion, it does provide a rough index of evolutionary progress in the primate line. The most advanced hominids of 2 million years ago had brains more than half again as large as those of their earliest known ancestors, and are classified as the first members of the genus *Homo*. The continuing expansion of the brain and the rise of *Homo sapiens* more than 1.5 million years later were intimately connected to the rise of increasingly complex social organizations and methods of obtaining food. Our kind began to dominate the scene about 100,000 years ago, and ever since then cultural evolution has been moving at an accelerating rate.

The final phase of prehistory, the last two hundredth or so of the long journey from woodland-savanna newcomers to modern people, includes the oldest traces of art and religion, long-distance exchange, the formation of band societies, and the appearance of elites, individuals regarded as superior to the ordinary run of mortals. It also includes the high point in the development of the hunt, the mass killing of herd animals by cooperating bands, the first hints of tribal confederations. After that, there was a decline of the hunt as an activity essential to the community, a decline which began some 10,000 years ago with the invention of agriculture. The invention of writing about four or five millenniums later may be taken as the official end of prehistory.

Something unprecedented happened during the course of these and subsequent events, something that acquires special meaning in the light of all that happened before the appearance of human beings. Their evolutionary position involves two apparently contradictory truths—namely, that they have much in common with other animals (far more than is generally realized) and, at the same time, that they represent another order of being. Humans are not merely a new species but the pioneers of an entirely new kind of evolution.

All previous species, some 500 million extinct as well as the 10 million or so surviving forms, evolved by mutation, the gene-shuffling process known as recombination, and natural selection. And all species, from whales and giant redwood trees to tadpole-shaped viruses so small that several billion of them would fit comfortably into a sphere no bigger across than the period at the end of this sentence, share certain basic similarities at the molecular level. They transmit their characteristics from generation to generation in the form of genes, discrete and highly organized molecules of hereditary materials known as nucleic acids, almost always the one known as DNA (short for deoxyribonucleic acid).

New species are formed in isolation, under conditions which permit a measure of independent evolution. In the vast majority of cases, the first steps take place when geographic barriers, anything from a stream that cannot be crossed to an ocean or a range of mountains, divide parts of the ancestral species from one another. The separated subpopulations begin to undergo distinctive changes. Mutations which would formerly have spread throughout the ancestral population now accumulate on either side of the barrier. Furthermore, since no two environments are exactly alike, the adaptations called for on either side of the barrier will differ in certain respects.

After a sufficient number of generations, the net effect is two genetically incompatible subpopulations. The differences between them have become so great that even if the barrier is removed or crossed they can no longer interbreed to reproduce generations of viable offspring. At this point a new species is said to have arisen. Darwin studied such a case on the Galápagos Islands, which lie in the Pacific Ocean about 600 miles from the nearest mainland, the coast of Ecuador. The islands were inhabited by more than a dozen species of finches, all of them the descendants of a colony of finches presumably blown to the islands by high winds and all of them sufficiently isolated from one another to develop different adaptations and species status.

The Galápagos finches provide a good model for the origin of species throughout the course of evolution; new species are still being formed. The Grand Canyon in northern Arizona separates two kinds of squirrel which had a common ancestor centuries ago and have been diverging genetically ever since. The question is whether the squirrels have yet become sufficiently different to be classified as different species, but they seem to be heading in that direction.

Human beings are subject to the same evolutionary forces that shaped and are shaping their fellow species. The geography of their speciation, the specific barriers that isolated hominid populations at various times in the past, is unknown. But there were barriers, and we are the result of them. Like all other creatures, we arose by the processes of mutation and natural selection, and we continue to depend on our genes. The big difference is that in other creatures genetic evolution plays the major role, while in us cultural evolution has developed to an unprecedented degree.

The things other species need to survive, to escape and kill and adapt, are generally built in as part of their bodies. Their genes determine the growth of fur, horns, scales, claws, wings, and so on. We learn and pass accumulating knowledge as well as genes from generation to generation; we make a wide variety of shelters and weapons and, to an increasing extent, our own environments. Culture permitted our ancestors, a single species, to spread throughout the world, to live and reproduce in high mountain valleys, semideserts, tropical rain forests, and subzero Arctic regions. Of course, genes continue to operate in us, just as learning may play an important role among other species. After all, we inherit our brain, and it, more than anything else, makes us human. But in our world, learning and tradition have acquired a new order of importance.

This is a relatively recent trend. In the earliest hominid days on the savanna, our ancestors were still very much genetic creatures in the sense that heredity played a far greater part in their activities than it does in ours. The way was prepared for new possibilities sometime during the development of social organization and the accompanying expansion of the brain during the past few million years. About 100 millennia ago, culture began overtaking genetics as the major determinant in human behavior.

The most important development of all, a kind of overgrowth or hypertrophy of culture, is even more recent. All other species basically stay put. They tend to live today very much the way they lived yesterday, assuming, of course, that the environment does not change. Given reasonably stable conditions, a favorable climate, plenty of food, and no human beings in the area, even chimpanzees—the animals most like us—would continue living in the same way indefinitely. The point is that they adapt, and in the process of adapting, they do not change their forests. This is what we mean by saying they are in balance with nature.

The same cannot be said for us as we have evolved in our times. Stability is not for us. When we settle down, forests are felled and earth is moved and the world begins changing radically. As the only species to produce major changes in the environment, we try to adapt in a difficult and unique situation. In effect, we create increasingly complex environments, which demand continual adaptations and readaptations. Moreover, the tendency is not to minimize change but to seek it out and discover and invent it. We have created in ourselves a new chronic restlessness, a process which continually works against equilibrium, an antihomeostasis.

Science offers no problem more complex than that of reconstructing the events and forces which have produced this condition, perhaps the outstanding characteristic of human evolution. This book is concerned with prehistory, with nomadic hunters and gatherers. It follows their evolution to the point when they are just beginning to settle down on farms. Subsequent events mark the coming of writing and records, the end of prehistory. The first part of the book deals chiefly with archeological evidence about extinct species, with artifacts and fossils and other material dug out of the earth. The second part, starting with Chapter 12, focuses on another important and closely related area of study, living prehistory, which provides clues to the past as revealed by the behavior of existing species.

Much can be learned from other members of the order of primates, which includes monkeys and apes. Recent investigations show that they have traditions, often rather sophisticated traditions, and leaders and hierarchies, and they spend an appreciable amount of time trying to maintain or improve their social status. When an opportunity arises, some of them will break their vegetarian diets and eat meat, even hunting upon occasion. The survival techniques that savanna-dwelling monkeys have evolved against predators may well have been used by early hominids.

As wildernesses vanish, investigators are taking a look at the last surviving bands of hunter-gatherers, people still living much as our ancestors lived 40,000 or more years ago. They still endure without agriculture in desert places, where they have been forced to live and where they fare much better than one might expect, thus demonstrating once again the capacity of humans to make their way under demanding conditions. Investigators are also studying people in cities and suburbs. New knowledge about such things as the bond between a mother and her infant, the nature of language and how children acquire it, and mass aggressiveness as a predominantly male characteristic inevitably deepens the understanding of the past because it is rooted in the past.

Contemporary research in living prehistory and archeology looks in both directions. It is relevant to the present and future as well as to the past. The study of prehistory presents modern times in a wider perspective so that we see ourselves more dispassionately in the light of remote origins, and above all so that we may rid ourselves of at least a few of the clichés and preconceptions that hold us down. We live with the past and always, to some extent, in it; we explore it to learn more about ourselves and what we may become.

chapter *1*

Primate Beginnings

More than a decade ago two excavators made an important find on Purgatory Hill, not far from the Fort Peck Reservoir in northeastern Montana. Leigh Van Valen of the University of Chicago and Robert Sloan of the University of Minnesota were working at a bone-dry and eroded site. Long ago a stream flowed there through abundant forests. Animals died near the banks. When the banks collapsed or heavy rains came, they were swept downstream to a place where a large, slow eddy had formed. Their bodies swirled on the lee side of the eddy, sank, and settled on a bed of clams. Over the ages sediments filtered down to cover everything.

Today the site is a compacted rocky conglomerate of clam shells, minerals, and bits of fossil embedded in a silty matrix. Van Valen and Sloan tossed chunks into 100-pound sacks and rolled the sacks down the steep hillside to a truck at a nearby reservoir. They poured the rock into fine-mesh screens, washing it in the lake until the matrix dissolved. The remainder went to a University of Minnesota laboratory to be dumped into a bathtub-sized vat of dilute acetic acid. The acid dissolved the clam shells, leaving a mixture which included, among other things, the fragmentary remains of extinct species.

The Montana project yielded important prehistoric remains after scientists had removed more than 30,000 pounds of rock from Purgatory Hill and sifted through the debris. The most striking find consisted of half a dozen molar and premolar teeth, bits of bony fossil 65 million years old, each about the size of the head of a paper book match. These were traces of the earliest known primates, the order that includes monkeys and apes and humans. Since then other investigators have been working sites in the same geological formation as that repre-

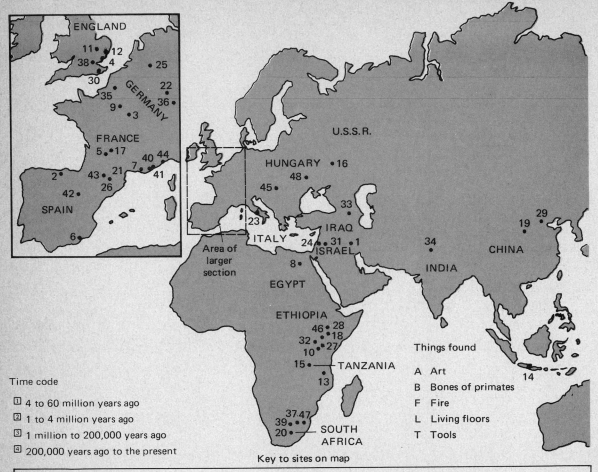

Time code

① 4 to 60 million years ago

② 1 to 4 million years ago

③ 1 million to 200,000 years ago

④ 200,000 years ago to the present

Things found

A Art

B Bones of primates

F Fire

L Living floors

T Tools

Key to sites on map

1. Ali Kosh ④ L, T	18. Lake Turkana site ② B, T	35. St. Acheul ③ T
2. Altamira ④ A, T	19. Lantian site ③ B	36. Steinheim ④ B
3. Arcy ④ B, F, L, T	20. Makapan ② B	37. Sterkfontein ② B, T
4. Clacton-on-Sea ③ T	21. Mas D'Azil ④ A, T	38. Swanscombe ④ B, T
5. Combe Grenal ④ F, L, T	22. Mauer site ③ B	39. Taung ② B
6. Cueva de Ambrosio ④ B, F, T	23. Monte Circeo ④ B, T	40. Terra Amata ④ F, L, T
7. Escale cave ③ B, F, L, T	24. Mt. Carmel ④ B, F, T	41. Lazaret ④ F, L, T
8. Fayum Depression ① B	25. Neanderthal ④ B	42. Torralba-Ambrona ③ B, F, L, T
9. Pincevent ④ A, F, L, T	26. Niaux ④ A, T	43. Tuc d'Audoubert ④ A, T
10. Fort Ternan ① B	27. Olduvai Gorge ② B, L, T	44. Vallonet cave ③ B, T
11. High Lodge ④ T	28. Omo ② B, T	45. Vertesszöllös ③ B, F, L, T
12. Hoxne ④ T	29. Peking Man ③ B, F, T	46. Lothagam ① B
13. Isimila ④ F, L, T	30. Piltdown (discredited)	47. Swartkrans ② B
14. Java site ③ B	31. Qafzeh ④ B, F, T	48. Molodova ④ B, T, L, F
15. Kalambo Falls ④ B, F, L, T	32. Rusinga Island ① B	
16. Kostenki ④ A, B, F, L, T	33. Shanidar cave ④ B, F, L, T	
17. La Chapelle-aux-Saints ④ B, T	34. Siwalik Hills ① B	

Major prehistoric sites: Europe, Africa, and Asia

sented at Purgatory Hill. William Clemens of the University of California in Berkeley and his associates have found more than a hundred teeth and two dozen lower jaw bones of the early primate genus known as *Purgatorius*.

PANGEA AND THE FIRST MAMMALS

The coming of primates has its own prehistory. It was part of a much earlier sequence of events which includes the rise and fall of reptiles, the rise of mammals, and a global splitting up of continents. Reptiles dominated the earth some 225 million years ago, when the first dinosaurs appeared along with the first ancestors of mammals. At the time, the world was literally one world. No separate continents existed, only a great single land mass or island in the midst of a great single ocean, a supercontinent known as Pangea.

But divisive stresses were already at work. Cracks or rifts were appearing deep in the earth, under the land mass and under the ocean. The earth started splitting into some 20 huge blocks of land or plates, along flaw lines possibly built into the planet during its formation 4 to 5 billion years ago. The first plate to break away from the supercontinent of Pangea was India–Antarctica, which formed a single block. By 200 million years ago there were three plates, India and Antarctica having drifted apart, while South America–Africa was attached to North America–Europe–Asia at only one place, Gibraltar. In one of the most recent developments, North America separated from Europe–Asia and attached itself to South America, which had previously separated from Africa. (The process is continuing; within 10 million years or so, parts of Somaliland–Kenya–Tanzania are scheduled to become a huge island, an island continent off mainland Africa, and a piece of southern California including Los Angeles will have broken off and started drifting toward San Francisco.)

These changes had a major impact on all subsequent evolution. The breaking up of Pangea produced an island effect, creating huge blocks of land and isolating large groups of species from one another. Isolation is one of the main factors promoting rapid and diverse evolution. Such conditions favor the appearance of new adaptations and new orders of creatures, since they have a chance to develop on their own in many different environments. Certainly the class of mammals spread widely and produced a rich variety of orders, more than 30 including the primates.

The first mammals, the remote ancestors of whales and tigers and human beings, were beady-eyed, bewhiskered, long-snouted creatures no bigger than your little finger. They may have existed for 130 million years before beginning to increase about 70 million years ago. They scurried and snuffled through fallen leaves and undergrowth for their food, which was chiefly insects. They probably also devoured anything else that was edible. Most seem to have been night feeders who spent the day huddled in nests and burrows. Unimpressive and inconspicuous, they had good reason to walk small. Giants were abroad.

Triceratops, a three-horned plant eater of about 5 tons with a head 7 feet long, and other dinosaurs dominated the earth. Studies by a number of workers including Robert Bakker of Harvard University suggest that not all dinosaurs were the sluggish, lumbering, cold-blooded animals described in textbooks. Some

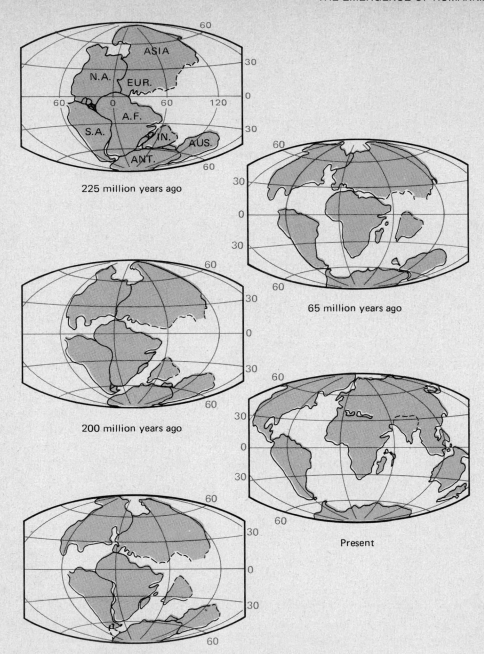

225 million years ago

65 million years ago

200 million years ago

Present

135 million years ago

Breakup of the universal continent, Pangea

of them at least may have been swift-running and warm-blooded, like the reptiles which gave rise to mammals. They vanished some 65 to 70 million years ago, and they were not alone. About half the world's genera, many mollusks and marine reptiles and microscopic plankton, vanished along with the giants.

We do not know why the extinctions occurred. But there are a number of theories. Those who think in terms of sudden catastrophe have a new scenario to replace the old and generally discredited Hollywood–Disney notion of panic-stricken dinosaurs fleeing from exploding volcanoes and inundated en masse in waves of white-hot lava. One currently proposed catastrophe is even more dramatic—an asteroid some 6 miles in diameter and weighing 10 billion tons hitting the good earth head-on, leaving a crater more than 100 miles across, and creating a lethal dust cloud that blotted out the sun for several years. Other investigators, including Bakker, offer a rather more peaceful theory. The dinosaurs faded gradually from the terrestrial scene in relatively quiet times "with the draining of shallow seas on the continents and a lull in mountain-building activity in most parts of the world." Incapable of changing with changing times, they produced fewer and fewer offspring in successive generations. Mammals finally came into their own after more than 100 million years in the shadows.

PROSIMIANS: THE FIRST PRIMATES

The earliest primates, small rodentlike creatures known as prosimians or pre-monkeys, lived in a time of extensive forests. Today's dwindling forests, stretches or patches of woodland among cities and deserts and eroded regions and farms, are mere remnants of what used to be. A belt of almost continuous tropical and subtropical forests thousands of miles wide extended from Seattle and Vancouver to southern Argentina and Chile, from London to Cape Town, from Japan to southern Australia. In the Sahara, woodlands and savannas and lakes existed where desert is now. There were crocodiles, palm trees, and swamps in England, France, and the northwestern United States.

Prosimians had to adapt in the dense foliage and branches and canopies of the forests, and how they did it is of direct concern to humans. Humans are forest creatures to the extent that their basic structure—brain, sense organs, limbs, and reproductive system—evolved in the forests. Later developments generally called for modifications and elaborations of those structures rather than for totally new ones. Preadaptation, the evolution of features in one environment which also happen to be as appropriate or even more so in a future environment, has been important in the shaping of all species, including humans.

Life in the trees offered interesting evolutionary possibilities, largely because it was not a complete exploitation of the third dimension, as is the flight of birds. Flying, which puts a premium on lightness, produced small and highly specialized species. As with flying machines, every fraction of an ounce of weight that could be dispensed with was. One result has been a brain that incorporates, within a small space, circuitry far more compact than anything yet designed by engineers concerned with minicomputers and solid-state physics. It coordinates elaborate nesting and mating behavior, communications, keen eyesight, and swift maneuvers in space. It gained compactness at the price of some flexibility, though—bird behavior tends to have a set, stereotyped quality.

Life on the ground provided another range of opportunities. Proceeding at a different pace, it did not need to be as automatic. It permitted the development of big bodies and big brains and offered the possibility of flexible, adjustable

First mammal: 200-million-year-old insect eater, about the size of a little finger, as reconstructed by Robert Bakker of Harvard University

behavior based to a greater degree on learning. There was time on the ground for watching, pausing, and a measure of preparation. Species could prowl about and lie in wait. Lying in wait demands control and the delay of reflexes and, at the same time, a readiness for swift responses. Inhibition achieved through regulatory centers in the nervous system serves the survival of animals that can bide their time. On the other hand, the challenge and complexity of general navigation, hunting, and escaping were not as great on the ground as in three-dimensional free flight.

Dime-sized jawbone: evidence from southern Africa for first mammal

Mouse lemur: first primate may have looked something like this

Life in the trees combined certain features of earthbound and aerial modes of existence. Species could evolve with brains large enough to handle considerable learning and to accommodate the built-in circuitry for advanced visual powers and sensory and muscular coordination. Even more significant, life in the trees introduced a unique feature, a new and chronic psychological insecurity or uncertainty. The ground is reasonably broad and solid, a dependable platform; the air is consistently insubstantial and must be coped with accordingly. The uncertainty in the trees stemmed from unpredictable changes between solid and aerial states. The environment was full of discontinuities, surprises. From a ground dweller's point of view, such a life would be roughly equivalent to speeding through tall dense grasses without being able to see more than a few feet ahead and suddenly coming upon a gaping hole too wide to cross. Such hazards, numerous and scattered at random over the terrain, require frequent swift decisions about how far to jump and in what direction. To live in trees, with such gaps between branches, is to be confronted continually with emergencies.

In addition, branches are never absolutely reliable as launching or landing sites, or even as resting places. A branch may be firm and solid as the ground itself, or it may sway, give, or break because it is too small or brittle to bear weight. One of the most amazing recoveries from a serious and seemingly unavoidable accident has been described by Ray Carpenter of Pennsylvania State University, a pioneer observer of primate behavior. One day in Thailand he saw a female gibbon swinging out on a limb and preparing for a take-off leap to another tree. At just that instant, the limb snapped off, leaving a stub about 6 inches long. The ape was suspended in space for a split second. "As the limb broke and fell, the gibbon recovered by turning almost in midair and catching the remaining stub of the branch. With extreme rapidity she swung around under and then on top of the [stub] and then, with only a slight loss of time and momentum, jumped outward and downward 30 feet to an adjacent tree top.''

A supreme trapeze artist, the product of hundreds of thousands of generations of evolution, the gibbon had managed to avoid trouble by a swift and superbly executed maneuver. While such agility in three dimensions is typical of many tree dwellers, the prosimians that took up life in the forests about 65 million years ago had some unique traits. Probably, almost from the beginning, they had fingers rather than the claws which are characteristic of such primitive species as the present-day long-tailed tree shrews of Southeast Asia. Tree shrews, incidentally, resemble both rodents and primates, so that paleontologists have shifted them from one order to the other several times. The latest and probably final decision is that they are not primates. Some tree shrews go abroad only at night, and all of them are vicious fighters and voracious eaters, consuming their own weight or more in food each day.

A theory by Matt Cartmill of Duke University accounts for a number of early primate developments. He believes that the hands and feet of prosimians evolved as aids in the food quest—the grasping feet developed before the hands, because ''grasping devices are basically for security'' and in climbing you want to have a footing before reaching upward to higher branches. It was an adaptation that favored ''cautious well-controlled movements in pursuit of prey on slender

Water hole at Amboseli: early humans lived on such savannas

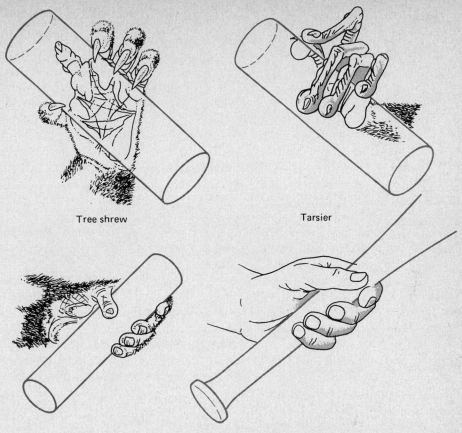

Tree shrew

Tarsier

Macaque

Human

Shrew and primate grips: from claws to human grip with fully opposable thumb

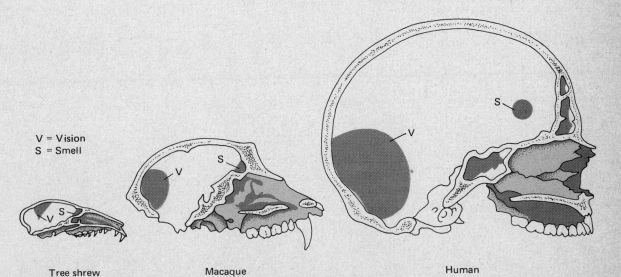

V = Vision
S = Smell

Tree shrew

Macaque

Human

Expansion of visual centers in primate evolution: relative decline of old "smell" brain (shrew brain included for comparison)

supports." The prey consisted primarily of insects, and the slender supports included creeping vines and small branches, which would be encountered while foraging among shrubs, bushes, and trees. As a grasping element, a thumb capable of moving opposite to the other four digits to form a locking grip was useful for predation. By the way, the adaptive value, if any, of fingernails and toenails, the result of rolling claws into flat plates, remains obscure.

Other changes came with the increasing exploitation of insects and forest environments. While preprimate mammals tended to have small eyes on the sides of an extended and tapering snout, in prosimians the eyes became larger, perhaps as an adaptation to let in more light and improve nighttime vision. Furthermore, the eyes moved forward like twin headlights as the snout retreated, which results in better depth perception, an enormous advantage complementing the use of hands and fingers for close manipulative work. Although three-dimensional vision is limited to distances of about 10 feet, it contributes also to accuracy and sure-footedness in leaping from bough to bough.

These and other developments were intimately connected with the development of more elaborate brains. In particular, moving about in a rich three-dimensional arboreal environment favored the expansion of the cerebral cortex, or outer bark of the brain. This structure arose in response to an earlier adventure in evolution, a rudimentary pinhead-sized patch of cells on the brain surfaces of the first creatures that came out of the sea and took up life on land. But with the rise of mammals, the cortex really began coming into its own as an organ for coordinating highly complex behavior, analyzing messages flowing in from the sense organs, and sending messages of its own to the muscles.

Although the prosimian brain was only the size of a pea in a 2-inch skull by this stage of evolution, the cortex had spread like a gray tide over the brain's surface, and it consisted of a thin sheet of millions of nerve cells. One cortical area was located toward the front of the head. The most important part of the so-called smell brain, it had a long and respectable history dating back to creatures which guided themselves primarily with the sense of smell. The newer part of the cortex, located at the back of the brain, had expanded to deal with the increasing amount of visual information involved in the successful performance of arboreal acrobatics.

Improved grasping preceded improved thinking, in line with an ancient evolutionary tradition. Muscle and the special senses such as sight and smell, movement and sensation, are primary, and nerves evolved to serve them. The predominance of the brain and of intelligence, language, and discovery is a very recent development.

MONKEYS APPEAR ON THE SCENE

A major turning point in the history of primates occurred about 30 to 35 million years ago. Prosimians had been highly successful for millions of years, multiplying, spreading widely, and dominating the vast forests of the times. Then they began declining rapidly, probably because of intense competition from other primates, from monkeys and apes. Geological changes that had begun long ago and had helped accelerate the passing of the dinosaurs were approaching a climax.

The weight of sediments accumulating on the floor of the great sea that stretched from Spain to Malaya caused a sagging in some places, an upward buckling in others, and the appearance of island ridges which were to become the Alps. Mountain-building processes elsewhere gave rise to precursors of the Himalayas, Rockies, and Andes. The net effect was a further splitting up of the lands, continuing a process that dates back to the beginning of continental drift. New land masses came into being, creating new environments and zones for new species. A similar fragmenting affected parts of the forest belt; the trees dwindled in various localities, giving way to open grasslands which also offered zones for new species. All the changes offered new evolutionary opportunities. Elephants, deer, rhinoceroses, and other modern mammals appeared together with monkeys and apes.

In this period, the Egyptian coast of the Mediterranean extended some hundred miles farther inland, so that part of the Spain-to-Malaya sea covered areas where Cairo and the Pyramids stand today. Coastal plains and savannas merged with thick and humid tropical forests through which sluggish swamp-lined rivers moved to the shallow sea. The rivers carried the bodies of many animals, and their sands buried the bodies. In relatively recent times lava from the depths of the earth forced its way to the surface, and cracks in the earth's crust formed steep cliffs and ridges.

The region called the Fayum Depression, a wasteland on the eastern edge of the Sahara, is one of the world's richest fossil-primate sites. Between the turn of the century and 1960, collectors had found only 7 pieces of primate remains in the Fayum, but since then about 1000 specimens have been found in expeditions headed by Elwyn Simons, director of the Duke University Primate Center. Among the finds is part of a lower jaw, which may represent the earliest known ancestor of living monkeys, a diagnosis based largely on tooth studies. It had 32 teeth, like most present-day monkeys, as compared with 34 teeth for most prosimians, and a special four-cusp pattern also typical of monkeys (although this pattern is absent from the molar teeth). It was probably about the size of a house cat, which is large enough for a prosimian, although not for a monkey, in accordance with the general trend toward increasing size among primates.

Within 10 million years, monkeys had spread throughout the forests and developed the basis for an entirely different kind of viewing and dealing with the world. Every change was part of a complex of interrelated changes, part of an emerging evolutionary pattern. The sense of smell declined in importance. A generation or two ago, investigators said that this decline was due to the impossibility of making or following clear-cut scent trails in the trees and that arboreal primates could not use the sense of smell to detect sharply defined, coherent, and directional patterns in the broken-up context of leaves and branches and the gaps between them. This turns out not to be the case, since primates and other arboreal species mark out clearly defined territories and trails by urinating at strategic spots, and they distinguish friend from foe by these odors.

In comparison with sight, however, the sense of smell assumed a secondary position. The olfactory nerve, which carries signals from nose to brain, decreases in diameter, a development indicated by comparative measurements of the holes in the nasal part of the skull through which the nerve passes. (This is recapitulated

Fayum Depression, Egypt: searching for fossils

in human growth: some olfactory-nerve cells begin dying off even before birth, and about half of them have died by middle age.)

Hands and sense organs evolved together, each development accelerating the other in an involved feedback relationship. Hands acquired a considerably richer supply of nerve cells and fibers concerned with the sense of touch. Fingers became more and more mobile and capable, not only of moving faster but also of assuming a far greater variety of positions. They were used increasingly for getting food and, even more important, for picking up objects, bringing them closer, and turning them around to examine them from all angles. The ability to manipulate in this way was new in the history of terrestrial life, and it reached a high point in the monkey family.

In fact, from one point of view the monkey's universe was the first to contain full-fledged-objects. The very notion of objects in an environment made up of separate and distinct things, some of which could be moved for one's own purposes, came with the simian way of life, with a superbly developed visual sense and advanced manipulative powers. The world was objectified, or fragmented into things which stood out from the background, as it had never been before. Eyes placed at the sides of the head see landscapes as two-dimensional, flat sheets and respond to motion across the sheets; they are poorly designed to detect what does not move or what moves slowly and directly toward the observer rather than across the field of vision.

A more and more complete picture of reality, a revelation, came with the movement of the eyes from a side to an up-front position and with color vision, which developed to an advanced stage among monkeys. Imagine that you can see things in two dimensions only. You are standing on a plain looking toward a

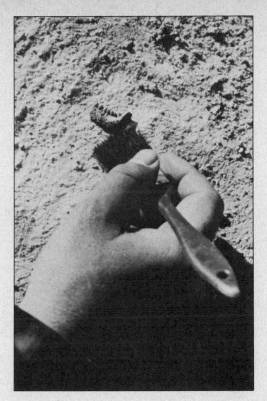

Fayum Depression, Egypt: fossil being prepared for removal

place where animals move among tall grasses and shrubs, and everything has a flat, stage-set quality, some of the animals merging in part with the landscape and others well camouflaged and entirely invisible.

Then, as you watch, you acquire stereoscopic and color vision, and the scene changes. The scene begins to take on depth, slowly at first and more rapidly later, as shapes and shadows seem to move forward and backward and assume their natural places. Animals and objects which were visible but not in full perspective begin to stand out more completely as distinct entities. Animals and objects invisible in two-dimensional, black-and-white viewing become increasingly visible with the appearance of a richer and richer variety of colors, so that even at a distance you get the feeling of almost being among them.

Something like this happened gradually during primate evolution. Color vision may have helped considerably in finding and selecting foods, color patterns serving as clues to the ripeness of fruits, for example, or as markers to identify poisonous plants. Marcel Hladik and Georges Pariente at the National Museum of Natural History in Brunoy, France, are interested in the possibility that color vision played and plays a role in food choice. Studies of different species of monkey sharing the same forest areas in Sri Lanka and Burma indicate that they tend to exploit foods of different colors. Color vision may also have helped in detecting predators and, later, as primates themselves became increasingly predatory, to detect prey.

Our visual apparatus is a direct heritage from life in the trees. It has changed little since the days when monkeys were the earth's highest primates. The structure of the monkey brain reflected the increasing emphasis on vision. The cortex expanded considerably, perhaps about two to three times, burying most of the old smell-brain centers. Although a large part of the expansion involved the visual cortex at the back of the brain, other areas were affected; for example, certain areas concerned with the control of finger movements—a tiny strip of cortex on the right side of the brain controlling the fingers of the left hand and a corresponding left-side strip controlling the right hand. The degree of detail on the map of the cortex depends on the evolutionary status of the species.

Judging by contemporary prosimians, ancestral forms must have operated their fingers en masse, in one gross movement. That is, they could not move fingers individually but moved them all together as a single mechanism. When they curved their hands to make a grip, nerve signals passed from the finger-control maps on the brain's surface to appropriate muscles in the hands, and the muscles contracted. Such generalized action did not require an elaborately organized map and consisted mainly of a general five-finger area. But judging by observations of living species, monkeys evolving 30 million years or more ago moved their fingers far more freely and independently; among other things, they could bring thumb and forefinger together to pick up small objects such as insects and seeds. Their cortical maps evolved accordingly, including, instead of one five-finger area, five separate one-finger areas for more precise digital control.

Generally speaking, the finer the detail, the larger mapping area required, a principle which applies to the wrist, arm, foot, toes, and other parts that became more mobile among monkeys. Furthermore, as the skin incorporated a richer supply of nerve cells registering the sense of touch, touch maps also became larger and more detailed. The expansion of the cortex was the net effect of the expansions of many kinds of maps. It also included large association areas, areas devoted to the swift analysis of information flowing from many sense organs, those recording the state of affairs within as well as outside the body, and from noncortical brain structures such as the cerebellum, attached to the brain stem at the back of the head, which coordinates balance and the tensions of more than 150 pairs of opposing muscles.

The brain, in short, was modified to serve the needs of a new kind of animal. It included structures designed to coordinate at extremely rapid rates the movements of muscles and sets of muscles involved in complex manipulations, climbing, leaping, chasing, and being chased. These structures could take orders from the cortex. But they also had to be capable of automatic operations on their own, because monkeys are restless, agile, and lightweight, and they often move so fast that there is no time for deliberation. Their entire behavior pattern represented and represents a special and highly dynamic adaptation to the forests.

THE DAWN APE

There were other kinds of primates in the trees. The pressure is always on in evolution. Life does not stay put but tends always to become more diverse, to

Aegyptopithecus: representative of earliest known apes (as excavated)

develop new forms adapted to new and varied conditions. Sometimes it is a matter of occupying new places, filling hitherto empty living zones—as, for example, when fish invaded the land more than 350 million years ago or when prosimians and some rodents took to the trees. In other cases it may involve a new time zone, as when certain species of early mammals exploited the possibilities of nocturnal feeding. Another type of adaptation, another major variation of the primate theme, arose at about the same time monkeys appeared on the scene or perhaps somewhat later.

The Fayum Depression has also yielded remains of what Simons calls "the dawn ape," a candidate for the common ancestor of apes and humans, dating back 30 million years. *Aegyptopithecus* was far more monkeylike than apelike. Cat-sized, like some of the early monkeys, it had a tail and walked monkey-style along tree limbs, on all fours. Only its molar teeth bear the mark of the ape, a characteristic five-cusp pattern, the extra cusp presumably used for more effective grinding and crushing. Also, it had a 30-cubic-centimeter brain, about the size of a golf ball and hardly impressive by human standards (the modern brain averaging between 1300 and 1400 cubic centimeters), but still the largest brain for its times—and perhaps representing an early hint of the primate trend toward larger brains.

We know something about the dawn ape's way of life, not only from Fayum fossils but also from studies of the anatomy and behavior of living primates,

Aegyptopithecus: the "dawn ape" (reconstruction)

including between 500 and 600 prosimians representing some 20 species at the Duke Primate Center, the world's only center with such a wide variety of prosimians. Studies show that nocturnal species, species which feed by night and sleep during the day, tend to have large, dark-adapted eyes designed to catch and bring to a focus as much light as possible.

The tarsier, a tiny nocturnal prosimian, has huge eyes for its size. If a human's eyes were proportionately large, they would be about the size of grapefruits. If *Aegyptopithecus* had been nocturnal, its eye sockets would measure an inch or more in diameter, while the actual figure is less than three-quarters of an inch, a significant difference which implies a daytime life style—and that, according to Richard Kay, another Duke investigator, implies a degree of social organization.

The chances of developing complex societies are greater among daytime foragers than among their nocturnal relatives. A wider range of possibilities is open to them under conditions of good visibility. They can evolve an extensive repertoire of visual signals, everything from skin-color changes that convey information about sexual receptivity to threat stares and yawns and submissive grins and crouching, which indicate status and ranking in dominance hierarchies. Kay stresses another clue to the nature of *Aegyptopithecus* troop organization. Males were bigger and heavier than females, perhaps 20 percent more on the average; judging by observations of living prosimians and other living primates, such a difference argues for a troop consisting of more females than males and sexual competition among the males, a state of affairs supported by the fact that *Aegyptopithecus* males had much larger "fighting" canine teeth than females.

Aegyptopithecus has inspired a transient controversy spiced with a certain measure of invective. Kay, Simons, and a number of their associates, including John Fleagle of the State University of New York at Stony Brook, regard the earliest ape as a tree dweller living in forest environments. Adriaan Kortlandt of the University of Amsterdam disagrees, suggesting that the Fayum was almost treeless scrub country and the earliest apes were ground dwellers. Moreover, Kortlandt says, those who believe otherwise are "not familiar with the everyday life of primates in the wild," a remark which annoyed Fleagle, who protested that he had "observed (and filmed) the naturalistic behavior of 31 species (17 genera) of nonhuman primates on three continents."

The arguments pro and con are too detailed to list here. They are presented in the March 1980 and December 1982 issues of the *Journal of Human Evolution,* and are well worth reading. I can summarize them, however, for those who do not have back issues handy—Kortlandt is wrong.

Ancestors of the earliest known members of the ape family evolved a different approach to the forest world, a large part of the difference involving ways of using branches to obtain food. Most of the food in trees hangs at the ends of branches, where it lies beyond the reach of many animals and has the best chances of not being eaten. (This is its evolution for survival.) But apes have an ingenious way of getting at such places. A characteristic posture of an ape in a tree is roughly that of a monkey which has slipped and saved itself by hanging on with its hands.

What represents an emergency for the monkey has become an important form of behavior for the ape. In the structure of their wrists, arms, elbows, and shoulders, they are adapted for hanging suspended full length under branches and for walking on top of them as well, as monkeys generally do. In fact, feeding far out on slender branches is easier for apes than it is for monkeys; monkeys are lighter, but they must go on four feet. Sherwood Washburn of the University of California in Berkeley, a leading investigator of primate evolution and behavior, points out that an ape can distribute its weight strategically among three branches by holding fast with two feet and a hand and reaching out for a succulent piece of fruit with its free hand; "This is a distinctive behavior pattern of apes which can hang comfortably with one arm and do things with the other arm. Only an ape could have any possible reason for designing a bus or a subway train with straps."

But no other ape is as good as the gibbon at swinging along through the trees. Using its powerful arm and shoulder muscles, it can propel itself 30 feet or more in one fluid movement, one of the most spectacular aerial maneuvers among nonflying animals. But in the course of evolving such talents, it had to stay small for the same reason that birds are small, to assure lightness and maximum mobility. (Gibbons are lighter than many monkeys, weighing only about 10 to 15 pounds.)

If all apes had gone the way of the gibbon, today's most advanced primates would be master aerialists rather than intellectuals. Some species followed another line of development, involving an evolutionary compromise between body weight and acrobatic skill. The most obvious advantage of being big was to discourage predators. The smallest prosimians and monkeys are fair game for the most abundant carnivores, small carnivores like snakes and eagles and jack-als. (If they have any choice, large carnivores do not bother to eat such small game.) But only leopards, lions, and other big cats take on orangutans, chimpan-zees, and the largest monkeys such as baboons. And nothing goes after gorillas but humans, who go after everything.

APES IN TROUBLE AND THE EXPANDING BRAIN

There may have been another reason for becoming bigger. The fossil record indicates that apes began spreading widely in Africa about 25 million years ago, reached a peak about 10 million years later with a record number of species, mostly relatively small forms, and then went into a sharp decline. The reasons for the decline are not at all clear. The number of species of arboreal monkeys seems to have increased enormously as the number of ape species decreased, which is somewhat surprising, since apes had better brains. Apparently, superior intelligence is not always enough.

Monkeys may have evolved more advanced social organizations than apes, perhaps because their troops tended to be larger and demanded more discipline and coordination. Another possibility, suggested by Robert Martin of University College, London, is based on observations of present-day species. Monkeys generally use food more efficiently than apes, grinding plant materials more thoroughly and thus permitting more complete digestion. Some species have compartments in their stomachs which are specialized to break down leafy foods; others, like the baboon, aid processes of digestion by softening food in cheek pouches before swallowing it. When competition for food is intense, as it might well have been 15 million years ago in African forests, any advantage in obtaining energy from food pays off handsomely in terms of survival.

So apes may have become bigger in the course of competing with monkeys and in self-defense, a point reinforced by the fact that in Asia, where arboreal monkeys are few, apes have remained relatively small. In Africa, gorillas and their ancestors may have specialized in highland-mountain living, while chim-panzees foraged mainly in lower woodland-orchard regions. Big primates roamed more widely and spent more time on the ground as well as in the trees, partly because they had less to fear and partly because they needed food and had to travel farther for it. (Most monkeys possess home ranges of a fraction of a square mile to 3 square miles or so; apes move over a territory of 15 to 20 square miles, except for the little gibbon, whose range is at the low end of the monkey scale.) In other words, they encountered a wider and more varied environment.

Their evolving anatomy permitted a greater variety of movements. New nerve pathways developed in consequence—the cerebral expression of new pos-sibilities. New cortical pathways appeared. The possible routes along which nerve signals may pass from sense organs to muscles increased enormously. The cortex is in part an organ of analysis, a dense tangle of billions of nerve cells which lies between stimulus mechanisms and response mechanisms, between experience and action. Its complexity reflected the new complexity of the apes' world.

The ape brain responded to a new way of life and expanded with increased body size. As usual, the cortex expanded most. In early prosimians, as in most present-day prosimians, it tended to be a smooth gray sheet, since it lay almost entirely on the surface of the brain. But among apes it became wrinkled and folded primarily because of increasing variety of movement; the increasing role of hand-eye coordination demanded more nerve pathways for the transmission and analysis of information. To meet this demand, natural selection favored the maximum cerebral tissue within the confines of a given skull capacity, so that the cortex spread down into crevices in the underlying white matter, a process already evident among monkeys. Perhaps 25 to 30 percent of the ape cortex is buried in the crevices, as compared with 7 percent for monkeys.

The evolving cortex expressed another important trend, a greater and greater stress on inhibition, on the art of not doing things. This is implicit in the multiplicity of alternatives confronting advanced species. Choosing a course of action demands the ruling out of many possibilities. It also demands time, deliberation, and delay. Life becomes less automatic and depends to a greater extent than ever before on learning, and learning is an inevitable consequence of complexity in evolution. It became increasingly important among higher species whose environments offered a wider and wider range of choices.

Many forces shaped primates during the period from 10 to 70 million years ago. Important parts of the record are still missing; for example, we do not know what happened during the transition time when prosimians evolved into monkeys and apes. The earliest known species, represented by fossils in deposits of the Fayum, had obviously done considerable evolving before that.

But the record is clear on one point. Primates were evolution's most promising way of adapting mammals, inheritors of the earth after the decline of the dinosaurs, to the uncertainties and challenges of life in the trees. Something more happened in the process of adaptation. Some species were equipped not only for forest dwelling but also for a new and bold adventure, the invasion of open country which foreshadowed the coming of humans.

SUMMARY

The human story starts with the appearance of mammals some 200 million years ago, a time ripe for widespread evolutionary change. Pangea, the ancient super-island consisting of the entire earth's land mass locked up into a single block, was beginning to split apart, forming the continents—and creating new environments, new mountains and valleys and rivers, new living spaces for new species.

The first mammals lived in the shadows of giants. Rodentlike creatures measuring no more than a few inches long, they subsisted mainly on a diet of even smaller prey, insects. They lived in the age of reptiles and did not come into their own until the dinosaurs vanished about 70 million years ago. Then they began spreading everywhere. Some of them, the primates, had their homes above ground in the trees, in the vast stretches of almost continuous tropical and subtropical forests that covered most of the earth.

Our earliest primate ancestors, known as prosimians or premonkeys, differed from the original mammalian stock in a number of significant ways. Their eyes had moved up front instead of being located at the sides of the head, providing three-dimensional vision, an important adaptation to an aerial life in the trees and the detection of insects and other small prey. Their brain, although no larger than a pea, included a thin sheet of gray cells at the surface, a cerebral cortex or outer bark, the precursor of nerve centers that would become increasingly important in the development of higher intelligence among higher primates.

When higher primates arose 30 to 35 million years ago, the prosimians vanished from most continental forests. The competition was too intense—for example, from monkeys which were generally larger, swifter, more dexterous, and smarter. Remains of the earliest known ancestors of living monkeys can be distinguished in the fossil record by various features such as teeth with a characteristic four-cusp pattern. The cerebral cortex of the monkey brain was perhaps two to three times larger than that of the prosimians.

Another kind of primate, closer to the human line, appeared at about the same time—and a prototype is recognized in the extinct species known technically as *Aegyptopithecus* and popularly as "the dawn ape." Monkeylike in most respects, it can be distinguished mainly by characteristic five-cusp molar teeth. Species like this gave rise to a wide variety of apes, including today's gibbons, orangutans, gorillas, and chimpanzees.

chapter *2*

First Members of the Human Family

Remember that an important double truth holds for the course of human evolution. Everything we are learning reinforces the notion that the human species is closely related to the apes, even more closely than Darwin himself recognized—that much of human behavior is shaped by our animal heritage. But it is equally and rather more interestingly true that we represent an evolutionary quantum leap, something utterly new under the sun, separated forever by a cultural abyss from other animals. The great problem is to understand how, given the original similarity between apes and the earliest hominids, this enormous difference came into being.

It all started with the breakup of Pangea. There is no telling what sort of animal would be dominating the earth today if the supercontinent had remained in one piece. It might be a 50-ton dinosaur, a tree-dwelling primate, a sophisticated whale or dolphin adapted to the universal sea, or perhaps an unimaginable creature like none of these. The odds are that it would not be a human being. Certainly there would have been no extensive glaciers and no ice ages. The fragmentation of Pangea triggered a chain of events which changed the entire climatic pattern of the planet and had a great deal to do with the emergence of hominids.

THE CIRCUMPOLAR CURRENT AND PRIMATE EVOLUTION

The crucial process was the gradual isolation of Antarctica. A relatively lush temperate land warmed by a steady flow of subtropical waters, it was still attached to Australia and South America some 55 million years ago. It featured green hills and valleys, rain forests of tall beeches and evergreen trees, and a variety of wildlife probably including such primitive mammals as the egg-laying duckbill platypus and the ancestors of modern kangaroos and wombats and bandicoots. What ultimately plunged the continent into its present-day barren deep-freeze was the cutting off of its lifeblood, its warm and warming subtropical current—a process which, according to James Kennett of the University of Rhode Island, occurred in two stages.

First, Australia broke away from Antarctica, opening up a passage for deep and frigid waters streaming in from the Indian Ocean. By 40 million years ago some Antarctica glaciers previously confined to high inland mountain places had advanced to the coastline. The second stage took place 5 to 15 million years later. It completed the isolation of Antarctica, as South America drifted off in the form of a great plate, floating away like a water-lily pad and opening up another stretch of ocean, the Drake Passage. Antarctica was now enclosed in an icy ring, the so-called circumpolar current representing the flow of more than a thousand Amazon Rivers, a clockwise-flowing current of cold water encircling the continent. "You had what amounted to a gigantic, fast-running river," Kennett explains, "a river 300 to 900 miles wide and a mile or two deep, driven by west winds racing at speeds of 100 or more miles an hour."

A further development triggered the final stage. According to one theory, a deep current of relatively warm and salty waters flowed across the North Atlantic into the polar region, raising temperatures about 3 to 4 degrees Fahrenheit, enough to increase precipitation. Ocean waters evaporated and fell back on Antarctica in the form of snow, and the snow remained where it fell season after season, piling up layer upon layer for millions of years. Glaciers in separate mountain-valley systems merged and were covered up with more compressed snows until the entire continent, 5 million square miles, lay buried beneath a sheet of ice more than 3 miles high.

That happened about 15 million years ago, and the whole world felt the chill. Worldwide temperatures fell, perhaps by as much as an average of 5 degrees Fahrenheit or so—and the ice sheet began changing the course of primate evolution, as well as the evolution of a good many other species. A broad forest extended from the west coast of Africa to the East Indies, but not the solid unbroken landscape of former times. Cooler and drier climates brought about a dwindling of the forests. The savanna was on the move. Parts of dark forests were turning into open country exposed to the sun. Grasses spread in a slow tide, displacing dense stands of trees. Dry plains appeared, wide as oceans, particularly on the lee sides of highlands, and interspersed among the plains and solid forests were stretches of open woodland.

LIFE IN A MOSAIC WORLD

New animals appeared in this new patchwork landscape, this mosaic of mixed environments. They were in the process of adapting to the edges of things, to a more varied life in and at the margins of dense forests, in more open woodland terrain, and on wide-open savannas. Among antelopes, for example, forest-adapted species diminished with the diminishing of forests, while species that adapted to the new scheme of things flourished. Among the diminishing species were small duikerlike animals, moving alone or in small groups through forest undergrowth, equipped with hooves splayed for walking on soft ground, and teeth low-crowned for browsing on a selective diet of tender leaves and shoots. Antelopes exploiting more open lands were often bigger, gathered in large herds on more compact hooves designed for moving over hard, sandy, sun-baked ground, and had high-crowned cheek teeth for grazing on coarse, fibrous, and gritty grasses that had to be ground up and crushed before being digested.

Other creatures were adapting to the forest-woodland-savanna complex of environments along with the antelopes, expanding as open country expanded, the forerunners of many latter-day species: ancestral ostriches and aardvarks; slender and short-necked and short-limbed giraffes-in-the-making; miniversions of elephants; relatively puny prehyena species, one of which would become as large as a grizzly bear, with a 3.5-foot skull and canine teeth up to 8 inches long— and later arrivals perhaps, lions and other big cats. Our remote ancestors were there, too, faces in a great crowd, part of the growing menagerie of new species, seeking places in a brave new mosaic world.

Remains of one interesting primate have been found in a churned-up part of East Africa, the region around Fort Ternan in Kenya about 40 miles east of Lake Victoria, where violent movements of the earth have formed a heavily eroded system of hills and valleys. The Leakeys, Mary and the late Louis of the National Museums' Center for Prehistory and Paleontology in Nairobi, dug there for three seasons starting in 1961, on the slope of one of the hills at a site discovered by a local orange grower who was looking for minerals and found fossils instead. An area about the size of a large living room yielded some 12,000 bones representing a wide range of species; half a dozen specimens out of the whole lot, jaw fragments and teeth, represented a primate individual whose place in the evolutionary story has been a matter of debate. Louis Leakey had no doubts, and considered it an unqualified hominid. Today we think differently.

Geologists at the University of California in Berkeley have dated the fossils by dating samples of volcanic rock found with them. Atoms of radioactive potassium in the rock break down spontaneously into the inert gas argon, which is trapped in rock crystals after the lava cools (there is no gas to start with). It accumulates at a steady rate which can be measured with the aid of devices capable of detecting fractions of a billionth of an ounce of material. According to this radioactive-clock technique, which has also been used to date crystalline rocks brought back from the moon, the Fort Ternan primate lived about 14 to 15 million years ago—which, remember, happens to be about the time of formation of the Antarctic ice sheet.

Louis Leakey hailed the primate find as an entirely new species that would help fill "an enormous gap in the panorama . . . of development," the gap between ape and human being. The announcement proved of special interest to Elwyn Simons, then at Yale University, whose digging in the Fayum region of Egypt is only part of a long and continuing investigation of primate evolution. He had spent considerable time studying hundreds of fossils from sites throughout the

Pygmy chimps, mother and child: earliest hominids may have looked something like this

world in an effort to avoid the bad habit which affects paleontologists as well as others—overestimating the importance of one's own work. Since it is generally more satisfying to discover something new than to confirm someone else's discovery, paleontologists often make too much of their finds. The tendency is to interpret small differences in tooth size and other factors, differences that fall within the normal range of individual variation, as signs of a new genus or at least a new species. In an extreme case, North American grizzly bears, now recognized as members of a single species which also includes Old World varieties, were once divided into more than 20 species.

Aware of a similar tendency in primate studies, Simons recognized the Fort Ternan specimen as important but not as a new genus or even a new species. He pointed out that the collection at Yale's Peabody Museum included an upper-jaw fragment and four teeth of the same sort of creature which a native worker had found about three decades earlier in foothills of the Himalayas, in the Siwalik Hills of the Punjab Province of northern India. Furthermore, he had already reconstructed the jaw and estimated the size of a missing canine tooth by the size of the empty socket. This hypothetical tooth turned out to be an almost perfect match with a real canine tooth found at the Kenya site.

Not long after the Fort Ternan announcement, Simons launched a more intensive survey of previously found material stored in museums, and gained as much fresh information as had been obtained during the previous search for new evidence in the field. For one thing, he "discovered" still another specimen of the same hominid species. That is, he reclassified an upper-jaw fragment which had been found in the Punjab hills about half a century ago, kept in the Calcutta collection of the Geological Survey of India ever since, and identified only as belonging to an extinct ape.

At this point the reexamination of old finds took a new turn. Simons noted that the three specimens, one from East Africa and two from India, were all parts of upper jawbones, a curious observation because collectors generally find more lower jawbones, which are denser, more compact, and hence more resistant to decomposition. He began to wonder whether some lower jawbones had actually been found and duly tucked away on museum shelves, but not recognized for what they were. As frequently happens in research, asking the right questions is more than half the battle. No sooner had Simons decided on what to look for than he found it, and in his own museum.

The Yale collection included three specimens, all lower-jaw fragments with molar teeth, all found in India years ago, all classified as a remains of a special genus of fossil ape, and all apparently related to other Indian finds and the Fort Ternan find. In fact, Simons conceived of a broad inclusive category and suggested that all the specimens represent a single species which he called *Ramapithecus punjabicus*. (*Rama* is the name of a hero in Hindu mythology, the incarnation of the deity Vishnu; *pithecus* is Greek for "ape"; and *punjabicus* signifies the part of India where typical material was first discovered.)

Subsequent discoveries and analyses have resulted in a still more inclusive and more diverse category. Further finds in India by David Pilbeam, formerly a colleague of Simons at Yale and now at Harvard, and other investigators indicate the existence of a number of related species which may be referred to collectively as ramapithecines, and lived from about 15 to 8 million years ago. They were widely distributed. Specimens have been collected not only in Africa and India but also in the Jura Mountains of southern Germany, in Turkey, Hungary, and Spain. By far the richest sites exist in the coal beds of Hunan Province, China, which have recently yielded hundreds of specimens, including complete skulls, and promise to yield further material as the search intensifies.

A MATTER OF DIET

Ramapithecine species represent a new development in the primate line. We know them chiefly by their fossil teeth and jaws—big-toothed, especially the molars, probably up to 20 percent bigger than the back teeth of similarly sized apes and with enamel layers as much as two or three times thicker; premolars "molarized" with flatter and more rounded cusps; canines often short and small rather than long and tusk-like, as in many primates; thickened and heavily buttressed mandibles; short-faced (a somewhat reduced muzzle)—a pattern which gibes with the picture of primates adapting to mosaic environments. Subsistence depended increasingly on woodland and savanna fare, including tough-stemmed grasses, roots, tubers, seeds, and nuts as well as softer leaves and fruits. Nowadays investigators generally agree with the conclusion of Milford Wolpoff of the University of Michigan: "The outstanding feature of the remains we now have of the ramapithecines is the masticatory apparatus adapted for a diet requiring powerful or prolonged grinding and crushing, permitting the exploitation of otherwise unusable dietary resources in new ecozones."

This is a rather recent consensus. It represents a change in outlook, a significant break with Darwin, not as far as the fact of the ape-to-human transition is concerned, but with regard to its course and causes. The focus on diet in general and plant eating in particular as central elements in the transition is due in large measure to studies which Clifford Jolly of New York University conducted more than a decade ago. Diet was implicit in Darwin's thinking as well. But he emphasized the hunt, the increasing consumption of red meat on the hoof, and the regular use of weapons to kill and dismember prey, and to provide defense against big cats and other competing carnivores.

Bipedalism, or the fully erect two-footed gait, a uniquely hominid characteristic among primates, arose as the hands were being freed for more effective weapon wielding. The key dental mark of the change was reduction in the size of canine teeth, the idea being that weapons made long slashing-ripping canines unnecessary, and they shrank by default and disuse. At one point the presence of small canines was accepted almost by itself as presumptive evidence for weapon use, and by implication for upright walking and probably for hunting too—in other words, for the entire Darwinian model. Jolly did not accept this model. He saw reduced canines not as a primary change but as an indirect effect of new dietary patterns; his view makes considerable sense in light of mounting evidence that bipedalism was an early development in the hominid story and hunting a relatively late development.

BIOCHEMICAL TIME SCALES

Another deduction from ramapithecine canines involves not their absolute size but the relative size differences between males and females. Richard Kay draws attention to an interesting correlation among living apes. Where a number of males may compete for estrus females, or females may choose males during courtship, male canines may be as much as two or three times larger than female canines, as in the gorilla. On the other hand, male and female canines are practically equal in size among gibbons, where monogamous pair-bonding is the rule.

Ramapithecines are considerably closer to the gibbons on the sex-difference canine scale, male canines being 15 to 20 percent larger than those of the female. Kay uses this finding to infer that they also may have been monogamous. Incidentally, on this scale present-day humans, with a 5-to-10 percent difference, are even more monogamous than ramapithecines, if somewhat less so than gibbons. Incidentally, the latest evidence, including facial specimens from China and

Greece, indicates that *Ramapithecus punjabicus* was a remote ancestor of orangutans rather than hominids.

The common ancestor of ape and hominid may have been a ramapithecine—that is, a primate making the most of life in a mosaic forest-woodland-savanna setting. The question remains as to when the blessed event occurred, the appearance of the first members of the human family, and the answer as usual depends on your criteria, what you will accept as the minimal evidence for a hominid. If it is the complex of tooth-and-jaw features associated with the mosaic-world adaptation, then the event took place 15 or more million years ago. If you require the added criterion of advanced bipedalism, then it could have happened much more recently, perhaps no more than 5 or 6 million years ago, although that remains to be determined.

And it does make a difference. The long time scale suggests a gradual transition from ape to hominid, and is thus in line with the general tendency of evolution to proceed by little steps. It is also rather more satisfying to people who still in their hearts agree with what one Victorian said upon learning about evolution: "Let us hope that it is not true, but if it is let us pray that it will not become generally known." Given such feelings and the weight of the evidence supporting Darwin's views, the next best thing is to push the emergence of our kind as far back as possible into the remote past, the inference being that we have come a long way during the past 15 million years and have clearly left our animal origins far behind.

The long time scale fits in nicely with a notion which was a good deal more popular during nineteenth-century Manifest Destiny times than it is today, after two world wars and a holocaust: the notion that evolution and progress are one and the same thing. According to this point of view, all is well with the world, and the human species is headed for even better things, having surpassed beast and subhuman, savage and barbarian, in its continuing development toward civilized status and beyond. In other words, our prospects have something of the automatic and inevitable to them. We are by our very nature self-improving, on the rise, and can enter the future with anticipation if not complete equanimity.

The short time scale has different implications. For one thing, it raises the serious possibility that the appearance of hominids may have been a sudden phenomenon, that is, sudden in evolutionary terms—say, within half a million years or so, which is very sudden indeed considering all that has happened since. On the philosophical side, it suggests a more immediate scenario. Humans may not be as remote from their prehuman past as one might like to suppose, not quite as remote or different from other primates. Our animal legacy, being more recent, may exert a more appreciable influence on our current behavior, in which case achieving something approaching civilization would demand considerably more than doing what comes naturally.

An important clue to the problem of time scales involves research conducted more than 15 years ago by Vincent Sarich and Allan Wilson of the University of California, Berkeley. They took advantage of the fact that the more closely two species are related, the closer the chemical composition of their blood proteins.

To test the degree of closeness, they mixed albumin proteins extracted from the blood of a number of primates with antibodies made by injecting rabbits with human albumin. The strength of the reaction between the antibodies and the albumin of a particular primate and the completeness of the albumin-antibody union, marked the evolutionary distance between human and primate. In other words, the human antibodies provided a standard of closeness with which various primates could be compared.

For example, the reaction between human antibodies and monkey albumin was about 80 percent complete, indicating an appreciable gap between ourselves and our simian relatives. The antibody reactions against the albumins of the Asian apes, the gibbon and the orangutan, was more complete, 88 and 92 percent respectively. The albumins of the African apes, the chimpanzee and the gorilla, produced by far the strongest and most complete effects, a reaction of more than 96 percent. It turns out that from a biochemical standpoint the chimpanzee and gorilla are actually closer to us on the evolutionary ladder than they are to their Asian cousins.

Similar findings have been reported by other investigators, notably Morris Goodman at Wayne State University in Detroit. Such findings also check with more recent comparisons of human, chimpanzee, and gorilla DNA, which reveal that the species share nearly 99 percent of their hereditary material or, to put it another way, that nearly 99 percent of the genes in a chimpanzee or gorilla ovum are identical to the genes in an ovum that will develop into a human being. The relationship is so close that there has been some speculation as to whether the crossing of a human and a chimpanzee would produce viable offspring. (The general opinion is that fertilization might take place but, because of differences in morphology, or body structure, the fetus would probably abort at about the third or fourth month.)

Another sign of the genetic similarity between humans and African apes, incidentally, comes from studies of their mutual parasites. Certain ultraselective varieties of fleas, lice, and mites live on humans, chimpanzees, and gorillas, but leave gibbons and orangutans strictly alone. Certain organisms causing malaria in humans cannot produce the disease in Asian apes, although the African species may not be immune. It seems that many of the parasites infesting humans, chimpanzees, and gorillas today had a common ancestor which was distinct from the common ancestor of gibbon and orangutan parasites, and a similar family tree applies to the primates themselves.

So the work of Sarich and Wilson was very much in line with other research. They took things a step further, however. They not only measured the distance between ape and human, but also suggested the existence of a protein "clock" for dating the origin of hominids. Assuming that primate proteins, including albumin, change at a steady rate during the course of evolution, they stated that "the time of divergence of Man from the African apes . . . is 5 million years." This announcement reduced previous estimates by 10 or more million years, and ran directly counter to estimates based on the fossil evidence as it was interpreted at the time, in 1967. As a result, the general response ranged from indifference to outright scorn, mainly because of the unfamiliar, unexpected source of the estimate—a biochemistry laboratory rather than a physical-anthropology laboratory, a study of species-specific compounds rather than ancient bones. Among prominent investigators, only Washburn took the announcement seriously.

The situation has changed in many ways since then. As will be pointed out in Chapter 3, the case for a short time scale—that is, shorter than originally believed—is somewhat stronger today. Too many theories have been forwarded, discarded, reforwarded, and modified for anyone to be certain of anything without more fossil evidence. Going on the basis of the evidence currently available, molecular and anatomical, from living as well as fossil primates, Pilbeam believes the first hominids appeared 6 to 10 million years ago, probably in tropical Africa.

LIFE STYLES IN THE BEGINNING

This development, the start of an entirely new direction in terrestrial evolution, may have come at a bad time as far as the apes were concerned. They seem to have been on the way out. The span from 30 to 15 million years ago represented a boom period for them. After that the number of species decreased sharply, species which had committed themselves to life in dwindling forests vanished, and the odds are that changing conditions would have wiped out all the apes even if we had never come along to hasten their passing. In fact, as a final irony, it was probably our appearance that saved the day for the ape family. In a sense, we are the apes that made it, the only breed that adapted successfully, and then some, to the change.

We are not sure about what actually happened. But one reason, according to a recent theory offered by Owen Lovejoy at Kent State University, is that the apes were not reproducing their kind efficiently. An ancient trend in primate and preprimate evolution has been toward more space between births, longer periods of infant dependency, older ages for sexual maturity, and away from litters to single births. Apparently the strategy of putting a premium on one precious infant at a time was not working out, even in relatively safe and abundant forests. Among present-day chimpanzees about half of all newborn infants die before the end of their first year, largely because mothers must range widely to obtain sufficient food, carrying their helpless infants most of the time and subjecting them to risk of accident, disease, and predation.

This ancient and continuing problem was solved by certain ramapithecines at large in African mosaic environments. There must have been intense fighting and violence at times, as different species competed for living space, but all species that survive operate on the principle that survival depends on minimizing conflict, and that is where the second split comes in. Some ramapithecines, the ancestors of contemporary gorillas and chimpanzees, adapted by settling for a predominantly forest life. Others committed themselves to no single environment but exploited the mosaic of environments, concentrating more and more on open country—and evolved into the first hominids.

These apes, perhaps because they were under more pressure for subsistence and from predators, adopted a reproductive strategy new for primates. "They did what mammals often do when offspring survival becomes critical," Lovejoy points out. "They started to call on the services of troop members who were unemployed as far as child rearing is concerned, namely, the males. For most primates, no one knows who the father is and no one cares. Mother does all the work. But in the pinch, selection favors direct participation of the male, thus doubling the number of actively involved parents for each offspring."

It was the beginning of monogamy, the formation of a firm male-female bond, the family circle complete with built-in male. Everyone came out ahead. Father gained a measure of assurance concerning the paternity of mother's offspring. In order not to compete with her for food, he tended to go farther afield and do more and more of the long-distance foraging—which, of course, meant less moving about for her and for the young, more attention and a safer upbringing. Strife within the group, always and still an important problem (probably more important than the danger of predation), declined as males competed less violently and less frequently for receptive females, a change reflected anatomically in smaller canine teeth. Walking upright evolved not as Darwin thought, in the process of freeing the hands for tool making and tool use, but to carry food back to mate and offspring.

Monogamy came early, according to the Lovejoy version of the remote past, and established a solid family unit. In fact, if the strength of the male-female bond is any index, modern humans could be said to represent devolution rather than evolution in at least that respect. Survival then depended on a close-knit male-female relationship to an extent that no longer applies. In a strictly biological way, the until-death-do-us-part notion made a lot more sense when hominids were in the minority and the struggle to survive meant more than it does today, now that we have become, for better or worse, the planet's dominant species and survival may depend on achieving zero population growth.

Lovejoy's scenario emphasizes reproduction as well as the food quest, thus widening the scope for further inquiry and research. But it is not the only scenario, and it has not gone unchallenged. To cite only one example, Wolpoff points out that there is no clinching evidence to support the notion of infrequent births and high infant death rates as a major factor among the earliest hominids or prehominids. It could have been, but we have no proof. An equally plausible and at least as likely an assumption is early death among adults.

A large proportion of our ancestral populations may have been orphaned at an early age. Wolpoff estimates that by the time a first-born offspring reached puberty the odds were about 7 in 10 that its mother would have died. If that was the case, if many offspring were indeed parentless at and before puberty, raising the next generation would be a serious problem, especially when you consider that early hominid offspring were probably among the most slow-maturing of all primates at that time, the least able to cope unaided with their environment.

Monogamy might have helped, of course, increasing the chances that a child would have one surviving parent. But it can be argued that throughout the long course of evolution monogamy has never been part of a natural way of life, at least not until recent times with the rise of urban society. Wolpoff feels that "other mating systems may not only improve provisioning strategy and consequently survivorship, but may also be more in accord with what we know of modern human and chimpanzee societies.'' What we know suggests another possible way of multiplying more efficiently, of saving more offspring.

There are lasting kinship relations among contemporary chimpanzees, one of the most interesting observations of Jane Goodall of the Gombe Stream Research Center on the shores of Lake Tanganyika, Africa. Also, mothers spend most of the time alone with their infants or else in "nursery parties," groups of other nursing mothers. Combining these two features might have led to the establishment of kinship-based nursery parties, among early hominids, related females caring for infants together, so that if a mother dies, her place as child rearer will be taken by a daughter or sister acting as surrogate mother. Under such circumstances a hominid male could take over as provisioner and protector for a group of related females and offspring, resulting in a harem or polygamous situation instead of monogamy.

We can think up other scenarios, other hypotheses about the possible social organizations and life styles of early hominids. But at present we do not know which one of them, or which combination of them, represents what actually happened. Although we may never know for sure, the challenge is to arrive at an explanation that seems to be most plausible in relation to all the other things we learn from studies of fossil bones, biochemistry, and environmental conditions. Certainty may elude us, but uncertainty is only an incentive to conduct more intensive and sophisticated research. In any case, a new kind of evolution had begun with the appearance of primates which were something more than apes and still a good deal less than full-fledged human beings.

PRIMATE TOOL USERS

Pilbeam thinks of the first hominids as creatures which looked more like chimpanzees than any other existing species—but perhaps slenderer and with longer limbs—creatures under increasing pressure to adapt in their own way to a changing forest-woodland-savanna world. The pressure was selective in the sense that it favored certain hitherto unexploited characteristics already present in an incipient or latent form among prehominids; but not previously necessary for survival, so-called preadaptations. One of the most important of such traits was the capacity to use and make tools.

Goodall was the first to observe this activity taking place among wild apes, thereby laying to rest the assumption, held by many investigators from Benjamin Franklin to Friedrich Engels to modern anthropologists, that only the human species was clever enough to do that. Chimpanzees make tools to obtain one of their favorite foods, termites. During most of the year, termite hills are covered with a thick concretelike shell to protect them from birds, monkeys and other termite eaters. But in late October or early November, just before the onset of the rainy season, worker termites drill holes through the shell, destroying all but the outermost fraction of an inch—so that they can emerge quickly when the rains come, begin their nuptial flights, and found new colonies.

While the termite operates by instinct, chimpanzees operate by insight. They have learned when a termite hill is ripe for exploitation and where the

Prehuman tool user: Gombe chimpanzee probing for termites

thinly covered holes are. Then they take a bit of vine or a slender stick, trim it neatly and carefully by pulling off leaves and side shoots, break it off to a length of 6 to 12 inches, and approach the hill. After licking the probe, they poke it through the shell and into one of the holes, and wait a moment or two. When they draw the probe out, termites are clinging to it, and the chimpanzees lick them off as gleefully as children with a lollipop. (Incidentally, Goodall has eaten termites and finds them "rather flavorless.")

In such foraging, chimpanzees may plan ahead. For example, they do not always find a promising termite hill and then proceed to make a probe. They may make the probe first, anticipating a meal of termites, although neither termites nor termite hills are in sight. One chimpanzee carried a suitably prepared stick in its mouth for half a mile, inspected eight hills without finding a good one, and then dropped the tool. So these apes seem to have the basic concept of a tool as something to be shaped for a situation that has not yet materialized, and there is reason to believe that our earliest ancestors were at least as ingenious.

Incidentally, whether or not chimpanzees use tools regularly to get their fill of termites may depend on the nature of their home foraging range. University of Tokyo anthropologists have an observing station south of the Gombe Stream Research Center, also on the shores of Lake Tanganyika, and Toshisada Nishida and Shigeo Uehara frequently see one troop, identified as group B, probing for the insects—while the so-called K group living nearby also consumes large quantities of termites and yet hardly ever uses probes (generally smashing the top off a mound and going after the insects with bare hands). The explanation: the group-B range is drier and more like mosaic open-woodland terrain than the group-K range, and in addition happens to include a tasty termite species which, because of its life style, is particularly vulnerable to the probing approach. So in this case the environmental situation definitely favors tool use.

Of special interest is the Japanese investigators' suggestion that in several cases a B-group chimpanzee may have used a digging stick. They are not sure because they did not actually observe it. They simply noted that the surfaces of several underground termite mounds seem to have been gouged open, and the gouge marks were too deep and too broad to have been made by fingers. The point here is that chimpanzees are perfectly capable of using, and perhaps even making, tools for digging, and there is plenty of food beneath the surface besides termites.

In fact, it has been estimated that any species systematically going after underground plants could double its food supply. Although I know of no reports of chimpanzees observed in the act of digging for such dietary items, savanna-dwelling baboons often do it. During dry periods when sustenance is scarce, they may spend as much as half an hour using their fingers to dig holes in hard ground up to 15 inches deep and 2 feet across to get at succulent roots and tubers, some of which may weigh 40 or more pounds. As far as we know, however, they have never picked up a sharp rock or a stick to make the job easier, just as they never use termite probes, although they relish termites and watch chimpanzees at work. Tool use is apparently beyond them, at least in the wild.

Apes have a different background, a different brain. When chimpanzees and gorillas are aroused, they often grab a nearby stick or branch and swing it about in a vigorous, random flailing motion. Goodall reports that on rare occasions playing with branches may take on a strange, ritualistic quality. A big male chimpanzee may become tremendously excited, break a branch off a tree, brandish it about, and rush down a mountain slope (often on two feet) dragging it behind him. Then he rushes up the slope and repeats the action several times. The significance of this behavior is not known, but sometimes other males will join the fun in a mass "branch-waving display . . . calling, tearing off and waving large branches, hurling themselves to the ground from the trees."

Branch waving plays a less mysterious role when chimpanzees are frustrated or angry with one another, in which case shaking branches is part of displays that may include slapping or stamping on the ground and high-pitched screaming. They have been seen charging at one another with sticks in their hands, and although in general they simply threaten and do not strike, they sometimes use sticks to attack one another. The apes also show a special concern with branches when they climb into a tree where they expect to spend some time, either to build a nest for a night's sleep or to play with other chimpanzees. They move from limb to limb, breaking off dead branches and dropping them to the ground below, as if clearing away deadwood to make the tree a safer place for maneuvering.

Apes thus demonstrate an ample repertoire of object-handling activities and manipulations which they use in different combinations and sequences under different circumstances. If necessary, they could probably use weapons in defense or to drive off prowling carnivores. Although no one has ever reported seeing a real-life encounter between an armed ape and a predator, Adriaan Kortlandt produced an analogous situation experimentally in the Congo. He arranged things so that a stuffed dummy leopard could be pulled out of some shrubbery and into a meadow when a troop of wild chimpanzees was being observed.

Here is how he describes one such confrontation when the stuffed leopard appeared with a chimpanzee-doll victim in its claws: "There was a moment of silence first. Then hell broke loose. There was an uproar of yelling and barking, and most of the apes came forward and began to charge at the leopard. . . . Some charges were made barehanded; in others the assailants broke off a small tree while they ran toward or past the leopard, or brandished a big stick or broken tree in their charge, or threw such a primitive weapon in the general direction of the enemy. . . . Both when attacking and when looking at the leopard, the apes again and again uttered a special blood-curdling type of barking yell."

For all the sound and fury, however, it was more a mobbing type of display calculated to harass the leopard and make it go away than a practiced and skillfully directed use of weapons. Clubs were brandished and hurled, but there were no actual hits. The interesting thing about all this is that the chimpanzees were forest dwellers, and attacks from leopards and other predators tend to be infrequent in forests. In later studies Kortlandt reports far more direct action among wild chimpanzees living in the sort of open savanna country in Guinea, where predators are more common. There was no doubt about the chimpanzees' objectives under these conditions. They beat up the dummy leopard with repeated and well-aimed heavy blows using clubs up to 6 feet long. Goodall has seen chimpanzees throwing stones at baboons; they seldom hit their targets, although some individuals are more accurate than others.

We must be careful about using the chimpanzee as a model for the first hominid, particularly the chimpanzee's tool-wielding capacities. Contemporary chimpanzees, like contemporary humans, are the products of more than 5 million years of evolution from a common ancestral stock. Our earliest relatives may have been somewhat smaller than chimpanzees, and spent more of their time in trees. On the other hand, they were probably climbing down frequently for bush foods, and it is in this context that their special characteristics developed. In any case, life in the trees involved certain preadaptations for the coming of tools.

Part of the story, of course, concerns the sort of dexterity required to grasp and pull branches and to swing along from branch to branch. But the coming of stereoscopic color vision was an even more important factor. As indicated in Chapter 1, objects acquired a new meaning, a new reality, with the appearance of highly advanced visual mechanisms. Objects were viewed in full perspective and tended to leap out of the background more completely and vividly for primates than for other, visually inferior animals. To put it another way, primates acquired richer and more detailed perceptions, and it is precisely this faculty more than anything else which created a heightened awareness of objects as distinct and clear-cut entities capable of serving as display elements and ultimately as tools.

For example, Lovejoy suggests that the need to bring quantities of food back to living places put a premium on some kind of container, perhaps a broad leaf or animal skin or a curved piece of bark, and at the same time on bipedalism for more efficient carrying. Carrying infants may have been as important as carrying food. If bipedalism produced a foot designed primarily for support and with greatly reduced grasping capacities or none at all, infants could no longer have clung as effectively to their mothers and would have to be carried. In fact, the one case that I have seen of upright walking among baboons involved a mother who from time to time was forced to move a few steps on two feet so that she could support her infant.

Bipedalism may have had other advantages. It resulted in a continuous and more panoramic view of the savanna, an increased ability to see things coming and to detect and anticipate danger. Looking ahead from an elevated position may have extended a sense of the future. Furthermore, it may have helped discourage the most dangerous predators, the big cats. A predator knows its prey from repeated encounters and repeated successes and failures in the hunt, and part of that knowledge in early hominid times must have been a firmly ingrained image of prey as four-footed animals. Hominids were unfamiliar in the sense that they did not fit into this age-old pattern. George Schaller of the New York Zoological Society, who has observed tigers in India, lions in Tanzania, and gorillas in the Congo, comments on this possibility:

> Some big cats turn into man eaters, a form of behavior interesting chiefly because it is so rare. They hunt by lying in wait or approaching stealthily and bounding on the victim's back, and they bite at the neck. A human is bipedal and thus does not furnish a good target, a good horizontal plane for the cats to jump on. Perhaps that is one thing that deters them today, and deterred them in the past.

It should be clear that the story of the earliest hominids is still largely speculative. Whether or not they used tools, how they walked, the nature of their social organizations—all this remains a matter for continuing research and debate. We only know that they were coping with changing environments, with a drier mosaic world, that under such conditions tools and two hands would have been helpful and perhaps necessary for survival, and that contemporary apes are clever and have potentials which do not seem to be fully exploited in their forest homelands. There is much plausibility in our arguments, but that is no substitute for solid evidence. So the search continues.

SUMMARY

The formation some 15 million years ago of a vast ice sheet in Antarctica brought about a major change in primate evolution. Acting as a kind of air-conditioning system, the 3-mile-thick sheet lowered worldwide temperatures an average of 5 degrees Fahrenheit, reducing rainfall and resulting in a dwindling of forests. Mixed environments replaced solid stretches of forest, a patchwork landscape of open woodlands and spreading grassy savannas in addition to remnant forests. A complex of new breeds of ape, known as ramapithecines, were among the species adapting to this new mosaic world.

Adapting meant, above all, consuming a wider variety of dietary items, a major change reflected in face, jaw, and tooth alterations—extra-large molars with thick enamel layers, premolars with flatter and more rounded cusps, canines often short and small, heavier mandibles, and a somewhat reduced muzzle. These features add up to more powerful grinding and crushing action, in line with a subsistence pattern that included not only forest fare such as leaves and fruit but tougher open-woodland and savanna fare such as seeds, nuts, roots, and tubers.

One of the ramapithecines may have branched into two lines, becoming the precursor or common ancestor of modern apes and hominids, representatives of the human family. But we are not sure when the split occurred, when the first hominids appeared. Some investigators believe it happened 15 or so million years ago, a viewpoint more widely held during the 1970s than it is today. A later date, based on biochemical as well as fossil studies, is more in keeping with the current consensus of 5 to 10 million years ago (with the odds favoring the more recent end of that range).

There are speculations also about the life style of the earliest hominids. According to one theory, they developed a form of monogamy, long-lasting male-female bonds which provided better care for slow-maturing infants; another theory suggests "harem" societies with a single male taking over as monopolist-protector for a group of females. The notion that early hominids made tools is based on inference only, on observations of chimpanzees making probes to pry termites out of nests and using hammerstones to break open nuts. Bipedalism, or upright walking, may have evolved for more effective carrying of tools, food, and infants.

chapter *3*

The Australopithecines

A major gap exists in the fossil record of the human species, a gap of some 10 million years. The earliest known ramapithecine, the Fort Ternan find, dates back more than 14 million years. After that, as far as the hominid story is concerned, there is hardly anything to go on, only half a robust, age-blackened mandible about 2 inches long with one thick-enameled molar tooth in place, from a site known as Lothagam Hill in Northern Kenya, plus two lone molars, from two other sites in Africa. Not until 3.5 to 3.8 million years ago, as measured by the potassium-argon clock, do we have traces of the first creatures generally accepted as true hominids—and at this stage the evidence is overwhelming.

In 1975 Mary Leakey announced the new finds from northern Tanzania, from a stretch of barren and sun-baked badlands known as Laetoli, a region she and her husband had investigated some four decades previously without finding much of interest. This time she and her associates had better luck. They collected a number of important fossils, jaws and teeth representing at least 11 individuals, hominids without a doubt, and subsequent digging yielded more than a dozen further specimens. But by far the most spectacular discovery was yet to come, a set of footprints preserved by a near-miracle combination of circumstances and recovered by some highly skilled excavating.

THE OLDEST HUMAN FOOTPRINTS

So we have marks made by our remote ancestors, prehumans moving across a grassy savanna. They were walking in the rain, in a light shower, perhaps in late September or early October at the beginning of the wet season. The ground was

Hominid footprints: more than 3.5 million years old

not soaked, not slippery-muddy, just damp enough to hold the pattern of their footprints. Not long after (before heavy downpours or passersby could erase the marks), the sun came out, and, in the words of Tim White of the University of California in Berkeley, one of the team working at Laetoli, baked the footprints "hard as a concrete freeway." Then they were covered and protected by ash falling gently from an active volcano to the east.

Mary Leakey's searchers came across the evidence nearly 4 million years later. The eroding action of wind and rain had exposed only the barest trace of the record, part of a heel impression. The rest of the trail lay buried beneath deposits which had to be removed fleck by fleck with specially designed spatula-like wooden tools, knives, dental picks, and paintbrushes. Grass and acacia-bush roots had to be snipped away without destroying the fragile features; in some cases, the uncovering of a single footprint took two or three days.

The trail consists of more than 70 footprints made by three individuals heading north, one an estimated 4 feet 9 inches tall, another slightly shorter, and a third measuring 4 feet 1 inch; all this information can be deduced from the lengths of the footprints. No one knows whether the tracks were made at the same time, whether the individuals were going some place together. But if they were, they might have been parents and child. No one knows where they were coming from, because whatever remains of the southernmost part of the trail will not be excavated for some years. Where they went will always be a mystery, because the northern part of the trail ends abruptly at the edge of a canyon. We only know they were not alone. The excavated surface also includes tracks of elephants, rhinoceroses, giraffes, hares, ostriches, and a lone beetle.

The extraordinary thing about the footprints, aside from the fact that they endured for us to excavate, is how human they look. Complete with well-developed arch and big toe pointing straight ahead rather than sideways, as among apes, they could have been made by present-day children, and they provide solid evidence for an upright stance and gait. The walkers had progressed toward a human stride, a development involving a series of precisely controlled and timed operations. The stride starts with arch and toes acting as a lever, lifting the body gradually until it rises several inches above its standing height. Measurements show that at this peak point the average person remains in a delicate balance for about two-tenths of a second as the entire weight rests on the foot. Then a final push, which lasts less than half that long, propels the body forward so that the other foot slides in for a smoother rather than a jarring landing.

WALKERS, CLIMBERS, OR BOTH?

Many investigators were surprised that such human-looking tracks appeared so long ago. The assumption was that these early hominids had a fully human gait. In fact, Owen Lovejoy speculates that they walked even better than we do. Their pelvic region may have been in better balance as they shifted their weight from foot to foot, so that they swayed less and used less energy in striding. For a number of reasons, including the widening of the birth canal to permit the delivery of larger-brained infants (Chapter 7), Lovejoy suggests that we might walk somewhat less efficiently and must upon occasion endure low back pain and childbirth difficulties. Other investigators, also assuming a fully human gait, measured the distance between footprints and deduced that the walkers were in no hurry, striding along at a leisurely pace.

William Jungers of the State University of New York at Stony Brook disagrees with Lovejoy. Studies of foot, ankle, hip, and hindlimb bones of early hominids have convinced him that they were not yet fully upright. The hindlimbs in particular point to this conclusion, according to his argument. They are much shorter than ours in proportion to the rest of the body, suggesting a less efficient, bent-knee, bent-hip gait and a naturally shorter stride—and, incidentally, challenging the notion that the Laetoli individuals were strolling. Their short strides may have been the result of anatomy rather than choice.

Also, even though they were apparently capable of upright walking, that by no means implies a full-time ground-dwelling existence. Jack Stern and Randall Susman, also at Stony Brook, have analyzed skeletal remains of our earliest known ancestors of some 4 million years ago and note, among other things, a marked curvature of the toe bones—a feature which suggests climbing and clinging and an appreciable proportion of time spent in the trees. The New York investigators speculate that if and when traces of a still earlier hominid or pre-hominid are discovered, it will be extremely difficult to distinguish the species from "a generalized ape."

The early hominid hand is also interesting. The finger bones are also curved, again suggesting climbing and branch-grasping. But Mary Marzke of Arizona State University notes some human features like the thumb which is more robust than the chimpanzee's thumb and a shortening of the fingers relative to the thumb, indicating "the potential for a firm grip and skillful manipulation of objects between the thumb and the side of the index finger . . . a three-jaw chuck grip"— the preferred grip for tool use and throwing. She suggests that such behavior contributed to evolutionary selection for an upright posture and gait.

SITES IN THE RIFT VALLEY

Human evolution proceeded in a period of major geological unrest, as it still does. Laetoli, the southernmost site in a south-north chain of sites, has yielded specimens of ancient hominid and contemporary species. Less than 20 beeline miles to the north lies the Olduvai Gorge, the main fossil-hunting grounds of the Leakeys for about half a century, and other fossil-rich areas have been tapped near Lake Turkana (formerly Lake Rudolf) in Kenya and still further north in Ethiopia. The chain marks one of the most spectacular series of upheavals in the history of the earth. Southern Africa remained quiet, geologically speaking, having had its period of fire and brimstone some 150 million years ago, when volcanoes erupted everywhere and buried it beneath more than 6000 feet of lava. But trouble came in more northerly regions, where the earth's interior was rumbling and unstable and where there were and still are marks of the continuing splitting up of continents.

Traces of what happened can be seen today in Kenya, less than an hour's drive out of Nairobi, from the edge of a cliff overlooking a valley 50 miles across.

At the other side is another cliff, and in between, on the valley floor 1500 feet below, are signs of a time when the earth tossed like an angry sea. Here the waves and the churnings are frozen in solid rock: Mount Eburru, black and craggy and flat along the top, a volcano that may become active again; Mount Longonot, with its peak hidden in clouds and long sloping terraces formed by ancient lava flows; domes like the tops of bubbles about to burst and craters where bubbles burst ages ago; and Lake Naivasha, with no visible outlet, drained by deep fissures.

This shattered landscape, one result of the drifting of land masses throughout the world, is part of a far-flung fracture zone, the Great Rift Valley, extending about 4000 miles from the Zambezi River area of Mozambique in the south, up through East Africa and Ethiopia, and north as far as the Valley of the Jordan in Israel. The Jordan River, the Dead and Red seas, Lakes Edward and Albert and Tanganyika and Malawi are some of the places where water has filled steep, parallel-sided valleys along the fracture lines of the Rift.

The rifting reached its height between 2 and 5 million years ago. The earth has not yet recovered; it still trembles and heaves in response to forces deep inside. Steam hisses from vents and fissures on the slopes of Mount Eburru, and local farmers use it to cook potatoes and, in condensed form, to water livestock. Some 2000 miles away, in the floor of the Red Sea offshore from Mecca more than a mile deep, are cracks out of which flows water at temperatures as high as 133 degrees Fahrenheit and ten times saltier than the sea water above it, cracks associated with continuing Rift activity. The Rift Valley has been called "an embryonic ocean," because it is widening at a rate of about half an inch a year and eventually part of Africa will break away (the island-continent-to-be mentioned in Chapter 1)—and a vast stretch of waters will roll between.

As regards human evolution, the effects of rifting in Africa are more difficult to specify than the effects of the increase of deserts and semideserts—but the movements of hominids were certainly altered. Traditional migration routes had to be abandoned and new ones established. Before the rifting, Africa was essentially a broad plain created by the erosion of ancient mountain ranges, a plain rising gradually to heights of more than a mile. The top of the rise formed a continental divide running north and south, waters of the Congo Basin draining west off the slopes into the Atlantic Ocean, and other waters draining east into the Indian Ocean. Rivers tended to separate hominid populations from one another, to restrict their movements to zones running east and west. (Apes are afraid of water when they cannot see bottom, and, as a rule, they will not cross a stream that is more than 1 foot deep and more than 20 feet or so wide.)

Rifting changed that pattern. Instead of flowing in a west-to-east direction from the divide to the Indian Ocean, rivers tended to flow north and south along Rift lines and drained internally in Rift valleys. So hominid bands could also move more freely along new north-south migration routes, although the all-important question of timing remains to be answered. Did populations of advanced hominids evolve on the plains of southern Africa and spread to the north when the rivers shifted; did they evolve in East Africa and spread south; or did they evolve in both regions and mingle? Some investigators suspect that post-

Rift migrations were from south to north, but the evidence is so sparse that no one really knows.

The picture becomes even more complicated when one considers that rifting closed certain routes while it opened others. In pre-Rift times a land bridge connected Asia and Africa, so that it was possible to move directly from Egypt or the Sudan or Ethiopia across Saudi Arabia into Iran and India. But that bridge was broken by the formation of the Red Sea. Furthermore, studies of closely related species of trees, mollusks, and birds now separated by 500 miles of hot, dry terrain suggest that the rising of Rift mountains cut West Africa from East Africa and isolated populations that once mingled freely.

Fossil remains like those at Laetoli have turned up more than 1000 miles

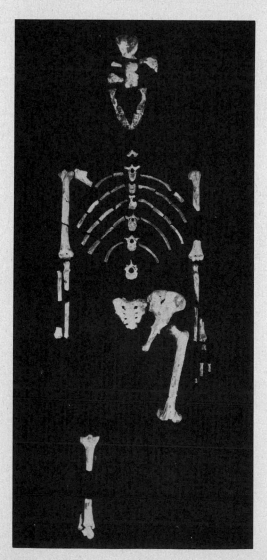

Australopithecus afarensis: Lucy, 3.5 to 4 feet tall

away in the northernmost of the Rift Valley chain of sites, in the "hot spot" near the Red Sea and the Gulf of Aden where the earth is still splitting at the seams. Ethiopia's so-called Afar Triangle has been described as "some 60,000 square miles of volcanic rubble, multi-grabened lowlands and blistering saltflats," a region featuring cliffs more than 2 miles high, deserts below sea level, flat-topped craters, and temperatures which may soar above 130 degrees Fahrenheit. This is where an expedition led by Yves Coppens of the Museum of Man in Paris, Donald Johanson of the Institute of Human Origins in Berkeley, California, and Maurice Taieb of the National Center of Scientific Research, also in Paris, found one of the most highly publicized hominids of recent times—Lucy, an arthritic female represented by some 50 fossil bones (40 percent of her entire skeleton), aged about 20, standing some 3.5 to 4 feet tall, and weighing an estimated 55 pounds. Another find was a "paleograveyard," consisting of at least 13 individuals, 9 adults and 4 juveniles killed en masse as the result of a natural catastrophe, perhaps trapped in quicksand or a flash flood.

AUSTRALOPITHECINES, EARLIEST KNOWN HOMINIDS

In the latest if not the last reconstruction of the genealogy that leads to ourselves, today's hominids, Johanson and Tim White believe that the creatures unearthed at Laetoli and Afar represent a single species, which they have christened *Australopithecus afarensis*, or "southern ape of Afar" (although it could just as well have been *Australopithecus laetolensis*). *Afarensis* was certainly en route to human status, judging by the transitional nature of its hands and feet.

Its teeth are also transitional. For example, in a sample of 18 lower third premolars, 8 have a flattened, clearly defined double-cusp pattern, the rest having either a single cusp or a rudimentary second cusp. An equal number of chimpanzee lower premolars would probably include no more than 2 or 3 double-cusp teeth, while there might be 15 or 16 in an early *Homo* sample. Analysis of other teeth supports the general impression, that, dentally speaking, this was an in-between species. On the basis of extensive studies of australopithecine faces, Yoel Rak of Tel Aviv University suggests that *afarensis* was "not at all far from the generalized pattern of the chimpanzee or the gorilla."

Judging by size, the brain is not impressive, although, as already pointed out, size alone tells us nothing about complexity of cerebral organization. Careful measurements by Ralph Holloway of Columbia University indicate that one of the largest *afarensis* individuals, an adult male, had a cranial capacity of some 500 cubic centimeters, and Lucy's brain was considerably smaller. This puts the species well within the chimpanzee range of about 300 to 500 cubic centimeters. The implication is that, for whatever reasons, locomotion and manipulation came first among our ancestors, and that the high order of intelligence which distinguishes us now was a later development.

According to Johanson and White, the *afarensis* breed split into two major branches perhaps some time after 3 million years ago: a "brain" line, which, despite an uncertain future, has managed to muddle through so far, with us as sole representatives; and a "brawn" line, equipped with increasingly powerful chewing mechanisms, only to become extinct with the past million years or so, perhaps because its members were outclassed and outcompeted by their less specialized and cleverer contemporaries. Of course, this is not the final word on the subject of family trees, and could not possibly be. After all, out of the billions of australopithecines who lived and died over a period of several million years, we have the remains of only 600 or so individuals, a mighty small sample, small enough to guarantee that the years ahead will see important modifications of our current notions. Indeed, the fact that so much can be deduced, that such an elaborate superstructure of theory can be built from so little, is a tribute to human ingenuity.

CONTROVERSY AND THE PILTDOWN HOAX

So it should be no surprise that our concepts are perishable, subject to change without notice. What is rather more surprising is how bitterly some investigators fight for their theories, and against one another. Mary Leakey and her son Richard, for example, disagree with the Johanson-White family tree and believe the Laetoli individuals may be members of the genus *Homo* rather than australopithecines, which is fair enough. But the debate among the parties concerned quickly developed into a feud which has been described, with only slight exaggeration, as "a furor . . . unleashed," "Machiavellian," and a clash between "prima donnas." Although most investigators go about their business with less fuss, fireworks are often par for the course, traditional behavior in the history of research on human evolution.

Controversy and injured feelings surround the man who coined the term *Australopithecus* and first recognized the importance of this genus more than half a century ago, about a generation before the time was ripe for acceptance of his ideas. Remains of these creatures were discovered by Raymond Dart, professor of anatomy at the Medical School of the University of the Witwatersrand in Johannesburg. One afternoon in 1924, he received two crates filled with fossil-bearing rocks collected by a miner at a limestone quarry in the village of Taung ("place of the lion" in Bantu) near the edge of the Kalahari Desert, about 200 miles away. He was expected at a wedding and was wrestling with a stiff winged collar at the time, but he promptly tore if off and began examining the material.

The quarry had already yielded the skull of a baboon, among other things, and there was always the possibility of finding something more interesting—the remains, say, of a more advanced primate. This is precisely what happened. A large block which had been blasted out of a tunnel-like cave in a limestone cliff contained the cast of a large brain case and major parts of a skull and jaw. Dart speculated that "the face might be somewhere there in the block." He went to work with hammer and chisel, and for the most delicate work he used knitting needles.

In a subsequent report he recalls the long process of separating the fossil bones from their matrix of sand and lime:

No diamond cutter ever worked more lovingly or with such care on a priceless jewel—nor, I am sure, with such inadequate tools. But on the seventy-third day,

December 23, the rock parted. I could view the face from the front, although the right side was still imbedded. [The complete extraction process took more than four years.] The creature which had contained this massive brain was no giant anthropoid such as a gorilla. What emerged was a baby's face, an infant with a full set of milk teeth and its permanent molars just in the process of erupting. I doubt if there was any parent prouder of his offspring than I was of my Taung baby on that Christmas.

About five weeks later, the South African anatomist announced his find in a paper published in the British journal *Nature*. The report noted that the canine teeth of the Taung specimen were small and that, in line with Darwin's notions, this implied an upright posture and increasing use of the hands and the probable use of tools and weapons. It also noted the significance of the fact that the specimen had been found in a desertlike site where life must have been difficult and must have required "enhanced cerebral powers" for survival. Dart described the specimen as that of an "ultra-simian and prehuman stock," "a manlike ape," and named it *Australopithecus africanus*, the representative of a new species.

His report also made a strong case for Africa as the continent where humans first appeared, another point emphasized by Darwin. More specifically, it suggested that humans arose in dry and grassy savannas rather than in dense tropical forests, as many anthropologists believed. Food was so abundant in the forests and life so easy that apes faced no major challenges and remained apes. "For the production of man a different apprenticeship was needed to sharpen the wits and quicken the higher manifestations of intellect—a more open veldt country where competition was keener between swiftness and stealth, and where adroitness of thinking and movement played a preponderating role in the preservation of the species."

These general conclusions were not so far from the mark, but they came at the wrong time as far as getting a reasonably unbiased hearing was concerned.

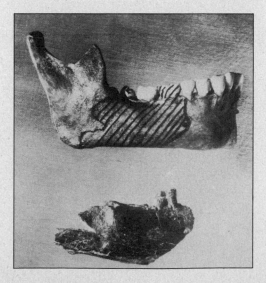

Lothagam fossil: modern jawbone showing location of fragment (top); *Australopithecus* jawbone fragment more than 5 million years old (bottom)

The ramapithecines had not yet been identified, and no one was thinking of an ape, even a clever ape, walking on two feet, much less using and making tools. Much to Dart's dismay, most investigators, including his former teacher, Elliot Smith of University College in London, regarded the Taung baby as an ancestral chimpanzee or gorilla rather than a hominid. They were less interested in discussing its evolutionary status than in noting the fact that it had been found so far south and in a semidesert region.

Furthermore, all eyes were turned to Asia, where the earliest traces of humans known at that time had been found. As far as most anthropologists were concerned, Dart was working in the wrong part of the world. They also felt that he had found the wrong kind of human ancestor. *Australopithecus* had a small brain weighing perhaps a pound, only about a third as much as the modern brain, and that did not fit in with prevailing theory. According to Smith and to most of his colleagues, the brain was a kind of pacemaker in evolution. *Homo* had arisen from a species endowed with big brains to start with, and then had proceeded to take advantage of this favorable beginning by evolving to human status.

There was some evidence for this theory. In 1912 the British lawyer and part-time antiquarian Charles Dawson reported that he had discovered the remains of an individual with a human skull and an ape-like lower jaw in a gravel pit in the village of Piltdown near the eastern coast of England. The face was missing, but the jaw included the first and second molars with a kind of flat wear never seen in apes but quite plausible for humans. Dawson also reported the finding of crude stone tools in the same pit and, next year, a highly worn canine, apelike in form but showing human-type flat wear—plus fragments of a human skull and an ape-like molar found in 1915 in a field 2 miles away. The material puzzled many investigators because the contrast between the humanness of the skull and the apishness of the jaw was so great. But since the remains tended to confirm the prevailing theory of brain as pacemaker, they were generally accepted at face value.

Dart had to wait until the time was ripe for his point of view, until the weight of accumulating evidence and the exposure of the Piltdown specimen as a fraud forced other workers to recognize that his southern apes were actually full-fledged hominids. The first confirmation came a dozen years later from a site nearer home, 30 miles west of Johannesburg. It lies in the Transvaal with its wide, dry, rolling plains, waist-high golden grasses, clumps of trees, and a dryness so prevalent that there is a joke about what to do when you fall into a South African river—you get up and brush yourself off.

The land here, as in many parts of Africa, is itself a prehistoric relic. It must have looked much the same in the time of *Australopithecus* and earlier, though the grasses are less hostile now, lions and other predators having been driven out and confined together with their prey to game reserves far from the city. One of the few wet waterways of the region, the Klip River, winds through a broad valley and rises from a swamp. Not far from the swamp, on a farm known as Sterkfontein, is a kopje, or little hill, with a long history.

The hill is a block of limestone formed some 2 billion years ago when Africa was submerged beneath a shallow sea, covered by more than 6 miles of sediments

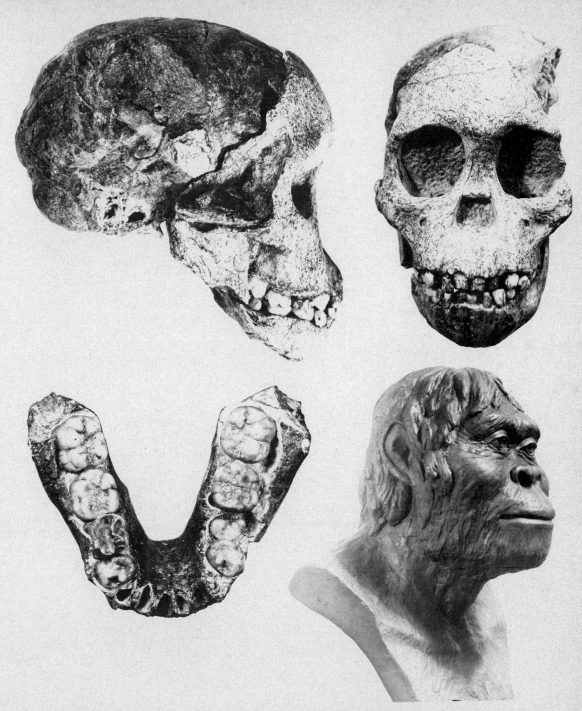

Dart's "Taung baby": the original *Australopithecus* discovery (top, left and right)
Australopithecus africanus: lower jawbone and teeth (bottom, left)
Australopithecus robustus: artist's conception of head (bottom, right)

and lava, and then exposed by erosion. Waters seeped down through cracks in the rock and dissolved away deposits containing calcium, producing small cavities at first and later a system of deep caves. One of the caves still exists; the others have crumbled away. Limestone quarriers moved into its several hundred yards of underground passages more than 60 years ago. There they found fossils, many of which were sold to tourists on Sundays when the mine was open to the public. Also on sale was a guidebook, which included an invitation: "Come to Sterkfontein and find the missing link."

One Sunday visitor took the invitation literally—Robert Broom, a Scottish-born physician and paleontologist who lived in South Africa. Among other things,

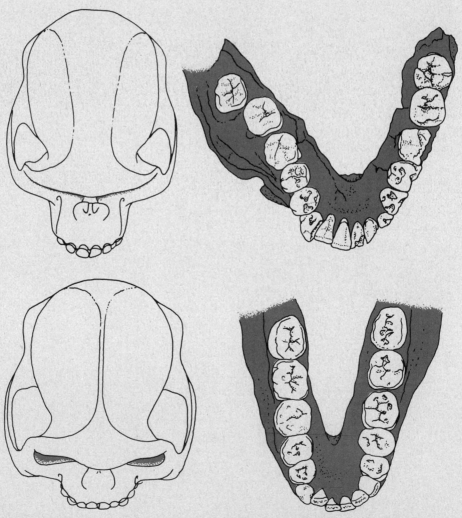

Australopithecus skulls, top view, and jaws: *africanus* (top) and *robustus* (bottom)

Early hominids, as they may have looked 5 or 6 million years ago

he was noted for digging in all weather wearing a formal business suit complete with tie and high starched collar. Broom immediately recognized the significance of Dart's specimen. In 1936 he came to have a look at Sterkfontein, where, as at Taung, baboon fossils had recently been discovered. (As fellow ground dwellers, the ancestors of humans and baboons shared life on the savanna.) It was the start of a second career for the 69-year-old investigator. Within two weeks he found pieces of the skull of an adult *Australopithecus*, and he decided to concentrate on the search for early hominids.

During the succeeding years, Broom and his young assistant John Robinson, now at the University of Wisconsin, conducted excavations at Sterkfontein and two nearby sites. It was slow work. The deposits of sand, earth, bone, and shattered rock containing fossils were cemented together by lime salts and as hard as concrete. The only practical way to get at the material was to drill holes in it and blast it into chunks with sticks of dynamite and later in the laboratory to pick away at the chunks or treat them with mild acid.

The procedure yielded several dozen new specimens, including the remains of another kind of australopithecine, which also walked upright but was considerably more rugged than *Australopithecus africanus*. This brawn-line representative was heavier (100 to perhaps 150 pounds or more as compared with perhaps

Baboons, like early humans, keeping lookout over savanna

75 pounds for *africanus*) and taller (about 4½ to 5 feet as compared to a typical 4 feet). Classified as *Australopithecus robustus*, it had a more massive skull, which, like the gorilla skull, often developed a special bony ridge running along the top from front to back, a crest designed to provide an anchoring platform for massive jaw muscles. Its teeth were formidable tools, pulverizers featuring supermolars as much as twice as large as ours with a grinding surface about as big as a postage stamp. Comparing *africanus* with later, more robust species, Rak sees a tucking-in of the dental arcade and a moving forward of the origin of the chewing muscles to apply better leverage and more power.

Meanwhile, Dart sent students to another rich site he had heard about during the 1920s located about 150 miles away in the Makapan Valley. At one end were red cliffs and a waterfall. It was the valley of a lost world, as wild in appearance today as it was when our ancestors wandered there more than 20,000 centuries ago. Makapan included a network of caves under a domed roof larger than a football field and some ten stories high.

Familiarly, Dart was led to the ruins of this huge cave system in 1945 by a limestone quarry, abandoned long ago, and the finding of a fossil baboon. Two years later, one of his students recovered the back part of an *Australopithecus* skull from the quarry dump. A year after that, it was a lower jaw and, within another four months, part of a face and several other pieces, including parts of a skullcap, upper jaw, and pelvis. The evidence was piling up, and none of it checked with the notion that humans had a big brain from the beginning or with Dawson's increasingly baffling Piltdown remains.

Finally things reached a point where it had to occur to someone that the chances of the Piltdown find's being genuine were somewhat less than the chances of its being a fake. The someone was the late Joseph Weiner of Oxford University. Driving from work one afternoon in 1953 and mulling over the peculiar remains, he suddenly considered deception as a serious possibility. Special studies conducted at Oxford and the British Museum of Natural History quickly removed all doubts. The Piltdown skull fragments belonged to a modern human, the jawbone and teeth to a modern ape. The material had been filed down, chemically treated, and otherwise tampered with to make it appear ancient and authentic. Then someone had planted the doctored specimens in the gravel pit.

The job was done quite skillfully, but not all that skillfully—not so skillfully that the experts could not have spotted fraud readily if they had been forewarned in any way, if they had had any reason to be suspicious. As it was, a number of them could never accept Piltdown; they remained puzzled and unconvinced, but also unsuspicious, until Weiner's fatal analysis. They were unable to conceive of a creature with a skull so human and a jaw so apish. The culprit was probably Dawson himself—a likely candidate who, it recently turned out, had participated in at least one other fraud, the discovery of inscribed bricks supposedly dating back to Roman times but actually fired in the twentieth century.

But the case will never rest there. It has been a field day for investigators dissatisfied with such a simple explanation. Most of them concede that Dawson was actively involved but cannot accept the affair as a straightforward one-person job, and are convinced that Dawson had one or more accomplices. Various speculations based on the study of old letters, the statements of people long since dead, and an involuted body of circumstantial evidence implicate various combinations of half a dozen of Dawson's associates in an elaborate plot. The motive remains anybody's guess—a joke carried too far to confess, an easy way of becoming famous, a compulsive drive to fool and make fools of the experts.

In any case, exposure of the skulduggery at Piltdown alerted anthropologists to the possibility of deception. As a result, the odds against their succumbing to another major hoax are enormous. Furthermore, discrediting once and for all the theory that people were created big-brained and fully human cleared the way for more plausible insights based on a wealth of new evidence.

Investigations still under way, including increasingly intensive analyses of material gathered during the past two decades, are paying off in the form of more sophisticated notions about what happened during the remote prehistoric past. The past may turn out to be rather less remote than most experts suspected, at least if the short time scale is the correct one. There is a feeling, and it is no more than a feeling, that *afarensis* as we know it from specimens nearly 4 million years old lies just on the borderline, a hominid without a great deal to spare. The implication is that any much earlier and much more primitive species would probably be classified as an ape. The nonhominid species preceding *afarensis* may date back only 5 or 6 million years at most. On the other hand, an important factor here is how long it took to develop full bipedalism and a human-type hand, and that has not yet been determined.

THE GENUS *HOMO* APPEARS

Looking in the other direction, to the earliest descendants of *afarensis* rather than to the ancestors, it seems that the transition was gradual. In 1964 Louis Leakey, going on the basis of skull fragments unearthed in the Olduvai Gorge, identified a new species, the first member of the genus *Homo*. *Homo habilis*, "handy" or "skillful" man, is distinguishable chiefly by a brain of about 650 cubic centimeters, some 30 percent more than the maximum acknowledged for *afarensis*, and can be regarded as the first true human being. It is about 1.8 million years old.

Nine years later Richard Leakey, surveying in his region near the eastern shores of Lake Turkana, reported another individual, perhaps a *habilis*, known by its catalog number 1470 and fated to be represented on a 1977 cover of *Time* magazine together with Richard himself, a distinction attained by no other fossil hominid. The saga of 1470 started with the finding of several bone fragments at the bottom of a steep gully, and the sifting of vast quantities of sand to gather several hundred fragments, some as small as rice grains. In a superjigsaw operation, mainly due to the patience and ingenuity of Alan Walker, now at Johns Hopkins University, some 150 of the pieces were fitted and glued together to form a nearly complete skull with an estimated cranial capacity of 775 cubic centimeters, nearly half again as large as a large australopithecine brain and more than half the modern average. The *Time* cover featured a Kenyan volunteer wearing a Hollywood-made rubber-mask-plus-wig based on one version of what 1470 might have looked like.

Less in the limelight but also of some importance are numerous other specimens from Kenya—and from the Omo River Valley of southern Ethiopia, the searching grounds of an expedition organized by Coppens and Clark Howell of the University of California, Berkeley. The valley yielded abundant hominid remains, including more than 200 early teeth, half a dozen lower jawbones, an exceptionally well-preserved forearm bone (the first complete specimen found in Africa), and parts of two skulls, as well as thousands of fossils representing more than 150 nonhuman species.

Work is going on at long-known as well as newer sites. Present-day investigators are revisiting the scenes of some of the most important discoveries of a generation or two ago, and have come up with new material and new interpretations of old material. To cite only one example, Charles Brain of the Transvaal Museum in Pretoria, South Africa, is doing further excavating at a site previously excavated by Broom and Robinson, the Swartkrans Cave, located less than a mile and across a valley from Sterkfontein. His research has been especially important in establishing the place of early hominids among their nonhominid contemporaries, and laying to rest the man-the-mighty-hunter myth.

For a time Swartkrans supported the myth. It contained fossil bones representing some 75 hominids and a mass of bones representing many other spe-

Who killed the Swartkrans hominid?

cies—everything from mice to baboons and other monkeys, hyenas, pigs, por-
cupines, and leopards—some 15,000 specimens (3000 collected by previous
workers, 12,000 by Brain). In the old days, say 20 or so years ago, such associated
remains were generally accepted as evidence that hominids were the killers and
all the other animals their victims. Here is how Dart expressed it: ''Man's
predecessors . . . seized living quarries by violence, battered them to death, tore
apart their broken bodies, dismembered them limb from limb, slaking their rav-
enous thirst with the hot blood of victims and greedily devouring living writhing
flesh.''

OUR REMOTE ANCESTORS—PREY, NOT PREDATORS

This picture, even minus the melodrama, is more science fiction than fact. Although it has been suggested that the main killer in the crowd was *Australopi-*

thecus robustus, whose remains have also been found in the cave, Brain regards most of the bones as the leftovers of meals consumed by ancient carnivores. He believes that hominids contributed very little to the total debris, mainly because only a small proportion of the bones are shattered to bits, the typical hominid practice. Furthermore, the observed finding of many intact lower-limb bones and

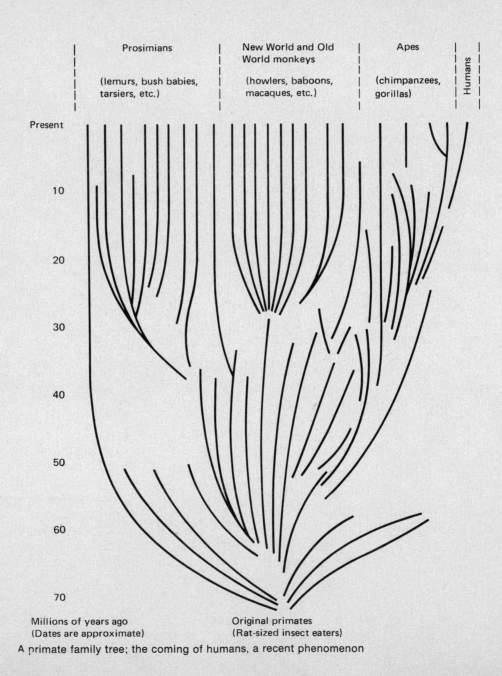

A primate family tree; the coming of humans, a recent phenomenon

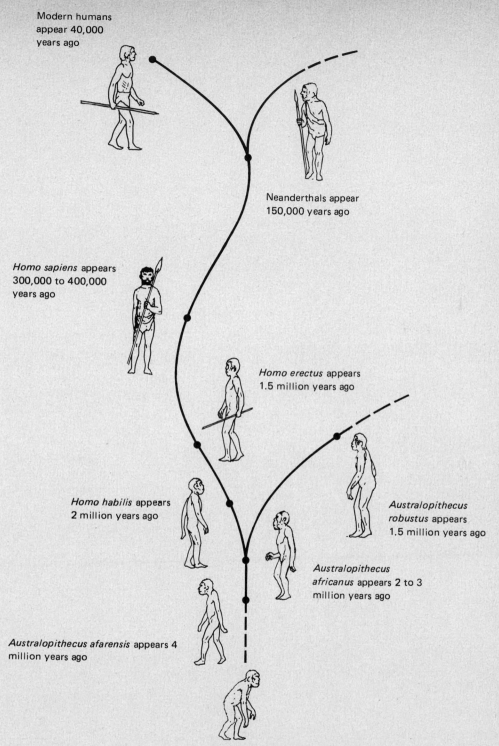

Modern humans appear 40,000 years ago

Neanderthals appear 150,000 years ago

Homo sapiens appears 300,000 to 400,000 years ago

Homo erectus appears 1.5 million years ago

Homo habilis appears 2 million years ago

Australopithecus robustus appears 1.5 million years ago

Australopithecus africanus appears 2 to 3 million years ago

Australopithecus afarensis appears 4 million years ago

Ramapithecines appear 15 million years ago

One version of human evolution; the first hominids appear 6 to 10 million years ago

few vertebrae fits in with what is known of the eating habits of leopards, and indicates that they were effective predators then as now.

Brain has even reconstructed the scene of the action. The Swartkrans Cave apparently had a vertical shaft leading from the surface down into its underground chambers, the sort of location where trees often grow today because of the association of trapped water and springs with caves. Combining this observation with the observation that leopards often drag and carry their prey into trees where they can eat undisturbed by hyenas and other meat-eating competitors, he suggests that prehistoric leopards did the same. According to Brain, the remains of their meals, discarded bones, fell through the shaft into the chambers below and contributed to the accumulating piles of garbage.

He also has an explanation for the presence of most, if not all, of the hominids among the cave's animal fossils. They were prey rather than predators, hunted rather than hunters, victims of leopards along with other sources of meat on the hoof. More than 40 percent of the Swartkrans australopithecines were apparently young, immature individuals, the sort predators most commonly go after. As part of his evidence, Brain offers a piece of the skull of a young *robustus* individual. The skull has two puncture holes in it, 33 millimeters, or about an inch and a third, apart, which is about the distance between the lower canine teeth of an adult leopard.

Caves have long served as centers of activity, dark and dangerous and attractive places. A number of species used different parts of Swartkrans at different times—owls roosting in the cave's twilight zone, bats swarming in by the hundreds to cling and sleep on high walls during the daytime, troops of monkeys asleep near entrances at night, hyenas on the prowl for what the leopards left and for kills of their own. Animals were crossing paths and competing with one another and there, among them all, hominids were also seeking food and shelter, but by no means always and automatically the single dominant species as Dart, and Darwin and others before him, had taken for granted.

Perhaps a warning is in order here. If the record suggests that early hominids were not the mighty killers envisioned in the reports and textbooks of times past, they were not puny nonentities either. It makes sense to take them down a peg or two, and we cannot argue on the basis of sheer plausibility and assume hunting abilities, impressive or otherwise, without solid proof. It might be a mistake, however, to swing too far in the other direction. There is always the risk of overdebunking. Our ancestors were more than fair game for carnivores, not scourges of the animal kingdom, not yet serious threats—but in the process of becoming nuisances and serious competitors. They had not arrived by a long shot, but they were certainly on the make.

SUMMARY

Some spectacular finds have provided insights into hominid origins, and, if we have not yet found the first representative of the human family, we are at least quite close. The most unexpected find comes from northern Tanzania, 70 footprints which look completely human, indicate an upright gait, and date back more than 3.5 million years. On the other hand, an appreciable body of fossil evidence, including some curvature of finger and toe bones, suggests that early hominids were also climbing and spending time in the trees. In short, they were still apelike, so much so, perhaps, that it might be difficult to tell whether fossil remains more than 4 or 5 million years old were those of apes or hominids.

As things stand now, we have fossil remains representing about 600 individuals, including the highly publicized Ethiopian female known as Lucy. Creatures like her presumably made the ancient footprints and belonged to a recently named species *Australopithecus afarensis—Australopithecus* meaning ''southern ape'' (a term suggested during the 1920s, when we knew less about our ancestors), and *afarensis* referring to the Afar region of Ethiopia where Lucy and other important specimens have been found.

Some time after 3 or so million years ago *afarensis* gave rise to two lines: *Australopithecus africanus*, a small species believed to be on the direct line to human beings; and a heavier, massive-toothed species *Australopithecus robustus*, which became extinct about a million years ago. These hominids are known collectively as australopithecines. *Homo habilis*, ''handy'' or ''skillful'' man and the first primate of our genus, appeared about 2 million years ago.

It has taken half a century to arrive at this interpretation of current evidence, and we can expect new evidence and new interpretations in years to come. Investigators of human origins have been and still are prone to bitter arguments. But there seems to be general agreement on at least one major point—we have tended to overrate the hunting abilities of our earliest ancestors. It seems that far from being successful big-game hunters, they were often victims of four-footed killers, more often prey than predators.

chapter 4

Interpreting the Evidence

Our remote ancestors left more than their bones behind, more than the broken and scattered remains of a few individuals preserved ages before the invention of burial and burial rites. We know some of the places where they stopped for a while to eat, to break bones with rocks, perhaps in the shade of trees near lakes and rivers, some of the caves and rock shelters where they slept or were dragged in by predators. They were only part of the savanna scene. They changed the wilderness only slightly, but enough so that signs of the changes have endured in certain places for more than 20,000 centuries.

A LONG SEARCH REWARDED

One of the places is the Olduvai Gorge, where the Leakeys found remains of *Homo habilis* and a great deal more, and it deserves special attention as an unusually rich source of information about the life of early hominids. It is located about 350 miles from Nairobi, past Mount Kilimanjaro and fever trees and herds of antelopes, giraffes, and zebras; past cliffs as high and steep as the Hudson River Palisades; past an extinct Rift Valley volcano, Ngorongoro, with a 12-mile crater; and down the other side into the Serengeti Plain, one of Africa's great game reserves.

Buried deep beneath the Serengeti is another plain. Runoff streams flowing from mountains to the south and east fed a brackish lake 5 to 8 miles across, whose fossil shorelines are visible today as rippled margins of black sand and whose central portion is marked by clays, transformed muds that are still soft. Many generations of hominids foraged near the lake and the streams in a region that had already seen some spectacular geological displays. About half a million years before the coming of our ancestors, the entire top of Ngorongoro, some 2 miles of mountain, had collapsed to form the recent crater.

Later, during hominid times, a peak in the south, probably Mount Olmoti, became violent and expelled a *nuée ardente,* or glowing cloud, a huge mushroom of red hot particles rising thousands of feet high. Then the particles started falling back to earth, rolled down the sides of the mountains at speeds of more than a mile a minute, and buried part of the lake and probably all the lakeside dwellers beneath 15 feet of ash and molten fragments. (In 1902, a similar volcanic avalanche on Martinique Island killed 28,000 persons in the town of Saint-Pierre, the sole survivor being a prisoner locked in an underground dungeon.)

This was the first of a series of major events. Another glowing cloud burst out of the mountain, or perhaps a flow of hot volcanic mud. Then things became relatively peaceful for a time, only to stir up again with the onset of Rift movements in the region and a dramatic change in climate. Before the change, the lake expanded considerably (to about 15 miles across), as indicated not only by the black-sand shorelines but also by the remains of crocodiles, which require an abundance of fish and deep waters. After Rift-produced dislocations and cracks formed in the earth's crust, traces of the lake disappeared and 20-foot deposits of wind-blown sand and volcanic ash marked the prevalence of desert conditions. Then there were alternating wet times, when the lake reappeared, and dry dust-bowl times, when sand dunes dominated the landscape and the lakes shrank or turned into a system of ponds and swamps or vanished entirely.

As a result of all this activity, the original plain, thousands of square miles of fossil wilderness where populations of hominids lived and died, is inaccessible. It lies under some 300 feet of volcanic ash and sand and lake sediments, except for one area in which nature has carried out a large-scale excavation. About 50,000 years ago, rifting produced a series of cliffs over which swift rivers cascaded, gouging down through accumulated deposits and exposing part of the old plain. The torrents created a miniature Grand Canyon, the 25-mile-long Olduvai Gorge.

The gorge has been explored largely through the efforts of Louis Leakey, who was born in Kenya and grew up with his two sisters and brothers as the only European children in a Kikuyu village (his parents were English missionaries). He devoted his life to the discovery and excavation of African sites. From the beginning, he felt there was something special about Olduvai, even before it yielded anything extraordinary. Within a few hours after arriving there for the first time, he found stone tools on the slope of a side gully less than a hundred yards from his tent, and determined on the spot to start a continuing search for remains of the tool makers.

That was in 1931, a generation after a German entomologist discovered Olduvai, when the trip from Nairobi took the better part of a week. Leakey returned again and again over the years, accompanied by Mary Leakey. Season after season, they camped not far from the edge of the gorge, walked down into canyons to explore areas as much as 10 miles away, and shared a water hole with rhinoceroses and other big game. ("We could never get rid of the taste of rhino urine,'' Leakey recalled, ''even after filtering the water through charcoal and boiling it and using it in tea with lemon.'')

They found many concentrations of tools and animal bones and sites to be excavated some time in the future, if sufficient funds and help became available, but few hominid fossils—until one July morning in 1959. The Leakeys were digging on borrowed time, having exhausted current research funds and drawn on the next year's budget. Prehistorians in the field never stop looking, and Mary Leakey happened to be walking along the same slopes where her husband had first found tools nearly three decades before. Only this time a recent rock slide had exposed previously buried deposits. Mary noticed a bit of skull and, stuck firmly in the face of a nearby cliff, two very large and shining brown-black premolar teeth whose size and cusp pattern indicated a primate more advanced than a monkey or ape.

It took the Leakeys 19 days to free the teeth and parts of a fossil palate from the soft rock, sift tons of rubble and dirt, and gather a total of more than 400 bone fragments. Some months later at a scientific meeting, Leakey, whose flair for showmanship matched his flair for anthropology, invited a few privileged colleagues to an advance hotel-room preview of a new find. He opened a black box and removed the beautifully reconstructed skull of an 18-year-old *Australopithecus*, known as ''Zinjanthropus,'' ''the nutcracker man,'' or ''Zinj'' for short. Not long afterward, the National Geographic Society began supporting his work, providing funds for workers and equipment. During the next 13 months, about 7000 tons of dirt and rock were moved, more than twice as much as had been moved during all the previous digging seasons.

Since then, Olduvai has yielded a number of important and surprising discoveries, including the first absolute date for such early sites. The South African sites are believed to be from 1 to more than 3 million years old. But they have not been dated accurately, because the only sufficiently accurate radioactive clock currently available, the potassium-argon technique, depends on the analysis of volcanic materials, and volcanoes were not erupting in South Africa during hominid times. But there are such minerals at Olduvai, and the deposits containing the 1959 skull turned out to be about 1.75 million years old, nearly twice as old as had previously been estimated on the basis of geological studies. The Zinj find made headlines, and brought welcome financial support not only for the Leakeys but for their colleagues throughout the world.

HOW SKILLFUL WERE THE TOOL MAKERS?

Fossils, especially fossil skulls with wide, empty eye sockets, attract publicity, and cash for research. But African sites contain a variety of other clues such as tools and living-floor patterns, patterns in the positions of tools and bones. Even unworked material, rubble or natural chunks of rock which have not been shaped or altered in any way, may have something to tell us about prehistoric activities and purposes. The stones may consist mainly of lava and quartz which do not come from the immediate vicinity of the site itself. At some of the older Olduvai sites such stones, known as manuports, have been carried in from places several miles away, perhaps to hurl at marauding animals or to hold down animal skins. If the hominids slept on the ground rather than in trees, as Leakey believed, stones could have been placed on damp surfaces under straw and grasses to make a dry bedding.

As far as actual tools are concerned, the record illustrates beautifully a phenomenon well known in science and other pursuits—namely, that what we see or fail to see depends to a large extent on our beliefs, on what we are prepared to see. At one time archeologists saw nothing at all. For many years they reported no stone tools from any of the South African sites—hardly a surprise, considering that they were looking hard for fossils and expected no tools. They assumed that tool making was beyond the capacities of relatively small-brained hominids, although the use of ready-made objects, unworked items, was conceded as a possibility.

That position had to be abandoned later when unmistakable tools were repeatedly found together with hominid remains. But the tenor of the times was still grudging, and the effect at every stage of discovery was reluctant retreat, conceding as little as possible. Granted that the hominids made tools, the general expectation seemed to be that they must have been extremely crude tools, and only extremely crude tools were recognized and reported. As a matter of fact, the tools found were so crude that it would be impossible to identify anything much cruder as artifacts.

One of the tools most commonly reported among the rubble was an item known as a "chopper," a cobblestone with flakes knocked off both sides, apparently producing a rough cutting or bashing edge. Such pieces must be studied on a statistical basis to be identified positively as artifacts. If they make up an appreciable proportion of the total stone assemblage, then one can be reasonably sure that they were made by human hands. But the finding of a few flaked stones that could be tools means nothing at all, because they could also have been produced by nature rather than humans.

Desmond Clark has walked along English beaches at Dover and elsewhere, examining stones chipped and broken by pounding surf. Many stones showed the removal of a single flake from one side, and some had flakes removed from both sides or both ends. Revil Mason of the University of the Witwatersrand in Johannesburg once examined 20,000 stones collected at Makapan. A number of them looked as if they were worked tools, but after considering the assemblage as a whole he realized that there was no solid evidence for the presence of artifacts. Nature had done the shaping, such as it was. So categories grade off into one another, and at the most rudimentary level it is not easy to distinguish accidents from artifacts. The late Abbé Henri Breuil, one of France's foremost prehistorians, expressed the problem as follows: "Man made one, God made ten thousand—God help the man who tries to see the one in ten thousand."

Later opinion swung about as far as possible away from the no-tool or crude-tool position. People began seeing more, more than was actually there, as a matter of fact—and it was argued that early hominids had a fairly versatile tool kit. An analysis of items collected from a site at the bottom of the Olduvai Gorge, for example, convinced Mary Leakey that hominids made 11 different kinds of

Revil Mason, University of the Witwatersrand archeologist, took this photograph of the late Brian Maguire trying to identify human-made tools among chipped and broken stones at Makapan *Australopithecus* site

stone implements such as engraving-gouging tools, quadrilateral chisels, large and small scrapers, and other special-purpose tools often crafted ingeniously of difficult-to-work lavas and quartz. "At first the tools were a great shock to us," she commented, "and we had a hard time believing it. After this, it should be easy to believe anything."

That was more than a decade ago. Today interpretation has swung back to a more conservative and, it is hoped, more realistic position, and the general feeling is that Mary Leakey exaggerated a bit. For one thing, the making of stone tools may have been a relatively sudden development. Glynn Isaac of the University of California at Berkeley speaks of a "threshold phenomenon": "There may not have been a long, gradual increase in the complexity of assemblages.

The discovery by hominids that stone fractures in a predictable way when struck may very well have given rise immediately to a wide range of forms.''

He suggests that the flakes struck off selected stones were at least as important as the remaining cores, which may have been used as choppers: ''The untrimmed, thin slivers . . . that comprise the so-called waste material are a far more versatile set of potential utensils than the more massive core-tool set. Even the least highly organized techniques of stone-knapping generate a great array of shapes with variously curved sharp edges, spurs and points. Items can be picked out from among these that will be suitable for use in any task involving such basic operations as cutting, piercing, shaving, whittling, etc. Opportunistic tool production of this kind remained important among some stone-using peoples right down to the ethnographic present.''

WHAT WERE THE TOOLS USED FOR?

Most of the cores or choppers among the older Olduvai collections are about the size of a tennis ball. But there was a much smaller kind. I have seen walnut-sized objects made of greenish lava, and although the hand of early hominids was smaller than ours, it was not so small that such miniature items would fit it comfortably. Perhaps the aim was to obtain extra-small flakes for some special purpose. The pieces must have been held in a three-fingered grip, thumb and ring and index fingers, and used for fine work like extracting fruit or nuts from hard shells, or bits of marrow or meat from bone fragments.

There are also spheroids, rounded and faceted stone balls which were once interpreted as parts of a bola, a weapon consisting of several stones tied to connected ropes or thongs. You swing the stones lasso-style over your head, and then let go at the feet of running animals to trip them up and entangle them for easy killing. A somewhat more plausible explanation is offered by John Whitthoft of the University of Pennsylvania. He believes the spheroids are much-used hammerstones, tools to make tools and ''the basic implements used by Stone Age people.'' The hammerstone often has a roughly spherical shape to start with, and it tends to become increasingly spherical as it is used to knock off more and more flakes, since irregularities and projections generally wear away faster than other surfaces.

Our remote ancestors also used bone tools upon occasion. At Olduvai, for example, there is a flattened and highly polished rib bone of a zebra or some other horselike species; the bones might have been rubbed against hides to make them smoother and more pliable. A similar tool has been found at Sterkfontein. A few years ago Charles Brain, excavating some of the deepest and oldest deposits at Swartkrans, discovered together with *robustus* teeth about half a dozen long-bone tools, pointed splinters which may have served as digging sticks. The area today contains abundant undersurface supplies of a bulb about the size of a small onion and widely eaten by primates, human as well as nonhuman. Baboons use their fingers to get at the bulbs in soft sandy terrain, but they cannot get at plants buried in rocky slopes, and this is where a digging implement would have come in handy for prehistoric hominids.

Recent research makes it possible to deduce the use of materials other than stone and bone, even though no actual traces remain. Tools made of wood have never been found at early hominid sites. Wood is far too perishable for such endurance records, although half-rotted fragments have been unearthed in deposits several hundred thousand years old. Now, however, there is a suggestion of woodworking dating back 1 to 2 million years, at sites in Kenya's Lake Turkana region, where the 1470 skull was found (Chapter 3). By examining the wear on ancient stone tools under scanning electron microscope, which produces detailed three-dimensional images at magnifications of 100 to about 2000 times, and comparing these markings with markings produced experimentally with replicas of ancient tools used to shape known materials, Lawrence Keeley of the University of Illinois at Chicago Circle has identified the telltale signs of worked bone, meat, hides, wood, and grassy plants.

Wood, for example, leaves a distinctive type of polish on the surface of tools made of flint and similar materials. Viewed under the microscope, the surface of such a tool is hardly the smooth, level surface one sees with the naked eye. It has a rugged "microtopography," appearing as peaks and depressions, and when wood is whittled or sawed, the peaks are gradually worn down to produce a typically bright whitish polish. This is precisely the pattern observed by Keeley and Nicholas Toth at Berkeley on the surfaces of tools made of chert (a rock consisting mainly of fine-grained quartz) more than 1.5 million years ago, presumptive evidence for past woodworking, perhaps to make picks or digging sticks.

The firmest date for the appearance of stone tools is about 2 million years ago, a figure based on potassium-argon studies of artifact-bearing deposits in the Omo Valley. Still older tools may have been discovered in the Afar Triangle: choppers and flakes which lie just above volcanic-ash layers dated at 2.8 million years ago, and which may be 2.5 or more million years old. In any case, it is interesting to note that, as far as what we can tell from the archeological record, early hominids seem to have gotten along without relying on stone tools for several million years. If so, one wonders what circumstances, what new environmental and survival demands, ultimately called for this technological advance. In the most general terms, it seems to imply more intensive subsistence strategies, a wider range of food items, some sort of basic dietary change.

ARCHEOLOGY IN ACTION

Insights into such strategies come from places where objects representing hominid activities are not only preserved but preserved in context, in practically the same positions they occupied ages ago. It is nothing new that evidence of this sort may be preserved at more recent sites representing the days of early civilizations with elaborate purposes and elaborate structures to match—palaces, courtyards, and battlements. The ashes of Vesuvius, which buried Pompeii only yesterday, A.D. 79, left houses and floors and furniture and bodies in place. But few investigators suspected that there were living patterns of any sort 2 or more million years before Pompeii, much less that they could possibly have survived ancient eruptions and subsequent geological changes.

Yet such patterns do exist. Objects covered gently by volcanic ash or fine lake sediments may be moved little or not at all, and such living floors survive almost in mint condition like intricate three-dimensional mosaics. Archeologists are always on the lookout for intact sites like the one Clark discovered at Kalambo Falls (see Prologue), places where erosion has laid bare the remains of prehistoric people. Or they may inspect miniature mesas, flat elevated areas surrounded by steep erosion gullies. If tools and fossils are abundant in the gullies, it is possible that the uneroded highlands may include sealed-in layers containing undisturbed traces of the distant past.

Once a first-rate site has been found, the chips are down and investigators are committed to a stretch of hard work which will last for months or years. They apply digging methods developed chiefly during the past century by archeologists in Germany, Denmark, England, and other countries for the excavation of farm and village sites dating back 4000 to 5000 years. A site is approached with almost surgical care and precision. First the outer cover of very recent rock and soil must be removed; pains must be taken to expose but not cut into underlying layers. The soil itself may contain valuable evidence, including tiny plant and bone fragments which can be extracted by flotation techniques (see Prologue). Then the job is to obtain as complete a picture as possible of the patterns preserved in the layers.

Every item, every piece of bone and rock, worked or unworked, and chips

Looking down 300 feet into Olduvai Gorge, where prehumans lived 20,000 centuries ago

and flakes as well as tools, must be exposed and cleaned, but not moved. Every object is part of the pattern of objects; it means nothing by itself. Its position is all-important. The digging rate varies depending on how much material lies on the living floor. But in a reasonably good spot, it may take one person an entire eight-hour day squatting in the dust under a hot sun to excavate 2 or 3 inches deep in an area the size of the top of a bridge table.

Much of the time is spent doing paperwork. Using a steel rule or a yardstick, one measures the position of every single one of several hundred pieces of material, their location on the exposed floor, and the depth beneath the surface of the site where they were found. One may also record the direction in which the piece is pointing, because, among other things, that may help check on whether or not the site has actually been disturbed. If a large proportion of the pieces are pointing in the same general direction, it may mean that they have been moved by flowing water; while unmoved pieces tend to be oriented at random. All this information is written in a notebook together with the number of each piece and its type—that is, whether it is a tool and, if so, what sort of tool. Later the pieces are washed and numbered for identification, with a fine pen and India ink.

As far as the nonspecialist is concerned, the older the site, the less interesting or impressive the objects uncovered. A classical site can yield pottery, necklaces of gold, teacups of iridescent glass, bronze statuettes. Figurines and

Louis and Mary Leakey examining early Olduvai living floor

animals carved out of ivory and delicate engravings on stone may date back 25,000 years or more, and beautifully worked tools of flint and obsidian come from sites many millennia older than that. But to the nonspecialist, pieces collected at the Olduvai sites usually appear to be hardly worth collecting. Archeologists who have brought such material to show to their nonscientific friends are familiar with the disappointment lay people try to conceal by polite interest.

So at the root of discovery, in archeology as well as in every other branch of science, there is tedium—the painstaking and sometimes grim accumulation of data, often under the loneliest of conditions. Tedium is and must be the guts of scientific endeavor because nothing worth coming by comes easily. Each excavator is part of a team that moves tons of dirt and rock. Day after day may be spent brushing dirt off artifacts, measuring their positions, marking them, entering the data in notebooks. The full story, what the site has to tell us about life in prehistoric times, may not be revealed until months or years later, when the data have been analyzed and the maps and charts drawn.

NEW LINES OF RESEARCH

Analysis generally takes at least as long as excavation, and often a great deal longer. Artifacts have always been studied intensively, examined and reexamined in the laboratory and then classified; practically everything measurable has been measured, from size and shape and weight to angle of cutting edge. Current procedures, such as Keeley's painstaking investigations of microscopic wear patterns, are more thorough than ever. The study of bones, once commonly neglected because they were not as "interesting" as tools, has become if anything even more intensive. In fact, an entire branch of research known as "taphonomy" (the word has the same root as "epitaph"—from "taphos," Greek for "tomb") is devoted to analyzing how bones change after an animal dies.

The research of Pat Shipman at Johns Hopkins University illustrates the taphonomist in action. One of the first sites she investigated was Fort Ternan, where Louis Leakey found half a dozen ramapithecine specimens out of 12,000 fossil bones (Chapter 2). Some 3400 of the lot were identifiable as to type of animal, and she examined every one of them. Furthermore, she and several coworkers collected an additional 1500 bones from a previously unexcavated part of the site, plotting the position of each item along with its state of preservation, position, size, type of breakage, and more than two dozen other features.

Among other things, Shipman was able to discount Leakey's explanation for the presence of so many bones in so small an area. He had suggested that it was a place where waters, and occasionally poisonous gases, rose from fissures deep in the earth, and that a sudden release of the gases killed animals coming to drink. If so, if the animals died such a death, all ages should be represented proportionately among the remains, since catastrophe is not selective and affects entire populations en masse. Predators, however, are selective. They tend to go after younger and older animals, more rarely animals in their prime, a bias reflected in Shipman's analysis of the Fort Ternan remains. Also, after being killed, the bones of the prey were concentrated in a clearly defined channel, a sign that they had been swept together there in a kind of mud slide.

Intact sites where bones and stones have not been moved much are ideal for archeological sleuthing. Reading the map of a carefully excavated and exposed site floor is something like trying to decipher a code or translate a manuscript in a strange language; the symbols are the patterns in the positions of the objects. Reading the record is often a matter of interpretation and, as in the case of identifying the earliest stone tools, it often depends on what one is ready to believe.

For example, a site at the bottom of the Olduvai Gorge includes a most interesting feature. The positions of many chunks of unworked and individually undistinguished stones, some of them quite large, were plotted one by one, and only gradually did it become apparent that many of the stones were arranged in a definite pattern. The pattern shows up clearly in a map prepared by Mary Leakey, who learned the art of precise digging from work at a hill-fort site in Devon, England. It consists of piles of rock in a rough semicircle or horseshoe formation around a slightly depressed area.

Incidentally, the site has been dated by the potassium-argon method and also by another radioactive-clock method which depends on the analysis of bits of volcanic glass scattered over the area. The glass contains traces of U-238, the radioactive form of uranium used in early atomic weapons, whose atoms split at a regular rate and leave fission tracks in the glass. The tracks look like tiny grooves under the microscope, and can be counted to provide a measure of time elapsed since the glass cooled. According to results reported by General Electric investigators, the stone semicircle is 2.03 million years old, plus or minus 280,000 years.

The question is—What does the pattern represent? A few years ago the answer was unequivocal. It was definitely something made by hominids, the stones being arranged deliberately, serving perhaps as a windbreak to protect sleepers or as a hunting blind, and that remains a possibility. But now that our ancestors' hunting prowess has been somewhat downgraded, some investigators

Pebble tool and a chopper, first stone tools made by our ancestors

Remains of what may be the oldest known structure, possibly a windbreak, uncovered at foot of Olduvai Gorge

are having second thoughts. Noting that the site is part of a 2-mile stretch where flooding took place, they suggest that the structure may be natural, that the stones might have been moved into the arc pattern by water rather than by hominids, although no one has yet reported a likely explanation of how that might have happened.

In any case, the skepticism indicates a policy of looking more carefully before making inferential leaps, a new rigor in the analysis and interpretation of what the archeologist unearths. Another sign of the times is the current discussion about what was going on at the Zinj site in the Olduvai Gorge. A map of the 3400-square-foot floor shows the positions of more than 4000 artifacts (including 60 tools) and fossils (including at least 16 types of large mammals and 31 hominid specimens), and features an area about 15 feet in diameter, with shattered bone and flaking debris everywhere—and everything, according to one comment, "bash, bash, bash." Outside this area the amount of material drops off sharply until one comes to another area off to one side, a few feet from the main concentration, a place containing larger pieces of bone and a number of unshattered jaws and skulls.

THE QUESTION OF HOME BASES

Until recently this pattern was regarded as a home base pure and simple, a place where people camped and some members of the band remained, including infants and children and elderly caretakers, while others went out to hunt and gather plant foods—a highly human arrangement and a real departure for primates. Monkeys and apes often return at sundown to the same clump of trees they slept in the night before, but at sunrise they all depart and go foraging together and never leave individuals behind to "keep house" while awaiting the return of the breadwinners. So the Zinj site represented a giant step forward, a quantum leap toward home life. The bash-bash-bash area was a dining place where hominids smashed bones to get at the marrow inside; the nearby concentration, including unbroken jaws and skulls, was a garbage heap; and an almost-bare arc-shaped area in between was the location of a windbreak of branches or a barrier to discourage predators.

So much for the old, pre-1982 version of the Zinj site. According to the current version, it is not a home base at all but something rather less advanced. The conclusion is based largely on the work of taphonomists and observations of Eskimo butchering strategies reported by Lewis Binford of the University of New Mexico (Chapter 16). He has frequently commented, pointedly and ungently, on the tendency to overrate our ancestors, to present the early hominid male as a schizoid Jekyll-Hyde character, a combination of killer ape and "a kind of middle-class genteel protohuman who shared his food, took care of his family, and was on his way to being emotionally and intellectually 'human.' "

Taphonomy reveals that hominids and other species, notably carnivores, interacted closely and in complicated ways, as Brain deduced from his research at Swartkrans (Chapter 3). Shipman and Richard Potts of Yale University used the scanning electron microscope to examine thousands of Zinj-floor and other Olduvai fossils and, after a series of extensive studies, learned to distinguish inanimate from animate bone-marking processes. Stone tools leave characteristically long grooves, V-shaped in cross section. Some of the grooves have fine parallel scratches inside, a sign that the tool was used for slicing. Chopping produces V-shaped grooves with tiny fragments of crushed bone at the bottom, while scraping leaves parallel scratches over wide areas of bone and not just in the main grooves.

Metal tools used by archeologists may also leave scratches and grooves. So may the roots of plants which eat into bone surfaces, the abrasive action of windborne or waterborne particles, and bumping against rocks in a fast-flowing stream. But these effects can be distinguished from those produced by stone tools. They can also be distinguished from the gnawing and scratching effects of carnivores, which also produce grooves, but the grooves are generally flat or rounded at the bottom rather than V-shaped and do not show the parallel scratches characteristic of slicing and scraping. Such clues provide basic information for inspecting material found at archeological sites.

As far as the remains on the Zinj floor and several other Olduvai sites are concerned, the transported stones and artifacts, mostly flakes, were clearly brought in by hominids. The bones were heavily worked over, gnawed and broken and otherwise exploited, by hominids or carnivores, and sometimes by both. There are "overlays" on about half a dozen out of some 75 marked specimens—that is, carnivore marks on top of hominid marks, or vice versa. Also, about half the observed hominid marks are on the lower leg bones of antelopes and other bones which have no meat on them, a hint that our ancestors were going after tendons and skins as well as meat, presumably to tie and wrap things and to make containers.

On the basis of such observations, Potts suggests a new scenario to explain the Zinj and several other Olduvai sites. First of all, he emphasizes that these were very dangerous places, located perhaps near or en route to water holes where game was plentiful and carnivores prowled. Understanding his case somewhat, he points out that "hominids would have benefited by not using these sites for sleep or camping." To put it more bluntly, the human family would have been wiped out long ago if our early ancestors had been dim-witted enough to pitch their figurative tents near carnivore hangouts.

Potts believes that Zinj-type floors may represent "cache sites—re-usable, quick-order sites." The idea is that hominids put their bipedalism to good use, and invented a foraging strategy new to the animal kingdom. They brought stones ahead of time to places not far away from certain "hot spots" where animals were frequently killed, anticipating future occasions when meat might become available, and anticipating the need for artifacts already at hand for rapid use. Presumably that would expedite the dismembering of prey, making it possible to transport the spoils rapidly to safer eating places.

INTERPRETING SITE 50

Another focus of hominid-carnivore activity has been discovered about 10 miles inland from the eastern shore of Lake Turkana, in the region explored by Richard Leakey, Isaac, and their associates. Known as Site 50, it is 1.5 to 1.6 million years old, and lies at the bend of a stream in a spot which includes a small promontory extending out into the water. No hominid fossils have been found there, but among the excavated materials are 1405 pieces of worked stone (most of them waste chips and flakes), 59 tools and cores, 76 brought-in cobbles or manuports, and about 2100 pieces of bone. Many items seem to have occupied about the same positions they occupied in prehistoric times. Some of the bone fragments lay close together and were put back together to reconstruct the original bone almost completely (a jigsaw-puzzle operation which is also possible at the Zinj site), and similar reconstructions have been achieved with pieces of worked stone.

As at the Zinj site, carnivores and hominids left their marks among the bones. In a continuing research project similar to that of Shipman and Potts, Henry Bunn of the University of California at Berkeley found typical V-shaped grooves made by stone tools on about a dozen Site 50 bone specimens. He also found a fragment of an antelope limb bone which had probably been smashed with a hammerstone, at least judging by comparison with experimentally broken bones. Another interesting observation involves a site 20 miles to the southwest which has only bones, about 200 fragments, 10 having tool marks. Bunn points out that since the nearest source of stones suitable for tools lies at least 5 to 6 miles away, and since there are no tools or tool-making debris, the hominids may have come with tools already made.

Site 50 may have served hominids as a cache site, a favorite or transient

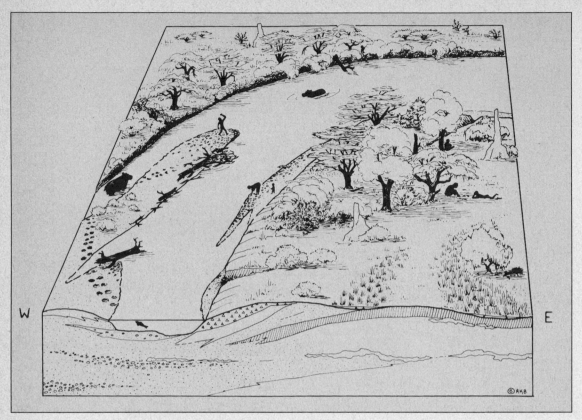

Site 50: early hominid camp (reconstruction)

eating place in the shade of stream-side trees, or a spot used only once. The other site might represent meat come upon suddenly and exploited quickly on the spot. We do not know enough to be sure. Progress in such cases has been mainly negative, in the sense that the odds seem definitely against the home-base notion. Hominids were not yet homebodies maintaining themselves and their families in semipermanent or seasonal locations. They were still more "animal" than that, probably living in troops and on the move like most primates. On the other hand, something uniquely intelligent was going on. Our ancestors were already innovating and actively competing for meat with more highly specialized and longer-established meat eaters.

SUMMARY

The glamor, controversy, and sheer hard work of research on human origins is illustrated by the work of Mary and Louis Leakey and their colleagues over the years. What stands out above all the fanfare is the dedication which kept them returning to the Olduvai Gorge season after season for nearly three decades in a search for elusive remains of early hominids. Success finally came in 1959 with the discovery of an almost complete australopithecine skull—and with the financial support that followed.

Excavations at Olduvai have yielded tons and tons of stone artifacts as well as the remains of extinct species—evidence which, together with similar finds from other African sites, is being studied with increasingly sophisticated techniques. A new technique, microwear analysis, makes it possible to tell from characteristic patterns of grooves and polish on stone-tool surfaces whether the tools were used to work bone, hide, wood, or grassy plants.

Finding artifacts, of course, is not enough in itself. The search is always for very special kinds of sites containing intact living floors, areas which have been preserved in undisturbed or only slightly disturbed condition. Everything is mapped in such sites, the precise positions of every piece of bone and stone, and insights may come from the patterns revealed. A striking example at Olduvai is a rough semicircular wall of rocks which may be the world's earliest known structure, perhaps a windbreak or hunting blind.

Early sites are being looked at more critically than ever. Until recently it had been assumed that sites containing large numbers of artifacts and animal fossils along with hominid remains represented home bases, long-term occupation sites. Now we are not so sure. It remains to be proved whether a given site is a collection of items washed together by stream action, a place frequented mainly by hyenas and other nonhuman carnivores, a caching site where hominids stored stones ahead of time for future use, a simple home base, or some complex combination of these possibilities.

chapter 5

The Food Quest and Meat Eating

To a large extent species are shaped by the food they eat, and the human species was no exception. Changing tooth patterns provide most of the earliest signs of the coming of hominids and prehominids—extra cusps, thick enamel, massive molars and jaws buttressed to support them, all of which affected the contours of the head and face. The changes made for a more effective bite or, rather, for a variety of more effective bites. It was a matter of versatility, of not being committed to a single type of bite, a single chewing style.

An evolutionary niche was open for a primate equipped with an all-purpose, built-in tool kit, a dental apparatus suitable for crushing or grinding or cutting or ripping apart as the situation demanded. The spread of open country, the increasing expanses of woodland and savanna, meant an increase in the number of open-country species. There were specialists, like herbivores and frugivores and insectivores and carnivores, and generalists—omnivores adapting a wide-choice or "broad spectrum" strategy in the food quest. Our ancestors lived as omnivores almost from the beginning, and they seem to have become more and more omnivorous with the passage of time. The challenge is to try to reconstruct their diets and their ways of organizing themselves for subsistence survival.

Everything points to plant foods as the staple in early hominid diets, the most reliable and predictable source of nourishment. That is, everything but direct evidence. We have not recovered samples of fossil plant remains, fossil pollen, or plant opals which may have endured at some sites and would almost certainly help in identifying vegetarian elements consumed. The circumstantial evidence, however, is overwhelming. All 188 living species of primate, ourselves included, rely predominantly on plant foods. So do all recent hunter-gatherers, except those living in Arctic or subarctic climates, and a similar state of affairs very probably existed in the remote past.

Indirect signs indicate what may have been going on, clues in observations of nonhuman primates. If baboons dig with their fingers to get at roots and other abundant underground items, it is probably safe to credit our ancestors with comparable ingenuity, given sufficient subsistence pressure; perhaps they used digging implements of bone or wood like those suspected at Swartkrans and Lake Turkana respectively (see Chapter 4). Lawrence Keeley's microwear studies of Lake Turkana tools 1.5 or more million years old show not only typical wood-working polish but also the sort of extra-shiny polish of "sickle sheen" produced by cutting grasses or reeds. We have no way of telling what the plants were used for, whether for their edible parts, for the manufacture of some kind of container, or for some other purpose. But such observations serve to keep investigators on the alert for further evidence.

THE MEAT-EATING MYSTIQUE

The role of plants in australopithecine and early *Homo* diets has attracted far less attention than the role of meat. As a matter of fact, to read some accounts of the way things were, you would think that meat rather than plants represented the mainstay of early hunter-gatherers. There are a number of interesting reasons for this mistaken impression. For one thing, as indicated in the Prologue, the most widely aired scenarios were written by male investigators who took it for granted that the species became human because of the initiative of males, and that females had little to do with progress besides contributing a steady supply of fresh males.

Over and above the sexism, however, is a more intangible element, a special mystique about meat eating and everything that is assumed to go with it. The chase, the tracking and killing of other species, especially difficult-to-corner and dangerous species, aroused mixed feelings of excitement and success, as if it were a test of daring and virility, and at the same time a vaguely evil, forbidden act. An old tradition has it that meat eating is corrupt, something to be guilty about, a sign of how far we have fallen from a state of original innocence. A seventeenth-century theologian, looking back to a fictitious past, described "those artless Ages, when Mortals lived by plain Nature. . . Men were not carnivores . . . and did not feed upon Flesh, but only upon Fruit and Herbs." More recently William Golding, in *The Inheritors,* a novel about prehistoric life, writes of the guilt people felt as they tore into a doe and of "the rich smell of meat and wickedness."

Chances are exceedingly slim that we will ever learn how early hominids felt about eating meat. But, guilty or not guilty, they certainly ate it. Furthermore, after all has been said about sexism and male egos and psychological associations, there remains a very good reason for devoting special attention to meat eating—it became increasingly important during the course of human evolution, a development unique among primates. We see its beginnings some 1.8 million years ago, not only at the Zinj site and a number of other Olduvai locations, but also near a low hill called Fever Tree Ridge in the Lake Turkana region, where a patch of flakes, several choppers, and hippopotamus bones attests to hominid butchering.

The question is not whether meat eating took place, but what kind of meat eating. Was it hunting or scavenging? Were our ancestors killing in their own right, or living off the kills of other species? Here again what actually happened remains elusive, although considerable information exists about what could and might have happened. There was certainly plenty to be scavenged. Within the boundaries of shrinking twentieth-century game reserves some evidence suggests the extent of prehistoric abundances. George Schaller has estimated that "well over 500,000" wildebeest were living on Tanzania's 10,000-square-mile Serengeti Plain in 1970, with at least as many more zebras, gazelles, impala, buffalo, and so on. Out of that population perhaps 200 to 300 animals die every day of natural causes and disease, and competition for the "free meat" carcasses is intense.

Vultures, among the most voracious of scavengers, are eyes in the sky for other scavengers. Riding rising air masses, thermal updrafts, they wheel and glide at altitudes of 1000 or more feet, scanning the landscape below for dead animals or animals about to die or to be killed—and when they start swooping down, landlubbing meat eaters take heed and head for the spot. "I have seen hyenas reacting to the whistling sound of air through the feathers of an alighting vulture," reports Hans Kruuk of Oxford University, another Serengeti observer, "suddenly waking up, looking at the vulture, then running to the place when it alighted. The mere sight of the large birds plummeting from the sky is enough to bring hyenas galloping miles to a carcass they could not possibly have seen (because it was behind a rise) or smelled (because the wind was in a different direction)."

Lions use the same cues. Looking upward from wide stretches of treeless savanna, they can see vultures at distances of several miles. Jackals and packs of wild dogs often join the race for food, and human scavengers as well. Members of the Gond tribe of north-central India are experienced vulture watchers, running to the death spot and ready to take the spoils even if a tiger has arrived ahead of them. Standing at a safe distance, they wave their hands and shout and toss stones. Generally the tiger, annoyed by the hubbub, leaves within a few minutes, and the tribespeople move in to devour every scrap of meat and break up every bone, leaving only the stomach contents.

It should be pointed out that the food quest, especially the quest for meat, involves a complex of animals watching and being watched by other animals, monitoring the changing scene ceaselessly because survival depends on it. Vultures see everything, and their abundance indicates that in the long run they gain more than they lose. Aloft, they keep a close eye on big cats stalking prey, and glide in swiftly, ready to snatch what they can soon after the final pounce. If they get there first, they swarm like huge maggots over a carcass in a commotion of wings and darting beaks, and may strip away the best meat in a matter of minutes.

As far as hunting is concerned, the big cats and other carnivores have evolved a number of strategies, including group or cooperative hunting. According to Schaller, if a herd of gazelles is grazing on the bank of a stream, lions may attempt a pincer movement, one lion circling to the left, another circling to the right, and perhaps two or three others advancing at a very slow pace frontally—

that is, directly toward the stream and the herd. As you might expect, such strategies pay off. Lions stalking and attacking in groups of two or more have a success rate of more than 30 percent, which means they make a kill about once in every three tries; the batting average for loners is less than half that figure.

Studies of wild dogs hunting on the Serengeti Plain show that they are highly successful, to a large extent because they employ group tactics. Surprisingly, gazelles have not yet learned to flee soon enough from these predators. They start running away only when a dog approaches within 600 to 800 yards, at which distance the dog can generally overtake them. Even so, a gazelle has a reasonably good chance of escaping from a single dog by a series of rapid zigzagging maneuvers, but it rarely escapes from a pack, which can attack from several directions at once.

Packs have also evolved ways of hunting wildebeest calves. The objective is to separate a calf from the herd, which means first of all snarling and snapping and coming as close as possible to the edge of the herd until the bulls charge. The dogs avoid the charge of the large antelopes, and then dart in to harass the mothers and calves in the core of the herd. As long as the core group remains together, the pack can do nothing. But the instant a calf becomes panicky and breaks away, the entire pack goes after it. The mother may try to defend the calf for a while, but she soon runs off to join the stampeding herd.

HUNTING BY NONHUMAN PRIMATES

Early hominids presumably had the capacity for hunting together, at least judging by the behavior of nonhuman primates today. Baboons provide clues to life on dry, wide African savannas. Pioneer studies of these large monkeys have been conducted by Irven DeVore of Harvard, Jean and Stuart Altmann of the University of Chicago, Thelma Rowell of the University of California at Berkeley, and John Crook and the late Ronald Hall of the University of Bristol, England. (Hall died in the summer of 1965, probably of a virus infection, after a laboratory monkey had bitten him on the hand.)

Primates, including baboons, live chiefly on plants. But many of them are omnivorous and, given the right circumstances—the need or the opportunity—eat meat with enthusiasm. In fact, even the browsers and grazers turn to meat if they are sufficiently hungry; there are reports of meat-eating deer. If a baboon happens to come across a nest of fledgling birds or newborn rodents, it may on rare occasions scoop up the contents casually, without breaking stride as it continues foraging. In other words, meat eating may be an act performed in passing.

It may also be considerably more than that, however. A male baboon was observed pursuing a hare in a zigzag, dodging course for about 70 yards in a chase that lasted more than a minute. The hare finally jumped over a log and froze motionless on the other side, only to be picked up and devoured by its pursuer. Such a tactic may fool many predators with poor color vision, and baboons may use it themselves, but in general it plays into the hands of primates, whose highly developed color vision helps them detect motionless objects.

Baboons may become meat eaters on a regular basis, a fact reported by

Carnivorous primate: baboon eating young gazelle

Robert Harding of the University of Pennsylvania and Shirley Strum of the University of California in San Diego. Harding discovered the practice while observing a troop foraging on cattle ranches in Kenya's Rift Valley, about 75 miles northwest of Nairobi. In more than a thousand hours of observation, he saw the baboons kill 47 animals, mainly the infants of Thomson's gazelles (or Tommies) and other antelopes, as well as hares and birds. Killing was predominantly a male activity. There were only 3 to 5 adult males in the 50-member troop, and they accounted for 44 of the 47 victims. Adult females accounted for the other 3 victims. Often the killers walked into a field where gazelles were grazing and deliberately criss-crossed the area in search of helpless infants.

Later observations by Strum revealed important changes in predatory patterns. The number of kills by adult males and females more than doubled, and younger troop members participated in the killing for the first time. Even more significant were the first steps in the development of cooperative hunting, which Strum witnessed one day. An adult male, Rad, went after a herd of Tommies, succeeding only in scattering the group while grabbing at a dodging baby, which he missed. Just as Rad was tiring, Sumner, the troop's oldest male, took over the pursuit, joined by Big Sam, a younger male, and Brutus, a newcomer from another troop. "The chase turned into a relay," Strum reports, "one male running after the baby and another taking over when the first tired. Finally, Big Sam chased the young antelope into Brutus' grasp. The baboons obviously learned from the experience. More and more frequently I witnessed hunting in which one or more baboons chased a Tommy toward another hunter. The success rate climbed sharply.''

Jane Goodall first observed cooperative hunting among Gombe chimpanzees more than two decades ago: "It happened most unexpectedly. . . . The prey, a red colobus monkey, was sitting in a tree when an adolescent male chimpanzee climbed a neighboring tree and remained very still as the monkey looked toward it. A second adolescent male chimpanzee then climbed the tree in which the colobus was sitting, ran quickly along the branch, leapt at the colobus and caught it . . . presumably breaking its neck, as it did not struggle or call out.'' The other chimpanzee, a confederate, then jumped into the tree to share the kill. A second maneuver, observed several years later, started with four male chimpanzees walking at a "silent, purposeful, almost stealthy pace,'' and ended with the screaming and death of a young baboon.

Since then many similar chases have been observed. Geza Teleki of George Washington University reports that "Gombe chimpanzees do pursue various prey species . . . in a coordinated manner, with two to nine adults positioning and repositioning themselves to maintain an enclosure, sometimes for an hour or more, to effectively anticipate and cut off all potential escape routes of the prey.'' He has records of 167 "predatory episodes'' over a 10-year period, with an estimated success rate of about two kills in every five tries.

Predation is not a frequent practice among chimpanzees, but it takes place often enough to indicate the evolutionary possibilities. There seem to be meat-eating crazes, periods when hunting and killing are notably more frequent than usual. One incident may be enough to serve as a trigger. Perhaps there is a brief and bloody encounter with a bush pig or some other small animal, and other members of the troop see and become excited and increasingly aware of meat and potential victims, in a kind of blood-lust atmosphere. A chimpanzee craze may last for a month or more, during which time dominant males generally get the lion's share of the meat, and then the excitement peters out until the next episode.

Systematic running down of small game, and sometimes not so small, may have been one of the early methods of obtaining meat. Many animals are swift runners in relatively short spurts. But then they tend to slow down and stop as if assuming that the spurts would be enough to shake off or discourage pursuers. Even larger animals, such as kangaroos, zebras, and wildebeests, can be run down by species that do not give up after the first dash but follow persistently— for example, wolves, wild dogs, and humans.

One archeologist observed a chase of this sort a few years ago while he was looking for artifacts on a rock-covered hill in Zambia. An African was running at top speed over and around the rocks, chasing a young antelope about the size of a collie dog and losing ground as the antelope darted over a slope and disappeared. But the African kept running and came back a while later with the live animal in his arms. (He took it home, fed it, and later killed it.)

Members of the Poka tribe on the Nyika Plateau of northern Malawi use similar tactics to catch elands and the francolin or spur fowl, a kind of partridge.

Chimpanzees eating meat: note hand outstretched in begging gesture

This bird operates on a built-in, almost automatic schedule consisting of three flights, each flight being shorter than the one before it. When first startled, the francolin flies away swiftly for a hundred yards or so before coming to earth; then, if it is still pursued it soars off for perhaps half that distance. But a third approach will send it flying only a few yards away, and that is the final stage. At this point the bird is through escaping. It freezes, huddling close to the earth wherever it happens to land, in the grass or fully exposed on bare ground—an easy catch for anyone in the vicinity. We do not know whether or not early hominids were clever enough to figure all this out. But quantities of francolin bones are found among their leavings at Olduvai sites.

Louis Leakey studied primitive hunting techniques and tried many of them himself in an effort to understand better and perhaps reconstruct prehistoric strategies. He actually learned an effective way of running down hares:

> When you see a hare, it runs straight away, and you run after it. It has its ears back as it goes, but not all the way back. The ears move all the way back when it's about to dodge, a sharp right or a sharp left. Now if you're right-handed you always dash to the right anticipating a dodge to the right. That means the odds are fifty–fifty, and you should catch half the hares you chase right off. If you've guessed correctly, the hare runs by instinct directly at you and you can scoop it up like fielding a fast grounder. Even if it happens to get past you, you haven't necessarily lost it. Stop and watch. It will probably dart under a bush and freeze there, assuming it has gotten rid of you. Then you can go over and simply pick it up.

Such examples suggest a less apologetic attitude toward human-style locomotion than has been the fashion. Bipedalism used to be regarded as a byproduct, or secondary effect, in the sense that the really important adaptations were supposed to be tool making or the ability to carry things or stand upright in tall prairie grass to watch for predators. The tendency then was to indicate that something may have been lost in the process, because humans are so much slower than other animals. This notion has been challenged by Donald Mitchell of the State University of New York in Buffalo, a marathon runner as well as an anthropologist.

His point is that human locomotion can stand on its own as an adaptation favored by positive selective forces. As far as endurance is concerned, the average person with an average amount of training—and our wilderness-dwelling ancestors were presumably in top-notch condition—can run 7 to 8 miles an hour for 20 to 30 miles, quite a respectable pace.

When it comes to the short run, to chases or escapes, the average human can maintain a speed of more than 15 miles an hour for 200 or more yards. Mitchell points out that this makes evolutionary sense, since the fastest predators are good for no more than a few hundred yards and cannot catch a human who has a reasonable head start. Furthermore, the speed differences between men and women are smallest (perhaps 10 percent or less) for the shortest distances.

ACCENT ON SCAVENGING

The debate continues as to whether early hominids were killers or scavengers. More often than not, it boils down to a debate of the heart rather than of the head, in the sense that the debaters are talking about something else, in effect expressing their opinion about the basic nature of the human species. If you tend to be romantic, optimistically inclined, and have a fairly high regard for the species, and for males in particular, you will probably picture and argue for early humans as hunters primarily. On the other hand, if you happen to be a bit more hard-headed, less inclined to see a rosy future, and sick and tired of unproved scenarios, you will lean in the other direction and put our ancestors in a more humble position among their fellow beasts. So the extremes in the debate are early big-game hunting versus predominant scavenging, and low-grade scavenging at that—primarily, the extraction of marrow from bones the scavengers left.

Actually, there is no need to take sides or even to enter the debate. In the absence of solid evidence either way, one can go on the assumption that both scavenging and hunting were involved. Most scavengers are also hunters. Hyenas, for all the unfavorable publicity they receive, hunt more than they scavenge. And hunters also scavenge. Lions, for all their reputation as killers, frequently go after the kills of other carnivores, notably hyenas. The odds are that early hominids at Olduvai, Lake Turkana, and other African sites were also opportunists and took everything they could get by any means, that they obtained most of their big-game meat by scavenging and most of their small-game meat by hunting. As a sheer guess, I would venture that most of their overall supply, measured in pounds, came from scavenged big game, perhaps from animals weighing 200 pounds and up.

In any case, they were certainly behaving like no primates today. We can imagine them, as scavengers, coming from a distance to a death site along with a variety of other vulture watchers, beating or scaring off as many of their competitors as possible, and presumably carrying chunks of meat into trees or shelters high on the sides of rocky slopes where they could eat in peace. They had many good reasons to fear lions and other large predators. But if they were indeed reasonably successful scavengers, they also benefited from the killing prowess of their competitors.

Schaller and Gordon Lowther of York University, Toronto, once spent a week camping by a river bank in the woodlands of the Serengeti Plain, about 70 miles west of the Olduvai Gorge. The investigators did some experimental scavenging, five days on foot and two days by car, with reasonable success. They came across four freshly abandoned lion kills which would have provided prehistoric people with brains and bone marrow. One day, guided to a thicket by circling vultures, they found a bull buffalo that had died of disease or old age; the vultures and hyenas had been at work, but more than 500 pounds of meat and skin still remained. Another source of scavenged meat would be the prey of wild dogs, highly effective hunters that are surprisingly easy to chase away from their kills.

As far as doing their own killing was concerned, the investigators counted it a kill if they could run down or stalk an animal and come close enough to hold on to its tail. This happened on two occasions. Once Schaller saw a zebra foal standing alone, gave chase, and after a brief sprint, caught up with it and grasped it firmly by mane and tail. Judging by its awkward gait while trying to escape, and by the fact that it had been abandoned, the foal was suffering from some disease; it was released, but undoubtedly fell prey not long afterward to carnivores who were playing for keeps.

Later on the same day Schaller stalked a young giraffe until he was directly in front of it, looking into its eyes. It was blind, and dashed off after he grabbed its tail. During another meat-gathering experiment, this one carried out on the open grassy plains instead of in woodlands, a hare and a number of crouching gazelle fauns were encountered and could have been killed without much trouble. Dismembering any prey could readily have been accomplished with the aid of sharp-edged rocks conveniently lying about.

Notice that in all cases the animals were very young, small, sick, old, or dead. Capturing a large, live, healthy individual presents an entirely different problem. On one occasion Schaller ran full speed at a group of wildebeests with a stick in his hand, and succeeded in cornering an adult male. It was a fleeting triumph. The animal promptly turned and lunged at Schaller, who wisely stopped in his tracks and decided to leave well enough alone. Hunters ready to risk their lives, and perhaps working with a companion or two, might have outmaneuvered and eventually killed the angry bull. But then again they might not have.

Schaller and Lowther conclude:

The means by which scavenging and hunting hominids might fit into the ecological community without competing too extensively with other predators pose

Schaller on the Serengeti: zebra foal "kill"

a number of questions. Their primate heritage suggests that they were diurnal, and selection pressure from their primate and carnivore way of life undoubtedly favored a social existence. The only other diurnal social carnivore is the wild dog, which hunts at dawn and dusk, and favors prey weighing 60 kilograms or less (about 130 pounds). An ecological opening exists for a social predator hunting large animals and scavenging during the day, an opening some early hominid may well have filled, assuming that none of the saber-toothed cats did so.

The past few years have seen a trend that is likely to continue during the years ahead, a concentrated effort to go beyond it-stands-to-reason arguments (it seldom does) in reconstructing the behavior and social systems of times past—in short, an expanding search for more direct evidence. The taphonomists' successful search for distinguishing hominid traces on bone, based on hours upon hours of close-up examination and experiment, is a case in point. Given sites with cutmarked bones, even without tools or hominid remains, they can now deduce the active presence of hominid foragers and, more than that, something about the probable objectives of the foragers.

CLUES TO DIET, MAINLY TEETH AND BONES

Of course, we would like to know a great deal more than that, ideally what the foragers were eating, how they hunted and gathered, and how they organized themselves. Obtaining such insights calls for increasingly detailed examinations of a wider range of excavated remains. As an indication of the intensity of current research, consider the full-scale study under way by Alan Walker at Johns Hopkins. The study involves teeth, long a source of general information about diet and specific information about individual health. For example, the size, shape, enamel thickness and other features of ramapithecine teeth reflect ancient adaptations to mosaic environments and the origins of the hominid line (Chapter 2).

The teeth of 18-year-old Zinjanthropus show that his was not an easy life.

The enamel of permanent teeth builds up layer by layer and year after year like tree rings during a child's development, and periods of illness show up as abnormalities, tiny hollows resulting from retarded growth. An acute illness like measles or chicken pox, which usually runs a brief course, may leave shallow hollows. But the hollows in the Zinj teeth show that he was a sickly child. They are deep and suggest that he had a disease that lasted for many months, probably gastroenteritis caused by malnutrition. Furthermore, he suffered three major attacks of the disease—at the ages of 2, 4, and 4½.

Walker's work, which exploits the advantages of the scanning electron microscope, demands closer examinations than have ever been conducted on a systematic basis. Walker obtains precise latex-rubber impressions of fossil tooth surfaces, uses the molds to make epoxy replicas of the teeth, and then coats the surfaces with ultrathin gold-palladium layers, a technique providing images projected from the microscope on to a television screen, with resolutions of about 0.00001 inch. (Pat Shipman and Richard Potts followed the same procedure for some of their bone studies, described in Chapter 4.)

A major objective of Walker's research is to find scratch-and-pit patterns characteristic of different species and different dietary adaptations. For example, one species of hyrax, a small mammal which looks something like a cross between a woodchuck and a chipmunk, is a wet-season grazer and its teeth show typical scratches produced by a diet heavy in grasses which contain many abrasive plant-opal particles. The teeth of another hyrax species, an all-year-round browser on leaves, twigs, and shrubs, show far less abrasion. In general, browsing animals have only about 5 microscratches per square millimeter (less than 1/600 of a square inch) of tooth surface, as compared with some 300 for grazers.

Walker is building up a collection of microwear patterns associated with species whose diets consist mainly of fruits or meat, and bone crushers like hyenas, as well as browsers and grazers. He is transferring the information to magnetic tape for processing in a computer, mainly for high-speed comparisons of known animal and human patterns with the patterns on the teeth of extinct hominids. Preliminary studies of the teeth of ramapithecines and robust australopithecines reveal the sort of low scratch pattern found in mandrils, chimpanzees, and orangutans, fruit eaters all. This is not 100 percent proof of fruit as the major food in the diets of these early hominids, but it is good evidence and it rules out heavy dependence on grasses, leaves, or bone crushing.

Further clues may come from studies based on the chemical composition of bone, specifically on amounts of the trace element strontium. Strontium occurs in practically all foods, but there is about three times more of it in plant than in animal tissues. Also, it tends to concentrate in bone. Given these facts, and analytical methods which depend on burning small samples of bone and measuring the intensity of spectral radiation emitted by strontium atoms, it should be possible to distinguish individuals who live primarily on plant foods from individuals who include appreciable proportions of meat in their diets.

This assumption has been confirmed in animal studies comparing herbivores and carnivores. In human studies Margaret Schoeninger, a colleague of Shipman's and Walker's at Johns Hopkins, found that the strontium levels in bones of adults buried at a Mexican site varied inversely with social status. The mean level for low-status individuals, individuals buried without any grave goods, was 700 parts of strontium per million parts of bone, suggesting diets high in plant foods. The level for individuals of distinction buried with items made of jade, a mark of high status, was 532, an appreciable drop suggesting diets richer in meat. Notice that this result involves an inference, namely that well-off people generally ate more meat than their less affluent brethren, as is the case today. But it is a strong inference.

No one knows whether such studies can be used to investigate the diets of early hominids and prehominids. The Mexican bones date back only 2500 to 3000 years. A major problem is that the chemical composition of bone may change appreciably over longer periods because of factors which may mask the effects of diet, such as contamination by waterborne minerals. If the changes are predictable, they can be allowed for. Using X-ray diffraction methods, for example, Schoeninger has found that strontium levels in Neanderthal fossils from the Tabun site in Israel decline in a regular fashion over the period from 30,000 to 70,000 years ago, and she is now investigating still older specimens.

Another technique, still under development, uses teeth which are chemically more stable, more contamination-resistant than bones. On African savannas grasses are more efficient than leaves, twigs, and shrubs in extracting carbon dioxide from the atmosphere during the course of photosynthesis, a difference reflected in higher C^{13}/C^{12} ratios for grasses, C^{13} representing a rare carbon isotope and C^{12} representing the common variety. Jonathan Ericson, Charles Sullivan, and Noel Boaz of Harvard, the University of Arizona, and New York University, respectively, report a relatively high ratio for a tooth of a fossil horse, presumably a grazer like contemporary horses, indicating a diet consisting of about 60 percent grasses, while a lower ratio for a tooth of an extinct giraffe, a presumed browser, indicates less than 7 percent grasses in the diet. Since these specimens are about 2 million years old, studies of early-hominid teeth can be expected to yield similar information.

A more direct way of determining early diets, potentially the most direct way, is the examination of "coprolites"—feces fossilized as hard rock and containing fragments of foods digested and excreted. Perhaps the most pressing problem at the present stage is to obtain enough samples. According to Boaz, who has been investigating this approach, Omo excavations have yielded many coprolites more than 2 million years old, several of which may be hominid specimens (judging by shape and contents), including one "about 90 percent certain." He has also collected a number of specimens, not yet completely analyzed, from desert sites in north-central Libya.

Coprolites may contain a wide assortment of ingredients, anything from bits of charcoal, cracked seed, shell, insect, and bone, to yeast cells and hair and plant fibers. The very variety of possible food elements may turn out to be a sign indicating the tastes of omnivorous hominids. Another important sign is the state of coprolite contents. Hominids were primarily food crushers, more so even than hyenas. Hyenas crush bones, but only slice and cut meat and plant fibers. Our ancestors used their large, thick-enamel teeth to crush and pulverize practically everything.

An entirely different sort of problem goes one giant step beyond identifying sources or kinds of food. Although meat eating can be inferred from cutmarks on bone, that does not answer the all-important question: Was the meat hunted or scavenged? Again, in a search for direct evidence, Elizabeth Vrba of the Transvaal Museum emphasizes a significant difference in bone assemblages found at cave sites. Hunters, hominid and nonhominid, prey to a large extent on young animals, and that should show up in an age analysis of bone assemblages. As far as the assemblages of scavengers are concerned, however, the remains of young animals should be few and far between because predators usually consume them so quickly and completely that there is nothing left to scavenge.

On the basis of this difference and others, Vrba suggests that the assemblages in certain levels at Sterkfontein and Swartkrans represent hominid hunting because of the predominance of smaller animals and the presence of hominid remains and stone tools. The trouble with such deductions is related to the weakening of the home-base notion. If we cannot bank on continuous occupation of an early site over an appreciable period, then any conclusions about how meat was obtained remain highly tentative. The same thing goes for Potts' suggestion that, although you may not be able to tell for sure whether animals were hunted or scavenged, distinguishing early and prompt access from late access to carcasses might be helpful.

Forelegs and scapulas are generally taken first and hind legs next, with vertebrae and ribs tending to be left at the death site. Forelegs and hind legs predominate at the Zinj site, for example, with the former outnumbering the latter three to one. All of which would be fine if we could only be sure that most of the remains were brought in by hominids, which may not be the case. In any event, the investigator who finds a reliable method of distinguishing scavenged from hunted remains will earn the undying gratitude of co-workers and something even rarer, academic tenure.

THE ULTIMATE QUESTION

After considering what might have happened and what actually happened, there is still the question of why it happened, the most elusive and important question of all. We confront a still formidable mystery, the nature of the forces responsible for the shift from ape to hominid. Studies of our closest relatives, the higher apes, only serve to deepen the mystery. Their story from the standpoint of human evolution can be summed up as follows: they can, but they never did. They probe and dig for food underground, using tools of sticks and stones. Indeed, as we shall see in Chapter 14, they can if sufficiently motivated make stone tools. Chimpanzees hunt, hunt cooperatively, and even share meat.

But all this does not seem to be true survival activity. The putting together or synthesizing of capabilities into more effective procedures is conspicuous by its absence. Chimpanzees do not need to use tools as weapons or, for that matter, to share meat. As far as we know, they do not even need to hunt or eat meat in the first place. Like human vegetarians of the twentieth century, they can get along very well without meat. There is an enormous difference between what they can do and what they have to do. Their skills can be regarded as potentialities only, preadaptations in evolutionary lingo, more than sufficient and not strictly essential.

That was certainly never the case for the apes whose descendants became the earliest hominids 5 or more million years ago. Something important happened which transformed a whole set of preadaptations into adaptations, unnecessary "bonus" capabilities into capabilities essential for survival. Imagine in more remote times many species of apes living in dense forests, and a few species more or less adapted to woodlands and savannas—a period followed by the coming of cooler, drier climates which brought a dwindling of forests and forest species, together with an expansion of open lands and open-land species.

Such conditions may have seen a spread into all available evolutionary niches, with our ancestors taking advantage of the diurnal scavenging-hunting niche. In this connection, it may be significant that several million years passed without any signs in the archeological record of the use or making of, or presumably the need for, stone tools (Chapter 4). Perhaps the appearance of stone tools 2.5 to 2 million years ago marked a change in the ways of obtaining meat. Hares are among the animals whose remains are found at a number of Olduvai sites, and they can be killed and dismembered in a few moments with teeth and bare hands.

These direct tactics would not work for other small game. The skins of young antelopes, for example, are so tough that they can be penetrated only with sharp cutting tools, and an increasing reliance on such game may well have led to the regular use of stone tools. The result may have been a new pattern of behavior, as Louis Leakey demonstrated on a number of occasions. One Christmas Eve at his Olduvai camp, an audience of attentive Masai tribe members watched him spend half a minute making a chopper and flakes out of a handy rock, and 20 minutes skinning and cutting up the carcass of a freshly killed antelope.

Dietary needs not only called for technological innovations in the gathering of plant foods as well as in the pursuit of meat. Even more significant, they called for social adaptations. We can infer a complex of interrelated and interacting changes. There was competition for food in open country, fuller exploitation of underground plants and meat, bipedalism and the freeing of the hands, the use and making of stone tools, and more and more turning to such capacities as cooperation and sharing, already evident in rudimentary form among apes—with an accent on something that was less evident among other primates: planning and a heightened sense of the future.

SUMMARY

The food quest played a major role in human evolution. It seems that from the very beginning our ancestors subsisted primarily on plants, following an ancient primate tradition inherited from the days of widespread forests. Foods present on a large scale in woodland-savanna settings included not only such tough items as seeds and tubers but also another increasingly important source of nourishment—meat.

Meat was there for the taking in abundances difficult to imagine today in a world no longer dominated by wildernesses and great herds. But even allowing for the decline of herds, an estimated one million wildebeests, zebras, gazelles, and other game are living on Tanzania's 10,000-square-mile Serengeti Plain. Some 200 to 300 animals are dying of natural causes every day, and the numbers must have been considerably greater in prehistoric times.

Competition for available carcasses is still intense in the Serengeti and other African game reserves. Vultures, eyes in the sky, scan large areas and swoop down waiting for death and ready to feed. Four-footed predators, seeing the vultures, follow to join the feast. There is hunting as well as scavenging by lions, hyenas, and other carnivores—often cooperative hunting, which produces higher yields than solo efforts.

Primates also eat meat, even hunting cooperatively upon occasion. But only *Homo* eats meat regularly, a practice that may have started with a concentration on small game. As far as big game is concerned, early hominids were probably scavengers, and low-grade scavengers at that, obtaining leftover bones, perhaps to get at the marrow inside. The appearance of stone tools two or more million years ago may mark an increasing dependence on meat.

We cannot yet prove or disprove this scenario. But research is under way to determine to what extent an assemblage of excavated bones represents the work of hominids or nonhominids, scavengers or hunters. In any case, it was in a context of mosaic forest-woodland-savanna environments and intense competition from other species that hominids turned increasingly to foraging for meat in broad daylight, when most other predators were resting.

chapter *6*

Out of Africa

A major surprise of the 1963 digging season at the Olduvai Gorge occurred one January morning. An African worker, part of the Leakey search team, announced he was going out to find a fossil man, and then did precisely that—returning sometime later with a matchbox containing a few badly broken hominid teeth. He had spotted them in the middle of a track made by cattle belonging to local Masai tribe members, which meant that a valuable specimen, as it turned out perhaps the most complete skull of its kind yet discovered, had probably been trampled to bits. In fact, hundreds of further fragments were recovered after some two months of scraping, sweeping, and sifting mud.

One result of this episode was a top-level meeting. Masai elders, government agents, and the Leakeys came to an agreement—namely, that dams and watering places would be provided for the Masai on the condition that they kept their herds out of the gorge. Another result was a specimen known officially as OH16, the sixteenth hominid found at Olduvai, and unofficially as Poor George (or, at the suggestion of an anonymous punster, Olduvai George from Olduvai Gorge). I saw the specimen one day at the Leakeys' home outside Nairobi. Mary Leakey removed it from a safe in her office and placed it on a folded blanket, as carefully as an antique dealer with a fine vase. Poor George's skull, a reconstruction of more than 100 glued-together pieces, is about the size of a softball with prominent brow ridges.

Ten years later the shattered remains of another hominid were sieved out of the sands of a little Lake Turkana gully, and investigators were confronted with another superjigsaw puzzle. The product of many hours of fitting and gluing, this specimen is catalogued as No. 1808, a female practically all parts of whose skeleton are present, although no part is complete. She measures about 5 feet 4 inches from head to toe, a very respectable height for our ancient ancestors, but apparently she was not well. Shortly before she died she suffered from a severe inflammation of the periosteum, the tough fibrous membrane surrounding bone, causing a deposit of coarse bony tissue more than a quarter of an inch thick on her arm and leg bones. Alan Walker speculates that she might have died from an overdose of vitamin A, which can kill if consumed in unusually large amounts and is highly concentrated in the livers of lions and other carnivores.

A NEW HUMAN SPECIES IN THE OLD WORLD

Poor George and No. 1808 are among the oldest representatives of *Homo erectus,* a species rather more human than *Homo habilis. Homo erectus'* brains were bigger and its teeth smaller, more like ours. It first appears in the record more than 1.5 million years ago and, according to Philip Rightmire of the State University of New York in Binghamton, survived "exhibiting little significant morphological change during a span of well over a million years." *Homo erectus* is important as the transition species between early hominids and *Homo sapiens.* We have only the briefest, most tantalizing glimpses of what these people did, the barest hints of what must have been enormous changes in life style.

Important questions remain unanswered. Why did pioneering hominid groups leave home territories in Africa at all—and why not until a million or more years ago? After all, they had been around for 4 or more million years before that, without entering the vast Eurasian continent. At least that is what the present archeological record tells us. Although the finding of earlier or contemporary remains in India or China, for example, could call for radical revisions of our theories, to date all the earliest hominid remains have turned up in Africa.

Geological changes certainly affected the movements of hominids and other animals, and the last 2 million years or so mark not only the rise of our kind but also one of the most unstable climatic periods in the earth's history. As indicated in Chapter 3, large-scale northward migrations may have become possible for the first time after the formation of the African Rift Valley removed water barriers by shifting the courses of major rivers from a general east-west to a north-south direction.

The coming of glaciers also had at least an indirect effect on the timing and course of migrations from Africa into other continents. Prehistory features what Karl Butzer of the University of Chicago calls "one of the rare spasms of extensive and recurrent glaciation affecting the planet." Indeed, no human being has yet lived under conditions which, considering the prevailing climates of the past, can be regarded as normal. The previous spasm had come and gone more than 200 million years ago. The latest one was preceded by a relatively quiet period, a long calm before the storm.

More than 60 million years ago, in prosimian times, long before the appearance of modern monkeys and apes, the earth consisted mainly of tropics. Vast forests and grasslands were widespread; alligators and other reptiles splashed about in steamy swamps as far north as Montana and Wyoming. The average year-round temperature of central Europe was about 70 degrees Fahrenheit. Temperatures held fairly steady for about 20 million years and then started falling, and this is believed to be related to a comparatively late event in the breaking up of the supercontinent Pangea. As indicated in Chapter 2, the formation of the circumpolar current in Antarctica produced a drop in ocean temperatures. Gradually the whole planet became cooler, average temperatures in Europe dropping some 20 degrees Fahrenheit.

Mountain building also had a widespread effect on climates. For example, when India split off from the Antarctica–Australia–South America land mass, it drifted on a collision course with Asia. The impact, which occurred about 40 million years ago, created, among other things, the great Himalaya ranges and shifts in worldwide air-circulation patterns. (The collision, incidentally, is still under way; the Himalayas are uplifting at the relatively rapid rate of about 40 inches per century; at this rate, if it continues, another mile will be added to Everest and other peaks by the year 3500.)

The stage was set for a spectacular phenomenon. About 2 or 3 million years ago climates started to oscillate, temperatures falling to subfreezing levels and rising and falling again in a series of cold spasms. As happened earlier in Antarctica, snows in North Pole regions and on the highest mountains no longer melted away during summer thaws, but piled up season after season to form great ice masses or glaciers. During cold periods ocean levels fell, as more and more water was locked up in glaciers, which advanced from the poles and covered large portions of the earth. The process reversed during warmer periods, ocean levels rising again as the glaciers melted and retreated.

We do not know why the oscillations occurred. In fact, James Kennett believes that they represent "one of the major unsolved scientific problems of the century." It is a double problem. First, investigators are seeking periodic processes which could trigger periodic worldwide temperature changes, such as long-term changes in solar radiation and long-term cycles of upheavals from still-

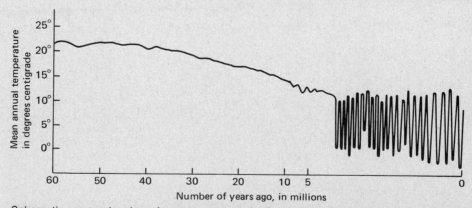

Schematic curve showing slow temperature decline and recent oscillations in central Europe during past 60 million years; time scale greatly exaggerated for the past 5 million years

active volcanoes that are perhaps related to colliding continental plates which created the Alps and Rockies as well as the Himalayas. Beyond that, there is the problem of accounting for the existence of cycles, because we know of no obvious reason why solar radiation, volcanoes, or any other contributing factors should vary in a periodic way.

Questions of how many oscillations there were, and how many glacial stages and warmer interglacial periods, are still wide open. The traditional number of four, based on older observations, is still cited in widely read texts. But new research, most of it conducted within the past decade, has changed the picture entirely. Studies of fossil pollen, sea-floor sediments and sedimentation rates, and changing concentrations of oxygen isotopes in microscopic marine shells point to more than 20 major advances and retreats of great ice sheets, 8 during the last 700,000 years alone and, according to many experts, the next to come within 2000 years or so.

Africa was far from the steep fronts of mile-high ice masses that moved like giant bulldozers down from polar regions. But its highest mountains felt the cold, and during glacial times, the snow line on the slopes of Mount Kenya extended some 5000 feet lower than it does today. More widespread effects are suggested by pollen studies which indicate that the Ice Age influenced climates all over the world, conditions being cooler and wetter in Africa when glaciation was most extensive in polar regions.

The new work draws attention to possible relationships between such changes and barriers to free migration. For example, increased rainfall during the first glacial stage may have created steppes, savannas, and lakes in the Sahara and opened up routes across previously impassable desert. Later the routes may have closed again, during the drier times of the subsequent interglacial stage. The Kalahari Desert to the south may have spread extensively; 40-foot-thick sand and ash deposits covering some of the hominid remains and traces of a broad, deep lake at Olduvai indicate a long stretch of arid conditions in East Africa. So climate produced at the poles influenced the movements of our ancestors in and out of traditional living zones.

Social forces—critical changes in evolving human behavior patterns—may have been at least as important as geological forces in early migrations from Africa. Although crowding can be a relative thing, as we are learning today, perhaps crowding or the feeling of being crowded has remote prehistoric origins. Perhaps small groups of younger individuals felt an urge to live well away from the old folks at home and moved on to the next valley, and their children or their children's children kept moving on until hunter-gatherers had spread throughout Africa and beyond.

But why during a particular period, and not before or after? There is no shortage of possibilities or bright ideas; there rarely is. The problem remains to figure out what sort of evidence could prove or disprove a particular theory, and then to go out and find the evidence. In general, such work has not been done. So we continue to speculate about the forces which sent groups of our ancestors into and across the Sahara and out of Africa. Desmond Clark has excavated a number of their African sites which lay along a route toward the vast Eurasian continent, on a treeless plain in the northern highlands of Ethiopia about 135 miles south of Addis Ababa.

One of the sites, located on the banks of an ancient stream, has yielded 7000 unworked cobbles and 3000 tools, some of them made from the volcanic glass obsidian, which could only have come from Rift Valley sources more than a mile below and at least 60 miles away. The site is probably between 1.5 and 1 million years old and, according to Clark, furnishes part of the evidence suggesting "a relatively sudden radiation out from the original homeland of the hominids in the warmer and drier habitats within the Rift, on to the high plateau montane forest and grassland regions. . . ."

TRACING THE SPREAD OF *HOMO ERECTUS*

Erectus fossil remains were first discovered outside Africa as a result of what one anthropologist has called "the greatest story of serene confidence I have ever heard."

About 90 years ago, Eugene Dubois, a young Dutch anatomist, performed the highly unlikely feat of deducing where hominid remains should be found, and then going out and finding them. His argument was that one should look in the tropics, specifically in the East Indies, where apes still lived and where no glaciers had come to disturb possible sites. By 1892, he had extracted part of the jaw, skull, and other fossil bones of a "missing link" from the bank of the Solo River in central Java near the village of Trinil; it was a creature which he regarded as more advanced than an ape and not quite a human.

Considering the tenor of the times and the tradition of heated disbelief which still prevails upon occasion among present-day fossil hunters, Dubois encountered a reasonable measure of respect for his ideas, although he did not see it quite that way. By his own count, out of 19 experts 7 viewed the Trinil creature as a human, 7 agreed with him that it was a transitional species between ape and hominid, and 5 considered it an out-and-out ape. To be sure, this fell short of unanimity. But it represented far more support than the Taung baby was to receive three decades later, or than the first Neanderthal find had received three decades or so earlier (Chapter 8).

The situation became clearer following excavations in China, which started during the 1920s as the result of a strange series of events. For centuries, expeditions had gone out into the remote mountain gorges and caves of Mongolia, China, and Indonesia and brought back tons of fossils annually, but not in the name of science. The expeditions were led by traders supplying the enormous demand for dragons' teeth, which, according to Far Eastern folklore, had potent medicinal effects. Chemists and apothecaries ground the bones into a fine sour-tasting powder and used it in a variety of elixirs and tonics probably no more ineffective than many over-the-counter preparations currently for sale in the drugstores of the Western world.

Paleontologists aware of these practices had long been shopping for fossils at local apothecary stores and inquiring about the locations of promising sites. One such inquiry led from a human tooth purchased at a Peking store to a large

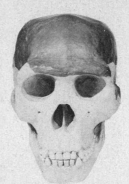

Homo erectus: reconstructed skull and artist's conception

debris-filled limestone cave in Dragon Bone Hill, about 30 miles from the city, where excavations were carried out between 1923 and 1937. By the time digging stopped, workers had reached a depth of some 160 feet without hitting bedrock and had unearthed 14 Peking-type skulls, about 150 teeth, and other remains representing more than 40 individuals who resembled the Java individual.

These discoveries more than vindicated Dubois. In fact, they showed that he had been too conservative and that his Java find was not a prehuman but a full-fledged human. But by that time Dubois had become a secretive, conservative, and eccentric old man. He went into virtual hiding, belittled the significance of the Chinese excavations, felt his colleagues were plotting against him, and buried his fossils in a chest in the ground beneath his dining-room floor. It happens

Artist's conception of *Homo erectus* foraging in wilderness of Java half a million years ago

that all the material on Peking individuals, which had taken so long to find, was lost without trace during World War II.

According to a recent version of what occurred, the remains had been packed in crates and were en route to the United States for the duration of the war as part of the personal luggage of a young doctor in the U.S. Marines heading for home in 1941. Intercepted by the Japanese, he managed to leave the crates with Chinese friends and Swiss and French officials before being imprisoned until the end of the war. Despite recent efforts to trace the material, a search that involved many leads and a $150,000 reward, chances of recovery now seem slim.

Fortunately, the record remains and includes fine plaster casts of the skulls, although the original specimens would be much more useful in continuing studies. During the past 15 years, digging has resumed on Dragon Bone Hill. Workers have found tools, animal bones, and some further fragments of Peking individuals in deeper levels of the large cave as well as in nearby caves. Digging has continued in Java, and two skulls and skull fragments have been found in the central part of the island, not far from the site where Dubois made his original discovery.

Further traces of *erectus* have been found in many parts of the Old World. In 1963, the year when Poor George turned up at Olduvai, an expedition led by Woo Ju-kang of the Chinese Academy of Sciences unearthed the lower jawbone of an individual referred to as Lantian man, after Lantian County in northwest China. The specimen was embedded deep in a 100-foot deposit of red clay and, judging by its size, Lantian man was probably a woman. The following year Woo and his associates reported the skull of another Lantian individual, also probably a woman and more than 30 years old.

In Africa remains have been found not only in the Olduvai and Lake Turkana regions but also, among other places, near a Mohammedan cemetery on top of a sand dune in Algeria, and on an ancient shoreline of Lake Chad in the Sahara. The oldest specimen in Europe may be a lower jaw found in a sandpit near Heidelberg, Germany. Other remains come from a Hungarian limestone quarry in the village of Vertesszöllös, about 30 miles from Budapest. In a valley where a tributary of the Danube once flowed, investigators have excavated a sealed-in site which includes hearths, burned bones and charcoal, many tools, several teeth, and part of a skull.

Most of these sites were probably occupied between 400,000 and 500,000 years ago, although some of the Java fossils date back 750,000 or more years. According to one estimate, all *erectus* specimens together represent more than 100 individuals. Other promising sites exist which do not have human remains but are old enough to fall within the *erectus* time range. There is the Vallonet cave in southeastern France, found some time ago by a young schoolgirl among frost-shattered rocks and deposits sealed in by stalagmites. The evidence is scanty but clear-cut. It consists of five pebbles chipped on one side, two of them choppers like those found at Olduvai; four flakes, two of which show use or working on the edges; and the bones of brown bears, oxen, rhinoceroses, elephants, and horses, several of which seem to have been broken deliberately.

Another site, the Escale cave, contains traces of hominid activity, but no hominid fossils. In 1960 workers dynamiting a road through the valley of the Durance River not far from Marseilles exposed the rear chambers of the buried cave and noted old bones among the limestone debris. Excavations conducted since then have uncovered traces of charcoal and ash, fire-cracked stones, and fire-reddened hearth areas up to a yard in diameter—direct evidence for what may be the earliest known use of fire. Clark Howell believes Escale includes relatively undisturbed living floors, and rates as one of the most important sites yet discovered in Europe.

Moving into new lands called for a degree of sophistication perhaps too great for the likes of the australopithecines. The *erectus* wanderers who frequented places such as the Escale and Vallonet caves had to deal with unfamiliar conditions, notably with glacial winters. One of their probable routes into Europe was through northeastern Africa and Israel and then across the Dardanelles in Turkey, where there was either a land bridge or else very narrow straits with slow tides, although even a relatively easy water crossing would have represented a challenge and an adventure. There was so much of the planet yet to explore, such wild wildernesses.

The most direct route, across Gibraltar, had tremendous tides associated with a deep submarine canyon and was a formidable barrier. Based on migration rates in more recent times—and the estimates are very rough—it might have taken hunter-gatherer bands 3000 to 4000 years to spread from East Africa to southeastern France, moving and occupying a new region for a time and moving again, generation after generation, at an average rate of about a mile a year. The

Vallonet cave near Monte Carlo, oldest known campsite in Europe

spread into the Far East, into Java and China, via southwestern Asia, Iran, and southern India may have taken more than twice as long. The enhanced ability to adapt to new environments reflected one of the most spectacular developments in human prehistory, the expansion of the brain from the earliest australopithecine times to *erectus*.

This phenomenon is a good example of what George Gaylord Simpson of Harvard calls quantum evolution, an explosive appearance of new adaptations. Of course, explosiveness is a relative thing. Simpson warns that "considerable imagination must be used to conceive of an explosion that makes no noise and goes on for several million years." A process which lasts that long is fast only on an evolutionary time scale.

According to one study, the average cranial capacity of early australopithe-cines was about 450 cubic centimeters, as compared with perhaps 650 or so cubic centimeters for *Homo habilis*. The cranial capacity of *erectus* averaged about 1000 cubic centimeters, and some specimens reached the 1300-plus level, which overlaps the range for modern humans (from less than 1000 to some 2000 cubic centimeters). In other words, some *erectus* individuals had brains rather larger than many people living today. The brain had increased two to three times in about 3.5 million years.

Powerful selective forces were at work, putting a premium on the emergence of larger brains. Something happened to step up the pace of change, or, to put it another way, something interrupted the customarily slow pace of evolution. As usual, a significant factor was the basic quest for food, and, also as usual,

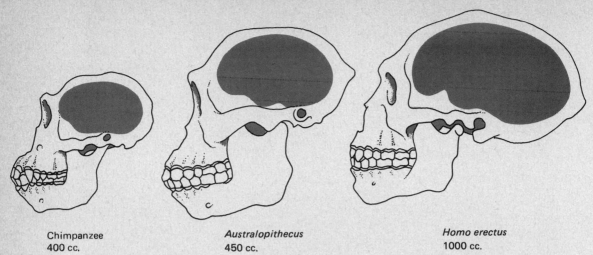

Chimpanzee
400 cc.

Australopithecus
450 cc.

Homo erectus
1000 cc.

Average cranial capacities, indicating more than doubling of brain size from *Australopithecus* to *Homo erectus* (chimpanzee cranial capacity included for comparison)

evidence is lacking for changes in the early exploitation and preparation of plant foods. The evidence for hunting, while hardly abundant or clear-cut, is somewhat more satisfactory. At least findings at a number of sites indicate that *Homo erectus* was in the process of becoming a better hunter. Although no single site offers proof beyond the shadow of a doubt, the overall picture is certainly suggestive.

Two extraordinary features distinguish the site of Olorgesailie, located in the African Rift Valley outside Nairobi and dating back between 400,000 and 700,000 years. It contains a heavy concentration of stone tools, and an even more impressive concentration of the remains of 90 giant baboons, some of them almost as big as a man and almost all of them clustered in an area not much larger than a tennis court. Pat Shipman, Wendy Bosler of St. Thomas' Hospital Medical School in London, and Karen Lee Davis of the State University of New York in Binghamton have studied the fossils recently—and, after taking into account the effects of carnivores and weathering and other factors, suggest that hominids very probably butchered the animals and perhaps killed them as well.

They note, among other things, an unusual type of bone breakage. More than 90 percent of the baboon thigh bones had a characteristic oval hole or pit at the upper front end, a feature which has never been observed "on the thousands of bones we have examined, including hundreds gnawed by two species of modern hyenas, leopards, wolves, bears and jaguars." Dismemberment by humans is the most likely explanation, specifically by a sharp blow with a stone tool to detach muscle. Another significant observation: the sample is heavily biased toward young animals, 76 of the 90 baboons represented being juveniles, most of them probably in the age range from 6 months to 3 years. This is in line with traditional predator practice of going after the most vulnerable individuals preferentially, although it does not tell us whether the killers were human or nonhuman.

WHAT HAPPENED AT TORRALBA-AMBRONA?

Further traces of butchery come from a site perhaps 300,000 to 500,000 years old on top of the arid plateau of Old Castile in north-central Spain, near the village of Torralba. Like many prehistoric sites discovered by people excavating for nonscientific reasons, this one was discovered by railroad workers who were digging a trench for a water main in 1888, and found fossil bones and stone tools. Starting in 1907, a Spanish nobleman, an amateur archeologist, spent 5 years excavating not far from the now-abandoned railroad station. Although his findings indicated that Torralba was an important site, no one thought seriously of any further digging until 1960, when Clark Howell spent an investigatory day there.

Howell located the overgrown trenches and back dirt of the old excavations, collected a few tools and bone fragments in adjoining fields, and decided that further digging was called for. He and his associates, including Leslie Freeman of the University of Chicago, worked in the region for the next three summers, 34 weeks in all. They excavated a total of 20,000 square feet to an average depth of about 8 feet; collected more than 500 pollen samples, 2000 stone tools and waste pieces, and uncounted fossil bones; and mapped more than 20 surfaces containing concentrations of bones and tools. Their current consensus, based among other things on recent examinations of cutmarks on bone, is that Torralba served as a prehistoric abattoir, a place for butchering and meat processing. Concentrated in a relatively small region are the remains of at least 30 elephants, 25 horses, 25 red deer, 10 wild oxen, and half a dozen rhinoceroses.

In one 270-square-foot area much of the left side of a large adult elephant was found, with tusks and bones unbroken and in place, as if put together for an exhibit. The pelvis was missing and so was the skull, although the lower jaw was left intact. Four flake tools that might have been used for cutting were also found. In another, somewhat larger area nearby, some of the bones of this same elephant were found, most of them shattered. There was a broken right-leg bone, some vertebrae, and fragments of ribs, upper jaw, and collar bone, as well as two stone cleavers and more flakes.

Freeman and Howell suggest that the two areas were used for different purposes. The elephant was killed and dismembered in the area containing its left side and the unbroken bones, and large pieces of meat were carried to the nearby area for further butchering and processing. In two other areas, finer splinters and fragments were found, together with a cleaver and a number of heavy side scrapers. It is more difficult to deduce what was going on here, but people may have been eating their share of the spoils—perhaps cleaning all the meat off the bones with the aid of the scrapers and then, as their African ancestors had done more than a million years previously, smashing the bones for the marrow inside.

Much remains to be learned from these traces. Especially intriguing is the arrangement of the large elephant's left-side bones, which were found in what had been a swamp, indicated by clay silt deposits. But they had not been left in place. They are not completely articulated, not all fitted neatly joint to joint. Also, they have all been turned over. It seems that after the animal was completely butchered, someone took some of the big bones and vertebrae and laid

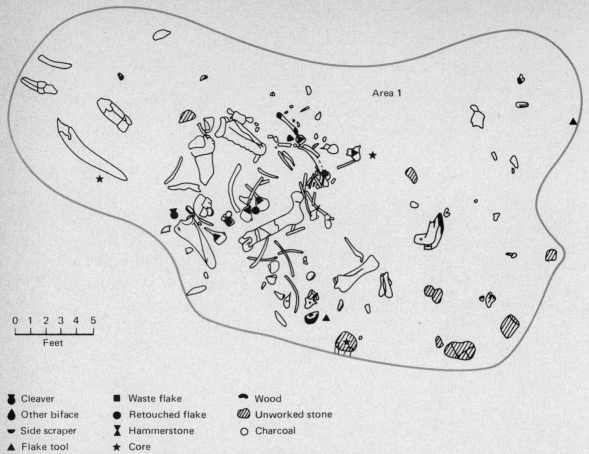

0 1 2 3 4 5
Feet

♨ Cleaver	■ Waste flake	⬿ Wood
♦ Other biface	● Retouched flake	⬔ Unworked stone
⬗ Side scraper	✕ Hammerstone	○ Charcoal
▲ Flake tool	★ Core	

Living-floor map, showing location of objects unearthed at Torralba

them down side by side to produce a partially reconstructed skeleton. Why anyone would have bothered is another question. It may have been a game, joke, or ritual, but there are no clues to support these or any other guesses.

Taking the site as a whole, Freeman and Howell believe that game drives may have occurred there. Torralba lies in a steep-sided little valley which includes the headwaters of a main tributary of the Ebro River. Even today under generally dry conditions places exist where the water level rises to within a few inches of the surface and where a heavy animal could break through and sink. The terrain was wetter when the elephants died. Fossil pollen indicates that there was a pine forest on the plateau, a sluggish, meandering stream in the poorly drained valley, and seasonal swamplands with dense reeds and sedges.

Bits of charcoal scattered over a wide area may represent wind-dispersed hearths or natural fires, but Howell suggests another possibility: "Whoever lit those fires was apparently burning grass and brush over large areas for a definite purpose. My guess is that the purpose was to drive the elephants along the valley

Excavators at Torralba hunting and butchering site

into the swamp.'' Freeman expands on this theme, speculating that a number of charred pieces of wood served as torches to drive fire-fearing elephants and other game into the swamp and that heavy stones found in the butchering area were used to stone the mired prey to death.

Howell discovered another major site in the region, or rather rediscovered a site where, according to old records, preliminary excavations had been carried out half a century ago. The records merely stated that the work was done in Ambrona, a village in the same valley as Torralba and less than 2 miles away, but that was not enough information to locate the site. Then one day in 1962 Howell asked his workers whether they knew of any places with fossil bones, and a man answered: ''Yes, in my field.'' It turned out to be the missing site. Subsequent investigations uncovered deposits of about the same age as the Torralba deposits, remains of the same kinds of animals, with elephants again predominant.

One area included most of the skeleton of a huge bull elephant—an old animal, judging by his very worn molar teeth—together with a few isolated bones of an infant and a young female. The bones, left in place just as they were excavated, are now housed in a little museum built on the spot. The area also contained bones of other elephants as well as horses, red deer, and wild oxen, all in deposits which had once been deep swamplands; scattered clusters of charcoal and carbon; and cleavers and other tools. The same activities were apparently going on here as at Torralba, perhaps involving the same people.

Not far away is another puzzling feature. The tip of an elephant tusk more than 4 feet long has a pencil-sharp point, perhaps shaped by a prehistoric whittler or broken off during a tusk-to-tusk fight between ancient elephants. But that remains pure speculation; this is one among many features which may or may not be identified during the course of future studies.

Howell and Freeman returned to Ambrona during the summers of 1980 and 1981. They found more stone tools and more elephant remains, including 19 tusks and pieces of worked bone and ivory—the remains of what they interpret as three separate periods of human occupation. They also found more cutmarks on bones, enough evidence in all to support their earlier notion that game drives and butchering took place at the site.

Another warning, the usual one, is in order here. Recent studies in Africa and elsewhere indicate that many sites are a great deal more complicated than we realized as recently as a few years ago. Richard Klein of the University of Chicago has examined every one of the 2000 or so fossil bones found at Torralba and reports that a large proportion of them were very heavily rolled, some so much so that they amount to bone "pebbles." This suggests the smoothing and

Elephant remains, including large tusk (front) and boundary of long bones (rear), excavated at Ambrona

rounding of water action as the bones tumbled about in stream beds, perhaps being transported some distance from the original death sites.

In other words, the picture of intact living floors throughout may not hold for Torralba. The site has been disturbed to some extent by natural forces. Furthermore, Klein points out that the number of animals has been overestimated, the total being about 45 instead of nearly 100, and about 15 elephants at the most instead of 30 or more. As at the Zinj site in the Olduvai, which has turned out to be a product of mixed animal and natural forces (see Chapter 4), humans and carnivores left their marks at Torralba, but we are at a loss when it comes to understanding what they did. This is the problem confronting Klein: "I do not think that Torralba is a straightforward living site. But what is it? If I could tell you, I'd be satisfied. But I can't, and that's what worries me."

EXCAVATING A HOME BASE

Such frustration, always temporary, is the sign of learning. The general impression for this stage of human evolution is of an increasing proportion of meat in the diet and, perhaps associated with that, a somewhat more organized life style. As far as places to live are concerned, our ancestors seem to have become more socialized as they became more carnivorous. The home base, that uniquely human institution among primates, probably appeared during *erectus* times. The typical early-morning pattern for baboons is for all members of the troop to move away together when leaving the trees in which they slept, and to return together at night. Weak or sick or injured members must try to keep up, and if they cannot they are left behind. Within hours after the troop has gone, and probably before its heart stops beating, the deserted baboon may be devoured by a predator. (Lions and other carnivores prey largely on incapacitated animals.)

Sherwood Washburn emphasizes the role of the home base in survival:

> The whole evolutionary impact of disease and accident on the human species was changed when it became possible for an individual to stay in one place and not have to take part in the daily round of the troop. Certainly one of the reasons why it has been possible for man to migrate without building immunity to local disease is that his way of life allows him to be far sicker than a baboon and still recover. Injuries to the legs are common and are far more serious, of course, for a biped than for a quadruped. It is the home base that changes sprained ankles and fevers from fatal diseases to minor ailments.

Archeologically speaking, a home base is a site with an intact, single-occupation level having signs of continuous occupation—say, one or more hearths, tools and tool debris and the cores from which the tools were made lying close together, and an accumulation of bones bearing stone-tool marks and representing selected parts of animals slain elsewhere. Investigators rarely encounter a site of this sort. Vertesszöllös, a possible home base, includes four living floors with tools made of several different materials, abundant animal remains, and a number of presumed hearths consisting of distinct clusters of burned bone.

The main cave in Dragon Bone Hill near Peking may have been a home base. A great deal happened there over long periods, and many species were in on the act. There are signs of a long struggle between humans and other carnivorous frequenters of the cave. Some of the deepest and oldest deposits feature the remains of large predators such as giant hyenas and seven members of the cat family (including a sabertooth tiger), together with the bones of their prey. Other layers sandwiched between the animal layers contain only human remains, indicating that the carnivores had been driven out of the cave for a time. No animal layers exist in the uppermost deposits. Peking individuals eventually won in the struggle. Their favorite meat seems to have been venison, deer fossils outnumbering the fossils of all other species by three to one.

Fire was a feature of the site, a dominant feature in certain areas. The site contains deposits of solid ash, one more than 20 feet thick and, according to one account, occurring "not in piles, but spread out in even layers, apparently the result of water movement." These layers could have resulted from fires set by accident, long-smoldering fires such as those found in marshes and peat bogs. Signs of possible hearths include concentrations of burned antler, seams of finely divided charcoal, and areas of baked red and yellow clay. Although we cannot be sure, it is a good bet that *erectus* ate and slept here.

One of the first undisputed home bases dates back to somewhat more recent times. Probably no more than 300,000 years old, it is an open-air hillside site in Nice on the French Riviera, on a dead-end street called Terra Amata overlooking the Mediterranean. Luxury apartments stand there today. But in 1966, when the apartments were being built, bulldozers uncovered some prehistoric tools, and work stopped for five months while Henry de Lumley of the University of Aix-Marseilles, his associates, other investigators, and student volunteers spent 40,000 work-hours excavating an area of about 1100 square feet. The Mediterranean was higher several hundred thousand years ago, and 80 feet of water covered the site of today's boulevards, hotels, and beaches. Surf broke high among the hills on the shores of other beaches, and a band of hunter-gatherers camped on one of them, on a bay near the mouth of a small river where animals came to drink.

Terra Amata is a rich site. Excavators unearthed and recorded about 1300 shaped tools; thousands of waste flakes (some of which can be "conjoined" or reassembled into the original cores); at least one pyramidal pebble which served as a platform or anvil for tool making; and lumps of red, yellow, brown, and purple ocher, some pointed like pencils at one end. There were also signs of meat eating, and the remains of a variety of game from rabbits and wild boars to deer and elephants, as well as structural features such as post holes, hearths, large flat limestone blocks, and a wall of stones.

Out of all these findings de Lumley has reconstructed an imaginative scenario. Posts were driven into the ground and supported by rocks wedged against them. They in turn supported a number of oval huts 20 to 50 feet long and 12 to 18 feet wide, probably made of sturdy branches bent so as to interlock at the top, with an entrance at one end and a "chimney" hole at the center to let smoke escape. The wall is located so that it could have protected hearths from prevailing

Reconstructions of Terra Amata: (top) actual hearth as excavated; (middle) reconstruction of the hearth being used 400,000 years ago; (bottom) reconstruction of the hut exterior, showing chimney and entrance

northwest winds. There are 11 fairly thin occupation layers in the area, suggesting that hunters, perhaps members of the same band throughout, visited and revisited the site for brief periods during 11 consecutive seasons. That they came in the spring is indicated by their coprolites, or fossilized feces, which contain the pollen of plants that blossom in the late spring and early summer.

The huts may have housed 10 to 20 persons. The areas closest to the firesides are clear of debris, indicating that people slept there, a practice still observed among hunter-gatherers in Australia and southern Africa. Hints of other activities include the flat limestone blocks which could have provided convenient surfaces for sitting or breaking bones (similar to some found at Torralba and Ambrona), as well as traces of what may be the earliest container yet discovered, a wooden bowl with a rough-hewn bottom. The lumps of red ocher, found in a corner near the bowl, were possibly used to color the body in preparation for some sort of dance ceremony.

This scenario, this set of interpretations, implies that most of the material recovered was relatively undisturbed, that it lay in about the same positions which it occupied when hunters abandoned the site for the last time millenniums ago. Paola Villa of the University of Wyoming, who studied artifacts collected at the site, is not so sure. She has found pieces of stone knocked off the same pebbles in layers separated by as much as a foot and a half, a sign of appreciable movement, especially when you consider that occupation levels may be only a few inches thick. In other words, the site, instead of resembling a photograph in sharp focus, may actually be just a bit "blurred," less clear-cut than de Lumley has assumed. Terra Amata still ranks as a highly probable home base, however, one of the earliest in the archeological record.

NEW TOOLS, HAND AXES, AND SYMMETRY

As far as tool making is concerned, certain features appear for the first time in the *erectus* record—for instance, the first direct evidence for the use of wood (a material very probably exploited long before by the australopithecines and earlier hominids). Torralba contains pieces of waterlogged wood preserved in clayey, boggy deposits and bearing the marks of whittling, gouging, and polishing. A few of the pieces may be parts of spears, which would make them the oldest suspected examples of this weapon. The oldest undoubted example is a 15-inch yew spear point found at Clacton-on-Sea, a site located on the eastern coast of England and believed to be at least 250,000 years old.

As compared with the earliest stone tools dating back 2 or more million years (see Chapter 4), the *erectus* kit represented an important increase in sophistication. Appearing half a million to a million years later, it included something brand-new in addition to the choppers and flakes of earlier times. People began making tools with a great deal more cutting edge. Instead of striking a few flakes off one end of a pebble to obtain a rough edge of perhaps 2 to 3 inches, they began trimming both sides and all around the pebble, increasing the cutting edge four or more times. Eventually the working-around procedure seems to have resulted in the first shaped tools—notably the so-called hand ax, which came in various forms such as almond-shaped, teardrop-shaped, or with a tapering point and a heavy butt end.

Despite its name, the hand ax was not designed for chopping wood. It probably served as a prehistoric "Swiss pocket knife," a compact multipurpose tool which could be used to dig, cut plants or meat, scrape hides, and so on. Above all, it is especially significant as a mark of foresight among our ancestors. It required an extra investment of time and energy (perhaps 25 to 65 blows as compared to only 2 or 3 to make a crude chopper), although the point should not be pushed too far. *Erectus* stone knappers could probably turn out a respectable hand ax in a few minutes, but it was still a big step beyond earlier "expediency" tools, made on the spot for immediate use and then tossed aside. It represents a measure of planning, a new sense of the future, if only the immediate future.

The hand ax also marks the appearance of standards of symmetry, things made in a disciplined way according to preconceived patterns. We would like to know whether other kinds of rules and traditions went together with the establishment of these rules and traditions, whether set ways of doing things emerged in activities other than tool making. The hand ax may be part of a development broad enough to include other imposed behaviors as well, such as food taboos, kinship customs, and perhaps ways of communicating. It also hints at a desire for something beyond utility. Some hand axes are so much more beautifully shaped than others that a budding esthetic sense was almost certainly involved.

SIGNS OF SOCIAL STABILITY

Analysis of tools found at *erectus* and pre-*erectus* sites raises some challenging questions. The oldest known tool assemblages—named Oldowan after the Olduvai Gorge, where they were first identified—were used over a long period. They have been found not only in deposits on the floor of the gorge but also in higher, more recent deposits up to the bottom of the thick layer of wind-blown sand and volcanic ash which buried early remains (Chapter 4), a time span from 1.8 to 1.2 million years ago. No traces of hominids and their works appear in this sterile layer. But above the layer, after an interval of many thousands of years, the Oldowan assemblage is found again, with some changes. The number of choppers decreases sharply, while the number of spheroids increases three to four times. Also, there may be a few roughly shaped hand axes.

An intriguing complication enters the picture at this point. Another tool assemblage appears for the first time above the sterile layer at sites contemporary with, but separate from, sites featuring the Oldowan assemblages. Named the Acheulian, after the French site of St. Acheul in the Somme Valley where it was originally found, it often includes a high proportion of hand axes (40 percent or more) but may have none at all and simply feature extra-large flakes. The assemblages at Torralba, Ambrona, and Olorgesailie are Acheulian, with a particularly dense concentration of hand axes at the latter site.

The big question is what the two assemblages mean, what can be deduced from the fact that two different tool kits were being used at the same time in the same general region. It may have had something to do with where people lived.

Olduvai Gorge camps containing Oldowan tools were located on flatlands next to lakes, at the mouths of streams fed by runoff from nearby mountains. On the other hand, African camps containing early Acheulian tools tend to be found away from lake shores along seasonal streams. These upstream sites have an abundance of large stones washed down from the mountainsides, and tools made from correspondingly large flakes, cleavers as well as hand axes, are common in Acheulian assemblages. Such stones are rarer at lakeside sites, however, and Oldowan assemblages rarely include tools made from larger flakes.

In other words, people tended to use what they had in the neighborhood to do their food processing. Thus, one reason for the difference between the two kinds of tool assemblages would be different kinds of local resources. Different occupational patterns may also be involved. Assuming that the spheroids were simply much-used hammerstones rather than items made deliberately for a special purpose, spheroid-rich Oldowan sites may have been used for relatively long periods—sites where tool making took place on a large scale. Acheulian sites, on the other hand, may have been located near places like water holes where game congregated regularly, and where people came with tools ready-made for butchering.

There is certainly more to the problem. One view is that two traditions coexisted, two different groups of people or tribes, each with its own customs and way of life. In any case, Oldowan tool kits, featuring a variety of choppers and lacking cleavers as well as hand axes, have been found at sites dated to about 100,000 years ago, while Acheulian tool kits lasted until about 75,000 years ago. These facts suggest extremely stable living conditions.

Considering that some hunter-gatherers left Africa 1 to 2 million years ago, the picture is one of little change for hundreds of thousands of years, at least as far as the stone-tool record goes. It seems to have been a time of established subsistence tactics, repetitive behavior patterns. Lewis Binford sees people continuing to sleep in trees when hyenas and other predators were about, waking up in the morning and perhaps seeing vultures circling in the skies, picking up prefabricated hand axes and heading fast for the spot, perhaps to a carcass

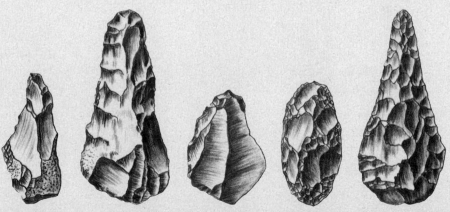

Acheulian tool kit showing flake tool (middle) and various forms of hand ax

abandoned near a water hole—and then competing for meat with other scavengers.

According to Binford's scenario, hunting on a regular basis was still a long way off. Our ancestors were probably quite capable of dealing with almost any species that was worth hunting. But they were still very much animals compared to later human breeds, still limited to short-term planning and to sequences of action performed semiautomatically. They were not all that different from the earlier hominids of Olduvai, Lake Turkana, and Hadar. Compared to the pace of things to come in due course, it was a lull before the storm.

SUMMARY

After at least four million years in Africa, our ancestors turned up in the rest of the Old World. Representatives of a new species, *Homo erectus,* they appeared in the African record about 1.5 million years ago and spread into Europe and Asia some half million years later. Their movements may have had something to do with unstable climates and early ice ages which may have opened up barriers to migration.

First traces of *erectus* outside Africa were discovered nearly a century ago in Java, and some of the richest evidence has come from China, from a limestone cave near Peking. *Erectus* individuals were distinguished by a brain averaging about 1000 cubic centimeters (as compared with an average of 450 for early australopithecines), with some specimens reaching the 1300-plus level, which is within the modern size range. They were quite probably better hunters than their predecessors, although proving the point has not been easy.

The problem is illustrated by two neighboring sites in Spain, Torralba and Ambrona, which have yielded many artifacts and bones, including the remains of elephants and other big game. The excavators believe these were butchering sites where animals, probably driven into swamps, were slaughtered—a scenario that implies advanced planning by several cooperating bands. Other investigators note that a large proportion of the bones have been rolled smooth, suggesting that they were concentrated by flowing waters rather than human activity.

Erectus times saw the earliest known hearths and home bases. They also saw another notable development, the first appearance of an esthetic element in the archeological record. New tool kits included symmetrical hand axes, tools carefully worked into almond or teardrop shapes which often seem more beautiful than necessary for strictly utilitarian purposes—and which may indicate the beginnings of standardization in some aspects of social behavior as well as in tool making.

Acheulian tool kits generally including high hand-ax proportions and Oldowan kits featuring a variety of choppers were used for hundreds of thousands of years. Whatever the *erectus* life style, it was apparently quite stable.

chapter 7

Organizing for Survival

By this time humans had almost completed their evolutionary journey. It was only a few hundred thousand years away from the twentieth century, out of some 5 to 10 million years of hominid development, the equivalent of the last 15 minutes or so of a jet flight from New York to Paris. The brain of *Homo erectus* was already well within the size range of modern brains. But the hominid way of life was far from modern. The future had hardly begun.

Looking back, the great question remains unanswered. We still do not have much of an answer for the humanist who complained: "I ask what is man, and you tell me he was an ape." We know only that a near-ape became a human being, and in the process developed an oversized brain. But why and how it happened is still elusive. It all started back in the forests; our basic heritage is a forest heritage.

The food quest was all-important from the beginning, 65 or so million years ago, when the first primates and preprimates took to the trees. Their life style was based on finely tuned perceptions, and an enhanced ability to detect and manipulate small objects. Their diet included insects, tiny moving targets which had to be spotted, tracked, picked up—activities putting a premium on stereoscopic color vision (probably at the expense of the sense of smell) and mobile fingers.

OMNIVORES IN SMALL GROUPS

Images played a vital role in behavior, as they do now. As monkeys and apes evolved more varied diets, the emphasis was increasingly on a multiplication of strategies. Insects and leaves are everywhere. But ripe fruits, highly favored items, tend to be dispersed, occurring in patches, and are generally available for restricted periods only. Also, it pays off if they are closely monitored. Species capable of keeping tabs on the ripening process can be there on the spot and ahead of less punctual fruit eaters when fruit is most desirable and nourishing.

Varied diets are a form of insurance. The more foods you exploit, the less your chances of going hungry if one or more sources fail. Gombe chimpanzees go in heavily for fruits, but Jane Goodall has seen them eating leaves, seeds, stems, blossoms, honey, bark, and eggs, not to mention seasonally available termites. Moreover, they not only rate as omnivores, but are potentially even more omnivorous. The fact that they eat meat, and even share meat, upon occasion suggests the possibility of adapting to regular meat eating as a source of sustenance if circumstances so dictated, which is presumably what happened during the course of hominid evolution. A mark of their potential for sophisticated manipulating and thinking is the use of crude tools to go after termites and crack open palm nuts (see Chapter 2).

Put such species, and such talents, in a world of dwindling forests, and you have some of the prerequisites for the emergence of humans. Cooler and drier climates brought a spread of sparser woodlands and savannas, and the rise of new species to occupy expanding evolutionary niches. The old dense-forest adaptations would never do in such exposed settings. One type of adaptation took full advantage of the power of large numbers. Wildebeests, buffaloes, and other close relatives of creatures that went about alone or in small groups in the forests massed together out in the savanna, expressing a herd instinct so strong that a mother would leave her offspring if necessary to keep up with the crowd.

Then there was the small-group adaptation, the troop made up of dozens of individuals at the most instead of the thundering herd made up of hundreds or thousands. It is a deep difference, worthy of serious comparative studies. For one thing, the spatial dimensions are so different. In a troop there is no forced movement in the sense of being pushed along by bodies jammed shoulder to shoulder; opportunities are more frequent to communicate by subtler line-of-sight signals over a distance. Troop living permits somewhat more individual action perhaps, more scope for the free play of curiosity, for time spent away from the smells and sounds of one's fellow species.

Our ancestors took the small-group way. They were part of it all, part of the great movement into wide open spaces. One of their uniquenesses involved putting already existing manual capacities to work in a new way, an anatomical division of labor in which the hind limbs took over the entire job of walking, and the forelimbs became full-time manipulators and carriers. So much that was possible among preadaptive apes came into its own among fully bipedal, visually oriented hominids. For one thing, tool use probably flourished, perhaps on a regular basis. Also, conditions were right for a form of silent communication, by gesture and facial expression, as well as communication by sound.

Change may have come slowly, more slowly than we believed a few years ago, but it was nonetheless significant. If the australopithecines and their early successors did not have full-fledged home bases, if they had not yet found it necessary to eat and sleep in the same place, they had reached a fairly impressive level of organization. Alone among savanna species, they not only used tools—and stone tools at that, made deliberately to obtain rough cutting-bashing edges—but they went a step further.

THINKING AHEAD

Cache sites such as those described in Chapter 4 imply a measure of planning. They are at least as interesting as home bases for what they indicate about the nature of early hominid societies. We can picture a foraging area which included a number of known "hot spots," say groves of trees near water or clumps of dense vegetation along perennial herd migration routes, where animals were frequently ambushed and killed. Cache sites would have been located very close to these places. Richard Potts suggests the existence of "a dual transport system"; selected stones were brought in ahead of time, and later chunks of meat and scavenged bone were brought in for processing.

Cache sites presumably called for monitoring or tending. Individuals approaching stations near carnivore hot spots would have to be sure that suitable stones had been provided for immediate use. The providers would not necessarily be the scavengers. There might have been a division of labor and perhaps what Potts calls "some sort of reciprocity," in the form of expectations that meat and marrow would be shared at eating places located safe distances away from cache sites. Of course, stones to help in processing meat and breaking bones would have been brought in ahead of time, during peaceful periods when neither predators nor prey were about. All of which called for cooperation and a measure of foresight, a somewhat extended sense of the future.

Early *erectus* times may have seen a marked shift in human diet, and in human evolution. Preliminary results of Alan Walker's studies of the microwear on fossil teeth suggest that until then hominids, presumably like some of their ancestral apes, were concentrating chiefly on fruits and that full-fledged omnivorousness—including the eating of rising proportions of seeds, grasses, and leaves as well as meat—came later. In any case, if interpretations of the remains at Torralba and Ambrona and Terra Amata hold up in the light of continuing research, *erectus* had the ability (which was perhaps greater than the need) to exploit big game, and was eating larger amounts of meat.

Hominids were probably in the process of becoming wide-ranging foragers. The difference between them and other primates must have been considerable, since meat eaters generally have to cover more territory than herbivores. Furthermore, they were becoming bigger, averaging, according to an estimate by Milford Wolpoff, about 5.5 feet tall and 170 pounds, as compared with 4.5 feet and about 115 pounds for the australopithecines. The bigger the body, the more food it needs and the more territory required to provide the food. As far as foraging terrain is concerned, *erectus* was more like a full-time carnivore, like the wolf or wild dog, than a primate.

Some small monkeys and gibbons, the smallest of the apes, spend a major part of their lives in a tenth or less of a square mile of forest (about 50 acres),

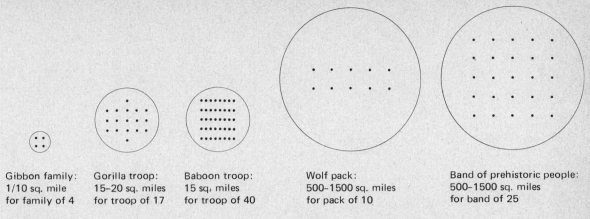

Gibbon family:
1/10 sq. mile
for family of 4

Gorilla troop:
15–20 sq. miles
for troop of 17

Baboon troop:
15 sq. miles
for troop of 40

Wolf pack:
500–1500 sq. miles
for pack of 10

Band of prehistoric people:
500–1500 sq. miles
for band of 25

Home ranges

while gorillas have a range of 15 to 20 square miles. Wolf packs may cover from 500 to 1500 square miles, and early savanna-dwelling hominids may have had territories of comparable size. According to Sherwood Washburn, "the most minor hunting expedition covers an area larger than most nonhuman primates cover in a lifetime."

BRAIN AND MEMORY

Foraging range, body size, and diet are among the key factors related in complex ways to the evolution of the brain. Body size increased in many mammalian lines including the hominid line, and the brain tended to expand with it. In other words, some of the brain expansion can be accounted for as part of a simple increase in overall dimensions. But it went further than that. The brain increased in relative size as well as absolute size. It outpaced the rest of the body, showing an extra enlargement, more than what would be expected on a strictly proportional basis, particularly in the dimensions of the cerebral cortex.

Leonard Radinsky of the University of Chicago traces similar changes among extinct South American ungulates, or hooved animals, and indicates the significance of the process: "The strongest indication we have that increased relative brain size was selected for, has adaptive value, or confers increased reproductive fitness, is that it evolved independently so many times in different groups of mammals (as well as in birds and sharks)."

The human phenomenon is even more impressive. It involved an increase in relative brain size along with other species, but more so. The human brain expanded out of all proportion, even allowing for and beyond the disproportionate increases characteristic of mammals in general and primates in particular. Noel Boaz estimates that our brain is about six times larger than it would be for a nonhuman primate of the same body weight.

Diet certainly played a role in accounting for this unusual development. Fruit eating may have put a special premium on intelligence, specifically on learning and memory, from the very beginning. Fruit-eating primates may be contrasted with primates who live primarily on foliage, leaves, and stems. Since foliage is everywhere while fruit tends to occur in dispersed patches and ripens at different times, fruit eaters generally have larger ranges and must travel greater distances in their daily food quest. As a rule, their search is considerably more complicated than that of the foliage eaters, or, to put it another way, they must register, store, and process considerably more information.

Information processing became even more important for our omnivorous ancestors, who went after foliage, leaves, fruits, insects, and meat among other things. Today's hunter-gatherers observe the places where plants grow with special care and in intense detail. Elizabeth Marshall Thomas points out that in an area of hundreds of square miles the Bushmen know "every bush and stone, every convolution of the ground, and have usually named every place in it where a certain kind of veld food may be even if that place is only a few yards in diameter, or where there is only a patch of tall arrow grass or a bee tree." They do not read or write, but they learn and remember. If all their knowledge about their land and its resources were recorded and published, it would make up a library of many volumes.

They can tell from tiny, hair-fine shoots when succulent plants will appear (and be there on the spot before competing species); from the tiniest buds whether next season's fruits will be scarce or abundant; from the shape of a leaf or the color of a berry which species are poisonous. They use sharp-edged tools to cut and shred fibers, pointed sticks to pry out roots and tubers, stone hammers to crack nuts, and containers of skin to carry food back to camp. Early hominids presumably developed similar techniques. Nuts, incidentally, not only satisfied immediate needs but represented nourishment for the future. These packets of naturally stored protein and fat could be gathered in large quantities and shared and eaten later on.

Survival depended on communicating such knowledge. Language evolved in the interests of transmitting increasingly complex information with increasing efficiency. George Silberbauer of Monash University in Australia, who has spent more time among the Kalahari Bushmen than any other investigator, stresses the importance of communicating about plants:

> As most food plants are distributed rather thinly, there is an unavoidable waste of time and energy in searching for them and in moving from one patch to another. This wastage is minimized by the expertise in field botany which is . . . passed on to girls while they are out gathering with their mothers and the other women of the band. Any individual moving about the band's territory, whether a man on a hunting trip or a band member migrating to a new campsite, takes note of the state of growth of food plants and passes this information on to others in the band. This constant updating of intelligence more narrowly defines the possible areas in which food plants might be found.

Bushmen are intimately acquainted with the life styles of more than 50 animals. The focus is always on the feeding habits of potential prey, their escape tactics, where they sleep and hide, and the things they do automatically which often lead to their undoing (for example, the three reflex flights of Malawi francolins and the telltale flattening of the ears in hares trying to avoid Louis Leakey's clutches, described in Chapter 5). Bushmen are master trackers. They can follow a herd of antelopes, even over brick-hard ground which holds only the faintest impressions of hooves, and can detect the differences in hoofprint patterns that distinguish a wounded or sick animal from its fellows.

Hunter-gatherers everywhere pay special attention to predators as well as to prey. Predators are dangerous competitors, and it is generally wise to keep at a safe distance from them, at least most of the time. Naturally, when the objective is scavenging, when people try to chase big cats away from a kill, it becomes necessary to come closer. As already indicated—whether it is a vulnerable antelope, a freshly killed carcass, a grove of just-ripened fruit, or a stand of seed-bearing grasses—the big thing is to get there first, before all the competitors, and to be ready for action. Remember those suggested cache sites at Olduvai, stocked beforehand with stones suitable for fast butchering (see Chapter 4). Also, the Acheulian hand ax, the first shaped tool prepared carefully and in advance, may represent increased meat eating and increased efficiency in beating out other predators (see Chapter 6).

We do not know all the elements that went into the humanizing of an ape. But it was a new world for primates, this walking upright on the lookout over extensive stretches of wilderness, a world of new experiences and possibilities. There can be relatively few surprises during a lifetime spent in a fraction of a square mile of forest. Horizons widen with widening ranging, with life in mosaic landscapes, dense forests, gallery forests along waterways, open woodlands, grassy plains, and semideserts. Wider roving exposed hominids to a wider variety of events, thus increasing their chances of encountering and dealing with novelty throughout life. That in effect extended their youth as compared with the youth of nonhuman primates, whose chances of encountering novelty or being surprised decreased much faster after childhood because of their restricted ranges.

The disproportionate expansion of the brain reflected this state of affairs. The brain expresses in its tissue, its biological structure, the world view of the species. Somehow it includes in the interconnections among its billions of nerve cells a micromodel of the world and its processes, and the interconnections multiply with multiplying experiences. Every new experience, every new insight and association and strategy, is represented by a new cell-to-cell pathway or net of pathways. The hominid brain became more complicated with the increasing complexity of the hominid world. As our ancestors roamed more widely in search of more kinds of food, they observed more and had more to remember and analyze. A further possible effect of the food quest, suggested by Robert Martin, is outlined in Chapter 4.

Research such as that of John Young at University College, London, hints at the anatomical basis of memory, the nature of the memory unit or mnemon. It can be thought of as a small cerebral circuit consisting of perhaps half a dozen interconnected nerve cells. Its main component is a classifying cell which receives nerve impulses from a sense organ and has two extending fibers which transmit messages to appropriate muscles. Impulses transmitted along an "advance" fiber cause the animal to approach, while the "retreat" fiber carries avoidance messages only.

We are designed to be optimists, to have great expectations, to approach things and life with high hopes. The mnemon is designed with a built-in positive bias so that an object seen for the first time is apt to be attractive and stimulate the sending of signals along the advance fiber of the classifying cells to the muscles. If the object turns out to be dangerous, however, the advance fiber is blocked chemically and subsequent signals from the classifying cell pass along the retreat fiber. Actual behavior is based on the interplay of many mnemons, but in general this seems to be how we learn that discretion is the better part of valor.

So evolution added more mnemons, more nerve cells, and the brain grew like a benign tumor at the head end of the spinal cord. Of course, it was far more than a mere increase in gross size. Subtle changes were taking place in internal organization—especially in the nerve circuitry required to inhibit or control the not-doing of things (Chapter 1). The mnemon, with its advance and retreat fibers, is the anatomical expression of an elementary choice between alternatives; depending on experience, one of the two fibers will be blocked. The multiplication of mnemons is the anatomical expression of the increasing complexity of hominid society, the multiplication of possibilities, alternative behavior patterns.

Restraint did not come automatically. Every choice, every course of action selected to the benefit of the individual and the group, had to be learned and remembered. Events weeded out those with an inferior capacity for learning and remembering. Obtaining food demanded patience and waiting, waiting for prey at water holes or salt licks, waiting for an animal to look away as you stalk it, waiting at the carcass so that you do not devour all the meat on the spot but save most of it for others waiting at the home base. Hominid evolution is a story of increasing restraint as well as increasing action.

There was also waiting for the fulfillment of sexual urges. Younger males who could bide their time and control themselves in the presence of aggressive, dominant males outlived those who could not. In anatomical terms, selection favored a rewiring of the brain so that increasing numbers of inhibitory retreat fibers ran from the highest control center, the cerebral cortex, to subcortical centers which released sex hormones and aroused sexual urges. The controls did not work perfectly. Robin Fox of Rutgers University indicates that the control of adolescent flare-ups demanded intensive initiation ceremonies and other social devices.

HELPLESS INFANTS

The expansion of the brain had a major social impact. It affected the relationship between the sexes by exaggerating a trend already evident in primate evolution, a lengthening of the period of infant dependency. A fundamental problem in the design of the female body involved the optimum dimensions of the female pelvis. From a strictly engineering point of view, the obvious way of allowing for the delivery of bigger-brained infants is to enlarge the pelvic opening or birth canal and widen the hips, and evolutionary pressures were at work which favored this solution. The difficulty is that individuals with wider hips and related modifications lose a measure of mobility. As far as speed is concerned, the ideal pelvis is a male pelvis. Women cannot generally run as fast as men, a disadvantage in prehistoric times when flight was called for frequently.

Another theoretical way of meeting the problem is to go to the other extreme and avoid the necessity for widening the hips. If the infant is born sufficiently early in its development so that its brain is still small, delivery difficulties can be minimized or eliminated. The limitation in this direction, however, concerns the danger of being brought too immature into the world; the earlier the infant is born, the smaller its chances for survival. The death rates for premature infants, weighing 5.5 pounds or less, are about three times higher than for full-term infants.

Confronted with these alternatives, nature in effect did a little bit of both, achieving a not altogether happy compromise. Natural selection arrived at a solution in which the hips were indeed widened sufficiently to permit delivery of an infant with a brain somewhat larger and sufficiently developed to ensure a reasonable chance of survival. On the other hand, the brain was by no means fully developed. It was still immature and small enough so that the hip widening did not reduce the mother's mobility to a dangerous extent. So the brain had to do most of its growing after birth. A rhesus monkey is born with a brain that has already reached nearly three-quarters of its adult size, but the brain of a newborn *Homo erectus* infant had probably completed only about a third of its growth.

Delayed maturity, of course, means extending the state of infancy, and that had crucial repercussions. Most mammals are ready to fend for themselves only a few months after birth, but a unique type of growth was established among primates and accelerated among hominids. Monkeys remain helpless for about a year, apes for 2 to 3 years; *Homo erectus* was in a similar condition for perhaps 4 to 5 years (as compared with 6 to 8 years for modern humans). Indeed, the first human infants were not only helpless longer than the infants of other primates, but they were also additionally helpless since they could not cling to their mothers.

Another trend in primate evolution is away from large litters and toward single births, or at least litters consisting of no more than two or three offspring. This development, like the development of stereoscopic vision and other features, is mainly a consequence of life in the trees, where it is considerably more difficult to care for infants than on the ground or in dens and burrows. One result is that prenatal growth can proceed at a more leisurely pace. Among species with large litters there is competition for nourishment and space within the uterus, a condition favoring relatively rapid growth and a short gestation period. Since higher primates typically give birth to only one infant, however, such competition does not exist and a slower rate of growth is possible. The focus has been increasingly on the infant as an individual, in a way that can never be the case among species with large litters. A single birth is more special, and can receive more care and attention.

Perfect solutions are rare in evolution. Prolonged infant dependency certainly increased the chances of suffering early psychic traumas, a fact which psychoanalysts have interpreted as highly significant, even regarding dependency itself as an inevitable and therefore universal trauma. But elementary biological considerations suggest that this may possibly have been a price worth paying, that in us as in other species something of value was gained as well as lost. It is at least arguable that selection was taking place for something rather more directly advantageous to the species than an increased susceptibility to neurosis.

Prolonged infancy is only part of an evolutionary process which has brought prolonged childhood, prolonged adolescence, and prolonged life, part of the slower pacing of things in a species which relies more than any other species on learning. It is difficult to imagine the young of a rapidly maturing species learning to behave appropriately in a highly organized band. An individual that could run, fight, and feed itself within 6 months or less after birth would probably not excel at the art of learning complex and flexible social responses. It would find itself too busy being a vigorous animal.

Growing up, human style, demands a delay in such activities. It is well served by early immobility and dependency which permit observations, listening, and contemplation of a sort, before full-time commitment to active doing. For example, although the circumstances under which language arose are unknown, it was probably evolving in important ways during early hominid times—and a connection may have existed between slow maturation and the ability to acquire new linguistic skills. A docile infant and an experienced adult must have made an effective combination for the establishment of social communications.

Evidence is accumulating to indicate that culture was already of some importance in *Australopithecus,* a notion originally proposed by Raymond Dart more than a generation ago. In a key investigation of molar-tooth development, Alan Mann of the University of Pennsylvania points out that the first, second, and third permanent molars erupt at about 6, 12, and 18 years respectively, in both *Australopithecus* and modern humans. On the basis of this observation, he suggests that "the growth stages of *Australopithecus* are comparable to those of *Homo sapiens* and [that] childhood development is similar in both groups." The implication is clear that hominids have long depended on "a large complex of learned behavior, or culture."

FEMALE AND MALE ROLES

Marks of the new societies involved the food quest and the division of labor between the sexes. Among today's hunter-gatherers all members of the band contribute what they can, animal or vegetable. Women may kill small game and birds when the opportunity arises, and they are at all times on the alert for tracks and other signs of bigger game; men may do their share of the picking and carrying when the time comes to collect large quantities of nuts and fruit. As a general rule, however, obtaining meat is mainly a male activity and gathering a female activity.

This arrangement is dictated mainly by the fact that human beings are born helpless and remain helpless for years. There can be no gambling on the care and feeding of offspring. That is primarily the mother's job, and she naturally exploits those resources which are most reliable and tend to be closest to home base, namely, plant foods. One result in remote prehistoric times may have been the development of an effective carrying technology. Sally Linton of the University of Colorado speculates that "two of the earliest and most important cultural inventions were containers to hold the products of gathering, and some sort of sling or net to carry babies." She also speculates that the invention of baby-carrying devices came first, and led to food-carrying devices and perhaps, still later, to the development of chopping and grinding tools for preparing food.

The evolution of the foot supports this notion, a point stressed by Adrienne Zihlman and Nancy Tanner of the University of California in Santa Cruz. Infant monkeys and apes have gripping feet that are half-hands and have mobile and opposable big toes designed to bend around and cling to the mother's hair as she moves along with the troop. *Australopithecus* infants did not have that option. Their feet were already so specialized for walking that clinging was no longer possible. As a result, there was considerable pressure on mothers to invent devices so they could simultaneously carry offspring and engage in gathering food.

The scavenging and hunting activities of males made it possible for hominids to exploit the savanna to the fullest extent. They were free to leave for long periods, and they learned from and improved on stalking strategies of lions and other rival competitors. Lions, for example, apparently do not know that their scent will not be detected if they approach prey from the upwind side, a fact which our ancestors were probably intelligent enough to deduce. Experience gained during the search for meat may also have enhanced the male's role as defender against the attacks of the big cats and other predators. Zihlman and Tanner estimate that meat may have made up about 1 percent of the diet among the earliest hominids, and perhaps 5 percent for the earliest representatives of *Australopithecus*. By *Homo erectus* times the proportion may have risen to a third or more.

Lionel Tiger of Rutgers University suggests that as men went after more game and a wider variety of game, they developed closer ties with one another. They went away in groups, ranged widely, and stayed away perhaps all night and perhaps on occasion for several nights. They began forming the all-male associations which more recently have led to such things as clubs, lodges, athletic competition, secret initiations, and an assortment of stag institutions.

Differences and stresses intensified within the male community between younger and older males. This was nothing new among primates. Goodall observes that among chimpanzees the young male has hard lessons to learn. Early in adolescence, which starts between the ages of 7 to 8, he becomes independent of his mother and increasingly capable of dominating the females, who used to dominate him. But this is also the time when larger, dominant males become increasingly aggressive toward him, and tend to keep him away from females. His frustration may be expressed by charging through the troop dragging branches and throwing rocks, but even here he must learn to be careful because all the hubbub may get on the nerves of the dominant males. Or he may wander off alone into the forest.

Making it, getting into the club of dominant males, was as important to hominid as to chimpanzee adolescents, only rather more complicated. The institution of hunting probably provided new ways for adolescents to take out their frustrations—to prove themselves. It was one further step in the accelerating development of symbols as hunting and the eating of meat acquired new values and meanings.

Such developments dramatize the very special position of hominids in evolution. They provide an example of species being put to the severest of tests. All species survive by adapting, but the adaptations of hominids were far more elaborate, and have become increasingly so. The divisive forces of the past, which tended to create new and conflicting groups within groups, represent only part of the story. The existence of society is possible because such conflicts served to accelerate the building up of powerful counterforces in a continuing interplay of tensions and the relaxation of tensions. Our ancestors became the only primates to scavenge and kill regularly for a living, and the only primates to share regularly on a day-to-day basis involving the entire group.

Evolution worked to establish a secure, stable social framework in a milieu of potentially disruptive forces. The new framework had to be strong and flexible enough to include male-male as well as male-female associations. The problem has not yet been solved to the complete satisfaction of either sex, but early steps toward a solution included changes in patterns of sexual behavior that were designed to reduce new tensions and anxieties.

The typical pattern among mammals involves regular bursts of sexual frenzy which take precedence over all other activities. At every ovulation or immediately after, all nonhuman females, including occasional nursing females, come into estrus or heat. Sexual activity is so concentrated and intense during such periods that it tends to interrupt the care of the young and all other forms of behavior. This sort of all-inclusive estrus ensures effective reproduction among most mammals which have rapidly maturing offspring, but not among primates. If all the females in a primate troop were subject to three days of sexual mania every month or so, it might be to the detriment of their slow-maturing infants. Natural selection brought about a modification in monkeys and apes, to the extent that estrus ceases during the later part of pregnancy and the early part of nursing.

A modified form of estrus is fully compatible with the primate way of life— that is, with the way of life of nonhuman primates. The human female is the only mammalian female in which estrus has disappeared entirely. This development may have started with the appearance of first hominids, which occurred 5 million or more years ago. It was probably established among the hunting-gathering bands of *Homo erectus*. Estrus cycles may simply have made less and less sense in a species with single births spaced further and further apart as the period of infant dependency lengthened. A new reproductive rhythm was being established; estrus no longer served an evolutionary purpose, and it went by default, as it were.

More positive forces may have been at work to speed the departure of estrus. The female of the species became sexually receptive at practically any time rather than during estrus only, eliminating periods during which male competition and aggressiveness reached a peak and contributing further to the stability of life. Extended sexual receptivity on the part of females served also to extend the period of their attractiveness to males and may have helped counterbalance the new appeal of male-male associations. The changing pattern of female behavior helped to tie males more securely into the group.

The increased possibility of choice in the timing of sexual relations had long-range repercussions. Estrus, even as modified among nonhuman primates, is essentially beyond the individual's control. Its presence and absence are determined by the automatic turning on and turning off of sex-hormone secretions, presumably by a kind of biological clock in the brain which keeps track of the passage of time and periodically triggers the activity of centers concerned with the arousal of sexual urges. Under such conditions, the sexual act among early hominids tended to be relatively impersonal and mechanical, as it is among contemporary monkeys and apes.

When sexual urges came under a measure of voluntary control, it became possible to select not only the time and place for mating, but also the mate. According to Zihlman and Tanner, it may have been another step in the continuing socialization, domestication, or taming of the male: "A male could attract a female's attention by disruptive displays or through friendly interaction, including greetings, grooming, playing with her offspring, food sharing, protecting, or simple proximity. Females preferred to associate and have sex with males exhibiting friendly behavior, rather than those who were comparatively disruptive, a danger to themselves or offspring. The picture then is one of the bipedal, food-sharing and sociable mothers choosing to copulate with males also possessing these traits."

Personal preference acquired a new meaning. For the first time more enduring male-female-offspring relationships became possible, which ultimately led to the family as we know it. These were the opening phases in the prehistory of love, at least love in the human sense, which includes homosexual love, a by-product of the male-male associations in hunting bands, as well as heterosexual love. Of course, both were by-products of the replacement of automatic hormonal control of social behavior by a measure of free selection of partners.

Changing sexual patterns brought new orders of social complexity, new things to be learned and remembered, new inhibitions and prohibitions, and wider relationships. As we shall see in Chapters 12 and 13, nonhuman primates are highly organized. But their organizations are primarily internal, within the troop. Their foreign affairs are rather less ordered than their domestic affairs. Troops generally either ignore or avoid one another, or else fight. Human beings alone form organizations, tribal unions, confederations. *Erectus* probably did not go very far in this direction. The possibilities were there, however; in a sense, the groundwork had been laid.

FIRE— REVOLUTIONARY CHANGES

The entire process of human evolution was complicated, enriched, and accelerated by the greatest technological advance of the times, the use of fire. The first force of nature to be domesticated, fire gave human beings a new degree of independence. By bringing fire to the places where they lived, they created zones of warmth and light in the darkness, halo spaces, caves of light. The wide wilderness became a little less wild and less lonely. They achieved a way of keeping the night and nighttime prowlers at bay and the freedom to explore new lands with harsh climates.

Judging by the evidence at hand, still largely negative, our ancestors first put fire to work on a regular basis to keep themselves warm somewhere along the route out of Africa across the Sahara and into Europe. Hominids must have been familiar with fire in Africa. They lived with it, and perhaps died by it, during volcanic upheavals associated with the formation of the African Rift Valley. They probably moved away when volcanoes were active, and returned when the earth became quiet again, being no less persistent than people today who keep returning to areas devastated by floods, earthquakes, and other natural disasters.

No early-hominid hearths have been found in Africa. But John Harris of the University of Wisconsin in Milwaukee and other investigators are looking for, and may already have found, clues to the use of fire in remote times. For example, a number of sites, among them Desmond Clark's Ethiopian site which yielded 3000 tools (Chapter 6), include patches of clay baked and discolored by fires that burned long ago. But we do not know precisely how long ago, or whether these features are the result of ancient campfires or fires produced by natural forces such as lightning or volcanic action. Some answers can be expected within the next few years, with more intensive studies of how fire affects bone and stone as well as clay.

In any case, ample evidence for fire exists in later and colder times and, as pointed out in Chapter 6, the earliest known hearths burned some million years ago in the Escale cave of southeastern France. Humans had wandered about as far north as they could at the time without starving and freezing to death. They were living where no normal primate should be, nearly within the shadows of alpine glaciers.

Fire was probably first obtained ready-made from natural sources. (The first sign of artificial fire making is an iron-pyrites ball with a deep groove produced by repeated striking to create tinder-igniting sparks; it comes from a Belgian site only about 15,000 years old.) The notion that Prometheus stole fire from the heights of Mount Olympus is not as widely believed as it once was. But Prometheus has a certain relevance if, as seems likely, volcanoes were a major source of fire in early prehistory. According to Kenneth Oakley of the British Museum of Natural History, other sources were available in less turbulent areas: "Man could also have relied on accidental fires started by lightning in dry brush or grassland or where there were seepages of mineral oil and gas. Occasionally in damp environments coal or shale-oil deposits might be ignited by spontaneous combustion, and during the last century one such fire burned for four years in Dorset."

Perhaps people camped near fire, a natural resource like game, water, and shelter. They may sometimes have left otherwise favorable areas when fires began petering out. If so, they had to take it with them when they moved away. It had to be kept burning like the Olympic flame, fed and nursed like a newborn infant. Each band may have had a fire bearer; perhaps one of its older members was responsible for carrying and guarding embers in a cup of clay covered with green leaves and breathed the embers into flame when the band found a new place to live.

Fire provided more than warmth. It soon became another factor in setting humans apart from other species. With it our ancesters could move more freely, and instead of having to avoid other predators, the predators got out of the way. Fire must have kept predators as well as cold weather at a safe distance. On icy wilderness nights, big cats and other predators, attracted by the smell of meat and light, stayed outside the protective circle of the fireside. Perhaps people observed that on occasion the animals scrambled even further away when sparks flew at them out of the flames. They may have learned to produce the same effect by hurling glowing pieces of wood at animals' heads. In any case, they eventually began using fire more aggressively, in a shift from defense to offense.

The earliest known hearths were located in caves, originally occupied by stronger and longer-established killers. Before fire people often had to be content with second-best sites, rock shelters, and overhangs and less effective protection. Fire, however, could help them drive other killers out. Bears, hyenas, and many other cave-dwelling animals shared the Escale region with early humans but stayed out of their caves. Fire probably enabled Peking individuals to take permanent possession of Dragon Bone Hill cave. It is no coincidence that the first layers which provide evidence that people had moved into the cave also happen to be the layers which contain charcoal fragments, burned bones, and other traces of fire. Only after they had learned to tame fire could they become regular cave dwellers whenever conditions demanded it.

They also used fire to become more and more effective predators themselves, to stampede animals and to produce more effective spears. The Australian aborigines charred the tips of their digging sticks lightly, a treatment which hardens the core of the wood and makes the outer part more crumbly and easier to sharpen. People were acquainted with this technique at least 80,000 years ago, as indicated by a yew spear with a fire-hardened point found at a site in north Germany. Some investigators feel that equally advanced treatments had been developed as far back as the days of Peking individuals.

Cooking is also believed to date back to these times, mainly on the basis of indirect but convincing evidence involving teeth, sensitive indicators of evolutionary change. As described in Chapter 2, one argument for dietary changes among the earliest hominids is that they had small canine teeth instead of the large canines characteristic of many other primates. But molar teeth, which serve chiefly for grinding and heavy-duty chewing, tended to remain large until *Homo erectus* times, when they began to become smaller, perhaps because people were eating softer, cooked foods.

Regular cooking may have helped reshape the contours of the human face, in a kind of chain-reaction process. According to one theory, softer foods put less of a strain on the jaws and jaw muscles, which became smaller along with the molar teeth. This in turn had an effect on the design of the rest of the skull. Thick bony protuberances on the side of the skull had evolved largely as platforms to which powerful jaw muscles could be attached, and massive overhanging brow ridges may have served as shock absorbers to take up stresses transmitted upward through jaws and cheeks from incisor and canine teeth. These structures were reduced as jaw muscles dwindled in size. Furthermore, the skull itself became thinner, perhaps one of the changes involved in expanding the cranium to house a bigger brain.

As for the origin of cooking, no one has yet been able to improve on the basic point of Charles Lamb's story about the suckling pig that was done to a turn when a house burned down. There were no houses half a million years ago, but a forest fire could have done the job just as effectively. Or perhaps a careless hunter dropped his share of the day's kill into a blazing fire and relished the meat when it was recovered. Such accidents must have happened many times before man finally made a practice of roasting tough foods.

There were psychological as well as physical changes. Cooking played a part in promoting more restraint. With the advent of cookery people tended to spend less time devouring freshly killed game on the spot and more time back at the cave eating with the rest of the band around a hearth. The domestication of fire was one more step in human domestication. Inhibition is as much a mark of evolutionary advance as action itself.

And above all, fire was light. It increased the length of the day, created a new kind of day, independent of the movements of the sun. Life became less routine. People no longer rose and slept with the rising and setting of the sun. They had become independent of one great natural rhythm, the internal rhythm of estrus, so now they were independent of the external rhythm of day and night. The hours after dark were hours of relative leisure, time for the evolution of more sophisticated ways of communicating. Language, the most human form of human behavior, must have taken a tremendous spurt when hunting was on the rise and fires burned brightly past sunset. There was so much to share—the day's adventures, a herd or a band sighted at a distance while out gathering, tall tales about the big one that got away during the hunt, and tomorrow's food quest.

The fireside became an institution, a cohesive force bringing members of the band closer together, old as well as young. Other primates also had their patriarchs and matriarchs, but now age acquired a new importance. Now individuals too old to fight, carry heavy things, or walk long distances became important because they remembered things beyond the memories of others— particularly things that happened rarely, such as floods and other catastrophes, and things that required special knowledge, such as the settling of territorial disputes and the treatment of illnesses. The elders took their places at the fireside and were consulted and listened to.

Finally, fire presumably played a role in early mystical experiences. A tendency to engage in rituals can be seen in our closest living relatives. Goodall has observed chimpanzees engaging in elaborate displays or ''rain dances'' during tropical storms. On one occasion seven adult males performed before an audience of appreciative females and juveniles that climbed into the trees to watch. The males moved to the top of a grassy slope, divided themselves into two groups of three and four members, and took turns making sudden charges down the slope and springing into a tree, tearing off branches, hurtling themselves to the ground, and dragging the branches along while barking and hooting.

They were responding to the elements. The entire performance, which lasted about half an hour, was carried out in the midst of a heavy rain to the accompaniment of thunderclaps and bolts of lightning. According to the British observer, "against the green grass they looked black and very large, like primitive men displaying their strength." It requires no great stretch of the imagination to think of early hominids responding with their own varieties of ritual to the forces of nature. Fire may have served a double purpose, to arouse excitement as well as to provide warmth and light.

Such effects may have very ancient origins. Oakley emphasizes "the deep subconscious or sensual appeal" of fire, noting that the appeal may be traced back to the earliest days of primate evolution: "The fact that the Philippine tarsier has been named *Tarsius carbonarius* on account of its propensity for picking up hot embers from camp-fire sites suggested to me that man's prehuman ancestors may have been attracted to natural fires and toyed with burning matter." Fire may be a stimulant as potent as drugs in arousing visions and previsions, and as such it would have served the purposes of priests and priestesses, the cultural descendants of the fire bearers of *Homo erectus* times.

Fire, like tools, had a double impact. It kept predators and the cold away and at the same time drew people closer together. It served material needs and at the same time helped create a new way of life and a new kind of evolution. Tracing cause-and-effect patterns in such a context becomes exceedingly difficult. Though we make inferences which go beyond the evidence, the effort is always to speculate along lines compatible with the evidence.

I wish we knew more about the life style of *erectus,* the daily grind. There is so little direct evidence that Arthur Jelinek of the University of Arizona characterized the period from about 1.5 million to 100,000 years ago as a time of "unimaginable monotony," that is, archeologically speaking. The record is frustratingly silent. A great deal must have been happening, and we have no choice but to make the most of inferences based largely on observations of the only living material available, nonhuman primates and recent hunter-gatherers. The dangers of inference are well known. Real life jibes all too rarely with even our most convincing speculations—which, of course, is one good reason for keeping minds open and theories tentative.

SUMMARY

Survival for all species depends primarily on the food quest, and there is an advantage in not being too specialized, too fussy. Forest-dwelling apes like the chimpanzee prefer fruits in season. But they are omnivores, ready to eat practically anything edible—leaves, seeds, insects, bark, honey, meat—a strategic form of insurance. If preferred sources of food fail, there are always options, and early hominids were similarly versatile.

They confronted some special problems. Since food tends to be far more widely dispersed in open woodlands and savannas than in forests, they presumably had to cover larger areas than their forest-dwelling ancestors. Gibbons, the smallest apes, spend most of their lives in a home range of a tenth or less of a square mile (about 50 acres), while hominids may have exploited 500 to 1500 square miles.

That called for extensive monitoring, knowing the locations of food sources, water holes, "hot spots" where carnivores did most of the killing and where stones might be cached for anticipated scavenging. It called for a measure of planning and foresight and sharing, restraint as well as action, qualities which put a premium on memory and on some relatively advanced form of language or prelanguage. It was under such selective forces that the brain tripled in size from early australopithecine to *erectus* times.

Life became more complicated with expanding brains. The dimensions of the female pelvis limited the head size of newborn infants; most of the brain's growth took place after birth, and slowly. As a result, *erectus* infants remained completely dependent for perhaps the first 4 to 5 years of life, as compared to a 2- to 3-year dependency for the offspring of modern apes. Extended infant care, mainly the mother's responsibility, intensified division of labor between the sexes. It also gave rise to social forces which, among other things, brought about a loss of estrus, increasing the period of sexual receptivity.

Social change was further accelerated by another major development, this one cultural rather than biological. *Erectus* was the first hominid to use fire, and that had repercussions which could not have been foreseen. Originally used to provide warmth, fire served a number of other purposes. It lengthened the day, drove predators out of their caves, helped establish secure home bases and cooking practices—and eventually played a central role in game drives, and perhaps in promoting ritual and ceremony.

chapter 8

The Pace Quickens

"Unimaginable monotony"—the phrase bears closer analysis. It applies not only to the persistence of the hand ax and other shaped Acheulian tools, but also to the morphology, the skeletal features, of the tool makers. As pointed out by Philip Rightmire (Chapter 6), *Homo erectus* seems to have changed little over a period of more than a million years.

That may be a record of a sort. Some investigators regard this vast stretch of time as a period of stagnation, a low point in the steady march of human progress. It does not look that way, however, if you consider what makes species successful. If adaptation is the business of evolution, if the objective is to achieve equilibrium, to find and settle into a secure ecological niche, then this period represents the high point in the story of the genus *Homo*. Judging by the current state of affairs, our kind may never achieve a comparable equilibrium, certainly not in the foreseeable future.

We do not know why the pace of change picked up, but the first signs are found in the fossil record. The earth was hardly a crowded place, but crowding can be a relative thing, and certain regions were more densely occupied than others. The population centers of *Homo erectus* were the richest grasslands, which attracted the largest herds and the greatest number of predators, including humans. Bands presumably crossed paths from time to time, and exchanged wary glances or signaled greetings as they proceeded on their ways. Perhaps they met now and then for seasonal get-togethers or for the occasional game drive, but the odds are that they did not stay together long, because the larger the group, the more frequent and intense the fighting. Our species has always found danger in large numbers.

OUR KIND OF HOMINID

Climate was one of the factors playing a role in the transition to *Homo sapiens*. The change may have occurred at different times in different parts of the world, notably in northern lands which called for new and more complex adaptations in the vicinity of glaciers. A gravel pit in the English village of Swanscombe, not far from London, has yielded important fossil clues, as usual through a combination of searching and luck, in this case luck triply compounded. The Thames Valley site is a well-known collectors' paradise, possibly a place where hunters camped to kill big game coming to drink from the river. Several hundred thousand stone tools must have been found there during the past century or so. But no human remains had appeared until one Saturday noon in June 1935, when local cement workers who had stopped digging for the day noticed a piece of bone protruding from a gravel bank. It turned out to be part of the skull of a prehistoric individual, probably a female who had died in her early 20s.

A second lucky find occurred the following March near the original find, another bone fragment which was not only human but also happened to be part of the same skull. The two pieces fitted neatly. The final discovery, representing something of an anthropological miracle, occurred one moonlit evening during World War II. A fleet of trucks came to the Swanscombe pit and removed hundreds of tons of gravel as part of the top-secret Mulberry harbor project to make concrete caissons, or floating docks, for the Allied invasion of Normandy. How many prehistoric remains were ground up for the concrete will never be known, but at least one important object was left behind and found after the war in 1955—a third skull fragment. This specimen turned up about 75 feet from the original find and, by remarkable coincidence, belongs to the same individual as the other two specimens; furthermore, it fits together with them to form the entire back half of a skull.

The relative age of these remains has been fairly well established. As pointed out in Chapter 6, after some 60 million years of comparatively mild and stable climates, Europe experienced a number of climatic oscillations, during which mean annual temperatures varied from 50 degrees Fahrenheit to below-freezing levels. Geological studies show that the gravels which contained the Swanscombe remains were laid down during a period of glacial retreat, a so-called interglacial stage which dates back perhaps 250,000 years.

Swanscombe people enjoyed a comfortable climate. In fact, as far as the weather is concerned, that was the time to be in England. Elephants and rhinoceroses, which had come from Africa over the Dardanelles land bridge, browsed in warm Thames Valley forests along with wild boar, deer, and other woodland species. But cooler times were on the way. A decrease in the number of these species and an increase in the number of open-grassland species, such as giant oxen and horses, indicate that the forests were beginning to recede, a prelude to the coming of another glaciation.

Swanscombe people represent a distinct advance over their fossil predecessors, although the extent of the advance has been debated. Examination of the three fragments and reconstructions based on them indicate that they had large brains; their cranial capacity is estimated at about 1300 cubic centimeters, which lies well within the modern range (see Chapter 6). Furthermore, there is a general suggestion of rounded and expanded skull contours, somewhat like the modern shape. These features have been interpreted as evidence for an apparent evolutionary leap, the sudden appearance of a human being who was nearly fully modern. On the other hand, the relatively low brain case and certain other characteristics suggest that the specimen may be a less advanced form, intermediate between *Homo erectus* and modern people.

Supporting the latter viewpoint is another fossil skull found in 1933 in another gravel pit, near the village of Steinheim in western Germany. This specimen includes the face and upper jaw, which are lacking in the English specimen, and it may have something to tell us about Swanscombe people, assuming, of course, that the two were contemporaries (both skulls were found in interglacial deposits) and were members of the same species or subspecies. In any case, Steinheim people were modern in back but not in front. They had sloping foreheads and very large brow ridges; it was argued that Swanscombe people may have been at the same stage of development.

These impressions have been put to the test by Joseph Weiner, the man who exploded the Piltdown hoax, and Bernard Campbell of Cambridge. They turned to statistical techniques, which depend on carefully selected measurements of corresponding areas and curvatures of different skulls. For example, one problem was to ascertain as precisely as possible the area of the neck region at the back of the skull, an area which tends to become smaller and smoother during the course of human evolution, reflecting the expansion of the brain and a decrease in the size of face and jaws.

In all, 17 measurements were made between points on the Swanscombe skull. For purposes of comparison, similar measurements were made of some

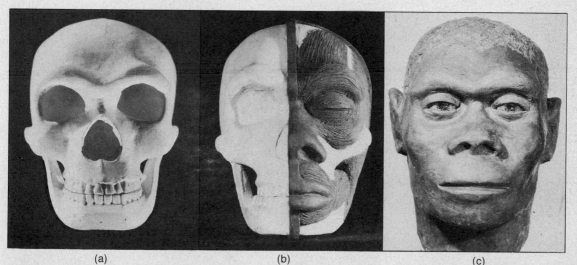

(a)   (b)   (c)

Stages in reconstruction of Steinheim people, one version of early *Homo sapiens*, front view: (a) skull in plaster; (b) building up muscles and skin with clay; (c) completed bust

500 male and female skulls excavated from a 4000-year-old communal tomb in southern Israel, about 60 skulls of contemporary races and 10 fossil specimens, representing finds from 250,000 years ago (the Steinheim specimen) to 35,000 years ago. This information was used to calculate the so-called distance functions, numbers which indicate how closely the different fossil skulls are related to modern skulls. The task required millions of calculations and would have taken years using desk-type adding machines, but it took only a few minutes using an electronic computer at Oxford University.

TRANSITIONAL SPECIES

Judging by the results, the Swanscombe individual meets the general specifications for a transitional species, a species on its way but not yet arrived. Like the Steinheim specimen, it is definitely *Homo sapiens,* but very early *Homo sapiens,* embodying certain relatively primitive as well as modern features. In short, the individuals are just about right for their time, the products of a gradual and continuing process rather than a sudden spurt. The same thing goes for the skull of a 20-year-old man excavated by Henry de Lumley at a cave in the French Pyrenees, and for a skull found embedded in the wall of an almost inaccessible chamber of a cave in the village of Petralona in eastern Greece. That such specimens may represent early precursors of modern humans is by no means a new notion; some investigators had already arrived at it without benefit of statistics. But the main point is that other investigators had arrived at quite different interpretations on the basis of the identical evidence; the study provides a relatively objective evaluation of the evidence.

The early forerunners of modern people probably lived pretty much the same as late representatives of *Homo erectus* lived. At least, stone tools and other excavated materials suggest no obvious differences. Although their work may have been somewhat superior, Swanscombe people were not radical innovators and they made the same basic Acheulian-type tools that had been made for hundreds of thousands of years—hand axes, notched and saw-toothed implements, scrapers, engravers, and so on. There are characteristics, however, which might represent differences in behavior if we only knew enough to interpret them. Why did the Swanscombe tool kit include nearly twice as many hand axes as the tool kits of Torralba and Ambrona predecessors? Why did Swanscombe people use an unusually high proportion of hand axes with a wide base, tapered to a point at the apex, and an unusually low proportion of ovate or egg-shaped hand axes? Current opinion is that these different tool kits may reflect different activities (see Chapter 9), but evidence for the specific nature of those activities is still lacking.

Another English site at Hoxne, about 65 miles northeast of Swanscombe and of about the same age or slightly more recent, provides further evidence. It contains rich deposits of clay, which mark the place where a huge mass of ice broke off a retreating glacier perhaps 300,000 years ago and melted slowly to form a small lake. (At another site near Birmingham, England, a block of ice about 50 feet across took more than 30,000 years to melt.) Ever since the eighteenth century the clays have been used to make bricks and terra-cotta pipes.

In 1797, the English antiquarian John Frere visited the site and made a remarkable observation.

People do not see what they are not prepared to see, and since the notion of a remote prehistoric past simply did not exist in those days, a variety of involved theories were invented to explain away traces of this past. Flint tools, some of them beautifully shaped, were considered natural accidents, like shapes seen in drifting clouds or in the gnarled branches of trees—things that had been formed either by thunder in the clouds and then fallen to earth or by lightning as it struck and shattered flint lying on the ground. Frere knew better. He found hand axes and other tools in the Hoxne clay deposits and recognized them as human-made implements dating back "to a very remote period indeed, even beyond that of the present world." (Frere, by the way, has the added distinction of being Mary Leakey's great-great-grandfather.)

Modern excavations at the site reveal a Swanscombe type of Acheulian tool kit, including the same unexplained high proportion of pointed hand axes with wide bases. Another finding emerges from fossil-pollen studies conducted by Richard West of the University of Cambridge. Pollens recovered from gray clays and muds deposited before the coming of humans show that thick oak and elm forests surrounded the lake. But signs of a different environment are found in overlying brown-green clay layers containing tools and other human traces. A decline of oak and elm pollens and a sharp rise of grass pollens indicate that open grasslands replaced the forests.

Geological research rules out the most obvious explanation for this change, a change in climate, for the climate was generally mild throughout. Another possibility exists, however. Charcoal has been found in the occupation layers, suggesting that the deforestation was caused by fires which were originally set during a dry summer, and then raged out of control. In any case, the forests returned soon after the people left, first temperate oak and elm forests and later forests of dwarf willows and other trees found in arctic environments. Another major glaciation had begun.

Little evidence exists for the course of human evolution during this period, which lasted more than 150,000 years. This is a particularly tantalizing state of affairs, since other information, such as the fact that surprising anatomical changes appeared later following the retreat of the glaciers, suggests that important developments were taking place. A number of French sites provide evidence of human activity. One workshop area, no larger than a living room, has yielded thousands of flint tools and in the archeologically rich Somme Valley region near Amiens, associated pieces, including various types of hand axes and cleavers as well as an assortment of scrapers and knives.

There is another interesting site in England at High Lodge, not far from Cambridge, where people camped by a lake during a time of temporary relief from Arctic conditions. (The climate was not stable in glacial periods, fluctuating from very cold below-zero temperatures to cool conditions rather like those encountered in mild winters today.) Many of the tools recovered from clay deposits marking the location of the lake are remarkably similar to tools found at the Somme Valley site.

Some clues about the people who made the tools come from the Lazaret

(a)

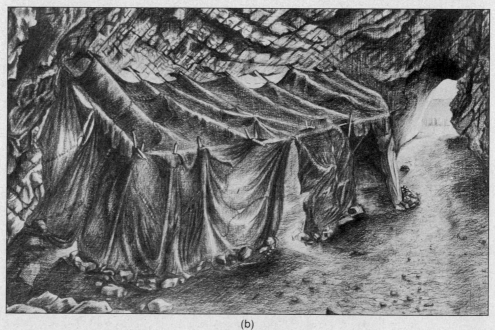

(b)

Lazaret cave: (a) excavators at work; (b) reconstruction of tent-like structure inside cave, as it may have looked 125,000 years ago; (c) tent-like structure, interior view

(c)

cave excavated by de Lumley and, like his Terra Amata site, also located in Nice on the French Riviera. One of the earliest patterned sites known, it dates back some 125,000 years and includes a sleeping area identified by the presence of clusters of small marine shells, a variety found attached only to seaweed; de Lumley believes the shells may have been brought in to provide a comfortable padding. Two hearths suggest a short-term occupation by two families, a total of no more than ten or so individuals. Shattered marrow bones were found near the hearths and, further away, intact vertebrae and other bones presumably discarded as garbage.

Piles of rock may have held up posts supporting a structure inside the cave, perhaps a tent or windbreak or a rack for the drying of hides. There are also wolf remains, including a skull at the cave entrance, interpreted by de Lumley as a kind of Keep Out sign to warn off intruders when the occupants were away. Binford has a less imaginative and perhaps more realistic explanation, namely that nonhuman predators used the cave at some later time: "I am confident that there was at least a minor occupation of Lazaret by wolves."

DOWNGRADING THE NEANDERTHALS

The next glimpse of humans comes from the next interglacial stage in Europe, the period from about 125,000 to 75,000 years ago. England and Ireland were part of the Continent then. Broad valleys existed where the English Channel and Irish and North seas are now, and great rivers flowed through the valleys, rivers which included the Seine, Thames, and Rhine as tributaries.

The people living among lions, hyenas, elephants, and other European animals of the times were not what one might expect of our evolving ancestors. They were definitely *Homo sapiens,* but they belonged to new subspecies, or races, and in certain respects a strikingly more primitive subspecies. Although their brains were about as large as the brain of Swanscombe and Steinheim people, their massive receding jaws and faces were actually closer to *Homo erectus* then to *Homo sapiens.* Their remains have been found in a limestone crevice in central Germany, in deposits on the left bank of a tributary of the Tiber near Rome, and at several other sites in Europe, the Soviet Union, and Israel.

Even stranger breeds of humans arose later. The bands hunting in western Europe during most of the subsequent cold period, the next-to-last glaciation, were made up of individuals anatomically more remote from modern people than were their predecessors from some 6000 or 7000 generations before. They had appreciably larger brains, one of the features by which they are ranked as *Homo sapiens.* They also had heavier brow ridges, a sloping forehead, large nasal cavities, forward-projecting nose and teeth, and a lower cranial vault which tended to be flat at the top and bulging at the sides. Rugged long bones, heavily reinforced where muscles were attached and with huge joints, indicated that their bodies were stocky, short, and massive-limbed.

This combination of features is based on specimens accumulated since 1856 and representing about 350 individuals. It marks the classic Neanderthal people. Erik Trinkaus of the University of New Mexico emphasizes their extraordinary strength. Their bones were 10 to 20 percent heavier than ours, denser and more solid, with smaller-bore marrow channels running lengthwise down the center. Their shinbones could withstand bending and twisting forces that would snap our shinbones like dry twigs. They had a hand grip two or three times stronger, and their strongest individuals could probably lift weights of a ton or so.

Their extraordinary muscularity tells us that they were performing on a habitual day-to-day basis physical work of the most strenuous sort—probably including walks of 20 miles or more through snow and over ice and rough terrain, and coming back with loads of meat, plant foods, and firewood. Even allowing for their exceptional strength, it is still difficult to understand how they survived, moving long distances through deep snows, apparently without snowshoes or any other specialized equipment. They provide perhaps the most impressive example of the adaptability of the human species, the ability to cope and endure even in the absence of a sophisticated technology.

The Neanderthal physique is believed to have been shaped in part by climate. The large nasal cavities helped warm extra-large volumes of inhaled air, and were located an extra distance in front of the brain to protect that organ from low temperatures. The massive muscles produced extra heat during activity. Also, Trinkaus points out that the shinbone was relatively short compared with the thighbone, an adaptation which serves to reduce heat loss to the extremities. A similar difference, although somewhat less marked, holds for the forearm in relation to the humerus. In general, individuals with short, stocky builds conserve heat better than lean and lanky individuals.

These people were respectable mentally as well as physically. There is no anatomical sign that they were inferior to us cerebrally. Their forehead does slope backward, for example, but not enough to diminish appreciably the size and presumably the quality of their frontal lobes, the most advanced brain centers. Yet even the best novelists who write about prehistoric times, as well as a number of anthropologists who should know better, seem to think otherwise.

The Neanderthals in Golding's *The Inheritors* speak in only the simplest here-and-now phrases like "I am hungry," "I ate meat," and "I have a picture," the latter phrase usually prefacing painful and generally unsuccessful efforts to think ahead or grapple with abstractions. In a more recent work of paleofiction, *The Clan of the Cave Bear*, they have undeveloped vocal cords and brains "with almost no frontal lobes." They use only a few gutturally uttered words, and communicate mostly by sign language.

The Neanderthals will always be surrounded by fiction. The strangest thing of all about them, stranger even than their unique physical characteristics, is the revulsion they aroused among their nineteenth-century descendants. They come to mind whenever cave dwellers are mentioned, and they inevitably serve as models for artists depicting our early ancestors. They have become symbols—for good reason. As the first fossil people to be discovered, they made a powerful impression on a world that was not ready to accept the notion of evolution or its implications. The discovery and the reaction to it mark one of the most significant and revealing episodes in the annals of science. It was the beginning of the study of prehistory, and the atmosphere was one of bitter debate and intense emotional involvement, bordering at times on a hysteria that still lingers in some quarters.

In 1856, when human bones were found in a small limestone-quarry cave in the Neanderthal, a valley near Düsseldorf, Germany, practically everything discussed in this book was unknown and the rest was ignored. Some investigators recognized the importance of the remains from the beginning, but they were a very small minority. The predominant opinion, which people were ready to accept, was that the bones represented not an extinct breed of humans, but a modern, freakish, and sick individual. A prominent anatomist reported that the fossils were those of an idiot who had suffered from rickets and other bone diseases and had a violent disposition. The flat forehead and heavy brows, he explained, had been caused by blows on the head.

According to other authorities, the bones were those of a Cossack who had perished during Napoleon's retreat from Moscow, a victim of water on the brain, "an old Dutchman," "a member of the Celtic race." Everyone wanted to disown this human specimen. An English scholar was responsible for one of the most melodramatic diagnoses: "It may have been one of those wild men, half-crazed, half-idiotic, cruel and strong, who are always more or less to be found living on the outskirts of barbarous tribes, and who now and then appear in civilized communities to be consigned perhaps to the penitentiary or the gallows, when their murderous propensities manifest themselves."

These and other reactions amounted above all to a violent rejection of the Neanderthals as legitimate human ancestors and, at a more basic level, a violent rejection of the notion that we have arisen from less-human species. Evolution, biological change, was an alien and heretical concept. It had long been taken for granted that species were immutable, that all living things had been created in their final perfect form in the beginning, and that nothing important had happened since. In the sixteenth century, for example, this belief was so firmly established that people simply refused to concede the existence of fossils of any sort.

Fossils implied extinctions, and extinctions, in turn, implied that the creator had designed species so poorly that they failed to endure. So the general attitude was to regard the objects which kept turning up, objects that looked very much like skulls and teeth and vertebrae and the imprints of ferns and seashells, as mere illusions produced by the action of thunder and other forces. In other words, fossils, like flint tools, were believed to be natural accidents. A less widely supported and slightly more realistic theory allowed that fossil bones were actually the remains of dead animals. On the other hand, the animals were not believed to be extinct; they still lived in unexplored parts of the world or in mammoth caverns deep beneath the earth's surface.

The theories had changed somewhat by the mid-nineteenth century. Extinction was recognized as a fact of nature, but the notion of perfect and unchanging species was preserved. According to prevailing ideas, fossils were the remains of creatures wiped out during the Flood (not having been passengers on the Ark) and not related to existing forms. Indeed, the whole past was a Biblical past. Genesis, Eden, the Flood, were not myths but familiar historical events, and very recent events at that. Different interpretations of the Scriptures gave different dates for the creation of the earth, 3700, 4004, or 5199 B.C., but authorities generally agreed on a past so brief as to allow little time for evolution of any sort.

Furthermore, the world was in many ways a simpler and cozier place than it is today. There were no eons, no vast stretches of geological time to make the past remote and evoke a feeling of infinity and other worlds. The past was close at hand and had a special aura to it, a glow like that surrounding a long-lost childhood. Although there were vague notions of barbarian times, the emphasis was on golden ages, knights, and chivalry. Modern living seemed shoddy by comparison.

In such times and against such a background of beliefs, the discovery of Neanderthal people came as a terrible shock. It might have created less of a scandal if other discoveries had been made in the proper evolutionary sequence, if the way had been prepared during preceding generations by finding *Ramapithecus* first and then *Australopithecus* and finally *Homo erectus*. The discoveries came in precisely the reverse order, however, which was partly to be expected by the nature of things. The laws of chance favored the possibility that fossil humans would be found first in western Europe, where population densities were highest and quarries most numerous, and that the first people found would be Neanderthals because Neanderthal remains seem to outnumber all other human fossil remains in this region.

Neanderthals came into the world of the Victorians like naked savages into a ladies' sewing circle. In the eyes of the Victorians, Neanderthals were beasts. Neanderthals suggested not only that the past may have been less golden than the Scriptures implied, but also that disturbing forces were at work in the present. They reminded people of the Jekyll-and-Hyde qualities and the animal side of human nature. We who live with our knowledge of fire bombs and Hiroshima and gas chambers and napalm can afford to be tolerant of the Victorians' horrified response to the sort of self-understanding that evolution offers. We are much closer to them than we like to think.

Attitudes began changing somewhat not long after the original 1856 discovery. The publication of Darwin's *On the Origin of Species* 3 years later provided a biological basis for evolution in general, and the discovery of more fossils provided new evidence for the evolution of humans. Between 1866 and 1910, half a dozen sites in France and Belgium yielded Neanderthal remains associated with flint tools and the remains of woolly rhinoceroses, mammoths, cave bears, and other extinct species. There was no longer good reason to regard the Neanderthals as mad or diseased moderns. It was widely agreed that they had vanished tens of thousands of years ago.

But most investigators were slower to recognize the Neanderthal breed as advanced human beings, and much less as *Homo sapiens,* than they were to recognize its fossil status. As recently as the 1920s Neanderthal people were considered far more remote from modern people and far closer to the anthropoid apes than a reasonably sophisticated analysis of the evidence could possibly justify, half-monsters of a kind, ungainly, ugly, and brutish. This picture was based to a large extent on a highly respected and highly misleading study of a skeleton found in 1908 near the village of La Chapelle-aux-Saints in southern France.

The study is one of the most amazing phenomena in the history of humankind's efforts to downgrade its ancestors. On the basis of casts of the inner surface of the skull, the study concluded that the convolutions of the brain had been simple and "coarse" and resembled the convolutions of the "great anthropoid apes or microencephalic man" more closely than those of modern people. Furthermore, it presented an outlandish view of Neanderthal posture and gait. It not only pointed to a supposed "simian arrangement" of certain spinal vertebrae and stated that the Neanderthals walked slumped over and with bent knees, but suggested that their feet may have been grasping organs like the feet of gorillas and chimpanzees.

Until 1957, this study was still being cited as a major source of information about the nature of Neanderthal people. In that year, however, the La Chapelle-aux-Saints skeleton was reexamined by William Straus of Johns Hopkins University and Alec Cave of St. Bartholomew's Hospital Medical College in London. They found that it was hardly typical, belonging to an old man between 40 and 50 suffering from arthritis of the jaws, spine, and perhaps lower limbs, and concluded with the following somewhat ambiguous statement:

> There is thus no valid reason for the assumption that the posture of Neanderthal man . . . differed significantly from that of present-day man. . . . If he could be reincarnated and placed in a New York subway—provided that he were bathed, shaved, and dressed in modern clothing—it is doubtful whether he would attract any more attention than some of its other denizens.

SURVIVAL IN AN ICE AGE

So anatomical evidence fails to support the stereotype of Neanderthal people as subhuman brutes. The trouble is that myths die hard, and it will take years before the popular image coincides with the scientific image. It should be no surprise that, as one of the subspecies of *Homo sapiens* occupying the Old World from about 100,000 to 35,000 years ago, they walked fully erect. After all, their ancestors had been doing that for several million years. What calls for an explanation, however, is that their distinctive set of characteristics should reappear, in the sense that this was reminiscent of earlier human forms, and that they seem to have confined themselves largely if not entirely to western Europe.

One possibility is that the Neanderthals were cut off from their contemporaries. The longer and more completely that breeding populations of a single species are separated from one another, the more widely they differ. Brief and partial isolation, such as that imposed by the institution of royal families, may produce such characteristics as the well-known protruding lower lip of the Hapsburgs. These characteristics, of course, are not sufficient to create new races. Longer periods of isolation, occasioned perhaps by geographical as well as social factors, may eventually produce differences so great that the result is distinct species such as *Australopithecus africanus* and *Australopithecus robustus*.

The conditions which gave rise to the Neanderthal subspecies may have been somewhere between these extremes. Clark Howell has suggested that they may have been caught in a kind of ice trap in western Europe, a glacial pincers movement. During the coldest periods, glaciers crept southwest from the great Scandinavian ice sheet into central Poland, and at the same time glaciers from the Alps moved northeast toward the Carpathians and the Danube. It was by no means a complete trap. The ice masses never met, and there was always a corridor several hundred miles wide between them. But routes through the corridor may have been few and hazardous enough during periods of severe cold to isolate many Neanderthal populations and bring about the appearance of a new subspecies.

Moreover, there are traps more effective than the geographical variety. The Neanderthals were fully adapted to their environment, as reflected in the very shape of their bodies. Their massive jaws may have evolved as adaptations to a diet of tough meat—that is, raw or lightly cooked meat. They probably felt no greater urge to pack up and leave than Eskimo tribes feel today. People still tend to remain in their homelands, even where it is an unending struggle merely to keep alive, and bonds at least as strong may have formed among prehistoric hunter-gatherers.

One can only wonder at the ability of the Neanderthals to endure the intense cold of western Europe during the next-to-last glaciation. Their loneliness, for example, is something difficult to imagine. In today's densely populated world, news travels fast and there are always rescue parties on the way. But there were no rescues in that world, and every band was alone and on its own. As already emphasized, moving through the snow must have been a major problem, since people probably had to get along without snowshoes and sleds and no one moved during blizzards when snows were highest.

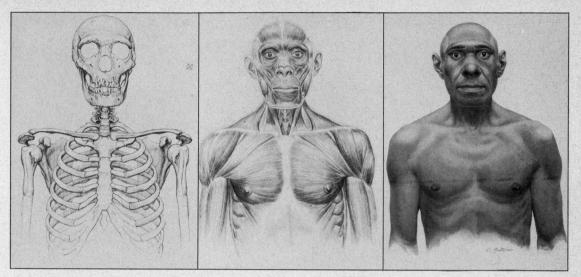

Three stages in a reconstruction of a Neanderthal male (© Jay H. Matterness)

Survival would have been impossible without reserves of food and fuel. The chief hunting grounds must have been snow meadows, wide flat areas swept by icy prevailing winds, where the snow may be only a foot deep and edible grasses grow under it. Today, in Canadian subarctic regions, such places are a major source of food for herds of caribou and caribou hunters, and similar regions helped feed reindeer and Neanderthal reindeer hunters some 50,000 years ago. Small game also provided a major share of meat; many traps must have been set along snow trails, the habitual routes of animals on the move.

But winter hunting could never have provided enough food by itself. According to one estimate, it takes about 800 to 900 pounds of lean meat to feed ten people for a month, and Neanderthal winters may have lasted 4 to 5 months. Such conditions demanded stockpiling, and extensive stockpiling. The people may have used underground cellars, pits hacked out of permanently frozen ground known as permafrost, as Eskimos use today, or "blue ice caves," or ice-cliff formations, could have served as deep-freeze lockers.

Prehistoric natural refrigerators of this sort have not yet been found, although a study of where Eskimo hunters locate their storage places today might furnish clues for archeologists in search of evidence of prehistoric practices. The record suggests that at least one family had a special larder for its winter food. A pit in a Neanderthal cave on the island of Jersey off the western coast of France apparently contained a liberal supply of large chunks of meat ready for cooking. It had been dug through deposits next to a cave wall, and three rhinoceros skulls and the remains of at least five mammoths had been found.

Fuel was another problem, to collect as well as to store. When wood was scarce, the Neanderthals burned bones, and they may even have learned to use fat. They and earlier people also had ways of promoting efficient burning. Soviet investigators have discovered "tailed" hearths, basins with a narrow trench or furrow extending out from one side. Actual tests indicate the reason for the trench. Apparently it provided a kind of flue or draft through which air was drawn to produce more complete burning.

THEY BURIED THEIR DEAD

Archeological excavations rarely provide direct information about the feelings of our remote ancestors; usually we are reduced to guesses, shrewd or otherwise. But now and then the past leaves patterns whose significance cannot be mistaken. During the early 1900s such evidence was uncovered at Le Moustier, about 30 miles west of La Chapelle-aux-Saints, which shows that these people had developed a new way of thinking, a new attitude toward life and death. A boy about 15 or 16 years old had been buried in a cave. He had been lowered into a trench, placed on his right side with knees slightly drawn and head resting on his forearm in a sleeping position. A pile of flints lay under his head to form a sort of stone pillow, and near his hand was a beautifully worked stone ax. Around the remains were wild-cattle bones, many of them charred, the remnants of roasted meat which may have been provided to serve as sustenance in the world of the dead. (The old man of La Chapelle-aux-Saints was also buried in a trench and surrounded by stone tools.)

Not far from the Le Moustier site is a cave which was discovered by a road-building crew and probably served as a family cemetery. The number of people buried there is unknown. Some 21 mounds and pits have been found in the cave, 6 of them containing skeletons representing 4 children and 2 adults. The other 15 may also have contained skeletons which were looted or disintegrated over the years. Or they may have held meat and other perishable material for the use of the dead in other worlds. One mound, part of a pattern of 9 neatly arranged mounds, included the skeleton of a very small infant, perhaps a stillborn infant, and three flint tools. A nearby pit was covered by a triangular limestone slab and included the bones of a 6-year-old child and, again, three flint tools.

The record includes symbols which we cannot decipher. Near Monte Circeo, on the Mediterranean coast between Rome and Naples, is a deep cave whose innermost chamber contained a circle of stones, at the center of which was a human skull with a hole bored into the base. There are also signs that animal rituals were practiced along with burials. A cave in a steep ravine in the mountains of Uzbek in Central Asia held the shallow grave of a young boy; half a dozen pairs of ibex horns were stuck in the earth around the head end of the grave, indicating that an ibex cult may have existed here among Neanderthals more than 50,000 years ago, as it does today among people living in the same region.

Other rituals apparently involved cave bears. A mountain cave in eastern Austria contained a rectangular vault holding 7 bear skulls all facing the cave's entrance; while material excavated from Regourdou, another site in southern France, represents perhaps the most elaborate bear-cult burial known. It included a skeleton complete except for the skull (which had probably been taken by an amateur collector), stone drains, a rectangular pit covered by a flat stone slab weighing almost a ton, and the remains of more than 20 cave bears.

One of the most revealing of recent discoveries comes from a site in the

Artist's conception of Neanderthal burial at Le Moustier

Near East, the Shanidar Cave in the Zagros Mountain highlands of Iraq, about 250 miles due north of Baghdad. Kurdish goatherds still live here, as they have for generations, making fire with steel and flint in brush huts under a vaulting roof which encloses an area about the size of four tennis courts. The site was excavated by Ralph Solecki of Columbia University. He hit bedrock at a depth

Artist's conception of Neanderthal people: home base, limestone shelter, at beginning of rhinoceros hunt

of 45 feet and, in deposits up to 100,000 years old, found skeletons of eight Neanderthal individuals, one apparently recovering from a spear or knife wound in the ribs.

A man with a badly crushed skull was buried deep in the cave with special ceremony. One spring day about 60,000 years ago members of his family went out into the hills, picked masses of wild flowers, and made a bed of them on the ground, a resting place for the deceased. Other flowers were probably laid on top of his grave; still others seem to have been woven together with the branches of a pinelike shrub to form a wreath. Traces of that offering endure in the form of fossil pollen collected from the burial site, the remains of the ancestors of present-day grape hyacinths, bachelor's buttons, hollyhocks, and yellow-flowering groundsels. The man was probably buried between late May and early July, which is when these flowers are in bloom today. (There are no signs of radical climatic changes in the region since prehistoric times.)

These findings, the graves, and the patterns around them, mark a great change in human evolution. Death, and presumably life, had become something special. No comparable evidence appears in earlier records, and as far as we know, before Neanderthal times, humans and the ancestors of humans had always died as other animals did, being abandoned when they were too weak to keep up with the band or wandering off to wait alone for the end to come. Burial

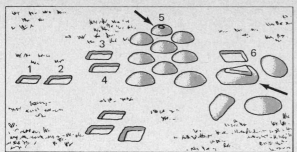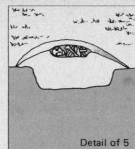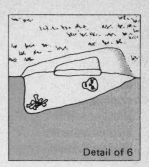

Multiple Neanderthal burial, possibly a family cemetery (numbers indicate places where skeletons were found)

implies a new kind of concern for the individual, and, according to one theory, it arose as part of a response to bitter glacial conditions when people needed one another even more than in less demanding times and formed more intimate ties and cared more intensely when death came.

THE BEGINNINGS OF RITUAL

Severe climates may have had something to do with the new spirit. Certainly considerable evidence exists in our own times to suggest that people living under the most depressing circumstances often have the highest hopes for the future, in another world if not in this one. But there had been hard times before, and death must always have been a mysterious phenomenon. The new element was the evolution of a brain capable of framing questions, arriving at answers, and establishing rituals—which, by the very fact that they were practiced regularly, reinforced the validity of the answers. Ritual expresses the belief or hope that a connection exists between repetition and truth, the notion that if a possibility is stated often enough it becomes a certainty.

There may have been another reason for an emphasis on burial. Perhaps the Neanderthals, like many hunter-gatherers in recent times, believed in ghosts and in the haunting of places where people have died and preferred to move away or dispose of their dead at some distance. If so, these practices might not have been possible during glacial winters. They could not move far through deep snows, and besides, their home bases probably included large stockpiles of food and fuel. So perhaps they had to stay put, bury their dead nearby or even inside their caves, and devise special ceremonies to appease ancestral spirits.

Neanderthal people invented, or at least formalized, illusion when they invented burial. The belief in an afterlife says in effect that death is not what it seems; that it represents an apparent ending only, an ending only as far as the evidence of the senses is concerned; and that in this case, the crude evidence of the senses is wrong. Reality involves not observed and observable facts, but an abstraction, the idea that death is actually a passage from one world to another. In this respect the burial ceremonies of prehistoric hunters expressed the kind of thinking used today to develop theories about the structure of the atomic nucleus or the expanding universe, things we cannot see but have reason to believe exist.

Further clues to the nature of Neanderthal society have come from continuing studies of Shanidar Cave burials, which date back at least 45,000 years. One individual, a 40-year-old male identified as Shanidar 1, was afflicted with a withered right arm and shoulder, a condition probably present at birth. Yet he lived a long life as a member of the band before being killed by rocks falling from the roof of the cave, clear indication that the Neanderthals found places for persons who could not fend for themselves without the support of the band.

Shanidar 1 has more to tell us. For more than a generation investigators have noted that there was something strange about the shape of his skull. It was unusually flat at the front and unusually curved at the back, an observation that made no sense until Trinkaus heard that a number of strangely shaped fossil skulls found in Australia had been deformed artificially. With that information in mind, he decided to restudy the Shanidar 1 cranial vault, comparing its contours with those of other Neanderthals, and learned that it was indeed way out of line—that the chances of those combined front and back features occurring naturally were vanishingly small.

That notion, plus the discovery of similar distortions in the skull of Shanidar 5, another adult male buried in the same archeological level as Shanidar 1, argues strongly that the Neanderthals also deliberately altered the head shapes of some of their offspring. Judging by tribal practices in modern times, this could have been accomplished by repeatedly pressing the infant's head manually, like molding clay, or else by binding the head with a flexible band for 6 to 12 months. In any case, it testifies to the existence of what Trinkaus calls "a sense of personal esthetic." The Neanderthals were already doing on a small scale what we do everywhere and on an enormous scale today—actively changing things, including their bodies, to suit their own purposes. It was the beginning of efforts toward evolution by human direction rather than natural selection.

The Neanderthals were human, all too human, in another way. Along with their spiritual ideas and aspirations they exhibited a talent for organized violence. Person killing person became more common. Some sort of mayhem took place at Krapina, a sandstone rock shelter overlooking a river in northern Yugoslavia, where at the turn of the century investigators recovered more than 500 bones and bone fragments representing at least a dozen individuals. A number of the bones are charred, suggesting that cannibalism may have been practiced, while other bones show definite signs of having been cut and scraped. Similar evidence has been unearthed more recently in a French cave not far from the Mediterranean.

Unfortunately, excavators did not work as painstakingly then as they do now, and no living-floor patterns were reported. But the mass killings hint at fighting among neighboring bands, a possibility strengthened by the findings at other Old World sites of a flint projectile point in a rib cage, a pelvis with a spear hole in it, and skulls bashed and penetrated in various ways. It seems that not only did the Neanderthals believe in an afterlife, but they were also active in speeding the departure of their fellow beings to the other world.

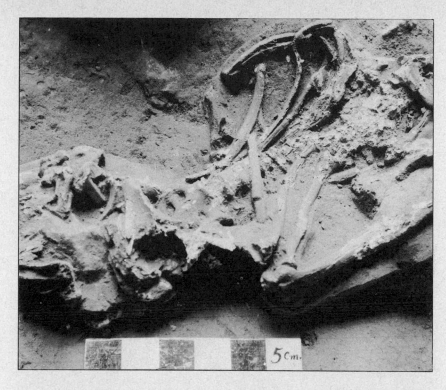

Find at Shanidar: ribs and pelvic region of a Neanderthal man of about 40 years who lived at least 44,000 years ago (top); skull, as unearthed, of some individual, probably killed in a rock fall (bottom)

SUMMARY

After several million years of relatively slow evolution, things began stirring some time after 300,000 to 250,000 years ago. Fossils like those found in the English village of Swanscombe represent the first signs of our kind of hominid, *Homo sapiens,* large-brained individuals with rounded head contours. As indicated by computer-aided analyses, however, they still retained features characteristic of *erectus* specimens. The Swanscombe people were definitely a species in transition.

More advanced humans were discovered in Germany in 1856, a memorable date not only in human evolution but also in the record of human error. The Neanderthals aroused strong reactions, predominantly on the negative side. After all, theirs were the first traces of earlier hominids ever found—and in those days investigators were not prepared for the notion that we arose from less-advanced species. The stocky, beetle-browed, heavy-boned Neanderthals were generally regarded as recent barbarians, modern cripples, or subhuman half-apes.

Fragments of the myth linger, but we now recognize the Neanderthals as fully human. Physically, they were exceptionally strong compared to us, as shown by the solidity of their bones. Their stocky build and other features are believed to be adaptations to cold climates. Their brain was at least as large as ours, indicating a high order of intelligence, which served them well in coping with the climates of western Europe more than 100,000 to about 35,000 years ago.

Survival in glacial times demanded some sort of food storage, perhaps in natural "ice lockers." It takes an estimated 800 to 900 pounds of lean meat to feed ten people for a month, and Neanderthal winters may have lasted from 4 to 5 months. Wood for burning must have been stockpiled, and it is difficult to imagine people getting around in deep snows without snowshoes. But evidence for such adaptations is still lacking.

As far as we can tell from the archeological record, the Neanderthals were the first humans to bury their dead. Furthermore, they placed tools and perhaps chunks of roasted meat in the graves, as if to prepare the deceased for journeys into another world. The belief in an afterlife, in the notion that death is not what it seems, not an ending but a continuation of some sort, represents a new feature in the human story—a creative interpretation of reality, the beginnings of theory building.

chapter 9

Neanderthal Studies: The Beginnings of Diversity

Even without evidence of the burials and beliefs, striking marks of change after more than 1 million years of apparent evolutionary stability, the record of the Neanderthals would be sufficient to indicate that something important was happening. For one thing, there was the lithic technology. Neanderthals made a new variety of tools, and much of what we know about the tools comes from one of the most beautiful parts of France, the region surrounding the village of Les Eyzies, more than 300 miles southwest of Paris.

Rivers have gouged the countryside out of a great limestone plateau. There are remote gorges and side valleys, wide-open valleys bounded by steep cliffs several hundred feet high, and in the cliffs, scooped-out places under massive overhangs and caves, many small ones and others that extend deep into the rock.

A CENTER OF PREHISTORY

This is an ideal land to live in, and has been for a long time. Much of the local activity takes place near the cliffs which dominate the landscape. Farmers plow to the edges of the cliffs, and some of their farmhouses are fitted so snugly into the hollows of overhangs that they seem to be growing out of the limestone. Indeed, cliff dwelling is an old tradition in these parts. In medieval times the nobility built castles on and into the cliffs, using natural caves for arsenals, storehouses, and wine cellars. Roman legions came before farmers and feudal lords; remnants of the walls they made have been found underneath ruined stables and towers.

But the Les Eyzies area is most widely known as a center of prehistory.

157

Le Moustier cave, Les Eyzies region, early burial site

For all that has happened since, for all the conquests and pageantry, its richest records and deepest mysteries involve people who flourished a thousand centuries before the Romans, Neanderthal people and their ancestors and descendants. Walking where they walked, one feels their presence everywhere, like ghosts. In good weather, they camped and lived outdoors; their flints can be picked up by the dozen in plowed fields near rivers and in the shadows of the cliffs and on the plateaus above the cliffs. Traces of hearths as well as flints are found in the mouths of caves and under the overhangs used for homes in glacial climates.

The record in this region demonstrates the human's extraordinary ability to adapt, to live practically anywhere. Here, people probably encountered glacial climates more rigorous and demanding than their ancestors had ever encountered, and yet they managed to cope with icy temperatures, blizzards, and accumulating snows. Certainly they could never have endured without making the most of natural resources, and the land around Les Eyzies offered a unique combination of advantages.

Shelter, of course, was provided by the cliffs, eroded structures formed by the lime-containing remains of tiny animals deposited and consolidated more than 100 million years ago in the warm, shallow sea that covered most of Europe. The cliffs provided raw material as well as shelter. Embedded in the limestone were large quantities of fine-grained flint in the form of nodules which, like the limestone, consist of the remains of microorganisms (in this case, colonies of single-celled animals with shells containing silica). Water was also available, runoff from mountains in the Massif Central, where the Dordogne and Vézère rivers rose and joined a few miles below Les Eyzies and passed through on their way to the Bay of Biscay, as they do today.

Above all, there was an abundance of game during the coldest times, chiefly reindeer, which seem to have been created in large measure for the nourishment of humans and other large carnivores. Wild horses, for example, will not stay long in areas where they are being heavily hunted. But reindeer such as the caribou of the Canadian Arctic are creatures of habit, and vast herds tend to return to the same general regions year after year, often along the same well-rutted trails, across the same mountain passes, lakes, fords, rivers, and high gravel ridges. Judging by the quantities of reindeer bones found at numerous sites in the Les Eyzies region, prehistoric reindeer were equally predictable and equally vulnerable. Groups of Neanderthal hunters, working together rather like wolf packs, must have stalked and killed individual animals.

So people found many resources they could use in the glacial climates of southern France. They must also have had a feeling for the beauty of the land and for the hard-won security of standing with a solid wall at their backs and looking out over a river valley. Some 200 prehistoric sites have been reported within a radius of about 30 miles of Les Eyzies, including Le Moustier and

Les Eyzies, center of prehistory

Regourdou and other burial sites mentioned in Chapter 8. Many more sites are known but unreported, since every investigator familiar with the area has a private list of places he or she hopes to excavate some day.

Most archeologists feel reasonably certain that several hundred undiscovered sites exist in the area. The great majority of reported caves, rock shelters, and open-air locations with prehistoric remains have been found within a mile or two of well-traveled routes, modern roads which often follow the original courses of old carriage roads. No one really knows what lies beyond. From the tops of the highest cliffs one looks into the distance and sees inviting backcountry valleys and other cliffs which have not yet been thoroughly explored and which almost surely contain the living places of prehistoric people.

THE STORY OF COMBE GRENAL

A site that has yielded a great deal of information about the Neanderthals, and promises to yield a great deal more, lies in the little valley of Combe Grenal, about 14 miles from Les Eyzies, on the side of a hill not far from the Dordogne River. A dirt road leads there, or rather a pair of ruts marking the remains of a dirt road; and off to the left, along a rising path hidden by trees and bushes, lies the site, a gouged-out place resembling an abandoned quarry. Higher up on the cliff and within sight of the excavations is a mine which provided flint in prehistoric times. Medieval stone workers also came there to obtain huge flint slabs for millstones.

Combe Grenal was excavated by the late François Bordes, director of the University of Bordeaux's Institute of the Quaternary (the period covering the last one million years of evolution). He began digging at the cave in June 1953, expecting to complete the project in short order, probably by the end of the summer, because a colleague told him that since bedrock had already been reached, only a small area remained to be exposed. But it soon turned out that the bedrock sloped sharply downhill, and Bordes and his associates followed the dipping rock line deeper and deeper season after season without hitting bottom in the form of a level floor. When the work finally came to an end in 1964, they had made a huge hole in the ground, digging to a maximum depth of some 40 feet and uncovering 65 separate layers of geological and archeological deposits.

The oldest and deepest layers can be dated approximately, by geological methods. They include a clayey red soil, the clay representing muds formed during thaws of the next-to-last glaciation. (The red color is rust resulting from chemical reactions between iron-containing minerals and oxygen, reactions which are limited in cold climates and took place during the subsequent interglacial stage.) These deposits are estimated to have been laid down 125,000 to 150,000 years ago, about the time when prehistoric pioneers explored the area, looked over the cave, and decided to move in.

The first occupants left no fossil remains. But they may have been people rather like those represented by the skull fragments found at the Swanscombe and Steinheim sites, definitely on the way to being modern people. They had

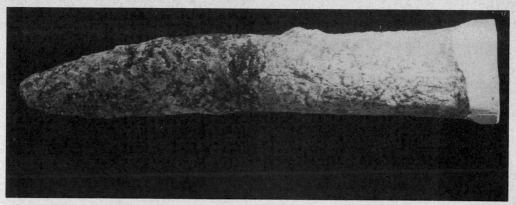

Plaster cast of posthole, Combe Grenal

Acheulian-type tools, like some of those unearthed at Swanscombe, including hand axes designed according to the same basic pattern used by their remote Olduvai ancestors hundreds of thousands of years before. Judging by the fact that about 80 percent of the bones found among their tools were reindeer bones, their diet included ample supplies of venison.

Combe Grenal's richest and most important deposits lie directly above the red Acheulian deposits, furnishing an almost continuous record of Neanderthal occupation from about 40,000 to 90,000 years ago. There are a few sterile layers without artifacts or any traces of human beings; the climate may have become too severe, even for the Neanderthals, and chunks of rock from the roof remained where they fell, since probably no one was around to clear away the debris. Combe Grenal was a center of activity most of the time, however, for groups of individuals who lived and died there over periods of many generations.

Archeologists are continually on the alert for any unusual features, which inexperienced excavators often miss entirely. One day, Bordes uncovered a flat stone of about 4 inches across, nothing much in itself. But it turned out to be one of a series of flat stones arranged as if to cover something. The soil under the stones was finer and looser than the soil surrounding the stones, the sort of pattern which may indicate that a hole had been dug and refilled. Careful removal of the fine soil revealed a basin-shaped pit, probably the funeral pit for a very young child. The presumed grave was empty, a fact difficult to explain since it had not been disturbed by looters or scavenging animals. Most likely the skeleton was destroyed by the bone-dissolving action of waters seeping through layers containing sand and ashes and rock; also, young bones are not fully calcified and may tend to disintegrate faster than adult bones. Three smaller pits near the grave, also empty, may have held meat and clothing for the dead child.

Another unusual feature was exposed in a higher, more recent layer. One of Bordes' co-workers noticed a dark circular patch of fine soil in an ashy layer. He scooped out the soil, taking care to leave the ashy material intact, and ended with a hole about 2 inches in diameter and 8 inches deep. Then he poured plaster into the hole, obtaining a cast which resembled the pointed end of a stake. This may have been one of several postholes at the mouth of the cave, where stakes were driven into the ground to support skins or woven branches which provided shelter from wind, rain, and snow. It may have supported a meat-drying rack (this is discussed later).

Combe Grenal is especially important for its tools, which Bordes analyzed statistically. Since excavating his first site at the age of 14 in a valley not far from Les Eyzies, he examined some 1.5 million tools, most of them turned out by Neanderthal flint knappers; he would note lengths and angles of cutting edges, types of retouching, signs of use, and many other features for each tool. Furthermore, he was an accomplished flint knapper himself. This accumulated experience served him well in compiling a list of more than 60 different kinds of tools, including backed knives, points, scrapers, borers, denticulates with several notches forming a row of sawlike teeth, and single-notch tools probably used, among other things, to scrape bark off branches in making stakes and spear shafts.

Bordes saw the tool making of the Neanderthals in an evolutionary context, as a stage in the ability to think abstractly. Associated with their work is a technique known as Levallois flaking (named after a site in Levallois-Perret, a

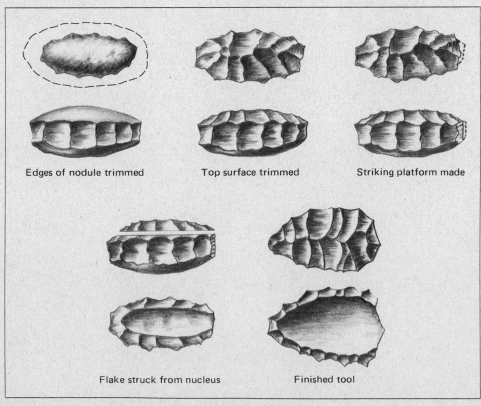

Edges of nodule trimmed   Top surface trimmed   Striking platform made

Flake struck from nucleus   Finished tool

Stages in making Levallois flakes, top and side views

suburb of Paris). It involved a series of steps. First you take a flint nodule or nucleus, trim it around the edges to obtain a roughly oval shape, and flatten it a bit on top by further trimming. Then you make a narrow, flat section at one end, the all-important striking platform. After these preparatory steps, you are ready to produce flakes. By directing sharp, precise blows against the platform at just the right angle, you can successively knock off a series of sharp, thin flakes in a kind of slicing operation, finally shaping the flakes into specialized tools.

According to Bordes, this was the third of a three-stage evolutionary process. Stage 1, the ability to see that "inside the rock there is a cutting edge, ready to be released by some blows with another stone," can be traced back at least 2 million years to crude African choppers. Stage 2 comes half a million to a million years later with the emergence of symmetry in the hand ax, which depends on the ability to see not only a cutting edge inside the rock, but a shape as well.

Bordes' stage 3, the invention of the "prepared nucleus," or Levallois technique, demands a higher order of insight and foresight. It involves seeing a cutting edge and a shape and, beyond that, a way of controlling the shape before striking off a single flake. It calls for a roundabout procedure instead of direct, head-on action, an inhibition of the natural impulse to simply knock a flake from a convenient rock; instead, in the name of increased efficiency, a preparatory step is taken first.

Prehistoric tool makers invented this procedure more than half a million years ago, probably as the result of accidents in fashioning hand axes. If you are trimming an almond-shaped piece of flint and strike it at too sharp an angle, you may knock off a large flake consisting of most of the hand-ax face instead of a small chip, and thus ruin the job. The Levallois technique, which deliberately produced large preshaped flakes, could easily have evolved from such mistakes. It was exploited widely by the Neanderthals.

A DEBATE ABOUT TOOL KITS

Bordes went far beyond the analysis of individual tools. He discovered patterns among the tools, a number of unique and characteristic patterns which tended to recur in different Combe Grenal occupation levels. Different layers contain different proportions of tools—different tool kits—which hint at basic differences in prehistoric living. The patterns occur among 19,000 Neanderthal tools collected at Combe Grenal. There are four basic tool kits:

1. *Quina:* 50 to 80 percent side scrapers, featuring a nicely shaped heavy-duty variety with delicate retouching along a curved edge; rare Levallois flakes or none at all; hand axes also rare or absent (0.5 percent at the most). The Combe Grenal posthole was found in a Quina layer. Another variety of this assemblage, Ferrassie, has many Levallois flakes. Quina and Ferrassie are the names of important sites in the Les Eyzies region.
2. *Acheulian tradition:* 5 to 40 percent hand axes, 5 to 20 percent side scrapers, many denticulates, notched tools, and backed knives.
3. *Typical:* a balanced assemblage, generally containing roughly the same

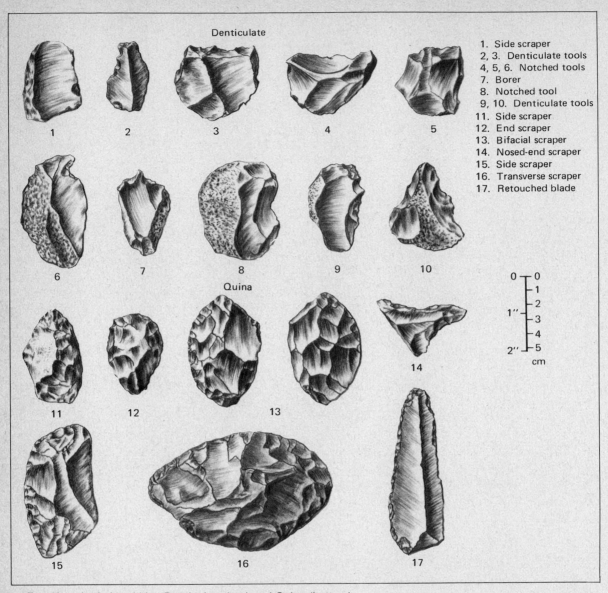

Denticulate

Quina

1. Side scraper
2, 3. Denticulate tools
4, 5, 6. Notched tools
7. Borer
8. Notched tool
9, 10. Denticulate tools
11. Side scraper
12. End scraper
13. Bifacial scraper
14. Nosed-end scraper
15. Side scraper
16. Transverse scraper
17. Retouched blade

Two Neanderthal tool kits: Denticulate (top) and Quina (bottom)

proportions of most tool types, except for low frequencies of backed knives and rare hand axes.

4. *Denticulate:* up to 80 percent denticulates and notches, few side scrapers (usually less than 10 percent), very few or no hand axes.

These tool kits and their variations point to widespread patterns in Neanderthal ways of life. In general, an occupation layer yielding a large enough sample of tools for valid statistical analysis includes just one of the characteristic

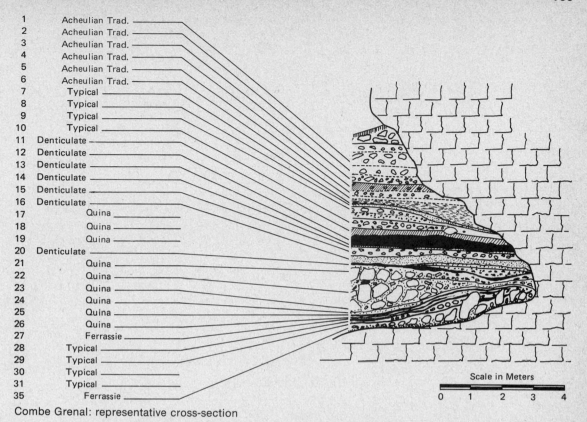

1	Acheulian Trad.
2	Acheulian Trad.
3	Acheulian Trad.
4	Acheulian Trad.
5	Acheulian Trad.
6	Acheulian Trad.
7	Typical
8	Typical
9	Typical
10	Typical
11	Denticulate
12	Denticulate
13	Denticulate
14	Denticulate
15	Denticulate
16	Denticulate
17	Quina
18	Quina
19	Quina
20	Denticulate
21	Quina
22	Quina
23	Quina
24	Quina
25	Quina
26	Quina
27	Ferrassie
28	Typical
29	Typical
30	Typical
31	Typical
35	Ferrassie

Scale in Meters
0 1 2 3 4

Combe Grenal: representative cross-section

kits. That holds not only for Combe Grenal and other sites in France but also for the great majority of sites in the rest of Europe and in North Africa and the Near East. Something basic was going on, something basic and rather subtle, for this is another case where the experts disagree.

Bordes interpreted the four tool kits as marks of four cultures, four tribes with different origins and customs, perhaps with different languages or dialects and different kinds of clothing. For example, he traced the Quina Neanderthals to a tradition that existed nearly 100,000 years before them at the High Lodge site in England, where people had used similar tools, including finely worked Quina-type scrapers (see Chapter 8). The Acheulian tradition people had a tool kit stemming from industries which first appeared more than a million years previously (see Chapter 6), a hand-ax line passing through intermediate stages such as those observed in the remains at Torralba and Ambrona and, more recently, in the lowest layers of Combe Grenal itself.

According to this way of looking at things, the Neanderthal tribes led relatively isolated lives. All of France probably contained no more than a few thousand persons, perhaps a few hundred bands or so; encounters would therefore have been rare, brief, and generally unexpected. Furthermore, distrust of strangers ran even deeper in prehistoric times than it does today, suggesting that the tribes tended to avoid one another. "A man may well have lived all his life without more than a rare meeting with anyone from another tribe," Bordes pointed out, "and it is very possible that these contacts, when they did take place, were not always peaceful and fruitful."

A totally different interpretation was offered nearly 20 years ago by Lewis Binford. He believes that the tool kits represent, not four tribes or peoples, but the same people everywhere doing different things. This is a functional rather than a cultural approach. It implies that the Neanderthals did not have different traditions, but simply used the same site for different purposes at different times. Binford recalls his first all-out exchange with Bordes in the latter's laboratory: "Our arms began to wave. . . . We must have argued for more than an hour, our voices getting higher and higher, standing up, sitting down, pacing back and forth, leaning over the charts."

The argument has not been settled yet, because the actual situation seems to be rather more involved than either of the proponent's viewpoints. But right now investigators are leaning toward the functional viewpoint in interpreting the artifact patterns at Neanderthal sites, as well as at earlier and later sites. At Combe Grenal there is evidence that denticulate kits are often associated with people specializing in horse hunting, and the large proportions of denticulates and notched tools may be used not only in woodworking but in some sort of food processing—say, shredding strips of meat for drying or smoking. The side scrapers predominating in Quina kits may have served in the large-scale cleaning of hides obtained during summer hunting trips and worked into clothing for long, hard winters to come. Also, three of the four Neanderthal kits turned up on different parts of the same living floor of a cave in northern Spain, indicating distinct activity areas within the camping ground.

Still, the last word has not been said. Bordes conceded that some of the differences in tool-kit composition may support the notion of different activities. But he knew, and Binford also knows, that function cannot account for many important observations. Different parts of France, for example, feature certain tool kits over periods of many generations. Sites in the Provence region bordering the Mediterranean have no Acheulian tradition kits at all, while sites some 350 miles to the northwest in the Charente district feature Quina kits almost exclusively.

It does not make much sense to think of one area where only one class of activity is practiced, and another where an important activity is bypassed entirely. These and other points argue for territorial factors and a cultural element. Imposed upon strictly functional or utilitarian patterns—patterns which may predominate under certain conditions—we also find expressions of style, socially accepted and socially dictated ways of working and behaving. Bordes appreciated the fundamental nature of the problem: "As ever, reality is more complicated than was thought at the beginning."

CONTINUING RESEARCH

An important source of clues to the behavior of prehistoric people is the recent and current behavior of people who still live by hunting and gathering. They are by no means relics of the remote past, having evolved in many ways along with the rest of us. Furthermore, they do not live in a pristine, untouched state; their world has been changed irrevocably by waves of foreign explorers and settlers. Yet even allowing for all that, certain practices endure, and some striking parallels exist between past and present.

Chapters 15 and 16 consider such observations in some detail, but one example here will demonstrate a direct application to the understanding of Neanderthal times. As part of an effort to learn more about what happened at Combe Grenal and elsewhere, Binford has completed a series of intensive studies among Eskimos living in the Brooks Range region of north-central Alaska, about 250 miles from Fairbanks. In one of his recent archeology projects, he excavated the site of a house occupied by Eskimos 80 to 90 years ago.

Among other things, he found caribou lower jawbones, all of which had been cracked open, a practice explained to him by Eskimos who remembered what their fathers and grandfathers had done. It had been a time of near-famine— and the jawbones contained patik, a fibrous tissue eaten as a starvation food in times of great hunger. The Neanderthals may have faced similar emergencies, since all but one of several hundred reindeer, horse, and ox-cattle jawbones found in Combe Grenal layers were also cracked open. Also, it seems that Eskimos and Neanderthals may have shared related beliefs. The Alaskan hunters had a taboo against eating material from the jawbones of bears, foxes, wolves, and other meat-eating animals—and not a single one of the two dozen or so bear, wolf, cave lion, and hyena jawbones found at Combe Grenal had been shattered.

The analysis of bones (fossil bones and fresh bones studied experimentally) will contribute increasingly to our understanding of the past, not only as far as early hominids are concerned (see Chapter 4) but also for all subsequent developments. Another new direction will involve the selection of sites for excavation. Until now the focus has been mainly on big sites, sites with thousands of tools and many levels, like Combe Grenal—all of which is fine for the statistical analysis of bones and tool kits covering periods of centuries and millenniums.

But there is a catch to such excavations. The general assumption has been that each level is a relatively intact home-base living floor, the result of a single occupation. This may not always be the case. A single-occupation level would tend to have a number of different activity areas, as at Lazaret, clusters of flint and bone representing places where people knapped flint, ate, slept, and so on. On the other hand, activity areas would be less clear-cut, less distinct, in a site visited not for one long stay, but many times and briefly. Since people would not camp in exactly the same spot during each visit, there would be a "smearing" effect from the imperfect superimposition of several living patterns; a mixing of artifacts would result. This situation may hold for Combe Grenal, according to a recent report by Binford.

So a great deal remains to be learned from selected smaller sites like Vaufry, a cave in a cliffside so steep that you need iron rods as handholds to get up and down. Excavated under the direction of Jean-Philippe Rigaud of the University of Bordeaux, the archeologist in charge of investigations in the Les Eyzies region, it has yielded evidence which is still being analyzed. For example, one level made up of perhaps three or four separate occupations contains about 150 Levallois flakes and retouched pieces, most of them concentrated in a small area. Some of the tools were made on the spot from local flints, while others, made of flints from quarries more than 30 miles away, were brought in ready-made. Helle Jensen of the University of Aarhus in Denmark is studying the toolmakers' reasons for their selection of raw materials.

What we know about the Neanderthals has been deduced from many sites throughout the world, including one located in northeast China near the Great Wall. Soviet investigators are digging at rich sites along river banks in the Crimea and elsewhere and have found traces of elaborate burials and semipermanent dwellings. One of the dwelling sites—Molodova, in the eastern Soviet Union, more than 250 miles from Kiev—includes a large ring of mammoth tusks, perhaps used for supporting posts; inside the ring are bones of horses, rhinoceroses, bison and brown bears, 29,000 pieces of flint, and 15 hearths.

There has even been increased activity in Greece and Italy, where archeological interest has hitherto focused almost exclusively on classical sites. The late Eric Higgs of Cambridge University and his associates have located more than 50 prehistoric sites in red erosion gullies among the mountains of northwest Greece (as compared to less than half a dozen such sites reported previously for the entire country). Work at one site yielded a number of living floors, as well as some unusual remains such as tool assemblages with a high proportion of microliths—points, bladelets, scrapers, and other miniature implements usually from half an inch to an inch long. Research continues in Africa, where the world's richest hunting grounds existed throughout prehistory. According to one study, during Neanderthal times there may have been two or four times as many people in southern Africa alone than in all of Europe.

A FEELING FOR PEOPLE

Bordes had definite feelings about the men and women whose artifacts he uncovered. They were still alive for him. As he dug in a rich Quina layer and found one superbly worked scraper after another, he was impressed not only with the handiwork but also with the fact that the artisans were working in an almost automatic fashion, as if they had perfected their techniques and had stopped inventing: "They made beautiful things stupidly. Digging Quina layers can be very boring. For the first week you are impressed with the tools, but after that you see scrapers and more scrapers and still more scrapers until you are sick of them!"

These people seem to have done most of the burying of the dead. At least most Neanderthal graves in France are associated with the Quina-type tool kit, an observation which leads Howard Winters of New York University to suggest that the tools may have been used during a time of year when bodies were interred in caves and rock shelters rather than elsewhere. If the tools represent activities carried out during the depths of glacial winters, for example, permafrost conditions might have demanded on-the-spot burials within living sites. In any case, here as elsewhere a great deal remains to be explained, and Winters wonders "why there are so few Neanderthal remains in these heavily used sites."

Acheulian tradition layers hint at a different set of circumstances. They include some hand axes and a relatively high proportion of knives, especially backed knives, blunted on one side for a firm and comfortable grip. Bordes believes that Neanderthals using such tools were far more inventive than those using tools of the Quina type. "They had some imagination. They made all sorts of backed blades and offbeat tools which you can't classify, including some combination tools, prehistoric versions of today's Swiss pocket knives with scissors and screwdrivers and nail files as well as regular blades. They experimented a great deal, and their experiments worked."

Whatever the final outcome of the Bordes-Binford debate, it demonstrates that in archeology as in other disciplines investigators whose basic viewpoints differ can nevertheless achieve productive results. The problems at issue demand a tribal or cultural approach and a functional approach as well. Archeologists concerned primarily with cultural factors tend to dig deep, to go back as far as possible into time, and to obtain a long record of successive changes. Functionally minded archeologists, on the other hand, tend to dig wide and to excavate broad areas at sites which cover more space and can reveal more about the organization of camping places and the variety of activities under way.

This difference of emphasis itself may express a cultural difference. After all, it is natural for Bordes and other investigators of Old World nations with long histories and established traditions to approach prehistory in cultural terms, and it is natural for Americans, as members of a nation whose history is brief and whose pioneers and prehistory are recent, to stress the practical aspects of how things are done and for what purpose. Prehistory is sufficiently complex to benefit from both approaches. The best excavations are both deep and wide.

One summer evening a number of years ago François Bordes played a recording for me in an old farmhouse not far from Combe Grenal, his home during the excavating season. He called the recording "The Song of the Neanderthals." It was a New Caledonian war chant, sung loud and deep and partly shouted to the beating of drums—sung with feeling but strangely without pattern. There was no sustained rhythm, only occasional and random intervals of rhythm which came like interruptions. For a few moments the chanters would sing in unison, and their voices and the drumbeating seemed to gain in power and purpose, and then the rhythm would break again. The song, with its flashes of harmony and style and its feeling of community and aspiration, represented a foreshadowing of things to come in prehistory—but not under the aegis of the Neanderthals.

WHAT HAPPENED TO THE NEANDERTHALS?

They started fading from the scene perhaps 40,000 years ago, and vanished some 5 or 6 millenniums later with the appearance in Europe of a different breed of *Homo sapiens*. The newcomers are referred to collectively as the Cro-Magnons,

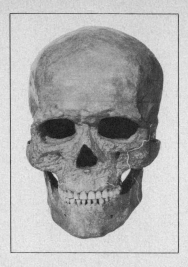

Reconstructed skull of a Cro-Magnon man

after the Cro-Magnon rock shelter located in a limestone cliff of Les Eyzies, where more than a century ago workers building a railroad through the Vézère Valley discovered five skeletons. (Incidentally, the cliff that includes the site is still inhabited, providing a ready-made rear wall for one of the village's tourist hotels.)

If sheer physical strength were the only criterion, the Cro-Magnons would have to be regarded as an evolutionary comedown. Although somewhat taller than the Neanderthals, they were considerably less rugged. Their arm and leg bones were relatively lightweight. Their jaws were also lighter and less jutting, their brow ridges lighter and less prominent. They were weaklings compared to the Neanderthals, or, to put it another way, they were more gracile, which means "gracefully slender," beauty of course being in the eye of the beholder.

The comparative quality of their brains is still an open question, although we like to think they were more intelligent than the Neanderthals, since they were essentially like ourselves, completely modern-type people. In a sense, the investigators who name fossil hominids have already prejudged the issue. The Neanderthals, officially designated as *Homo sapiens neanderthalensis,* rate only a single "sapiens," while the Cro-Magnons rate as doubly wise *Homo sapiens sapiens.* As indicated in Chapter 8, however, there is nothing in the cranial anatomy of the Neanderthals to suggest that their brains were different from ours.

Why they vanished is still a mystery. About the only thing we can say definitely is that no simple answer will do. There are two general theories, neither entirely satisfactory and neither subscribed to in their extreme forms; Trinkaus refers to them as the local-continuity and the replacement models. The local-continuity model rests on the notion of independent origins, the notion that Neanderthals evolved into Cro-Magnons at different times in different parts of the world. The replacement model, sometimes referred to as the Garden of Eden theory, holds that *Homo sapiens sapiens* arose only once in a single region and spread out from there.

The local-continuity model finds support in observations from a number of regions. There is a cave in Israel, on the slopes of Mount Carmel overlooking the Mediterranean near Haifa, where excavators unearthed the skeleton of a short, stocky individual with heavy limbs and bony brow ridges, clearly a Neanderthal but apparently not the kind that was living in western Europe. The brow ridges were less massive, the skull somewhat more rounded. Furthermore, near the cave is a rock shelter which served as a cemetery for people who lived in the area several thousand years later, and who were even closer to modern people. The ten skeletons recovered there had longer limbs than their predecessors, more prominent chins, and smaller faces.

Inland and about 50 miles from Haifa, not far from Nazareth at the narrowest part of a pass to the mountains of Lebanon, is another site of transitional people—the huge Qafzeh Cave, where the remains of at least seven individuals resembling those excavated at Mount Carmel were found more than 30 years ago. This site, which was blown up by British troops during the 1940s as a suspected ammunition depot, has since been revisited. After about six weeks spent removing the debris of the explosion, tons of fallen rocks, investigators uncovered two beautifully preserved skeletons, enclosed them in blocks of plaster, and flew them back to Jerusalem by helicopter. Since then about half a dozen more individuals have been recovered, all very closely related to Cro-Magnons.

Further evidence for an entire spectrum of hominids, ranging all the way from skulls with heavy brow ridges and jaws and sloping foreheads to more gracile forms approaching the double-*sapiens* pattern, comes from a variety of Old World sites, from the most recent Shanidar burials and from similar finds in China. Fossil remains, although fragmentary, suggest that transitional Neanderthals, people anatomically closer to the Cro-Magnons, lived in Czechoslovakia and other parts of eastern Europe, while David Frayer of the University of Kansas reports that early European Cro-Magnons retained a number of Neanderthal-like features.

Another kind of observation has been used to support the local-continuity theory. It was once believed that the Neanderthals and Cro-Magnons could be distinguished by their tool kits. Now that no longer holds. At Qafzeh, representatives of *Homo sapiens sapiens* were using, and presumably made, Neanderthal-type tools. More recently the site of Saint-Césaire, about 60 miles north of Bordeaux near the Bay of Biscay coast, has yielded the remains of an individual somewhat on the gracile side, but definitely Neanderthal, in an occupation level containing the sort of blade tools generally associated with Cro-Magnons. In view of such findings a number of investigators, Bordes among them, have come out in favor of what is essentially a multiorigin or multitransition theory, since it implies that modern people evolved from Neanderthal ancestors independently in several regions, in western Europe and the Near East, among other places.

It so happens that there is also plausible evidence for the Garden of Eden theory. For one thing, the Saint-Césaire find, and a similar find in Yugoslavia, can also be used to support the replacement theory, the notion that modern humans did not evolve several times in several regions, but only once in one favored region. The specimens are relatively recent, probably about 32,000 years old—too recent, according to Christopher Stringer of the British Museum of Natural History and some of his colleagues, to have evolved into full-fledged *Homo sapiens sapiens* within a few millenniums, which is when our kind appeared on the scene. In other words, even allowing for the gracile features of the last Neanderthals, they could never have made it the rest of the way to modern humans in the time remaining. It seems that Neanderthals and Cro-Magnons may have co-existed for a short period.

This line of reasoning argues for the replacement theory. It suggests the migration into Europe of an advanced population which had evolved elsewhere, took over, and was largely responsible for the extinction of the Neanderthals. The newcomers may have arrived from the Near East, or perhaps thousands of miles away at Klasies River Mouth, east of Cape Town on the south coast of South Africa. Specimens there, remains of anatomically modern humans, have been dated to at least 65,000 years ago, although that has yet to be proved.

The scenario that follows from such observations is one of a movement out of Africa, reminiscent of the movement of *Homo erectus* more than a million years earlier, into the rest of the Old World. A look at the record of vanishing minorities in our times may help us guess at what may have happened then in Europe according to the replacement theory. In some places the Neanderthals may have been wiped out violently, like the Tasmanians during the last century, by newcomers with superior weapons and ideas of racial superiority. A more likely course of events, however, is that the natives were the victims of various forms of "assimilation" such as those currently being experienced by Eskimos, Kalahari Bushmen, and Australian aborigines. In any case, all of us have an appreciable number of Neanderthal genes.

In the last analysis it is not a matter of choosing between replacement and local continuity. The replacement scenario fails on a number of counts. For example, it cannot explain the existence of various transitional forms of human which support local continuity. The latter scenario, on the other hand, cannot explain what forces brought about the relatively rapid transition. Trinkaus indicates how much we have to learn: "It has become increasingly apparent that neither of these schemes is an accurate reflection of the origins of modern humans. . . .The transition . . . was an extremely complicated one, involving all the known processes that come into play during periods of rapid, within-species evolution. These involve regional continuity, local population replacement, and substantial levels of gene flow [interbreeding]."

For some time now there has been a serious unbalance in research on the rise of our species. Most of the money and most of the publicity have gone to studies of the remote past, focusing on the selective processes that transformed ape into hominid. Without underrating the importance of this transition, the later transition discussed in this chapter represents the other major turning point in the human story and certainly deserves equal attention, which it has not yet received. Specifically, understanding the Neanderthals is particularly important, because in them we see the launching of an accelerating phase of human evolution which really takes off in later times (see Chapters 10 and 11).

SUMMARY

One of the most important sources of information about the Neanderthals is Combe Grenal, a cave site excavated by the late François Bordes of the University of Bordeaux. In a decade of excavations there he exposed 65 layers of deposits, in some places 40 feet deep, and covering the period from more than 125,000 to about 40,000 years ago.

Neanderthal toolmakers exploited a technique invented at least half a million years ago, a new stage in the evolution of stone-working technology. The earliest toolmakers of 2 or more million years ago produced effective cutting and bashing edges; their *erectus* successors created the hand ax, the first symmetrical tool. The Neanderthals' innovation, known as the Levallois technique, involves a special way of preparing a selected stone so as to obtain by successive blows a series of similarly shaped flakes.

Bordes discovered that each Neanderthal layer at Combe Grenal contained one of four basic combinations of tools (tool kits): (1) the Quina kit, 50 to 80 percent side scrapers, featuring a heavy-duty variety with fine retouching; (2) the Acheulian tradition kit, featuring 5 to 40 percent hand axes and 5 to 20 percent side scrapers; (3) the so-called typical kit, containing roughly the same proportions of most tools; and (4) the denticulate kit, featuring up to 80 percent notched tools.

These kits occur not only at Combe Grenal but also at other Neanderthal sites in France—and, beyond that, in the rest of Europe and in North Africa and the Near East. Bordes believed that the four kits represent four cultures, four tribes each with its own customs and tool-making traditions—the cultural viewpoint. Other investigators, notably Lewis Binford, emphasize the functional viewpoint—the notion that the four tool kits represent four different activities, four adaptations to different living conditions developed by members of a single culture. The issue is complex and has not yet been settled.

We do not know why the Neanderthals vanished. It happened between 40,000 and 30,000 years ago, and the newcomers were the Cro-Magnons, modern-type people like ourselves, members of the "doubly wise" species *Homo sapiens sapiens*. According to the replacement theory, the Cro-Magnons evolved somewhere outside of Europe, perhaps in Africa or the Near East, and spread from there throughout the world. The local-continuity theory holds that Neanderthals evolved into Cro-Magnons at different times in different places.

chapter 10

An Evolutionary Explosion

The gradual, slow-fuse phase of human evolution came to an end with the earliest known burials and burial patterns. More than a million stable Acheulian years and a span of at least 100,000 years for the Neanderthals were followed by a phenomenon which had all the impact of the breaking of a logjam, a period of unprecedented change, known as the Upper Paleolithic and lasting from about 35,000 to 10,000 years ago. This period saw the emergence of modern human beings, people like ourselves. It included dramatic developments across the board, on all fronts, affecting all aspects of behavior and technology.

PREHISTORIC PIONEERS

Something was released which had not been expressed before, perhaps a preadaptive capacity for detailed planning and forecasting. If variety is the spice of life, then life was certainly getting spicier. We see it in the tools of the times, in the works of artisans exploiting to the fullest extent and for the first time many different designs and strategies. We see it in the food quest, which called for organization on a hitherto unknown scale, in the decline of mobility, and in the establishment of communication networks. Along with all this was a crumbling of egalitarian traditions, the rise of hierarchy and status—and a thrust into new lands.

Two of the great voyages in the human record occurred during late Neanderthal and early Upper Paleolithic times. One of them started somewhere off the coast of Southeast Asia. It was the last of a series of landfalls, the last lap of an island-hopping process that has been going on for generations, past the shoals and reefs of archipelagos now submerged beneath the South China Sea and adjacent waters. Navigators set out from the shores of the final island into open ocean, guided by birds in flight and the behavior of the sea itself and perhaps by the stars, until they saw new land looming dark and low on the horizon, pulling up at last on an alien beach. The voyage covered a distance of only about 50 miles. But it took place 40,000 or more years ago in a bark or dugout canoe or on a raft, and it opened up the island continent of Australia.

The other voyage led from the easternmost tip of Siberia into Alaska. Like the route to Australia, it could have required a trip across open water by raft or canoe, since the Bering Strait, which separates Asia from America and has always separated them during relatively warm interglacial times such as ours, is also about 50 miles wide, with two islands in between to make the crossing easier. It would have been easier still during glacial periods, when ice sheets locked up so much water that the oceans were several hundred feet lower than they are today, and a tundra plain more than a thousand miles wide connected the two continents. We do not know when hunting-gathering bands first entered the New World, but they had certainly made it by about 15,000 years ago, and perhaps 10 or more millenniums before that.

NEW TOOLS, NEW TOOL KITS

Striking changes in life style took place throughout the world—in the Near East, on the wide Iranian Plateau, in India and China and Southeast Asia. But the story is best known in western Europe, the most intensively studied region. Among other things, there was a boom in toolmaking. More tools were being made than ever before, more kinds of tools, made from more materials, and with a notable increase in efficiency and finesse. The Upper Paleolithic featured a special blade technique which may represent a refinement of the Neanderthals' Levallois technique (see Chapter 9).

The first step in both cases was to select a suitable nodule of flint and prepare it, not for making a single tool, but for striking off a number of flakes with controlled shapes, each a blank for a separate tool. The Cro-Magnon procedure involved the preliminary forming of a roughly cylindrical core, say 4 or so inches in diameter and half a foot long, with one flattened end used as a striking platform. A sharp blow, often delivered with a "soft" hammer of bone or antler rather than stone, directed at a spot at the edge of the platform, produced a long, narrow, and thin sliver or blade of flint.

That was the beginning of an ingenious peeling-off process. Another blow directed near the striking point, which was used to detach the first blade, produced a second blade—and successive blows continuing around the circumference of the striking platform produced further blades one after the other in a sort of spiraling-in pattern as the core became smaller and smaller. The end result, in the words of John Witthoft, was a series of "highly specialized long chips which have been split from cores as precisely as one might split shingles from a bolt of oak."

In all, the technique commonly resulted in 40 to 50 blades from a single core, each a blank which would be worked into any one of a number of different tools. According to one estimate, making an advanced Upper Paleolithic knife required some 250 blows, more than twice the total required for a Neanderthal knife. The technique paid off, however, in terms of a notable increase in flint-knapping efficiency, yielding about 40 feet of cutting edge per pound of flint as against the 40 inches yielded by the Levallois method, and a mere 2 to 8 inches for the Acheulian hand ax.

The number of different tools also increased markedly, from the 60-odd items which made up Neanderthal kits to more than 130, and that comparison tells only part of the story. Actually no single site contains every tool in the list of possible tools. A typical figure for a Neanderthal site might be 15 or so different kinds of tool, while the average Cro-Magnon site might contain 40 to 50 kinds.

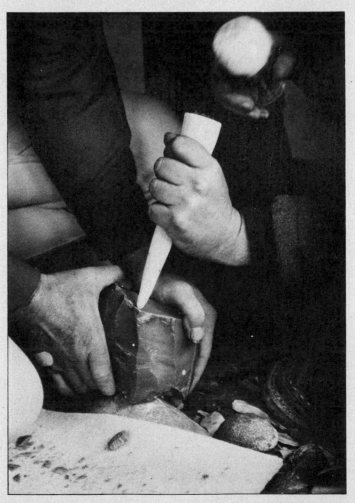

Punched blade technique: using bone punch

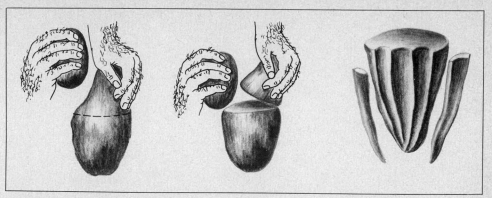

Stages in making punched blade tool

Tasks apparently involved longer sequences of operations, being broken down into a greater number of discrete steps, many of which required specially shaped tools.

Of all the new special-purpose tools unearthed at Upper Paleolithic sites, the burin is perhaps the most representative, certainly one of the tools produced in the widest variety and associated frequently with innovative design. It was designed for applying pressure concentrated at a point or across a narrow edge, for achieving variously shaped grooves, for carving, engraving, chiseling, and gouging. Rare in Neanderthal tool kits, the burin is one of the most common items in many later assemblages, occurring in more than a dozen different forms, more than a dozen readily recognized and standardized "models," which implies a whole range of new operations.

Considerable effort went into the making of microliths, tiny tool elements, some measuring less than three-quarters of an inch long, about half as long as a paper match. They had a long prehistory, being used more and more frequently with a definite trend toward increasing miniaturization starting in France about 25,000 years go. Many microliths are beautifully worked, with delicate trimming and retouching which can best be appreciated only when viewed through a magnifying lens. Collections include fingernail-sized end scrapers as well as star-shaped multipointed borers, knifelike bladelets, bladelets notched with saw teeth on both sides, and triangular, trapezoidal, and rectangular bladelets. Also rare in Neanderthal times but more common later was the combination two-in-one tool, generally a blade with a burin at one end and a scraper at the other.

Toolmaking became more sophisticated, more complicated. People went in increasingly for the exploitation of favored quarries, selecting particular types of stone for particular tools. Upon occasion, instead of taking the material ready-made in its natural state, they improved its quality. A kind of stiff liquid made up of interlocking silica microcrystals, flint can be modified by annealing, heating followed by slow cooling. This relieves or relaxes internal strains built into the crystal structure, producing a softer, more elastic material which can be shaped and trimmed with less applied pressure.

The Upper Paleolithic brought not only more tools and more kinds of tools, but also more tool materials, part of a more complete use of animal resources. Hominids had been using bone for some 2 million years (see Chapter 4), but not to the fullest extent, not as a raw material in its own right. They generally treated it as if it were stone, knocking off flakes with hammerstones and generally turning out hand axes, cleavers, and other traditional items. The Cro-Magnons were more aware of the unique properties of bone as well as of antler and ivory; being less brittle and softer than stone, these animal materials could be worked more readily into a number of special shapes.

Hafting became more important. The Neanderthals seem to have done some setting of blades into wooden handles, but their successors used the technique far more extensively. That was part of the reason for the manufacture of microliths. Although you can do effective work with some of the tiny tools by gripping them with your fingers, especially with bladelets backed or blunted along one edge for holding, many of them were designed to be inserted into grooved or slotted handles of wood or antler. Set firmly in place with a resin cement, they often served as replaceable teeth, or cutting and piercing elements, in harpoons and other composite tools.

All this takes time. A reasonably skilled flint knapper can make a burin or backed bladelet from a blank in 30 seconds or so, but preparing an effective handle may take more than an hour. Mark Newcomer of the Institute of Archaeology in London suggests that hafting may have resulted in a changing attitude toward tools: "Having put the extra effort into a tool, you become literally more conservative. The handle represents an investment, acquiring a special value as something long-lived that you want to keep." Hunter-gatherers who are frequently on the move tend to travel light, holding the number of items that must be carried to a minimum. But tools with handles are not readily discarded. They represent something to hold on to, an early form of private property.

French investigators have distinguished four major types of Upper Paleolithic tool kit. The kits have been dated by a technique which, like the potassium-argon clock (see Chapter 2), depends on the steady decay rate of a radioactive element, in this case a radioactive form of carbon known as carbon 14. The technique has provided the following approximate durations for the kits:

Perigordian: from more than 35,000 to 23,000 years ago; named after the Perigord, the 2700-square-mile region which includes Les Eyzies; featuring a number of distinctive flint points.

Aurignacian: from about 35,000 to 20,000 years ago; named after the Aurignac site in the Pyrenees; featuring nosed scrapers and bone points with beveled or split bases.

Solutrean: from about 20,000 to 17,000 years ago; named after an open-air camp near the village of Solutré in east-central France; featuring finely worked points.

Magdalenian: from about 17,000 to 10,000 years ago; named after the La Madeleine rock shelter some 3 miles from Les Eyzies; featuring harpoons, a variety of microliths and burins, and spearthrowers.

A warning about this sequence: it is deceptively straightforward. For ex-

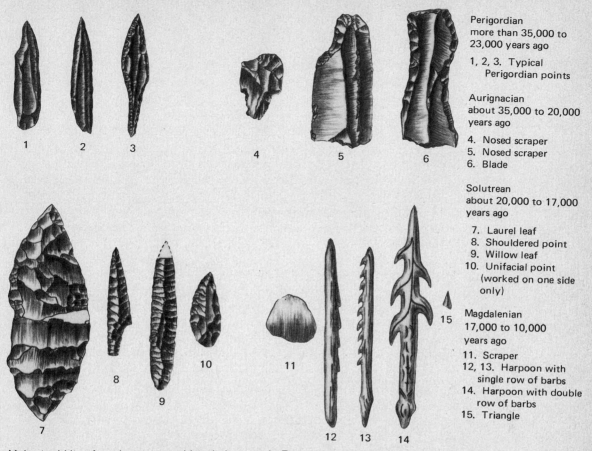

Perigordian
more than 35,000 to
23,000 years ago

1, 2, 3. Typical
       Perigordian points

Aurignacian
about 35,000 to 20,000
years ago

4. Nosed scraper
5. Nosed scraper
6. Blade

Solutrean
about 20,000 to 17,000
years ago

7. Laurel leaf
8. Shouldered point
9. Willow leaf
10. Unifacial point
    (worked on one side
    only)

Magdalenian
17,000 to 10,000
years ago

11. Scraper
12, 13. Harpoon with
    single row of barbs
14. Harpoon with double
    row of barbs
15. Triangle

Major tool kits of modern-type prehistoric humans in Europe

ample, the Perigordian and Aurignacian kits raise the same sort of problems that have arisen in the case of François Bordes' Neanderthal kits (see Chapter 9). Do the kits represent different cultures, people with different backgrounds and traditions, or different functions, the same people doing different things?

Supporting the functional view is the observation of Denise de Sonneville-Bordes, of the University of Bordeaux, that Perigordian tools are found in sites with relatively thin deposits, suggesting brief or intermittent occupations. Also, the sites are generally scattered throughout the Les Eyzies region and located in different kinds of terrain. Aurignacian kits, on the other hand, tend to be concentrated in narrow valleys or against cliff walls providing clusters of neighboring shelters, and are usually found in thick layers, implying more people or longer occupations or both. These features can be interpreted as reflecting different activities carried out in different settings.

There are arguments on the cultural side. As far as the Les Eyzies region is concerned, the Perigordian and Aurignacian tool kits do not actually overlap in time as they may elsewhere. Jean-Philippe Rigaud points out that in this region the Aurignacian kit was present from about 33,000 to 28,000 years ago, but not the Perigordian kit, which turned up some distance away to the southeast. He suggests the possibility of population displacement, rival groups or tribes—the Perigordians and Aurignacians—competing and supplanting one another.

INNOVATION AND SURVIVAL

The Solutrean period, although brief compared to the others, was something special. If the Upper Paleolithic as a whole was a time of take-off, its Solutrean phase represents an evolutionary spurt, a definite stepping up of the rate of change. It was a time of great stress, of maximum glacial advance. Conditions were probably colder then than at any previous time during the past million years or more. The Scandinavian ice sheet covered Scotland and most of Ireland and, together with other glacial systems, held so much water that sea levels fell sharply. As in previous glacial periods, there was no English Channel and no North Sea; a plain connected England and France, and the Baltic Sea was a vast fresh-water lake.

People living in southern France had to contend with severe climates, with winters which may have lasted 8 or 9 months and brought average temperatures as low as 10 degrees below zero Fahrenheit. Under intense survival pressure, the Solutreans made a number of major innovations. The archeological record indicates that they were the first to make sharp-pointed bone needles, containing eyes which must have required piercing with tiny flint awls, and implying the emergence of "tailoring," the wearing of fitted clothing made of hides sewn together, presumably with sinews.

They probably invented the spearthrower, a device designed to amplify muscle power and still used today by the Australian aborigines. Generally about 2 feet long and made of wood or antler, it had a barb at one end which hooked into the butt end of a spear shaft. Held over the shoulder with shaft in place and snapped forward by a sharp jerk of the wrist, it imparted considerable extra force to the spear, producing a swift flight and flat trajectory. Using a spear alone, it is rarely possible to kill a large animal unless you are close enough and fast enough to make repeated thrusts. Equipped with spearthrowers, the aborigines can hit a target, say a kangaroo, three out of four times from more than 100 feet away, and kill from 30 to 50 feet.

The bow and arrow may also be a Solutrean invention. Some time ago Eduardo Ripoll-Perello of Barcelona University dug in a cave in the mountains of southeast Spain, the Cueva de Ambrosio, and found an assortment of points closely resembling arrowheads found by the thousands at American Indian sites. Indeed, if the same points had been uncovered at one of these sites, they would have been identified without question as arrowheads. Similar points have been found in other Spanish caves, and they provide the earliest indirect evidence for the invention of the bow and arrow. (The earliest direct evidence, from a 10,000-year-old open site in Denmark, consists of two arrow shafts preserved in water-logged deposits with tanged arrowheads still in place.)

The Solutreans were virtuoso flint knappers. Along with scrapers and burins and quantities of other ordinary items, their kits included some of the most beautifully shaped tools ever made. To cite only one example, they produced laurel leaf blades—slender, symmetrical, flat pieces tapering to a point. Dozens of different kinds, long blades and short blades, thin and thick ones, were produced, all variations on the same basic theme. Some sites contained so many laurel leaves and other finely shaped tools that they may have been special workshops organized for a flourishing export trade. Incidentally, as pointed out by Roy Larick of the State University of New York at Binghamton, the toolmakers favored a special translucent chalcedony, a fine-grained quartz, for these points.

"Like the puffing-out of a candle"—this is how one investigator described the abrupt disappearance of the Solutreans or, more strictly speaking, the Solutrean tool kit. This passing set the stage for perhaps the most spectacular development of the period, the rise and rapid expansion of the Magdalenian tradition. Part of the record has been found at the site for which the tradition is named. It lies on the banks of the Vézère River, in the hollow of a massive limestone cliff overhang. To reach it one climbs up one side of a ridge rising above the river valley, passes a ruined medieval abbey at the top, and then goes down the other side of the ridge along the long face of a cliff to a place surrounded by a high wire fence with a sign that says, "Abri de la Madeleine—Fouilles Interdites" (digging prohibited).

The setting is remote, hidden in the trees on a hairpin loop of the river with water rushing past and meadows nearby. But things hummed here during prehistoric times, perhaps 13,000 to 14,000 years ago. Collections from this site feature tools made of bone and antler and ivory, often decorated with engravings of reindeer, horses, bison, mammoths, abstract spiral designs, fish and stylized fish motifs, and, more rarely, crude human figures. Magdalenian tool kits include shaft straighteners, spear points, wands of unknown purpose, and, above all, the first harpoons—a rich variety of them, long and short, with single and double rows of differently shaped barbs.

The combination two-in-one tool makes up 2 or 3 to 10 out of every 100 tools in some of the Magdalenians' assemblages. There are also bone needles, first seen in Solutrean deposits but by now developed and used in quantity. Another prominent item, another possible Solutrean invention, was the spearthrower, probably often made of wood but surviving only in bone and antler. This device disappears toward the end of Magdalenian times in France, most likely because the bow and arrow was beginning to be used on a widespread basis. These times also saw what Bordes called "an explosion of microliths."

Such varied kits reflect an enormous increase in the variety and complexity of Upper Paleolithic life styles. Scrapers used to prepare hides and needles for sewing indicate how some of the tools were used in the daily grind, and other studies point to significant changes in the food quest. For one thing, there must have been an increasing sophistication in plant-gathering techniques, although this part of the record is notable chiefly for being widely neglected. Soil samples from prehistoric sites, which contain plant fragments and fossil pollen and crystalline phytoliths, or plant opals (see Prologue), represent a largely untapped source of information, particularly in western Europe.

But we have hints of what was going on. The origin of agriculture as a way of life lay thousands of years in the future, but there can be little doubt that the people of the Upper Paleolithic would have known enough to turn to farming if reasons to do so had existed. Some of the evidence comes from Duruthy, a Magdalenian site in the southwest corner of France, not far from Biarritz. Robert Arambourou of the University of Bordeaux, who has been excavating there for more than 20 years, describes it as a "seasonal village" where some 100 hunter-gatherers lived during the fall and winter, probably moving to high grasslands during the summer.

Something strikingly unexpected turned up in late deposits perhaps 11,000 to 12,000 years old. Arambourou examined more than 1500 tiny backed blades, and found that about half of them had lustrous, shiny surfaces along the front or cutting edge. This feature has not been reported from any other site in southwestern Europe (although Bordes also noted it at one of his sites), but it is familiar enough in later tool assemblages of other regions—for example, the Near East. Known as "sickle sheen," it results from the polishing action of the silica-containing stalks of cereal grasses during reaping, and indicates that some of the Magdalenians at least were harvesting plants which may or may not have been domesticated.

BIG-GAME HUNTING ON THE RISE

Subsistence techniques were just as advanced when it came to meat eating. The odds are that hominids had the capacity for killing big game at least 300,000 years ago and perhaps rather earlier (see Chapter 6). But apparently they put their talents to use chiefly on an opportunistic basis, when a herd happened to be spotted heading for a river crossing, into a dead-end canyon, or into some other natural trap where escape might be difficult. Going after big game on a regular, organized basis, exploiting herds systematically, seems to have been practiced in the main during the Upper Paleolithic.

There is some evidence that scavenging remained an important source of meat during late Neanderthal times. Studies of cutmarks on bone are suggestive in this connection. During the course of his work among the Brooks Range Eskimos of Alaska (see Chapter 9), Lewis Binford noted differences between the butchering of freshly killed caribou and caribou scavenged long after their death—specifically, in early spring, when meat is scarce and local hunters search out the frozen carcasses of animals that had died during the winter. The front legs of a freshly killed animal, for example, are flexible, and the lower end can be severed with a quick cut at the joint, at right angles to the upper end. It is quite a different problem to sever a limb frozen and flexed. That calls for two well-directed chopping strokes at a different angle.

Such cutmarks have been studied on fossil specimens. Clive Gamble of the University of Southampton in England has found the frozen-limb variety on bones from late Neanderthal sites, mainly on the bones of horses, wild oxen, and other large animals. The bones of small red deer, on the other hand, have cutmarks typical of fresh-kill butchering. Binford reports similar cutmarks on bones from the *Homo sapiens sapiens* Klasies River Mouth site in South Africa (see Chapter 9). He believes that practically all animals weighing over 90 pounds were scavenged, probably from lion kills. Some 30 to 40 percent of the under-90-pound animals may have also been scavenged, the rest being obtained by hunting and trapping.

A different pattern emerged during the Upper Paleolithic. The accent was more on planning, less on spontaneous, spur-of-the-moment hunts, a tendency documented by findings reported from a number of recent and continuing excavations. Archeologists are still putting together a picture of activities at the Abri Pataud, a site located at the base of a cliff overlooking the main street of Les Eyzies, and excavated under the direction of Hallam Movius of Harvard University. Bedrock was reached at a depth of more than 30 feet after six seasons of digging, which uncovered 14 occupation layers, more than 50,000 worked pieces of flint, and thousands of bones.

Like the great majority of Upper Paleolithic sites, the Abri Pataud indicates that Cro-Magnon hunters killed more reindeer than any other species. Out of 498 identifiable bones uncovered in its lowest layer, an Aurignacian occupation, 484 are reindeer bones. The extent of concentration on reindeer is an Upper Paleolithic characteristic, representing a marked shift from Neanderthal practices. One of the upper Abri Pataud layers includes a row of hearths at the rear of the

Artist's conception of Cro-Magnon community, showing tents in rock shelter

shelter's rocky overhang and protected by a row of limestone blocks, some weighing half a ton or more. They form a solid barrier, except for a gap at one end which may have served as the doorway into a long house for a community of several families.

Another major site or, rather, complex of sites, is a 25-acre Magdalenian area known as Pincevent about 35 miles southeast of Paris, not far from the palace of Fontainebleau. After more than 3 years and 300,000 hours of digging, André Leroi-Gourhan of the University of Paris and his associates uncovered about 5 acres of what seems to have been a summer and fall camp for reindeer hunting. One of half a dozen living floors consists of three hearths and three sleeping areas, all of which may have been enclosed in a large tent made of skins. The entire site is in a remarkable state of preservation and includes considerable pollen and animal remains as well as hearths. Things have been so little disturbed over the millenniums that tiny chips have been found and fitted to the blades from which they were removed, and the source of the blades, the original flint core, has also been recovered nearby. An open-air museum has been built at the Pincevent site.

A stampede which took place in Colorado some 10,000 years ago illustrates the sort of techniques applied increasingly during the Upper Paleolithic. Joe Ben Wheat of the University of Colorado describes what happened in a gully about 150 miles southeast of Denver, basing his reconstruction on the articulated remains of a bison herd at the Olsen-Chubbuck site:

> Animal after animal pressed from behind, spurred on by the shower of spears and the shouts of the Indians now in full pursuit. . . . The bison, impeded by the calves, tried to jump the gully, but many fell short and landed in the bottom of it. Others fell kicking, twisting and turning on top of them, pressing them below even tighter into the confines of the arroyo. In a matter of seconds, the arroyo was filled to overflowing with a writhing bellowing mass of bison, forming a living bridge over which a few animals escaped. Now the hunters moved in and began to give the coup de grace to these animals on top, while underneath the first trapped animals kept up the bellows and groans and their struggle to free themselves, until finally the heavy burden of slain bison above crushed out their lives. In minutes the struggle was over. One hundred ninety bison lay dead in and around the arroyo. Tons of meat awaited the knives of the hunters—meat enough for feasting, and plenty to dry for the months ahead—more meat, in fact, than they could use. . . .

Such clear-cut evidence of a single mass-kill episode is lacking for Europe. We do not know whether the remains of more than 200 mammoths at a site on the Russian plain, or the remains of more than 1000 of the giant creatures at a Czechoslovakian site, were the victims of similar stampedes or simply the accumulations of many generations of small-scale hunts. But such finds contribute to the general impression of all-out hunting, hunting on a mass-production scale.

The most spectacular accumulation of all exists at Solutré, the Solutrean-type site discovered more than a century ago, at the foot of a steep cliff. Extensive

Artist's conception of camouflaged Magdalenian hunters stalking reindeer

deposits more than 3 feet thick contained bones representing 10,000 to 100,000 horses, either driven to their deaths off the top of the cliff or ambushed in a narrow pass down below. Recently Randall White of New York University has drawn attention to findings made half a century ago at an important open-air site in southern France. Located on a terrace overlooking a river valley and at the foot of a steep 100-foot cliff, Badegoule provides abundant evidence of organized mayhem—340 pairs of antlers, piles of reindeer vertebrae, and articulated feet (including some 1600 toe bones), 5000 molar teeth, and the articulated remains of the front part of a mammoth in a huge fire pit. These animals were not killed and carried up from the valley floor or down from the top of the cliff. They were driven over the cliff to their deaths.

THE MOST DANGEROUS KILLERS

White emphasizes the importance of large-scale hunting, and the food quest generally, in determining the choice of a place to live. On the basis of visits to some 185 out of more than 200 sites within a 30-mile radius of Les Eyzies, he notes a significant pattern. Whereas the Neanderthals occupied upland sites, high on regional plateaus, the people of the Upper Paleolithic moved down into the

Mass slaughter: reconstruction of bison being stampeded over cliff

Artist's conception of ibex game drive

valleys for easier access to food resources, a trend which may have begun 20,000 or more years ago. Furthermore, all large Magdalenian sites lie in major river valleys at naturally shallow places or fords formed, millions of years before the appearance of humans, by geological upheavals and the outcropping of erosion-resistant rocks.

The location of Upper Paleolithic sites near fords has also been reported in Hungary, and in the Soviet Union along the Lena River in Siberia near the Arctic Circle. It is part of a time-tested "head 'em off at the pass" strategy. In Canada's Northwest Territories present-day Eskimo hunters still lie in wait at such places, observe caribou moving by the thousands along river banks in search of easy crossings, and then close in for the kill as the animals swarm helplessly in the water.

The location of many prehistoric ambush sites near modern caribou crossings suggests that the animals are using some of the same migration routes today that they used thousands of years ago. White notes similar features in the Perigord. Large quantities of the bones of reindeer, Old World relatives of caribou, tend to be concentrated at large Magdalenian sites near fords. Fords also represent ideal locations for weirs, traps and nets used in harvesting fish, notably salmon—the "caribou" of riverine species as far as mass migrations and predictability are concerned.

Locational studies suggest further refinements in the art of planning kills on a large scale, of restricting the mobility or escape options of prey. Most digging tends to be close-to-the-cliff digging, either inside or just in front of caves and rock shelters occupied by the hunter-gatherers of the Upper Paleolithic, which makes some sense unless you are interested in learning more about mass killing. As White emphasizes, the evidence for that probably lies at some distance away from cliffside camping places.

The odds are that concentrations of bones and tools would be found out in the open fields of dry valleys, or "combes," many of which are narrow with steep cliffs at the sides and at one end. They provide ideal traps, natural dead-end enclosures into which herds can be driven and slaughtered on the spot, or perhaps corraled and kept for future slaughtering. The overwhelming majority of Upper Paleolithic sites, 88 percent, are located in or near (within about 275 yards) of dry valleys.

Notice how mass hunting, and the entire Cro-Magnon life style, may have played a central role in changing hominid anatomy. From the beginning, from australopithecine times, our ancestors have been rugged specimens, and the robust Neanderthal physique continued in that tradition. We can imagine that the Neanderthals did less planning than their successors, that they walked through snows in search of big game more often than they gathered at ambush points and waited for the game to come to them—and that they came in close for the kill, near enough to attack with spear and lance and club, jabbing and thrusting, often in physical contact with an animal fighting back for its life.

Presumably close encounters of this kind were rarer during the Upper Paleolithic. The spearthrower provided increased power, at a distance. The bow and arrow not only increased power and range beyond that, but also increased

Mass slaughter site: fossil bison remains from Olsen-Chubbuck site, eastern Colorado

the possibility of stealth. To hurl a spear you must spring out of your hiding place and give your position away. You can stay put with a bow and arrow, and shoot a second or third time if you miss on the first try. Game drives and stampedes, although posing risks of their own, reduced the incidence of direct human-vs.-animal combat. The net effect of these and other developments, substituting strategy for strength, probably helped transform the heavy-boned, massive-muscled physique characteristic of previous hominids to the gracile modern physique.

(Opposite page) The art of archeological reconstruction. Plateau site in southwestern France: exposed living floor, prehistoric objects in place; map showing pattern of distributed objects; reconstruction, interpretation of the pattern.

The irony is that as humans became weaker, they also became enormously more dangerous to the rest of the animal kingdom. As a general rule, there are two patterns among bones excavated at large kill sites. If the fossil specimens represent animals at the extremes of the age scale predominantly, the old and the young in a so-called bimodal distribution, the odds are that selective predation was involved—since early human hunters, like their carnivorous competitors the lions and wild dogs and hyenas, probably tended to go after the most vulnerable individuals in a herd, avoiding adults at the prime of life and focusing on those less capable of fighting back.

An all-ages pattern, on the other hand, implies the working of more impersonal forces. Floods, earthquakes, volcanoes, and other devastations do not operate selectively. They wipe out entire populations, the strong as well as the weak and everything in between. It may be that for hundreds of thousands of years, as long as our ancestors were capable of killing large animals, they were bimodal killers, hunting in the ancient tradition of their nonhuman contemporaries. The all-ages pattern became increasingly common during the course of the Upper Paleolithic. *Homo sapiens* had come a long way in their game drives. They were no longer killing like a normal predator, like a respectable carnivore— but like a natural catastrophe, an act of God.

REDUCED MOBILITY, SEASONAL VILLAGES

Developments in tool and subsistence technology, however dramatic, represent only a small part of the story. The nature of society, the deep structure of living styles, was being transformed. Mobility patterns changed. The Upper Paleolithic featured migrations into new environments, new lands, and at the same time signs of a settling-down, settling-in tendency. Nomadism, a characteristic of hunting-gathering bands from early hominid days, had started on its long period of decline.

A number of sites took on a more solid, somewhat more permanent quality. They became "stonier." Stone as a mark of the change was brought in not just for tool making but also for structural reasons, to modify the site, to make it more convenient for living. Things began to get interesting during Neanderthal times. Some of the Neanderthal open-air sites feature prominent "rock-scatter" pavements of a sort, made up of thousands of cobblestone-like pebbles. The purpose of these artificial surfaces remains unknown; one suggestion is that they somehow made getting about more convenient during and after rainstorms.

A whole complex of unexplained features, undeciphered patterns in stone, appeared after the Neanderthals. An open-air site at Solvieux, not far from Bergerac, includes 16 Upper Paleolithic occupation levels covering the period from about 30,000 to 14,000 years ago. James Sackett of the University of California in Los Angeles has spent more than a decade digging there, and has unearthed a wealth of patterns, everything from rock-scatter pavements to stones placed in straight and curving lines which may or may not be footpaths. There are rectangular and circular patterns of stones, once identified as mysterious symbols, purportedly of magical or ritual significance, and now regarded more prosaically as the remains of huts, being used to hold down the ground-level edges of skins placed over wooden frameworks. Solvieux also includes large, circular block structures made up of flattish chunks of limestone, which no one has yet been bold enough to interpret.

The Cro-Magnons were generally choosier about where they lived than the Neanderthals. For one thing, they showed a preference for caves and rock shelters with a southern exposure. White notes that 54 out of 79 Magdalenian occupations are "at least partially south-facing," 26 of them directly oriented to the south, a tendency evident for all Upper Paleolithic sites. Southern exposure offers a number of advantages in addition to solar heating, such as more light, drier living floors, and better protection from prevailing winds.

According to Bordes, there was also a difference in fuel economy. Neanderthal home fires usually burned directly on flat living-floor surfaces, spread out over a relatively large area with perhaps a stone or two set up to protect against the wind. The fires of the Cro-Magnons were more compact, placed in prepared hollows, commonly encircled with stones, and often featuring a narrow channel or "tail" scooped out at the bottom to create a draft and hotter burning, a feature invented more than 200,000 years ago but not found in Neanderthal sites. Cro-Magnons frequently used bone for fuel; it is difficult to ignite, requiring wood as a primer or starter, but, once ignited, burns at high heat.

There is a suggestion of more elaborate sites, and of the first assemblies of hunter-gatherer bands, probably on a seasonal basis. Some 27,000 years ago, at a site known as Dolni Vestonice, on the rolling glacial plains of south-central Czechoslovakia, people drove wooden posts into the ground near a stream (traces of the postholes are still visible as faint soil discolorations), supports for the walls and roofs of a cluster of four huts, the largest measuring 50 by 20 feet. Posts of the long bones and tusks of mammoths formed the framework for a brush-and-dirt wall surrounding the huts, the earliest known palisade, presumably to keep out animals and icy winds. Another streamside cluster of dwellings complete with palisade, located not far away and perhaps a millennium or two more recent, may have housed 100 to 125 persons. No Neanderthal sites of comparable complexity have been found.

The existence of one seasonal village has already been noted. La Madeleine, the Magdalenian type site, definitely fits into this category. Rich and thick occupation layers, as yet unexcavated, extend out to the Vézère River, and the original site probably occupied an area of several acres. About 20 miles farther downstream along a 2-mile stretch of the Dordogne River is another row of shelters which housed an estimated 400 to 600 persons. This sort of housing pattern is often associated with the Magdalenians, particularly during their later stages.

Along with larger aggregations and reduced mobility, reduced nomadism, came a need for monitoring wider regions. As a general rule, efficiency demands a broader base of operations, knowledge of resources not only in the immediate area but further afield—because sooner or later the group will have no choice but to move away. Sooner or later, within a decade at best, the area will be hunted out; animals will avoid the area or be wiped out. Under such conditions it is wise to know in advance where to set up a new home base, and that implies keeping tabs on abundances of game, wild cereals, fruit and nut trees, and other resources in wider areas.

This is what modern hunter-gatherers do. Binford has records of one band of 36 Brooks Range Eskimos with a total territory of some 8700 square miles, or about the equivalent of a circle with a 53-mile radius. That is the band's so-called extended range, the land it considers its own. But the people never exploit the whole territory at any one time. They live in and confine most of their hunting activities to one of about half a dozen smaller and partly overlapping annual or residential ranges within the larger territory, shifting from one to another (the most abundant) as local resources dwindle. In other words, when the time for moving comes, they are ready. They know everything they need to know about subsistence conditions throughout their extended range, because they visit all parts periodically.

Cro-Magnon bands, and hunter-gatherer bands confronting similar problems everywhere, probably practiced similar strategies. Far beyond that, they were in the process of forming wider associations with other bands monitoring and exploiting other extended ranges. The Neanderthals lived relatively self-contained, relatively isolated lives in the sense that, as far as we can tell from the archeological record, societies made up of a number of affiliated bands were not a major feature of the times. Compared to what came later, individual bands had only casual relationships with one another. Compared to what came later, the Neanderthal world was fragmented, loosely coupled.

The people of the Upper Paleolithic evolved along radically different lines. They were forming new contacts, new frontiers and outposts, building themselves into networks extending over greater and greater distances. The archeology of affiliation includes observations such as those made by Larick working under Rigaud's direction at the Flageolet rock shelter not far from Combe Grenal. One level of deposits, from 2 to 6 inches thick yielded about 700 tools in an excavated area of about 50 square feet—and the raw materials used for the tools, the flints and other stones, came from at least 17 different sources, some more than 50 miles away.

Quantities of so-called chocolate flint, a rich brown material extracted from clays in a mining region of central Poland, were carried as much as 250 miles to sites in Russia, Germany, and Czechoslovakia, in some cases exchanged for supplies of jasper and obsidian, a dark volcanic glass. People also traveled for items of show, or display pieces, personal adornment being another brand-new feature of the Upper Paleolithic. In the Ukraine, lumps of "the golden glowing stone," or amber, a fossil substance formed from resins produced 30 million years ago in primeval forests, have been found at sites 100 or more miles from the nearest source. Collecting marine shells, a common exchange or trade item throughout Europe, required trips up to 400 miles, or about three weeks of walking.

BAND SOCIETIES AND THE FIRST ELITES

All this, the variety of raw materials and the large-scale use of ornaments, is something completely unknown in Neanderthal times. Martin Wobst of the University of Massachusetts in Amherst is studying the dynamics of network formation. Bands as well as individuals need one another. They must come together to carry out large-scale hunting and harvesting operations, exchange raw materials, share information about where the food quest is likely to be most successful, and obtain mates. This has always been the case, only far more formalized relationships became more urgent during the Upper Paleolithic.

In part of a continuing theoretical analysis, Wobst considered associations of bands, each consisting of 25 members. It so happens that 25 is a good representative figure, a widely noted "magic number," for the logistics of living together. Among the Australian aborigines most bands are made up of 25 individuals, with a range of from 20 to 70, and similar figures have been reported in a series of studies of the Kalahari Bushmen, the Andaman Islanders, the Birhor of northern India, and other hunter-gatherers. A 25-person band includes about a dozen adults, which is generally sufficient to carry out the day's work.

Using a computer, Wobst followed the histories of a number of simulated band societies year by year for an average of 400 years (some five minutes of computer time per simulation), and calculated the chances of survival under various conditions. Mating rules are a major factor in determining the size of the tribe, the population needed to insure its survival by providing mates for all eligible individuals. Assuming that members of a band generally have to go outside the band for mates, that there is a taboo against incest, that a man marries a woman younger than himself, and that the wife moves in with her husband's family, then a tribe would require at least 475 people to provide an adequate mating pool, or a mating network of nineteen 25-member bands.

That result is of special interest. Another magic number involves the notion of "dialectical tribe," groups of affiliated bands all speaking the same dialect. Census studies among modern hunter-gatherers indicate that while a tribe may have as few as 200 members or as many as 800 or more, most tribes operate at about the 500 level. The theoretical level of 475 is reasonably close to that real-life figure. As an interesting sidelight, there is an architect's rule of thumb to the effect that the capacity of an elementary school should not exceed 500 pupils if the principal expects to know all of them by name. Also, it has been stated that when a group exceeds 500 persons, it requires some form of policing.

Band societies need organizing—rules, punishments for breaking the rules, and people to see that the punishments are carried out. One result was a breakdown of one of the oldest and most widespread of hunter-gatherer traditions, the first signs of an accelerating departure from egalitarian principles that seem to have prevailed for many thousands of millenniums, as long as there were any principles at all. Present-day hunter-gatherers live by democratic principles, by an ethics of complete equality. There is a policy of ephemeral or dispersed leadership among the Bushmen of Africa's Kalahari, a semidesert region as large as France, different individuals being heeded under different circumstances. The best story teller may take over at the end of the day around campfires, the best hunter carries extra weight in planning the search for meat on the hoof, the best shaman is consulted when people need consoling or healing. No single member of the band serves as official big man or full-time chief.

Egalitarian principles also apply to the notion of ownership. If Kalahari men or women acquire valuable or beautiful objects, say a fine hunting knife or a colorful blouse or sweater, they are torn by conflicting emotions. They appreciate and treasure the object, and yet they feel exposed and threatened by having something which others do not have. The object becomes a psychological hot potato, something to be concealed for a while and gotten rid of as soon as possible. It will have been given to another member of the band within a few days, and within another two or three weeks it will probably be found in another band miles away. People tend to feel more comfortable not having an outstanding possession, and thereby sinking back into a less-conspicuous and less-envied position within the group.

An ethics of sharing and egalitarianism is also observed among the Australian aborigines and other hunter-gatherers. We cannot be certain that prehistoric bands lived by similar principles. But the record is clear-cut about one point. It contains no evidence for differences in status until the Upper Paleolithic; then we begin to get the first archeological traces of inequality. The evidence is striking. A site 20,000 to 25,000 years old, known as Sungir and located about 125 miles northeast of Moscow, contains a complex of four burials, two adults identified as man and woman, and two boys. Only a skull remains of the woman,

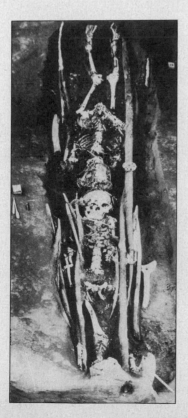

Sungir: boys buried with ivory spears

who had been buried in a grave sprinkled with red ochre. The man, broad-shouldered and in his middle 50s, was laid to rest in state, dressed in some sort of garment decorated with hundreds of pierced mammoth-ivory beads, wearing several bracelets and a headband also made of mammoth ivory.

The boys, aged 7 to 9 and 12 to 13, were buried face up in the same narrow trench in a head-to-head position, and with an even more impressive array of grave goods—some 8000 ivory beads, Arctic-fox canine teeth, assorted rings and bracelets, and 16 spears, darts, and daggers. Several spears demonstrate a high order of craftsmanship. More than 6 feet long, they are made of mammoth tusk, which is naturally curved. They had to be straightened, softened, and unbent step by step, probably steamed or immersed in hot water, a process which may have benefited from experience gained in the straightening of reindeer antlers. A set of graves excavated in the Grottes des Enfants, on the Italian Riviera, also includes two young children with large clusters of perforated shells around their midsections, presumably the remains of decorated clothing, as well as an adult wearing a shell headdress. A child about 7 years old was buried in the La Madeleine rock shelter, powdered with ochre and decorated with rings of strung-together shells on its head, neck, elbows, wrists, knees, and ankles.

The Grottes des Enfants site may have served as a special cemetery for people of distinction, perhaps members of a single extended family. It contained a total of some dozen burials, all with a variety of shell decorations. In addition, a number of the burials featured flint blades extraordinary for their length, 8 to 10 inches, requiring not only exceptional skill in the making but also carefully selected materials. Similar blades have also been found at another site located not far away, next to a skeleton with stones placed on its hands and feet, as if to keep the individual from leaving the grave.

A great deal of effort went into these burials, and into the appropriately elaborate ceremonies which must have accompanied them. Such honors are not for everyone, only for special people, indicating the beginnings of formal social distinctions. The burying of young children suggests further developments. Leaders who earn their positions by actual deeds need time to win recognition as hunters or shamans. They must keep proving themselves, and when they can no longer do so, they are replaced by someone who can. But the existence of children buried with high honors before they are old enough to do anything outstanding raises the possibility of status by heredity rather than achievement. Notice that this is only a possibility, since elite parents may simply choose to bury their offspring with special honors.

In any case, the appearance of people of distinction represented an enormous change in the rules of the game. Where life had probably proceeded largely along low-profile lines with no big men, or chiefs, and members of the band almost competing at times to remain inconspicuous, there was now room at the top. Instead of staying small and equal, a few individuals became very unequal indeed and proud of it, taking on the special responsibilities and privileges of leadership, enjoying the glamor of open recognition. Instead of giving things away, the most valued things the most quickly, they accumulated possessions for public display, as marks of status.

A set of new problems emerged with this shift in outlook, in ethics, a situation hinted at in the nature of Upper Paleolithic tool kits. As already noted, tools tended to become standardized, but not on a universal basis. Different areas each had their own toolmaking traditions; tools were shaped according to a number of distinctive local styles. In other words, toolmaking diversity decreased locally and increased regionally. The pattern is significant. It suggests a shift from the life styles of small hunter-gatherer bands to something rather more complicated. Along with larger and closer-knit groups came sharper differences among groups, the rise of new unities and, at the same time, new tensions and a new restlessness.

SUMMARY

The Upper Paleolithic, the period from about 35,000 to 10,000 years ago, saw a burst of innovation, new developments in every phase of life. It was the beginning of an acceleration of change which continues at a quickening pace today, among us. New lands were discovered in voyages to the Australian continent and the New World. People invented a new and highly efficient peeling-off process for making flint blades; new tools, some of them hafted, were made of bone and antler and ivory as well as stone.

New tool kits turn up in the archeological record, notably the Solutrean kit, which existed from about 20,000 to 17,000 years ago, and Magdalenian kits dating back some 17,000 to 10,000 years. Innovations of the Solutrean period included bone needles, spearthrowers, beautifully worked laurel-leaf blades, and perhaps the bow and arrow. The Magdalenian period included all these plus barbed harpoons, wands or rods for purposes unknown, and special blades which may have been used in harvesting cereal grasses.

A significant change in the food quest occurred during the Upper Paleolithic. Recent evidence suggests that scavenging of big game provided an important source of meat until late Neanderthal times. The Upper Paleolithic accent was on mass killing, apparently the first exploitation of herd animals on a regular basis. Sites featuring enormous accumulations of single species, mammoths or horses or reindeer, attest to the use of organized game drives.

Increased reliance on hunting was a major factor in speeding social change. It called for the location of sites near strategic points where game concentrated, near shallow river fords and narrow passes. It may even have affected human anatomy. The use of planning and mass-kill strategies instead of the sort of brute force involved in direct human versus animal combat may account for the fact that the Cro-Magnons were considerably less rugged and muscular than the Neanderthals.

People were becoming less and less nomadic, living for longer periods in seasonal villages. Theoretical considerations hint at the appearance of band societies, groups of interacting families perhaps averaging about 500 individuals. A sign of increasing communications among band societies was the first long-distance trade. Above all, the Upper Paleolithic saw the end of egalitarian traditions, the first elaborate graves marking the appearance of elites.

chapter 11

Art, Symbol, Society

No site in France, no site in all of Europe, can match Lascaux, a cave located in the woods on a plateau above the valley of the Vézère. The way in leads through a metal door, down a flight of concrete steps, through another metal door, to the threshold of the hall. You stand there for a moment in pitch darkness, and suddenly the lights are turned on. Without prelude or preparation, before the eye has a chance to become intellectual, to look at any single feature, you can take it in all at once. You see it whole, painted in red and black and yellow, a burst of animals, a procession dominated by huge creatures with horns. The animals form two lines converging from left and right, seeming to stream into a funnel mouth, toward and into a dark hole marking the way into a deeper gallery.

Then the experience breaks into parts. The animals become individuals in a frieze along an overhanging ledge formed by the scooping-out action of an ancient river, along a wall that curves in front of you like a panoramic motion-picture screen. Four bulls in black outline with black sweeping horns dominate the procession; one of them, the largest cave painting yet discovered, measures 18 feet long. Two of the bulls face one another, and five red stags fill the space between them. The frieze also includes six black horses, a large red horse, three cows, an enigmatic animal which guides and investigators alike persist in calling the "unicorn" although it has two horns and resembles no species known in real life or fable, and a number of other animals which are difficult to distinguish because they are partly covered by more recently painted figures.

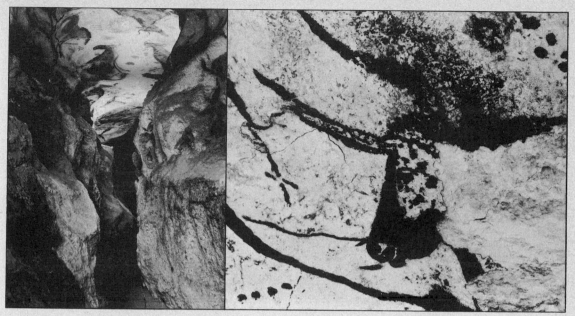

Lascaux cave: (left) ceiling paintings in one of the galleries leading off the main hall; (right) close-up of head of largest bull, about 18 feet, in the main hall

VARIETIES OF ART

The most spectacular mark of the Upper Paleolithic, the first explosive phase in human evolution, was the sudden appearance of art—and of all the art, Lascaux provides the most spectacular example. Lascaux is one of more than 225 art caves and rock shelters in western Europe, about 90 percent in France and Spain. Most of the sites are concentrated in three regions: the Bay of Biscay coast of northern Spain, the foothills of the central Pyrenees, and, the biggest cluster of all, in the Les Eyzies area. A total of 10,000 to 15,000 paintings and engravings have been reported to date.

The figures are mainly animals, as might be expected of people living wilderness lives in a world dominated by other animals. It is difficult for us, living in lands where the sight of a wild animal is becoming increasingly rare, to imagine the psychology of our ancestors, members of a minority species at large among herds numbering in the thousands or tens of thousands. Human beings rarely appear in cave-wall panels, and when they do they are often, though not always, drawn crudely and strangely distorted. Human hand prints are more common.

Many geometric patterns appear among the animals and humans. Their names are legion—claviform or club-shaped, tectiform or roof-shaped, scutiform or shield-shaped, tessellated or checkered, bell-shaped, tree-shaped, quadrangular, rayed, barbed, branched, and serpentine scrawls known as meanders or

Lascaux: close-up of part of main-hall panels

"macaroni." Some look vaguely like huts, corrals, traps, flying objects and have been interpreted as such. Some are so complicated that words fail. We have no idea what they mean. But we know they were full of meaning for the people of the Upper Paleolithic.

Reaching the art is part of the experience, part of a most effectively staged buildup. Some of the paintings and engravings are magnificent for any time and any place. Even relatively crude figures have a powerful impact come upon suddenly, the marks of humans deep underground, in some of the most unlikely and difficult-of-access places. No matter how many caves one has explored, the art always comes with a catch of the breath. It may be a bull or a bison drawn larger than life or an engraved horse no bigger than your little finger. It may appear high in a fissure or down close to the floor, on wide, exposed surfaces for all to see or in private crawl-in spaces, painted in bare red or black outline or in rich polychrome, starkly grand or delicate in a low key—a variety of locations and styles, and yet all part of a single tradition. The world's first "art movement" endured for some 20 millenniums.

Upper Paleolithic art includes a great deal more than paintings and engravings. Low-relief sculptures have been found on rock walls, near cave mouths; in many cases, the figures are on blocks, chunks of limestone that have fallen off

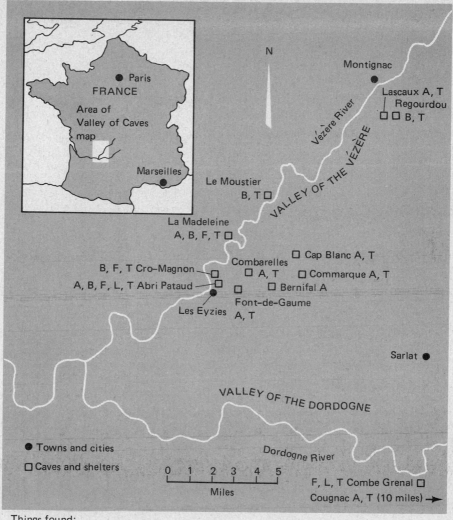

Things found:

A Art   F Fire   T Tools
B Human bones   L Living floors

"Valley of Caves" *Homo sapiens* sites, in Les Eyzies region, France

the walls. Angles-sur-Anglin, an unreported rock shelter at the foot of a cliff in a gorge some 150 miles south of Paris, contains part of a frieze on the grand scale. Covering an expanse of wall 10 to 12 feet high and more than 65 feet long, it features a beautifully carved horse looking back over its shoulder, a group of three women, a grazing horse, vulva signs, and a niche enclosing a composition of three ibexes and at least ten bison. Traces of color indicate that some of the figures may have been painted red with black eyes.

Cast of so-called Venus figurine found at Willendorf, Austria

There is another kind of art, widespread and involving different techniques, so-called portable, or mobiliary, art, objects generally small enough to hold in the hand and perhaps carry about—statuettes, figures engraved, carved, or painted on tools, limestone slabs, or plaquettes, as well as on odd pieces of bone, antler, stone, and ivory. The most famous are highly stylized statuettes of women, so-called Venus figurines found at a number of European sites and as far east as the Lake Baikal region of Siberia. I know of no official count of portable items, but they must number in the tens of thousands. Sites in a single province in the south of France have yielded about 2500 duly recorded pieces—that is, pieces described in publications. But excavators have probably unearthed four to five times as many items, and tucked them away in private collections.

The outpouring of Upper Paleolithic art is all the more impressive considering that it appeared with a bang, without a hint, in the archeological record, of its coming. There is nothing, absolutely nothing, to prepare us for the phenomenon. Can we detect a faint, very faint, flicker of the esthetic sense among Olduvai Gorge toolmakers of nearly 2 million years ago? They went out of their way to obtain and work a special kind of green lava. They also seem to have been attracted by smooth pink pebbles, apparently to look at and perhaps feel, since the pebbles show no sign of working. However you interpret such evidence, the toolmakers certainly had an interest in color.

Something more was involved 500,000 years later in the making of the hand ax, the first symmetrically shaped tool, described in Chapter 6. A number of these items required so much more effort than others, so much more attention to forming attractive contours, that the odds definitely favor esthetic considerations. Hand axes far too big to wield, 2 or more feet long and weighing 25 to 30 pounds, suggest the possibility of symbolic, ceremonial use. An unusual hand ax found in England includes a natural decoration, a fossil scallop shell embedded in the flint and left in place for appearance's sake.

The possibility of deliberately used color exists at Terra Amata, also described in Chapter 6. People may have brought lumps of colored ocher to the site to decorate artifacts made of such perishable materials as wood or hide, or perhaps to decorate their bodies. Some of the lumps, the ones sharpened at one end like pencils, suggest cosmetic motives. Neanderthal sites commonly include similar lumps of ocher and black manganese, as well as pieces which seem to have been scratched to make powder. A concern for pattern and the esthetic is also expressed in burials of Neanderthals laid to rest in circles of antlers or, as at Shanidar, with flowers (see Chapter 8).

The search for pre-Upper Paleolithic art has been intense, and continues. But it has yielded nothing. One of the oldest interestingly marked objects known to date comes from a site in southwestern France. François Bordes, who found it more than a decade ago, once showed it to me. A piece of ox rib about 6 inches long and 200,000 to 300,000 years old, it has markings on the surface, including what looks like a pair of curved lines running parallel to one another. Viewed under the microscope, however, each line is actually a carefully incised double line, and the pattern does look purposeful. But it depicts nothing recognizable, and hardly rates as a work of art.

Le Combel, southern France: red dots on ceiling, meaning unknown

DISCOVERY AND DISBELIEF

There is nothing ambiguous or uncertain about what happened during the Upper Paleolithic. The art is often so "advanced," so strikingly beautiful and fresh, that at first the experts would not accept it as genuine. The first man to present a good case for the antiquity of cave art was laughed out of court. In 1875 Don Marcelino de Sautuola, a nobleman and amateur archeologist, started investigating a cave called Altamira, discovered near his estate in the village of Santillana del Mar on the northern coast of Spain. He worked on and off for four years, often with his young daughter Maria for company, collecting bones and artifacts not far from the mouth of the cave and not far from a side chamber with a very low ceiling. He had gone into this chamber a number of times on his hands and knees, always looking down in an unsuccessful search for a place to dig.

One summer day, according to a story which has become legend, Maria—aged 5, 7, or 12, depending on the story teller—wandered into the chamber, now known as the Great Hall, and looked up and saw paintings by candlelight. The ceiling is an undulating, vaulted surface of hills and valleys and "ripples" in rock, something like an upside-down relief map of low rolling country. Inside the hollows and on top of the swellings, using natural rock contours to impart a feeling of three dimensions and animation, artists had painted a grand composition.

The paintings are mostly bison, all of them big, from about 4½ to 6 feet long, in various positions: standing, walking, lying down with head turned looking back, crouched and curled up, head raised and bellowing, and one drawn with no head. Also, painted over the body of a hind is a 5-foot horse and next to it a wild boar. The largest figure is another hind measuring more than 7 feet from muzzle to tail. In all, the 1800-square-foot ceiling includes some 25 polychrome paintings, vivid black and red and pink and brown, about 20 of them in good condition, perhaps three to four times as many faded or fragmentary paintings, and many engravings among and in between and underneath the paintings.

We do not know precisely how much Sautuola and Maria saw, how deeply they penetrated past the Great Hall, which is just one of the branches off the main gallery. This gallery extends nearly three football-field lengths deeper into the earth, zigging to the left, zagging to the right, and including many more

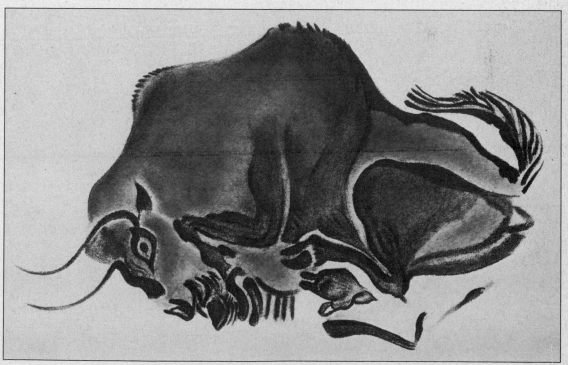

Altamira: curled female bison

figures—oxen, bison, and horses engraved and painted in black outline, two black ibexes at the back of a side chamber, a feline of some sort hidden in a niche, a tangle of lines traced with fingers on a clayey section of ceiling, and in the midst of the tangle the head of an ox.

After a stretch of walking and seeing nothing, one comes to a dark hole, the entrance to a tunnel, a long and narrow "tail" which gets narrower and lower the further in you go. In the beginning you can walk stooping only slightly, but soon you must go on hands and knees. This is the innermost gallery of Altamira. The way leads past animal figures, around a hairpin bend, past more animals, and then to the left one of the cave's most unusual features, a natural rock formation shaped something like the prow of a boat, with eyes painted on either side and a suggestion of a beard down below, forming what some investigators interpret as a human face or "mask" viewed head-on.

There is a similar figure nearby, also on the left wall and, directly opposite, a set of abstract quadrangular shapes with ladderlike and crisscross patterns inside. The last part of the tunnel includes still another face, again on the left wall, and another set of abstract shapes opposite, as well as some ten deer and ibexes all clustered within an area about the size of a newspaper page. The tunnel dead-ends in a tight crawl-in space, with a final panel of black forms.

The events which followed the discovery of Altamira demonstrate how, given a certain set of prevailing beliefs, one could avoid discovering practically anything. Caves have always been exciting places—surprises and dangers underground, shapes high in the rocks, colors and moving shadows, miles of winding galleries in which to get lost, water dripping into pools so black they seem solid, chambers so large that lamps do not reveal the ceilings, and winds rushing past as on a mountainside. The urge to explore this unexpected world runs as deep in us as it did in our prehistoric ancestors.

Local people and tourists, who had been going into art caves for generations, often saw the paintings and engravings, but the experience simply did not register. Only the mildest sort of curiosity was aroused. During the early 1800s, a guide to the Niaux cave in the French Pyrenees, which contains many beautifully executed pictures, told museum officials in the area about the art. As far as we know, nothing ever came of it. In 1864, an archeologist visited the cave and entered the following comment in his diary: "There are some paintings on the wall. What on earth can they be?" And nothing came of that either.

Sautuola had no trouble answering this question; he was convinced on the spot. The figures on the ceiling at Altamira were very much like those he had seen the year before at the Paris World's Fair, figures engraved on pieces of bone and antler and already identified as the work of prehistoric people. (One engraving found at La Madeleine not only depicted an extinct animal, a woolly mammoth, but was done on a fragment of mammoth tusk which had been fresh at the time it was worked.)

Most authorities found this line of reasoning too direct. They were ready to accept engravings on bone, but not engravings or paintings on cave walls. They balked at the notion that people who wore skins and used stone tools went deep into underground places equipped with pigments, brushes, lamps, and other artist's supplies—and with the purposes and imagination required to create fine polychrome paintings. A Spanish artist offered the following argument to prove that such work must have been done by one of his contemporaries:

> There are perhaps twenty figures, some life size, in profile on the vault of the roof, attempting to imitate antediluvian quadrupeds. Their execution shows no sign of primitive art. . . . By their composition, strength of line and proportions they show that their author was not uneducated. And though he was not a Raphael he must have studied Nature at least in pictures or well-made drawings. As is seen by the abandoned mannerism of their execution, such paintings have none of the character of either Stone Age, Archaic, Assyrian or Phoenician art. They are simply the expression of a mediocre student of the modern school.

Within a year of the Altamira find, prehistorians attending an international congress in Lisbon challenged the claims of Sautuola for a number of reasons, most of them quite plausible. The paintings seemed far too sophisticated to jibe with current ideas about the sophistication of Cro-Magnon people; the pigments were amazingly fresh; the limestone crumbled so readily that it was difficult to understand how the painted surfaces had remained intact; and so on. A Spanish professor administered the finishing touch by dismissing the paintings as forgeries and revealing to his assembled colleagues the identity of the presumed forger, an artist who had been living at Sautuola's estate for a number of years.

PAINTED CAVES—THE LIST GROWS

Sautuola was finally vindicated in 1895, but by that time he had been dead 14 years. What won the day was the discovery by the French of cave art in France. A prominent French prehistorian, one of those who had attacked the Spaniard's claims most bitterly, investigated an art cave near Les Eyzies, found engravings sealed by prehistoric deposits, and later published an apology of a sort to the Sautuola family. From then on resistance to the notion of cave art began crumbling. There were still mutterings about fakes and forgeries, but it was the last gasp.

The following generation or so saw a mounting search for more art, discovery after discovery. More than half a dozen sites turned up in the Altamira region, including two of the caves in Monte Castillo, a great honeycomb of underground galleries and, in the south of Spain some 40 miles northeast of Gibraltar, La Pileta, with its miles of galleries and figures and a pit 240 feet deep at the end. Among developments in the Pyrenees was the official rediscovery of Niaux, and two caves at opposite sides of the same hill—Tuc d'Audoubert, featuring two beautifully sculpted clay bison preserved for 15,000 years, and Trois Frères, famous for panels covered with engravings and its ''sorcerer'' or ''horned god,'' possibly a prehistoric shaman.

For concentrated cave art nothing surpasses the Les Eyzies region. Just outside the village, a group of prehistorians, led by a local farmer, found pictures at Les Combarelles, a long narrow passage with some ten right-angle bends and

Tuc d'Audoubert cave: bison modeled in clay

more than 300 engravings, and at Font-de-Gaume, about a mile away. Font-de-Gaume, which has about 200 paintings and engravings, must be visited several times. Many of its greatest painted friezes of mammoths and other animals have faded and are overlain by calcite layers, some more than half an inch thick, and it takes time to see and appreciate what is there.

For example, the only clear features on one wall are two long, black, curving antlers and a black line sweeping up from them and to the left, enough to convey the form of a stag. To the right and below the antlers is a red area, nothing, at first glance, but a large smudge. I stood in front of this panel for a long time. What emerges as the eye finds traces of other lines, and the mind fills in the gaps between the traces, is a black stag, head bent down and nuzzling or licking the head of a doe, painted red with black markings and kneeling in front of him. The scene is typical of Font-de-Gaume. Paulette Daubisse, who with her husband has

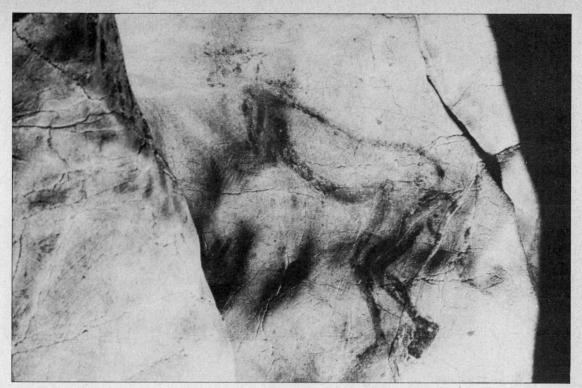

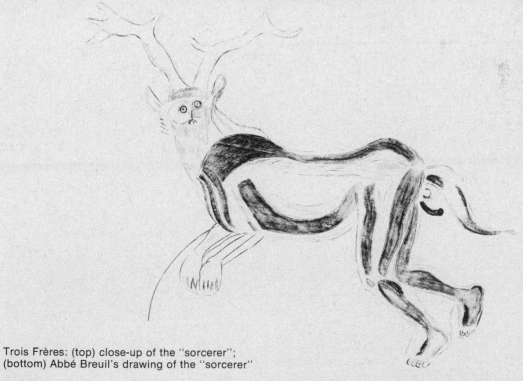

Trois Frères: (top) close-up of the "sorcerer";
(bottom) Abbé Breuil's drawing of the "sorcerer"

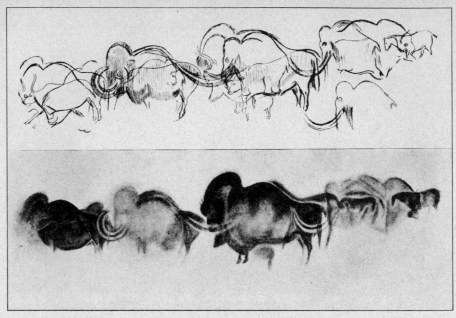

Font-de-Gaume cave: frieze of mammoths, deer, horses, bison

been in charge of the cave for more than a generation, compares the general mood and style with the Lascaux paintings: "The painted animals at Lascaux are grandiose and violent. Here they are at rest and at peace, more gentle, more realistic."

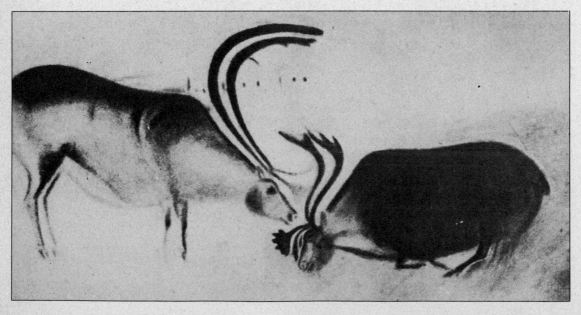

Font-de Gaume cave: facing male and female reindeer

Some of the smallest and most seldom visited sites contain figures of special interest. Commarque, one of my favorites, lies at the foot of a cliff topped by the ruins of a medieval castle. Explored during World War I, it features a large horse's head, engraved in profile, which may be difficult to find. During my first visit to the cave I could not find it for more than half an hour, even though I had been told it was on the right-hand wall of a small gallery. Then it suddenly appeared, clear and animated as if flashed on a screen, in full detail—staring eye, a natural pit in the rock used for the nostril, and a natural swelling used to depict the swelling cheekbone. I had shifted my lamp down and to the side, in just the right position to reveal the engraving.

The search for more art accelerated after the discovery of Lascaux in 1940. Even with knowledge of Altamira and other stand-out sites, no one had expected a gallery of such superb paintings so well preserved. Adding to the excitement was the widely circulated story of the find, one of the great real-life adventure stories of childhood. Four boys on a treasure hunt came across a small hole in the ground where a tree had been uprooted during a storm. They proceeded to widen the hole, cutting away earth and undergrowth with penknives, dropping

Commarque: Christian Archambeau and friend searching for prehistoric art

in rocks from time to time, and listening to the echoes as the rocks bounced into the depths.

When the opening was large enough, they slid feet-first down a rocky slope, their way lit by a homemade kerosene lamp, and landed in the hall with the bulls. Jacques Marsal, one of the original four, has been associated with the cave ever since as official guardian-protector: "I never went back to school, and I'll never leave." His attachment is easy to understand. Lascaux is almost unbelievably rich. Over and above its frieze of converging animals, more than enough to put it in a class by itself, is an art-crammed side gallery and a side chamber. The gallery contains some 60 figures, among them a large leaping cow and, on an arched ceiling, a composition of three red cows and a "Chinese" horse, so named because of the delicacy of the drawing.

In some respects the side chamber tops all other parts of the cave for sheer remarkability. A high-vaulted complex of spaces and surfaces used for some especially important purpose, it is known as the "apse" and resembles a small chapel. A great deal has faded here. But the remains of a frieze of painted deer are still visible, including a wounded stag with large red antlers and black hooves and legs buckling as it collapses from the impact of a spear driven into its side.

There is a mystery scene at the back of the chamber. One passes through a narrow cleft to a 15-foot pit, known as the "shaft of the dead man," the edge worn smooth and shiny, indicating that many persons slid down during prehistoric times, probably with the aid of a rope. (Fragments of three-ply rope have been found in the cave.) Now the descent is by an iron ladder, and the scene is painted in black on a ledge at the bottom—a bison wounded in its hindquarters and attacking a stick-figure man with a bird's head and penis erect. The man is falling over backwards, and just below him to the left are a pole with a bird's head on top and a two-horned rhinoceros.

The scene has been called the most "suggestive" in cave art, but what it suggests is something else again. Among many interpretations, none of them provable or disprovable, that of François Bordes is one of the most direct, and he offers it partly with tongue in cheek as a piece of science fiction: "Once upon a time a hunter who belonged to the bird totem was killed by a bison. One of his companions, a member of the rhinoceros totem, came into the cave and drew the scene of his friend's death—and of his revenge. The bison has spears or arrows in it and is disemboweled, probably by the horns of the rhinoceros. This is how it was."

The publicity involving these and other features and the prospect of more tourism put local people on the alert for more sites. A few months after the discovery of Lascaux, stonemasons repairing a collapsed wine-cellar wall in a village 40 miles away came upon a cave, joked about finding another prehistoric art gallery, lit matches, and saw the first engraving in a passage now known to house more than 220 engravings. Another cave was discovered partly through the good graces of a dowser using a plumb line whose pendulum started swinging back and forth over various parts of a hillside, supposedly a sign of running water and possible caves. The list of sites has been growing ever since.

The major part of the task of authenticating, recording, and copying the art

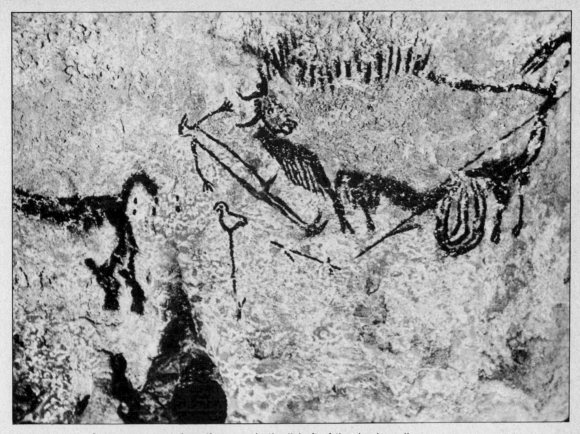

Lascaux cave: enigmatic scene in the "shaft of the dead man"

fell to an investigator who dominated the study of early art as completely and almost as long as Louis XIV dominated France. From the turn of the century until his death in 1961, the Abbé Henri Breuil, a Catholic priest, dedicated his life to "the land of dark caverns . . . and the harsh intoxicating silence of the painted rocks." At the age of 69 he wormed his way through a difficult 200-foot rat-hole passage in a cave southeast of Paris, although he got stuck at one point and had to be pulled loose. From 1900 through 1956 he spent a total of more than 700 days in 73 caves.

The priest was a jealous leader. At meetings he would shout down younger investigators who disagreed with him, and after a while they learned to keep their thoughts to themselves. One of his former students and a close friend for 30 years once dared to suggest in the mildest terms that Breuil had not been entirely correct about the authenticity of the art in a certain cave, and he never spoke to her again. Another close friend summed things up as follows, after Breuil's death of course: "As he got older and perhaps less sure of touch in his intuitions . . . he did not become less pontifical and it became more personally difficult to disagree with him."

THE CASE FOR PLANNING

Currently the most influential investigator of Upper Paleolithic art is André Leroi-Gourhan, excavator of Pincevent and a number of other sites (see Chapter 10). More than a generation ago he and a team of colleagues launched a large-scale study of 72 art caves and rock shelters, noting different styles and mapping the positions of more than 2100 animal figures and hundreds of signs: "I did not find the cultural chaos I was expecting—works scattered over the walls in disorder by successive generations of hunters. Neither Lascaux nor Altamira struck me as a welter of epochs; rather, I was impressed by the unity each of the sets of figures embodies."

His final report, a formidable volume of more than 500 pages, includes many new observations, one of the most striking being a tendency for certain animals to be placed in certain parts of the caves. For example, 92 percent of the oxen, 91 percent of the bison, and 86 percent of the horses appear in central zones, among panels in main chambers and halls. Other animals occur more commonly near entrances, in passages connecting major parts of the caves, and in the most remote chambers. All of which suggests some sort of organized symbolism. Furthermore, there seems to be a pairing tendency, or dualism, horses or ibexes frequently drawn together with bison, oxen, or mammoths and Leroi-Gourhan interprets this in sexual terms, horses and ibexes representing males, bison and oxen and mammoths representing females. He also classifies the abstract forms or signs into male and female symbols.

This report has aroused a measure of controversy. Some investigators are not convinced that the overwhelming majority of animals and signs are sex symbols, although the basic point of an underlying dualism seems to hold. But what stands out in the report, what has determined the course of much subsequent research, is the general message of the Leroi-Gourhan study. A major stress ever since has been on a search for broad patterns among the figures, on each cave as a unit, a "composition" in itself.

Among those engaged to the hilt in the search is Alexander Marshack, a New Yorker specializing in the study of cave art. His first publication, which appeared nearly two decades ago, describes a set of 30 painted dots on the wall of a Spanish rock shelter and, at another Spanish site, another set of 29 painted strokes and circular blobs. He interpreted these and two other sets engraved on a reindeer bone and on the tip of a mammoth tusk as lunar notation involving the phases of the moon. Also, he indicated the existence of many similar patterns: "The evidence is neither sparse nor isolated; it consists of thousands of notational sequences found on the engraved 'artistic' bones and stones of the Ice Age and the period following, as well as on the engraved and painted rock shelters and caves of Upper Paleolithic and Mesolithic Europe."

His work has inspired other counts. A Soviet investigator, for example, has noted sets of markings that are multiples of five and seven, without offering an explanation. A British report relates counts of 63 notches on selected pieces of mobiliary art to the period of 63 days, or about nine weeks, for "ear emergence, flowering and ripening" of certain possibly edible grasses, and Marshack himself has suggested the possibility of another set representing the 11-month pregnancy period of the horse. Playing the numbers game can be dangerous. There are so many periods and cycles in nature that one can see patterns everywhere and find significance in practically any combination of strokes and notches. On the other hand, such studies do hint at purposeful activity; Marshack now regards lunar-type notations as only one of more than a dozen symbol systems.

An entire complex of symbols, something brand-new, was discovered recently in an unexpected place. El Juyo, a small single-chamber cave located at the end of a bumpy dirt road a few miles from Altamira, seemed to be a traditional Magdalenian camp, and was being excavated as such by Leslie Freeman, one of the Torralba-Ambrona excavators (see Chapter 6) and J. Gonzales Echegaray of the Altamira Museum and Research Center in Santander, Spain. The 14,000-year-old site acquired a new meaning with the uncovering one morning of a flattish limestone slab about 6 feet long, half a foot thick, and weighing nearly a ton.

Beneath the slab was a row of 25 bone spear points, and still deeper a structure like nothing else in the prehistoric record, a mound more than 3 feet high built up of half a dozen alternate layers of colored mosaics and burnt offerings. The mosaic layers consisted of earthen columns, apparently made by filling containers with earth and turning them upside down like buckets used in building sand castles by the seashore. The columns were arranged in rosettes, a central column surrounded by a circle of six others, each smeared on top with red, yellow, green, or black clay. The offering layers included deer bones, ashes, and lumps of red ocher.

The most surprising feature of all turned up a few feet from the mound—a stone face carved on a chunk of rock. Crude in execution, it was half human and half feline. Engraved lines suggested a beard and moustache on the right side, and a fang and muzzle and whiskers on the left. According to Echegaray and Freeman, the face expresses a dualism, perhaps male and female, or the savage and socialized sides of human nature. It was placed so that the human side could be seen from a distance near the cave entrance, but viewers had to come quite close to see the feline side. Face and mound and associated features were part of a carefully worked-out design. The whole structure must have been thought out in advance, and probably built step by step according to some sort of paleolithic blueprint. The excavators think of it as a sanctuary with "an esoteric meaning accessible to all who entered . . . and an occult, esoteric significance known only to those who had been shown its mysteries."

Not all the designing was done underground. People also worked in open-air settings, although only the barest traces remain, such as the puzzling mammoth-bone constructions at Mezhirich, located in a river valley about 90 miles southeast of Kiev and a millennium or so older than El Juyo. According to Olga Soffer of the University of Wisconsin, the site includes four oval-shaped dwellings, one of which had an outer wall with a facing of 95 V-shaped mammoth mandibles placed in a circle and stacked one on top of the other in a herringbone or chevron pattern. The outer wall of another dwelling had a mammoth skull with a scapula-scapula-pelvis alignment on each side. These and other arrangements are further evidence of a feeling for pattern and design not found in earlier times.

Perhaps the most ambitious and difficult study currently under way involves an analysis of signs and figures at Nerja, a huge multilevel system of twisting galleries on Spain's southern coast not far from Malaga. Lya Dams of the Royal Belgian Society of Anthropology and Prehistory, who with her former husband, Marcel, has been among the most active investigators of cave art, is concerned not only with individual figures but with complexes of figures, their precise positions on cave walls, and the way they must have been seen by Upper Paleolithic viewers.

For example, Nerja's lower gallery includes a recess about 16 feet long and featuring to the right as you enter a "drapery" formation, limestone sheets in vertical folds something like a hanging curtain. The recess is narrow and has only one entrance, so there is only one way to walk through, leading you past a sequence of red figures on the curved sides of the folds facing you. Then you come to a dead end where, on the floor and barely visible, there is a large ibex painted in red. On the way out you see another sequence of figures on the other sides of the folds. The question arises whether the figures, two animals and more than 100 signs, were meant to be seen in that order and, if so, whether we can ever hope to "read" the messages.

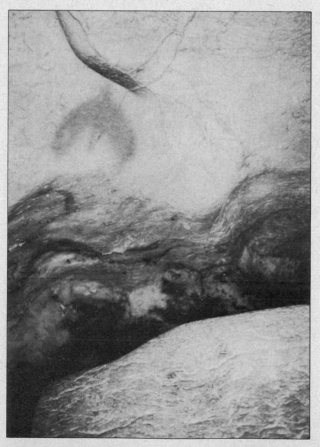

Le Portel, French Pyrenees: mysterious "flying object" sign

The assumption behind these and related studies is that little if anything was done casually. The bulk of the cave art represents detailed planning—the selection of a cave and a part of the cave, the selection of figures and combinations of figures, the decision whether to paint or engrave or both, the choice of colors, the placement of figures. Some of the figures are complete and easy to recognize. Others are fragmentary, perhaps a pair of horns only or an isolated head or body; still others are so ambiguous that investigators argue whether they depict horses or oxen or something else. The caves contain distorted figures such as horses with long snakelike necks, monsters, and imaginary animals like the unicorn in Lascaux.

Le Portel: horse about 16 inches long

According to Denis Vialou of the Institute of Human Paleontology in Paris, it was all part of a highly organized effort to exploit every possible effect in the cause of making naturally strange settings stranger still: "There are no unfinished or unachieved figures, if the implication is that the artists began something and were unable to complete it for some reason, that they failed in some way. They knew their animals down to the finest detail, and were perfectly capable of drawing striking likenesses. We must assume that every incomplete figure, every ambiguous and imaginary figure, was drawn with a purpose."

CONTROLLING CONFLICT

That defines the issue squarely, and confronts us with the key question. Why, after more than 2 million years of human evolution, did art appear suddenly some 30,000 years ago? The most widely cited theories turn out to be of little help. The art-for-art's-sake theory ascribes the paintings and engravings to pure self-expression, the products of people concerned primarily with their own thoughts and feelings. Two other theories focus on more materialistic, more practical, objectives. Some investigators think in terms of the food quest and hunting magic. They suggest that the animals, particularly those depicted with spears or arrows in their bodies, were drawn and killed ritually to ensure successful hunting, reminiscent of the voodoo practice of making wax statues and sticking pins in them. There is also the fertility-cult theory that the drawing of pregnant animals and sex organs served to ensure a continuing abundance of big game.

Such notions indicate possible motives, but do not explain why the art appeared when it did. *Homo sapiens* had existed for 200,000 to 300,000 years without art, so something special must have happened during the Upper Paleolithic to account for an entirely new form of human behavior. In the days when most investigators considered the Neanderthals mentally inferior to the Cro-Magnons, art was viewed as a natural product of a more complex brain. But a reexamination of Neanderthal remains fails to provide solid evidence for any cerebral difference (see Chapter 8).

Recent studies point in another direction, emphasizing social rather than biological factors. More than painting and engraving was going on in the caves. Flutes have been found there, and bull roarers, which make a high whining hum when whirled from a string. Patterns of footprints in Tuc d'Audoubert clays and a few drawings of high-stepping humans suggest dancing and probably singing, as well as music and sound effects. Preserved over the millenniums, the art represents the most vivid and by far the most abundant evidence for complex activities carried out in remote secret places, all that remains of intensive and elaborately staged ceremonies.

So the question of why the art emerged when it did becomes a broader question: Why the burst, the explosion, of ceremony? For part of the answer we can turn back to events described in Chapter 10. Art and the arts were not isolated phenomena. They were part of it all, part of the forces driving people to change their life styles, and part of the response to those forces. People were coming together in larger and larger groups, organizing ambushes and stampedes and mass kills, and staying together afterwards to celebrate and share the spoils, and all the time building themselves into tribal societies, wider trade and communication networks.

This is the great strength of the human species, our unprecedented flexibility and capacity for cooperation. But nothing in evolution is ever an unmixed blessing. The irony is that people do not find it easy to get along with one another, and that conflict soars in the very act of getting together. We see this not only in our cities but also among the Australian aborigines and other recent hunter-gatherers currently in the process of trying to adapt to larger groups characteristic of the settled life (see Chapter 15).

There is an arithmetic of conflict. The amount of tension, measured in crime rates or alcohol or drug consumption, for example, soars with the size of the group, specifically with the number of possible two-person relationships, or dyads. Dyads increase exponentially with population. The formula is $(N^2 - N)/2 = D$, where N is the number of individuals in the group and D is the number of dyads. There are 3 possible relationships among 3 individuals, 6 among 4 individuals, 300 among 25 individuals (a typical hunter-gatherer band), 19,800 among 200 individuals (a typical village population), and so on—and the level of conflict rises in the same way.

If this relationship held then as it does today, ceremony could well have served as part of the effort to control conflict. The idea was to use ritual and myth to help create wider "families," feelings of unity among all members of larger groups, loyalties over and above loyalties to kith and kin. Instilling a common system of beliefs is a socializing process that must start young, and one recent observation suggests that this is indeed what took place. Of the more than 1000 prehistoric footprints known from art caves, including those at Tuc d'Audoubert, more than a third are the footprints of children.

TRANSMITTING THE TRIBAL ENCYCLOPEDIA

It may seem strange that ceremonies designed for essentially educational purposes, for the entire group, should be held in hidden places underground. But there was good reason for that. Individuals had an enormous amount to learn, and it had to be learned thoroughly. Stability and security depended on it. The details of creation myths, the doings of ancestors and supernatural beings, the meanings of animal figures and abstract signs depicted on cave walls and on bodies and portable art, dance steps, tunes and rhythms, the words of sacred songs—all this had to be imparted, and much, much more. The innovations of the Upper Paleolithic meant the crumbling of traditions and entirely new sets of rules, ways of behaving with other people, an etiquette of things done and not done, and masses of practical knowledge as well, everything from hunting strategies and the habits of prey to the art of making and using the spearthrower and the bow and arrow.

There was a mountainous pile-up of things to be learned, a swift and sudden expansion of the tribal encyclopedia. The explosion of art and the arts, the explosion of ceremony, reflected an information explosion, the world's first. Furthermore, and this is the crucial fact, it came in a time without writing. Everything had to be memorized. In the absence of books or computer circuits for the storage of information, the contents of the tribal encyclopedia had to be imprinted, intact and indelibly, in the human brain.

The Neanderthals also transmitted information from generation to generation, but it was only a small fraction of what the Cro-Magnons had to transmit. The difference called for nothing less than new ways of implanting information, a brand-new technology of mnemonics, and that is where the caves came in. If you want people to remember everything you tell them, an important first step is to take them away from familiar surroundings and put them in a strange, unsettling environment. It helps if they are also a bit scared, or more than a bit, because what one hears under such conditions may never be forgotten.

Caves provided ideal environments for this sort of indoctrination. But the elders or shamans of the Upper Paleolithic, whoever were responsible for the transmission of information, did not take the caves as they found them. They created settings and a wide variety of devices calculated to enhance the strangeness, the unforgetability, of natural underground settings. Imagine being brought suddenly out of pitch darkness into the Lascaux main hall or into the Trois Frères sanctuary, and at the same time hearing weird echo-chamber sounds and songs and rhyming words repeated over and over again to the beat of dancing feet and probably of drums. You would retain what you learned there for a long time.

Ceremonies held in caves involved all the arts to bombard the senses with impressions that would endure. They also involved—demanded—people of status and the end of egalitarian traditions. To obtain absolute, unquestioning acceptance of the tribal encyclopedia, absolute belief and obedience, the messages must come from superior individuals who can overawe novices by basing their authority on the sanction of supernatural forces. Nothing short of that would have sufficed. The objective was to reduce conflict through ceremony, and that was as essential to the survival of the species as eating and reproducing.

ART AFTER THE MAGDALENIANS

The Upper Paleolithic, art and all, ended with the passing of the Magdalenians some 10,000 years ago. Societies had come and gone before, but this one had reached such a high point that subsequent developments seem somehow like more of a letdown. What happened is plain in the record. Occupation layers at the major Magdalenian sites are thick, extend far out beyond the area immediately in front of caves and rock shelters, and contain many tools and varieties of tools. They represent the remains of a powerful, creative, and imaginative people.

By contrast, the layers on top of the most recent Magdalenian deposits are meager. They tend to be thin, so thin at certain sites that early excavators frequently missed them entirely. They contain far fewer tools and more limited tool kits, including characteristically flat harpoons, and microliths very much like those generally found in sites throughout the world. (A steady decrease in the size of tools was a widespread tendency in prehistoric times.) These meager layers mark a kind of retreat, or pulling back; living quarters were confined to spaces close to the cliffs and under sheltering rocks. These are the remains of a shrinking population, the so-called Azilians, named after the Mas d'Azil cave in the French Pyrenees, who lived literally with their backs to the wall. If they ever visited the art caves of their predecessors, they must have wondered at the pictures on the walls. They left no such traces of their own.

All we find at their sites are abstract signs painted on pebbles, a comedown from the cave paintings, although of some interest in their own right. In a study of some 2000 pebbles, Claude Couraud of the National Museum of Antiquities in Paris discovered special patterns in the signs. There are just 16 different signs including dots, wavy lines, chevrons, crosses, ovals, and circles. Most of the pebbles feature ''binary associations''; that is, they contain two and only two of the signs. Furthermore, out of 246 possible pairs among 16 signs, only 41 are used—and some signs are always associated with one another, while others never appear together. The Azilians were using some sort of system, conveying messages which Couraud hopes some day to decode. But it was not art.

A world had passed, and for a surprising reason. The climate improved. The continuing retreat of the glaciers brought milder weather to the region. Species of grass which had adapted to glacial conditions and provided food for reindeer followed the glaciers north, the reindeer followed the grasses, and most hunters followed the reindeer or moved to coastlines and lived on other herd animals and seafood. The Azilians were descendants of those who stayed behind to carry on in the new environment, and, all things considered, they did well.

The world's earliest art died out locally, but other works turned up elsewhere. For example, art flourished between 5,000 and 12,000 years ago in eastern Spain in the so-called Spanish Levant, where some hundred sites have been found in cliffside rock shelters, most of them unmarked by signposts and tucked away in back country far from roads. Lya Dams notes that the artists went several steps beyond their predecessors and possible cultural ancestors, the Magdalenians. They introduced scenes and a feel for composition where previously there had been isolated individual animals almost exclusively. Motion, pursuit, and action are also featured for the first time in the art of the Spanish Levant.

Climatic changes in the Les Eyzies region brought about a new and ingenious way of life. Herds of game on the hoof were no longer around to be killed en masse by hunters lying in wait along traditional migration routes. The problem was to deal with more elusive forest animals which moved about in small groups and were agile, swift, and camouflaged. Snaring, trapping, and other techniques that had played secondary roles in reindeer times were refined and used more intensively; the bow and arrow may have been more important than ever. The Azilians also relied more heavily on fishing and acquired new food tastes, for snails as an example, which must have taken some doing after a diet of venison; presumably snails became delicacies at a later date. (Stone picks similar to those found at Azilian sites are still used on occasion along the northern coast of Spain to open mussels.)

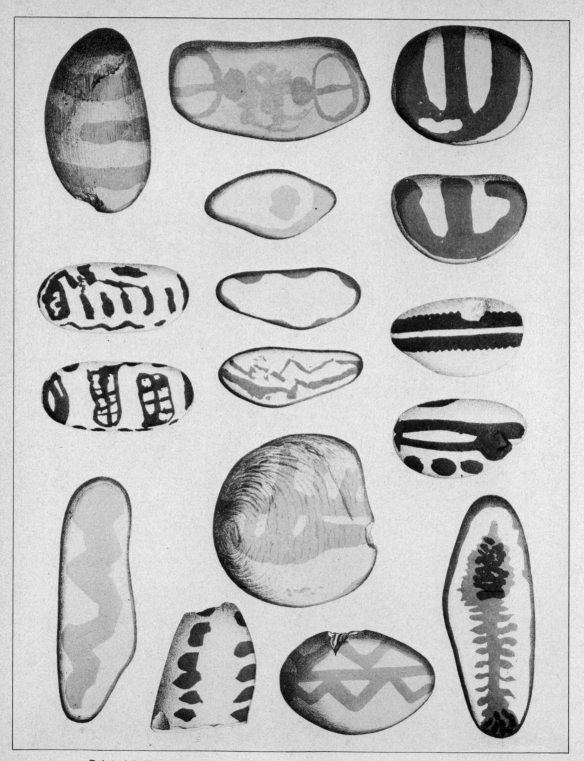

Painted Azilian pebbles

THE AGRICULTURAL REVOLUTION

Up to this point people had lived chiefly on what food the good earth happened to offer in the form of wild plants and wild animals. The story of the Magdalenians shows how much could be achieved when conditions were right and remained that way for long periods. But it also shows how vulnerable people were to changes beyond their control, as long as they depended on natural abundances for survival. If they had not "cheated" by tinkering with the natural order of things, by producing food instead of collecting food ready-made, the world would be a much simpler place. We would probably all be hunters and gatherers still.

As indicated in Chapter 10, people probably knew a good deal about agriculture thousands of years before they started giving up the hunting-gathering way of life some 10,000 years ago. They changed, not because they wanted to, since hunting-gathering was generally an easier and more reliable way of obtaining food. They changed because they had to. The full explanation remains to be worked out, but one major factor was overpopulation and the threat of famine. The world contained an estimated 10 million persons 10,000 years ago, which is hardly crowded in terms of twentieth-century populations. But considering that it took several square miles to feed a person by hunting and gathering, and that most of the best terrain was already occupied, the pressure was mounting. Furthermore, melting glaciers and rising seas submerged large areas of coastal plains, so that land was scarcer.

Another factor may be important in accounting for the origins of agriculture. John Speth and Katherine Spielmann of the University of Michigan and the Smithsonian Institution, respectively, point out that people can sicken and sometimes starve to death from "protein poisoning" if they rely too long on a diet consisting predominantly of meat and very low in essential carbohydrates, fats, and sugars. This problem may arise in Arctic regions, particularly in the spring, when caribou and other game animals are in poor condition, having used up most of their winter fat reserves. The result is nutritional stress, on a seasonal basis. But if long-term climatic changes such as severe cold or spreading deserts brought about chronic stress, chronic carbohydrate shortages, survival might have demanded "increasing reliance on plant foods," forcing people to take the first steps toward domestication.

At present the evidence indicates that the world's first farmers appeared in the Near East, and perhaps in India and China as well. Agriculture associated with farming villages dates to about 7500 B.C. in the so-called Fertile Crescent along a 2000-mile arc starting in Israel and Jordan, extending up the eastern Mediterranean coast, swinging around through southern Turkey and then southeast, and following the Zagros Mountains of Iran to lands bordering the Persian Gulf. A side branch of the arc runs 500 miles due west along the coast of Turkey. The region included wild goats, sheep, pigs, and cattle as well as massive stands of such wild grasses as wheat and barley. During the next five or six millenniums farming villages also appeared in Egypt, Mesoamerica, South America, and other regions. People were now creating artificial abundances. The land was now producing more than 50 times the amount of food that nature had provided in the form of wild species. Populations soared everywhere.

From this period on, changes came one after the other at an accelerating pace. Villages grew large and split into clusters of villages, and still larger centers took shape among the clusters. In most parts of the world, early cities arose within 3 or 4 millenniums after the first farming villages. The first cities were small by modern standards, numbering perhaps 10,000 to 30,000 inhabitants; but that was enough to create enormous new complexities and new problems. Above all, people had to be organized to work long hours, not only for their own subsistence, as in hunter-gatherer days, but for the subsistence of others—notably to provide emerging elites with the best of everything.

Such demands were often made in the name of serving the gods. Great temples and plazas were built for ceremonies on a grander and grander scale. One result was an explosion of symbols, the invention of writing, the coming of records and archives and myths preserved word for word. This was the end of prehistory and the beginning of a race between rising populations and food supplies, a race against famine, which continues in our own times.

SUMMARY

The most spectacular mark of the Upper Paleolithic is the sudden appearance of art 35,000 to 30,000 years ago—and of all the art the most spectacular is the frieze of brilliantly colored animals depicted on the walls of Lascaux, a cave in southwestern France. Lascaux is one of more than 225 art caves containing paintings and engravings, mainly figures of animals and abstract signs, many of them hidden deep in remote chambers and passages. There are also low-relief sculptures, as well as portable or "mobiliary" art, consisting of statuettes and a variety of engraved objects.

The first cave to be recognized as a prehistoric art site was Altamira in northern Spain; it featured a ceiling covered with some 25 large polychrome animals, mostly bison. Altamira was discovered in 1875, but most investigators considered it a complete fraud and acceptance did not come for another 20 years when similar figures were found in French caves. After that, discovery followed discovery, and new art caves continue to be reported.

One of the most challenging problems in prehistory is to figure out why art appeared suddenly at the start of the Upper Paleolithic, and why it flourished some 10,000 years later during Solutrean-Magdalenian times. We still have a great deal to learn, but an important clue came with the recognition that the art caves were the result of detailed planning—that each cave represented a kind of composition.

Recent research suggests that the art became important when people began living in larger groups and for longer periods. Conflict increases exponentially under such conditions, according to a "conflict formula" based on observations of people in present-day settings. Art seems to have been part of intensive ceremonies designed to reduce conflict by creating an atmosphere of common beliefs and new loyalties over and above loyalties to blood relatives. Ceremony served to pass traditions on from generation to generation in the absence of writing, to imprint the expanding body of information—the contents of the tribal encyclopedia—indelibly in memory.

The cave art passed with the passing of the Upper Paleolithic, the high point of the hunting-gathering way of life. As populations grew, people no longer had the easy option of moving away into uninhabited regions. They had no choice but to settle down, to subsist locally on domesticated plants and animals. The agricultural revolution brought still larger groups, cities, writing, and the end of prehistory.

chapter 12

Living Prehistory: Primate Studies

The story of human evolution, the rise over a period of 5 to 10 million years of our kind from breeds of bygone apes, has been based chiefly on dead material dug out of the earth. Most of the evidence involves analyses of remains and artifacts of creatures that have long since perished. It comes from fossil bones, soils, pollen, worked flints, paintings and engravings, burial sites, and living floors in "mint" condition as people abandoned them ages ago.

Studies of living material—baboons, chimpanzees, lions and other carnivores, and hunter-gatherers of the twentieth century—have been cited to help interpret archeological findings, to support arguments bearing on the development of erect posture, tool use, scavenging and hunting, and social organization. The stress has been on the use of behavior directly observed as an aid in interpreting the behavior of extinct hominids. For example, I have noted lasting kinship relationships and tool use among chimpanzees (see Chapter 2); meat eating among baboons and the hunting strategies of lions, wild dogs, and humans (see Chapter 5); and comparative foraging ranges and the Bushmen's intimate knowledge of their land (see Chapter 7).

HOMO AND OTHER ANIMALS

But information about living species is of major importance in its own right, and it is accumulating at a formidable rate. The preceding chapters have drawn on only a fraction of the research being conducted on mammals, including nonhuman primates and the entire spectrum of human primates—from Australian aborigines, the Kalahari Bushmen, and other tribal groups to people living in high-rise apartments and condominiums. A fuller account of such investigations, and the philosophy behind them, is essential in the effort to understand human origins and possible futures.

That effort depends on seeing animals, ourselves included, as objectively as possible. We tend to read so much into the behavior of our fellow species. They may be viewed as cute and cuddly, a bit bumbling and foolish (the Br'er Rabbit or Disney approach); or as noble, wise, and innocent; or as brutes and innate killers; and so on. Such attitudes are messages in disguise, preconceptions rather than principles deduced from the evidence. Writers often use animals to make a point, to tell you what they think they know, not about animals but about people. For example, if a writer belongs to the noble-and-innocent school of animal behavior, the odds are that he or she is commenting on the Fall of Adam and the corruption of the human species. The temptation to moralize, to attribute all sorts of irrelevant characteristics and motives to other species, is strongest when studying primates, our closest relatives, the creatures which have most to teach us.

Research on animals demands, above all else, carefully controlled observation, and plenty of time. Considering that entire careers are being devoted to the study of such relatively simple species as ants and bees, and that a great deal remains to be learned, think how much further work will have to go into the study of mammals and, among mammals, into the study of primates—and among primates into the study of the most subtle breed of all, *Homo sapiens*. One evolutionary trend across the board seems to have been toward increasingly complex and close-knit groups. The broad features of this trend have been analyzed by John Eisenberg of the Smithsonian Institution in a survey of nearly 500 investigations. He describes four grades or levels of mammalian social organization:

Grade 1—female-young unit: A mother caring for her offspring is the most elementary of all mammalian social units, a bare minimum in the sense that no species could endure with anything less. The wood rats of North America, for example, live alone in nests of twigs and come together only for mating. The female provides shelter and food and protection for her litter, and attacks and drives away males which come too close.

Grade 2—mother-family groups: Here again mothers and offspring make up the basic units, but they may aggregate into large groups, a situation found among red deer. Fifteen or more hinds, each with two or three young, live together throughout the year under the leadership of an older female. A hind goes off alone to give birth, rejoining her group after a few days when the calf can walk and follow. The stags live separate lives, wandering more widely and foraging in loose all-male herds; during the breeding season a stag will associate himself with a female group and defend it against other stags. Stags and hinds may come together in good feeding grounds during the winter.

Grade 3—permanent male-female group: More than one male is generally associating with a number of females. Certain primate societies represent this grade of organization, living in troops that may include more than a hundred individuals and that are generally closed to outsiders. The males may act collectively in defending females and offspring. In such groups conflicts involving the individual and the organization may arise in acute form and demand new and complex control mechanisms.

Grade 4—male-female pair bond: This rare situation includes a wide variety of specialized living arrangements, the common element being that the male is part of the basic family social unit, and that both male and female provide food and care for the young. Among wolves, for example, the male not only shares in protecting the litter but he is also the provider and may join with other males in hunting. At the kill site, he will swallow chunks of meat without chewing them, and disgorge the food back at the den for family consumption.

Eisenberg points out that relatively unspecialized or low-grade social structures are typical for representatives of new orders among mammals, populations engaged in finding places for themselves in a world of established species. The newcomers were often small and inconspicuous, lived in the shelter of forests rather than in open terrain, and did their foraging at night—all characteristics which favor grade 1, female-young units. Developments which appear later in evolution may have the opposite characteristics. Species frequently became larger in the process of adapting successfully, acquired greater freedom of movement, and foraged actively during daylight hours. There is also a trend toward larger brains and more complex sense organs. Such changes favor the formation of more and more elaborate social organizations.

Similar patterns may be seen in the evolution of primates. The first prosimians, forerunners of monkeys and apes, were small forest dwellers, probably nocturnal. They depended largely on the sense of smell for communicating with one another and for detecting danger. Like some surviving prosimians, they probably lived solitary lives and were dispersed over wide areas. The trend has been in the opposite direction ever since, toward increasing brain and body size, increasing importance of sight and hearing in communications, and the formation of permanent troops. These developments are relevant to our own origins. In the words of Paul Bohannon of Northwestern University, "Whether we like it or not, anthropology is a branch of primatology."

A PRIMATE LIFE STYLE

The first systematic study of wild primates came in 1931, when Ray Carpenter began observing howler monkeys in Panama. But extensive research did not start until the decades following World War II, a conflict which gave rise to second thoughts about the quality of human primates and brought about a new and harder look at human origins. Powerful observation techniques were developed by investigators studying fish and birds, notably by Niko Tinbergen of Oxford, who made a special point of the value of animal research in the analysis of motives and purposes: "The fact that animals cannot tell us what urges them to behave as they do might well be a blessing in disguise; at least they cannot tell

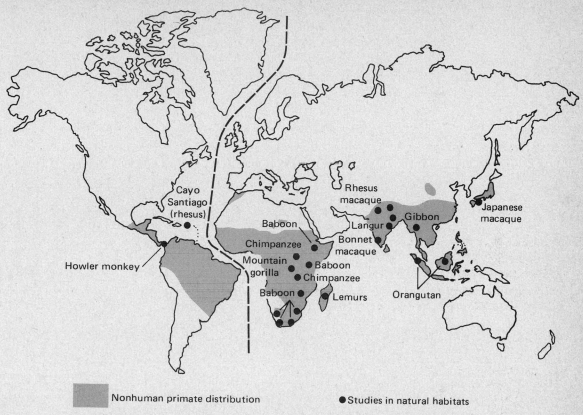

Nonhuman primate distribution ● Studies in natural habitats

World distribution of contemporary nonhuman primates

us conscious or unconscious lies. They just behave." Tinbergen focused attention on repertoires of behavior patterns, repeated actions and reactions, and their interpretation in evolutionary terms.

This sort of work encouraged a new interest in primates, and for the first time observations in the wild became a major research activity. Continuing investigations have involved more than 200 field studies in a score of countries including Japan, India, Kenya, Uganda, and Borneo. Nearly 25 years ago, pioneer researchers, among them Jeanne and Stuart Altmann and Irven DeVore (see Chapter 5), noted broad behavior patterns which served as the basis for later and more detailed studies. Perhaps the biggest surprise in the beginning was the low level of aggression in primate troops—that is, the low level compared to what had been expected.

Anthropologists and zoologists entered wildernesses expecting mayhem, mainly because most reports written during the decades after Darwin's discoveries represented a kind of turning away from Darwin. Instead of venturing into the great outdoors where the facts were, where primates could be observed living freely, early researchers went indoors to observe monkeys and apes locked in the cages of laboratories and zoos. Under such conditions the animals engaged in numerous and bloody fights, often to the death, and indulged in a variety of bizarre sexual behaviors, all of which might have been predicted if only by analogy with the actions of people in prison.

These findings were definitely in line with the Puritan and Victorian views of people as Jekyll-Hyde creatures, part disheveled, lustful, and violent animals and part well-groomed and restrained gentlefolk. The discovery of Neanderthals scandalized the Victorians because they saw them as Mr. Hydes built into the human past. The moral, of course, was that if only the beast in us could be curbed, life would proceed in a lawful and orderly fashion. But putting animals in cages had practically guaranteed that they would exhibit a high level of aberrant behavior, the "bestial" behavior generally expected of nonhuman species. It was almost as if observers were deliberately creating conditions under which the gap between humans and other primates would appear as wide as possible.

In any case, fighting occurred so infrequently compared with what had been expected that at first investigators doubted their own results and made a special point of reexamining the evidence—perhaps the species they were observing represented an exception to the rule of violence, or the animals were members of unusually amicable troops. Later they compared notes and realized that they had not been dealing with exceptions but with a common state of affairs. Wild primates and most wild animals tend to avoid fighting with one another. Survival is too serious a business to allow for the luxury of frequent violent dissension within the ranks. If primates behaved as aggressively in the wild as they do in cages, they would have become extinct long ago.

Something about the human past may be deduced from the behavior of primates at large in grassy savannas, African baboons in particular. These monkeys originally received special attention, because they have adapted to the same sort of exposed environments which our hominid ancestors encountered. Among the earliest baboon studies are those of DeVore and his co-workers in Nairobi Park and the Amboseli Game Reserve of Kenya, and the rest of this chapter is devoted mainly to their basic findings, and to the recent and continuing research of current observers.

Getting acquainted or accepted is an important part of primate observing. DeVore became practically an honorary member of several troops. He came to know some 80 baboons by sight and had names for all of them. He understood what they were saying to one another, a skill which helped considerably in interpreting their behavior—and, on at least one occasion, in interpreting his behavior to them. Baboons are reasonably tolerant of scientists, but one thing you must never do is frighten an infant. DeVore did just that by accident one day, the infant yelped, and immediately several large angry males dashed to the spot, slapping the ground and lunging at him. Fortunately, he knew the appropriate signal. He smacked his lips loudly, which is a pacifying gesture among baboons and can be translated roughly as follows: "Sorry about that. It was a mistake. No harm intended."

DeVore followed troops all day for many days before he began to recognize some basic features of their way of life. Their comings and goings, which seem so haphazard at first, are actually quite predictable. Each troop confines its

Irven DeVore establishing contact with baboons

movements largely to a definite territory, a home range of about 10 to 15 square miles. The boundaries of the range are marked by an invisible fence, signs which we do not see but which are very real to troop members. Baboons become tense and watchful as they approach this line; they move away, and cannot be driven across it. They are not familiar with what lies on the other side. Novelty is always a reason for caution, and when the novelty is too great, it can be a powerful repellent.

Nairobi Park and Amboseli baboons move in diurnal cycles, locked in as it were to the clockwork rhythm of sunrises and sunsets. Their home range contains two or three core areas where the troop spends more than 90 percent of its time and does more than 90 percent of its traveling and feeding. Each core area includes at least one stretch of a stream or river with trees growing along the banks. Baboons sleep in trees, halfway out on the branches, and begin to stir with the first light of day, generally around five in the morning, often in a groggy state somewhat reminiscent of more advanced primates like ourselves. "They tend to awaken very sluggishly," DeVore noted, "and you get the impression that what they need most is a cup of coffee."

Then the time comes for leaving the trees, and it is at this point that one becomes aware of something which corresponds to a collective wisdom and decision-making mechanism in the troop. We have no idea what determines the day's first destination, but a decision has obviously been made. First to leave the trees are certain adult males and juveniles corresponding roughly to older

Baboons on the move: (top) feeding near trees; (bottom) at water hole

Grooming group, infant holding leg of dominant male

teenagers in human groups. They move rapidly in a beeline, as if they know exactly where they are going, and they do not look back. The rest of the troop follows.

Several feeding places may be visited on the way to the main feeding place, located from a few hundred yards to several miles from sleeping sites and containing enough food for as much as two to three hours of intensive eating. Sometimes, particularly during the dry season, it is amazing how much food baboons can obtain from apparently barren areas. They pull up everything in plain sight, and then scan the ground for withered stalks and other signs of succulent plant runners that extend like tiny pipes just beneath the surface. They also detect almost invisible wisps, hairlike filaments marking the location of deeper-lying tubers, bulbs, and roots.

The troop rests at midday, usually not far from the main feeding place in a shady spot. It is a relatively relaxed time, a time for grooming. Typically, one baboon sits or lies on its back as another baboon parts and searches through its fur, picking or licking off every speck of alien material. The groomer scans the fur intently, area by area, while individuals being groomed close their eyes or look to the side and wallow in contentment, always avoiding a direct look at the groomer, because that is a sign of aggression. Grooming almost certainly serves a hygienic function, ticks and other parasites being abundant. But above all it seems to be a source of sensual pleasure and affection.

Midday is also playtime. By the age of 2 to 3, baboons chase and tumble over one another, dodging and wrestling. Special signals distinguish play from fighting. In fights the pursuer may come on with a rush, loud grunts, and eyes fixed on the pursued, who dashes away screeching with fright. Play tends to be silent, and the approach is made with a characteristic bouncing or hopping gait, baboon sign language for "this is just for fun." When it builds up too intensely, play may merge into real fighting, especially among male infants and juveniles who play longer and harder than females, and must be watched with extra care.

THE WISDOM OF THE TROOP

Adult males are the chief watchers, keepers of peace in the troop (when they are not occupied in asserting status among themselves). A dominant full-grown male is an effective policeman, and has a wide sphere of influence. If he strides toward trouble, head up and leading with his chin, his presence may be felt at quite a distance. A hard stare was once sufficient to break up a fight between two juveniles some 60 feet away and, on another occasion, to make a misbehaving infant scream and fall over as if it had been hit.

After the midday interlude, the troop moves toward another feeding place, which more often than not lies on the way back to the trees where it will spend

Male baboons, play-wrestling

Glare threat of adult male baboon

the night. Tension may rise as the afternoon wears on and the sun starts sinking; lions and other big cats generally do most of their hunting in the dark. Baboons are safest when they have reached their sleeping trees. Shortly after sunset, the day has come full circle and they are dozing off. The troop, which may consist of a dozen to more than 150 members, move about 3 miles a day on the average, often returning to the same trees it left early in the morning. Normally every troop member is in sight of other members, and many baboons spend their entire lives within a few miles of the places where they were born.

As far as the daily round is concerned, DeVore stressed problems with predators. Survival depends on being alert, a state most evident when baboons are feeding, which is most of the time. A baboon moves its head and shifts attention periodically. It feeds with head down, scanning the ground and missing nothing as it passes, pulling up grasses and shoots, digging for juicy roots in the dry season, snatching eggs out of nests, occasionally turning over rocks for insects. But it is not built to concentrate too steadily. Every five to ten seconds it stops, looks up, and glances about for a second or two before resuming feeding. At any given instant about half a dozen individuals in an average-sized troop will be surveying the landscape.

A baboon troop on the move makes a formidable array and is attacked only rarely and only by lions. Its early-morning trek is from a few hundred yards to a few miles to reach the day's main feeding place, where eating may go on for as much as two or three hours after the area has been surveyed for possible predators. Often you come across a troop feeding together with a herd of impalas in a natural and effective association, since baboons have fine eyesight and impalas have a fine sense of smell. Between them they can detect practically any predator and give the alarm in the form of warning barks. As a rule, it seems that baboons recognize and respond to the alarm cries of many other species.

DeVore recalls observing an encounter between predators and a troop which was already within sight of its sleeping place in a shallow valley. One baboon stopped eating and turned to look in the direction of a clump of trees about a hundred yards away; gradually, over a period of a minute or so, every monkey was sitting and looking in the same direction, that is, all but two infants that started playing and were promptly slapped down. Suddenly an old male baboon grunted twice and walked toward the trees. Almost immediately, he was joined by about half a dozen other males, big adults and juveniles that advanced with him side by side in a tight line. At this stage DeVore first saw what was upsetting the baboons, the heads of two cheetahs sticking up out of the grass near the trees and only a hundred feet or so ahead of the line. The line advanced until it was only about 60 feet away, when several of the baboons broke out of formation and made a lunging charge directly at the cheetahs. The big cats turned and ran off, and the baboons behind the line started eating again.

As an organic repository of information, a baboon troop knows more than any one of its members. The unique and unusual experiences accumulated by older individuals affect the troop's behavior. One example of group learning has already been described in Chapter 5—about two years after Robert Harding discovered meat eating among Kenya baboons, his colleague Shirley Strum found the practice widespread among troop members, who also developed cooperative hunting.

Once an investigator studying parasitic diseases shot two Nairobi Park baboons from a car. More than eight months later the troop was still giving cars a wide berth, although it had previously been quite approachable, and although the odds are that only a few of its 80-odd members saw what happened. Other primates also develop traditions of a sort. Macaque monkeys on Kyushu Island in Japan sometimes walk 30 yards or so from the forest to the beach to wash dirt off handfuls of sweet potatoes provided by scientists to entice the animals into open country where they can be observed. This custom was learned about 25 years ago, and it spread rapidly and has been practiced ever since.

Such experiences may be remembered for years or generations and become part of the troop memory, a simple form of culture. In fact, the larger the troop, the greater is its store of accumulated information, its security from predators, and its general knowledge about the environment. If these were the only or the major factors operating, the forces of natural selection might well have produced larger and larger baboon troops and perhaps considerably more advanced social organizations. But DeVore pointed out that other factors limit group size. When a troop has more than a hundred members, it tends to split. One of the reasons is a rise in tensions; when there are too many large dominant males they begin to form two rival groups. Also, when the population increases beyond the capacity of the land to provide food, part of the group must move away to less intensely exploited areas.

Yawn threat of adult male

Every baboon receives a more or less continuous flow of information about the state of mind of other baboons and transmits information to them about its own feelings. The air is alive with signals. Lip-smacking and soft grunts are the most frequent signals and indicate peaceful intentions. As already indicated, hard direct stares are the most powerful gestures of all. Threatening yawns revealing large canine teeth are typical of baboons who are standing stiff with shoulders hunched and neck hair raised. Every now and then there is a chase accompanied by loud grunting and screeches of fear. Little harm comes of the commotion. Most threats do not lead to a chase, for the threatened individual makes some sort of submissive gesture, such as moving away slowly or screeching loudly with lips curled in a grin of appeasement. When chases do occur, they generally end with the fugitive pressing its body to the ground and the pursuer holding it there for a moment and then walking off. Bloodshed is rare, serious injury even rarer.

MALE AND FEMALE HIERARCHIES

As a rule, quarrels last less than half a minute. They can be interpreted as letting off steam or maintaining a certain level of excitement and alertness among individuals that really have little else to do. The net effect is to achieve stability through a sort of regulated turbulence. All this activity goes on within the framework of a rigid social system, a hierarchy in which every adult member of the troop has a place. An individual's position in the hierarchy can usually be figured out by noting which of two individuals gives way when both approach food or a shady resting place or a female in heat. Status also shows up during episodes of so-called redirected aggression. This is the baboon version of what happens when a man who has just been called down by his boss comes home and snaps at his wife—who then slaps her child, who, in turn, kicks the dog. The result is a flow of aggressive energy downhill through the troop's hierarchy. A dominant male usually starts things by chasing a subordinate male, who promptly expresses his feelings by chasing a still more subordinate individual. Low monkey on the totem pole during such activity is rarely an adult male, but often an adult female—the highest-ranking female still occupies a position below that of the lowest-ranking male. Sometimes baboons will even release their aggression on an inanimate object, bouncing against a tree or tugging at a large rock.

This sort of behavior may take place on a large scale when the troop has been frightened. The mere sight of a leopard, the most dangerous predator to baboons, was once followed by an extended burst of activity, dominant males chasing subordinate males, and subordinate males chasing females, to the accompaniment of much screeching and nipping. The episode lasted for more than five minutes before simmering down to a flurry of grunts, threatening yawns, and lip-smacking. It was something like waves and ripples dying out in a pond after gusts of wind. On another occasion a lion charged at a troop, and it took a full hour for the baboons to relax.

The hierarchy is not always a simple matter of A dominating B, B dominating C, and so on down the line. In one troop, for example, the strongest individual and the best fighter was Kula, an "aggressive, fearless, dominance-oriented" adult male in his prime. Kula could almost certainly have beaten any of the other adult males of the troop in single combat. But he never received privileges commensurate with his abilities because three older baboons, including a very old and formidable veteran, stayed close to one another most of the time and acted together in putting down the challenges of others. In other words, Kula was the victim of the establishment, or central hierarchy.

The Establishment: (top) adult male threatens two members of central hierarchy, who turn and chase him (bottom)

These are among the earliest in-the-wild observations of primate behavior, and an enormous amount of information has accumulated since then. New studies have featured a much greater emphasis on the inner dynamics of troops, on some of the more subtle interrelationships among individuals, together with a more balanced picture of the place of aggression and an increasing effort to get at the underlying factors which determine individual behavior and social organization. Also, we know more about more species. Out of about 200 species of primates, perhaps 80 to 90 have been studied in some detail—for at least a year or two.

On the other hand, the total includes no more than half a dozen or so truly long-term studies including research commitments of years rather than months—and that represents a serious limitation, because time reveals many basic social patterns which would otherwise be missed. For example, during a short-term study it is all too easy to overemphasize the role of males. One cannot help being impressed with the swagger, confident bearing, and effective policing actions of a top-ranking male.

But he will be displaced sooner or later, and so in due course will the male who displaces him, and so on. It turns out that in the long run the female hierarchy, although generally ranking below the male hierarchy, is far more stable. In most species male primates emigrate to join other troops, while females stay put and represent the continuity of the troops as a social unit. Furthermore, there is evidence that, among baboons and macaque monkeys at least, females may inherit their mothers' dominance ranks—and for life.

MOTHER-INFANT RELATIONS

Insights into the female role are now coming from a number of field investigations, among the most outstanding being those of the Altmanns. Their research on Amboseli baboons has been going on for more than 20 years, and includes a 7-year study of births, deaths, and reproductive behavior, with an especially intensive focus on mother-infant relations. Method is crucial in such work. The objective is to go beyond anecdotes and impressions to solid knowledge, and that is always a difficult and tedious proposition. It is sometimes more fun just to sit back and think, but that gets you nowhere.

The mother-infant study involved the following schedule of observations: 2 days at least a week apart during the last month of pregnancy; the day of birth; the fifth day of infant life; 2 days during the infant's second week; a day a week for the next 24 weeks; and 2 to 3 days a week for the next 6 months—a total of 80 to more than 100 days. On every one of those days Jeanne Altmann watched two females alternately, each for 15 minutes per hour from 8 in the morning until 5 in the evening (with an hour's time out at noon).

At four times during each 15-minute period she noted the mother's behavior (whether grooming, feeding, walking, and so on), all the mother's neighbors within 2 meters and more than 2 to 5 meters away, the distance between mother and infant (four degrees, from direct contact to more than 20 meters away), and whether the infant was playing or in contact with any other troop member. In addition, she had a list of behaviors, including chasing, crying, eyelid displays, lip-smacking, suckling, and more than 40 others, which she used in recording

Mother-infant bond: infant in mother's arms

interactions during each 15-minute session. All this and more for each of 14 mother-infant pairs yielded a large body of information, supporting evidence for some interesting and unexpected observations.

One impression after following baboon troops for a few weeks or so is the difference between male and female behaviors, males representing the chief locus of aggression and tension in troop and aggregated females with their infants representing the locus of affection. Indeed, for the first month or so mother and infant are practically a single organism. The infant is either in her arms nursing, being groomed, or clinging to her belly upside down as she moves with the troop.

Although this impression still holds, more intensive studies reveal less obvious but nonetheless significant tensions among groups of mothers and infants. "The general problems that face most human and nonhuman primate mothers are in many ways similar," notes Jeanne Altmann, and she might have added that the similarity probably extends to prehistoric as well as contemporary mothers. For one thing, there is the sheer stress of feeding. The average adult female in a baboon troop spends more than half of her time obtaining nourishment for herself and her infant, and spends most of her life, perhaps as much as 75 percent, taking care of a dependent infant.

TENSION AMONG MOTHERS

Competition for food and social position may be intense. It is basically the old problem of keeping up with the Joneses or at least trying hard to get along with them and, unsurprisingly enough, high status pays off handsomely. Mothers ranking high in the female hierarchy are more successful, more confident, than subordinate mothers, notably when it comes to rearing healthy and well-adjusted offspring. Their infants are groomed more frequently by other members of troops, perhaps as a way of currying favor. Also, they are more permissive, allowing their infants to move away from direct contact earlier, ignoring or rejecting their infants earlier, and so on.

Low-ranking mothers tend to be far more restrictive and protective—and with good reason. Their infants are in greater danger of being pulled away, mainly by higher-ranking females, "sometimes . . . with sufficient force to produce counter-pulling by the mother, screeching by the infant, and other signs of distress in both." Jeanne Altmann notes another striking feature related to status. High-ranking female baboons in Amboseli may give birth to more daughters (19 daughters out of 29 recorded births), while low-ranking females produce more sons (15 out of 22 births), a phenomenon which remains unexplained but presumably represents the effects of differential stress. Joan Silk of the University of California in Davis has observed similar tendencies in a group of captive macaque

Infant baboon looking for reassurance before exploring

monkeys, where low-ranking mothers are harassed and injured more than high-ranking mothers, and their infants have less chance of surviving past the age of 6 months.

What it all adds up to is that motherhood, which makes up most of the lives of adult females, represents a high-risk, high-stress condition. Every mother competes directly with every other mother in a food and status quest for herself and her infant. An interesting exception has been noted among baboons in Tanzania's Mikumi National Park. According to Samuel Wasser of the University of Washington, cooperation may exist among mothers nursing offspring up to about three months old, apparently a critical period during which infants gain most in social development by associating with their peers. Before and after that period pregnant females and nursing mothers tend to avoid one another.

There is nothing simple about fatherhood either. Fatherhood as well as motherhood in primates, human as well as nonhuman, is a thing of paradoxes. An infant is an important factor in binding the troop together and creating a close-knit social unit. "It is scarcely possible to overemphasize the significance of the newborn baboon," DeVore points out. "It becomes the center of interest, absorbing the attention of the entire troop. From the moment the birth is discovered, the mother is continuously surrounded by other baboons, who walk beside her and sit as close as possible when she rests." An infant is likely to come at a time of relative abundance. DeVore noted that about four out of five offspring were born between October and December, at the onset of the rainy season in Kenya, when the food supply is about to reach a peak.

Child rearing is essentially a group activity. Mothers aggregate at the center of the troop, and other baboons, drawn by the enormous attraction of the infants, join the cluster. Juveniles and adolescent females come near and smack their lips and reach out to touch the infants, although mothers try to prevent any outside contact for the first week or two. Adolescent females approach, and learn how to care for the infants they will bear by carrying and fondling the infants of others. The odds are that if a mother dies, one of them, probably a relative, will adopt the infant. The central nucleus is ideally designed for the learning process, and infants born into primate societies have a great deal to learn.

MALES IN THE FAMILY

Males are also powerfully attracted. As a matter of fact, primate males are outstanding among mammalian males for their "mothering" inclinations. At the same time, however, and under special circumstances, their behavior may be ambiguous or worse. One day in the Amboseli Reserve an adult male was in a high dudgeon, running rampant through his troop, going after females and juveniles and practically every individual in sight. He had just lost a fight to a higher-ranking member of the hierarchy, and had a lot of steam to let off. Another male, seeing the aggressor heading in his direction, quickly picked up a nearby infant and began to groom it, as if he knew that he would probably be immune from attack with an infant in his arms. That is what happened. The aggressor passed him by for another victim, after which he promptly released the infant.

This sort of behavior has been observed on many occasions. It is highly complex, and raises a number of questions. From one point of view it can certainly be interpreted as pretense or deceit, a peculiarly primate behavior pattern. It is seen in no other order of creatures. On the other hand, the infant was directly in the aggressor's path and might well have been mauled, in which case the action of the other male could be interpreted as protective rather than, or as well as, downright deceitful. Sometimes behavior which appears selfish can at the same time benefit the community along with the individual and thus serve the cause of group survival.

A grimmer aspect of male behavior has been documented by Sarah Hrdy of Harvard during studies of langur monkeys in India. On one occasion, for example, the lone adult male in the troop she was studying was driven away and replaced by another male—a change accompanied by the disappearance of an adult female and all six of the troop's infants. Subsequent observations in this troop and others indicate what had happened: the newcomer had attacked and killed the infants. Since then infanticide, predominantly the work of usurping males, has been reported in more than a dozen primate species including baboons, macaques, and chimpanzees. For reasons to be discussed in Chapter 14, the killings may represent a rather perverted form of fatherhood, as if the killers wanted none but their own offspring in the troop.

There are, of course, certain presumably outweighing advantages to having males around. They have been known to care for an infant, carrying it the way its mother does, by letting it cling to the hair on their bellies. (Fortunately, it has a firm grip.) In at least one case a sickly female infant whose mother had died after nursing was adopted not by a female relative but by a dominant male, a member of the central hierarchy. Indeed, adult males may continue to protect a young baboon after its mother no longer does. After 2 years or so, when she is busy with her next offspring, they will come to its rescue for another 6 months or longer.

It should also be emphasized that infanticide might be rather more common if it were not for males apparently acting as defenders. Judging by observations of baboon troops in Botswana, Curt Busse and William Hamilton of the University of California in Davis are convinced that some males carrying infants are not trying to appease high-ranking males, but are probably protecting their own offspring. In 28 of 29 confrontations the threatening male outranked the infant carrier, but did not choose to fight and the infant was not injured.

Reproductively active females, females either pregnant or nursing, have males with whom they prefer to associate, a pattern that has been reported often and is thoroughly documented by another Harvard primatologist, Barbara Smuts. Her 16-month study of a baboon group living on a 45,000-acre cattle ranch in Rift Valley northwest of Nairobi features periods of extremely detailed observations comparable to those used by Jeanne Altmann. If a male ranked number one or two as far as most frequent grooming and closeness to a particular female were concerned, he was rated as her "Friend."

By these standards 29 out of the 31 females observed had at least one Friend. Females like to be close to their Friends, within limits. Smuts' analysis reveals that "although females preferred to be near the males with whom they had special relationships," they did not in general want to be too near. They were mainly responsible for maintaining distances of 1 meter up to 15 meters from Friends, but males usually took the initiative in coming still closer, in bridging that last 1-meter gap.

A female benefits from association with a preferred male, particularly right after the birth of her infant, when he may act as protector and occasional caretaker. Also, aggression between the sexes is part of the social life of baboons, and she gains by additional protection. Adult males, "infrequently but routinely" bite adult females and, being twice as large, rarely pay a price for their attacks, which sometimes result in serious wounds. The aggressors in these encounters are usually "non-associate" males; the defenders are usually Friends. In general, "when a female establishes a special relationship with a male, she and her immature offspring acquire an ally in the troop—an ally who, because of his larger size and superior fighting ability, may make a significant contribution to the fitness of the female and her offspring."

Such relationships would not exist unless the male also had something to gain. If the infant is his, by no means a certainty, his benefits include an enhanced probability that his genes will be passed on to succeeding generations. It seems that many but not all Friends are the infants' probable fathers. Also, the preferred male has access to an infant whom he can carry to help reduce the risk of injury to himself during aggressive encounters with other males. Perhaps the most important benefit, however, is access to females who, after their reproductively active periods, may mate preferentially with their former partners.

The more we study primates in the wild, and many major problems remain unsolved, the more we appreciate their capacities. "In searching for answers to difficult questions," Smuts concludes, "we may finally begin to give baboons, and other nonhuman primates, their due as psychologically sophisticated creatures whose social relationships approach our own in complexity and in intensity of emotion." The baboon troop exists as a compromise, a successful compromise, between individual competition and cooperation. For all the tensions, for all the chasing and attacking and biting, most of the day consists of peaceful feeding, resting, and grooming. Affection represents the pervading force, and the power of affection is indicated by the troop's durability and continuity.

It is difficult to think of an organization better designed for the protection of infants, the rearing of the next generation, than the baboon troop with its inner cluster of mothers and resident males. Yet less than half of all infants born survive beyond their second year; the rest become victims of injury, disease, and predators.

An infant's death illustrates the persistence of affection, and also how abruptly it may cease. A mother may carry a dead infant for several days, clutching the corpse to her belly, letting it drop from time to time and then going back and picking it up again. When the ultimate separation comes, it may be striking for its complete lack of apparent emotion. After clinging to her infant for four days, one mother simply let go of it without even breaking her stride or looking back, as if she were unaware of what had happened.

Circumstances call for the shutting off of deep concern. The laws of necessity dictate that affection cannot be attached too strongly to any single individual. Death is too frequent. But affection itself must outlast all the endings and letdowns. In the case of the female, it must always be revived by the sight and touch of her next infant and the infants of others. The troop owes its existence to the fact that evolution and natural selection have made this enduring renewal possible.

SUMMARY

We learn about human evolution from living material as well as dead material, from present-day species, human and nonhuman, as well as from ancient bones and artifacts. The problem is to see ourselves in the context of developments that hold throughout the animal kingdom. Among new orders of mammals, the earliest species tend to live in the simplest social units consisting of a mother and her infant, with males kept strictly at a distance. Species which appear later tend to form increasingly complex social systems, eventually including males.

The past few decades have seen a notable increase in research on our kind of animal, wild primates. Baboons are frequently studied, partly because they live in open country and can be readily observed, and partly because it is in such terrain that the earliest hominids evolved. Baboons live sunrise-to-sunset lives. They sleep in trees, wake with the first light of day, head for the main feeding place, find a shady spot around midday where they can rest and groom one another and play, and then head back for their sleeping trees as the sun sinks.

The baboon troop includes male and female "pecking orders," or hierarchies made up of dominant and subordinate individuals. The male hierarchy dominates the female hierarchy in the sense that low-ranking males generally outrank high-ranking females. But the status of males changes relatively frequently and the status of females less so, so that the female hierarchy represents the stable, long-term core of the troop. Child rearing is primarily the mother's job, and recent studies indicate that the average adult female may spend as much as 75 percent of her life taking care of a dependent infant.

The more we learn about baboons, the more complex their behavior appears. There is cooperation among individuals, and conflict too. If a mother dies, another female may care for her infant. But competition is intense for food and social position, and low-ranking mothers are harassed and injured more than high-ranking mothers. Males often groom and protect infants, but they may also kill infants for reasons that are not at all clear.

Individuals do not find it easy to get along with one another, but in the last analysis they manage. Otherwise, the species could not survive.

chapter **13**

Chimpanzees: Our Closest Living Relatives

A high order of intelligence is generally associated with independence, individual initiative, and a capacity for novel and creative behavior. This implies that the more intelligent a primate is, the greater the difficulty of limiting its freedom in the context of rigid hierarchy. We see that tensions and frustrations have been observed even among baboons, and such behavior might well have caused more serious stresses among more intelligent prehuman apes. Severe conflict was probably a basic feature of the hominid line from the very beginning as a direct result of savanna life and the need for rules and discipline.

Baboon society provides a model of primate life in the grassy savannas of Africa, the sort of world our ancestors encountered when they moved out of open woodlands. They, like baboons, may once have lived sunrise-to-sunset lives, slept in trees for safety, and headed by dawn's early light for the first feeding place of the day (see Chapter 12). Probably their sons also played rough-and-tumble games, while their daughters were attracted increasingly to infants and the care of infants. They also had hierarchies, an establishment, and the perennial problem of building individuals into stable social systems.

But the comparison can be carried just so far, and no further. Other species have adapted in other ways to exposed conditions. Ronald Hall found that the patas monkeys of Uganda, perhaps the most terrestrial of all nonhuman primates, survive by scattering rather than aggregating as baboons do. Individual troop members are often separated by distances of more than a hundred yards, on the principle of offering predators isolated rather than concentrated targets. Built like greyhounds, they are outstanding for their fantastic running and dodging abilities;

247

they show little aggression. Much remains to be learned about survival in the savanna.

OBSERVATIONS IN THE WILD

As for life in open woodlands, where the human family is believed to have originated, attention focuses on the chimpanzee. Of all living primates, the chimpanzee is most like people and, therefore, the most difficult to observe objectively. In recent times, it has been described as a creature living in a state of primal innocence and as "a diabolical caricature of ourselves . . . as common, as vulgar, as no other animal but a debased human being can be." In less gaudy terms, it ranks high on the primate intelligence scale, with a brain about twice the size of the baboon brain. It spends much of its time on the ground and reveals an impressive capacity for complex and enduring social relationships. Moreover, observations suggest the sort of forces that might have transformed the life style of a forest-dwelling chimpanzee into a hominid-savanna life style.

The wild chimpanzee prefers to keep its distance, at least in the beginning; this usually presents far more problems in forests than in savannas for investigators observing primates. In 1960, when Jane Goodall started her studies in Gombe Stream Reserve forests, she would arise daily about half-past five in the morning and spend most of the day on top of a rocky hill overlooking the forests and Lake Tanganyika, where she could observe and be observed as a harmless and unassuming fellow primate.

Social acceptance was slow in coming. Some days she spent 12 hours in the field, climbing up and down slopes and forcing her way through dense undergrowth without seeing a single chimpanzee. She often heard calls in the distance, but the animals had moved off by the time she managed to make her way to the area. "It wasn't just fear," she explains. "It was also resentment of your presence. Like people in an English village, they don't care to be stared at." During the first few months they would run away upon seeing her at distances of as much as 500 yards.

The apes became tamer as they learned her ways, and as she learned theirs. Part of her strategy, for example, was pretending not to pay attention. Often a group that seemed nervous and about to take off when being watched intently would calm down and stay if she started doing something else, such as eating leaves or digging a hole. Gradually she was able to come closer and closer—to within 50 yards by 8 months and within 50 feet by another half-year or so. In general, males were bolder than females, "displaying" for five or ten minutes on occasion as they would to a fellow chimpanzee—that is, engaging in behavior such as screaming, hitting trees, and shaking branches. Then they would ignore her and go about their business.

Chimpanzees enjoy a social life which is strikingly flexible compared to that of baboons. They are more human than baboons, or rather they jibe better with the way we like to picture ourselves, as freewheeling individuals who tend to be unpredictable, do not take readily to any form of regimentation, and are frequently charming. (Charm is relatively rare among baboons.) Although baboon troops usually remain together with all members clustered in a single area, this is rarely the case for chimpanzees. According to Vernon Reynolds of Oxford University, who studied chimpanzees in the Budongo forest of western Uganda, they move about in four types of bands: adult males only; mothers and offspring with occasionally a few other females; adults and adolescents of both sexes without mothers or offspring; and representatives of all categories mixed together. The composition of a party may change a number of times a day, as individuals wander off and groups split or combine with other groups.

Chimpanzees live in such an easy-come, easy-go style that both Goodall and Reynolds commented on their apparent lack of permanent social organization. Japanese investigators were the first to note the existence of loose but nevertheless definite troops. In 1967, Junichiro Itani and Akira Suzuki of the University of Kyoto, working in Tanzania some hundred miles south of the Gombe Stream Reserve, reported the same invisible-fence phenomenon that was found among baboons (see Chapter 12). Lines exist in the forest, boundaries which human eyes cannot detect and which chimpanzees do not cross, turning back as if obeying No Trespassing signs.

Chimpanzees are nomads. They generally sleep in different trees every night and travel in individual core ranges or circuits depending on sex and the abundance of food. Studies by Richard Wrangham of the University of Michigan suggest that males tend to forage together in the same areas during times of abundance, and disperse when food is scarce. Females are dispersed at all times, except when sexually active. Chimpanzee paths are everywhere in the forests, miles and miles of them, including tunnels through the densest stretches of undergrowth, tubes just about big enough for an individual to scramble through on all fours. (Many animals have such tunnels, perhaps the most spectacular being the great elephant tunnels of northern Bengal, long corridors 10 feet high that wind through tangled places in jungles along the foothills of the Himalayas.)

MEAT EATING AND FAMILY TIES

There is nothing nonhuman for chimpanzees to fear in the forest. The most formidable predator, the leopard, tends to concentrate on other game. Chimpanzees hunt more often than they are hunted. Geza Teleki, whose analysis of their predatory episodes is referred to in Chapter 5, has estimated that, on the average, a community of 50 chimpanzees may go after prey four or five times a month, and that the cooperation of 2 to 5 individuals is involved more than half the time. As among human bands, females rarely participate in hunting when adult males are around, but they may hunt in the absence of males. An interesting pattern is reported by William McGrew of the University of Stirling, Scotland, who describes meat eating among chimpanzees in a 3100-square-mile reserve in Senegal. There the primates prey chiefly on bushbabies and pottos, nocturnal prosimians that sleep by day in dense foliage, tree hollows, and other hiding places.

Meat eating and sharing seem to go together. Adult nonhuman primates rarely share plant foods, although mothers may share certain items with their infants. But a successful hunt creates situations which definitely encourage giving or at least permissiveness. According to Shirley Strum, among baboons adult male-female and mother-infant pairs may eat the same piece of meat side by side: "Frequently, one individual moves to allow another access to the meat." This mild or passive form of sharing is also found among chimpanzees, together with rather more active and more elaborate forms. Out of 579 "exchange interactions" which Teleki observed during 12 kills, 395 were requests for meat. These included peering intently at or reaching out to touch the meat or the eater; emitting soft whimpers or "hoo" sounds; and extending an open hand, palm upwards in the classical begging gesture. About a third of the requests produced results; most of the time they were firmly and not always gently ignored.

Hunting and sharing chimpanzee-style are highly significant. As James Chisholm of the University of New Mexico emphasizes, although meat makes up only a small proportion of the apes' diet (probably less than 1 percent), it calls for the first steps toward a new and complex level of sociability—in effect, a kind of high-grade inhibition. When an adult male chimpanzee has a freshly

Chimpanzee mother playing with son

killed animal in his grasp, he is temporarily king of the hill. He may occupy a low position in the established hierarchy, but his superiors waive rank and request food from him instead of grabbing it away and terrorizing him. They recognize that the possession of an extremely valuable resource somehow changes the rules, and that in the long run there is more to be gained by restrained, polite, and submissive behavior than by aggression. This quality probably developed to a high degree when our hominid ancestors relied increasingly on meat as part of their survival on the savanna.

Chimpanzees may become highly aroused at the mere sight of a killing, screaming loudly as they watch the action, and running about and throwing their arms around one another. In fact, a variety of conditions can throw them into a frenzy. As mentioned in Chapter 7, they may perform rain-dance displays to the accompaniment of thunder and lightning during tropical storms, and one of their most outlandish rituals is the carnival, when as many as 30 individuals come together in a period of fantastic noisemaking which may last several hours. The sound is difficult to believe even when you have heard it.

Reynolds has described what it is like to be caught in the middle of a carnival: "The noise is terrific, like a tornado or an audience-applause machine turned way up. It can be very frightening, because there is also a great deal of running back and forth, and the ground shakes, and you hear high shrieking and the thud of heavy feet coming toward you and violent drumming on the trees." No one knows what unusual events start such bursts of mass excitement. They may represent reactions to a killing of some sort, elaborate greeting ceremonies between two communities that have not crossed paths for a long time, or perhaps responses to the presence of human observers.

Another sign of more complex social behavior is that the mother-offspring bond is more enduring among chimpanzees than among baboons. Chimpanzees mature far more slowly, requiring a prolonged period of infant dependency. The first separation between mother and infant, the first break in physical contact, does not occur for 16 to 24 weeks, as compared to about 4 weeks among baboons. Although juveniles no longer need to be nursed after they are 4 or 5 years old or so, they may share their mother's nest for another three years; they are dependent until about the age of 8.

Increasing independence, however, does not mean the severing of family ties. As indicated in Chapter 2, one of the most significant discoveries about chimpanzee behavior in the Gombe area, a discovery that would never have been made without long-term observations, is that family ties probably last throughout life. One mother estimated to be nearly 50 years old had two sons, both over 20, who often kept her company and groomed her. The two top-ranking males in a seven-male group support each other in times of trouble, apparently obtain extra-large portions when there is meat to be shared, look alike, and are probably brothers. Other examples of close ties, including brother-sister bonds, indicate the complexity of social relationships within the community.

The period of extended youth provides ample opportunity for many kinds of play. As among baboons, this consists in the main of silent chasing and wrestling. The chimpanzee is unique among primates, however, in the amount of

Chimpanzee family: sister nuzzling brother in mother's arms

time it spends playing with objects. It seems to have a special predisposition for manipulating certain kinds of objects, notably sticks and twigs, and manipulating them in a certain way, by poking and probing. Such a built-in bias helps to ensure that learning will not proceed at random but along broad, genetically guided lines.

TOOL-USING CHIMPANZEES

One of the Gombe chimpanzees' outstanding accomplishments is inserting probes into termite-mound holes to extract the edible insects from underground nests (see Chapter 2). This is by no means a simple technique, as Teleki discovered during long periods of observation of an adult male (named Leakey after the Olduvai investigator). For one thing, finding the covered holes demands considerable experience. Leakey would inspect a mound briefly, and then flick away a bit of dirt, almost invariably exposing an opening. Teleki never learned where to flick, nor could he detect any cracks, bumps, or depressions which might mark the location of a hole.

Leakey unhesitantly selected stalks or stems suitable for efficient probing, neither too stiff nor too flexible, while Teleki, who never mastered this trick of instant choosing, spent frustrating hours learning how to insert the probe into twisting channels and vibrate it gently so that termites would be aroused to attack the invading object by biting onto it firmly. Such difficulties are not surprising, considering that Teleki had only 2 or 3 months to learn, while Leakey had had a lifetime. The point is that nonhuman primates need and have an impressive ability to acquire elaborate new skills, to expand their repertoire of behavior patterns.

Another skill demonstrated by Gombe chimpanzees represents the anthropoid equivalent of drawing water from a well. The well is the crotch of a tree where rain water has collected, and the problem is to get a drink. Thirsty juveniles and young infants bend over and squeeze their faces into the hollow, but they get nothing because their faces are too big. An experienced chimpanzee knows precisely what to do. It strips some leaves from a convenient plant, chews them just enough to form a crumpled ball, dips the ball into the hollow, and then withdraws the soggy mass and sucks the water out of it. In other words, it makes a kind of artificial sponge.

The full range of tool use among wild apes is just beginning to be appreciated. Itani reports that chimpanzees in western Tanzania, occupying territories up to a hundred miles south of the Gombe Reserve, scoop honey out of honeycombs with twigs, use sticks to attack one another (see Chapter 2), and crack hard fruits with stone hammers. Chimpanzees in Guinea forests not far from the coast of West Africa have evolved rather more sophisticated nut-cracking techniques. They not only use a hammerstone to open palm nuts, but first place the nuts on another stone serving as an anvil. Even more interesting, they may reuse the same selected stones over periods of months.

Human beings go chimpanzees one better. They are also long-time eaters of insects, including termites, and one night Teleki had a chance to observe the methods of local Tanzanians. They took two short sticks, started drumming rhythmically on the top and sides of a termite mound, and then scraped off part of the mound with a machete, exposing swarms of termites which were promptly dumped into baskets. The purpose of the drumming? ''We do that to imitate the rain.'' The regular beat sounds like raindrops to termites nesting deep underground, and they are fooled into climbing to the surface. Thus, baboons wait until relatively late in the rainy season and have about 2 weeks of termite eating; chimpanzees go to work early in the season and have 2 months or so; and human beings by creating a fake rainy season, have at least 4 months.

Methods of catching termites are a measure of the intellectual capacities of baboons, chimpanzees, and human beings. Baboons have an avid appetite for termites and will watch intently as chimpanzees use probes to eat the insects by the thousands; sometimes baboons will pick up sticks, but that is where it ends. There is a world of brainpower between baboon and chimpanzee. The concept of a tool, the notion of using an object to make up for their own limitations, does not occur to baboons under these circumstances. They have never been observed trying to use probes, and they seem completely incapable of making a connection between the sticks they hold in their hands and the activities of the chimpanzees they are watching. Instead they wait until later in the season when termites are swarming and grab what they can on the ground or in mid-air, a far less efficient process.

SIMILARITIES AND DIFFERENCES

Similarities between people and chimpanzees may be as striking as differences. Chimpanzees use familiar gestures to express their feelings. Upon meeting in the forest, old friends kiss and embrace, or one individual may reach out and pat the other on the head or shoulder. Another common form of greeting is to rest the hand on the thigh or genitals. This gesture may also signify reassurance, and men as well as chimpanzees have used it for that purpose. (In the Bible, for example, laying a hand on a person's thigh is a way of sealing a bargain, of swearing to do what the person asks.)

There are other actions one would have no difficulty in interpreting; for example, chimpanzees scratch their head when trying to make up their mind. Before picking a piece of fruit off a tree, chimpanzees may squeeze it gently to test its ripeness, like a person selecting tomatoes at the local supermarket. Goodall saw a male fidgeting and absentmindedly eating a flower while waiting for a companion, presumably female, and looking for all the world like an "impatient man glancing at his wristwatch." Chimpanzees are perhaps most human when they are at play. Infants may play tug-of-war with a stick; juveniles chase one another, and in the midst of a chase, the pursued may burst out laughing, presumably in anticipation of being tickled by the pursuer.

Four things that chimpanzees have never been observed doing indicate the nature of the gap between them and us—and also suggest that some of our most unusual characteristics may have appeared during relatively recent times. First, although chimpanzees may upon occasion go after one another with sticks, they do not regularly use weapons of any kind, either in the hunt or against one another. (The earliest evidence suggesting the possibility of armed combat among humans or at least violence is a 300,000-year-old Ethiopian skull which had apparently been scalped.) Second, they have never been observed ganging up to kill or pursue animals bigger than themselves, generally confining themselves to prey weighing no more than about 20 pounds.

Third, chimpanzees do not teach hunting techniques, or anything else for that matter, to other troop members. For example, it would be highly unchimpanzee-like for an adult to go through the entire probing-for-termites routine purely for demonstration purposes—that is, not out of hunger or appetite but simply to show a juvenile how to select and prepare suitable stalks, how to probe, and so on. Learning undoubtedly takes place, but it proceeds without deliberate instruction, by imitation only, which means lengthy periods of trial and error. As David Premack of the University of Pennsylvania has pointed out, we are the only species in which teachers watch novices; in all other species the novices do all the watching.

Weapon-wielding male chimpanzee

One result is a severe limitation on the effectiveness of culture as an evolutionary mechanism. Even among humans and with the very best of instruction, a great deal can be lost in efforts to transmit information. Master hunters or toolmakers always know more than they can impart, subtle innovations or insights which they are often not aware of themselves. The loss is considerably greater when there is no teaching at all, only imitating, and when the present generation must therefore relearn the hard way so much of what the previous generation learned.

All this has some interesting implications for evolution human-style, because it seems that teaching is something quite new in the record of our species. Judging by the sluggish pace of change for several million years until the onset of the upper Paleolithic (see Chapter 10), our sort of culture itself may be a recent innovation. In any case, the spurt of social evolution which began then may have been connected with efforts to apply pedagogical methods, probably quite rudimentary, for the first time on a systematic basis.

There is nothing easy or "natural" about teaching. Its appearance seems to depend on a special kind of selective pressure. It is certainly a rare phenomenon among recent hunter-gatherers. John Yellen of the National Science Foundation and George Washington University has spent more than 3 years living among the Kalahari Bushmen of Botswana and recalls only two cases of what might be considered teaching, both baby-care pointers to young children. Documenting the prehistory of teaching presents quite a challenge. Perhaps a relationship exists between teaching and the making of dolls and other toys, from which one might infer conscious attempts to prepare children for adult roles, although I know of no systematic studies of the origins of toys.

A fourth significant difference between our closest living relatives and ourselves involves the capacity for forming complex social systems. Although tension and aggression exist within primate troops, the troop itself generally manages to endure as an effective social unit. What has not been observed among nonhuman primates is anything approaching an alliance, a superorganization made up of two or more troops coming together for more effective hunting or for any other reason. More often than not, troops make a point of avoiding one another; if they fail to do this, the outcome may be disastrous.

The nine adult males of one Gombe Stream Reserve chimpanzee troop exterminated the seven adult males of a neighboring troop, one by one, over a span of some 3 years. The attacked chimpanzees each disappeared within a few days, and in several cases their mauled bodies were found. The same sort of thing may occur between gorilla troops. According to Alexander Harcourt of Cambridge University, "the result of a fight between strange males can be many square yards of blood-bespattered, flattened vegetation with the males bearing wounds that can take days, sometimes weeks, to heal."

Not all meetings have such catastrophic outcomes, however. As Reynolds reported, chimpanzee troops may come together with apparent enthusiasm in a "carnival" chorus of deafening greetings, and on rare occasions two troops will share a sleeping tree. Peaceful, even affectionate, episodes have been observed in the very midst of aggressive encounters. Individuals sometimes leave their native group and join the other group, possibly attracted by the presence of brothers or sisters who have already made the transfer and become accepted members of their adopted community. So despite conflict and imminent violence among neighboring troops, kinship ties permit a limited form of interchange and communication.

Relationships among chimpanzees may proceed at a subtler level, hinting at the possibility of something rather more complex. A number of years ago three distinct communities co-existed in the Gombe region, two with 40 to 50 members and one with 20 to 30 members, each occupying a separate territory. They were well aware of one another, frequently visiting checkpoints to make sure that trespassers were not at large. Richard Wrangham has observed "scouts" patrolling ridges which formed boundaries between troop territories: "The fact that parties sometimes travelled to the ridges without eating en route, and then returned after listening for 30 minutes or more, suggested that they were monitoring the boundaries. Prime or dominant males were invariably involved."

The troops in a given region may have a strict "pecking order," the troop with the most members generally rating No. 1 and so on down the line to the smallest troop. A hierarchy tends to minimize mayhem, since at the mere approach of a high-ranking troop lesser troops quietly give ground and move to another area a safe distance away. This is the closest nonhuman primates come to an organization of organizations. It amounts to cooperation of a sort, if only a negative "agreement" to recognize and abide by rules of status. Again, as in the case of teaching, it should be pointed out that formalized relationships among bands of affiliated human primates, fellow members of the species *Homo sapiens,* are relatively recent developments, having first become of major importance during the Upper Paleolithic (see Chapter 10).

Presumably primates resembling chimpanzees or the precursors of chimpanzees lived 15 or so million years ago, before the coming of hominids, in forests that still dominated the earth, stretching in a broad band from Africa to the Far East (see Chapter 2). If one can judge by observations of today's forest-dwelling chimpanzees, these prehuman apes had little to fear and were relaxed, relatively independent creatures, with social systems sufficiently flexible to permit appreciable freedom of movement and individual action. Most of them probably moved in and out of thick foliage and shadows, along well-worn ancestral trails.

A rather different life style was in the making, however, for primates adapting to less-sheltered settings, to spreading, open woodlands and wide-open savannas. One form of adaptation depended on mass aggregation. That was the way of many antelopes, wildebeests, and other hooved animals, originally forest creatures wandering solitary or in small groups among the trees, and now moving into a new complex of ecological niches. As emphasized by Richard Estes of Harvard, they were coming together for protection, safety in large numbers: "The herd was a passport to the grasslands. It substituted for cover, providing concealment for the individual." In other words, the herd adaptation submerged the individual in crowds numbering in the hundreds or thousands.

OPEN-COUNTRY VS. FOREST LIVING

The apes that became our ancestors never had to go that far. They came well equipped for life in the sun. They were large, agile, and sharpsighted; above all, they were intelligent and adaptable. But woodland-savanna terrain called for some fairly basic changes, not only physical changes such as thicker-enameled teeth (see Chapter 2) but also social changes. For one thing, predation can be more of a problem in open country. It is by no means the only danger and, as we have seen, primates may have as much to fear from members of their own species as they have from prowling carnivores—or perhaps more to fear.

On the other hand, early prehominids could not afford to travel through exposed places the way they had traveled in the forests, at ease and with an almost careless lack of alertness. They had to contend with other species occupying grassy plains and riverine groves by evolving predatory tactics, harassing, ambushing, stalking and killing, scavenging, cooperative hunting. A reasonable guess is that they did what all pioneers, human as well as nonhuman, must do when they enter hostile territory. They joined ranks to form tighter organization, traveling together in complete and more disciplined troops.

Landscape has a major impact on behavior. Think of the life of baboons as we have described it in Chapter 12—adult males in tight-line formation confronting cheetahs, troop members constantly on the alert while feeding, the feeling of controlled tension within the troop and among troops, the occasional outbreaks of aggression, individuals asserting rank or being submissive to their superiors. Given such observations, it is hard to believe what one sees in a different environment—for example, in the comparative safety of the forests of Uganda. According to Thelma Rowell, baboons there do not have rigid hierarchies, live far more relaxed lives, and move freely from troop to troop.

Baboon troops foraging on the edge of the Budongo Forest, where Reynolds did his chimpanzee watching, live strikingly similar lives. James Paterson of the University of Calgary studied one such troop in some detail and reports an apparent absence of "any sort of dominance hierarchy among the males or females." As for aggression, there was "virtually none at all. . . . The usual amount of play chasing and open-mouth threatening occurred among the infants and juveniles, but there was none of this in the adults, except that which was directed against the observer." He compared this troop to another troop of baboons that were foraging in open savanna country to the southwest—and exhibited the "normal" pattern of hierarchy, tension, and frequent fighting.

The landscape effect holds for chimpanzees as well as baboons, only it works the other way around. The contrast is so vivid between the uptight life style of savanna baboons and that of forest chimpanzees, who generally seem as casual and unconcerned as people on a Sunday stroll in the park, that it is easy to assume that these are built-in natural behavior patterns. But put chimpanzees in a more open setting and they may behave more like baboons. You can see the effect even in the forest, when they must negotiate small stretches of open terrain. Budongo chimpanzees amble along among the trees, but they are tense and vigilant when it comes to crossing a road, looking to left and right at the road's edge, running back into the undergrowth, and finally making a dash for the other side. Gombe chimpanzees become nervous on the slopes of hills where the forest thins out.

McGrew's Senegal chimpanzees are of special interest. They live in mixed, mosaic terrain containing everything from short-grass plateaus and woodlands to bamboo thickets and gallery forest. But open lands predominate, and of all chimpanzee ranges investigated to date, this one probably rates as the driest and most open, a feature reflected in troop size, composition, and behavior. McGrew notes that the apes seem more nervous with "a higher proportion of the community staying together at any one time" than is the case for chimpanzees in forest environments. Furthermore, parties including adult males are more common: "We think the threat of being preyed upon is greater in open areas, and that adult males deter predators."

Consider all this in terms of what might have happened in remote prehistory, as our ancestral primates underwent a gradual transformation. At first perhaps it was a matter of occasional crossings and the finding of new foods on the savanna, occasional excursions into savanna regions bordering forests, and back to the shelter of forests at night. Then there were moves farther and farther out into the open until the bonds between primate and natural shelter dissolved, and they left the wide forests for good and used tiny islands of forest, clumps of trees near waterways, for refuge and sleeping.

Such developments or something analogous, lasting several million or more years, produced the first hominids. A new way of life came into being, the beginnings of the amazing human phase of terrestrial evolution. But it was achieved at a high price. Life in the open could never be as casual, as easy, as it was in the forests. It demanded larger troops, more individuals forced to stay together for longer periods, a situation practically guaranteed to increase tensions, and requiring stricter discipline, tighter hierarchies, a higher level of alertness. In a sense, our ape-like ancestors became "baboonized," as usual for survival's sake.

So here at the very beginning of the human line we have hints of a problem that was to arise again in an entirely different context during near-modern times with the appearance of *Homo sapiens sapiens,* the problem of creating and maintaining order in the community. During the Upper Paleolithic it seems to have been at least in part a matter of increasing sedentism and population densities (see Chapters 10 and 11). In early prehominid and hominid times it had to do with organization for survival in a world of spreading woodlands and savannas.

Observations of wild primates supplement archeological findings in attempts to reconstruct life styles of the remote past. Archeology tells us that stone tools appeared more than 2 million years ago, perhaps in response to greater reliance on eating meat obtained by scavenging and hunting. Primate studies tell us that chimpanzees can make and use tools, hunt, share their kills under certain circumstances—latent talents ready to be exploited on a larger scale as a result of evolutionary pressures. Comparisons of baboon and chimpanzee behavior indicate the sort of social changes that may have been needed to cope with changes in the environment.

PRIMATES AT PLAY

Incidentally, it would be a mistake to overemphasize tighter organization and hierarchies in our early prehistory. There were other changes which in effect may have worked to keep things in balance, including the development at the same time of more frequent and more complicated play behavior. As already mentioned, chimpanzees spend rather more time than most primates in manipulating objects seemingly for the fun of it and indulging in a variety of relatively sophisticated games, all of which may have special significance as the continuation of a development which started long before the appearance of advanced apes.

Play is definitely something new under the sun. It appeared after 4.3 billion virtually play-free years, in Pangean times when the planet's surface consisted of a single great ocean surrounding a single land mass or superisland on the verge of splitting into continents (see Chapter 2). It appeared some 200 million years ago with the arrival of warm-blooded animals. At least this is one implication of a recent study by Robert Fagen of the University of Alaska, who points out that the evidence for play among reptiles and lower species is scanty and questionable, but abundant for higher animals, notably mammals: "The evolution of play mirrors the evolution of the brain. Play and a highly developed cerebral cortex go together." In general, the most intelligent animals, including primates and dolphins and dogs, tend to be the most playful.

Play is part of the primate bias for exploring, probing, examining, part of the continual monitoring of home territories so that anything unusual, anything unfamiliar, is duly noted and stored in memory. Place a new object in the path of a foraging troop, especially something shiny or possibly edible, and it will almost certainly be touched, sniffed, mouthed, bashed, bitten, and otherwise examined. Most of the time the item will be discarded after a thorough mauling. But now and then, out of a lifetime or several lifetimes of such encounters, one item may turn out to the benefit of the individual.

A case in point is that of Mike, a wild adult chimpanzee that Goodall observed in the Gombe forests, and who put a pair of newly discovered artifacts to good use. He discovered, first, that banging two empty kerosene cans together produced fantastic and unexpected racket; second, that the racket scared every fellow chimpanzee within hearing range; and third, the payoff, that if he rushed banging and hooting toward other chimpanzees, they would get out of the way in a hurry. Without the cans, Mike had been no one in particular, ranking near the bottom of his troop's dominance hierarchy. With them, he became No. 1.

Any consideration of play raises more questions than it answers, because the word itself is so misleading, amounting to an intellectual booby trap. It implies something useless and trivial, something not to be taken seriously. Yet everything we know argues that it is to be taken very seriously indeed, and I have more to say about its importance for primate evolution in a later chapter. Play has become something fantastically elaborate in us, giving rise to a diversity of unlikely activities which, at first examination, would seem to have little survival value. In the last analysis, however, it stands out as perhaps the most striking mark of the human species.

SUMMARY

In the case of chimpanzees, our closest living relatives, it is a matter of so near and yet so far. Chimpanzees resemble us in so many ways, in their gestures and the way they play, and yet the gap between us and them is enormous. We are still trying to account for the emergence of that gap, for our striking uniquenesses.

Wild chimpanzees live relatively relaxed lives. They use tools, including probes to extract termites from termite nests, and hammerstones to open nuts (see Chapter 2). The have few predators, and hunt more often than they are hunted. As indicated in Chapter 5, they may hunt cooperatively and share meat. They form strong family ties. One mother estimated to be about 50 years old maintained close relationships with two of her sons, both over 20, and there are signs of enduring brother-sister and brother-brother relationships.

Certain things that chimpanzees have never been observed doing, however, indicate the basic nature of the gap between them and us. Four differences are noteworthy: (1) they do not use weapons in going after meat or in fights among themselves, (2) they do not go after animals bigger than themselves, (3) they do not teach one another by deliberate instruction (learning proceeds by imitation only), and (4) they do not form superorganizations made up of two or more cooperating troops.

Continuing observations suggest how millions of years ago environment may have played a role in transforming a primate something like a chimpanzee into something like a hominid. In forests where chimpanzees have few predators and food is generally abundant, they can maintain a relaxed, loosely organized life style. But they behave differently in more open country, moving about more cautiously and in larger groups, more like baboons. (Baboons, by the way, apparently live more relaxed lives in forests than on savannas.)

Similar changes may have taken place when early hominids were adapting to open country. Part of the adaptation seems to have involved the development of toolmaking, hunting, and other features existing but not fully exploited among nonhominids. Tighter organization may have been part of the price paid for survival. But at the same time play became more significant, at least if we can judge by the observation that increasing play and increasing intelligence tend to go together.

chapter *14*

Primates and Other Species

For all we have learned and are learning, the deepest insights into the forces that shape primate behavior are yet to come. They will come from studies of captive as well as wild species, from an interchange of information between laboratory and field. The French biologist Claude Bernard used to tell his students that "observation shows and experiment teaches," a statement which certainly applies to primate research. Observations in the wild suggest hypotheses which can be tested by experiments performed in laboratory settings. Experiments, in turn, suggest patterns to look for when observing troops in their native surroundings.

The effort is always to widen the scope of things, to understand the behavior patterns not of one forest-dwelling primate but of all forest-dwelling primates—and, beyond that, of all 200 primates, savanna dwellers and others as well as forest dwellers. And, still further, the search continues for a wider and more inclusive understanding, for the common elements or universals involved in the social behavior of all species, humans included. At the broadest level the synthesis would ideally encompass the total of living forms, not in a hierarchy with us at the top (the current tendency), but in a single vast network of ecological interrelationships.

DEPRIVATION AND REHABILITATION

On the experimental side, one of the most extended series of studies took place in a colony of macaque monkeys established more than a generation ago. Harry Harlow of the University of Wisconsin originally intended "to provide a steady

Love for mother surrogate: (upper left) macaque infant clinging to warm terry-cloth surrogate; (upper right) reaching for milk on bare-wire surrogate; (bottom) using terry-cloth surrogate for protection against strange object

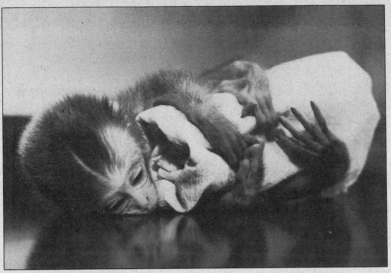

Macaque clinging reflex, prominent during first 2 or 3 weeks of life

Normal maternal behavior: (left) mother protecting infant; abuse of infant: (right) pathological maternal behavior of females reared without mothers

supply of healthy newborn monkeys for the intensive study of learning and intellectual development from the day of birth until the attainment of full capacities." But the animals never became progenitors of a brave new laboratory breed. Taken from their mothers 6 to 12 hours after birth and treated with as much care as human infants, they weighed 25 percent more than mother-reared infants and had a lower death rate.

By the end of their first year, however, all was obviously not well. The monkeys were physically fit but emotionally crippled. They sat motionless in their cages, staring into space or rocking, sometimes for hours at a time. Some individuals would start biting themselves as soon as they saw a human being approaching. Also, they were sexually incompetent. One male was aroused when put in a cage with an experienced estrus female who had grown up in the wild. He tried several times to mount her, but did not know how and finally gave up trying and began to attack her viciously. Females raised alone behaved similarly with experienced males.

Harlow and his associates, having unwittingly provided striking examples of the importance of the mother-infant bond, proceeded to investigate the elements of this basic relationship. They made use of mother surrogates—that is, effigies or dummies built to serve some of the functions of real mothers. In one test infants were brought up in cages containing two wooden-headed dummies, one made of bare wire and the other covered with terry cloth. When bottles of milk were strapped to both dummies, infants invariably went to the terry-cloth

Surrogate mother: English sheep dog "adopts" deprived rhesus monkey

Caged chimpanzee: vacant "1000-mile" stare

dummy. Even when milk was available from the wire dummy only they spent less than an hour a day there and 17 to 18 hours a day with the terry-cloth model. Softness and warmth were apparently far more important than food in determining the strength of an infant's early attachment to a mother figure.

Under certain conditions, strong attachments may be formed with nonprimate mothers. William Mason of the University of California in Davis reared rhesus infants for 1 to 10 months, first with their mothers or other infants or cloth surrogates, and then separated from these familiar figures. The deprived infants quickly learned to accept gentle female dogs as substitute mothers.

Unsurprisingly, the shock of deprivation leaves permanent marks. Individuals who grow up with surrogate mothers are practically as pathological as individuals reared in complete isolation. The few isolated females who eventually became pregnant, because of the persistence of males rather than their own initiative, showed no trace of affection toward their infants. They were indifferent and rejecting at best; at worst they attacked and killed their infants. What seems surprising, however, is that some of these females gave birth to a second infant and performed far more adequately as mothers the second time around. That a female can live through extreme deprivation and still be able to modify her behavior significantly indicates how strongly she is predisposed to function as a mother.

The ability to bounce back, to make up at least partially for early trauma, is demonstrated in studies by Linda Koebner of the New York Zoological Society and Tony Pfeiffer of the College of the Mainland in Texas City. They worked

Released chimpanzees: laughing together

Released chimpanzees: a dominant male asserts himself

with sick animals—chimpanzees originally used in medical research and then confined for extended periods in telephone-booth cages, a form of monotony-torture that produced stereotyped rocking behavior and other inevitable symptoms of severe mental disturbance. After being released on a small island in a Florida game park with some living space and in the company of other chimpanzees, however, the animals made incomplete but strikingly effective recoveries, behaving in many respects as they would have behaved in their native forests. Such studies are of special interest in a human context. They suggest that the impact of early deprivation, even the earliest and most severe deprivation, can be appreciably reduced, a view which runs counter to the views of some psychoanalysts.

EXPERIMENTS IN BEHAVIOR

Aspects of mother-infant relationships observed or hinted at in the wild may be investigated under controlled laboratory conditions. For example, a year-long study which bears on reports of competition among wild mothers has been conducted by Robert Hinde and his associates at the Sub-Department of Animal

Behaviour at Cambridge University, England. The study included four "isolate" pairs of rhesus monkeys, four mother-infant pairs living alone in large outdoor cages—and, as controls, nine mother-infant pairs, each living in a troop consisting of a male and three or four other mother-infant pairs.

Troop mothers tended to be restrictive, much more so than isolate mothers. They maintained physical contact with their offspring a greater proportion of the time and, when contact was broken, reestablished it sooner. Remember, this occurred in the absence of dangers encountered in natural woodland and savanna environments, notably in the absence of predators. In other words, there are dangers as well as advantages to group living, a problem to be discussed later in this chapter.

Further tests revealed an interesting asymmetry involving short-term separations of mothers and infants. It makes a big difference who is removed from home base and who is left behind. An infant left for 6 days without mother responds to her return with such signs of anxiety as frantic clinging, repeated distress calls, and temper tantrums, all of which tended to subside rapidly. But one response proved an exception to the rule: a fear of strangeness or novelty— for example, a room containing mirrors and other unfamiliar objects.

Infants exhibited this fear more than 2 years after their mothers' 6-day absence, and after living continuously with their mothers ever since. They were especially wary of strange objects such as a big ball or Hinde himself dressed in mask and black robe. It was expected that removing infants from their home cages for 6 days would prove even more traumatic, but leaving mother behind had just the opposite effect. The isolated infants were far less disturbed upon their return home, chiefly as a result of the fact that they had to deal with far less disturbed mothers. Mothers may be better adapted to separation than offspring, perhaps reflecting high infant death rates in the wild.

Another study with evolutionary implications concerns the emergence of self-recognition. Gordon Gallup of the State University of New York in Albany put full-length mirrors just outside the cages of four chimpanzees, two males and two females born in the wild, and observed their reactions. At first the image in the mirror was an alien thing, an object inspiring curiosity and fear, something to be bobbed and lunged at. (This mixed response was reminiscent of that exhibited by wild Congo chimpanzees confronted with a photograph of a chimpanzee in color and slightly larger than life.) After 2 days, however, the four apes clearly began to realize that they were looking at themselves. They were soon making use of the mirrors for such activities as picking their teeth, and, most interesting, they promptly noticed red marks that had been dyed on their eyebrows and ears under anesthesia. In other words, they noticed changes in their image and responded by touching the marks repeatedly.

Such behavior contrasts dramatically with the behavior of monkeys, who were similarly confronted with full-length mirrors for 3 weeks and at no time indicated that they connected the image with themselves. Gallup's research demonstrates that awareness of self is a sign of superior intelligence and advanced brain structure among higher primates. It has implications beyond that. Self-awareness must have developed further during the course of human evolution from the first hominids to early *Homo sapiens,* which raises the question of what new quality of self-awareness came with the appearance of modern humans within the past 50,000 years and with the first evidence of personal adornment and art. Perhaps it was a new kind of power, the realization that one can somehow change the order of things by changing one's image deliberately and by creating images and symbols outside oneself.

Apes may well have image-making capacities which are hardly called on in their normal lives, but which might be more fully developed in appropriately designed experimental environments and social structures. The same thing goes for tool making. Chimpanzees could probably make tools far more sophisticated than termite probes and hammerstones if they had sufficient reason to do so, at least judging by the accomplishments of a 5-year-old orangutan named Abang, a resident at the Bristol Zoo in England. Abang learned to make and use stone tools, his incentive being to have company and to please his teacher, Richard Wright of the University of Sydney, who was visiting England at the time.

In the first stage of the experiment Wright brought two items into the orang's cage, a smash-proof box of fruit, which could be opened only by cutting a tough nylon string, and a sharp flint flake, which was put on the floor next to the box. Abang put his heart into the game, trying everything from biting and tugging at the string to breaking the box and forcing the lid. At one point, he stopped and turned to Wright with an appealing what-do-I-do-now look on his face. Following several demonstrations of the flake being moved back and forth across the string, Abang got the idea—and had his first success after 69 minutes of training. From then on he had mastered the trick, performing it 15 to 20 times in a row.

The next stage involved the same setup, except that instead of a flake Wright put a large chunk of flint and a 3-pound hammerstone into the cage. It was up to Abang to make a cutting implement for himself by bashing the flint

Abang the toolmaker: (left) before knocking off flake; (middle) examining flake; (right) eating fruit from opened box

with the hammerstone and knocking off a suitable flake, a more difficult problem than learning to use a ready-made flake. After watching more demonstrations and tossing the hammerstone away at one point (his only sign of impatience), he took 134 minutes to learn the task; the total training period was about three and a third hours. Later for the benefit of British television he did it all over again in about 15 minutes.

WHEN ALTRUISM PAYS OFF

Such investigations provide a fuller picture of primate potentialities, the primate matrix out of which humans emerged. Further insight comes from research which has expanded rapidly during the past 5 years, and which involves an apparent paradox or contradiction in evolutionary theory. In its purest form, the theory is ego-centered in the sense that it focuses on the individual first and above all else, the assumption being that individuals act strictly out of self-interest. If so, the problem is how to account for altruism, risking or sacrificing one's life to save the lives of others.

Imagine baboons moving through their home range and suddenly coming across predators, as in the case of the troop that confronted two cheetahs on an African savanna (see Chapter 12). On occasions of this sort, one of the lead baboons may give a warning signal, an alarm bark, which alerts the other members of the troop, and also draws the predators' attention to himself. Or take another example from Chapter 12, the male baboon who picks up an infant, presumably to protect it from an angry and higher-ranking male. In all such cases altruists appreciably increase their chances of being killed and, according to theory, that should be enough to weed them out of all populations in the long run.

The paradox has been resolved by William Hamilton of the University of Michigan, who departed from the notion of strict self-interest and substituted the notion that individuals always act in the interest of their genes. Generally, as in the case of a one-to-one confrontation with a predator, that means saving oneself. But if there are others around, and if they are blood relatives, as often happens, then one's own death may pay off in terms of genes preserved and passed on to future generations. Known as kin selection, this is the same principle embodied in the following Arab proverb: "I against my brother; I and my brother against my cousin; I and my brother and my cousin against the world"—which, freely translated, means "me first, and after that my relatives in order of closeness."

According to the assumptions of sociobiology, which Edward Wilson of Harvard has defined as "the systematic study of the biological basis of all social behavior," there is a calculus of altruism, a calculus based on kinship. It predicts that a primate, or any other animal, will be more likely to defend or cooperate with an individual with which it shares half its genes (brother, sister, parent, offspring) than with one sharing only a quarter of its genes (uncle, aunt, nephew, niece, grandparent), and that it will favor quarter-gene relatives over those sharing an eighth of its genes (first cousins, great-grandchildren).

Sociobiology has stimulated a great deal of new research and interpretations of behavior that might otherwise make little sense. Again, we have examples from Chapter 12, in the possibility that the baboon males observed by Barbara Smuts in Africa's Rift Valley may be protecting their female companions in the interests of future preferential matings and the preservation of their genes. In other words, the role of protector is self-centered, or rather gene-centered, but at the same time of benefit to the troop as a whole, serving to increase the odds that infants and the species will survive. Evolution selects those "selfish" behavior patterns which also happen to promote the interests of the group.

On the darker side, consider the adult males who switch from one troop to another and kill infants sired by other males, an act observed on rare occasions among langurs, macaques, baboons, and chimpanzees. Some investigators believe this is an artifact, a byproduct of overcrowding, occurring among troops forced by the existence of nearby human settlements to live in severely restricted home ranges—a situation which always results in increased violence.

Other investigators see infanticide by newcomers in sociobiological terms, as the adult males' effort to wipe the genetic slate clean, to eliminate all but their own offspring, their own genes. From this standpoint, it is an example of me-first behavior that, if not counteracted by other forces, would work against the survival of the species. In any case, Sarah Hrdy comments that such infanticide is "probably the most extreme cost females pay for having males around."

Genetic payoff may also account for the finding that a mother's social position, her standing in the female hierarchy, can influence the sex of her offspring. The pattern has been observed among wild baboons and captive macaques and, most recently, among captive rhesus monkeys by Anne and Michael Simpson of the Sub-Department of Animal Behaviour. They report that between 1960 and 1981 high-ranking mothers gave birth to 53 infants, 38 of them daughters; low-ranking mothers had 86 offspring, including 54 sons.

One explanation depends on the following facts: (1) an offspring tends to inherit its mother's status; and (2) the females of these species tend to remain with their mothers and with their native troops for life, while the males generally wander off and join other troops. So it pays a high-ranking mother to have a daughter around to help in interfamily fights and preserve the family line, rather than a son who will eventually join another troop where he will not necessarily enjoy high status and be a successful breeder. On the other hand, it pays a low-ranking mother to have sons. Like daughters, they also inherit her undesirable status in the troop, with a significant difference. They move on to other troops where they have a fighting chance to improve their positions.

A big problem remains unsolved, however. What mechanism could possibly account for the effect of social rank on sex of offspring? A number of investigators refused to accept early reports, because they were unable to conceive of a plausible explanation, but John Hartung of the State University of New York has come up with some interesting suggestions. The chemistry of a high-ranking female might be different from that of a low-ranking female. For example she might have higher blood levels of the sex hormone testosterone, and that, in turn, might trigger a process more lethal to sperm bearing the Y, or male-determining, chromosome than to X, or female-determining sperm. (We know that the death rate among sperm is high, so that only a small fraction of the hundreds of millions in a single ejaculation ever reach the egg.)

COMPETITION—FEMALES FOR FOOD, MALES FOR FEMALES

Competition exists everywhere at all biological levels, among sperm en route to ova as well as among individuals acting on me-first principles and among troops. Indeed, Richard Wrangham emphasizes that competition within primate sexes may be the driving force in social evolution. He suggests that the female's primary concern when it comes to reproductive success is food, while the male's primary concern is females. So the key element, the factor upon which everything else depends, is the conflict of female against female for food to nourish herself and her offspring and the resulting distribution of females.

Compromise is the rule for social primates, as for all species. Groups of females, "female-bonded gangs," form when food is so distributed that the advantages of communal feeding outweigh the advantages of foraging alone. One favorable situation involves the existence of large patches of high-quality foods such as fruit which can be monopolized by larger gangs against smaller gangs. Furthermore, in times of scarcity there must be sufficiently large patches of low-quality foods such as leaves to support the larger gangs.

This is a common female subsistence strategy. It is a territorial strategy, and males must adapt accordingly. It seems that females in gangs can act effectively to minimize the disrupting harassment of competing males. At least that is one possible explanation for Wrangham's observation that territorial primates tend to consist of female-bonded gangs with a single male, while nonterritorial species tend to be organized in multimale troops. Note that the single-male group can be regarded as a "harem," although the term is rather misleading. "Harem" implies a group of submissive females under the domination of an all-powerful male, while the actual case among nonhuman primates is that the females in effect permit only one male in their midst, while other males must seek mates in other troops.

There are some interesting exceptions, however, including chimpanzees and by inference perhaps our earliest ancestors. Chimpanzees prefer a diet of ripe fruits, which are generally distributed in small and widely scattered patches rather than over larger areas. Since competition may be intense under such concentrated feeding conditions, females have less reason to form stable gangs and do most of their foraging alone or with dependent offspring only. In this case, it pays males to form gangs. The advantages of seeking mates alone are outweighed by the advantages of cooperating to control a territory which includes as many females as possible, and it is the females who switch most frequently from one troop to another.

If the first hominids descended from a chimpanzee-like ape, as many investigators believe, their societies may also have consisted originally of emigrating females and a core hierarchy of "resident" males, at least in the beginning. This raises the possibility of a significant shift in the structure of early hominid society as the result of the shift from exclusive forest dwelling to a life spent mainly in open woodlands and savannas (see Chapter 2). The change involved an increased amount of meat eating and meat sharing as well as an increased danger from predators, both of which may have swung things, if not toward the more common primate pattern of stable female hierarchy and emigrating males, then and more likely toward a "harem" group made up of a single male and several females.

Another line of argument points to a harem system. In a promiscuous troop with a number of males competing on a free-for-all basis for access to females, males are considerably larger and heavier than females, a feature noted by Darwin and others more than a century ago. Competing males also tend to have large canines serving as effective weapons and, according to a recent study by Roger Short of the University of Edinburgh, heavy testicles favoring frequent ejaculations with large numbers of sperm.

At the other end of the scale, competition is at a minimum in monogamous troops (about 20 percent of primate species are monogamous), where males tend to be about the same size as females and have small canines and small testicles. Promiscuous chimpanzees have testicles about five times heavier in proportion to body weight than the testicles of orangutans, who have a single-male breeding system. We lie between these extremes, much closer to the orangutan. All things considered the male of the human species rates as mildly polygynous or mildly harem-oriented, and our ancestors may have had similar mating patterns.

THE WAYS OF PREDATORS

The emphasis on primate studies in efforts to gain a wider perspective on our roots has sound reasons, the most obvious being that they are our kind, members of the same order. The problem is sufficiently complex, however, to widen research still further. For one thing, we can learn a great deal about ourselves from nonprimate species, notably from other predators. Of all predators none comes closer to our ideals of cooperation than the wild dog, which has been studied by many investigators including George Schaller, Richard Estes, and Wolfdietrich Kühme of the Max Planck Institute for the Physiology of Behavior near Munich, Germany.

Kühme spent more than three months studying a pack of wild dogs on the Serengeti Plain, the general area which includes the Olduvai Gorge. The pack consisted of 23 individuals, 6 adult males and 2 females, one with a litter of 4 and one with 11 newborn pups, all living together in a borrowed den, one of the numerous vacant burrows dug by aardvarks, wart hogs, and hyenas. The females nursed and cared for all 15 offspring on a first-come, first-served basis. They often competed for the privilege, even to the point of trying to steal one another's pups, a tactic which produced the only friction in the pack, mild bickering in the form of growls and snapping. Males were never seen fighting; there are no hierarchies among wild dogs.

Both sexes performed guard duty, usually the same individuals taking on the job of remaining with the young while the rest of the pack hunted. In other words, unlike nonhuman primates, the wild dogs had a home base where the very young and their guardians stayed while the rest of the pack hunted. When the hunters returned with pieces of unchewed meat in their stomachs, pups and guardians met them with a characteristic begging gesture, the beggar pushing its nose against the hunter's mouth or biting at the lips or jowls. The meat was then disgorged, and every pack member received its allotted portion.

Regular food sharing, a basic element in the pack's way of life, is unknown among nonhuman primates, as is regular communal hunting and division of labor in gathering food. However, as indicated in Chapter 13, a form of sharing has been observed among baboons, and chimpanzees share frequently. This is something which could be built upon and extended, given the proper set of circumstances. But human beings remain the only primates to go in for sharing and meat eating habitually and, whenever possible, on a relatively large scale.

Hunting in groups is another highly developed form of cooperation found among wild dogs and other carnivores. Estes used a Land Rover to follow a pack in the crater of Ngorongoro, the volcano on the way to Olduvai which collapsed sometime during the past three million years. Some 25,000 herd animals and their predators live on the 104-square-mile crater floor, an open plain providing ideal observing conditions. The investigator obtained most of his information during the predators' two regular hunting periods, which last about an hour or two and begin early in the morning shortly before sunrise and in the late afternoon.

During the stalking phase of the hunt, wild dogs move with shoulders hunched, ears flattened, and hind legs in ready-to-spring position, like a runner at the starting block. The objective is to get within 300 yards or so of a grazing herd, usually gazelles, before breaking into a run and stampeding the prey. The leader of the pack selects a victim from the fleeing herd, perhaps one of the slower individuals; one or two adult dogs follow at intervals of about a hundred yards, and the other members of the pack run behind at distances of as much as a mile.

Hunting strategies are simple and effective. Dogs running immediately behind the leader are ready to cut off the prey as it attempts to dodge, but as a rule by the time it starts dodging it is too tired to get away. At the end of the chase the victim is usually so exhausted and in such a deep state of shock that it does not fight back. Estes describes a large female antelope which "did little more than stand with head high while the dogs cut it to ribbons, looking less the victim than the witness of its own execution."

About 85 percent of all chases end successfully, that is, from the pack's point of view—not surprising in view of the fact that a wild dog can attain top speeds of more than 40 miles an hour, and run at an average speed of 30 miles an hour for several miles. Most chases last only about 3 to 5 minutes and cover a mile or two. Schaller has found that when game is plentiful, hunting packs on the Serengeti Plain kill enough animals to provide about 20 pounds of meat per dog daily, at least four times more than is needed.

Wild dogs have developed some amazing rituals. A typical prelude to the hunt might find them lolling about in the grass. One restless dog will begin romping with a few of its pack mates. Soon others join in, and gradually the play and the chasing build up into a wilder and wilder climax, with the entire pack milling around in a circle and emitting, in unison, peculiar bird-like twittering calls

Wild dog devouring young antelope

signifying a high degree of excitement. The procedure, which has been compared to a pep rally, brings the pack to a fever pitch for the hunt.

Kühme notes the existence of another ritual which serves to prevent violence within the pack. Adults forestall aggression by habitually assuming postures of humility toward one another when greeting or soliciting food. Again, it is a kind of acting. An adult male may pretend to be young and use the same begging gesture infants and juveniles use, pushing its nose against the mouth of another adult. At other times, adults behave like nursing pups, males licking the udders of females and females creeping under males as if seeking an udder. Such rituals achieve a "tolerance of competitors, which human beings find so difficult."

Research on wolves, hyenas, jackals, and wild dogs is providing a richer background of knowledge against which to view human behavior. The abandonment of stereotyped notions about other social carnivores may prepare humans to see themselves more clearly. For example, although hyenas have been too readily dismissed as uncourageous scavengers, the fact of the matter is that they function as effective hunters upon occasion. In early prehistoric times, hyenas probably preyed on savanna apes and prehumans at least as much as did lions and other big cats. As far as character is concerned, they display a rather subtle combination of shyness, persistence, and incredible gall.

A solitary hyena during the day is relatively harmless, and perhaps the animal's reputation as skulking coward is based on the behavior of such loners. But there is nothing more lethal than a pack of 20 or so hyenas at night. A lion will move away from its kill at the attack of a hyena pack, snarling but making no serious attempt to fight for its meat. Schaller once saw a pack that had worked itself into a state of excited aggression and was mobbing a large male lion. Under these circumstances the lion was anything but a king of beasts. It was plainly terrified.

The hyena is a superb waiter. According to Estes, "it will lie all day near an ostrich nest, anticipating the time when the eggs may be left momentarily unguarded . . . and cripples may be followed for days until too weak to resist." He also observed hyenas waiting hours for a pack of wild dogs to begin hunting, often crawling to within a few yards of the pack and staring almost purposefully at the dogs "as though urging them to get started." Furthermore, like jackals, lions, the Gonds of India, and other tribes (and perhaps like early hominids; see Chapter 6), hyenas scan the skies for circling vultures and dash to the spot to share in the carcass.

Parallels exist between the evolution of canids, members of the dog family, and primates. As related species evolve increasingly complex social systems, they require increasingly complex signals to establish and maintain individual relationships within the group. In other words, there is selective pressure for more sophisticated communication, and one result may be an increase in the mobility of the face and the number of possible expressions, a phenomenon being studied by Michael Fox of the Institute for the Study of Animal Problems in Washington, D.C.

He points out that wolves, highly social animals with a system of cooperative hunting and sharing at least as elaborate as that of the wild dog, exhibit a far greater variety of facial expressions than canids such as the red fox, which does not live in packs and tends to be a loner when it comes to hunting. Similar tendencies have been observed among primates; as a matter of fact, social canids and social primates share a number of basic expressions signifying a playful mood (the so-called play face), threats, submissiveness, and so on.

The behavior of the big cats is also of interest, and Schaller has spent a good deal of time among them, most recently during a three-year study of lions and other predators on the Serengeti Plain. His records show the advantage of hunting in groups. A lion alone, stalking its prey, lifting and placing each paw separately as it advances, and selecting a moment to rush from its hiding place, has a batting average of about 0.150, or a success rate of one kill in every six or seven attempts—considerably better than a one-in-twelve estimate for tigers, who always hunt alone.

On the average, a hunting group of from two to four or five lions is about twice as successful. As indicated in Chapter 6, lions use elaborate encircling tactics, but when a herd panics, they may simply move forward in an irregular line along a broad front and dash in for the kill. Sometimes, in the confusion, animals rush directly into the jaws of their predators. From the prey's point of view as well as from the predator's, there is an advantage in being a member of a group, provided the group is not too large. A zebra is far more vulnerable alone than in a herd, if the herd has no more than 75 individuals; but as herd size increases much beyond that level, so does inertia. It may take longer to get moving, flight is inhibited, and the success of a killer rises correspondingly.

Lions, like most carnivores, conserve their energies and do not bother to kill if they can get meat in some other way. On the open savanna, they do more scavenging than hyenas; about half their food comes from moving in and taking the kills of cheetahs and other predators. When lions are not hunting or scavenging, they do nothing in particular, spending about 20 hours a day lying down generally asleep. Incidentally, wild dogs spend even more of their time doing nothing, probably because their success rate in killing is so high; they lie down about 22 hours a day.

As a general rule, different species of predators tend not to get along with one another. Lions have been known to chase and kill leopards, cheetahs, and hyenas; leopards may kill cheetahs; hyenas may attack cheetahs and jackals; jackals may eat foxes. Furthermore, there may be within-the-species killing and cannibalism. Tigers may prey on tigers, lions on lions, and so on. Peace does not seem to prevail among carnivores. Such behavior contrasts with the behavior of antelopes, zebras, and other plant-eating herd animals, which normally live side by side without trouble; and the same thing is true within troops of nonhuman primates.

SEARCHING FOR PATTERNS

Basic patterns are found not only in primates and their predators but throughout the class of mammals. Alarm calls, for example, have been documented among ground squirrels living in a high 20-acre Sierra Nevada meadow. The warning call, a sharp staccato cry, is emitted at the approach of weasels and coyotes—and only by females, males having deserted the home burrow after mating. Paul Sherman of Cornell University has found that females with close relatives nearby (mothers, daughters, sisters) sound the alarm sooner and more often than females without close relatives.

Squirrels probably recognize these relatives on the basis of smell or sight signals imprinted in their memories at an early age. But the scope of their memories is limited. They do not recognize more distant relatives, cousins and nieces and granddaughters, a limitation which clearly restricts the complexity of the societies they can form. Presumably primates and other higher mammals are aware of more extensive kinship ties, although that remains to be demonstrated in controlled studies.

Also widespread among mammals is the incest taboo or, more precisely, incest avoidance, since the word "taboo" implies the deliberate imposition of rules. According to Norbert Bischof of the California Institute of Technology, the notion that mammals commonly commit incest is "a die-hard fable": "In the whole animal kingdom with very few exceptions no species is known in which under natural conditions inbreeding occurs to any considerable degree." He emphasizes that sex evolved as a way of achieving genetic diversity, of producing offspring with mixed and varied hereditary traits; that this effectively ensures species against sudden extinction in environments that vary continually and unpredictably; and that extensive inbreeding would run counter to this principle. Incest taboos among human beings serve to reinforce what evolution and biology favor in the interests of survival.

The search for patterns involving mammals in general has yielded important insights into the most striking feature of human evolution, the expansion of the brain. A big brain is always an advantage in the survival of the individual, and every species has the biggest brain it can afford for its size—that is, the biggest brain the female of the species can produce. A major limiting factor is her metabolic rate, how fast her body can move food through the gut and break it down into energy available to her unborn child. It turns out that animals with high metabolic rates have large brains, brains large in relation to their body size.

Robert Martin discovered this relationship recently in a study of relative brain sizes among 309 mammalian species, and explored some of its implications. One implication is that animals which concentrate on high-energy foods such as fruits would have larger relative brain sizes than those subsisting mainly on insects, leaves, and other low-energy foods. This appears to be the case for bats, fruit-eating species having larger brains and higher metabolic rates than insect-eating species. Capuchin monkeys, which are closer to us than chimpanzees with respect to relative brain size, go after moth larvae, palm nuts (which they bang against trees to open), and other rich dietary items. We do not know whether they have a high metabolic rate, but Martin's bet is that they do.

If today's chimpanzees are any indication, our prehominid and early hominid ancestors also preferred fruits and ranked high on the metabolic scale. Furthermore, they must originally have had access to plenty of fruit, a deduction based on the fact that the future of the species was invested chiefly in single, one-at-a-time births rather than large litters; this strategy demands abundance, a stable and dependable supply of high-energy food. Such conditions are typical of tropical and semitropical forests, but not of drier, grassy savannas, at least not unless a species goes after new foods with the aid of new techniques.

Many investigators believe our ancestors adapted to savanna living 5 or more million years ago. Martin believes it took longer than that. He suggests that reliance on forests and forest foods may have lasted until about 2 million years ago, when the first members of the genus *Homo* appeared, "the first hominid to show accelerated brain expansion." He also suggests that the problem of nourishing single, big-brained fetuses was ultimately solved by transforming the savanna culturally from an unreliable to a reliable source of rich food. Perhaps people were going after buried energy-rich tubers with digging sticks, and beginning to supplement diets which had hitherto consisted primarily of plants with appreciable quantities of energy-rich meat.

The continuing objective is to learn more about evolution and adaptation in the broadest sense, about "the biological basis of all social behavior." The underlying fact is the me-first principle, as individuals exhibit strategies calculated to pass their own genes on to succeeding generations. And yet societies exist. Moreover, the future belongs to the human species as far as the development of increasingly complex societies is concerned (assuming, of course, that we survive our own complexities).

Representatives of new mammalian orders, newcomers engaged in making places for themselves in a world of established species, often live dispersed, solitary lives ideal for maximum inconspicuousness. The ancestors of all existing mammals, at large in wildernesses some 200 million years ago, were probably nocturnal loners (see Chapter 1). So were the ancestors of highly organized insect societies. Judging by fossil specimens trapped in New Jersey amber, the present-day array of 8000 to 12,000 ant species descended 100 million years ago from solitary wasps.

New nonhuman societies may be evolving before our eyes today. For example, we think of the spider as a solitary creature, waiting alone and motionless in its web, ready to scurry across its gossamer net to entangled victims. But one Mexican species which weaves "a three-dimensional space web and catching spiral" exists at an in-between stage. Its members tend to be solitary when insect food is scarce, notably in desert settings. But they come together in aggregations of 5 to 150 individuals, with the largest groups occurring in moist tropical terrain where insects are abundant, and they build and maintain "a mass of interconnected webbing," a great communal web. Again, it is a matter of payoffs. A large web is so efficient in trapping insects that its advantages outweigh those of me-first, solitary predation. On the other hand, these gregarious spiders have not evolved to the stage where they share food and develop hierarchies—not yet.

The hierarchy is a common form of social organization. It probably evolved time after time in many extinct species, and it works now for a variety of species, from crickets and lobsters and whales to *Homo sapiens sapiens*. So we have a picture of millions of species in a kind of superweb of interrelationships, each occupying its niche in the scheme of things, each competing for living space— and each exerting a continual pressure to expand beyond its present niche, a force counteracted by the same pressure in all other species. One species, namely ourselves, seems to be in the process of breaking loose from these restrictions by moving increasingly into low-population territories, including outer space.

SUMMARY

Behavior observed in the wild can be investigated further under controlled laboratory conditions. Dummy or surrogate mothers made of wire and cloth have been used to explore the nature of the mother-infant bond, and the ability of primates, including perhaps humans, to compensate at least partially for the effects of early deprivation. Other experiments suggest that a new kind of self-awareness may have evolved in the ape line, since chimpanzees can—but monkeys cannot—recognize themselves in mirrors. Also, although apes have never been observed making stone tools in the wild, at least one captive ape, an orangutan, has learned the trick.

Sociobiology, "the systematic study of the biological basis of all social behavior," has stimulated considerable research. It emphasizes an apparent paradox in evolutionary theory—namely, how individuals acting predominantly out of self-interest, or self-preservation, can upon occasion become altruists, risking their lives to save the lives of others. The paradox can be resolved by assuming that individuals act not to preserve themselves but to preserve their genes, passing their hereditary characteristics on to future generations.

This principle, known as "kin selection," has been used in explaining why male primates protect their female companions, and why they may kill infants sired by other males. Kin selection helps account for the intriguing observation that baboon mothers ranking high in the female hierarchy tend to have more daughters than sons, while low-ranking mothers tend to have more sons. The competition of females against females for food, and of males against males for females, can also be interpreted in terms of kin selection—and suggests that early hominids may have lived in mildly harem-oriented societies.

A broader perspective on hominid evolution comes from studies of nonprimates as well as primates, and especially from studies of predators. Among wild dogs, hyenas, wolves, and lions we can see a variety of adaptations—guarding of the young in home-base dens, stalking tactics and the selection of vulnerable individuals in a herd, and, above all, the importance of cooperative hunting and communication.

There are principles that apply still more widely. Incest avoidance, for instance, is observed throughout the animal kingdom, since mating beyond one's blood relatives preserves genetic diversity in the interests of long-term survival. A survey of more than 300 mammalian species suggests a new relationship between diet and large brains.

chapter 15

Contemporary Hunter-Gatherers

Many flashes or episodes of behavior reminiscent of human behavior occur in the daily lives of monkeys and apes. We see ourselves in the baboon, top-ranking member of the hierarchy—in the male as he scans the horizon for danger, hesitates, and finally leads his troop across a stretch of savanna; in the mother-infant pair surrounded by solicitous females; in the rough-and-tumble play of male juveniles. We see ourselves in the chimpanzee with a mischievous twinkle in his eyes, scratching his head in perplexity or laughing out loud at a bewildered playmate. Such similarities reflect the fact of continuity in human evolution, the existence of patterns which humans and their ancestors share with lower primates.

If ancestral hominids still roamed river valleys, savannas, and coastal plains, bands like those whose traces are found at the Olduvai Gorge or at Terra Amata, investigators could obtain firsthand records of early hunting methods and social organizations. In the absence of such bands, however, we ourselves can serve as subjects for research in living prehistory. We provide a legitimate source of clues to the nature of prehistoric people. Much of what we do and think today is conditioned by what our ancestors did and thought long ago, when they were half wild and all the world was a wilderness. Investigators expect to learn more about how human beings behaved in the past from studies of contemporary human behavior.

Much can be learned from contemporary hunter-gatherers, people who live on wild plants and wild animals. They are by no means relics of the Stone Age. Like the rest of us, they have been adapting for millenniums and they are still

World Distribution of Hunter-Gatherers

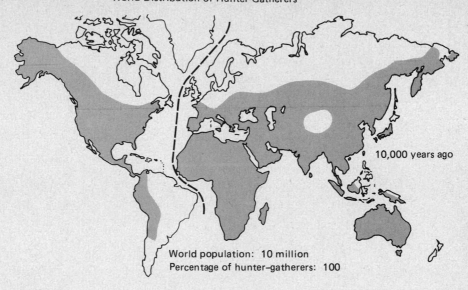

10,000 years ago

World population: 10 million
Percentage of hunter-gatherers: 100

Known Living Sites of Contemporary Hunter-Gatherers

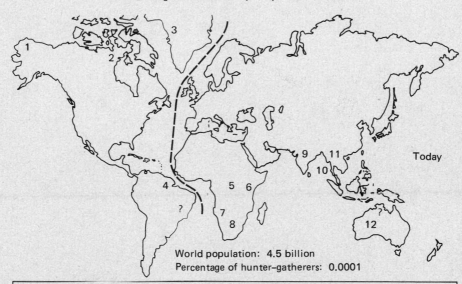

Today

World population: 4.5 billion
Percentage of hunter-gatherers: 0.0001

1. Eskimos; Alaska	8. Kalahari Bushmen; South Africa, Botswana
2. Eskimos; Northwest Territory	9. Birhar; Central India
3. Eskimos; Greenland	10. Andaman Islanders; Andaman Island
4. Akuri; Surinam	11. Mrabri; Thailand
5. Pygmies; Congo	12. Australian Aborigines; Australia
6. Ariangulo; Tanzania	13. Tasadays; Philippines
Boni; Tanzania	14. Sevnany; Malaya
Sanye; Tanzania	15. Kubu; Sumatra
7. Koroka; Angola	16. Panan; Borneo
Bantu; Angola	

Some living areas of contemporary or recent hunter-gatherers

trying to adapt, although the dice are loaded against them. On the other hand, of all existing societies theirs is closest to a way of life that prevailed for most of human prehistory, the simplest and most stable life style yet evolved. They are vanishing rapidly. Some 10,000 years ago, when Magdalenian times were coming to an end in western Europe, there were an estimated 10 million people in the world, all of them hunter-gatherers. According to a 1966 estimate, the number had dwindled to about 30,000 by then in a world total of 3.3 billion; today, in a population of about 4.5 billion, their numbers have dwindled further to perhaps 5000 or so.

The past treatment of hunter-gatherers and other tribal societies marks a low point in colonial history. As mentioned earlier, a common notion was that such people belonged to subhuman breeds, occupying "at best a middling position among the species," somewhere between apes and humans but rather closer to apes as far as mentality and morals are concerned. In the name of this belief, they were widely dispossessed, enslaved, hunted, raped, slaughtered, fed poisoned food, and otherwise exploited.

LIVING AMONG ABORIGINES

The classic case of this viewpoint in action involved the wiping out during the last century of 3000 to 5000 aborigines living on the Australian island of Tasmania. Rhys Jones of the Australian National University in Canberra comments on the process: "The fate of the Tasmanians constitutes one of the few examples in written history where an entire people has become totally extinct. . . . It is the example *par excellence* of genocide. . . . Savage and barbarian met face to face, and the savage died."

A later and somewhat more enlightened attitude, but one based on the same belief, was that they should be preserved together with other forms of wildlife as "living fossils" or lower species that never attained the evolutionary status of modern people. The report of a scientific expedition to central Australia in 1894 indicated the prevailing bias of the times toward members of all primitive societies, a bias found not only among the lay public but also among specialists.

In appearance [the Australian aborigine] is a naked, hirsute savage, with a type of features occasionally pronounced Jewish. He is by nature lighthearted, merry and prone to laughter, a splendid mimic, supple-jointed, with an unerring hand that works in perfect unison with his eye, which is as keen as that of an eagle. He has never been known to wash. He has no private ownership of land, except as regards that which is not overcarefully concealed about his person. . . .

Religious belief he has none, but is excessively superstitious. . . . He has no gratitude except that of the anticipatory order, and is as treacherous as Judas. He has no traditions, and yet continues to practice with scrupulous exactness a number of hideous customs and ceremonies which have been handed down from his fathers, and of the origin or reason of which he knows nothing. . . .

After an experience of many years I say without hesitation that he is absolutely untamable. . . . Verily his moods are as eccentric as the flight of his own boomerang. Thanks to the untiring efforts of the missionary and the stockman, he is being rapidly "civilized" off the face of the earth, and in another hundred years the sole remaining evidence of his existence will be the fragments of flint which he has fashioned so rudely.

Today's attitudes are generally more in keeping with times that have seen the undermining of white supremacy and the passing of an empire upon which the sun never set. Anthropologists make a special point of recognizing all extant hunter-gatherers as members of the club of *Homo sapiens sapiens*. They are people living exactly as we would be living if we had adapted to the same conditions. Their societies are much simpler than ours, but sufficiently complicated to warrant years, even decades, of investigation. (At that, we would still know only a fraction of what they knew.)

Among those involved in long-term studies is Richard Gould of Brown University. In March 1966, at a native reserve on the southwest fringe of the Gibson Desert in western Australia, he met an unusual two-family group of 13 aborigines (3 women, 2 men, and 8 children ranging in age from about 4 to 15). They were among the very few people in the world still making and using stone tools on a regular basis. A lost colony, one of the last remaining pockets of hunting-gathering existence in the twentieth century, entered the modern world from an isolation so complete that it had met its first white person only a few months before.

The aborigines soon had enough of the present and decided to step back into the past again, heading on foot for their homeland 155 miles away in the heart of the desert. Gould and his wife, Elizabeth, followed not long afterward in a Land Rover. They lived with this group and others for extended periods during the next 15 months, learning their language, sleeping at their campsites, and walking out with them in search of food.

Gould has returned to the Gibson Desert some half-dozen times since that 1966 meeting to renew old acquaintances, follow up earlier observations of individuals and groups, and analyze new records. This continuing investigation is the first of its kind ever undertaken. Trained as an archeologist, Gould made a special point of collecting "living" information of direct interest to archeologists concerned with understanding human traces at prehistoric sites and reconstructing prehistoric behavior. He mapped the distribution of bones and artifacts at sites occupied within the memories of his aborigine friends, excavated ancient sites with them, and consulted them about problems of interpreting living-floor patterns.

THE DAILY GRIND

The desert dictates the course and rhythm of daily activities. One of the world's most unpromising regions for human habitation, Australia's arid interior is 500,000 square miles of sandhills, miles and miles of parallel ridges one after the other which, according to Gould, extend to the horizon "like stationary waves viewed from the shore of a petrified red sea." It is a barren landscape dotted

Yutungka, drinking at clay pan

with scrub acacia trees, white-barked ghost gums, pale green clumps of spiky spinifex grass, occasional cliffs, and rocky outcrops. Summer temperatures may soar above 120 degrees Fahrenheit in the shade and drop below zero on winter evenings.

Water is the crucial resource. The Gibson Desert averages about 8 inches of rain a year, but that is a deceptive statistic. People live and die by actual rains, not averages. More than 40 inches of rain may fall one year and only an inch or two the next, and droughts lasting two or three years are not uncommon. Furthermore, there is no way of telling how any year's quota will be distributed. One territory may be in the throes of drought, while another 50 or 100 miles away flourishes, so that the desert may be a patchwork of localized environments, some bone-dry and others relatively lush.

In the lives of the aborigine families who were the Goulds' hosts, a typical December or January day, the height of the Australian summer, begins in darkness about half an hour before dawn. The people are awakened by nature's alarm clock, the sound of parrots, cockatoos, and half a dozen other birds bursting into song. They join the chorus with yawns, throat-clearings, and exchanges of morning greetings and banter. There is no formal, communal breakfast. During the next hour or so each member of the group eats from a supply of food prepared the night before, usually cakes and loaves of ground-up seeds or fruit.

Work starts at about six or seven, when it is still cool by local standards—that is, when the temperature is below 95 degrees. The group divides into two parties. The women are responsible for the gathering of plant foods and may walk 4 or 5 miles—with long wooden bowls of water balanced on their heads and nursing children carried on their hips or slung over their backs—perhaps to one of the areas containing bushes of ngaru, an abundant pale green fruit about the size of a small tomato. Dogs and children old enough to walk come along too; no one stays behind at the camp.

Meanwhile the two men from the family group go off together to attend to their job of hunting, a less dependable way of obtaining food under desert conditions. In general, they go to a place where they can ambush game instead of tracking and chasing it, especially in the summer heat. Perhaps they make use of a water hole as a kind of trap. They may travel a mile or two to the nearest creek bed, where they scoop out a pit or soak hole exposing a small pool, and then select a spot on the bank overlooking the pit about 15 feet away to build a circular blind or hiding place of bushes (preferably in the shade of a tree). They lie there and wait, ready to hurl their spears at a thirsty emu or, very rarely, a kangaroo or a wallaby.

Yuwi, the hunter

Stalking is done more rarely than waiting in blinds, but if an aborigine sees a possible kill, he loses no time in going after it. "That happened late one evening about twenty minutes before sunset," Gould recalls.

There was not much wind, the landscape was very red from the setting sun, and a kangaroo was browsing about a thousand feet away. One of the hunters started walking directly at it, moving over the sand with the graceful and smooth motion which is second nature to the aborigines as sea legs are to sailors. He kept his eyes fastened to the animal's head and ears, and the instant it started to look up he froze in his tracks, sometimes for 2 or 3 minutes until it looked down again and continued feeding. Then he moved forward again. After about half an hour of stalking he came to within 75 feet of the kangaroo—but missed his prey! He used a rifle, and many Gibson Desert aborigines are still very bad with rifles. He would never have missed with a spear.

Everyone is back at camp by ten-thirty or eleven. By that time the temperature may have risen to 120 degrees, and not even the aborigines go out in that noonday sun. The women return the wooden bowls empty of water and filled with ngaru fruit. The men are usually not as successful. Sometimes they manage

Gibson Desert "still life": a day's catch

to kill a large animal, but on most days they have little to show for their patience, perhaps only a single goanna lizard. Most of the aborigines' diet is made up of plant foods, gathered mainly by women; the meat consists chiefly of lizards, rabbits, snakes, birds, and other small game, also frequently provided by women. According to Gould, "about 90 percent of the time women furnish at least 80 percent of the food."

The midday resting period is devoted to sitting in the shade, taking naps, making tools, gossiping. At three-thirty or thereabouts the women go to another area for a fruit related to ngaru. At this time of year, the fruit is parched and looks something like large raisins. The two fruits provide more than half the aborigines' food during dry summer months. One man decides to try his luck at the blind again; the other considers that to be a waste of time and goes lizard hunting. The people reassemble at camp before dark, in 2 hours or so, and the women prepare food for the evening and the next morning. Fires are built even in the hottest summer nights to keep *mamu,* or night cannibal spirits away. There is much talking, and everyone is asleep by eight-thirty or nine.

ARCHEOLOGY IN THE DESERT

The remarkable adaptation of these people to desert conditions includes a technology that would have been familiar to a toolmaker living 30,000 or more years ago. A distinctive and common tool, the so-called adz flake with a thick and fairly steep edge, looks much like the sort of scrapers archeologists find at prehistoric sites the world over. The edge may be made by removing tiny chips with a hammerstone or a wooden stick or, most unusual of all, with the teeth— a technique first reported by the Spanish explorer Coronado in 1541 among the Great Plains Indians of North America. Evidence for the practice in more remote times exists in the form of tiny chips of quartz found in human coprolites, preserved feces excavated at a prehistoric cave in Utah.

The dental method involves placing the flake in a nutcracker position and nibbling with the side or premolar teeth. It requires teeth worn flat at the crowns to form an even working platform and exceedingly strong jaw muscles, both of which the aborigines have developed during years of using their teeth to chew tough meat, soften sinews, and rip the bark off branches. (They have no trouble in removing the top of a tin can by making successive bites along the rim.) Magdalenian and Azilian tool makers may have used this same method (among others) in the delicate job of fashioning microliths, very small scrapers and blades.

The need to travel light in the desert puts a premium on multipurpose or combination tools rather than elaborate tool kits. Of these the most impressive is the spearthrower, a flat wooden tool which in addition to its primary function of providing extra killing power at a distance (see Chapter 10), may also be used as a firemaker upon occasion. When an aborigine wants to start a fire, he splits a piece of wood, puts bits of dried kangaroo dung in the slot, and then rubs the edge of his spearthrower back and forth in the slot like a saw blade, hard and fast, until friction ignites the dung, a procedure that generally takes less than 20

Tjakamara, making a spearthrower

seconds. This versatile tool serves other functions, such as shaper and cutter, with the aid of an adz flake hafted to one end; mixing board for preparing pigments and a special blend of premasticated wild tobacco and ashes; and noisemaker for beating out rhythms at dances and other ceremonies.

Gould has devoted much time to a study of contemporary living floors, occupation patterns representing the activities of aborigines he knew well or the activities of their friends and recent ancestors. Such evidence can be used in interpreting prehistoric living floors not only in the Australian desert but elsewhere. For example he gathered considerable information during visits to Tika-Tika, a major open-air site covering several acres. The site includes ample supplies of fruit and berries in midwinter and late summer, small game and occasional kangaroos, and five water holes on a limestone flat, one of which can be counted on to furnish some water even during severe droughts.

One important feature of the layout here, and at other sites in the desert, is that the people never locate their occupation areas close to water holes. The general practice is to build camps at least 200 to 300 feet from the nearest source of water; if they were much closer, camp noises would frighten game away.

Aborigine women winnowing wangunu grass seeds

Another reason for having the water hole farther away is to reduce social tensions and preserve peaceful co-existence among neighboring groups. Under the system of rules that governs the behavior of relatives toward one another, for example, a man is strictly forbidden to talk with his mother-in-law, and if a family lived near a water hole it might be difficult to avoid awkward encounters.

In all, Gould and his wife spent the better part of a summer month living at Tika-Tika with the family group they originally followed into the desert. Shade is the primary concern during the summer season, when daily temperatures may average more than 100 degrees for 4 or 5 months in a row, and a typical shelter includes a basic structure of eight branches set into postholes about a foot deep and arranged in a rough semicircle. Thick clumps of grass piled on top of the branches provide protection from the sun, while the interior of the semicircle is scooped out to a depth of 2 to 3 inches to permit sleeping snug to the ground. The aborigines camped in two such shelters, making small fires just outside the entrances.

A winter visit to the same area called for different kinds of scooped-out shelters, for nights when the temperature may fall to freezing or below. One campsite consisted of a cleared oval area about 14 feet long with a windbreak of dense brush constructed along the windward side. A large hearth was located at one end of the clearing between the windbreak and bushes growing nearby; two small hearths burned at the other end. The aborigines make no clothing for cold-weather living, and their custom has been to curl up naked near hearths and

Nyampitjin, summer camp in the Gibson Desert

behind windbreaks. Dogs may furnish additional warmth when wrapped around the chest or legs like furs or blankets, a procedure which the animals seem to appreciate as much as the people.

A deserted campsite located nearby also had a windbreak and three hearths. What distinguished it was that the hearths were arranged in a row like those found at the Abri Pataud in France and at Kostenki in the Soviet Union. The aborigines explained the pattern. It was the sort of camp constructed by all-male groups, probably two men in this case, since one man usually lies in each of the spaces between hearths.

Artifacts collected from deserted sites at Tika-Tika included digging sticks, pieces of wooden bowls and spearthrowers, and an unusual pad made of emu feathers and designed to be worn on the foot during revenge expeditions (organized when a group of aborigines believes one of its members has been bewitched by another group's sorcerer). Of course, such items are perishable and may disintegrate within a couple of years under desert conditions, usually devoured by white ants. Among the durable items were grinding stones and slabs, several dozen adz flakes, and hundreds of waste chips, all of them made of various forms of quartz obtained from quarries 40 or more miles away. Such material may

Close-up of aborigine branch shelter

accumulate for many years, because campsites tend to be used over and over again.

Gould visited nearly a hundred sites, including sites occupied by only a few persons, complexes with clusters of as many as 20 camps and more than 80 persons, ceremonial sites, butchering sites, and ambushing sites. In all, his maps represent several hundred living floors and some new features of special archeological interest. At the dead end of a steep gully, he came across a ring of rocks which, on the side facing a nearby waterhole, were piled neatly to form a wall. A similar ring in another gully a quarter of a mile away and near another water hole had an even more carefully built wall almost 3 feet high.

Such structures had never been reported before, so Gould turned to the experts for an explanation. The aborigines identified them as blinds used by hunters at night. The gullies are natural traps for kangaroos and emus, and some hunters hide in crevices along the gullies and at the entrances, ready to intercept animals trying to escape. Large animals killed far from camp are roasted whole on the spot in earth-oven trenches (another archeological feature that may endure for many years). The animals are butchered and divided among the hunters, who may subsequently subdivide their shares among as many as 50 or 60 individuals back at camp.

Many of these activities presumably reflect the activities of times past. In the last analysis the similarities between recent and prehistoric hunter-gatherers are probably much greater than the differences. On the other hand, this emphasis

Aborigine hunting blind

can be carried too far. Differences must be recognized, otherwise even logical and convincing hypotheses will never match the facts. Perhaps the most obvious difference between the aborigines and prehistoric people living in western Europe 35,000 to 10,000 years ago is their different environments. The technologies and philosophies that evolved in glacial climates with abundant big game naturally differed from those evolved under desert or semidesert conditions.

Among the aborigines themselves, there were differences in prehistoric times between those who lived in the desert and those who lived along coasts and rivers, where food was considerably more plentiful. Changes occurred even more among the desert people. The original settlers of Australia probably did not have dogs, spearthrowers, stones for grinding food, and spears as well designed as those of modern times. Over the course of millenniums, they borrowed techniques from others and developed techniques of their own. In fact, Gould has discovered a procedure that seems to have come in quite recent times, a way of using rock slabs as foundations for shade-providing structures in summer camps. There are more than enough differences to keep investigators occupied for decades.

Meanwhile, the search for similarities goes on. The aborigines and the Magdalenians may or may not have had radically different religions, but what they have in common with one another and with us is more significant, a capacity for seeing beneath the surface of things and expressing their ideas in art and ritual, and a need to see the world as an orderly and meaningful place. More specifically, the similarities known to exist between some of the stone tools and living floors of prehistoric and recent times hint that further similarities remain to be discovered. Recognizing such things as rock blinds, rock alignments, earth ovens, and so on in the occupation area of the aborigines helps to free the mind when it comes to interpreting possibly related features of other living floors in Australia and elsewhere. According to Gould, "it suggests new possibilities and analogies to us, and helps us get unstuck from a limited range of ideas."

By the time he conducted his most extensive excavation, Gould had learned a great deal about aboriginal life styles in the region. He and a group of students dug for 11 summer weeks in a rock shelter at the foot of a steep cliff, under hot and dry conditions very much like those that prevailed in prehistoric times. Less than half an inch of rain had fallen there in 2 years, and all of it fell in a single day during the third week of the dig.

The shelter was first used about 10,000 years ago, and is still being used for brief visits today. In fact, within two years or so before excavating started, aborigines had left a number of stone tools at the site, tools like those made and used throughout the history of the site. The original settlers, perhaps two families, found an ample shelter 40 feet long and 15 feet deep. One day, after they had been living there for a long but undetermined period, and fortunately when no one was in the shelter, part of the roof collapsed, covering most of the living space with tons of quartzite debris. The people returned, however, and cleared two oval-shaped areas, presumably one for each family.

Gould drew on his knowledge about the behavior of living aborigines to help understand the behavior of their remote ancestors. The two oval-shaped areas are exactly the same size and shape and contain many of the same kinds of artifacts as 41 current-style camps which he mapped over a period of a few years, suggesting that then as now such areas were probably occupied by three to four persons. Some of the stone tools recovered from the site are identical to tools from other Australian sites dating back about 30,000 years, and to tools still being used today. Furthermore, microscopic studies reveal that the wear patterns of modern woodworking tools are identical to those of similar prehistoric tools.

Experience gained from living with aborigines also helped explain one of the most unusual features of the site. Next to the main rock shelter is a smaller one, too small to live in, but containing a pit 5 1/2 feet deep, with many thin tilted layers of differently colored soil, some containing ash or charcoal. Excavators were surprised to find moist soil within the pit, suggesting that it had served as a water source, a trap for moisture percolating down through cracks in the cliff.

Gould believes the pit is a "fossil" well, and he has seen similar structures actually being used by modern aborigines. They are dug down to the water table, sometimes 15 feet deep or more, and provide virtually permanent supplies of water. But it may be months or years between visits to a native well, and during that period the openings may be clogged with dense growth of grass and thorny bushes, which are cleared away by burning. The same procedure was probably practiced in times past, which would account for the thin layers of burned material found in the prehistoric rock shelter.

At times the shelter must have served as a place for magical and sacred activities, as indicated by rock paintings, quartz crystals, tektites, or glassy objects which may be the remains of shattered meteors, and other unusual stones brought in from surrounding areas and presumably used for charms and talismans. Also, some time between 7000 and 10,000 years ago, grinding stones and the charred remains of seeds and other plant parts appeared in excavated layers, perhaps a sign of more intense exploitation of local food resources.

For all the information that has come from the aborigines during past investigations, considerably more can be expected in the years ahead, as interest in living prehistory continues to grow. Findings in Australia already bear on problems encountered in the digging of European and Near Eastern sites. For example, Nicolas Peterson of the Australian National University and Carmel Schrire of Rutgers University have spent time in Arnhem Land along the north-central coast of Australia, the home territory of some 5000 aborigines. They present reasons for believing that the differences between tool kits found at coastal and inland sites and once attributed to different cultures actually reflect local adaptations to seasonal rains and flooding. In other words, the same people were doing different things at different times of the year, and comparable situations may have existed among prehistoric hunter-gatherers living at sites like Combe Grenal in southern France (see Chapter 9).

A LIVING LANDSCAPE

The aborigines lead a rich ceremonial life. They believe that in the beginning the world was chaos, not the hectic sort with everything flying about in a state of turmoil, but a dead, cold chaos of universal sameness, a level plain without features and without motion. "Everything was resting in perpetual darkness," according to one aborigine version of genesis. "Night oppressed all the earth like an impenetrable thicket. . . . As yet there was no water in it, but all was dry ground."

Everything that was yet to be lay underground. The sun, the moon, and the evening star were sleeping beneath the earth's crust, along with totemic ancestors and an embryonic gel-like mass of half-developed human infants. Then came the "dreamtime," a remote golden age when all the world was young green and abundant, and things began stirring. Sun, moon, evening star, and ancestors awoke and broke through the crust. The ancestors roamed over the earth in a variety of human and nonhuman guises, heroes bringing life and knowledge to the human mass and having adventures wherever they went. Every adventure was forever embodied in landscape, leaving its traces on a once-featureless plain.

In one tale the totemic lizard, running west to east to escape a band of hunters, found a hole and slid into it, leaving the tip of his tail sticking out. The hunters tried to pull him out, but he pulled them in and they all turned to stone—and a split in a steep cliff marks the spot today. This is only the smallest part of a long, long story, the last of a series of adventures that occurred during the lizard's wanderings, and each adventure is manifested as a distinct feature of the desert. Gould followed the entire lizard route in an airplane flying low over a line of cliffs, as an aborigine informant pointed out water holes, caves, hills, individual rocks and trees, and other features over a distance of some 200 miles.

The lizard track is made up of scores of places where adventures occurred. But the complete journey is far more complicated than that. Associated with each place, with each adventure may be up to a dozen or more secondary places and secondary adventures making up the full record of the totemic lizard's travels. And there are more complications. The lizard track with all its legendry is only one of a great number of tracks, and not the most important track at that. The tracks of the kangaroo and dingo (a breed of dog introduced into Australia about 3000 years ago) left traces which extend for hundreds of miles and feature thousands of adventure places, and other tracks include those of the emu, eagle, bat, marsupial cat, bush turkey, rabbit-eared bandicoot, rainbow serpent, spiny anteater, seven sisters, two men, and so on.

The entire desert is a maze of crisscrossing totemic tracks made by sacred ancestors during the dreamtime. The people have created a world for themselves and their descendants, a different world from ours. To us the desert is monotony incarnate, barren and unexciting, with few features and only scattered scrub trees and dry, sun-baked dunes to relieve the flatness. To the aborigine it is a land of infinite variety. The slightest rise or depression in an apparently level stretch of sand, the faintest change of color, the shape of a tree or a pile of stones or a clump of spinifex grass—all these and much more are prominent landmarks, vivid and familiar and loved. Theodor Strehlow of the University of Adelaide has described the aborigine's countryside as follows:

> He sees recorded in the surrounding landscape the ancient story of the lives and deeds of the immortal beings whom he reveres; beings who for a brief space may take on human shape once more; beings many of whom he has known in his own experience as his fathers and grandfathers and brothers, and as his mothers and sisters.
>
> The whole countryside is his living, age-old family tree. The story of his own totemic ancestor is to the native the account of his own doings at the beginning of time, at the dim dawn of life, when the world as he knows it now was being shaped and moulded by all-powerful hands. He himself has played a part in the first glorious adventure, a part smaller or greater according to the original rank of the ancestor of whom he is the present reincarnated form. . . . Today, tears will come into his eyes when he mentions an ancestral home site which has been, sometimes unwittingly, desecrated by the white usurpers of his group territory.

MAPPING AND MEMORY

Religion in the Gibson Desert works at many levels. The legends and the deeds of totemic ancestors who are not dead and gone but still alive, only sleeping, and the interlacing tracks everywhere, evoke feelings of design in nature and the universe, an underlying connectedness among all things, a reason for the lives the people lead. Their enriched desert also has another aspect involving problems of enduring in a harsh and severely demanding environment.

There can be no settling down in the desert. "A house is a good thing," an aborigine observed recently. ''You can lock it up, and go and live anywhere you please.'' Survival depends on ''chasing rain'': on arriving at the right place at the right time; staying as long as local supplies of water permit; and when the time comes for moving on again, knowing in what direction to go. Gould reports that one Gibson Desert band of a dozen persons moved nine times within a 3-month period, walking more than 250 miles from camp to camp in a foraging area of nearly 1000 square miles, and his records include many such cases.

People have no choice but to keep on the move. They must know where recent rains have fallen and where water is likely to have collected, not in any loose, hit-or-miss sense, but with the utmost precision, because you can die of thirst if you miss your target. They need a detailed and deeply rooted sense of place and, above all, maps. That is where the totemic tracks come in. The network of tracks is the equivalent of a complete set of large-scale maps which may cover an area 40 to 50 times the size of Manhattan Island.

The tracks are ''narrative'' maps. Every place is identified by what happened there in a dreamtime legend. Every place lies along the route to a water source or is itself a source of water—a rare spring or water hole, a claypan depression, a ''soak'' where water must be dug for, a billabong or stream bed with a few standing pools, a rock hole or cleft or a hollow place in a tree. An important part of every aborigine's education is to learn these maps—which, in

Water-snake pattern in aborigine rock shelter, illustrating a dreamtime legend

the absence of writing and printing presses, means to learn them by rote, holding images of the land intact and indelibly in memory.

The memorizing is accomplished with the aid of religion and ceremony and art, in what may well be evolved versions of systems invented in Upper Paleolithic times (see Chapter 11). The aborigines may be transmitting the contents of their tribal encyclopedia from generation to generation by mnemonic techniques similar to those used by the Magdalenians in the Les Eyzies region of southwestern France some 15,000 years ago. The rock art of the aborigines, figures

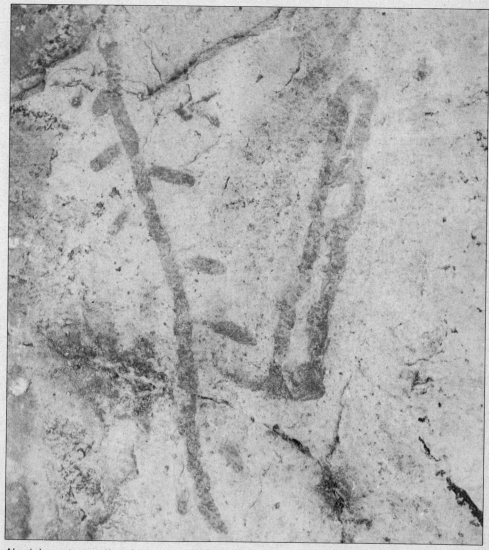

Aborigine art on rocks of a hunting blind: (left) kangaroo tracks and unidentified object

painted on boulders and the walls of shelters throughout the desert, is part of the learning process. It includes an extensive repertoire or "vocabulary" of designs, concentric circles and squares, zigzag and herringbone and hatched-line patterns representing sand hills, rock formations, totemic tracks and water holes, and other places along the tracks.

Similar designs are as common in aborigine lives as advertisements and road signs are in ours. Spearthrowers, for example, serve as memory aids as well as multipurpose tools. They may be carved with the same sort of patterns used in rock art, and also representing landmarks and tracks and water sources. In fact, a spearthrower can be regarded as a kind of map, its length of 30 inches or so depicting landscape features along a scaled-down track 100 to 150 miles long. The Magdalenians also had spearthrowers and also decorated them upon occasion, but the task of deciphering their symbols will be formidable.

Painted patterns are conspicuous in aborigine ceremonies. Body painting, again featuring many of the designs used on rock walls and spearthrowers, is a major art in itself, a complex of rituals which must be observed to the letter. There are strict rules specifying whether red ocher should be used or kangaroo dung (which provides a yellow-green color) or other pigments, how the pigments should be mixed and applied, where the patterns should be placed (some may be painted on the chest, others on the back, and so on), even the number and order of strokes. These and many other rules have to be memorized along with everything else.

EDUCATION BY RITUAL

Body painting itself is simply part of the preparation for further rituals, part of elaborate ceremonies. Education in the desert is a continuing process involving formal rites of passage conducted at various stages throughout life. One of the most memorable and effectively organized ceremonies, a key stage in the implanting of information, is the initiation of boys into manhood. It generally begins between the ages of 14 and 18, and ends with circumcision in public with a stone knife, an event all the more traumatic considering how easy the living has been up to that point.

Children are reared in a highly permissive atmosphere. They may be allowed to suckle until they are 4 or 5 years old, and routinely get away with outrageous behavior that would earn a solid smack in our families. Initiation marks the end of indulgence, a swift and sudden end. One day the boy becomes an outcast, the breaking of the bond between mother and son signalizing the beginning of indoctrination into the sacred life, which may last as little as a few months or as much as a year or two. Wrenched out of one world, the world of home and family and two sexes, he is thrust into an exciting and often bewildering all-male world.

The novice, in the charge of a man other than his father, works on a full-time schedule. He is taken into the desert, into places hitherto forbidden to him and forever forbidden to females, and shown some of the landmarks along the tracks of the dingo and kangaroo, the totemic ancestors of all tribal members. These are introductory visits only, just a fraction of what he will have to learn

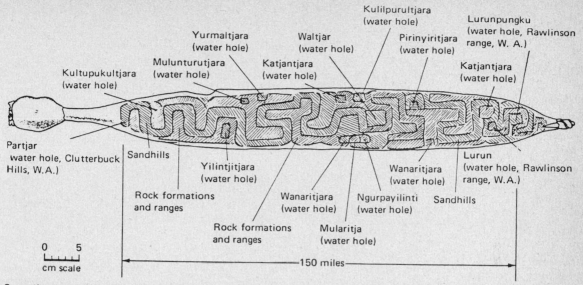

Kulilpurultjara
(water hole)

Lurunpungku
(water hole, Rawlinson
range, W. A.)

Yurmaltjara
(water hole)

Waltjar
(water hole)

Pirinyiritjara
(water hole)

Mulunturutjara
(water hole)

Katjantjara
(water hole)

Katjantjara
(water hole)

Kultupukultjara
(water hole)

Partjar
water hole, Clutterbuck
Hills, W.A.)

Sandhills

Yilintjitjara
(water hole)

Wanaritjara
(water hole)

Lurun
(water hole, Rawlinson
range, W.A.)

Rock formations
and ranges

Wanaritjara
(water hole)

Ngurpayilinti
(water hole)

Sandhills

Rock formations
and ranges

Mularitja
(water hole)

0   5

cm scale

150 miles

Spearthrower as "map": Gibson Desert landmarks and water sources along a 150-mile track of a totemic snake in the dreamtime

later on. He hears secret songs, repeated many times in their entirety, and participates in secret dances. All this and much more is preamble, part of a long and slow buildup, for the final day, the final ordeal, which includes a ritual wailing by women and children, the same loud cry that accompanies a death in the group and now proclaims the end of childhood, with manhood imminent.

Then there is the moaning-whining sound of bullroarers representing the

Nyapurula, aborigine mother and son

voice of the totemic kangaroo, and dancing performed to the beat of sticks pounded against the ground in imitation of the kangaroo's thuds as it hops along. Then all sounds cease at once, as the novice is placed on a "human table," a platform made up of the backs of men on their hands and knees, and circumcized. For several days to a week or two, as long as it takes the wound to heal, he remains silent. He returns to camp, relieved and proud, launched on his journey toward full adulthood.

Every step of the process, every ritual, is dedicated to the preservation of memory. Not a trick has been missed. What more could one do to ensure retention than start with young subjects, work them into a state of altered consciousness and readiness to accept, and conclude with an act of pain? Initiation combines many effects, all calculated to attach emotion to information, an aura of mystery and secrecy, the dark of night, images seen suddenly coming out of the dark, movement enhanced by body painting, information mythicized and sung and repeated to a beat, fear and fire, pain and the strange triumph of having come through suffering without crying out.

Further rituals lie ahead, some rather more painful. The desert contains so many places, so many tracks, so much to learn. It is no surprise that these people are never lost, that they know the locations of more than 400 places where water

Yutungka, in permanent water hole

Australian aborigines: boys being taught ceremonial dance, imitating rush of native brush bird

may be found. There are other things to be learned, such as the complex set of rules governing kinship and marriage and, in general, how to conform. Women also have secret ceremonies which, however, are not held as often or conducted with such prolonged intensity. Arranging and participating in major ceremonies is the men's job, probably their most important activity, at least in the Gibson Desert, where hunting is rarely successful.

It is a hard life, coping with the desert. Since breast feeding goes on for 3 or more years and women can neither carry nor nurse two offspring at once, they must upon occasion kill newborn infants. Although the aborigines do everything they can to minimize conflict, such as giving things away and living by an egalitarian ethics (see Chapter 10), controls may break down. There are murders, particularly when bands gather in larger groups, violence increasing according to the $(N^2 - N)/2$ formula (see Chapter 11). Raids may occur, and rare pitched battles. Also, a generation gap exists, a tension between the young men and the older men responsible for initiations—although, as pointed out by Annette Hamilton of Australia's Macquarie University, these feelings are less intense among desert aborigines than among those living to the northeast in Arnhem Land, where food and rain are abundant, and the elders commonly have two or three wives.

Ceremony plays a major role in reducing conflict, as it may have done during Upper Paleolithic times. At the broadest level, the aborigine life style represents an outstanding example of our genius for adapting. Wherever we live, we do what must be done in order to survive. That includes finding reasons to survive in the first place, creating a harmony between necessity and belief. Necessity dictates that the land be used as effectively as possible, especially in inhospitable desert regions; belief ensures that this does indeed happen. It is a mobile, nomadic life. When food is limited, people cannot live together in large,

Australian aborigines: ceremonial dance, Northern Territory

settled groups. If they did, they would soon eat themselves into extinction, consuming everything like swarms of locusts and ruining the land in the process. Survival depends on living in small groups over a wide area, and on remaining dispersed most of the time.

Although there are differences among the aborigines, the similarities are outstanding. In everything from artifacts to religious beliefs and practices, they tend to be extremely conservative, and their past demonstrates the strengths and weaknesses of extreme conservatism. For them everything had a completed quality; everything was accounted for, once and for all. The dreamtime was a kind of cultural high-water mark against which subsequent events could be measured, a lost golden age of heroes and heroic deeds, of abundance and easy hunting and gathering. Every change since then was a change for the worse, a step backward. The duty of the living was a rear-guard action to hold the line and prevent changes that would result in any further falling away from dreamtime days.

This system illustrates the fact, amply documented in all societies, that people can be programmed or indoctrinated with practically any set of beliefs, and that change itself can be put off if those beliefs are implanted deeply enough. The complexity of the aborigines' religion contrasts sharply with the simplicity of their technology, and suggests that they poured most of their creative energies into the dreamtime world. Their struggle to preserve things succeeded for a long time. It failed, not because of any change in themselves or in their land, but because of the coming of people who had been programmed to regard change as both possible and desirable.

SUMMARY

We ourselves are among the species that may provide insights into the life styles of times past. After all, members of the human family have been living as hunter-gatherers in the wild for all but 10,000 years out of more than 5 million years, so it should be no surprise that some contemporary behavior has prehistoric roots. Present-day hunter-gatherers demonstrate our unprecedented ability to adapt to practically any environment.

The aborigines of Australia's arid interior have adapted to deserts of scrub acacia trees, tough grasses, thorny bushes, and miles and miles of sandhills. Foraging on a typical summer day starts around six or seven in the morning, when it is still "cool" (below 95 degrees Fahrenheit); includes a break at midday, when the temperature may climb to 120 degrees, and ends around six in the evening. Men go after kangaroos and other large game, an unreliable food source. Women generally provide at least 80 percent of the food, mainly plants such as seeds and bush fruit, and small game.

The aborigines use hammerstones and adz flakes, steep-edged tools for cutting and scraping, as well as perishable items such as digging sticks, wooden bowls, and spearthrowers. The stone tools are identical to those excavated at sites 10,000 to 30,000 years old, when similar perishable items were probably also used. Aborigine informants have identified many features which archeologists could not explain—for example, a ring of rocks near a water hole as a hunting blind, and a pit near a rock shelter as a long-abandoned well.

The desert, a monotonous world to us, is alive with myths for the aborigines. A split in a certain cliff marks the spot where long ago, during the "dreamtime," hunters and their prey—a totemic hero disguised as a lizard—turned to stone. Legendary episodes are associated with every desert feature down to individual trees and clumps of grass and rock piles.

The landmarks collectively make up maps to be taught and remembered in often painful ceremonies which continue throughout life. The maps serve, among other things, to locate sources of water, a matter of life or death in desert surroundings. So ceremony is as essential to survival for the aborigines today as it must have been for their ancestors in Australia—and to the hunter-gatherers of the Upper Paleolithic.

chapter 16

The Behavior of Hunter-Gatherers

An ambitious, long-term objective of research in prehistory, in the social sciences generally, is the discovery of basic relationships among people and other group-living primates, independent of time and place—what James Moore of Queens College, New York, calls "the laws of motion in social life."

As indicated in Chapter 10, one such relationship may be hinted at in the size of nomadic hunter-gatherer bands, which average about 25 individuals, with a range of 20 to 70. This is somewhat higher than the range for gorilla troops (about 12 to 17), fairly close to that for Indian langur monkeys (18 to 30), and lower than the averages for baboons (about 40), forest-dwelling rhesus monkeys of north India (about 50), and African chimpanzees (40 to 50).

FRIEND OR FOE?

Notice that the human range is not radically out of line with the characteristic ranges for the order of primates. The number 500, on the other hand, represents something really new. As a common average for the tribe, defined as a group of bands speaking the same language or dialect, it is a purely human number in the sense that such organizations have not been found among other primates. It may reflect certain features of human communication systems. The unity of a hunting-gathering tribe, of a village or town or section of a city, depends on face-to-face meetings, a feeling of belonging to the same community.

The memory capacity of the human brain probably plays a role in this feeling, since that limits the number of people we can know by sight on a first-name basis, which may turn out to be of the order of magnitude of 500. When tribal populations rise much above that level, or when several tribes co-exist in the same region, people may need some way to identify themselves as friend or foe—markers, for instance, and they had better be easy to see. In a recent study of "stylistic behavior" in present-day Yugoslavia, Martin Wobst found that men of different ethnic and religious groups wear "items that are visible over long distances, such as from one mountain side to another, or over some distance along the road . . . [and] that allow you to decipher a stylistic message before you get into the gun range of your enemy."

Under conditions of stress Yugoslavs use hats to proclaim their loyalties from afar. The bazaar in Sarajevo, a city noted for conflict and competition among Serbians and Croatians and Muslims, offers "a large section of hatmakers in residence," while hatmaking is a minor craft in Zagreb, where the population is predominantly Croatian and life runs relatively smoothly. Ornaments serve different purposes. As close-up rather than long-distance communication items, they involve fine distinctions and convey information to a smaller number of individuals who are already recognized members of the community.

Similar conventions may have been invented, adopted for the first time, during the Upper Paleolithic, and for similar reasons. One of the outstanding developments of that explosive period, along with innovations in tool making and mass hunting and the first "seasonal villages," was the appearance of ornaments, personal adornments (see Chapter 10). Why would people who for some 2 million years, 80,000 generations, went all unadorned, suddenly begin to make necklaces, pendants, bracelets, anklets? Perhaps the ornaments were close-up identification markers, insignia of a sort indicating membership in a tribe and social status, which also made its first appearance during the Upper Paleolithic. As far as long-distance markers are concerned, friend-or-foe indicators, a number of cave-wall engravings and statuettes suggest that people were wearing identifying hats or headdresses and perhaps distinguishing coats and cloaks.

FOOD QUEST IN THE KALAHARI

Studies of contemporary hunter-gatherers as well as contemporary city dwellers can help put prehistoric society in perspective, with the emphasis increasingly on large-scale projects conducted in depth. One such project, the first of its kind, started in 1963 and involved a region in southern Africa where about a third of all the world's hunter-gatherers at the time were concentrated (about 9000 persons). It focused intensively on a very small area of unusual interest, a speck in the 350,000-square-mile Kalahari Desert of Botswana.

The area has a radius of less than 20 miles, is surrounded by vast stretches of waterless terrain, and included 11 permanent water holes and wells, between 400 and 500 plant and animal species, and about 450 Bushmen. Irven DeVore organized the project, which ultimately drew on the talents of investigators from Harvard University, the University of Michigan, the University of New Mexico, and a number of other institutions. They studied everything from the food quest to the role of ritual, and provided fresh insights into the effectiveness and complexities of the hunter-gatherer way of life.

Kalahari mongongo forest

Richard Lee of the University of Toronto has concentrated on the economics of that life style, on the amount of effort individuals put into the business of obtaining food. Local Bushmen are fortunate in having an abundant and dependable food staple, a staff of life, in the form of the high-energy, high-protein nut of the mongongo tree. Although some 85 desert plants are considered edible and may be used for variety or as second-best fare, this single species provides from 1/2 to 2/3 of the total vegetable diet. The selection of campsites is determined by the locations of mongongo forests found on the crests of long sand dunes or, more precisely, by the distances between the nearest water sources and the forests.

According to Lee, "the Bushmen typically occupy a camp for weeks or months and literally eat their way out of it." During January or February, when most of the rain falls, they may camp at a temporary pool within a mile or so of the nearest trees, and exhaust that supply of nuts in a week. Then on successive weeks they may have to walk 2, 3 and 4 miles to progressively more distant forests, all the time camping at the same pool. They will never walk more than 6 miles, however, since women, the main food providers, are not willing to undertake longer trips in a single day at temperatures averaging 100 degrees and carrying 20 to 40 pounds of nuts on their backs, plus infants or tired children.

This is the departure point, and the group will then move to another water source near other forests—that is, in relatively wet weather. But in the driest season, in October and November, there is no choice because all temporary pools have vanished and the people must stay near one of the permanent water holes. Most of them forgo mongongo nuts and other preferred foods, living on poorer fare which can be gathered within a few miles of their homes. Some hardier groups, however, travel up to 20 miles to mongongo trees in waterless places where they may camp for a week or two.

Life becomes exceedingly difficult under such conditions. Indeed, it would be impossible without a certain type of shrub that has bulbous root organs which are about the size of a football and store water in the form of milky juice. Even with these natural reservoirs, the campers barely make a go of it in dry seasons; so much of the water they get from the roots is needed simply to replace the water lost in the process digging for the roots, which lie a foot or two underground in the hard, compacted soil of basins between sand dunes. Incidentally, on one occasion Lee asked a group of Bushmen to go through this ordeal, even though he could easily have driven them to a mongongo forest and back again in his Land Rover. It is something like asking city dwellers to walk to work in a heat wave without using available buses and subways. But they promptly agreed after he explained that they were the only people in the world who could cope with the Kalahari at its worst, and that he and others wanted to know how they did it.

Kalahari dietary staple: roasting mongongo nuts

Food gathering requires only a bare minimum of equipment. The basic tools are a pair of unworked stone hammers to crack nuts with and a sturdy digging stick about 3 feet long and 3/4 inch in diameter, sharpened to a blade at the business end. The most important item of equipment is the kaross, a combination garment and receptacle made of antelope hide which women wear draped over the shoulder. It forms a pouch for carrying nuts, berries, edible roots and bulbs, ostrich-shell water containers, firewood, and babies. These three simple items, the two tools and the kaross, are all that is needed to obtain vegetable foods.

Going after animals demands more ingenuity and a correspondingly more elaborate set of tools—including bows and arrows, arrow poisons made from crushed beetle pupae, rope snares, nets, firemaking kits, knives, and a dozen other items. John Yellen has gone with Bushmen on hunting trips and studied their tracking techniques. Judging by a variety of scuff marks and indentations in the sand, they can tell the kind of animal as well as its size and sex and which way it is going. They can also tell how old the track is. Some tracks are so recent that sand is still falling into the hollow, while old tracks may be blurred and

Kalahari woman gathering food with child on back

faded. Such abilities are relatively routine, roughly the equivalent of reading and writing.

The finer points of the art come into play in deciding what the animal is doing and whether or not to go after it, decisions based on an intimate knowledge of the land and animal behavior. Yellen emphasizes that an eland's tracks may be only half an hour old, but if hunters feel it is "going somewhere far" and moving at a steady pace, they will not bother to pursue it. On the other hand, tracks several hours old may represent a call to action if they indicate that the animal is moving irregularly within a limited area, which may mean that it is stopping frequently to rest or keeping watch on a young offspring hidden in some bushes.

One of the most impressive things about these and many far subtler deductions is what they imply about the quality of the brain required for advanced forms of hunting. During the following of game trails one discusses the nature and meaning of tracks, assesses the probable merits of different theories about what is happening, decides on a course of action, and frequently checks and rechecks one's theories in the light of fresh evidence. One distinguishes clearly between fact and hypothesis. The hunter's brain is also the scientist's. Whether they are deciding where to gather the day's food or predicting the movements of game in a wilderness or of satellites in space, people everywhere use the same basic thought processes.

Big game is not as plentiful in the Kalahari as it once was, so considerable effort is devoted to smaller animals. The most commonly caught game, the springhare, is taken in its burrow with the aid of a flexible pole 13 feet long. The hunter pushes the pole into the burrow slowly as it bends to follow underground turns: he proceeds by "feel" and is ready to detect vibrations or sounds that indicate the location of the cornered prey. Then at the proper moment the pole is moved backward and then forward in a swift thrust, impaling the hare on a hook attached to the probing end. A digging stick is used to get at the animal and kill it.

Trapping requires expert skill and involves far more than merely finding tracks where snares may be placed. The trick is to influence patterns of animal movement, deliberately creating places suitable for snares. For example, when hunters notice antelope tracks on a sandy area of bush country, they sometimes toss some branches across them. When they come back to the area a day or two later, they note changes in the tracks and put down more branches. After a number of days there is a seemingly haphazard brush fence with gaps 2 or 3 feet wide. The next step is to add just enough branches to narrow the gaps still further, and then set nooses in them. By this time, and it requires considerable patience, the animals have been conditioned to walk right into the traps.

There is also a clever way of catching guinea fowl. If a hen sees that one of her eggs has rolled out of the nest, she tries to roll it back with her head and beak. This is an automatic reaction, triggered by the sight of the misplaced egg, and the way to take advantage of it is to remove an egg from the nest, place it about 8 inches away, and lay a buried noose around it. As soon as the hen returns to her nest and notices what has happened, she is doomed because she cannot help nudging the egg toward the nest and springing the trap.

How successful are the Bushmen's subsistence strategies? It has not been easy, providing a straightforward answer to this seemingly straightforward question. Part of the problem is the old, deep-seated swinging-pendulum tendency to think in extremes, to oscillate between belittling and glorifying our ancestors, between the putdown and romantic idealizing.

As far as making stone tools is concerned, for example, the dogma a generation ago had it that small-brained early hominids were incapable of such feats. A decade or so later, after stone tools had been found at their sites, it was a different story, with the stress on tool kits supposedly including sophisticated items like scrapers, engravers, and chisels (see Chapter 4). The same sort of overreaction occurred when some investigators abandoned the notion of early hominids as highly organized big-game hunters and pictured them as nothing but low-grade scavengers (see Chapter 7).

We now know that in both cases the truth lies somewhere between the extremes, and the same goes for the Bushmen's food quest. When Lee first visited the Kalahari some 20 years ago, he studied a band of about 30 persons camping near a water hole for 28 consecutive days in July and August, when food was neither exceptionally abundant nor exceptionally scarce. He found that the people were getting along on a balanced diet made up of 37 percent meat (mostly small game), 33 percent mongongo nuts, and 30 percent other vegetables, enough to provide each band member with 1.4 pounds of food a day—about 2140 calories, 165 more than the basic daily requirement.

These figures hardly jibe with a prevailing view of the times—namely, that hunter-gatherers were engaged in an unremitting struggle against starvation. Early reports have turned out to be overly idyllic, however. Lee himself emphasized that the Bushmen spent only 12 to 19 hours a week foraging for all the food they needed, a point which encouraged one anthropologist to describe them as representatives of "the original affluent society." But their total work budget, including preparing food as well as getting it, making and repairing tools, fetching firewood and water, and other duties (but not including child care), came to about 45 hours a week for men and 40 hours a week for women.

This more realistic assessment is still impressive, although there is certainly room for improvement in diet and general health. Nancy Howell of the University of Toronto, who has analyzed records of about 850 Bushmen, finds that populations have been increasing slowly over the years, and that death rates have been moderately low in the recent past and probably for a long time before Europeans came. Their maximum life span seems to be the same as it is for human beings everywhere, with perhaps one person in a million living to the age of 110; about 8 percent of the Bushmen are more than 60 years old. On the other hand, Edwin Wilmsen of Boston University has shown that a less than ideal diet is one factor reducing the fertility of Bushman women, and helping to account for the long interval between births, about 3.7 years.

A number of theories have been advanced to account for observed subsistence strategies. The optimal foraging model, for instance, assumes that people always behave rationally (always a dangerous assumption), that they will abandon a food-rich patch before it is fully depleted, and that they will collect foods on the basis of the most efficient energy expenditure. As applied to a hunter-gatherer tribe in eastern Paraguay, the model shows that a mixed take of 11 animal resources, including deer and peccaries, and 5 plant resources provides more calories per hour, 872, than any other mix.

The investigators who conducted this study, Kristen Hawkes, Kim Hill, and James O'Connell of the University of Utah, suggest that a similarly detailed analysis of Lee's data would explain why the Bushmen continue to spend considerable time hunting, although they often come back empty-handed. But the optimal foraging model breaks down when it comes to explaining other aspects of hunter-gatherer behavior. As an example, here is what Bruce Winterhalder of the University of North Carolina has to say about a nearly universal practice: "The division of labor, in which males pass up encounters with highly ranked plants and females do so for highly ranked animals, lowers the potential foraging efficiency of each. This indicates that foragers are not attempting to maximize their energy intake; genuine energy maximizers would not afford such cultural luxuries."

AN OLD PROBLEM—COPING WITH CONFLICT

So we continue to study a way of life which has vanished but which dominated most of our past. Hunter-gatherers were never affluent or noble, and they were never long-suffering savages either. They were and are merely human, which is rather more complicated. There has never been anything natural about living together, if by natural we mean easy or effortless. Every individual must devote an appreciable proportion of time and energy to maintaining a reasonably peaceful place in the scheme of things, to keep from rubbing other individuals the wrong way or being rubbed the wrong way. The continual boiling and spilling over of tensions is as characteristic of human groups as of baboon groups.

For all the fighting that goes on, people seem to be able to keep conflict at a relatively low level, at least in a hunter-gatherer context. Experienced observers are impressed with the fact that much less aggression exists among humans than among other primates, mainly because humans are indoctrinated, domesticated, along lines designed to keep conflict at a minimum. The overriding reason that people of the Kalahari have no full-time leaders and avoid the possession of valued objects is that they fear violence (see Chapter 10).

Any boasting or pompousness, even the faintest hint of arrogance or an attitude that might eventually lead to arrogance, becomes sufficient reason for a firm putdown. A hunter may come into camp with a fine antelope kill at a time when game is scarce and the people are craving meat, but if he merely utters a noncommittal "I have killed an animal," the response is likely to be "only one?" or some such mild disparagement which is only half joking. Lee himself was the victim of this treatment when he bought an ox for a Christmas feast, and was told repeatedly in a dozen different ways by a dozen different people that the animal was scrawny, that he had been cheated, and that there would not be enough meat to go around. Actually, it was a fine animal, and everyone had more than enough to eat. But the people were acting to avoid any show of pride: "When a young man kills much meat he comes to think of the rest of us as his servants or inferiors. . . . Some day his pride will make him kill somebody."

Accumulating things, another source of pride and potential domination, is also discouraged. The tendency is to keep a treasured object for a while only, perhaps a few days or weeks, and then pass it on to someone else who will eventually feel the same way and get rid of it. The passing-on has positive as well as negative aspects. The Bushmen are continually giving things away—skins decorated with beads, knives, arrows, cattle, sandals, safety pins. Goods of all sorts pass from relative to relative, from band to band, along gift or exchange networks that involve dozens of persons and may extend for as much as 300 miles. Polly Wiessner of the University of Michigan has studied these networks in detail and points out that they serve, above all, to establish good will over wide areas so that people in search of food, a new home, or simply of companionship will find a welcome in many places.

The shaping of behavior can be seen in the way Bushmen raise their children, a process based on customs and instincts which have evolved over many generations. Training in generosity starts a few months after birth; strings of beads are put around an infant's arms, neck, and waist; and not long afterwards, generally between the ages of 6 months and 1 year, the infant is provided with new beads and encouraged to give the old ones to a relative.

The Bushmen have widespread kinship networks which overlap extensively with their giving networks. Henry Harpending of the University of New Mexico studied 9 areas containing about 2300 Bushmen, and found that more than 40 percent of parents were born outside their current home-base areas, an index of the degree of outbreeding, genetic mixing, and "hypermobility." The band does not exist as a fixed group of individuals seeing the same faces month after month, living and moving together as one big family. It is a dynamic unit where people, singly and in groups, arrive and depart for a number of reasons.

The population of one typical camp fluctuated from 23 to 40, with a total of 76 different individuals, all during a single month. People often move because local food supplies are limited, and also upon occasion to get away from it all. According to Lee, it is one way of reducing conflict: "Unlike farming and city peoples, foragers have a great deal of latitude to vote with their feet, to walk out of an unpleasant situation. And they do so, not when their food supply is exhausted, but well before that point, when only their patience is exhausted."

A whole region, not a single territory or plot of land, is home for Bushmen. Patricia Draper, a colleague of Harpending's at New Mexico, has provided a vivid and quantitative picture of the intimacy of wilderness life. She kept records of the activities of some 35 children up to 14 years old, each of whom was observed in a series of spot checks for a total of three to four hours each over a period of 12 months. Taking the entire age range, from birth through 14 years old, children were in physical contact, actually touching another individual, about a third of the time. For the age range from birth through 5 years, the proportion of contact time was more than 50 percent, and in only four observed cases was the child unaccompanied—that is, without another person less than 3 feet or so away.

From the young child's viewpoint, the Kalahari camp is a self-contained world, an island in the bush which extends pathless in all directions with few obvious landmarks. The camp is a cluster of family groups and little beehive-shaped huts made of saplings, palm fronds, and grass and arranged in a circle or semicircle. In such a setting strangers are rare, and the response of Bushman infants to an unfamiliar face may be spectacularly intense.

Melvin Konner of Emory University tells how he and a British associate once stopped their Land Rover to pick up a family of Bushmen, including a mother with a sleeping infant. During the ride the infant woke up, lifted its head, saw the Britisher in the back seat, and unleashed an ear-splitting scream—the sort of scream babies emit when in extreme physical pain. Although infants of all societies generally begin to fear strangers at the age of 7 to 9 months, the response is relatively mild among Europeans and Americans. Among Bushman babies, however, the appearance of strangers is presumably a far rarer event, and an event that in times past usually meant trouble.

The atmosphere in a Bushman camp is typically low key, with few surprises. The child grows up in a close-knit group. Families sitting at night in front of their huts and around their fires do not have to raise their voices to speak with one another across the camping areas. A disturbance of any sort moves swiftly like a ripple through the group. There is little aggression and no sustained fighting among children. Potentially disruptive encounters are halted at the very start by an adult, usually but not necessarily one of the children's mothers, who is within arm's reach and, more often than not, separates the would-be antagonists casually, without interrupting work or conversation. "Aggression is never allowed to build up," Draper comments, "and children do not get a chance to learn the satisfaction of making someone cry or humiliating a person."

VIOLENCE, SEXISM, HEALING DANCES

Nevertheless, for all the training and traditions of humility and generosity, aggression exists in the Kalahari as it does elsewhere. Individuals get on one another's nerves, and there are arguments and fights and occasional killings. The homicide record illustrates the tendency of conflict to increase with the size of the group, which may have become a serious problem during the Upper Paleolithic (see Chapter 11). Lee found that in one group of Bushmen 18 homicides occurred during the period from 1920 to 1962: 15 in camps of 40 to 150 individuals, and only 3 in camps of less than 40.

A second major Upper Paleolithic change, the earliest traces of status differences, can also be seen in the Kalahari. As emphasized in Chapter 10, Bushman hunter-gatherers live by an ethics of equality, with no one in a position to lord it over others—at least as long as they go about in small nomadic bands. According to Elizabeth Cashdan of the University of Pittsburgh, however, democracy tends to break down among larger groups, which shift camps less frequently and supplement their wild-species diets with domesticated species. While there is still no formal social ranking or leadership under such conditions, a few individuals are able to accumulate wealth in the form of livestock and other items, and to afford several wives, all of which may set the stage for the future appearance of status.

A more settled life also seems to encourage sexism, a phenomenon observed by Draper in another agriculturally oriented group. Division of labor exists among nomadic Bushmen, as among all hunter-gatherers. As a general rule men do the hunting and women gather plant foods. But upon occasion men may collect mongongo nuts and women may come home with meat, usually small game. Fetching water is woman's work as a rule, but men and boys join the ranks of water fetchers when necessary. Attitudes about who does what are informal and flexible. When the occasion arises, members of either sex may take on some of the other's duties without making a fuss about it.

All this begins to change among less mobile, more sedentary Bushmen. For the first time pride and dignity become extremely important. Men who previously would not think twice about helping to fetch water now scorn such work as unworthy of their maleness, and boys are quick to take the cue from their fathers. We have here the emergence of contempt for what has become work for women only, and similar tendencies have been observed among recently settled Australian aborigines. We do not know the reasons for this sort of behavior, although it may have something to do with a loss of male prestige. After all, the male's standing as hunter and breadwinner may have been undermined when people depended increasingly on domestic animals.

There are many sources of tension among hunter-gatherers, and many ways of helping to relieve the tension. Perhaps the most significant source of relief is the healing dance, which, according to Richard Katz of Harvard University, represents the Bushmen's primary ritual, the core of their religion—and the core of the dance is the trance state of the healer. The medicine, which is believed to lie cold in the pit of the healer's stomach, can be released and transferred to ailing individuals by a laying on of hands. But first the medicine must be brought to a boil, which is the purpose of the dance.

Proceedings usually start in the evening as women, and often children, make a fire and sit about it clapping and singing. Soon some of the men move into the area to dance for brief periods in circles around the fire, shoulders hunched, feet stamping, and arms pressed against their sides in a casual sort of warm-up period that may last for two hours or so. Then the frenzy comes. A vacant stare appears in the eyes of the dancer, and he trembles, sweats heavily, and stamps hard on the ground. The trance is marked by moaning, shrieking, and intense physical exertion.

Sometimes a dancer, a novice as a rule, loses control and runs wild into the bush or burns himself by dancing through the central fire. One man described the experience as follows: "I see all the people like very small birds; the whole place will be spinning around and that is why we run around. The tree will be circling also. You feel your blood become very hot just like blood boiling on a fire and then you start healing. . . . When I lay my hands on sick people, the medicine in me will go into them and cure them." Healing generally hits a peak between midnight and 2 in the morning, simmers down for a while, hits a second peak at sunrise, and comes to a close around 10 or 11.

The healing dance involves the entire group. Healers are not members of a select, elite class. Women may be healers, and about half the men are considered "doctors." Katz stresses the importance of group participation: "The village

Beginning of Kalahari trance dance: preparing for laying
on of hands and healing

becomes a community healer. . . . [It] experiences a communal transformation.
Individuals are healed, and the village, as a unity greater than the sum of its
members, is also healed and set right in its environment." The healing dance can
be regarded as a kind of group therapy, an intensive session taking place about
once a week on the average and lasting 15 or more hours. That might not be such
a bad idea for the rest of us.

Did the Bushmen's remote prehistoric ancestors live in a similar fashion,
by similar traditions and with similar ceremonies? Studies still being conducted
by Yellen and Alison Brooks, also of George Washington University, suggest that
traditions do indeed endure for long periods. For one thing, Kalahari people seem
to have lived in the region far longer than was previously believed. The old notion
that they had been forced out of more abundant lands into refuge areas during
relatively recent times is contradicted by the discovery of typical Bushman sites
dating back at least 20,000 years and perhaps a good deal longer. The fact of
continuity in the desert encourages current studies designed to reconstruct prehistoric behavior patterns and social systems.

The George Washington investigators are comparing archeological remains found at these sites with remains found at sites abandoned within the past generation or so, and find no signs of radically different life styles. Furthermore, the Bushmen who excavated with them are helping interpret various findings, just as the aborigines of the Gibson Desert helped Richard Gould in his studies (see Chapter 15). The search is always for new insights, for patterns that may provide a more complete picture of behavior in times long past. There is a newly discovered pattern in recently abandoned Bushman camps. The camps include a central or nuclear zone where remains tend to be heavily concentrated, where people sat around communal hearths and performed the day's chores, everything from making arrowheads to cracking nuts and cooking. A definite mathematical relationship exists between the zone's area and the size of the camping band. For example, if the zone measures 1800 to 1900 square feet, it was probably occupied by about half a dozen families, 25 to 30 individuals.

As long as the band's population does not change, the zone stays the same size. But it is generally surrounded by another zone which is used for special, often messy, activities requiring extra space, such as cleaning and drying skins or roasting heads in pits—and which tends to grow larger the longer people occupy their camp. Thus, if the half-dozen families settled for about a month, the total area of their camp, nuclear zone plus special-activities zone, would gradually increase to nearly 5300 square feet. One of the problems confronting archeologists now is whether similar relationships hold for a wide spectrum of prehistoric sites.

ADAPTING TO GLACIAL CLIMATES

We have referred to some of the work of Lewis Binford and his associates in a rather different environment, but one which more closely resembles winter climates during Neanderthal and Upper Paleolithic times in Europe (see Chapters 4, 9, and 10). Time spent among some 135 Eskimo villagers in the Brooks Range of Alaska included an unscheduled adventure, which provided firsthand experience in dealing with emergencies and fortunately had a happy ending. No less than 7 feet of snow fell during one 6-day blizzard featuring temperatures of about 25 to more than 50 degrees below zero Fahrenheit and gusts of wind up to 65 miles an hour.

The community faced its most severe food shortage in decades. Snows covered everything, changing the landscape of familiar contours and paths and willow stands into a vast, blank, white expanse with all landmarks buried except for the tallest trees, the highest bluffs, and the mountains themselves. Migrating caribou, the major source of food, stayed in forests to the south, and people turned to strategies which had probably served their ancestors well in remote prehistoric times.

One group of hunters saw tracks in fresh snow, set 150 snares, and caught 65 Arctic squirrels, although as far as a square meal is concerned, a squirrel compares to a caribou as a young hummingbird compares to a Thanksgiving turkey. The hunters also decided to try ice fishing in a nearby lake, but gave it up after hacking a hole more than 4 feet deep into the ice without any signs that water was near. They had better luck, but not much better, finding meat put away in special places around the countryside for just such emergencies, locating two out of ten caches. Meanwhile women were beginning to tap another source of food, marrow bones and the frozen carcasses of wolves and foxes kept on the roofs of houses where dogs could not get at them.

At about this stage things started improving, and there was no need to turn to last-resort foods such as fern roots and the inner bark of willow trees. A herd of moose headed south for food in the forests; hunters saw their tracks and came back with 3700 pounds of fresh meat. Not long afterwards, as temperatures soared to 5 or 6 degrees above zero, the caribou finally showed up. But for nearly a month Binford had a glimpse of what things must have been like during prehistoric glacial emergencies, when the weather often did not improve, and hunter bands were wiped out. Even today and even given the favorable change in weather, the community would have suffered far more severely if he had not brought an ample supply of antibiotics with him, because all but half a dozen villagers caught influenza.

Living with Brooks Range Eskimos raises a number of interesting questions about prehistoric living. We may never know whether or not the Neanderthals had snowshoes and sleighs. The odds are that items made of wood and thong have disintegrated without trace. In any case, nothing has been found (although it makes sense to keep looking). And yet direct experience of blizzards and the task of getting around in deep snows makes it difficult to imagine how our ancestors could ever have survived ice ages without such inventions.

One of the most common Eskimo traps is the deadfall, a heavy roof stone forming the top of a boxlike structure with stone walls. The roof falls on any animal trying to get at bait inside and tripping the trap's "trigger." According to Binford, many archeological features identified as children's burials, ritual cairns, and storage pits may actually have been deadfalls. He knows of at least two such structures excavated at Neanderthal sites in the Les Eyzies region. Also, stone semicircles 7 to 8 feet across may represent hunting blinds like those the Eskimos and Australian aborigines use today (see Chapter 15) rather than small huts, a common interpretation.

There is more, much more, waiting to be deciphered in the archeological record. To date, practically everything we know has come from relatively gross studies of gross features—that is, from examinations of the more obvious characteristics of hearths, bones, artifacts, and so on. But a wealth of new information, amounting almost to a new archeology, is there to be discovered and interpreted. To cite only one example: major advances are under way in taphonomy, the art of "reading bones." Patterns of grooves and scratches in bony surfaces have already been used in the effort to distinguish hominid from non-hominid activity (see Chapter 4) and scavengers from primary hunters (see Chapter 10).

ESKIMOS AND NEANDERTHALS

This is an intensive wringing-dry operation calculated to squeeze every drop of data, every possible inference, from the evidence at hand. It calls for microscopic studies and experiments to duplicate patterns of markings and, ideally, firsthand "do-it-yourself" experiences among people who still subsist at least in part by hunting. Archeological sites take on a new dimension after such experiences. They come alive in the sense that instead of seeing only stone and bone features, you see people in your mind's eye, people going about their business, doing things. It is analogous to reading notes and hearing music.

Jean-Philippe Rigaud describes the impact of part of a summer spent in the Brooks Range: "Our ideas were static before. I had never seen a real hunting-gathering camp. Now we have a feel for social organization, the way people behave." Splinters of bone found at his Flageolet rock shelter (see Chapter 10) are recognized as the probable result of women's work, pounding bones on a stone anvil with a bone hammer to obtain marrow and bone grease. A pile of quartz cobblestones excavated at the site reminded him of a similar pile seen at an Eskimo camp where the stones had been brought in as "pot boilers" to be heated in a fire and dropped into skins containing snow or water.

Binford notes a number of subtler features. Of all wild oxen, horse, and reindeer bones recovered at the Neanderthal site of Combe Grenal, the part showing the most cut marks is the lower jaw. Specifically, the marks often consist of oblique scratches on the inside of the bone, generally opposite the second molar tooth. Marks similar to those made by the Neanderthals 50,000 or more years ago are being made today by Eskimos butchering male caribou. Circular cuts around the bases of ancient antlers from young reindeer in the Les Eyzies region are also found on the bases of antlers from young Brooks Range caribou, which Eskimos go after in the fall to obtain hides for winter clothing; characteristic marks on fossil reindeer vertebrae resemble those noted on caribou vertebrae after modern hunters have filleted the tenderloins.

There are hundreds and hundreds of already observed cut-mark patterns, and at least as many more yet to be discovered, a legion of clues to the behavior of people whose lives depend on hunting. Their tracking, killing, butchering, and caching and sharing strategies are based on millenniums of accumulated knowledge, and vary with the seasons, local abundances and scarcities, and other factors. These hunters have a kind of built-in calculus of subsistence, taking account of the shifting values of every caribou part. Their hunting behavior is shaped by the behavior and, ultimately, the anatomy of their main prey. A strict and precise relationship exists between the food quest and social organization.

All this information makes up only a fraction of what Eskimos must know in order to survive, a fraction of their enormous tribal encyclopedia. Like the Australian aborigines, and like the people of the Upper Paleolithic, they must transmit the contents of the encyclopedia intact from generation to generation, in the absence of writing. In other words, they must store the contents in memory.

To obtain an idea of how much is remembered, Binford asked one Brooks Range hunter to describe features of the surrounding landscape. The result was one description after another, with a story and remembrances to go with each feature. The man had a name for practically every visible feature, for every stream and stand of trees and hillock, for every rock on nearby and distant knolls, and, to go with every item, an account of times past—part fact, part legend, and part spontaneous embellishment (distinctions which are very difficult to make), going back as many as five generations. He learned all this and a great deal more starting as a boy after he had killed his first caribou, on long camping trips with his father and uncles, who pointed out places where memorable events had occurred.

Furthermore, frequent "refresher courses" take place, sessions during which old adventures are recounted and new ones added. "The first thing a man does when he returns from a hunting trip is to tell what happened in empirical detail," Binford reports. "He may talk steadily for 3 to 5 hours, with a glazed look in his eyes as the information pours out of memory—'I walked between the river and the opening of the valley and saw two wolf tracks and a raven circling overhead, and the snow was beginning to melt at the place where meat is cached. . . .' Everyone listens quietly and intently, men and women and children. The analysis comes after the narrative. There are questions and discussions and the old people recall what happened long ago at the same places."

PEOPLE IN RAIN FORESTS

The most recent study of African hunter-gatherers takes a very different approach. Still in its earliest phases and organized by DeVore, who also launched the Kalahari project, it is part of an expanding effort to see the human species in sociobiological terms as a member of the order of primates, to learn more not only about ourselves but about primates in general. Work is concentrated on the Ituri rain forest of northeastern Zaire, specifically on an area of some 2000 square miles which supports an estimated 450 pygmy hunter-gatherers living in association with 600 village farmers, members of the Lese tribe.

Investigators are in the process of compiling a prodigious quantity of information. A team including Robert Bailey and Nadine Peacock of Harvard University and Elizabeth Ross and Richard Wrangham of the University of Michigan has obtained vital statistics—age and birthplace, and kinship, marital, and reproductive histories, all duly entered on more than 1000 file cards representing as many individuals. In addition, the recorded height, weight, head circumference, and other physical measurements for 800 of these people, a procedure that will take place twice a year for as long as the project continues, which will probably be for more than a decade.

These records, while reasonably voluminous, involve basically routine procedures. Far from routine, however, are methods for observing human behavior, which demand data collection on a grand scale and techniques related to those developed by the Altmanns and other watchers of nonhuman primates (see Chapter 12). As a sample of the degree of detail involved, here is a bit of the special code used in observing the activities of No. 746, a pygmy mother named Botendi: A7Ø1ND-6MH5SO. Freely translated, this means "Botendi gave (A) a fellow member of the Andibundu band (7), an infant (Ø), her first-born (1), some plantain (ND), while she herself consumed 6 bites (6) of manioc root (MH) and 5 bites (5) of crushed manioc leaves (SO)"—all only a part of what was recorded during the twenty-sixth minute of one hour spent observing one individual.

The complete behavioral code is made up of between 150 and 200 shorthand symbols. The list includes symbols for 20-odd activity verbs (MK, make; CH, chop; WR, wrap; etc.), 50-odd objects (AR, arrow; KN, knife; HB, honey basket; etc.), a dozen forms of social interaction (FT, friendly touch; GR, groom; TK, take from forcibly, etc.) and about 15 postural states (z, sleeping; q, squatting; h, walking fast; etc.); Bailey's contribution included observations of some 20 male pygmies for a total of 32 hours each, 8 hours for each of four times a day (early morning, midday, early afternoon, late afternoon). Peacock compiled comparable records for pygmy women.

Wrangham and Ross obtained similar information about Lese tribespeople, 30 married men and 30 married women respectively. Every day for about 15 weeks they set out in opposite directions on observation circuits lasting some five hours, during which they made contact with the individuals under study. Since standardized techniques for noting the effect of the observing procedure on those being observed are still rather new, they devised a numerical code to record whether individuals knew they were under observation and, if so, whether and how they changed their behavior.

The Ituri investigators gathered considerably more raw data than I have indicated, and an enormous amount of computer-aided analysis remains to be done. But they have some interesting preliminary impressions. In measuring subsistence among the pygmies, Bailey and Peacock find that women provide nearly twice as much food by calories as men (about 66 percent and 34 percent respectively), while men contribute far more of the total protein in the form of meat (61 percent and 39 percent).

Also, some of Peacock's most important findings involve the extent and scope of women's work. Her study included a 32-member pygmy band with an abnormally low number of children, 6 as compared to an expected 18 or so—and even under these conditions, women spent about 75 percent of their time caring for the few children in addition to gathering, doing household work, preparing food, working in the village, and so on.

So if life is that busy in a few-children context, what would it be in a normal situation? Certainly a great deal closer to 100 percent occupied. Peacock emphasizes the only possible solution to the problem. More often than not men, when they are busy at all (about half the time), are engaged in a single task such as butchering or repairing a tool. Women, on the other hand, spend an appreciable proportion of their waking hours doing several things at once, stirring the pot and feeding the infant and tending the fire. In other words, women become multiple-task specialists.

As indicated in Chapters 10 and 11, the beginnings of the transition from foraging to a more settled village life was marked among other things by the first appearance of status in the archeological record of the Upper Paleolithic. An analog of this process may be seen in the Ituri rain forest. Status certainly exists among the pygmies, but only in an incipient, unofficial form which is rather difficult to measure.

Among Lese villagers, however, status can be measured. Wrangham and Ross developed a rating of the wealth of families based on counts of owned items—agricultural tools, household goods, clothing, chickens, and weapons.

Among other things, they found that the wealthiest men received more meat and honey and labor from the pygmies than men with fewer possessions, and had more children—and more wives. Incidentally, it is not only the men who benefit from polygyny. Co-wives also benefit by sharing the work and enjoying more free time than monogamously wedded women.

Perhaps the most significant point about these and other projects is the extent of our present-day ignorance or, to put it another way, how much remains to be learned about the human species. As far as hard data are concerned and after centuries of study and contemplation, we are practically starting from scratch, or so it seems after reviewing where things stand today. We seem to know so much more about nonhuman species than we do about ourselves, and the difference is more formidable the closer we come to hominids on the evolutionary scale.

Certainly the next generation, the next decade, can be expected to bring not only new knowledge but a new perspective on what being human means, a deeper awareness of our considerable uniqueness and at the same time of our basic biological ties to other primates, other mammals. The ancient aboriginal life styles are vanishing, and there are no "pure" hunter-gatherers any more, no people living in isolation on wild species (a state which probably passed many millenniums ago). But there is still ample material for research among people at large in modern societies, industrial and otherwise. We are close to our Upper Paleolithic ancestors in many respects, close enough so that our behavior may throw light on theirs, and vice versa.

SUMMARY

Comparative studies indicate that modern hunter-gatherers tend to form bands averaging some 25 members, with a range of about 20 to 70, not out of line with troop sizes for other primates. The number 500, however, represents something uniquely human—an order-of-magnitude figure for tribes made up of a number of hunter-gatherer bands. The appearance of ornaments during the Upper Paleolithic may have been associated with the appearance of such societies, perhaps to identify individuals as members of the group.

Among the most intensively observed present-day hunter-gatherers are the Bushmen of southern Africa's Kalahari Desert, with special attention paid to a group of associated bands numbering some 450 individuals. Survival means keeping on the move as people exhaust local food supplies, mainly plants including their staple, the nut of the mongongo tree, trapped small game, and large animals brought down with poisoned arrows. During the dry season bands move near one of the few permanent water holes, digging for water-rich roots in times of direst need.

Like most hunter-gatherers, the Bushmen live by a strictly egalitarian ethics. Sensitive to the relationship between status and conflict, they have no formal big men or chiefs. Boasting, accumulating possessions, anything that might arouse envy or arrogance, is socially unacceptable. Children are trained in generosity from early infancy. Adults are generally close at hand to nip playtime fighting in the bud, before it develops into something serious.

Adapting to subarctic conditions calls for special strategies. Caribou meat has long been the food staple for Eskimos living in the Brooks Range of Alaska, and when caribou do not come, as happened following a recent blizzard, they turn to last-resort sources—snared Arctic squirrels, emergency caches of frozen caribou meat, marrow bones, and frozen wolf and fox carcasses. Such practices suggest things to look for when excavating the sites of ice-age hunters.

A new large-scale study involves pygmy hunter-gatherers and village farmers living in the rain forests of Zaire. Basic data consist of physical measurements, life histories, and genealogies for 800 to 1200 individuals, and hundreds of hours spent observing and recording behavior patterns. Preliminary results include statistics indicating the different roles of men and women in the food quest, and insights into forces favoring the rise of status.

chapter *17*

Experimental Archeology

One way of entering a bit more actively into the lives of prehistoric people is to try doing what they did, to perform experiments designed to learn more about their techniques and strategies. Sometimes opportunities for experiments arise unexpectedly. One July evening in 1966 a group of excavators was camping in an isolated part of the Fort Apache Indian Reservation of eastern Arizona. Among them were William Longacre, an archeologist at the University of Arizona, and a group of students. They were engaged in digging an 800-room pueblo community dating back to the fourteenth century, a continuing, long-term project.

The camp routine was upset an hour before midnight when a student stringing up a hammock heard a rustling in the leaves and turned his flashlight on a big black bear who had been attracted by the smell of baking banana bread. The animal was fair game. The bear population in the area had increased rapidly, and the Apaches were losing cattle regularly. Several nights earlier, bears had killed a couple of calves at a nearby dam. The cattle manager for the Indians was called to the scene and killed the animal with a single 30-30 carbine shot.

RE-CREATING THE PAST

The problem of what to do with the carcass became a valuable lesson. It happened that the late Don Crabtree of Kimberly, Idaho, a specialist in stoneworking, was visiting the camp to demonstrate toolmaking techniques to the students. The bear represented an unprecedented chance to see his tools actually in use by an expert hunter and skinner, the man who had killed the bear. The expert, Gene Seely, gracious if not highly enthusiastic, obviously preferred rather more conventional methods, but agreed to give it a try.

Everything was ready early next morning. Crabtree had prepared a little kit of eight tools, all made of obsidian, a hard volcanic glass. The students had gathered around to watch, and there in the center of the circle were the dead bear and Seely, who was chewing tobacco and shaking his head skeptically. He took a backed blade and started the first cut from below the jaws down the chest, but he was shocked to find himself off balance in a peculiar way. On the basis of his experience with steel knives, his muscles were set to overcome a certain amount of resistance in cutting through the tough skin. The obsidian blade had gone through the skin as if it were butter.

From there on it was smooth sailing and a clear-cut victory for the stone tools. Seely, muttering to himself in surprise, completed in less than two hours a task that would have taken up to three and a half hours using his favorite Swedish steel knife. Of course, the one advantage of steel is its superior durability, although the volcanic glass can be resharpened in a few seconds by removing tiny chips along working edges. After the demonstration, Seely requested and received a kit of obsidian tools to commemorate the occasion.

Experimental archeology includes a wide range of projects. Under the general heading of tools and toolmaking, archeologists have tumbled unworked pebbles in cement mixers to find out whether random chipping and flaking can produce objects resembling human-made implements (it can), immobilized their thumbs to find out whether creatures without opposable thumbs could make crude hands axes (they could), and tested dozens of ways of duplicating and using prehistoric tools. Other experiments deal broadly with various aspects of the food quest, the methods of the cave artists, and efforts to live for a while in Upper Paleolithic fashion.

No matter how hard most investigators work at recording and reconstructing the past, their approach is necessarily passive. They are always on the outside looking in. But experimentally minded investigators find a way to enter, however briefly and superficially, the world of prehistoric people. An analogous process takes place in acting. When actors learn to move as they believe a character would have moved, they assume the gestures and intonations and garments and bodily rhythm of the character, they are beginning to feel another's feelings and to live another's life. We say they live their role.

Investigators have not gone to the extreme of immersing themselves that deeply into the roles of Upper Paleolithic hunter-gatherers. On a more restricted scale, experimental archeology has made efforts to re-create a small part of the past so as to obtain by direct action a measure of insight into what it might have been like to work in, say, Magdalenian times or earlier. It is primarily an active approach, a matter of trying out a technique to see how it works, modifying it if necessary, seeking fresh archeological and behavioral evidence, and trying again. Anything that helps translate hypothesis into action helps to make prehistory less remote, and thus serves teaching as well as research purposes.

MODERN FLINT KNAPPERS

Many experiments concern the making of stone tools, by far the most numerous traces of prehistoric people. Tools can be found in isolated places everywhere, on all continents, often in fantastic abundance. I have seen stretches of semidesert peppered with artifacts lying exposed on the sand, sites where you can still collect several dozen hand axes and cleavers and other tools within half an hour or so, even though amateur archeologists, professional archeologists, and tourists in search of souvenirs have been collecting from the area for 20 years or more. One part of South Africa alone, the Springbok Flats just outside Johannesburg, contains an estimated 17 billion artifacts.

No material is familiar to us in the way stone was familiar to our ancestors. Toolmaking was second nature to them, part of their daily lives, something like driving a car is today, only learned much younger. They acquired a feel for the qualities of stone, for the way it had to be held and struck and the way it broke; and every step of the shaping proceeded according to traditions thousands of years old. They accumulated a kind of muscular knowledge, only a fraction of which could be conveyed by words.

Prehistoric children probably learned mainly by watching and imitating rather than by verbal instruction, at least as far as most early tools are concerned. A number of experiments suggest that such instruction is not necessary to make reasonably good hand axes or, according to Gould's observations, to make the sort of tools produced by the Australian aborigines. On the other hand, when it comes to the most refined techniques and the shaping of such items as Solutrean blades and some of the projectile points to be discussed in the following paragraphs, experts almost certainly had to tell novices what to do.

Crabtree was a pioneer among modern flint knappers. He made more than 50,000 blades, arrowheads, scrapers, and other tools, and probably broke three to four times that many during the course of his research. One of the projects that occupied him off and on for years involves a beautifully worked flint tool found predominantly in the New World, a projectile point discovered in 1926 at a buffalo-kill site near the town of Folsom, New Mexico. Folsom points come in a variety of forms. But Crabtree concentrated on a type which, in his opinion, "reflects the very ultimate in working skill and control . . . being as thin and perfectly shaped as the technique would allow." It is an artifact generally about 2 inches long, shaped something like a rowboat, and featuring a full-length groove or fluting along each side.

There is and was no simple way of making the artifact. Crabtree tried 11 different methods, each calling for the control of up to 35 variables—from the selection of suitable flint to final retouching—and finally reached a stage where he could make a good replica in about 3 hours, with a failure rate of more than 50 percent. He knew that the American Indians of prehistory must have done much better than that, perhaps by a combination of pressure flaking—removing small chips with a wooden or bone tool placed hard against the flint and pushed forward sharply (probably another Solutrean invention)—and indirect percussion, using a punch to strike off chips.

In a recent follow-up of this work, and after much research and testing, Jeffrey Flenniken of Washington State University took the Folsom technique several steps further. He has developed a seven-stage process calling for initial use of a soft limestone hammerstone as well as indirect percussion and pressure flaking, and turned out 100 replicas made from Texas chert and Oregon obsidian. It takes him about 40 minutes to produce a Folsom point, with a failure rate of less than 37 percent.

Another Crabtree study arose from an observation made during the 1930s. He noticed that flint flakes collected at certain American Indian sites were greasy, shiny, and often pinkish, while samples of the same material in its native "fresh" form, as obtained from local quarries, were dull gray. Furthermore, the flakes were less brittle and much easier to work. Experiments soon revealed that they had been annealed, heated, and then allowed to cool slowly, a process which relaxes the strains built into flint crystals and results in a softer, more elastic material which can be trimmed and shaped with less applied pressure.

Subsequently François Bordes and other French investigators, alerted by such studies, looked for and found evidence for similar preheating at Upper Paleolithic sites—a further mark of our ancestors' sophistication. There is no single best heat treatment. Different sizes and types of flint require temperatures ranging from 400 to 1100 degrees Fahrenheit; temperatures must be held at various levels for hours or days; and various cooling schedules must be tried.

(Left) Don Crabtree demonstrating chest crutch to make Folsom point
(Right) Contemporary flintworkers: Don Crabtree and François Bordes in Crabtree's Idaho workshop

Four Crabtree-made Folsom points

Such procedures, which depend on trial-and-error experience and considerable technical knowledge, further swelled the contents of the memorized tribal encyclopedia (see Chapter 11).

Bordes and Crabtree met in a number of flint-knapping sessions, the former specializing in percussion flaking, the latter in pressure flaking. Each learned a great deal from the other. Bordes' theory that there were four Neanderthal tribes or cultures, a theory which opened the way for a new approach to the study of tool assemblages (see Chapter 9), arose directly out of his first-hand research on the use and making of stone tools. His analysis could have been carried out only by someone with a worker's knowledge and feel for the shaping of flints. Several years ago Bordes had a tool-making session with aborigines in northern Australia: "I chipped tools with them and taught them a lot of techniques they did not know. Of course, this comes a little late to change things. I also learned a lot from them."

Do-it-yourself procedures are also in order when it comes to figuring out the uses of prehistoric tools. A case in point is the dismembering of the Arizona bear described at the beginning of this chapter; another is Louis Leakey's Christmas Eve dismembering of an African antelope (see Chapter 5). In the same tradition, but on a rather more systematic basis, is an extended series of experiments, the first of its kind, conducted by Nicholas Toth, mainly with tools he made himself. His subjects included one circus elephant, one cow, part of an oryx killed by a lion, one pig, four horses, and seven goats.

Wielding replicas of Oldowan "choppers," Acheulian hand axes, and a variety of sharp-edged flakes, Toth went through the entire butchering process—from initial hide slitting, skinning, and dismembering to final bone smashing for marrow. His belief that a major reason for the appearance of stone tools two or more million years ago was an increasing reliance on hunted or scavenged meat confirms a general impression from other studies (see Chapter 5). Incidentally, in addition to butchering, he performed a number of other early-hominid chores: digging for plant foods and water, cracking nuts, scraping and drying hides, chopping wood, carrying cobbles, throwing spears, and so on.

STONE AND BONE ANALYSIS

Toth also managed to make some deductions about planning and foresight among early hominids, deductions based on a unique toolmaking project. A practiced stone worker, he made replicas of the more than 50 lava cores found at a site in the Lake Turkana region of Kenya where hominids ate meat some 1.5 million years ago (known as Site 50; see Chapter 4), counted all flakes 2 centimeters or more long, and divided them into six types according to different stages of the knapping process. On the basis of this and other experiments, he compared the number of flakes of each type, predicted from his own work, to the numbers of flakes actually found at early-hominid sites.

The predicted numbers tended to be too high, appreciably exceeding the actual numbers. Since there is no evidence at the sites of the sort of water action that might have carried flakes away, Toth suggests that some of the early hominids' stone working had been performed away from the sites, perhaps at quarries where they prepared pieces of roughly the required size to lighten their carrying load. An interesting clue tends to support this possibility. The type of flake formed prehistorically during the late stage of knapping generally occurs in higher-than-predicted numbers, which supports the notion of early stage work having been conducted elsewhere.

Kathy Schick of the University of California at Berkeley, also a practiced stone worker, is engaged in related investigations of site integrity, the degree to which the original, as-was patterns at various sites have been preserved. Her findings are based on 110 tookmaking sessions, during each of which she turned out cleavers, choppers, hand axes, and other early-type tools—and collected the thousands of flakes and waste chips more than a half a centimeter long. She noted standard size distributions, with more than 60 percent of all fragments measuring less than 2 centimeters, and smaller and smaller proportions in the 2-to-4-, 4-to-8-, 8-to-16-, and over-16-centimeter categories.

The next step was to compare these experimental distributions with observed flake-and-debris distributions at prehistoric Lake Turkana sites. Some sites were clearly disturbed. For example, those associated with ancient stream channels generally showed lower-than-expected proportions of small flakes, which flowing waters selectively wash away. Other sites, Site 50 among them, seem to be in a near-pristine, relatively undisturbed condition, with flake-size distributions close to experimental levels. Schick's work, involving a great many observations and measurements in addition to distribution statistics, is part of a continuing trend toward increased precision in the analysis of archeological sites.

Another line of research, already referred to in Chapter 4, focuses on the problem of deducing what tools were actually used for, since butchering experiments simply indicate possible uses. More than 30 years ago Sergei Semenov of the USSR Institute of Archeology in Leningrad began studying microwear, marks on tools which cannot be detected by the naked eye. Certain visible features such as gloss or polish, nicks and scratches provide hints. But a far more detailed and reliable record can be obtained by treating tool surfaces with metal powders or various chemicals, and then examining them under the microscope.

This procedure reveals an entirely new landscape of wear, something like the difference between viewing the moon from an earthbound telescope and from a telescope on a satellite in orbit near the lunar surface. For example, Semenov reexamined a Neanderthal tool which, on the basis of naked-eye inspection showing polish on both sides of the working edge, had been tentatively identified as a knife. The microscope showed a system of many fine grooves which, instead of running parallel to the working edge, as expected from a regular back-and-forth cutting action, ran at various angles, often crisscrossing one another. This was precisely the pattern produced experimentally with scrapers. Furthermore, the material involved was probably animal skin, since previous skin-scraping tests produced identical patterns.

Lawrence Keeley has refined the Soviet work to a point where identification can be made with a high degree of accuracy. On the basis of hundreds of comparisons between the patterns on prehistoric and experimental tools, he has learned to distinguish a variety of materials. Woodworking produces a characteristic bright, whitish polish, which Keeley found on tools dating back 1.5 million years (see Chapter 4). He can also distinguish the microwear patterns of dry hides (matt, dull-low-luster effect, with "linear features," a diffuse streaky kind of polish), wet hides (greasy luster, also with linear features), and plants (very bright and smooth, "melted" appearance, a few comet-tailed pits).

Identifying bone as the worked material involves patterns not yet understood. Tools that have been used on bone have a bright polish and one of two other features, either many micropits or peculiar pock marks, like the hollows in snow melting around the bases of trees. Working antler produces the same features, so it is possible to tell that a tool was used to work either bone or antler, but not to distinguish between the two.

Five years ago Mark Newcomer gave Keeley, then a graduate student still working on his thesis, a tough put-up-or-shut-up trial. Newcomer made 15 flint tools such as might be found at sites from 50,000 to some 2 million years ago, and simple retouched and unretouched flakes, which he used to work various materials, and gave the lot to Keeley for analysis. For Keeley it was a completely "blind" test; he knew nothing about what Newcomer had done. Yet he correctly identified the worked material in 10 cases, for a respectable batting average of 0.675, and he could do rather better than that today.

Bone can be at least as important as stone in yielding information about the life styles of times past. Taphonomy, the study of post-mortem changes in bones (see Chapter 4), has brought a new sophistication and a new caution when it comes to drawing conclusions from fossil remains. Not so long ago it was taken for granted that a relative scarcity of bone implies a low-meat diet, and that a predominance of the bones of small animals implies a diet heavy on small game.

Now the tendency is more to think twice. To check the first of these assumptions, Glynn Isaac dumped 55 large bones and bone fragments and some 60 bone splinters on a 1-square-yard plot in the African Rift Valley. Returning 4 months later to see what was left, he found that more than 70 percent of the material had vanished completely, destroyed and scattered by hyenas and other predators. As far as the second assumption is concerned, John Yellen observes that, in the Kalahari, large bones are often splintered for their marrow and that splinters disintegrate rapidly, while small bones may become buried and remain intact. In other words, many interpretations once recognized as "self-evident"— a booby-trap word if there ever was one—are currently recognized as things to be proved.

Taphonomy is still in its early stages, and experimental taphonomy perhaps even more so. Investigators can simulate as well as simply observe events that affect the condition and distribution of bone assemblages. The sorting-out action of water in dispersing the assemblages, tending to carry smaller bones further downstream than larger bones, has been studied in sluiceways serving as artificial streams. Hours have been spent in breaking bones in a continuing effort to deduce from the breakage patterns whether or not the breaker was a hominid, and in dismembering carcases in a search for marks on bone that could have resulted from human butchery and from nothing else. If it were possible, of course, much of this sort of research would be carried out in a real-world context, such as what Lewis Binford encountered when living among the Eskimos, where there is direct, on-the-spot exchange information with experienced hunters.

MORE DO-IT-YOURSELF RESEARCH

Those who have actually lived with people on a day-to-day basis gain a kind of firsthand knowledge that can be obtained in no other way. In his studies of the Bushmen, for example, Richard Lee had to learn their difficult language, which includes four different clicks and five tones. He has gathered mongongo nuts with them, and lived for three weeks on a diet consisting mainly of this staple. On one occasion he managed to keep up with hunters walking through the Kalahari at a speed of 5 to 6 miles per hour, although doing that as a regular practice was something else again. His most arduous experience was an effort to live as Bushmen live at the height of a drought, accompanying a group on an overnight hike to a mongongo forest where the only local source of water were the juices in deep underground roots.

This was too much for Lee. After spending hours looking for game and digging for roots and walking some 9 miles under the sun in temperatures of well over a hundred degrees, he realized that he would be a burden to the others. He felt feverish and dry, could not swallow, and decided to go back to the base camp near a permanent water hole. Upon his return early the next morning, Lee made a dramatic beeline for the nearest water bag and emptied it with evident relief, a sight that set the Bushmen laughing for an hour.

That was an experiment of a sort. A more direct approach is the one Louis Leakey used on numerous occasions—do the hunting yourself. One of his most successful performances occurred on open country near a lake outside Nairobi. Leakey saw a herd of nine fleet-footed Thomson's gazelles, or Tommies, about 250 yards away, and decided to stalk one of the group that was grazing apart from the others. First he fastened leafy branches to his belt as part of a crude camouflage, not to hide himself, but to break up the telltale silhouette of the human body. Then he started closing in: "The essence of stalking is to appear not to move."

The trick is to move directly forward and to move very slowly, because that way the shape of your silhouette does not change and the size increases imperceptibly. But any sideways movement, particularly of the hands, which are a sure sign of a person, changes body shape and may cause animals to flee in panic. So Leakey kept his hands against his sides, moved his legs straight forward, and kept his eyes on the gazelle he was stalking as well as on the rest of the herd.

As long as the animals were feeding, as long as their heads were down, he advanced steadily. But the instant they looked up in his general direction, he had to freeze to the spot, and he knew how to anticipate that instant: "There's a subtle movement just before a Tommy lifts its head. One shoulder seems to rise just a bit higher than the other." Leakey advanced in a series of stops and starts and changes of direction as his prey moved about. Several times he had to wait motionless for birds, which emit sharp alarm calls when startled, to fly away. Finally, after two solid hours of stalking, he reduced the distance between him and the gazelle from 250 yards to about 6 feet, and brought it down with a perfectly timed flying tackle.

During the entire period Leakey played two roles alternately. Part of the time he identified himself with the gazelle he was stalking, drawing air through his nostrils for the scent of predators, listening for a snapping twig or the rustle of branches, and anticipating, not only by overt signs but with a sixth sense for its rhythm of alertness, the moment to stop grazing and look up. When the animal pricked up its ears and turned suddenly, Leakey felt an uncertainty, a tension, that was not relieved until it resumed feeding. And a split second before the final tackle he felt the burst of fear and confusion of his prey.

At other times he was a prehistoric hunter, applying what he had learned as a child from Kikuyu hunters who lived near his home in Kenya. He observed a thousand details while frozen in position, noting things nearby as well as at a distance, particularly things that meant food—a large snail, an anthill, tracks and trails where snares might be set, and weaverbirds' nests lined with grass on the inside so that there are few openings and little light gets through, a sign that rats or mice have moved into the abandoned nests. "You try not to take risks, not to strike until you're quite certain," Leakey explained. "But I've failed many times and Stone Age man did, too, so he always noticed second-best foods as he stalked, in case his quarry escaped."

Prehistoric gathering has also been investigated experimentally. Some years ago Jack Harlan of the University of Illinois, a specialist in early plant domestication, joined an archeological expedition to southeastern Turkey, one of the Near Eastern regions where farming was first practiced. The region is still rich in plant foods. Harlan saw "vast seas of primitive wild wheats" still growing on mountain slopes, the same varieties of wheat used by early farmers some 10,000 to 12,000 years ago. One day, he went out into the fields to see how much grain he could harvest.

During his first tests, he used the simplest of tools, his bare "urbanized" hands, which soon became red and raw. But even so he had no trouble gathering an average of about 4.5 pounds of grain per hour. Then he made himself a crude sickle by gouging a slot in a sturdy branch and inserting a flint sickle blade obtained from a 9000-year-old early agriculture site in Iraq. The blade cut wheat about as well as a steel sickle blade, yielded nearly an extra pound of grain per hour, and spared his hands. His conclusion: "A family group . . . working slowly upslope as the season progressed, could easily harvest wild cereals over a three-week span or more and, without even working very hard, could gather more grain than the family could possibly consume in a year."

Harlan also tried various ways of preparing wild wheat. He removed hulls by using an Osage Indian mortar and pestle, a process made somewhat easier by pretoasting in an oven for 15 to 30 minutes at 350 degrees. The pounded material could be cleaned by passing it through a sieve of woven grass, or simply by winnowing it in the wind, and then made into a soup or boiled like rice. Harlan reports that wild wheat is nutritious as well as tasty, chemical analysis showing that it contains nearly 60 percent more protein than modern cultivated varieties.

Experiments involving the final stages of the food quest, prehistoric cookery, include the roasting of whole animals in their skins, an Old Australian aborigine custom. This recipe, which produces steaks ideal for those who prefer their meat slightly warm and well underdone, may have been conceived 500,000 or more years ago, during the days of *Homo erectus* (see Chapter 7). Cooking in water brought to a boil by the use of hot pot-boilers probably dates back to more recent times. American Indians practiced the technique as recently as a century or so ago, Basque shepherds in northern Spain do it upon occasion to boil milk or water, and, as Jean-Philippe Rigaud observed (see Chapter 16), so do Eskimos in Alaska.

One living floor at the Abri Pataud site in the Les Eyzies region includes smooth river pebbles, most of them broken and colored red or black by the action of fire. To test the notion that these were pot-boilers, Hallam Movius heated some river pebbles, tossed them into a pail of water, and observed that they produced effective boiling. He also observed that after being used three or four times, the stones split in two, and split into smaller pieces during subsequent plunges. When the pieces reached a certain size, they no longer split but burst into fragments, a phenomenon which undoubtedly startled prehistoric cooks as much as it did Movius. The tests produced shattered stones and fragments resembling those excavated at the site, implying the existence of some kind of skin containers or, more probably, wooden cooking vessels.

PREHISTORIC ART AND MUSIC

A whole series of investigations stems from increasing interest in Upper Paleo-lithic cave painting and the artists' techniques. Newcomer, an inveterate experimenter, has had a hand in these studies, too. The garden of his home outside London contains a collection of items that might baffle future archeologists. It includes assorted traces of simulated prehistory, relics of past and continuing tests such as flint in various stages of working, and a pebble painted with lines and dots using a frayed-twig brush, a copy of the painted pebbles found at Azilian sites (see Chapter 11).

In another part of the garden is a slate with six rectangular strips painted in various shades of red and representing six different paint preparations that cave painters might have used. Five of the paints contain red ocher, a natural mixture of clays and hematite, or iron oxide, combined with five binders—egg yolk and water, egg white and water, whole egg and water, saliva, and slightly heated mutton fat. The sixth is a mixture of egg yolk and water and pure hematite instead of ocher. The strips had been painted in 1976, and after seven years of exposure to the elements, five of the six mixes had faded considerably. Only the pure-hematite mix has retained its color.

One of Newcomer's most recent projects was a test of the cave artists' stone lamps. Starting from scratch with a set of homemade flint tools and a limestone slab, he spent 5 hours making a teardrop-shaped model about 7 inches long and hollowed out at the center, a copy of a prehistoric original. Filled with any one of various cooking or animal fats and oils, such as lard or peanut oil, and a wick of rolled-up leaves, grass, or moss ("anything that burns"), it provides five to six hours of light, enough to illuminate several square feet of wall surface. If you want more light, you can use several lamps or a single lamp with several wicks.

A lamp with two wicks was put to use for a time during an elaborately planned project—copying an entire frieze 23 feet long and 8 feet high and including ten mammoths, four bison, four oxen, and three horses, all done in black outline. The original frieze exists in a much-visited art cave in the south of France; the copy was painted with charcoal crayons on a selected wall of a nearby cave which tourists have never seen; and the artist was Michel Lorblanchet of the French National Center of Scientific Research.

Lorblanchet had studied the original for hours, so intensively that he was reasonably sure not only of the number of separate strokes in each figure but also of the order in which they were drawn. For example, in the case of one of the bison, he knew that the artist had started with a sweeping line at the head end, followed by successive lines for the back, tail, legs, and then to the head end again, exactly 30 strokes in all. Drawing time for most of the figures was from 1 to 4 minutes each, except for a number of schematic figures which required less than 30 seconds. The entire frieze took an hour or so, probably about the time required by the original artist.

Timing the art, going through motions similar to those of the creator—the same "gestures"—provides a feeling for the pace and skill of the work. Even more important, it provides a feeling for repeated patterns and elements of style, knowledge of which may help in deducing when different figures were painted. "Upper Paleolithic art is full of stylistic conventions from one period to another," Lorblanchet explains. "It is produced in line with special rules, a kind of code. We may never crack that code, but it is certainly worth trying."

Incidentally, Randall White discovered something interesting about Upper Paleolithic engravings during the course of experiments with burins, or engraving tools. Alexander Marshack has spent considerable time in the art caves and elsewhere examining engraved lines, and one of his main points is that different kinds of grooves represent the use of different burins, presumably made by different individuals at different times. White's work demonstrates that this need not be, and probably is not, the case. He notes that three different ways of using the same burin can produce three different patterns—a U-shaped groove, a symmetrical V-shaped groove, or an "offset" V-shaped groove with one arm of the V shorter than the other.

Having completed this analysis, White examined Marshack's microscopic photographs and observed the same three patterns. This finding runs directly counter to the assumption that different kinds of grooves were produced by people coming back to the same cave location to incise new marks, presumably for some sort of record-keeping. On the positive side, White stresses that it is a tribute to the sophistication of the engravers, since a variety of lines may be executed "in one sitting by the use of one tool": "Boldness or fineness of lines is directly related to mode of burin use. . . . Tools need not be changed, and lines can be produced in any sequence the artist wishes."

A unique and ambitious effort to learn something about prehistoric music is underway at Harvard University. Lyle Davidson, a musicologist and composer, has a replica of an Upper Paleolithic flute (made by Newcomer, of course, and one of about 20 found in the caves). Precisely 4.375 inches long with six stops, it is designed to be played clarinet-style by blowing through one end. It is pitched an octave above soprano at about piccolo level, and has a pentatonic, or five-tone, scale—which also serves as the basis for one form of Hindu music, Anglo-Saxon folk melodies, and certain music in the Japanese Kabuki theater. Davidson is impressed with the quality of Upper Paleolithic music:

The flute by its very existence and design indicates something fixed and planned about the melodies played, something fixed in the composer's mind. It is anything but haphazard, delicate and sensitive with a level of technological subtlety which implies a corresponding subtlety of use. Controlling it requires considerable exertion and practice. Of course, a modern flute also requires an enormous amount of practice, but it is designed to play music you know. You have mental templates of contemporary notes and scales, and can tell when you produce the right sound. But with this prehistoric instrument you have no such guidelines. You must figure out what it wants to do, discover what is difficult and what is easy or natural.

The process is something like working with a strange horse, not breaking it in but adapting to it, understanding its disposition and natural pace. At this stage it is clear that the music must have had an unusual, offbeat quality, since the two sets of stops produce two very different kinds of sound. The upper stops produce distinct and discrete notes, much like the notes in modern scales. The lower stops, however, yield notes with shorter intervals and almost the same pitch; it is the color or timbre, the resonant quality, that changes. The result is a more continuous, nearly steady tonal effect.

Taking the measure of the flute—testing its range and the sort of finger action to which it responds best, exploring its strengths and limitations—is still a problem. The ultimate objective is reconstruction. There are many graphic versions of what the artists did and how they did it, illustrations showing them at work engraving mammoth tusks, shaping figurines, preparing pigments and painting on cave walls, and sculpting animals in rock. It may not be long before Davidson and others take the first steps toward producing analogous versions of the music played in times past. In any case, he enjoys the challenge: "The music is very rich and warm, not at all light or airy—very serious. I am learning a great deal about the flutes of the world."

SOME STUDIES FOR THE FUTURE

Another type of experimental archeology with many unexploited possibilities, particularly in education and in evaluating excavating techniques, is the construction of simulated prehistoric sites. For example, a number of years ago John Chilcott and James Deetz made several such sites on the campus of the University of California in Santa Barbara. They used a machine to dig square pits 7 feet on a side and some 5 feet deep. They put artifacts and other materials in predetermined positions, filled the pits up again, and planted grass on the surface. Six months later, after the elements had aged the area, they returned to excavate.

One of the pits was designed to test the effectiveness of various digging techniques in recovering small objects, in this case glass beads about the size of BB shot. Among other things, the study indicated just how important the type of soil may be in this connection. Ninety-six percent of the beads placed beforehand in the natural silty soil of the region were recovered by simply scooping up the soil in a trowel and sifting through it. But the recovery rate dropped to less than 60 percent in damp earth formed by decayed organic matter, which is oily and tends to cling to the beads, a fact underlining the need for special measures when working in such soils.

A second site served as a proving ground for students. It had three made-to-order occupation layers, the deepest containing a hearth, scrapers, projectile points, and other carefully placed items that might be found in Indian deposits 6000 years old or more. Above this layer, the California archeologists arranged a more recent type of living floor, including coyote and human bones and pottery; and above that a modern or "historic" layer, with a beer bottle, pieces of glass, a metal blank, and other human remains. Five crews of students representing different age groups and different degrees of experience worked at five parts of the site. As expected, the more experienced students did a more careful job of excavating than novices (breaking fewer items and leaving more items in their

Solebury School students at experimental site

original positions). In other words, this sort of setup provides a good way of training and testing students.

There is no reason why such projects should be confined to colleges. Students in lower grades can also be involved, as demonstrated in an early experiment devised by trustees at the Solebury School in New Hope, Pennsylvania. They invented a game to be played between eighth and ninth graders. In the fall, eighth-grade students dug a large square hole about a yard deep, and at the bottom arranged a hearth with ashes, flint chips, a broken scraper, and some fossilized bones—representing remains as they might be found in an actual Indian site 10,000 or more years old. The students made a map indicating the position of each object, and then filled in the hole with earth.

Next spring ninth-grade students excavated the site, the aim being to plot the positions of the uncovered objects precisely enough to duplicate the map drawn by the eighth-grade students. Although the soil was clayey and difficult to dig, they managed to reconstruct appreciable portions of the original patterns. The experiment gave students a chance to think up their own living-floor patterns, and in the process to gain a firsthand feeling for the basic notion of living floors and the importance of slow and careful excavating. Similar games have been devised by William Turnbaugh of the University of Rhode Island, who is developing a variety of new ways of teaching archeology.

British investigators are conducting a rather more elaborate, long-term experiment. Peter Jewell of Royal Holloway College near London and his associates have built an experimental earthwork, or barrow, with a ditch and bank such as prehistoric people built to house their distinguished dead. Jewell and his colleagues placed inside it cremated human bone, numbered pieces of pottery, burned and unburned wood, leather, dyed and undyed cloth, and other items. The exact position of each item has been recorded. The project is designed to determine how, and how fast, materials decompose, how their positions change as a result of the heaving of freezing and thawing soils, and the action of earthworms and other burrowing animals. Some notable changes have already taken place. For example, pieces of unburned wood and undyed cloth have disintegrated, but not the burned and dyed specimens. The experiment will last at least a hundred years. The earthwork was built in 1960 and has been opened up half a dozen times since then, most recently in 1976. The next excavation is scheduled for 1992 and the last for the year 2088.

There is an advantage in trying to share a way of life, an advantage beyond coming closer to people and earning their confidence and good will. Although one can never learn to think as prehistoric people thought or learn exactly how they did things, every increase of knowledge adds a bit to reconstructions of times past. The problem of improving the reconstructions, of understanding human origins better, is sufficiently important to merit the exploration of every possible lead. Perhaps the ultimate step, the ultimate experiment in living archeology, is to "go prehistoric" for a time and live entirely on what you can get from the wilderness.

As far as I know, no one has yet undertaken such a project in an organized fashion, although there have been occasional efforts. One archeologist in his undergraduate days spent several months hunting and trapping alone in the wilderness, and provided very well for himself. But his motive was personal rather than scientific; he simply wanted to get away from people. And about a generation ago ten French investigators spent 3 weeks in a cave living off the land in what they considered to be the style of the Neanderthals.

The pioneer work of Errett Callahan when he was at Virginia Commonwealth University in Richmond represents a more systematic approach. For a number of years he has been developing programs in subsistence living, or living archeology. They are increasingly sophisticated efforts to learn more about prehistoric peoples by firsthand experience and by "resurrecting 'dead' information, information supposedly locked in time." High points of his studies occurred in the summers of 1974 and 1975 during experiments in living on a wild 1500-acre tract on the Pamunkey River 25 miles from Richmond, not far from the Pamunkey Indian Reservation.

Before moving into the area, Callahan and his students trained for the project by getting used to meals made up of wild foods and by weight lifting and daily jogging (a mile in less than 8 minutes). They lived on the land in the style of woodland Indians more than a millennium ago; they used tools they made themselves to construct shelters, traps, fish weirs, and a raft; and they contended with a drought during the first season and almost ceaseless rain during the second. It was an adventure, but no lark. Callahan, now doing experiments at the Lejre Research Center in Denmark, is still analyzing the results of this project.

Louis Leakey once had a living-archeology plan which he never carried out. It was intended to cover several million years of human evolution in 6 weeks, each week representing a different stage of development. The plan called for Leakey to live during the first week the way hominids presumably lived before the regular making of tools, say, some 3 million years ago. Equipped with clubs, rocks for bashing, digging sticks, and cord for snares and traps (made from the inner bark of trees), he would subsist chiefly on plant foods and small game which could be ripped apart with bare hands.

During the second week, the second evolutionary stage of perhaps 2 million years ago, he would make simple choppers and flake tools. That would permit systematic scavenging for the first time, because such tools make it possible to cut through tough antelope skin and separate joints and do general butchering, all of which cannot be accomplished with hands and fingernails and teeth (Leakey has tried). The third week would involve increasing independence of other killers; the decline of scavenging and the rise of big-game hunting; the development of hand axes, cleavers, and other heavy-duty butchering tools; and the invention of wooden spears with whittled and perhaps fire-hardened tips, or antelope-horn tips.

More and more advanced techniques were planned during the last 3 weeks, covering the period from 10,000 or 15,000 to about 100,000 years ago. Leakey would begin by making stone points and hafting them to spears with natural resins, gums, and sinews, and later turn to backed blades and spear throwers and harpoons. Up to this point all his weapons would be designed primarily to cripple animals and slow them down, but the final week would see the first case of shooting to kill with finely balanced spears and, above all, an efficient bow and arrow. Throughout the 6-week period he would live in increasingly advanced quarters: rock shelters; caves; crude tents, half-sunken pit houses, or artificial caves, and huts with solid walls and roofs.

Leakey had an explanation for never undertaking such vigorous living off African savanna lands: "I'd have done it long ago, but Mary wouldn't let me. She thought it was too dangerous." But a review of what has already been done and of what has not yet been done indicates that the time may be ripe for some such plan. Making tools, and using them to make other tools for butchering animals and gathering plant foods, trying out primitive hunting techniques, and many studies have all contributed blocks of information to our understanding of hunter-gatherers. But each study has been a piecemeal effort, isolated from the others and representing the skills, enthusiasm, and interests of the individual investigator acting pretty much on his or her own. The next step might well be a coordinated series of field expeditions where the objective would be to duplicate the complete range of actual Stone Age living as closely as possible by organizing volunteers into prehistoric-type bands and having them camp out in the wilderness for extended periods.

Experimental archeology, once mainly a casual sideline activity of a few investigators, is moving into a key position in prehistoric research. It is part and parcel of a whole complex of studies designed to supplement and illuminate archeological evidence. Used during the course of analyses of hunter-gatherer life styles, assemblages of fossil bones, and microwear, it brings the all-important do-it-yourself element into the picture, enriching our efforts to make the past come alive in a truly meaningful way. Furthermore, it offers as-yet-unexploited possibilities in education. Introducing the notion of evidence and experiment into the humanities can help students gain, among other things, a better understanding of human origins and of the cultural process itself.

SUMMARY

Part of the effort to understand prehistoric behavior involves the direct, do-it-yourself approach—experimental archeology. The idea is that by attempting to do some of the things our ancestors did, by dealing with some of their daily problems, we can come closer to them, if only a bit closer. There is so much to learn that everything must be tried.

Toolmaking is a case in point. François Bordes' skill as a master flint knapper served him well in identifying basic Neanderthal tool kits (see Chapter 9). Another master was Don Crabtree, an Idaho researcher who made tens of thousands of tools, and specialized in pressure flaking as practiced by American Indians. Among other things, he noted that the Indians sometimes heated their flints to obtain softer, easier-to-work materials, a practice that was later observed in tools made during the Upper Paleolithic in Europe.

Other investigators concentrate on earlier times, making choppers, hand axes, and other tools dating back 1 to 2 million years. They collect all the flakes and waste chips, compare the collections with similar collections unearthed at African sites—and deduce how early hominids may have made tools, and to what extent individual sites have been disturbed by erosion. They also use the tools to butcher animals, scrape hides, chop wood, shape spears, and so on. Experiments are under way in an effort to distinguish bones broken by humans from bones broken by other predators or by natural forces.

Other experimental techniques are more direct. Louis Leakey was an expert on early hunting techniques; among his feats was the stalking of an unsuspecting gazelle, finally brought down with a flying tackle.

Studies of Upper Paleolithic art include making and using limestone lamps like those found at various sites, mixing red ocher and other pigments, and actually painting figures on cave walls. A musicologist-composer is learning to play a prehistoric-style flute, an exact replica of one found in a French cave.

Some investigators have conducted more ambitious experiments, making shelters and traps as well as tools, and living on the land for extended periods. Leakey had plans, never carried out, to go through several million years of evolution in 6 weeks, starting with an australopithecine life style and ending up as a full-fledged Magdalenian hunter-gatherer.

chapter 18

The Human Infant:
A Study in Living Prehistory

The human infant is born primed for action, ready from the very beginning to reach out and make sense of the world and the people moving around in it. Infants start exploring almost immediately, not long after they leave the womb, just about as soon as there is anything worth exploring. Changes come throughout the course of life. But the swiftest and most spectacular changes of all come during the first few years, nature having arranged things so that we do most of our growing up when we are most helpless, most immobile.

Research on early development has a number of evolutionary implications. For one thing, by providing clues to the nature and pace of learning, it suggests ways of improving education, improving the species, and thereby guiding and accelerating future evolution. It also provides clues to the remote past. The human infant was to a large extent shaped in a world that no longer exists, adapted primarily for survival in vanished wildernesses among small bands of hunter-gatherers—which raises the possibility of deducing from its behavior something about the course of events in prehistoric times.

MAKING SENSE OF THE WORLD

Learning takes place rapidly during infancy, so rapidly that it is difficult to observe and analyze. In this respect, the human condition contrasts sharply with that of most other animals. Generally speaking, the lower a species ranks in the hierarchy of evolution, the more likely its young are to be born ready-made and prepared to participate in life with a minimum of learning. The leopard frog, for example,

343

comes fully equipped for keeping itself alive. Its brain and sense organs are built to perceive only those elements in the environment strictly necessary for survival, and to exclude everything else. It sees only what it is designed to see. Its world is a mere fragment of the real world.

Experiments conducted by Jerome Lettvin and his associates at the Massachusetts Institute of Technology show that a frog is blind to stationary insects. It actually sees nothing in its field of vision until the thing moves toward it. Insects moving away are invisible, and do not exist in the frog's world. Furthermore, the things it sees are not insects as we know them, creatures with six legs and wings and iridescent colors. As far as the frog is concerned, all that information is utterly useless. It sees abstracted insects stripped of everything but a few essential details, standardized symbols like the black dots used on maps to represent cities, small objects with curved front edges.

The frog operates largely as an automaton, and automata are notoriously vulnerable to experimental tricks. If a frog is put in a cage with freshly killed flies, it will starve to death unless it is rescued and provided with a supply of live flies. It cannot see motionless food. But in the context of evolution and adaptation, such behavior is a strength rather than a weakness. Frogs are admirably designed for their real world, where small objects that are curved in front and move are almost always insects. The probability of being confined in a place where the only insects are dead insects is exceedingly low, so low that the frog has endured for some 200 million years.

Whether or not humanity manages to survive that long, and there are powerful arguments on both sides, we are committed to survival by different means. Our forte is flexibility of behavior, which depends as heavily on inheritance as rigid behavior does. The marks of the past are deeply embedded in us. The past has given us a selective advantage that enables us to survive and multiply. Although the range of observed human patterns is vast, it is still only a fraction of the even vaster range of possible patterns. We do not move along narrow and strictly determined paths like robots on monorails; but neither are we completely at liberty. Like all species, we represent a compromise between freedom and constraint, with perhaps a rather larger proportion of constraint than we imagine.

The infant is born with enormous potentialities. Its brain will have a memory capacity recently estimated at some 10^{12} or a trillion bits of information, enough to fill a library of some 10,000 books each the size of a volume of the *Encyclopaedia Britannica*. It comes equipped with nerve centers and a kind of built-in switching circuitry which dictate the human way of life. In the last analysis we have no choice but to be true to our genes. It is as impossible for us to stand pat as a species, to resist the forces for change embodied in the brain, as it is for animals of lower species, such as frogs, to unlearn their built-in habits. We are born free in comparison with other animals. Our world is wider and richer in events because of inherited behavior patterns, products of an evolutionary process involving a hominid line that goes back 5 to 10 million years.

During their very first hour out of the womb, infants are active explorers. They spend 85 percent of that time alert, eyes open wide, taking in all they can, turning their head toward a voice, preferring a female to a male voice. Within a day or two they may track triangles displayed in their field of vision, following the outlines with their eyes. When a newborn baby is confronted with a plain black background, it may keep looking from side to side and up and down, apparently in search of something more interesting. It is designed to focus on edges and discontinuities, on marked differences of light, shade, and color, on any and all unusual features.

It also possesses remarkable and, until recently unsuspected, powers of imitation. Experiments orginally conducted at Oxford University and repeated last year at the University of Miami, Florida, indicate that infants smile in response to a smile, pucker up their lips and look down in the mouth in response to a doleful adult face, and open eyes and mouth wide in response to an expression of surprise. Furthermore, according to the Miami studies, all this may take place during the first 36 hours of life.

During the first 2 weeks there are certain "throwback" reflexes that may have been important during early hominid and prehominid times. Infants have a tenacious grip, in some cases strong enough to hang from a stick and support their weight for as much as 15 seconds or so, an ability that might have saved lives when our ancestors lived in trees. A more complex pattern which also involves grasping and has been called the embrace reflex may be a vestige of the infant monkey's efforts to obtain a firm hold on the belly of its mother as she rises to walk. These reflexes disappear within a few months.

By three weeks the human infant recognizes its mother's voice, associates her voice with her face, and distinguishes her voice from its father's. Experiments show that when mother stands behind her baby and speaks, it tends to behave rather matter-of-factly, as if expecting food or a diaper change; after all, mother is a familiar presence. Father, on the other hand, is more of a novelty and elicits a brightening of the eyes and the expectation of play. According to investigators at Harvard and the University of Denver, "a dramatic shift in face looking" takes place from 3 to 7 weeks after birth. The infant, which had always looked at the edges of its mother's face, now suddenly begins looking at her eyes, indicating a new perception of the face as a pattern and the beginnings of eye-to-eye communication.

EARLY SMILING

There is no human undertaking more important than the newcomer's first efforts to communicate. An infant starts out well equipped to enter into and maintain relationships, as well as to break them off if they turn out to be traumatic. Whatever happens later on, a baby has a positive bias to reach out and approach and bring things closer. Of all ways of reaching out, the smile is perhaps the most effective and certainly the most studied.

The fact that smiling is universal and appears in all human societies suggests that it has deep roots and that it arose in response to strong prehistoric needs and demands. Its development is a process of unusual interest to investigators as well as parents. The act itself, the mechanics of drawing back the corners of

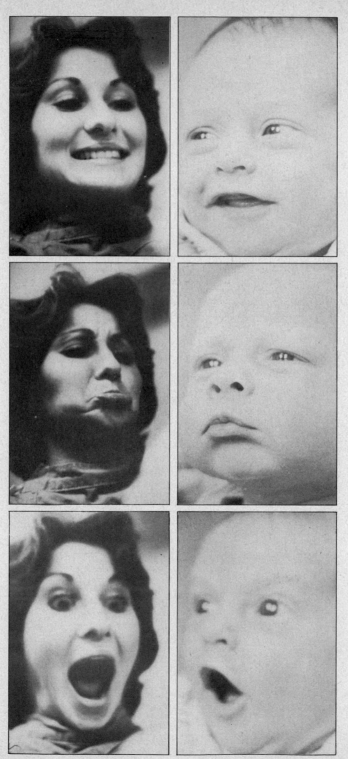

Infant imitating adult

the mouth and associated facial movements, appears very early in life. In fact, the first smile of the infant appears so early that it is usually never seen. Judging by observations of premature babies, it may occur in rudimentary form two or more months before birth. The role of subsequent learning is to attach that reflex to appropriate things in the environment and that involves other biases.

The first public smile comes several months later. It appears as early as the third week after birth, as late as the twelfth week, and in most cases between the fourth and sixth weeks. In the beginning the infant smiles not at its mother, but at a visual symbol of its mother, an abstraction related to her the way pictographs are related to actual objects. The symbol may involve sounds and physical content and other sensations. But the central factor is the sight of the face—and at first the sight of only a part of the face, the part which the infant, with its primitive capacity for seeing, finds most compelling, namely, the eyes, especially when the face is moved about a bit.

Studies indicate that an image of the eyes is a minimum requirement to arouse a smile in an infant. Investigators used masks to eliminate lips, nostrils, hair, and every feature other than eyes, and the infant still smiles. Both eyes are necessary; smiling stops when one eye is masked or when the investigator shifts from a full-face to a profile position so that the infant can see only a single eye. Two glass balls or any other pair of shiny objects will also produce smiling, as long as they have roughly the same size, shape, and spacing. Human eyes are most compelling, however, because they stand out against the more uniform background of the forehead and cheeks. They have color and movement, and reflect a high proportion of the light falling on them.

This reaction involves the decided preference for variety and contrast which babies seem to be born with. The reason an infant looks away from a black background is partly because of the monotony of a scene without features, and it naturally glances toward places where the action is, where there are edges and areas of dark and light. All shiny objects are of unusual interest, and the infant's world is full of them: keys, dishes, chrome-plated handles, and all highly reflecting surfaces of polished wood, glass, and metal.

But the infant goes beyond the mere taking of a general inventory. Out of the entire collection of attractive items it begins to learn to know the one that is and will continue to be most meaningful, the pair of bright objects which at first represents all it can notice of its mother. It picks out one image from all the rest, the one usually associated with soothing sounds and other pleasant sensations and answers that particular brightness with a brightness of its own, the brightening of its eyes when it smiles. The infant learns to smile at a selected image in its new world because of a built-in ability that will serve it throughout its life, an ability to sort things out and distinguish those of special importance.

A great deal is going on along with the subsequent development of a smile. After 2 months or so, an image consisting of two bright spots no longer causes the infant to smile. It requires something more before it will respond, the outline of a nose in addition to two eyes and later, a mouth and lips and hair and so on. In other words, the infant's impression or picture of the face is filled out in finer and finer detail until it becomes complete and is identified with a specific person, generally the mother.

This process has been investigated in some detail by Anthony Ambrose, former director of the Behavior Development Research Unit of St. Marys Hospital in London. His technique was to stand before a baby and simply look at it for 30 seconds without moving and without expression. Then he would step away, record observations of the infant's smiling responses and other behavior for 30 seconds, return to watch for another 30 seconds, and so on until he had completed a run of 12 consecutive observing periods. In one of the many experiments he conducted 30 runs, one a week, on four infants starting when they were 6 weeks old.

Among other things, he found that the total smiling time per run, a measure of response strength, changes in a characteristic way. For example, one infant did not smile at all during the first three runs, smiled only a few seconds during

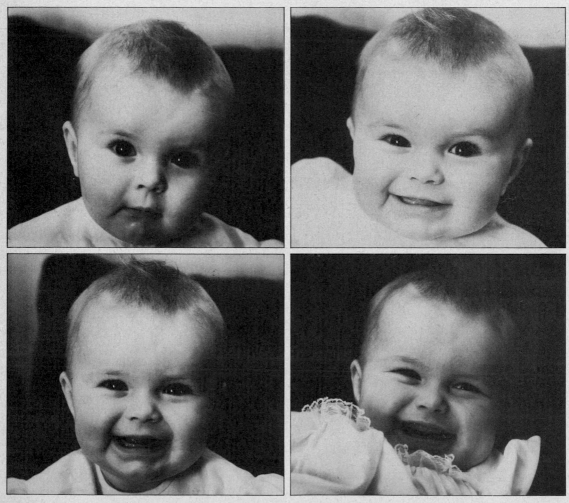

Smiles of human infant: straight face, low, medium, and high intensity

the fourth run, and not at all again during the fifth run. Practically nothing happened between the ages of 6 and 11 weeks, a situation which contrasted with the infant's response to the face of its mother, to which it smiled increasingly over this period—because the sight of her face was usually accompanied by movement and by her voice, touch, and warmth. So the first part of the experiment showed that during the early weeks, the image of a face alone, without movement or other accompanying sensations, produced hardly any response.

Then a striking change appeared in the record. The infant rapidly became more and more responsive until at the age of 14 weeks it was smiling more than 40 percent of the observing time, about two and a half out of six minutes, indicating that it had learned to react with feelings of pleasure to the image of a face by itself, isolated from voice, touch, and other sensations. At this stage, the infant was responding to a general, broad-gauge symbol rather than to a particular human being. Any appropriate image or properly designed mask besides that of its mother or Ambrose would have produced a smile.

The next change came even more rapidly; one week later there was a sharp decline of smiling. The infant smiled only fleetingly at Ambrose, and for no more than 20 seconds in all. The rest of the time it stared without expression, turned away, sucked its thumb, or whimpered. But during the same week its smiles had become even more frequent and brighter for its mother. The infant had passed the peak of indiscriminate and impersonal responding. Mother had suddenly become a unique individual. The image of her face had filled out in sufficient detail so that it could be compared with and distinguished from other faces. Later the infant's response to Ambrose reached a second peak, considerably lower than the first peak, that represented a level of habitual smiling reserved for all people not members of the family.

Infants differed widely as far as the timing and intensity of their changes were concerned, but they showed the same general changes in the same order. The sequence of little or no response, sharp increase in smiling, sudden decline, and so on turns out to be a basic pattern which involves not only certain built-in biases but also a bias to learn in a certain way. Ambrose used his observations and the observations of others to develop a theory of the origin of smiling.

THE EVOLUTION OF THE SMILE

The process started more than 65 million years ago among practically deadpan prosimians or premonkeys, the first primates to take up life in the trees. The most primitive surviving prosimians, such as the lemurs of Madagascar, simply do not have the proper equipment for a fine play of emotions. Their facial muscles consist mainly of broad bands of fibers which tend to contract all together and produce gross movements. It happens that lemurs are capable of only a single clear-cut facial gesture, the original primate expression. It consists of a drawing back of the lips to bare the teeth for biting, a sign of fear or anger.

Refinements of this fighting posture came with the reshaping of the face. The earliest prosimians had long snouts, like terriers, and they lived mainly by the sense of smell, as their ground-dwelling ancestors had lived. But chases and escapes and games played high in the trees favored the rapid development of vision at the expense of the sense of smell. The snout retreated, the face shortened and flattened somewhat, and the eyes shifted from the sides of the head to an up-front position. Evolution in effect created a kind of natural screen, or surface, for visual displays.

The muscles of the face became more specialized among higher primates and primates living in more complex social groups, forming small bundles of fibers which branched off from the broad bands like secondary roads and side lanes from superhighways. A particularly elaborate system of muscles developed around the eyes and lips, and nerves running to and from the brain permitted finer control and greater variety of expression. For example, laughter seems to have emerged in apes as a composite form of behavior. When a chimpanzee laughs it draws back its lips and bares its teeth as if confronted with a dangerous situation, but at the same time its muscles are relaxed and its eyes brighten as if it is playing.

These and other mechanical characteristics of laughter may be regarded as signs of ancient emotional conflict between opposing tendencies. The dominant tendencies were enjoyment and an attraction toward the object or situation being enjoyed; the subordinate tendencies were fear or anger and running away. This interpretation fits in with what we know about the arousal of human laughter, which generally occurs in response to a surprise of some sort—that is, to sudden or startling stimulation such as takes place in tickling or in mock attacks and chases during games. Of course, a delicate balance is involved. The lightness and good humor can vanish swiftly as a result of overstimulation—that is, from too much tickling or playful fighting that becomes too rough.

Ambrose suggested that smiling evolved from laughter and that the social smile, which is uniquely human, evolved as a special adaptation designed to strengthen bonds among people. The first and basic bond is with the mother. In prehistoric times, however, there were forces tending to weaken that bond, forces which became increasingly powerful as society became more and more complex. A critical point may have been reached some 2 million years ago with the appearance of the first members of the genus *Homo*, makers of early style stone tools.

The infant was still a major attraction. It was still carried practically 100 percent of the time during the first year or more of life, or in contact with its mother, judging by Patricia Draper's observations among the Kalahari Bushmen. But it no longer enjoyed quite as much undivided attention as infants had enjoyed in earlier times. Parents had more things to do—making and possibly caching tools, with men perhaps doing most of the scavenging and hunting, and women focusing primarily on gathering plants, preparing meals, talking. Furthermore, the infant found itself in a frustrating position, in a social setting which called for increased learning ability, larger brains, and a longer period of development and dependency after birth.

Not only was the infant born helpless, and not only did it remain helpless longer than the offspring of monkeys and apes, but it was physically ill equipped to do anything about it. Presumably, its mother had to put it down on occasion and walk off to perform a chore, if only for a few minutes. When that happened, it could neither cling to her nor follow effectively. It could only watch as she moved out of sight, a predicament guaranteed to produce emotional disturbances in the young of any primate. The tendency to explore was also frustrated, since the prehistoric infant depended completely on its mother for transport. Unless she carried it, it could not go where it wanted to go, nor could it establish contacts with new people and objects.

The smile may have evolved as a signal or communication to help make up for the handicap of infant immobility. Of course, crying could always be used to bring the mother to the spot. But crying alone was not enough. Infants of other primate species have vocal signals of some sort which indicate at a distance the nature and intensity of their distress; and something extra was called for to deal with the human predicament, something to hold the mother's attention longer and after the nursing and the burping were done. The infant represented only one of several alternative social contacts available to the mother. It had a high priority, to be sure. But it still had to compete for her time against other individuals and groups of individuals with demands of their own. Smiling became an essential way of meeting this competition.

The forces of natural selection come into play under such circumstances. Ambrose's research indicates that the smile is simply mild and low-intensity laughter minus chuckling and other sounds, and more relaxed. When it first appeared after nursing, mothers no doubt responded with cooing sounds, or the prehistoric equivalent thereof, and other forms of affection. Infants capable of making a ready connection between such pleasant responses and their mothers, who at this stage were seen merely as pairs of shining dots, learned to smile more and more and received more care and attention than other infants and prospered accordingly.

In other words, it was extremely important for the infant to form a deep attachment to its mother and to form it swiftly. Conditions existing in prehistoric times favored rapid learning at an early age. Judging by the records of contemporary infants, the process may have started during the third month of life with a sudden decrease in smiling at any human face and an increase in smiling at the mother's face. The odds are that if an infant had not formed a firm attachment by the age of 6 or 7 months, it never would. So the evidence suggests the evolution of a sensitive period, when the infant is particularly ripe for learning the smiling response and associated behavior.

Consider one of the ways a 4-month-old baby may behave when its mother comes into the room. It has just learned to distinguish her face from other faces, and as soon as she enters it turns its eyes on her, smiles, and tracks her while she moves about, looking and smiling intently all the time. This is an impressively powerful response, a silent response. The infant seems to be compensating with all its might for its immobility. It is doing with its eyes and its smile what other primates can do more directly by clinging or following—keeping in close touch with its mother. The tracking could hardly be more efficient if its eyes were actually connected with the target. Such observations indicate strongly that tracking can be regarded as a substitute for following, and that imprinting or something like it played a major part in the evolution of the human smile and continues to play a major part in the development of the smile during infancy.

The infant had much to gain by its positive reactions. The longer its mother remained close, the greater the chances that its immediate physical and emotional needs would be satisfied. So it would presumably be healthier, and even a small raising of the odds in that direction could have had an appreciable selective impact among populations in which more than half of all infants died before they were 12 months old. But helping to meet the demands of the moment was probably not the only or most important function of the smile.

Everything points toward its predominant role in a long-range social context, in promoting the capacity to get along with other individuals. The increase in complexity of social systems during hominid evolution put increasing pressure on the infant. Indeed, evolution seemed to be painting itself into a corner. It was shaping an infant which had to learn more and sooner, and which at the same time remained helpless longer. In such circumstances, its first close associations with an adult inevitably assumed an overriding importance.

WHY INFANTS SMILE

The uses of the smile reveal a great deal about the position of the mother in human societies and about her special meaning to the infant. One interesting response may occur after an infant tracks her movements around a room. Notice that such behavior implies that it is not hungry or cold or uncomfortable in any way. For such things, crying serves and has long served as a highly effective protest and summons. In this case, the infant wants something else, and what it wants is indicated the instant its mother comes over and picks it up and holds it in her arms.

At that point smiling usually ceases abruptly, almost as if shut off by a switch, in a gesture that says, more plainly than words, "mission accomplished." Then, secure in physical contact with its mother, it proceeds to look around the room. This is the exploring tendency in action. It is the beginning of an adventure, a brief adventure to be sure, but a prototype for all subsequent adventures. Later, when the infant crawls, it continues to use its mother as a base of operations from which to explore the mysterious world. It leaves her to play with things it cannot touch by reaching, and then comes back to her and leaves again. Still later there will be other departures and returnings.

The mother also has problems, problems more difficult to investigate and perhaps even more complicated than those of the infant. Evolution has confronted her with dilemmas. Her infant, who represented the ultimate in the primate trend from litters to a single precious birth (see Chapter 7), demanded an unprecedented measure of attention. Its increasing dependency increased her dependency as well. The longer it remained helpless, the longer she had to stay nearby and be ready to come at its call.

Mother love runs deep, but it is not without some ambiguity. Like infant love, it had to be learned and learned quickly. The mother's natural bias, like the infant's, was toward the positive, toward all feelings and actions that would

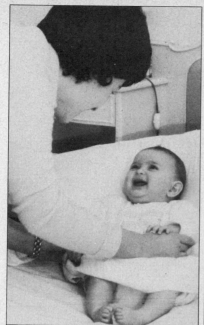
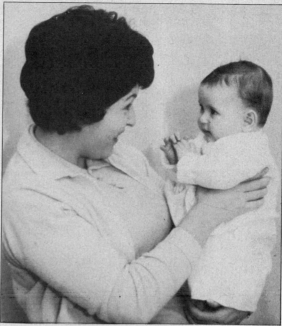

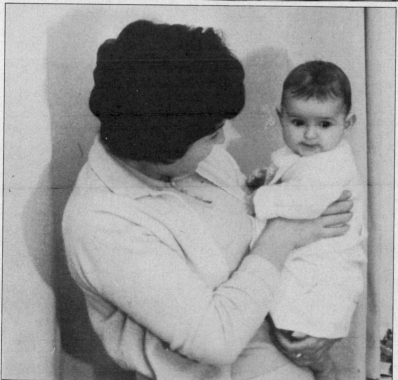

The smile in action: infant attracts mother with broad smile; mission accomplished, infant picked up, smile shut off; secure in mother's arms, infant unsmilingly explores its world

foster affection and coming together. Her smiling and associated behavior became part of a self-enhancing communication that worked both ways. But there were negative as well as positive aspects of infant care. Upon occasion, especially after prolonged crying, the mother came to her infant with resentment and anger, and one of the main functions of its smile may have been to help soften her feelings.

In the last analysis a fundamental conflict exists between offspring and mother, between offspring and both parents. Robert Trivers of the University of California at Santa Cruz emphasizes that parents are prepared to invest a certain amount of time and energy in rearing their young, with each offspring competing for all the attention it can get—which is always rather less than it wants. He sees the infant as "a psychologically sophisticated organism" surprisingly sensitive to adult behavior and determined to influence that behavior in its own behalf. (Trivers' ideas apply to all sexually reproducing species, from birds and rats to caribou and primates, nonhuman as well as human.)

Trivers has been working toward a broad sociobiological theory of the family, which recognizes the problems Freud recognized, but interprets them in a somewhat different way. He believes that within-the-family tensions are not basically a matter of Oedipus and Electra complexes: "The source of conflict is not repressed mating urges, but differences in genetic self-interest." In other words, he suggests that the conflict is among individuals competing and manipulating others to ensure that their own genes and not someone else's will be transmitted to future generations.

WHY INFANTS CRY

The smile may be regarded as one tactic in this continuing struggle. Crying also has evolutionary implications, although it seems to be more complicated than smiling, at least during infancy. For one thing, it is more difficult to classify. There are degrees of intensity and tone which make all the difference between hunger cries, pain cries, and so on. In addition, crying may come in regularly or irregularly spaced bouts, and distinctive patterns may exist within individual bouts. Preliminary studies suggest that it may be necessary to consider eight or more types of infant crying.

In most cases, however, the general message is clear and basic. Crying is designed to elicit a fast maternal reaction, and the faster the better. But the infant requires time to learn how effective its crying is, and to adjust its behavior accordingly. Mary Ainsworth of the University of Virginia reports that although the amount of crying varies widely during the first three months of life, from more than 20 minutes per hour to practically no crying at all, it has little to do with maternal responsiveness. At that stage, babies tend to cry at their own individual levels no matter what their mothers do.

Differences begin showing up during succeeding months. By the end of the first year, there is appreciably less crying among babies whose mothers are quick to respond than among babies whose mothers delay responding or do not respond at all. If myths were not so enduring, such findings would be enough to discredit once and for all the notion that a crying infant is trying to get away with something and, for the good of its character, must not be spoiled by getting too much attention.

The primal urgency of most crying, its deep-rooted nature, is revealed by the observation that what counts most is the promptness of the response. Some mothers know better than others why their babies cry and precisely what to do—whether to feed the baby, change its diapers, pick it up, or simply utter soothing words. But as long as she appears promptly, its crying will tend to decrease.

The real point of appearing promptly is what it does for the baby's expanding world view. Equipped with its appetites and desires and biases, it must identify objects and events, learn their regularities, and to some extent control their movements. When crying brings a dependable response, its world makes that much more sense—and making sense of things can be extremely difficult, perhaps even more difficult during infancy than later on. What happens outside and around the infant must often seem erratic and unpredictable.

Ainsworth's work indicates that a rather high proportion of mothers, perhaps a quarter or a third, frequently misinterpret infant signals or even overlook the signals entirely—and some investigators put the proportion even higher. Part of the problem is the tendency to underrate the communication capacity of infants, indeed to treat babies as if they were too immature to have anything meaningful to communicate. A baby may feel hungry and cry, but its mother, who may or may not be going by some sort of schedule, figures that the last feeding was too recent for another one just now. So she comes over with a toy. A while later the baby, having been distracted for a spell, is busy playing with the toy and suddenly finds it must stop, mother having decided the time is ripe for a feeding.

OBSERVATIONS IN THE LABORATORY

It is on the basis of such mysterious behavior that infants must learn to figure out the ways of attending adults, modify their wants accordingly, and build models of the real world. They often have major difficulties, an observation whose impact in later adult life has yet to be explored. Ainsworth and her associates have discovered a number of things about the complexities of the mother-infant relationship, and one of their most intriguing discoveries involves the strange and tragic behavior of one class of frustrated infants.

Ainsworth has developed a standard experimental procedure designed to study the infant's response to brief separations from its mother and to strangers. In the first part of the procedure, for example, mother and infant are brought into a room with chairs and toys, and the infant is free to explore for 3 minutes; then a stranger enters for 3 minutes, and then the mother leaves quietly for 3 minutes (or less, if the infant is "unduly distressed"). Observations of more than 100 cases show that the normal, most frequent response was to explore actively when mother was present, do little exploring when she left the room (about half the infants also cried), and greet her reappearance by intense looking at her and reaching out for reassuring hugs.

But some infants responded in an unexpected, "cold" fashion. For one thing, they showed little distress or none at all when mother left the room—and then when she returned, instead of reaching out for affection, they either looked at her and smiled casually, or else ignored her and actually turned or moved away. Mary Main, of the University of California at Berkeley, has filmed some 400 mother-infant reunions and notes a blank, "empty" expression among such infants, as if they were automatically shutting off any form of contact.

This turns out to be a defense reaction, a mark of suppressed anger and a way of avoiding painful encounters, saying in effect, better no communication at all than communication which hurts. On the basis of follow-up studies, Ainsworth characterizes the at-home behavior of the infants' mothers as "having an aversion to close bodily contact, angry, relatively wooden in facial expression, and compulsive." It is difficult to imagine more striking examples of mother-infant conflict and, unfortunately, such examples are by no means rare, occurring in about one out of every five cases.

Evolution may be in the process of weeding out this form of emotional pathology. If the mothers tend to have fewer than average offspring, and if the same holds for their offspring, then such individuals would eventually disappear from the species. On the other hand, the will to survive and the need for affection are powerful forces, and some babies who remain dry-eyed when their mothers leave, cry at the departure of strangers, indicating an enduring capacity to form deep attachments. Incidentally, according to Main, mother avoidance may be a uniquely human response, suggesting that it has already been bred out of our fellow primates.

CHANGING MOTHER-INFANT RELATIONSHIPS

Feeding seems to be a perennial problem. The notion of a strict every-4-hours schedule, originally promoted about a century ago without benefit of evidence by a discipline-minded physician, is no longer as popular as it once was. On the other hand, modern living conditions do not permit a baby to follow its natural inclinations, a point made by Nicholas Blurton Jones, of the University of California at Santa Barbara, who studied children in the Kalahari and in England. (He is the British stranger mentioned in Chapter 16, the sight of whom caused a Bushman baby to scream.)

Blurton Jones' comparative studies of a hundred mammal species show that the chemical composition of mother's milk provides clues to the frequency of infant feeding. Mother's milk containing high proportions of protein and a fat is characteristic of rabbits, who feed their offspring about once every 24 hours, and tree shrews, who feed their offspring about once every 48 hours. At the other extreme, among some rats, some marsupials, and most monkeys, the young are fed every half-hour or so; rat mothers have low-protein, low-fat milk.

Human mothers and chimpanzee and gorilla mothers have milk very low in these essential compounds, indicating that frequent, almost continuous feeding was the rule in the remote past. The same conclusions follow from the observation that frequent feeders tend to suck slowly, and human infants are very slow suckers. Judging by Melvin Konner's estimate for the Kalahari Bushmen, infants who are carried most of the time and have ready access to the breast probably feed at least twice an hour, each time for 30 seconds to 10 minutes.

Such behavior represents the result of intensive selection and suggests some of the fundamental characteristics which humans share with other mammals. It may serve the special purpose of developing a close bond between mother and infant. Blurton Jones asks the question: Why carry babies? His provisional answer, based on admittedly incomplete evidence: "The association in the mammals between frequent feeding and a following or carrying system of child care is not nutritionally necessary, but rapid onset of hunger and satiation in the baby would be a simple mechanism for ensuring that it stays with the mother."

The fact that the infant can adapt to a rich variety of feeding practices and schedules, most of which are hardly geared to its basic biases, is as significant an example of the unique flexibility of humans as is the capacity for surviving and multiplying in widely different environments. Studies of smiling, crying, and other forms of infant behavior reinforce the notion of the infant as an active participant in its own development. It is not waiting, unformed and undirected, for us to make impressions upon it. It takes the initiative in responding, approaching, and establishing relationships, and makes up for its physical helplessness by a surprisingly advanced ability to communicate.

Ainsworth emphasizes an interesting point in this connection—namely, that you can often tell a great deal about the quality of an infant's communications with its mother by watching its face. A highly mobile face, a face that shows a varied and vivid interplay of emotion, is usually a sign that the infant has established satisfactory and sensitive communications. On the other hand, less fortunate infants tend to be "pudding-faced," a bit on the deadpan side. It may be that prolonged infant dependency and the importance of a close mother-infant bond have a close evolutionary relationship with the increasing capacity for facial expression.

Research in living prehistory includes living infants and all representatives of *Homo sapiens,* not just members of the last remaining bands of aborigines in desert places. It was only a few hundred generations ago that we, the citizens of technologically advanced nations, were also hunter-gatherers. Contemporary people are close enough to those days to behave "prehistorically" upon occasion. Their behavior provides clues to the behavior of prehistoric people.

The differences between the most civilized and the least civilized among us are striking, but hardly basic. They are cultural differences chiefly, learned programs of behavior expressed and conveyed to us in traditional codes, and such programs are completely interchangeable. Any child from an American or Japanese family, for example, could be brought up to believe as firmly as the Australian aborigines in dreamtime beings and a world that can only change for the worse. What we want to understand better are things relatively independent of upbringing, the sort of biases all humans share, the built-in tendencies for all individuals to feel and think and react alike under comparable conditions.

The tendencies must first be identified and then accounted for in evolutionary terms. In the process of reconstructing the past through studies of contemporary behavior, we can also work things the other way around, using what we learn about prehistory to see ourselves more clearly here and now. It is a matter of obtaining new perspectives on life in our times. The present and the future are also part of human evolution, the part that must concern us most directly in times of accelerating transition. So it may help to turn in a serious and systematic manner to prehistory as part of our current efforts in self-understanding.

For example, evolutionary studies indicate that the mother-infant bond may not be as adaptive as it once was. In fact, any other conclusion would be amazing, considering how much the world has changed. Society was much simpler in prehistoric times. There were fewer people and fewer kinds of people. Not only that, but customs and traditions endured to an extent that we can hardly conceive. Individuals lived their entire lives in societies that had not changed appreciably for thousands of years, and would not change for thousands of years to come. They faced exactly the same dangers that their ancestors had faced.

Survival in this kind of world favored rapid learning and, even more to the point, once-and-for-all learning, the formation of relatively fixed actions and attitudes. It was a steady-state, predictable world, the sort we yearn for in our weaker and more nostalgic moments. Time and life had a monolithic quality. Expectations were high that everything would endure in its present form forever, that the future would continue to be very like the past. In other words, what the infant learned fast and early would in all probability serve it admirably for the rest of its life.

Ours is a different world, with the wilderness gone. Even danger is not what it used to be, and instead of predators we face diseases that tend to develop slowly and strike late in life, a kind of violence which is as uniquely human as mercy or tolerance, and the enduring insecurity of change itself. The emphasis must be increasingly on flexibility. The mark of the new evolution which sweeps us along is that unlearning and learning anew have already become as important to survival as learning used to be. What people know is far less important than their capacity for modifying or discarding what they think they know.

So self-examination includes a harder look at the mother-infant bond and the speed, depth, and intensity of early learning. Much of what the infant learns during its first years may block its ability to learn later in life and create rigidities, an outcome somewhat more appropriate for prehistoric than for modern societies. The question for the future is whether built-in flexibility, one of the most distinctive marks of being human, is great enough to permit the erasing if necessary of information learned early—whether in a sense we can be taught to forget as effectively as we remember.

SUMMARY

We are just beginning to appreciate the speed and complexity of infant learning. The infant comes into the world with behavior patterns shaped over an evolutionary past extending back at least 5 million years. It is busy making sense of its surroundings from the very start. Within a day or two it may turn its head toward voices (preferably female voices), scan the environment for interesting shapes, and imitate facial expressions. Within 3 weeks it recognizes its mother's voice, and soon begins looking at her eyes.

The infant needs help in learning, and of all behavior patterns the smile is most effective in obtaining that help, in attracting teachers. Most infants begin smiling 4 to 6 weeks after birth, at the sight of two eyes, or any two shining objects about the size of eyes and set about as far apart. Gradually it learns to smile at complete faces, and by 4 months it apparently recognizes its mother's face.

The smile has a long prehistory. The first tree-dwelling primates, the prosimians, who appeared more than 65 million years ago (see Chapter 1), were deadpan creatures, lacking the network of facial muscles needed to produce varied expressions. Laughter seems to have arisen perhaps 40 million years ago among apes—a strange pattern which combined the baring of teeth, originally a response to danger, with relaxed muscles and brightening, "playtime" eyes. The smile evolved from laughter in the hominid infant as a powerful way of obtaining attention and affection.

The mother's response also involves powerful behavior patterns. Mother love runs deep. But it is not possible to fulfill all the infant's needs. Crying is designed to elicit fast maternal responses and, above all, consistent responses. Controlled laboratory studies involving 3-minute separations provide insights into mother-infant relationships. In most cases, an infant does little playing or exploring after mother leaves the room, and reaches out for reassuring hugs at her reappearance. But some infants, apparently those who are not confident of securing affection, show little distress when she leaves and little emotion when she returns. These and many other patterns developed in prehistoric settings, during times of little social change for thousands of generations. Present-day adaptations call for increasing flexibility, the shaping of new patterns. Mother-infant relationships are still evolving.

chapter *19*

The Evolution of Language

More than half the people in the world can neither read nor write, but practically all individuals everywhere speak their native tongue. And, at the deepest levels, all languages are built according to the same fundamental blueprint. They all involve a very small number of basic voice or speech characteristics, about 15 or so ways of producing vowel and consonant sounds. These sounds are building blocks which in various combinations make up a very large number of words (several million words in the English language, which is increasing at an estimated rate of tens of thousands of words a year). The number of sentences, the hierarchies and patterns of words used, is infinite.

The origin of language is one of the great problems of science. If we understood how speech emerged from a system of calls—from the assorted grunts, barks, screams, hoots, and whimpers of nonhuman primates—many of the mysteries of human evolution would be solved. Such insights are yet to come. They demand nothing less than a step-by-step reconstruction of the evolutionary process, and for that the evidence is still lacking. There are no fossil clues to the nature of the earliest human languages and no living representatives of early stages on the way to present-day languages.

The theologians of the fourteenth and fifteenth centuries assumed that human beings were created a few thousand years ago, fully articulate, Adam and Eve speaking Hebrew in the Garden of Eden. A Scandinavian, dissenting from prevailing opinion, suggested that God addressed Adam in Swedish, Adam answered in Danish, and the snake tempted Eve in French. A complete list of all theories, variations on theories, and related studies has not been compiled, but a recent bibliography includes more than 6000 references. Papers barren of solid evidence were so numerous that the Linguistic Society of Paris banned all such writings in 1860 and again in 1911.

Clearly, the ban was not highly effective, although it may have spurred the search for evidence. In any case, the extent of the search was indicated in 1975 at a 4-day New York conference on the origins and evolution of language. Somewhat to the surprise of the organizers, hundreds of investigators and students packed a large hotel ballroom to hear some 50 reports on work in progress, discussions involving the linguistic capacities of animals, language development in the human child, and problems of neuroanatomy, the sort of brain required for language—all active approaches in current studies.

UNEXPECTED CAPACITIES AMONG MONKEYS

Animal studies have featured "talking" apes—notably chimpanzees, as the species deemed closest to us—and we shall come to them later in this chapter. But studies at least equally important concern a lesser primate, a species which ranks lower on the evolutionary scale and whose abilities were barely mentioned at the New York conference. It turns out that vervets, a breed of agile African monkeys foraging in groups of 10 to 40 individuals, have an impressively complex communication system. We know that system mainly from the original results obtained a generation ago by Thomas Struhsaker of Rockefeller University, and from the follow-up research of Dorothy Cheney and Robert Seyfarth of the University of California, Los Angeles.

Struhsaker reported three distinct alarm calls among vervets, signals warning about the threat of at least three distinct types of predator. The leopard alarm consists of sequences of sharp, short sounds which have been called "chirps"; a martial eagle arouses low-pitched, staccato grunts, while the snake alarm, generally uttered at the sight of a python or a poisonous snake, is a high-pitched hiss or "chutter." Cheney and Seyfarth have since found that the vervet alarm repertoire includes two further "acoustically distinct" calls evoked by two potentially dangerous primates, baboons and strange humans (usually members of the Masai tribe). Notice that these calls are reserved for only a few of the more than 150 birds, reptiles, and mammals familiar to vervets.

The Los Angeles investigators are currently extending other Struhsaker observations in a series of experiments among wild Kenyan vervets. One study focuses on a special, frequently uttered call, a low-pitched pulsing grunt or "woof"—or, rather, on what sounds to us like a single call. The vervet woof is actually a whole class of woofs which we hear as a single sound because our hearing is not tuned to detect what the monkeys distinguish readily as separate signals.

Cheney and Seyfarth managed to discover this set of grunts, even though they heard no differences, by using directional microphones and a tape recorder to obtain records of woofs emitted in a number of different contexts. Then, hiding speakers in bushes and tall grasses, they played back the tapes and watched the vervets' reactions, supplementing their impressions with motion pictures taken at the same time. All this is much easier to describe than to carry out in a field, in savanna-woodland settings among monkeys whose movements were not always predictable.

For example, here is what happened in response to the playback of woofs emitted by adult females and juveniles when they saw another vervet heading out of bush and tree terrain into open country, a move calling for vigilance because of the danger of predators. The warned individuals averaged about 7 to 8 seconds looking in the direction in which the speaker was pointing, as if to make sure that the coast was clear, and only about a second looking at the location of the speaker itself. This compared with more than 30 seconds looking toward the speaker in response to played-back grunts emitted by a dominant male.

Such tests reveal the existence of at least four distinctly different woofs, four distinct patterns of acoustic frequencies which sound the same to the human ear but which represent meaningful signals to vervets—not only woofs directed to individuals moving into the open and to subordinates by dominant males, but also woofs emitted by subordinates and by members of one group to members of another group. In other words, the evidence indicates that vervets are busy exchanging a great deal of information during the course of their daily lives.

Even more subtle exchanges are under investigation, social exchanges. Cheney and Seyfarth are studying three vervet groups, each of which lives in a region including at least five neighboring vervet groups, and playback experiments point to elaborate regional relationships based on voice recognition:

> Vervets seem able to identify with which group a particular call is associated, even when they have never lived in the same group as the vocalizer. The members of other groups are apparently not just recognized as strangers, but as individuals living in particular neighboring groups. Social groups are distinguished as discrete and separate units.

As far as relationships within a group are concerned, further playback tests hint at unexpectedly complex and detailed identifications. Communication extends beyond "egocentric discriminations," such as mothers recognizing the voices of their offspring. More remote blood relatives may also be recognized. There is reason to suspect that when it comes to knowing one's relatives, vervets are more discriminating than squirrels, who recognize mothers, daughters, and sisters only (see Chapter 14). Other studies suggest that monkeys may be able to recognize nephews, nieces and cousins as well. In any case, Kenyan vervets seem to be aware of matrilineal kin, kinship patterns based on descent through the female line. The stress among these primates, as among all social primates, is on "interpersonal" relationships, the most important thing in the vervets' world being other vervets.

COMMUNICATING WITH CHIMPANZEES

Research involving communication between humans and apes is another story. There the objective is to put primates to the supreme test, to find out how far the most advanced nonhuman species can go in acquiring language, to learn more about their capabilities and limitations—and in the process to learn more about our own capabilities and limitations. Current studies stem from the pioneer investigations of Allen and Beatrice Gardner, a husband and wife team at the University of Nevada.

Their first ape was a young African-born female chimpanzee named Washoe. For 5 years, starting in June 1966, when Washoe was 1 year old, she lived in a trailer with free access to a yard containing trees and a jungle gym. All her waking hours were spent in the company of one human being or more, usually the Gardners and their graduate students; but she never heard human speech. Observers never uttered words in her presence, only hoots and other chimpanzee calls. In addition, people made gestures based on those of Ameslan, the standard American sign language for the deaf.

There is a logic behind this unusual experimental arrangement. Chimpanzees cannot learn to talk, a point proved once and for all more than 30 years ago when another husband and wife team brought up another female chimpanzee named Viki. Viki learned to brush her teeth, dust furniture, open cans and bottles, and eat at the table with manners at least as respectable as those of the human children who were her only playmates. But she could utter only three words—*mama, papa,* and *cup*—and only with extreme difficulty. In fact, she often rocked back and forth and exhibited other symptoms of severe emotional distress when called on to say her words.

The Gardners designed their experiment partly as a consequence of seeing motion pictures of Viki's behavior. They did not conclude that the chimpanzee is inherently incapable of language, but simply that it is incapable of imitating

Nonhuman primate learns to "talk": Washoe says "drink" to Beatrice Gardner

human speech sounds and acquiring spoken language. On the other hand, gestures come quite readily to it, and it often imitates human gestures when playing. So it seemed reasonable to take advantage of this natural ability and explore the chimpanzee's linguistic potentialities by using sign language.

Washoe responded enthusiastically. She learned her first word at the age of about 15 months, an insistent *come gimme,* represented by a beckoning gesture with fingers or wrist. Her second word, *more,* which involves bringing the fingers of both hands together, came within another week or two. By the end of 1967 she communicated with 17 signs, including *funny* (tip of index finger pressed against nose, accompanied by a snort), *drink* (first and thumb extended, thumb in mouth), *sorry* (bent hand rubbed on chest), and *flower* (tip of index finger touching one or both nostrils). Eventually, she achieved a vocabulary of more than 175 words.

When Washoe was about 2 years old, she spontaneously made the *come gimme* sign and then wagged her tongue and touched it with her index finger, the sign for *sweet.* It was her first sentence. But even more significant, it was a creative sentence. Although she had learned the individual signs by imitating, the combination was not imitated and could not have been because Washoe had never seen that particular combination of gestures. The Gardners had never used sign language to ask her or one another for candy. Many of her subsequent sentences were also original combinations, such as *come gimme tickle, please up,* and *hurry open.* She has used five gestures in a single sentence *(more more more sweet drink)* and as many as four different gestures *(drink sweet please hurry* and *out open please hurry).*

Washoe recognizes herself in the mirror, an ability she shares with other chimpanzees such as those studied by Gordon Gallup (discussed in Chapter 14). The big difference is that in the case of the Gallup chimpanzees, the ability had to be inferred indirectly because they did not know how to communicate with people. In Washoe's case, the evidence is direct. While looking into a mirror one day, she was asked, "Who is that?" and promptly responded, "Me, Washoe" in sign language.

It is hardly surprising that Washoe acquired a special sort of word consciousness. One day when she went riding in a car with the Gardners, they used the sign for a dog in conversing with one another. When Washoe "overheard" the sign she looked out the window in search of a dog, indicating that she had acquired a kind of built-in cerebral dictionary which matches gestures and images. Washoe often "talked" to herself privately and made signs in her bedroom before going to sleep (an activity observed among human children) as she thumbed through a magazine or picture book or sneaked toward a forbidden part of the yard (using the sign for *quiet*) or ran for the toilet (using the sign meaning *hurry).*

After more than four years in Nevada, Washoe was transferred to the University of Oklahoma's Institute for Primate Studies under the direction of Roger Fouts, a former Gardner student. The move called for some readjustments. Washoe had seen another chimpanzee only once before, and now, living among half a dozen chimpanzees, she did not regard them as fellow apes. She apparently considered herself superior to them, calling them "bugs." This attitude was reminiscent of what happened during the 1940s when Viki sorted photographs of human beings and apes into two piles. Viki accomplished the task with 100 percent accuracy, until she came to a picture of herself; without hesitating, she placed it in the "human" pile along with Eisenhower, Roosevelt, and Joe Di-Maggio. There is a tragic element in both cases, an identity crisis leading to a denial of one's own kind.

Later generations of Gardner-reared chimpanzees have demonstrated a variety of intriguing talents. For instance, a young female christened Moja invented word combinations to name things never seen before—*metal hot* for a cigarette lighter, *metal cup drink coffee* for a thermos bottle, and *listen drink* for a glass of Alka-Seltzer. (Washoe's contributions along these lines included *water bird* at her first sight of a swan.) As an example of chimpanzees using the Ameslan gesture language to communicate with one another, Moja in the process of sipping soda pop through a straw was approached by Tatu, a younger female who obviously wanted to share the beverage and made the thumb-in-mouth sign for *drink*.

THE POWERS OF NONHUMAN PRIMATES

Also assured of a prominent place in the annals of human-ape communication is Sarah, the world's most "educated" chimpanzee and the most sophisticated linguistically. The protégé of David Premack of the University of Pennsylvania, she continues to contribute to primate research in her middle age, about 22. Her education started back in 1968 with a simple procedure. In the first step, designed mainly to achieve a good working relationship between ape and teacher, Premack put a ripe banana on a table and watched benevolently as she ate it.

Having established that routine, he put a banana just out of her reach and, within reach, a small pink plastic square with a steel backing. Sarah quickly learned that to get the banana she had to pick up the piece and place it on a magnetic language board. In similar fashion she learned that a purple triangle meant "apple" and so on, for a total of half a dozen different fruits and their corresponding plastic pieces. Confronted with two pieces and one fruit, two fruits and one piece, and various combinations, she showed that she knew which pieces and fruits went together, and had chances upon occasion to indicate her preferences.

The next stage was teaching Sarah a new class of words, the names of her different teachers. She found that to get a banana from Mary Morgan, a research assistant working with Premack, she had to place a plastic M on the language board and, under it—since Sarah writes vertically, Chinese-style—the square banana symbol. After learning the names of several teachers, she discovered that fruit would not be forthcoming unless she constructed a three-word sentence—for example, M for *Mary,* the purple triangle for *apple,* and, between the two, a third piece shaped something like a vertical bow tie and representing *give.*

Slowly, step by step, Premack built up Sarah's linguistic skills until she learned about 130 words—that is, plastic shapes that she manipulated to produce sentences on the language board. She learned to use proper word order—for

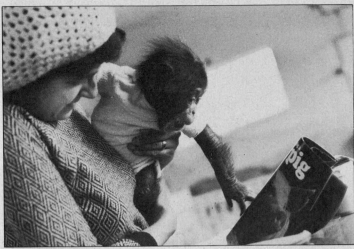

Tutu, age 3 months, sees a picture of a pig (top). First language signs appear at this age. Pili, age 1½ years, looking through his picture book (center). Signing between chimps: Moja, age 6, at left, and Tatu, age 2½, signing "drink."

Give

Chocolate

Sarah

Sarah and trainer: learning to "talk"

example, *Mary give apple* brought results, while *apple give Mary* did not. She answered *yes* or *no* to questions, asked questions, dealt with *if-then* sentences, and so on. Also, she made limited but basic comparisons, indicating whether two objects are the same or different.

Premack feels that up to this stage Sarah actually learned very little which was new to her: "Mostly our procedures had been merely teaching her the names for concepts she already knew." Since then, however, he has built upon those concepts and carried things much further. For example, Sarah now understands the meaning of *same* and *different* to the point where she knows which to match with a half-filled glass of water, half an apple or three quarters of an apple. Beyond that, she has been taught to comprehend still more subtle forms of sameness, matching such items as lock-and-key with can-and-can-opener as pairs of related objects.

Something very special is going on here. Notice the sort of thinking involved in recognizing, detecting, and comprehending, the essential similarity among a variety of functionally related objects—among hook-line-sinker, bread-butter, and chair-sofa, as well as lock-key and so on. It demands the ability to ignore a legion of attributes, any one of which might be of relevance in other contexts, the shapes and textures and sizes of related objects, and abstracting from all of them the notion of "used-togetherness." This is an ability rare in the animal kingdom, found only among species representing the very highest evolutionary reaches.

Sarah has learned to recognize problems and the solutions to problems. Shown a photograph of a human actor trying to get out of a locked cage or to play an unplugged phonograph, she has no trouble choosing photographs representing appropriate solutions, using a key or plugging a cord into an electrical outlet—actions she learned without being "told." Moreover, she will deliberately choose a wrong solution when the human actor is someone whom she has good reason, on the basis of previous training sessions, to dislike.

These are only a few of the tests which Premack has designed to explore the mental powers of Sarah and of four younger chimpanzee participants. There is a long list of high-priority projects already planned in some detail but not yet administered, to probe deeper into the apes' not inconsiderable capacity for lying and other forms of deception—an indication that they not only have well-defined purposes of their own but also can size up the aims of others and behave accordingly.

To a degree, and within definite limits to be discussed shortly, what an ape can be taught to do depends on the ingenuity and imagination of curious humans. Another long-term study is under way at the Yerkes Regional Primate Research Center in Atlanta, where Duane Rumbaugh, Sue Savage-Rumbaugh, and their associates work with chimpanzees living in rooms with rows of push buttons on one wall, each marked with an abstract symbol representing a word. By pressing appropriate buttons in the appropriate order, they can ask for a variety of things—candy, apples, bananas, milk, movies, slides, companions (humans, not apes). Similar buttons outside the room permit investigators to communicate with the chimpanzees.

One series of "blind" experiments—during which investigators could not see or be seen by the animals, and hence could not provide voluntary or involuntary clues—started with a relatively simple sorting problem and worked up, step by step, to more and more complex tasks. Austin and Sherman, aged 4 and 5 respectively, went through a preliminary training period, a kind of same-different task. After more than 1000 trials each, they succeeded in putting three edible objects (orange, beancake, bread) into one bin and three inedible objects (key, money, stick) into another, with 90 percent or better accuracy.

From there on, things became increasingly abstract. First, the chimpanzees learned to label the same objects with the proper lexigrams, or symbols, presented against a black background—a white circle flanked by two curves representing *food* and a white triangle-diamond pattern representing *tool*. Later they learned to label photographs of the objects rather than the actual objects with the appropriate lexigrams. Finally, they passed the supreme test with lexigrams of the objects substituted for photographs. Austin and Sherman learned the lexigrams for five foods (sweet potato, chow, M&M, corn, banana) and five tools (magnet, sponge, wrench, lever, string), and identified them with the correct food and tool lexigrams. According to the Rumbaughs' report, this "use of one symbol to classify another" was possible, because the chimpanzees had been trained to communicate with one another and not only with humans.

The study of primate language and communication is a continuing adventure, with many discoveries to come. It has already demonstrated the existence of capacities far greater than most investigators of a generation or so ago ever suspected. We know now that chimpanzees can name and classify features of the world around them, see relationships among the features, and discover relationships among relationships. Far from being conditioned-reflex machines responding automatically to repeated rewards and punishments, they are highly talented problem solvers and enjoy the challenges put to them. This should surprise no one; after all, they are fellow primates. We come from a distinguished line.

In a way, the capacities of lesser primates are even more intriguing. The vervets' four meaningful woofs, and there are probably more, represent only a fragmentary glimpse of a communication system whose full extent remains to be explored. A similar complex of signals has been reported among Japanese macaque monkeys, a set of seven "coo" calls which, as in the case of the vervet woofs, are indistinguishable to the human ear. The most significant thing about these signals is that they evolved spontaneously in the wild, to serve the animals' own purposes and in the absence of human trainers with purposes of their own. Given all this among mere monkeys, we can look forward to major findings among chimpanzees at large in their native wildernesses, and among gorillas and orangutans as well.

HUMAN LANGUAGE—NEW ORDERS OF COMPLEXITY

In the last analysis one's evaluation of the progress made to date is all a matter of perspective. If you consider our earlier expectations—which were unreasonably, not to say irrationally, low—the linguistic accomplishments of nonhuman primates have been nothing less than spectacular. A totally different and equally valid picture emerges, however, if you compare nonhuman with human capacities. It is strictly no-contest. The gulf between ourselves and the next most articulate primates may be a mite smaller than it once appeared, but it remains enormous.

Life begins in chaos or near chaos. As a newcomer, a recent arrival from the womb, the infant faces a problem it will never solve completely. It is born into a turbulence of noises and odors, smooth places that suddenly become rough, cold places that suddenly become warm, lights and shadows that rise, fall, appear, and disappear. Plunged into this commotion, the infant must start to find a way and a place for itself. Its job is to create out of all the random strangeness a system of familiar objects, landmarks, rhythms, and laws.

So the infant investigates because it must, because that is what it is designed to do. It seeks and sorts out the elements of its world, including the sounds. It distinguishes meaningful from meaningless sounds, which sounds to heed and which to ignore, and, among the heeded sounds, which have the precisely patterned qualities of words. And it eventually makes what is probably the greatest discovery it will ever make, a discovery which is no less great because it is made over and over again by every infant. It proceeds to discover language.

This is a true discovery in the sense that the child learns but is not taught. Most of us have little or no knowledge about the intricacies of syntax and semantics, and even if we did, we would not be able to impart such abstruse information to our offspring in the nursery. We play a vital but more passive role, supplying language to them as we supply food and shelter. We provide them with a flow of sounds, words, and intonations which they may imitate, and that is the full extent of their imitating. Given this raw material, this sample of developed speech—an estimated total of 50 million words overheard during the first thousand days of life in the utterances of older children and adults, including speakers on radio and television—they go to work and create language anew on their own.

Out of that massive barrage of words and sentences, the infant somehow deduces for itself the elements of speech and of effective communication with other individuals. The process, at least that part of it which we can observe, probably starts at about the age of 6 months with babbling, a kind of practice for producing basic sounds deliberately and for discovering and refining syllables and intonations. The infant utters its first words, mainly action verbs and nouns (more abstract words such as adjectives tend to come later), at 10 to 14 months its first sentences of two or more words at 18 to 26 months.

At this stage some basis, however fragile, exists for comparing child and chimpanzee, in particular as far as size of vocabulary is concerned. Some time before the age of 2, the child has a working vocabulary of 150 to 200 words, roughly the chimpanzee level—which also happens to be the chimpanzee limit, all it will ever learn. Then the human takeoff begins in what is probably the most dramatic example of high-speed learning in the animal kingdom. Vocabularies soar to about 1000 words at the age of 3, more than 8000 words at 6, and about 18,000 words at 8. Furthermore, since the ability to comprehend language outruns the ability to use it, you can double or triple each of these figures to arrive at an estimate of the number of words understood but not yet uttered.

The full-scale investigation of language development among young human primates is a demanding task, which may be one reason that until recent times it has been generally avoided. Roger Brown and his associates at Harvard University have summarized their problems, tape-recording the utterances of children between the ages of 2 and 3:

> There were those who warned that the child would be shy and speechless in our presence; this was not the case. Mothers told their children that visitors were coming and, in general, we were eagerly welcomed, shown a parade of toys and games, and talked to rather steadily.
>
> It became clear that the child expected a guest to put in some time as a playmate, and so the recording was a two-man job, with one of us taking data and the other prepared to play cowboy, horsie, coloring, trains, and the mule in "kick the mule." . . . We found that by about noon we needed a rest and so we went away for lunch, returning about two; the child took his nap in the interval.

The patience and endurance required to cope with such conditions have proved rewarding in a number of ways. For one thing, the evidence shows quite clearly that the child takes the initiative in learning language. Its first sentences, mostly strings of two or three words, are not formed at random. They indicate an inherent feeling for subject-predicate and verb-object relationships. Furthermore, they are often completely original. The child continues to surprise us with a rather high proportion of phrases—such as *that doed, more up, allgone shoe* and *hi, milk*—which cannot be the result of any parroting process, since it does not hear any such remarks from its elders.

Learning proceeds at an impressive rate. Brown's studies indicate that starting at the age of 26 to 34 months or so infants learn special ways of modulating simple sentences, expressing meanings. English-speaking infants, for example, begin to use the present progressive tense correctly in sentences involving activities under way here and now, as in *me going* and *me eating*. Next they master the use of *in* and *on;* then sounds of the plural forms *iz,* as in *roses; z,* as in *dogs;* and *s,* as in *cats;* then the past irregular *went* instead of *goed;* and so on.

The process seems to obey its own laws and develop according to a predetermined timetable, no matter what anyone does about it. According to Charles Hockett of Cornell University, language acquisition "is practically impossible to prevent, save through environmental insults so drastic that the child has little chance to survive at all. . . . The earliest steps, moreover, are remarkably alike for children in all different speech communities, suggesting that all the languages of the world are, and for a long time have been, erected on a single groundplan." On the other hand, the coming of language cannot be rushed. Children make progress when they are ready to make progress, and not before.

For example, at about the age of 3, when they are still learning the rules of negation, they tend to produce double negatives and, as the following exchange indicates, until they grow out of this stage nothing can be done about it:

CHILD: Nobody don't like me.
MOTHER: No, say "nobody likes me."
CHILD: Nobody don't like me.

This mother put up a game but losing fight. After the above dialogue was repeated word for word eight times in a row, she tried one last time:

MOTHER: No, now listen carefully; say "nobody likes me."
CHILD: Oh! Nobody don't likes me.

The double negative was ingrained in the child's mind. It could not change, because no matter how often its mother repeated the correct sentence starting with *nobody,* the child heard something else. It listened with its inner ear and heard not one but two words, *nobody don't.* Of course, within a month or two it had learned to hear differently and was producing perfect negatives. So let the teacher, parent or otherwise, beware. Individuals younger than we are may not always be ready to profit by our greater experience and wisdom.

There seems to be something critical about the age of 12 or 13. Before that, language comes as it should come, readily and swiftly. Children pick up second and third languages without an accent, and injuries to the dominant half of the brain (the left half in right-handed individuals) do not usually produce permanent language deficiencies. After the critical age, accents and permanent brain-damage deficiencies are common—and severely abused and deprived children never catch up, as in the case of Genie, who had been confined to a small, closed room at the age of 20 months, harnessed to a potty chair or restrained in a covered crib, and lived there without human companionship for nearly 12 years. Remarkably enough, she has learned to converse, but with chronic difficulties involving certain aspects of word order, tense, and other grammatical forms.

Language develops with the pace and sweep of a biological force, on schedule, like walking and puberty. By the age of 5 the child has completed most of its work, which means that it has learned the great majority of more than a thousand basic rules of grammar. To be sure, many fine points remain to be mastered. There are several thousand more rules and exceptions to rules, most of which are learned unconsciously by the age of 10 or so, although some people never learn some rules.

When it comes to such accomplishments, of course, we are light-years ahead of the apes. But it is interesting to investigate where the gulf begins, the lessons apes can almost learn but not quite, the precise nature of their limitations and failures. Sarah has some idea of number, as indicated among other things by her ability to match half a glass of water with half an apple, and she could probably be taught to count. But it would be a formidable task for her and for her trainers, calling for many thousands of trials and errors over an extended period. A child, on the other hand, counts at about the age of 4 and, according to recent tests, probably has some concept of number as early as age 2 or $2\frac{1}{2}$.

The same thing goes for one-to-one mapping—say, putting ten dolls on ten chairs—and also for ranking items on the basis of size. Given ten balls of different sizes and a brief demonstration of lining up the balls in sequence, with the biggest at the left and the smallest at the right, a child has no trouble lining up ten blocks in a similar fashion. Premack points out that these are borderline procedures, easy for the child and extremely difficult for the ape. It is as if something extra has been built into the human brain, a set of sophisticated short-cut circuits designed to eliminate entire complexes of individual step-by-step operations.

The way children acquire language hints at what might have happened in the remote past. "The two fundamental developments were naming and grammar," Ben Blount of the University of Georgia comments, "and these emerged out of increasing complexity in social behavior and cultural information. The same is true for children learning the words of their language and for the highly efficient organization of grammar. Just as our protohominid and hominid ancestors did, children create and discover finer and more precise ways of relating information about the environment and themselves to other individuals."

Another important point is that infants manage to communicate a great deal before they begin using words. Smiling and crying convey a wide range of feelings, some subtle and some not so subtle—hunger, pain, discomfort, anger, frustration, pleasure, the need for affection, the desire to explore. Emotion, intense expression without words, preceded the coming of language as we know it. According to Blount, imparting information dispassionately, the first steps toward "the freeing of utterances from affect," came later during the course of evolution.

This was a most significant change. Nonhuman primates, all animals, are ruled by emotion and emotion-triggered responses, an observation emphasized by Tony Pfeiffer: "Even relatively lofty chimpanzees wear their hearts on their sleeves. Leaders display in a burst of noise; individuals nearby scream and lose bowel control. Feelings are never far removed from the surface. By contrast, a human hunter can assert himself as much with words as with noise and bluster. Language permits people to interact with a minimum of feeling, with carefully directed feeling or, in some cases with disguised feeling." On the other hand, it is only in comparison with other primates that we may seem controlled and inscrutable. We are still evolving, and even today our capacity to engage in emotion-free communication is probably rather more limited than we imagine.

THE FIRST SPEAKERS

In any case, chimpanzee studies suggest that the potential for language, for labeling and naming, has been around for a long time. Even before the appearance of hominids 5 or more million years ago, the world was richer and more diverse for primates than for most other mammals. Equipped with an outstanding visual apparatus, they saw more objects more vividly and in finer detail. From one standpoint, objects did not exist in the fullest sense of the word before the coming of advanced stereoscopic color vision. The environment became richer, less of a continuum, less an uninterrupted expanse of blurred and merging forms, and more a system of distinct items.

It was a kind of slow-speed, low-key information "explosion" with more things to observe, more to communicate about. Social relations also put a premium on signaling. Only primates seem to be capable of deceptive behavior as described in Chapter 12—which describes how a male baboon, threatened by an angry and higher-ranking male, snatches up an infant and begins grooming it, apparently because he knows he is safer from attack with an infant in his arms. This form of pretense involves deliberate plotting, the use of symbols, and a second-nature familiarity with complex hierarchical relationships.

Even more significant, it involves a certain ability to disengage oneself, to stand apart and observe the relationships and exploit them for new ends. It amounts to an abstract "tool use" in which a behavioral pattern is displaced from its natural setting and put to work in the service of a special purpose. The grooming of an infant used as a device to turn away wrath demands a certain detachment not unlike that which became important in the evolution of language. Again, it is a matter of controlling emotion, reacting to sounds not as emotional here-and-now signals, but as abstractions referring to something that had happened or was about to happen.

Given a measure of detachment, together with the chimpanzee's linguistic capacities and a system of calls at least as complex as the vervet's, there is also the all-important element of play. As indicated in Chapter 13, play probably appeared with the emergence of warm-blooded animals and reached a high point in the primate line. Language seems somehow to have arisen from play, in a uniquely human spinoff process which has acquired a life of its own. (Playing with words, inventing new words and more and increasingly abstract symbols, is a feature of present-day hominid behavior.)

The implication here is that the offspring of early hominids were major innovators. Their repertoire of games must have included such perennial favorites as chases, mock fights, and various versions of hide-and-seek and king-of-the-hill. But perhaps some games were being played that had never been played before. Perhaps tool use encouraged something like the game of catch, which can be regarded as a watered-down or domesticated pursuit, a disguised target practice in which the participants take turns at throwing and being thrown at, at being predator and prey.

A ball game would have required some delay, some anticipation, as compared with earlier primate games. It calls for organization, perhaps a choosing up of sides, and an object—often a prepared object at that, something worked into a roughly spherical shape to remove sharp edges and projections. An elaborate system of calls could have evolved in such a context. Before the start of a play chase, many mammals approach with a kind of hopping gait, a signal that what is about to happen is all in fun, and perhaps an analogous point was conveyed vocally as a prelude to games with objects. Maybe the combination of a throwing gesture and a special excitement call could have meant "Where is the ball?" or "Let's play catch!"

At some later stage a child acting on the spur of the moment, or as the outcome of an accidental turn of events, may have invented a more complicated game—say, a game requiring throwing and then running—and uttered the calls for "throw" and "run" in that order. Perhaps the two-part action came first and inspired the two-part call, or it might have happened the other way around. In either case the result could have been a dual creation, a new game and a new sentence or protosentence—and, given enough time, such behavior could have built up an appreciable vocabulary.

The very nature of play makes for innovation in all forms of behavior, including language. Novelty flourishes wherever there is freedom and a certain lack of responsibility for taking care of the world's immediate problems. There must have been a long period of increasingly complex prelanguage signaling, and a stage when signals originally invented in the easygoing context of play acquired an adaptive value in the serious matter of survival. Linguistic habits carried over into adult life probably served well in hunting and gathering and getting along together, thus setting a prehistoric precedent for the notion that Britain's wars were won on the playing fields of Eton.

AN EVOLUTIONARY SPURT

The first or primordial spoken language is the subject of a bold theory offered by Mary Foster of California State University. She was led to the theory by "the accidental discovery that resemblances between presumably unrelated American Indian languages were too widespread to be due to chance or borrowing" and by the subsequent finding of further resemblances in the Indo-European, Turkish, Hittite, and other languages. She believes that people originally spoke a language consisting of 18 sounds, each of which had a distinctive cluster of related meanings.

The units were gestures of a sort, hidden gestures based on the mechanics of pronunciation, the way the tongue, lips, and other parts of the apparatus produce the sounds. For example, sounds such as *p, t* and *k* (stopped sounds), produced at the front of the mouth and requiring complete closure of the expelled-air channel for a fraction of a second, represented the general notion of movements away from or outward. Resonant sounds such as *m, l,* and *r,* produced further back in the mouth together with vocal-cord vibrations, represented a class of internalized or subjective meanings involving mental activity, beginnings, desire, and so on. Foster has reconstructed a theoretical basic vocabulary made up of more than a hundred primordial words built from various combinations of the 18 sound-meaning units, or oral signals.

Perhaps something like these units appeared in the process of trying to name more and more objects, activities and relationships. If the number of names increased rapidly to a point where there were no longer enough calls to go around, not enough sounds to be recognized as distinct patterns, the result would have been a threatened overloading of communication systems and a heightened risk of misunderstandings and ineffective or confused responses. Hockett suggests that hunter-gatherers dissected calls into their components, shifting attention from whole sounds to parts of sounds. What may have happened was the invention of a kind of vocal alphabet, a small set of acoustic units, vowels, and consonants, which could be combined into an indefinite number of words.

There is no generally accepted time scale for the evolution of language. In fact, the job of reconstructing the process seems formidable, although it would be a great mistake to underrate the ingenuity, imagination, and persistence of investigators. Yves Coppens, for example, recently noted an intriguing difference between markings on the inside surfaces of *Australopithecus* and *Homo habilis* skulls, faint imprints left by the networks of vessels supplying blood to the brain. The *habilis* network was more intricate, more highly branched—and especially at the side of the brain which includes centers associated with speech.

Another line of evidence, also derived from studies of fossil skulls, comes from Jeffrey Laitman of the Mount Sinai School of Medicine in New York, who discussed his ideas during a 1984 meeting at the American Museum of Natural History. Certain bone formations at the base of the skull suggest that *Homo habilis* and later *Homo* species, but not chimpanzees and australopithecines, had a vocal apparatus capable of "the sort of varied sounds produced in speech." Also, there is Ralph Holloway's observation of early "symbols processing" centers. These observations, along with related observations by Dean Falk of the University of Puerto Rico, suggest collectively that some form of language may have originated two million years ago among the first representatives of the genus *Homo.*

One factor stands out in considering the evolutionary pressures that favored this development. Of all primates, humans are the only ones in which groups of unrelated adult females may forage in the absence of one or more protecting males, a feature that struck Richard Wrangham during his work among Ituri rain forest pygmies and villagers. Only by his actual presence could a male hope to keep intruders away, monopolize females, and ensure paternity and the transmission of his genes to succeeding generations—that is, before the coming of language. But language might well make a would-be intruder think twice, even with no guardian male about, since females could readily identify him and his actions after the fact.

So language from the very beginning, by virtue of its emotion-controlling aspects, may have been important chiefly in helping to reduce conflict. As already indicated, the main problem for hominids, as well as for other primates and lesser species, is not to avoid predators but to get along with one another—and this problem almost certainly swelled to major proportions during the Upper Paleolithic. Some 35,000 years or so ago, when people started living together in larger groups for longer periods, the archeological record tells of a full-scale information explosion, an explosion of symbols with the appearance of art, and a sharp rise in tension and conflict (see Chapter 11.).

There is some evidence, indirect but intriguing, that language may have undergone phonetic changes, among others. Jane Hill of Wayne State University in Detroit notes that "the simplest phonetic systems reported for the languages of the world are those of the languages of Polynesia, where the profound isolation of individual island societies made meaningful development of area networks unlikely." The most complex phonetic systems, on the other hand, occur in areas of high ethnic diversity, rising population densities, and rising feelings of hostility toward aliens. The Upper Paleolithic must have seen similar conditions.

BRAIN AND LANGUAGE

Whatever level of sophistication or complexity language had attained before, it underwent an evolutionary spurt during the Upper Paleolithic. The period saw spectacular changes in everything from techniques of toolmaking and hunting to social organization, and a corresponding increase in the number of things to be named and related to one another. That meant a burst of new words, new rules of grammar, much more to remember. At the same time there may have been trends in the other direction, the invention of new words to save words such as *tools* and *plants* instead of lists of specific items.

Rapidly expanding vocabularies could have put a severe strain on memory and brought about, even forced, the development of rules to relieve the pressure. Suppose that the singular and plural of every noun had been represented by two entirely different words; for instance, *tree* had the plural *gluh,* and people invented the notion of adding *s* to the singular, thereby eliminating the need for a plural word. Suppose further that the same situation held for the present and past tenses of verbs, and people got rid of past-tense words by simply adding *ed* to present-tense words. Analogous changes may have reduced the pressure on memory storage during the Upper Paleolithic. They may also help explain why Cro-Magnon brains seem to have been slightly smaller than Neanderthal brains (by some 6 cubic inches, about 700 million fewer nerve cells).

In the last analysis, understanding the evolution and development of language depends on advances in brain research. The striking fact that 5-year-old children have vocabularies of thousands of words and an impressive command of grammar argues strongly for inherited cerebral structures, nerve circuitry specifying the behavior necessary to acquire language. According to Noam Chomsky of the Massachusetts Institute of Technology, language acquisition is essentially a hypothesis-forming process. We are designed to scan the environment from infancy on, and to seek and discover in all the hubbub of sensation certain very special kinds of order, the rules of grammar. We do this automatically and unconsciously by trial-and-error experiment, deducing from an analysis of the utterances of others certain rules and the annoying existence of exceptions like *went* instead of *goed*.

An even more strictly biological theory, with an even greater stress on the role of heredity, has been put forward recently by Derek Bickerton of the University of Hawaii. Basing his conclusions on the grammatical structures of creole languages, languages invented and being invented to make communication possible where races come together in the world's melting or boiling pots, Bickerton will have nothing to do with the notion of forming hypotheses. According to him, we do not deduce the most fundamental rules of grammar. They are built into us as "biograms"; "Children can only learn language because, in effect, they already know a language."

We have yet to learn what all this means in terms of the anatomy and physiology of the brain. Just enough is known to hint at some of the problems that lie ahead. The ability to associate things heard with things seen, one of the elementary requirements of language acquisition, is extremely difficult for most lower primates. In the words of one investigator, if you want to teach them to learn that certain sound patterns or words are the names of objects and persons, "you have to hit them in the guts." If you want a macaque monkey to associate the word *circle* with the image of a circle, you must subject it to considerable emotional stress. You must punish it for making mistakes by applying an electric shock or some other painful stimulus, or keep it hungry and then reward it with food. And even under such conditions the experiment may not succeed.

Anatomy suggests one of the most important reasons for the difficulty. A certain visual area on the surface of the monkey's brain, on the sheet of nerve cells forming the cortex, is concerned with the shaping of images; another auditory area is concerned with patterns of sounds. Learning to associate an image and a sound is primarily a matter of establishing communications between the two areas. But it happens that there are very few direct connections from one to the other.

The main pathways in the macaque brain take an indirect course. They include nerve fibers running down beneath the auditory area on the cortical surface to nerve structures which appeared relatively early in evolution and are involved in emotional and biological needs. The fibers then make connections with other fibers ascending from these structures to the visual area at the surface. Many problems encountered in the laboratory arise because such roundabout routes are involved in efforts to train monkeys to associate complex sounds and images.

The situation in people is entirely different. The human brain includes a rich system of direct routes, fibers within the cortex itself which bypass the depths and connect not only visual and auditory areas to one another but also both these areas to a similar area concerned with the feel and texture of things. In fact, the fibers are so numerous that a special switching station, a superassociation structure, has appeared during the course of hominid evolution. It is somewhat bigger than a half-dollar piece and occupies a strategic position on the side of the cortex, just behind the temple, at the junction of the three areas.

Medical research indicates that this structure may be involved in the development of language. According to Norman Geschwind of the Harvard Medical School, it plays a major role in the formation of connections which enable children to associate the image and the feel of a teddy bear with the sound pattern for the words *teddy bear*. Injury to the center later in life may produce strange disorders of language, the result of difficulties in establishing connections between things heard and things seen. For example, a patient may have only minor difficulties in speaking, but he or she may lose the ability to read or write. Recently Geschwind and Marjorie LeMay, also of the Harvard Medical School, reported that among right-handed persons, nerve centers in the left-hand side of the brain, regions long known as major language centers, generally tend to be larger than corresponding regions in the right-hand side of the brain—a difference which may be related to an increase in the size of the superassociation structure.

The anatomy of this structure helps account for something we know from observations of behavior. The calls of lower primates are bound to emotion, occurring almost invariably in response to immediate satisfactions and dissatis-

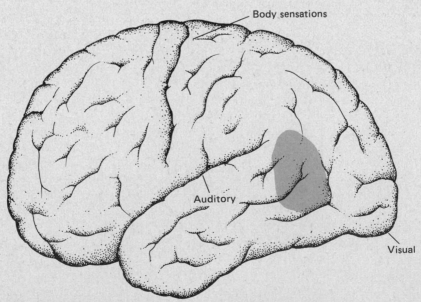

The "superassociation" center, a brain area believed to be involved in language acquisition

factions, a fact which makes sense considering the strong links that connect their visual and auditory areas to underlying nerve centers concerned with emotion. On the other hand, the fact that such links are much weaker in the human brain accounts for our ability upon occasion to communicate dispassionately. By the way, although the superassociation structure is absent or exists in only very rudimentary form in monkeys, it may be somewhat better developed in the chimpanzee, which helps explain the talents of Washoe and Sarah.

Here is an example, however hypothetical it may be at the current stage of human ignorance, of what it means to know. The point is not that we have an answer or a partial answer to our problems. Geschwind's ideas will surely have to be revised or they may well be discarded within a few years; but the approach, the fundamental nature of the search, is meaningful and appropriate. Sooner or later things must be confronted at the biological level; we must seek explanations in the behavior and organization of nerve cells.

We do not really know unless we know anatomically and physiologically, and in most cases even conceiving plausible models is enough of a problem. How would one design a brain so that it automatically classifies things? The information received through sense organs passes into some kind of sorting structure, some system of precisely interconnected nerve cells or molecules within cells. It must be categorized, arranged in hierarchies of classes, subclasses, subdivisions of subclasses, and so on. The information is stored in retrievable form so that answers can be given, usually in short order, to questions like "Have you ever eaten at the Golden Horn?" and "Do you know an elderly carpenter named Jim?" The anatomy of grammar will be better understood when we learn how the brain cross-indexes its remembrances of things past.

In general, it seems that the mechanisms involved are not primarily a matter of brain size. Size is important if only to provide sufficient storage space, and the elephant's famous long memory may be related to the massiveness of its cerebral hemispheres. But language may be acquired with surprisingly little nervous tissue. There are dwarfs with perfectly proportioned bodies scaled down to a height of $2\frac{1}{2}$ feet or so, and their brains weigh only some 14 ounces, the weight of the chimpanzee brain and about a third of the weight of the average human brain. They are mentally retarded, but they speak fluently. Their undersized brains still retain intact the uniquely human mechanisms which embody the capacity for language and probably arose early in hominid evolution.

These mechanisms have certain built-in biases, as indicated by the observation that all children acquire certain habits of using words. For example, Joseph Greenberg of Stanford University points out that in all languages studied to date, the word for *good* appears more often than the word for *bad*. (In English, *good* appears five times more often than its opposite.) The phenomenon may reflect at the linguistic level our tendencies to expect the best and to start by approaching things rather than turning away. But what are we to make of the fact that *long* occurs far more frequently than *short* and, similarly, that *many, deep,* and *wide* occur far more frequently than *few, shallow,* and *narrow*?

Also, the order in which rules of grammar are learned may be significant. For one thing, it may imply something about the nature and sequence of evolutionary events. The order in which children learn the rules may in some way reflect the order in which the species encountered and dealt with social problems. Perhaps language is full of such relics, clues to prehistoric experiences and ways of thinking. Perhaps language, like the brain itself, is a thing of many co-existing structures which are inherited from times past and can provide insights into our remote heritage. The past has not vanished or been discarded in the continuing process of becoming human.

SUMMARY

The origin of human language, by far the most sophisticated communication system in the animal kingdom, is one of science's great unsolved problems. One line of research involves the capacities of nonhuman primates. Vervet monkeys, for example, utter at least four different "woof" grunts, all of which sound the same to us, but have different acoustic patterns and different meanings for troop members. We have yet to take the full measure of monkey communications.

Apes are rather more talented. Washoe, a female chimpanzee studied at the University of Nevada, uses Ameslan, the standard American sign language for the deaf, has a vocabulary of more than 175 words—and, among other feats, invents word combinations, such as *water bird* to describe a swan. Other chimpanzees exposed to different kinds of training understand simple arithmetical relationships, and classify different objects, combinations of objects, and photographs of the combinations.

These and other studies reveal an impressive order of abstract thinking, far more advanced than investigators suspected a decade or two ago. But the gap between the cleverest ape and the average child remains enormous. A 2-year-old human has a vocabulary of 150 to 200 words, which soars to about 1000 words by the age of 3 and some 18,000 words 5 years later. Moreover, the child learns hundreds of basic rules of grammar in a particular order, rules which are not taught explicitly but learned by inference.

Language, like cooperative hunting and sharing and tool use, seems to exist in a rudimentary form among apes, and may have evolved to higher levels among early hominids, perhaps among hominid children at play. Later development favored the serious use of language to communicate rules of behavior and subsistence strategies in increasingly complex societies of hunter-gatherer bands. A possible sequence would start with simple word use among australopithecines 4 or more million years ago and a notable spurt during the Upper Paleolithic some 20,000 to 30,000 years ago.

Language comes to all humans automatically and on schedule, like walking and adolescence. During the first three years of life, the child hears an estimated 50 million words used in various combinations, and arrives at meanings and grammatical rules from an analysis of such raw data. Somehow this is accomplished with the aid of mechanisms built into the brain, association centers developed to a unique degree among human primates. Some major research breakthrough must take place before we can say much more than that.

chapter *20*

The Power of the Past

Everything that is being learned about human evolution points to the power of the past. Patterns of behavior that were developed in remote times, in the process of adapting to conditions that prevailed hundreds of thousands of years ago, continue to influence current behavior. To a certain extent we are all prehistoric, reenacting fragments of the past. We may respond prehistorically to present-day situations, thinking and acting in flashbacks, as it were, living upon occasion in a world that has long since vanished. We may at times turn back to a dreamtime of a sort, attempting to understand and handle contemporary problems as if we were still small-band members of a wild species at large in wildernesses.

The modern scene provides abundant examples of premodern behavior, basic and revealing insights into prehistory. There is a great deal to be learned not only from chimpanzees, the most human of nonhuman primates, and from hunter-gatherers in the Kalahari and the Ituri rain forest and the deserts of Australia, but also from those living far from wildernesses—in the spreading urban centers of industrial societies, in high-rise apartments, squatters' settlements, and suburban homes. Primitive behavior that has ancient roots and may, therefore, suggest how human beings once coped with ancient environments is widespread among all present-day peoples. In the words of John Hartung, "the degree to which modern cultural practices are vestiges of our past can hardly be overemphasized."

Real hostility: nonhuman primate

PRIMATE BEHAVIOR PATTERNS

We see flashes of the primate past in children. Some time ago Stuart Altmann spent two years studying some 400 rhesus monkeys on the island of Cayo Santiago off the coast of Puerto Rico, a colony imported from India nearly 40 years ago for research purposes. As part of his field work, he kept a detailed record of rhesus behavior, concentrating on the things a monkey does, identifying and noting its gestures, sounds, expressions, and movements. Similar techniques had been developed by zoologists in the study of insects, birds, fish, and other species.

Altmann compiled a catalog of the elementary behavior patterns of Cayo Santiago monkeys, listing such actions as "grooms," "gnashes teeth," "grimaces," and some 120 other items. This is a very restricted list in the sense that it contains only a tiny fraction of all the things a monkey is physically capable of doing. But since it does include most of the patterns which are known to serve in social communications and which thus make the survival of the species possible, it constitutes a list of behavioral patterns selected over millions of years of rhesus evolution.

Such lists have also been compiled for children. These lists generally include 125 to 150 separate items, a representative sample although by no means exhaustive. William McGrew has observed striking similarities among groups of human and nonhuman primates at play. He reports practically identical "flashing" or eyebrow raising and other common elements such as "play face," "play crouch," "gaze fixate," "kiss," "stamp," "beat," "hug," and so on: "I would estimate that at least 80 percent of the behavior patterns we have defined for nursery-school children have counterparts in nonhuman primates."

Similarities are also found in more elaborate activities. In many ways children's rough-and-tumble play is identical to the play of other primates. There are chases, fights, and wrestling, all typically preceded by a kind of I-dare-you posture and expression. A child about to be chased often stands side-on to the prospective chaser, slightly crouched and with a mischievous play face resembling the play face of the macaque monkey or chimpanzee under comparable circumstances; they display an open-mouthed smile with the teeth hidden. Another characteristic pattern jumping up and down on both feet, is reminiscent of the baboon's hopping gait in mock fights. There is also an open-hand beating movement, without actually hitting, an overhand movement very much like that used in throwing a ball or spear. Incidentally, boys tend to play harder and rougher than girls, a difference noted among baboons and other primates (see Chapter 12).

The patterns for fighting, including frowning, a cold stare, and real blows, are entirely different. In fact, the differences are greater and more clear-cut for

Real hostility: human primate

Play-fighting face: nonhuman primate

children than for the offspring of any other primate. Play fighting has been distinguished in a very special way, isolated and set apart from real hostility, identified by a system of signs so that the chances of misunderstanding are reduced to a minimum, which has a double implication for what apparently happened in the remote past. Hostility became especially dangerous, even lethal, in a species that wielded rocks and clubs and hurled missiles. At the same time, play acquired an extra importance not only as practice for real-life fights and escapes but also in the development of social competence and perhaps a mastery of language.

Nicholas Blurton Jones undertook child studies after observing fleeing reactions, threat and attack displays, and meeting ceremonies among chickadees and geese in England and seagulls off the Bering Sea coast in western Alaska. In one study he spent more than a hundred hours among children 3 to 5 years old in a London nursery school. He simply sat on a chair in a corner, notebook in hand, and began watching:

> On your first visit the children make an enormous fuss about you. They either stand and stare or run up and give you things, and then go away if your response is polite but uninvolved. They make a fuss again at the beginning of the second visit, but it does not last long. It takes about three visits to be completely ignored practically from the start.

Among other things, Blurton Jones noted a form of mother avoidance reminiscent of what Mary Ainsworth observed in one out of five middle-class American infants (see Chapter 18). At the end of a nursery-school day, an

Play-fighting face: human primate

avoiding child typically keeps its distance when its mother comes to take it home, and presents her with a new toy or some other object instead of rushing to her with open arms for a hug, the most common greeting. Older children often do the same sort of thing upon meeting a stranger, a mark of deep-seated tensions about which we know very little.

A basic source of such tensions may be the clash between the world as it is and the world as it was. The world as it is, notably the world of middle classes, may be working against some infant-childhood tendencies that evolved and were more meaningful long ago. For example, we may be putting too much stress on the mother-child bond, perhaps tying the bond too tightly. The child seems to be ready for close associations with other individuals, particularly its peers and older brothers and sisters, early in its second year—a good two years before nursery school usually starts.

This can be interpreted as preparation for the sort of environment or "home" setting which existed throughout the main course of evolution, during the 5 or more million years from the earliest hominids to recent times. Children once lived continuously in true groups, as individuals in intimate contact with many other individuals. This point suggests that life in remote times resembled life among today's hunter-gatherers and other nonindustrialized peoples in providing far more opportunity for the child, and also for the mother, to form a wider network of associations than is generally possible in present-day middle-class circles. Many tensions may be traced to the fact that different home settings have evolved and are still evolving, while we remain to an appreciable extent creatures of prehistory.

THE EVOLUTION OF PLAY

The past is also at work among us in play, a recent phenomenon in the history of life on earth and a major element in the evolution of highly intelligent species (see Chapter 13). Play, as a complex activity under intensive study, is not always fun. Corinne Hutt of the University of Keele in England has observed nursery-school behavior in a test situation. A familiar playroom included both familiar toys, such as a truck and a panda doll, and a brand-new object, a red metal box with four brass legs and a kind of four-position gearshift lever on the top. Under the conditions of one series of experiments, moving the lever operated a bell, a buzzer, and four clicking counters.

Children were set free in the room for six 10-minute sessions, usually 2 days apart, and their actions at first were decidedly not playful. At first they were afraid. When an adult was in the room with them, the fear did not last long and they approached the red box within 30 seconds or so, generally after asking what it was. But when they were alone, they delayed longer and approached more hesitantly, and never approached without bringing a familiar toy along. Boys brought the truck, girls the panda doll. And even then the children did not play.

As might have been predicted, they paid special attention to the new object, spending up to half their time with it, holding the lever in one position, listening to the noise, watching the counters, shifting positions rapidly, and trying to twist it and pull the lever off. Such activity might have passed for play in this study, as has been the case in many other studies, except for the key observation that the children did not seem to be having fun. There was a certain amount of tenseness in the air as they concentrated on the object with intent, earnest attention. The entire pattern of behavior, from the first hesitation on, was clearly serious business.

Novelty is a threat to children as well as to their elders. The fear comes from the remote past, when the sight of a stranger or an unfamiliar object had the impact of a criminal loose on the street or a house on fire. Children and adults may be reacting appropriately for that early world if not for their own. Working against the fear of novelty, however, is the tendency to approach and inspect and above all to remove the mystery and the insecurity. Novelty is also a necessity. It cannot be wished away. It can be assimilated and transformed into the familiar and made part of the environment. It can be built into the scheme of things as a landmark, as something dependable and therefore something that can usually be ignored. All this represents a special need for the human child who is dependent for so long.

Hutt's nursery-school children first hesitated and then investigated, an activity that tapered off rapidly after the third or fourth experimental session, after the red box had lost its mysteries. Now at last they were ready to enjoy themselves. Starting at the second session and reaching a peak at the fifth, their posture and facial expression relaxed, and they spent more and more time treating the box as a familiar thing. In effect, it became a toy for the first time. One boy ran around the room pulling the truck, and every time he passed the lever he shifted it to produce bell-buzzer sounds. He had finished exploring and had turned to play.

Hutt stresses the significance of the shift: "The emphasis changes from the question of 'what does this object do?' to 'what can I do with this object?' " Play is thus active in a creative rather than a purely exploratory way. It is a fragile thing, as fragile as joy itself, which vanishes with the first hint of fear or uncertainty. Play flourishes among familiar objects in a familiar setting, as at savanna feeding grounds where dominant males are nearby and at home bases. Among hominids it has become increasingly associated with pretending and acting and the invention of games, and perhaps of language. Regarding pretending, the boys in Hutt's studies did more of it more elaborately than the girls. She observed 20 out-of-the-ordinary cases of playing with the red box, such as using the gearshift knob as a microphone and crooning into it, and in 16 cases the player was a boy.

We can only guess at the conditions under which play evolved in times past. There is no easy explanation for the observation that it is confined largely to birds and mammals, although one factor may be that warm-blooded animals tend to spend more time and energy feeding and exploiting a wider variety of foods than cold-blooded animals. According to Robert Fagen, this difference might well favor play as a form of stamina-building scrimmages which prepare for active foraging in the future. Also, play may have prepared individuals to predict one another's behavior and to cooperate. Certainly powerful selective forces must have put a premium on the emergence of play, which had a number of serious disadvantages in the wild and would never have become prominent without important compensating advantages.

Fagen emphasizes that play tends "to put an animal in double jeopardy:

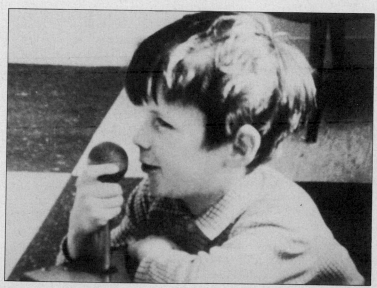

Make-believe crooning

First, the animal is penalized for not using its play energy for growth and main-tenance, and then it is penalized over and above this effect due to specific risks associated with play.'' In other words, play uses up energy which might be better spent in satisfying immediate needs, and also creates new dangers. Animals at play lower their guard and may not be on the alert. Absorbed in their make-believe fights and pursuits, they are notoriously vulnerable to the attacks of predators.

To investigate factors favoring the rise of play, Fagen used a computer to help evaluate comparative costs and benefits, simulating the life histories of hypothetical animals devoting various proportions of their time and energy to reproduction, play, feeding, and other activities. Certain results of the computer experiment check with well-known observations. Among simulated as among real-life animals, the young tend to play more than their elders. Furthermore, play appears more frequently among relatively secure species established in stable, predictable environments than among species under stress in the process of trying to adapt to short-lived environments. The cost-benefit analysis also indicated that the amount of time spent playing could vary enormously, not only among different species, but within different populations of the same species, a phenomenon noted in squirrel monkeys, for example, some troops of which play frequently and others not at all.

Other model studies suggest that although play may provide training for real-life situations, such as hunting, fleeing, and establishing social relationships with other individuals, its basic payoff is discovery. Most of what happens most of the time in the relaxed world of make-believe involves activities which are new to the individual but old to the species, tactics, maneuvers, and ideas which have been part of the species' heritage for many many generations.

But now and then something new arises, a new dodging strategem or a new mock alarm call or a new variation in an old game, and some of the things discovered at leisure (perhaps a very small proportion) turn out to have survival value later when the pressure is on, for example, when hominid life demanded more effective communications and the beginning of language (see Chapter 19). In Fagen's words, "play behavior might even be described as extraordinary scientific research performed by animals."

The implication is that basic research, human-style, has its roots in the sort of play that features problem-solving and the invention of problems. There may be an analogous relationship between play and the arts. The element of pretend-ing, of something standing for or symbolizing something else, is prominent in both play and art. So are the elements of surprise, adventure, pleasure, experi-mentation (in the sense of trying out new patterns and contrasts), and "useless-ness" (in the sense of not fulfilling any immediate biological function).

These similarities are emphasized in the studies of Ellen Dissanayake, an art historian in Kandy, Sri Lanka (formerly Ceylon). She believes that art arose in play and later went its separate way, acquiring formal and ritualistic qualities in the course of serving serious social needs (see Chapter 11). The precursors of art may have been a variety of representations used originally in games—pieces of wood resembling animals and infants, circles and other shapes drawn in the dirt with sticks and fingers, colored clays smeared on faces, pebbles, and cave walls. As far as the oral tradition is concerned, the origins of myth and legend, most children begin telling stories on their own between the ages of 3 and 4, using some of the elements of poetry—intonation, stress, and rhythm.

Art may have been associated with religion from the very beginning. The archeological evidence suggests that religion in its earliest forms arose at least 75,000 years ago (see Chapter 8), some 35,000 or so years before the first signs of painting and engraving, indicating that the earliest art, like the art of medieval times, may have been sponsored by individuals in charge of memorial ceremonies, burials, and other rituals. Art was probably also involved in teaching, in designing ornaments as marks of social status, and in arousing people to a pitch of excitement for hunting, fighting, and worshipping—and it probably continues to serve evolutionary ends. It continues to be a medium of assertion and rebellion, communication at the social level, as well as a form of exploration and a way to provide continual surprise and novelty.

LIVING WITH THE PAST

The past also exerts a strong influence in the way we form groups. Spontaneous social organization starts relatively young. In a study of more than 400 school children, Donald Omark and Murray Edelman of the University of Chicago found the first signs of hierarchies emerging among first-graders, "with boys being placed near the top, girls near the bottom, and considerable overlap in the middle." There were other interesting sex differences. Boys formed larger groups, generally at some distance from their teachers and other adults, and were more competitive and aggressive; girls "talked quietly in groups of twos and threes," generally closer to their teachers. Furthermore, when discussing their positions in hierarchies, boys tended to overrate themselves, exaggerating their true rank more than girls.

Hierarchies are widespread in the animal kingdom, from insects to humans (see Chapter 14). It apparently took an act of will, a strong tradition amounting to a taboo, to prevent the formation of hierarchies among hunter-gatherers, a tradition which began to be broken only during the Upper Paleolithic. There are no such traditions among lower primates. On the basis of studies among captive vervet monkeys, Michael McGuire of the University of California in Los Angeles notes a number of characteristic behavior patterns which hold for all primates.

For example, the larger the group, the more often the dominant male will be challenged by younger males and the more likely he is to keep them under control by means short of outright aggression—say, by frequent minor confrontations calling for submissive gestures, a pattern observable among humans as well as among vervets in the wild. "Among adult males competition for the dominant position appears to be an endeavor for which male animals are strongly predisposed," McGuire notes, "one which takes precedence over all activities, save remaining a group member."

Much human behavior, a good deal less than among other animals but probably a good deal more than we realize, has a strong hereditary bias. The power of the past is indicated by what comes easy to us and what comes hard. It is hard to think things through before acting, to develop long-range master plans and abide by them. It is easy to act quickly for quick results on a day-to-day basis. In certain respects we still behave like members of a small-band species with a small-band mentality; in certain respects we are still creatures wandering in close-knit groups through wildernesses.

It is easy to love family and a few friends, hard to love more widely, to care about anyone outside one's immediate circle and to trust people who look different. To be aroused to quick anger and a fight, even when the arousal works against one's interests, is easy; to become aroused actively about community projects is hard. As Edward Wilson points out, we respond too readily to the call of the wild: "We are ready at a moment's notice to explode, to escalate even a mild disagreement into a full-blown tribal conflict. If we could only cut that wire, the psychological bomb would be defused."

People interacting with one another show many of the characteristics found in troops of nonhuman primates. Direct stares, frowns, forward movements of the lips, and other expressions indicate aggression; hunching the shoulders, drawing the chin in toward the chest, closing the eyes, and moving away are among our natural flight reactions. People living together in groups in hospitals, homes, offices, and military units use such signs to establish hierarchies much like those observed among wild baboons, or to form a coalition of two or three individuals which becomes a dominant core or establishment (see Chapter 12).

The fact that we are partly geared to the past is reflected in physiological processes over which we normally have no control. Body temperature falls about 3 degrees Fahrenheit during the course of a night's sleep, reaching a low point at about four in the morning, and begins to climb sharply from then on. Blood pressure follows the same general pattern, and so does the concentration in the blood stream of certain adrenal-gland hormones which mobilize natural body fuels. During the last hour or two before we wake up, dreaming tends to increase and heart and breathing rates become more irregular.

This entire complex of changes, which exists in certain lower primates, has been interpreted as an alerting mechanism. Although humans no longer live in open country, sleeping on the ground or in trees or on rocky ledges, the brain, at least those parts of the brain responsible for such reactions, does not know about these changes. Morning after morning we are prepared for events that no longer occur, for responding to emergencies that confronted our ancestors, for the hours before sunrise on the savanna, which represent a period of special danger as far as stalking predators is concerned.

The past is with us also when we wake up and go about the day's business. Unpleasant encounters, frictions, a bitter argument at home, an accident barely avoided while driving, a belittling remark from a superior at the office—all can produce changes which prepare the body for violent and sudden exertion on the spot—for bursts of anger or fear and for attacks and flight. Many predawn reactions are accentuated; for example, a sharp rise in the output of adrenal hormones produces a corresponding rise in the blood level of fatty substances that can be burned or metabolized rapidly to provide energy for the muscles.

Usually people do not act impulsively because they have learned not to act; certain parts of the brain play an inhibiting role on other parts. But self-control may take a toll in the long run. Some investigators believe that if excessive fatty substances in the blood are ready for burning and do not burn, people may suffer as a consequence because, while most of the substances are excreted unused, very tiny amounts may accumulate and form deposits on the inner walls of arteries, including the arteries that bring blood to the heart itself. Consequently, as the deposits thicken, the arteries become narrower and narrower, until blood supplies are seriously reduced or cut off entirely, and a heart attack results.

Such attacks are far more common among men, since women burn fatty fuels more completely. Possibly, this is because women are brought up to be less ashamed of emoting and hence tend to release tensions more openly and directly. In a sense they live more in harmony with their metabolism and their inherited physiology. Probably, men emote less readily and are called on more often to disguise their feelings. They often encounter situations demanding inhibition, so they seethe inside, smile, and delay the settling of accounts. Vital statistics suggest that the woman's way may be healthier than the man's; she lives seven to eight years longer than he does.

Evolutionary factors may also be partly responsible for a number of other diseases that come increasingly after middle age. The body's immunity system reflects the notion that in the remote past people too old for hunting, fighting, and reproducing played minor roles at best in society. Active participation after the age of 40 or 50 is a relatively new phenomenon, and the body has not caught up with the times. It is precisely during this period that the immunity system, which not only combats bacteria and viruses but may also destroy abnormal cells, begins to go into a decline.

This amounts to a lowering of the guard. One result may be increasing vulnerability to a variety of infections which were held in check during earlier years, to cancer and other conditions involving uncontrolled cell growth. Robert Good of the Sloan-Kettering Institute in New York comments: "After all, nature is not basically interested in individuals who have passed the age of maximum reproductive efficiency. The coming of language and brains capable of intricate learning and long memories, factors that helped make old people important as bearers of tradition, is a very recent development in evolution."

Mental conditions may also involve evolutionary throwbacks, behavior patterns derived from responses traceable to remote times. Christopher Brannigan of the Department of Psychiatry at the University of Birmingham in England and David Humphries of the University of Aston reported an episode that occurred during a group therapy session in which one patient's homosexuality was being discussed. At the uttering of the word *homosexual,* another patient, Mr. X, responded with an involuntary gesture, a characteristic movement in which he placed his hand on the back of his neck. The gesture was a message, and the British investigators were prepared to read it because they had conducted studies of child behavior that, like those described earlier in this chapter, were based on detailed observations of gestures and expressions.

They had observed 136 separate elements including 42 hand-arm gestures,

17 eyebrow patterns, and 7 types of smile. The hand-to-neck gesturing of Mr. X made sense in the context of this silent language and its special vocabulary. It is related to gestures of preschool children who are preparing for fights and who raise their hands to a ready-to-strike position, assuming a so-called beating posture. As children grow older, usually starting at about the age of 5, they begin to modify this reaction; they are learning other ways of settling disputes, mainly exchanging well-chosen words instead of blows. But often they are unable to prevent early patterns entirely. At the start of trouble, the hand goes up by instinct; then, as controls take over, instead of moving forward for a blow, the hand retreats and hides, as it were, ending up concealed at the back of the neck.

The gesture in childhood is a sign in disguise, something like a message written in code. It can express hostility, feelings of being threatened, and a readiness to fight if necessary, and it is carried over into adult life. For Mr. X the word *homosexual* uttered in an open group discussion represented the threat of being discovered, and it came out later that he had strong homosexual tendencies. So the child appears in the adult, and the species appears in the child. The case of Mr. X is not only part of the history of an individual; it is also part of human history, since the hand-to-neck gesture is a pattern developed in remote times when words were just becoming a serious alternative to violence.

There are many other basic gestures of this kind, most of them yet to be interpreted with any degree of precision, and all of them making up the elements of an evolutionary sign language. The ability to read this language will advance our understanding, not only of emotionally disturbed persons but also of the forces that shaped prehistoric people and made them vulnerable to new varieties of mental disease. Other behavior patterns generally thought to be solely abnormal states with no particular evolutionary significance may also reflect prehistoric ways of life. One study suggests that epilepsy or something very much like it may once have served a useful purpose in human survival—if one can judge by the results of animal research.

Michael Chance, head of the University of Birmingham's Subdepartment of Ethology, conducted a special investigation of epilepsy in humans and other species, and pointed out that in many cases it can be better understood in terms of the prehistoric past. For example, laboratory tests show that certain strains of deer mice inherit a tendency to have violent epileptic seizures upon hearing sudden loud noises. The reaction is clear-cut, swift, and dramatic. Typically, an individual runs and crouches alternately, then lapses into a running fit, during which it runs blind and collides with anything lying in its path; then it attacks cage mates and inanimate objects, sinking its teeth in and holding on; finally it collapses, stopping dead in its tracks and going rigid all over. The entire reaction generally lasts only a minute or so.

This behavior appears to have nothing to do with survival mechanisms when observed among caged animals; investigators have usually dismissed it as the result of an undesirable mutation. But it makes more sense when one considers the behavior of deer mice in the wild. They do not make burrows. They live on the surface in sparsely wooded country where at any moment they may encounter a predator out in the open. Under such circumstances, chances for survival would be increased by a pattern of automatic flight, vicious fighting if flight fails, and, if fighting fails, freezing or playing dead. So epilepsy among hypersensitive deer mice, as well as among other animals, seems to be a hereditary and pathological form of normal defensive behavior.

The same principle may apply to human epilepsy. Early people also lived in open country with few places to hide and had to develop a variety of flight tactics. There seems to be a connection between this behavior and an observation of sexual behavior. According to the Kinsey report, about one out of every six preadolescent boys and a small proportion of men occasionally have violent convulsions during or after orgasms, which may reflect the well-known and very ancient association of sexual activities with flight and aggression.

Certain forms of seizure may have acquired special importance by helping to control the flow of fuel to various parts of the body. Brain cells demand liberal supplies of oxygen, and suffer irreparable damage when supplies fall too low. The threat of such emergencies must have arisen frequently 1 to 2 million years ago when the brain was expanding rapidly with the coming of *Homo erectus*. If so, epileptic attacks may have served a protective function by prostrating the body and increasing the flow of oxygen-rich blood to the brain.

PSYCHOANALYSIS AND AGGRESSION

The study of people as members of the order of primates and, more generally, as one among many social species, inevitably affects our notions about the underlying causes of human behavior. For example, take Freud's image of the original human family—a "primal horde" made up of an all-powerful, jealous, and aggressive father, a Jehovah-like figure who maintained a harem and drove his sons out of the household when they became sexual rivals, thus providing the basis for the original and all subsequent Oedipus and Electra complexes.

Certain elements of this picture apparently fit in with current ideas about the nature of prehistoric society. Something which looks like a harem arrangement may have arisen when generations of our ancestors gradually shifted from forest settings to open woodlands and savannas (see Chapter 14). The melodrama and the sex, however, tell us more about Freud and his contemporaries than about early hominids. Freud was influenced by Victorian attitudes toward sexual passions as the root of all evil, animalistic drives inherited from subhuman savages and in Jekyll-and-Hyde conflict with civilizing notions. Much of what he interpreted as the thwarting of incestuous mating urges seems rather to be an expression of "genetic self-interest," not a matter of Oedipus and Electra complexes, but of offspring competing for parental care and attention (see Chapter 18).

On the positive side, Robin Fox points out that Freud recognized what most biologists and few psychoanalysts recognize today—namely, that any theory about the origins of human behavior must be based on studies of the behavior of other primates. The best sources available to Freud during the early 1900s consisted of tall second- or third-hand tales about gorillas. Their basic social unit was supposed to include a single dominant male, a number of females monopolized by the male, and younger males continually trying to gain access to the females and continually being outfought.

That image, the source of the primal-horde notion, is not supported by the work of George Schaller and others. Gorilla bands usually contain more than one adult male; the head of the hierarchy may be completely unconcerned when other males copulate with receptive females, even when the males are newcomers to the troop; and younger males are not driven off. Intense aggression is rare. Males certainly compete and fight with one another, but, as Lionel Tiger has emphasized, they also form close associations (see Chapter 7).

Many familiar observations acquire new significance when one begins to regard groups of men in a strictly behavioral context, in the same spirit which guides recent studies of children and wild primates. The basic fact which emerges is that men seek each other out and find pleasure in being together. They engage in a wide variety of activities (all essentially male monopolies) from which women have long been excluded—war, the top councils of organized religion, finance, politics—in addition to their tendency at parties to converse in groups away from the womenfolk.

According to Tiger, men are attracted to one another, and the attraction is as powerful and deep-rooted as that between men and women or between mothers and infants. He suggests that the very pleasure involved in all-male associations, particularly in sports and fighting, is an index to the intensity of the attraction: "An emotional current or perhaps an esthetic excitement adheres to manly militant strength which seems biologically equivalent to the sexual excitement between men and women." In this connection, many ceremonies may play a role in male-male relationships analogous to the role of courtship in male-female relationships—for example, the circumcision rites of the Australian aborigines, initiations into fraternities and secret societies, and, at a somewhat less ritualized and communal level, businessmen's luncheons.

Men are predisposed to associate with men, another way of saying that the tendency has a genetic basis and a long prehistory. It may have arisen very early in hominid evolution, at least judging by certain observations of wild chimpanzees. One of the most remarkable features of chimpanzees' remarkably relaxed and informal life in the trees is the spirit of camaraderie which prevails among top-ranking adult males. Even investigators trained to avoid easy comparisons between apes and humans describe what they observe as friendship.

The biggest and most powerful chimpanzees in a given territory seem to enjoy one another's company, and often travel about together in groups of half a dozen or more individuals. Such behavior probably arose out of necessity; group action had an important selective value when it came to defending the troop in times of emergency. But eventually it may have come to serve some other function as well, perhaps helping to promote and maintain amicable social relations with the troop itself. In any case, the attraction of males for males continues in contemporary forests, even though dangers are few and chimpanzees have little to fear from predators.

One factor which brings out opposing forces is crowding. The larger the group, the greater the amount of conflict. In fact, conflict tends to increase exponentially with group size, and efforts to resolve conflict probably had a great deal to do with the emergence of art and ceremony during the Upper Paleolithic (see chapter 11). Charles Southwick of Johns Hopkins University reports that crowding has long been a major problem among rhesus monkeys in northern India. Encounters among the monkeys are particularly vicious in and near Hindu temples, where they occupy the same sort of position as pigeons do around churches and other buildings in American cities.

The monkeys are fed by local people and treated somewhat as pets; they multiply freely and produce larger and much more aggressive troops than those found in the forests. Fighting breaks out more often, not only within the ranks but among entire troops. There are dominant and subordinate troops, hierarchies of hierarchies, whose positions are usually determined by the number of members. Subordinate troops always retreat when they see a higher-ranking troop approaching.

But not infrequently, perhaps once every three or four days, sudden encounters take place. A subordinate troop may be so absorbed in its feeding that it fails to notice the approach of a dominant troop, and then violence flares up. Adult males generally begin the fighting, but females and juveniles also join in. According to Southwick, temple monkeys are particularly vicious aggressors: "These fights were ferocious and dangerous . . . often resulting in severe wounds, and most adult males bore wound scars around the face, shoulders, or rump. Wounded individuals were fewer among the rhesus monkeys in rural habitats and forest areas."

Most fights end after only a few minutes with the retreat of the subordinate and smaller troop. Now and then, however, the sides happen to be evenly matched and a pitched battle results, lasting as long as 15 to 20 minutes. On one occasion, part of the top-ranking troop suddenly came upon the entire membership of the No. 2 troop. The subordinates seemed to be enjoying a distinct advanatge until the rest of the dominant troop, like reinforcements of federal cavalry in a Western movie, arrived to save the day.

Such episodes are probably the closest that nonhuman primates can come to human-style fighting. Indeed, the case of the Indian temple monkeys suggests how collective fighting may have become an established thing among us, a part of our life style. As long as people foraged in small groups with freedom to move from group to group when things became too tense, conflict could remain at a relatively low level, a principle well known to hunter-gatherers. When asked why they live in small groups, the Bushmen of the Kalahari reply that they fear fights.

Trouble came with the larger groups of the Upper Paleolithic, and increasingly with the coming of agriculture. Settling down into village-farming communities apparently accelerated the growth of populations, bringing more people and more different kinds of people closer together than ever before. As if that were not enough, the quality of life was changing. There were schedules to be met, times for clearing the land, planting, weeding, harvesting, and planting again. Life for humans became tamer with the domestication of plants and animals, less spontaneous and perhaps less exciting, particularly for males, who, throughout the course of primate evolution, have been difficult to build into a family unit.

Boredom has yet to be given its due as a factor in influencing human behavior. It may well have had a special impact on men in agricultural societies. Deprived of hunting as a major source of excitement, prestige, and subsistence, and of wild species as a major focus of aggression, men may have begun playing the most dangerous game of all, going after one another instead, as if their peers were the only creatures clever enough to make hunting really interesting. (War has always been more exciting than peace, robbers more exciting than cops, Lucifer and hell more exciting than God and heaven.)

Considering the forces favoring aggression, we can hardly be surprised that violence flares up in today's crowds. The miracle is that cities can exist at all, that descendants of a long line of small-band foragers at large in wildernesses can endure in brightly lit places, bounded by walls and sharp corners, among noises mostly made by machines, within shouting distance of hundreds of persons, most of them strangers. The very existence of cities is a tribute to our ability to adapt, and we do it partly by creating special kinds of small groups, social islands in oceans of population.

PROBLEMS OF FORESIGHT

The readiness to form and join organizations has become more intense in urban settings. People tend to associate themselves with certain fellow workers at the office, and with a widening variety of community and special-interest groups outside the office—political action committees, country clubs and hobby clubs, historical societies, conservation movements, and so on. Each group has its hierarchy of presidents, vice presidents, treasurers, secretaries, executive committees. Each group is an artifact designed to limit and channel social contacts, permitting individuals to behave as if they were still living in an extended-family, small-band setting. The city is possible because so few people know one another. Being a stranger to all but a few, being impersonal to all the rest, has its evolutionary advantages.

Life is complicated by the fact that we have never yet been able to foresee many, if not most, of the consequences of the changes we must bring about. Major changes undertaken with the most conservative of motives have a way of thwarting our conservatism at every turn, as if we and evolution were chronically at odds. In all likelihood, the first fire users of perhaps half a million or more years ago simply wanted to keep warm, to curl up near red-hot embers on cold nights (see Chapter 7). Hardly revolutionaries, they simply wanted to make the world as they knew it more comfortable.

Our ancestors could not begin to know the consequences of their actions. They could not foresee the implications of the fact that light comes together with heat, creating a longer day for working and socializing. Nor could they know that the pain and fear associated with fire would be exploited to the utmost— that fire would be used more and more over the millenniums to drive other animals out of their lairs and caves into a variety of deathtraps; that fire would bring wonder at the flickering of shadows, visions among the shadows, and intimations of the supernatural. In short, the first fire users could not know that the innocent act of bringing warmth into their camps would transform their lives.

The same forces, the same limitations, continue to operate in our times, only in a far more immediate context. Take ecological chain reactions, for example. Some years ago, as part of a drive to wipe out malaria, World Health Organization workers sprayed the thatched-roof huts of Borneo villages with DDT. The foreseen result was a sharp drop in malaria—the unforeseen result, an increased risk of typhus and plague. The DDT had poisoned local cats, increasing the population of rats and rat-infesting lice and fleas. Part of the remedy was to parachute fresh supplies of cats into the villages.

In Egypt, a host of troubles followed completion of the billion-dollar Aswan Dam, one of the greatest construction feats of the twentieth century, and one of the saddest examples of ecological mismanagement. The dam is doing many of the things it was built to do: it is generating electricity, preventing severe floods along the Nile, and providing irrigation waters for about a million acres of land that once was desert and now yields up to three crop harvests a year.

But it also created new problems, among them a serious health emergency. In pre-dam days irrigation canals had contained snails carrying bilharzia, a lingering and weakening parasitic disease, but the canals dried up periodically and the snails died. Now that the canals are full all the time, snails are flourishing, and at one point the disease increased tenfold. Meanwhile, crop yields have been decreasing in certain areas. Salts which reduce soil fertility are accumulating, and the only countermeasure is to build a network of special canals to drain irrigated lands more efficiently. More than a hundred scientists have been engaged in an effort to deal with these and other difficulties.

There is no choice in such matters. We do what must be done. But that calls for a hitherto unprecedented degree of experiment and planning, a new order of foresight. All of which runs counter to some of our most deeply rooted instincts, the old tendency to do things now and quickly, to leap before looking. The tendency is to trust the future, assuming that things will take care of themselves naturally and come out all right in the end. It is a kind of lazy optimism.

MAGICAL THINKING, RESISTING CHANGE

In this respect we are all primitives, all magical thinkers, a point stressed in a somewhat different context by Richard Shweder of the University of Chicago:

> The theoretical consequence of the discovery of massive deficiencies in the intellectual performances of normal adults in our own culture has been a fascinating one. . . . What was once an arrogant and ethnocentric portrayal of the shortcomings of the primitive mind has today become universalized into a more humble and self-denigrating portrait of the limited rationality of normal adults in all cultures.

A realistic picture of human behavior is barely beginning to emerge from current research. What makes insight difficult, aside from the sheer complexity of things, is the intense and continuing resistance to such studies (see Chapter 12). The resistance is so powerful and so effective that it must have been of special value to the species, serving some vital adaptive need. Perhaps it was a matter of survival for early people to feel supremely confident, especially when the wilderness seemed most alien and daily routines most futile. Feelings of superiority are not easy to maintain in the face of too much self-knowledge.

In any case, if insight once threatened our security, today ignorance has become an even greater threat. Considering our biases and tensions and instabilities, one can no longer be quite so confident about the future as was the fashion before our most recent world war. The new study of humans starts off with a new realism. It avoids the unwholesome spirit that causes us to speak of black Americans as one-third middle class instead of two-thirds impoverished, and that impels us to put rouge on the faces of corpses and to suggest that the effects of nuclear radiation be measured in "sunshine units."

People are beginning to be watched as they have never been watched before. The elements of their behavior are being noted and the repeated patterns are being analyzed from an evolutionary viewpoint. And there is more to come. There will be further studies of people in schools, offices, homes, and churches as well as in deserts and jungles, along with studies of nonhuman primates and other animals.

Like all research designed to get at fundamentals, such work is tedious most of the time. The real work of sophisticated analysis starts only after information has been painstakingly coded and entered into computer memory. The results should be exciting and revealing. The search is for nothing less than basic patterns of behavior seen in broad evolutionary perspective—fresh knowledge about our origins and guidelines for the future.

SUMMARY

We are still subject to the power of the past. That our behavior is still conditioned to an appreciable extent by patterns inherited from prehistoric times stems from the fact that members of the human family have been living in small nomadic bands for five or more million years, and in settled communities for only a few millenniums.

We see flashes of the past in children. An estimated 80 percent of elementary behavior patterns observed among monkeys, actions such as "stamp," "hug," "kiss," and "flash" (raise the eyebrows), are also observed among nursery-school children. Nonhuman as well as human children engage in games, "pretend" activities such as mock fights and mock pursuits and escapes.

Close observations of human children approaching objects never seen before show that play has its serious aspects. Boys and girls tend to examine and handle new objects earnestly and with a certain tenseness before they relax and start playing. Novelty attracts, but it also arouses fear, a possible throwback to early times when something strange often meant danger. Play first appeared among mammals 200 million years ago (see Chapter 3). It has become especially important among primates and most important of all among human beings, perhaps as rehearsal for real-life behavior and for discovery in arts and sciences.

Vestiges of the past exert a strong influence on adult behavior. Intense competition among males, the formation of hierarchies, is an ancient pattern not only among primates but throughout the animal kingdom. Many things that we do "naturally," readily, seem to reflect the small-band life styles of prehistory—living mainly on a day-to-day basis, acting first and thinking things over later, caring deeply for family only and a few friends, distrusting strangers, quick to get angry and fight. The past affects patterns of health and disease, biological rhythms still attuned in part to wilderness living.

Primate studies throw new light on the forces, often irrational, which influence human behavior. Much of what Freud explained in psychoanalytical terms turns out to involve a form of kin selection (see Chapter 14), competition among offspring for parental attention. Similar forces may help explain the formation of all-male groups among nonhuman and human primates. Survival depends increasingly on getting along with one another in crowded cities, and on long-range planning—all of which puts a premium on our unprecedented ability to adapt.

Epilogue: Things to Come —Can We Make It?

The only thing we know for sure about the future is that we are moving into it faster than ever before. Practically everything worth predicting is unpredictable, including the key question of whether there will be a future fit for human beings to live in. The question arises now with a new nuclear urgency after 5 to 10 million years of evolution in the hominid line, after the transformation of a clever ape into a creature with unprecedented and increasing powers to create and destroy. As the only remaining members of the human family, we may or may not survive.

Certainly, as John Hartung reminds us, survival is uncommon in the scheme of things: "Adaptation by natural selection . . . operates primarily at the level of the individual. . . . Most individual lines become extinct, most social groups become extinct, and most species become extinct." On the other hand, there has never been anything on earth like the human species. Potentially it has the power to control its future, to change the rules and increase the odds in favor of survival. Anything can happen, assuming of course that we do not succeed in destroying ourselves.

The future remains obscure. But in a way we are already living in it, surrounded by and immersed in new beginnings, new technological and social developments that will shape the future—under, we hope, some measure of human control. Evolution proceeds at an accelerating pace, and the most vivid mark of the human take-off is the computer. A machine and something more than a machine, it is a "hot spot" focus of evolution human-style, hinting more forcibly than anything else at the nature of changes to come. We sense those changes already; we feel in our bones that they will dwarf the most radical changes of times past.

As far as unpredictability is concerned, the computer is the prehistoric fire story all over again. The story, low key and almost humdrum in the beginning, takes on the aspect of a major evolutionary adventure. The first electronic computer, a dinosaur of a machine, blazed no mathematical trails. A development of World War II, the so-called ENIAC (Electronic Numerical Integrator and Computer) was designed primarily to do something that had been done ever since the invention of big guns—to prepare ballistic tables indicating shell trajectories for different elevations, wind directions, and so on. Under peacetime conditions such tables had generally been produced by groups of mathematicians working at hand-operated desk calculators, but the war brought a serious shortage of operators, and the only alternative was to turn to automatic methods.

Yesterday's purposes and accomplishments are hopelessly mundane, hopelessly elementary, compared to what is already going on today. A new kind of relationship is being created between people and machines, a unique organic-inorganic union. Computers are strong where we are weak, and weak where we are strong. The hunter-gatherer life style did not foster an outstanding ability to do arithmetic. People cannot carry out even a moderately difficult series of calculations without making errors. For example, you might take some 5 minutes to multiply 3,696,437,692 by 9,731,991,327—but the odds are that you would not obtain the correct answer (35,973,699,559,339,897,284) on the first or second try. Computers not only operate without errors, but the fastest models can run for days or weeks doing 100 million or more such calculations a second.

Precision is fine, to be sure. But the real world is a sloppy place, and computers have considerable trouble with sloppiness. That is where we shine. We must be able to deal with sloppiness—we are built for it—because we are so sloppy ourselves. To take only one simple example: there are many ways of printing the first letter of the alphabet—a, A, large or small, italicized or unitalicized, in any one of hundreds of type styles. Furthermore, human handwriting is anything but precise, and any one of these letters may be written in a fast scrawl. Yet we can make out an almost infinite variety of scrawls and even cope with complete illegibility by our knowledge of context. For instance, the a in *strange* may be a meaningless blob, but we can figure it out because we know the word from the other letters. This is high-level pattern recognition, and it applies to recognizing faces, gestures, and words spoken as well as written, words in foreign as well as native languages, landmarks, and so on. It is beyond the capacities of any existing computer.

One big difference between us and computers, however, is that they are changing much faster than we are. ENIAC contained some 20,000 vacuum tubes and occupied a space about the size of a tennis court. Today engineers are cramming more computer power into microchips smaller than the letter *M* and about as thick as this page, and planning still further size reductions, as well as calculating speeds 100 to 1000 times faster than the fastest present-day machines.

Computers are becoming "friendlier," easier to communicate with, because of new software, programs designed for human-machine interaction in a conversational mode. Computer graphics involves images on computer screens, images in color and three dimensions, images of office-condominium complexes and space vehicles which you can walk around and through, video games played for architectural and scientific purposes as well as for fun. It is all part of our response to the continuing information explosion which began back in the Upper Paleolithic (see Chapter 11). In the field of chemistry alone, about 5 million substances are known with some 1000 new ones synthesized and named every day. In all, our current rate of learning has been estimated at 100 trillion new bits of information per year, enough to fill about 2 million volumes of the *Encyclopaedia Britannica*.

As far as electronic thinking is concerned, machines are evolving more slowly than we would like but, to reemphasize the point, at a pace far greater than hominids ever did. Within a generation, computers that play chess, representing the avant-garde of the programming art, have advanced from low-grade models which any good amateur could beat to present-day versions which defeat most human players with the greatest of ease and, upon occasion and with somewhat more difficulty, upset the masters.

Marvin Minsky, who is conducting research at the Massachusetts Institute of Technology, on artificial intelligence, predicts that within another generation "we should be experimenting on programs that write better programs to replace themselves." If that happens, if investigators arrive at a set of instructions which permit computers to learn from their mistakes, the trick will be to pit computer against computer until the machines play perfect games. In that event, chess, which is known to be a strictly determined game as trivial mathematically as tic-tac-toe, will lose its interest for humans, although they will certainly devise games with new orders of complexity, perhaps even too complex for the computers of the future.

The problem right now is that chess machines are not very intelligent. Theirs is chiefly a bulldozer, bludgeon approach which depends in the last analysis on examining millions of positions at prodigious speeds. Their limitations involve pattern recognition. The ability to size up complex chess positions on the basis of experience, to examine certain selected moves and countermoves and counter-countermoves to a look-ahead depth of a dozen or more plays, remains a human skill. But there is one interesting reason why present-day chess-playing computers may win in tournaments. It has primarily to do with our natural sloppiness.

It seems that even the world's best players make serious mistakes, and, even more to the point, their opponents may make the additional mistake of failing to notice the slip-ups. That much has been known as long as chess has been played. What we did not realize is how often such double errors occur. Computers have taught us that. They are not all that clever, but now and then, in a kind of ruthless "pouncing" action, they may detect and take swift advantage of the mistakes that cleverer humans make—and that is enough to bring victories.

Computer chess is important as a model for future advances in artificial intelligence, for its basic similarities to the playing of more serious games. For example, there is the "game" of medical diagnosis, often a matter of life or death. Master diagnosticians, like master chess players, draw on an enormous store of knowledge, thousands of hours spent with people describing their symptoms and sometimes telling more about themselves by gestures and expressions than by words, thousands of hours spent studying charts, X-ray pictures, electrocardiograms, electroencephalograms, and so on. Diagnosis is art as well as science, and even the best physicians, like the best chess players, make mistakes.

The pressure to call increasingly on computers as aids to diagnosis comes mainly from the information explosion. Information about diseases, new diagnostic methods and possible causes and treatments, is increasing so rapidly that no physician can hope to keep up with it. Even specialists find it more and more difficult to keep up with developments in their own restricted fields. It has been estimated that in making diagnoses most doctors use only about 70 percent of the information available, presumably because they are unaware of the other 30 percent.

Preliminary efforts to solve this problem are under way at a number of institutions. Physicians at the Tufts–New England Medical Center have worked with artificial-intelligence specialists at the Massachusetts Institute of Technology to develop a program involving one symptom to start—edema, or swelling. Given this program and the information that a particular patient is a young man with swelling of the feet, a computer types out, "First time? Infrequent? Occasional? Frequent?" When the doctor responds, "First time," the computer asks, "Painful? Not painful?" "Dyspnea (shortness of breath)?" "Is there jaundice?" "Is there varicose veins?" and so on. Upon completion of this "conversation," the machine types out three possible diagnoses, favoring by an 80-percent probability, in this patient's case, "idiopathic nephrotic syndrome," a kidney condition.

Similar interactions, programmed for abdominal pain, diseases of the nervous system, the care and treatment of cancer, and general internal medicine, call for storing the symptoms of more than 600 diseases in computer memory. Furthermore, the question-answer approach can be applied to fields other than medicine, wherever information has piled up to a point beyond the capacities of humans without computers—and that is practically everywhere. Investigators are preparing increasingly sophisticated software for increasingly sophisticated hardware in designing aircraft and space vehicles, in finding legal precedents (and loopholes), in planning long-term industrial policy, and so on.

These so-called expert systems are beginnings only. Today's most advanced designs will certainly be out of date within a few years, and that situation, a sign of how swiftly research is progressing, is likely to continue, the major problem for the future being pattern recognition. Even so, some people are beginning to feel threatened. Every report on computerized diagnosis, for example, includes repeated statements reassuring physicians that final decisions will always be theirs, that, in the words of a recent American Medical Association report, computers "will merely serve as expert consultants."

George Miller of Princeton points out "a human being assisted by a computer is still a human being." It is also true that the combination of a human being and a computer behaves more like a computer than a human being. In any case, we are in the process of transforming ourselves, and current developments indicate the extent if not the precise nature of future changes. For example, what are the limits of prosthesis, the use of artificial organs and tissues to replace defective body parts? Today in the United States alone some 3 million plastic, ceramic-glass, and metal parts are implanted in patients' bodies every year— everything from synthetic hip and knee joints, ear bones, pacers, and heart valves to tear ducts and nerve sheaths.

All such cases represent a kind of holding operation, the objective being simply to restore function, to make things at least nearly as good as new. It should be possible to go further, however, and improve on nature. Perhaps surgeons working with artificial-intelligence specialists will learn to implant compact microchip devices in the brain—say, a sleep enhancer that would permit getting along on only 3 or 4 hours a night, or a memory unit that would double or triple an individual's storage capacity. Whatever happens, the human body will include a higher proportion of prosthetic items. In that sense, our descendants are likely to be rather less "natural," less human, than we are.

A step in the same direction, only more so, is genetic engineering, deliberately altering DNA, the hereditary material. The general idea is to remove undesirable sections of DNA, some 2 yards of which are coiled up in the nuclei of human cells, and insert new sections in their place. As Sherwood Washburn indicates, changes at this molecular level would represent the ultimate in tinkering with nature: "Darwinian evolution is purposeless and very slow. It is difficult to demonstrate any change over the last forty thousand years. Genetic engineering is purposeful and fast, and that makes all the difference."

As if all this were not enough, a new breed of machine is about to come into its own, the robot. The most advanced models among us today do not live up to popular conceptions of the word. They are not nearly as ingenious as the creations of science fiction, neither metallic monsters capable of going berserk nor benevolent automatons like R2D2 of *Star Wars* fame. They are special-purpose automatic machine tools equipped with mechanical wrists and fingers, memory circuits, three-dimensional vision, and a sense of touch and motion—capable of picking up heavy pieces of metal and working them into precisely shaped parts, all under the direction of appropriately programmed computers.

It is ironic that Japan, where workers noted for their loyalty have enjoyed lifelong job security and sing company songs at assembly every morning, should be the world's current leader in designing and manufacturing machines to replace humans. According to one estimate, 20,000 robots are at work in Japanese factories, compared with perhaps 6000 to 7000 in the United States, and both nations, as well as European countries, have launched ambitious programs for future developments.

Second-generation robots will include more versatile and more mobile models, self-navigating walkers, talking and listening on a limited basis, handier in the sense of being able to make more varied and more precise manipulations. Third-generation versions, still more articulate and more versatile with the aid of built-in computer "brains," will learn from experience and be far closer than anything on the drawing boards of the 1980s to the androids of science fiction. As a sheer guess, I would expect the coming of superrobots some time after the year 2000 and before 2025. But one thing we can be sure of—by that time the general shape of things, technologically and otherwise, will be quite different from our most imaginative current speculations.

Whatever comes to pass, it is clear why *Homo sapiens sapiens* stands out as the representative of a brand-new kind of terrestrial evolution. All other species take the world pretty much as they find it, altering the environment minimally if at all. We are changing the environment with a vengeance, bulldozing and re-shaping landscapes, creating new environments. All other species survive by the powers they were born with. We are unique in expanding our inherited powers, amplifying vision with instruments that can see atoms and galaxies, amplifying intelligence and memory with computers, planning to build artificial "species" in the form of robots and to reshape heredity itself.

So much for the works of scientists and engineers, for the potentialities of basic and applied research. As has been evident for some time, and increasingly in recent times during the course of two world wars and a holocaust, science will not ensure the survival, much less the progress, of the human species. Every scenario about what this sort of technology may bring, every prospect for the evolutionary future, must come up short against the most crucial problem of all, the limited ability of humans, males mainly, to live less aggressive and less violent lives.

Fundamentally, the problem is to remake ourselves in another image, to become more human, closer to the sort of individuals we would like to be but are not yet. That means changing ourselves as effectively and creatively as we change machines. People have a natural ability to get along with one another, up to a point. As far as going forth and multiplying is concerned, they have been strikingly successful, at least so far. But that will be enough from here on, even if they achieve a steady-state zero population growth.

People living in the midst of rapid change will have to get along much better than they ever have before. They will have to reorganize themselves on the run, as it were, and there is nothing natural about that. It demands the development of new artificial environments as appropriate for contemporary populations as natural wilderness environments were for prehistoric hunter-gatherers. More intensive studies of people in groups, grownups as well as children, are under way in an effort to learn more about the effect of architecture on behavior.

One of the most imaginative designs for a city grew directly out of a consideration of human needs and the causes of human conflict. Some years ago Christopher Alexander of the University of California at Berkeley started from scratch with the notions that cities are meeting places and that the most elementary human need of all is the need for intimate contacts with other individuals. He defines intimate contacts as situations in which people see one another often, at least once a day, not in offices or public places, but under informal, at-home conditions.

Contacts of this sort were commoner in prehistoric times and in times not long past. Small farms and villages were commoner, as were homesteads with large families made up of representatives of three or more generations. Things never were idyllic. Life can be too close, too ingrown, encouraging the old tendency to regard outsiders and outside ideas with hostility. But the modern city, for all the variety and opportunities it offers, produces other kinds of alienation. For one thing, people become defensive among crowds, behaving impersonally and ignoring others as if the world were still a place of small groups (see Chapter 20).

Alexander approaches the problem directly with a plan for a new kind of made-to-order city, including, within densely populated areas, zones designed to encourage certain living features once provided by village-farm settings. He cites psychiatric studies suggesting that mental illness is especially likely to develop among persons with few intimate contacts or none at all, and that an individual needs at least three or four such contacts. The environment must be organized so that close friends can drop in on one another on the spur of the moment, which means that they should live no more than ten minutes apart. In today's cities, friends or, rather, potential friends usually live half an hour to an hour apart, enough to prevent casual dropping in.

These human requirements lead to certain design requirements. Each house must be located on a through street for automobile traffic, the street being a thousand feet long at the most and connected with a major traffic artery at both ends. Each house must lie within a hundred yards of 27 other houses, and have private bed-living rooms as well as a transparent communal room which opens onto a private garden and can be looked into from the street. Also, the entire residential area must consist of uncluttered countryside and rolling hills.

In all, there are 12 requirements or "geometric considerations"; a residential area that meets them all will include an artificial landscape where hills are constructed so that the highest and steepest may be nearest the theater-shopping-commercial center of the city, and the lowest and flattest are furthest from the center. All roads and houses in the area are underground, providing unbroken expanses of countryside. Each house is located so that while its street-side entrance is buried, its garden-side entrance lies on a hill slope and is wide enough to let in daylight for communal and other rooms.

According to Alexander, planners who start with his objective—namely, to create an urban environment fulfilling our need for one another—will arrive at a design that may differ from this one in details but not in any fundamental way. He is also stressing something even more important, a principle that holds independently of this or that particular plan. Architectural design is no cure-all; it cannot by itself solve problems of mental illness and violence. But it is not arbitrary either. It depends on and is determined to a large extent by human needs.

Evolutionary forces continue to change the design of institutions as well as urban environments—for example, changes in organizing people to get work done. The classical hierarchy, the pyramid with one man at the top and descending levels of vice presidents and lesser subordinates, is being viewed critically again. Hierarchy arose some 25,000 years ago during the Upper Paleolithic as a way of reducing large-group conflict. It flourished from about 10,000 to 5000 years ago with the coming of villages, cities, and states, reaching an all-time high in the person of the Egyptian pharaoh, no mere mortal but an absolute god. It has been on the decline ever since. For all their power, today's dictators and tycoons represent a considerable comedown from divine status.

In many cases, the hierarchy remains an effective way of getting things done. When the rules of the game are well established, when the job at hand is best carried out by doing things as they have been done before, it is generally the system of choice. But these times often call for flexibility, devising new and less hard-and-fast procedures in federal agencies, businesses, schools—and under such circumstances, hierarchies are about as inappropriate as living in caves.

Under such circumstances, in fact, hierarchies can be more harmful than they are worth. They can pit individual against individual. They encourage personal vendettas, the what-makes-Sammy-run syndrome that has been attributed to human nature, but turns out to be chiefly an artifact of social design, a product of institutions built on principles of all-out competition. Rosabeth Moss Kanter of Yale University spells out the problem in her outstanding study of "Indsco," a pseudonym for one of the largest American corporations:

Hierarchical systems of organization are often successful in fragmenting groups and leading them to believe that their interests lie in opposition, so that they blame each other for their problems rather than uniting to change the system. Attempting to keep the other group out, while ferociously improving oneself in the hopes that more advantage will follow, is a characteristically American approach to the problems stemming from inequality.

Recent times have seen a somewhat belated reform movement, a new emphasis on the importance of modifying hierarchies. Prompted more perhaps by increasingly tough competition at the international level than by conscience, managers are reexamining the notion that people might be more productive in a less cut-throat atmosphere. In some cases they have already taken preliminary steps to "flatten the pyramid," to decrease the distance between top and bottom, to distribute power and prestige more equitably.

Similar trends are under way in more intimate settings. The family is evolving into something less and less like the family of a generation or even a decade ago, and less and less like the families of other primates. Its ties are based more on the evolving needs of independent individuals than on strict rules of dominance and submission. The domestic hierarchy, of course, is in the process of being flattened, at least in countries where the woman shares the breadwinner's role or takes on the entire burden.

The bond between mother and infant may be as intense as ever but, at least after the period of infancy, it demands less of her time. This is the latest phase of a development that started in prehistoric times when women assumed the responsibility for gathering plant foods, cooking, and keeping the home fires burning. Her most important concern was still the infant, but it was not her only major concern, as it is for mothers in a chimpanzee or baboon troop. Today, for the first time, prolonged infant and juvenile dependency need not mean prolonged maternal dependency.

Meanwhile, the attitude toward having children continues to change. Overcrowding once existed somewhere else, in slums and across oceans. Now it is here among us marked by the dwindling of wildernesses and villages, traffic jams on Main Street, streams clogged with garbage—and, above all, by the prospect within a generation of half a dozen supermetropolises, cities made up of several hundred million people each. Parents will continue to be as proud of their children as they were before the population explosion, but they will be less proud of large families.

The primate trend toward single births, the concentration on a single precious infant, is being carried to a new extreme in China, where some 10 to 15 million families with only one child have signed pledges to have no more. As rewards they receive pay increases, extra housing space (enough for a two-child family), special health-care privileges, and other benefits—all of which are withdrawn if a family breaks its pledge and has a second child. A third child brings wage reductions of 10 percent or more. The present laws do not specify what lies in store for more prolific parents.

At some stage in China and elsewhere there may be a shift from voluntary to compulsory reproductive behavior. It is difficult to foresee the nature of future birth-control laws, or their impact on the family. Suzanne Keller of Princeton University has this to say: "Just as agricultural societies in which everyone had to produce food were once superseded by industrial societies in which a scant 4 percent now produce food for all, so one day the few may produce children for the many." Questions immediately arise as to which women would be selected for controlled motherhood, on what basis and by whom. The future is certain to be more complicated than the present.

Again, I am assuming that there will indeed be a future. There are a number of possibilities, and the issue will almost certainly be settled within the next 50 to 100 years. Most species have become extinct, and nuclear warfare could hasten us toward that end. But we cannot count on a sudden "big bang" extinction, a kind of mercy killing or mercy suicide. It would probably be a lingering death, the fading of a species that had lost will and purpose and the capacity for caring. Another possibility—humans might survive and attain an evolutionary plateau, an ultrastable stop-action state like the horseshoe crab and other species that have changed little for hundreds of millions of years, a dull but relatively safe prospect.

The most exciting scenario is one of ever-widening exploration. Stability, of course, would go by the boards. Humans would continue to try everything, to extend themselves to the limit and a bit beyond. It is the can-you-top-this psychology, play and more than play, the readiness to do anything providing it seems useless and has never been done before—everything from double- and triple-somersault ski jumps and tightrope walking between skyscrapers and group parachute jumps to wrapping cliffs in cellophane and attempts at levitation. A deliberate search for novelty, for instability, is characteristic of avant-gardes in science as well as in the arts, and it could continue into the indefinite future.

Human evolution proceeds right now as it has in times past, in an atmosphere of uncertainty, turmoil, and adventure. People are just beginning to explore outer space, the ultimate frontier, where they may yet catch glimpses of evolution on a cosmic scale. Intelligence at the human level or beyond may be confined to the planet earth, or it may be spreading like an epidemic throughout the galaxies. (There are plausible arguments on both sides.)

Again, the only sure thing is change and the struggle to adapt. Change may be painful, but it is bad only if you believe the past was good—only if you believe that our ancestors, prehistoric and historic, saw better days and that things have been sliding downhill ever since. That hardly seems likely.

Most of prehistory has been a record of small bands on the loose, the efforts of a minority species to survive in an alien and mysterious world. Most of history has been a record of increasing inclusiveness, of letting more and more people into the club of first-class citizens, commoners as well as kings, nonwhite as well as white, women and children, all minorities and pseudo-minorities—human liberation, if you will. The odds are that we shall continue to behave as we are designed to behave, proceeding positively on the assumption that we represent not an ending but a beginning.

Bibliography

Prologue: The Search for Human Origins

Bates, Marston, and Humphrey, Philip S. *The Darwin Reader.* New York: Scribner, 1956.
Beer, Gavin de. *Charles Darwin.* Garden City, N.Y.: Doubleday, 1965.
Binford, Lewis R. *In Pursuit of the Past.* New York: Thames and Hudson, 1983.
Braidwood, Robert J. *Prehistoric Men.* 8th ed. Glenview, Ill.: Scott, Foresman, 1975.
Cronin, J. E., et al. "Tempo and Mode in Hominid Evolution." *Nature,* 9 July 1981.
Foster, H. L. "How Not to Understand Human Evolution: A Layman's Guide." *Harvard Magazine,* July–August 1979.
Golding, William. *The Inheritors.* New York: Harcourt Brace Jovanovich, 1962.
Mayr, Ernst. *Populations, Species and Evolution.* Cambridge, Mass.: Harvard University Press, 1970.
Oakley, Kenneth P. *Man the Tool-Maker.* 6th ed. University of Chicago Press, 1976.
Osborn, Henry Fairfield. *Men of the Old Stone Age.* 3rd ed. New York: Scribner, 1925.
Pfeiffer, John E. *The Search for Early Man.* New York: American Heritage, 1963.
Pilbeam, David. *The Ascent of Man.* New York: Macmillan, 1972.
Reader, John. *Missing Links: The Hunt for Earliest Man.* Boston: Little, Brown, 1981.
Tanner, Nancy. *On Becoming Human.* New York: Cambridge University Press, 1981.

CHAPTER 1: PRIMATE BEGINNINGS

Alvarez, Luis W., et al. "Extraterrestrial Cause for the Cretaceous-Tertiary Extinction." *Nature,* 21 January 1982.
———. "Impact Theory of Mass Extinctions and the Invertebrate Fossil Record." *Science,* 16 March 1984.
Andrews, Peter. "Hominoid Evolution." *Nature,* 21 January 1982.

Bakker, Robert T. "Dinosaur Renaissance." *Scientific American,* April 1975.

Bown, Thomas M., et al. "The Fayum Primate Forest Revisited." *Journal of Human Evolution,* December 1982.

Calder, Nigel. *The Restless Earth.* New York: Viking, 1972.

Cartmill, Matt. "Rethinking Primate Origins." *Science,* 26 April 1974.

———. "Basic Primatology and Prosimian Evolution." In *A History of Physical Anthropology, 1930–1980.* New York: Academic Press, 1982.

Clemens, William A. "*Purgatorius,* an Early Paromomyid Primate." *Science,* 24 May 1974.

Eimerl, Sorel, and DeVore, Irven. *The Primates.* New York: Time-Life Books, 1965.

Fleagle, John G.; Kay, Richard F.; and Simons, Elwyn L. "Sexual Dimorphism in Early Anthropoids." *Nature,* 25 September 1980.

Hsü, Kenneth J., et al. "Mass Mortality and Its Environmental and Evolutionary Consequences." *Science,* 16 April 1982.

King, James E., and Fobes, James L. "Evolutionary Changes in Primate Sensory Capacities." *Journal of Human Evolution* 3:435–443 (1974).

Kurten, Bjorn. "Continental Drift and Evolution." *Scientific American,* March 1969.

Martin, R. D. "Ascent of the Primates." *Natural History* 84:52–61 (1975).

McKean, Kevin. "A New Ancient Ape." *Discover,* August 1981.

Officer, Charles B., and Drake, Charles L. "The Cretaceous-Tertiary Transition." *Science,* 25 March 1983.

Pilbeam, David. "New Hominoid Skull from the Miocene of Pakistan." *Nature,* 21 January 1982.

Simons, Elwyn L. "The Earliest Apes." *Scientific American,* December 1967.

———. "Primate Evolution—an Introduction to Man's Place in Nature. New York: Macmillan, 1972.

———, and Kay, Richard F. "*Aegyptopithecus* and *Propliopithecus.*" In *McGraw-Hill Year Book of Science and Technology,* (1981).

Tuttle, Russell H., ed. *Paleoanthropology: Morphology and Paleoecology.* Chicago: Aldine, 1976.

Van Valen, Leigh, and Sloan, Robert E. "The Earliest Primates." *Science,* 5 November 1965.

CHAPTER 2: FIRST MEMBERS OF THE HUMAN FAMILY

Bartholomew, George A., and Birdsell, Joseph B. "Ecology and the Protohominids." *American Anthropologist,* October 1953.

Cherfus, Jeremy, and Gribbon, John. "Updating Man's Ancestry." *New York Times Magazine,* 29 August 1982.

Goodman, Morris; Tashian, Richard E.; and Tashian, Jeanne H. "Progress in Molecular Anthropology." *Current Anthropology,* September 1976.

Hockett, Charles F., and Ascher, Robert. "The Human Revolution." *Current Anthropology,* June 1964.

Jolly, Clifford J. "The Seed-Eaters: A New Model of Hominid Differentiation Based on a Baboon Analogy." *Man,* March 1970.

Kay, Richard F. "*Ramapithecus* and Human Origins." In *McGraw-Hill Year Book of Science and Technology,* 1982–1983.

Kerr, Richard A. "New Evidence Fuels Antarctic Ice Debate." *Science,* 28 May 1982.

King, Mary Claire, and Wilson, A.C. "Evolution at Two Levels in Humans and Chimpanzees." *Science,* 11 April 1975.

Kortlandt, Adriaan. "New Perspectives on Ape and Human Evolution." *Current Anthropology,* December 1974.

Lawick-Goodall, Jane van. *In the Shadow of Man.* Boston: Houghton Mifflin, 1971.

Leakey, L. S. B. "Adventures in the Search for Man." *National Geographic,* January 1963.

———. "An Early Miocene Member of Hominidae." *Nature,* 14 January 1967.

Lee, Richard Borshay. *The !Kung San.* New York: Cambridge University Press, 1979, Appendix E.

Lewin, Roger. "Is the Orangutan a Living Fossil?" *Science,* 16 December, 1983.

Lovejoy, C. Owen. "The Origin of Man." *Science,* 23 January 1981.

Mann, Alan. "Hominid and Cultural Origins." *Man,* September 1972.

Peters, Charles R., and O'Brien, Eileen M. "The Early Hominid Plant-Food Niche." *Current Anthropology,* April 1981.

Pilbeam, David. *The Ascent of Man.* New York: Macmillan, 1972.

———. "Major Trends in Human Evolution." In *Current Arguments on Early Man,* New York: Pergamon Press, 1980.

———. "The Descent of Hominoids and Hominids." *Scientific American,* March 1984.

Sarich, Vincent M., and Wilson, Allan C. "Immunological Time Scale for Hominid Evolution." *Science,* 1 December 1967.

Simons, Elwyn L. "On the Mandible of *Ramapithecus.*" *Proceedings of the National Academy of Sciences,* March 1964.

———. "The Early Relatives of Man." *Scientific American,* July 1964.

Simpson, George Gaylord. "The Biological Nature of Man." *Science,* 22 April 1966.

Stanley Steven M. "Mass Extinctions in the Ocean." *Scientific American,* June 1984.

Vercors. *You Shall Know Them.* Boston: Little, Brown, 1953.

Washburn, Sherwood L., and Moore, Ruth. *Ape into Man: A Study of Human Evolution.* Boston: Little, Brown, 1974.

Wolpoff, Milford H. *Paleoanthropology.* New York: Knopf, 1980.

———. "Ramapithecines and Hominid Origins." *Current Anthropology,* October 1982.

CHAPTER 3: THE AUSTRALOPITHECINES

Brain, C. K. "A Hominid Skull's Revealing Holes." *Natural History,* 83 (10):44–45 (1974).

———. *The Hunters or the Hunted?* Chicago: University of Chicago Press, 1983.

Charteris, J., et al. "Functional Reconstruction of Gait from the Pliocene Hominid Footprints at Laetoli, Northern Tanzania." *Nature,* 9 April 1981.

Dart, Raymond A. "*Australopithecus africanus*: The Man-Ape of South Africa." *Nature,* 7 February 1925.

Gwynne, Peter. "Bones and Prima Donnas." *Newsweek,* 16 February 1981.

Hay, Richard L., and Leakey, Mary D. "The Fossil Footprints of Laetoli." *Scientific American,* February 1982.

Hays, J. D.; Imbrie, John; and Shackleton, N. J. "Variations in the Earth's Orbit: Pacemaker of the Ice Ages." *Science,* 10 December 1976.

Holden, Constance. "The Politics of Paleoanthropology." *Science,* 14 August 1981.

Howells, William. "Piltdown Man: His Rise and Fall." In *Mankind in the Making.* New York: Doubleday, 1959.

Isaac, Glynn L.; Leakey, Richard E. F.; and Behrensmeyer, Anna K. "Archaeological Traces of Early Hominid Activities East of Lake Rudolf, Kenya." *Science,* 17 September 1971.

Johanson, D. J., and White, T. D. "A Systematic Assessment of Early African Hominids." *Science,* 26 January 1979.

Jungers, William L. "Lucy's Limbs: Skeletal Allometry and Locomotion in *Australopithecus afarensis*." *Nature,* 24 June 1982.

———, and Stern, Jack T., Jr. "Body Proportions, Skeletal Allometry and Locomotion in the Hadar Hominids: a Reply to Wolpoff." *Journal of Human Evolution,* November 1983.

Lawick-Goodall, Jane van. *In the Shadow of Man.* Boston: Houghton Mifflin, 1971.

Leakey, Mary D. "Footprints in the Ashes of Time." *National Geographic,* April 1979.

Lewin, Roger. "Were Lucy's Feet Made for Walking?" *Science,* 13 May 1983.

———. "Do Ape-Size Legs Mean Ape-Like Gait?" *Science,* 5 August 1983.

Marzke, M. W. "Joint Functions and Grips of the *Australopithecus afarensis* Hand." *Journal of Human Evolution,* February 1983.

———. "The Morphological Basis of Hominid Manipulatory Behavior." Paper presented at the Fifty-Third Annual Meeting of the American Association of Physical Anthropologists, Philadelphia, April 1984.

Matthews, L. Harrison. "Piltdown Man: Shall We Ever Know the Truth?" *New Scientist,* 2 July 1981.

Oakley, Kenneth P. "The Piltdown Problem Reconsidered." *Antiquity,* March 1976.

Peacock, D. P. S. "Forged Brick-Stamps from Pevensey." *Antiquity,* June 1973.

Pfeiffer, John. "Current Research Casts New Light On Human Origins." *Smithsonian,* June 1980.

———. "Early Man Stages a Summit Meeting in New York City." *Smithsonian,* August 1984.

Pilbeam, David, and Gould, Stephen Jay. "Size and Scaling in Human Evolution." *Science,* 6 December 1974.

Rak, Yoel. *The Australopithecine Face.* New York: Academic Press, 1983.

Reeser, Lori A.; Susman, Randall T.; and Stern, Jack T., Jr. "Electromyographic Studies of the Human Foot: Experimental Approaches to Hominid Evolution." *Foot and Ankle,* May-June 1983.

Stern, Jack T., Jr., and Susman, Randall L. "The Locomotor Anatomy of *Australopithecus afarensis*." *American Journal of Physical Anthropology,* March 1983.

Susman, Randall L. "Evolution of the Human Foot: Evidence from Plio-Pleistocene Hominids." *Foot and Ankle,* May–June 1983.

———; Stern, Jack T. Jr.; and Jungers, William L. "Arboreality and Bipedality in the Hadar Hominids." *Folia Primatologia.* In press.

Swedlund, Alan C. "The Use of Ecological Hypotheses in Australopithecine Taxonomy." *American Anthropologist,* September 1974.

Tazieff, Haroun. "The Afar Triangle." *Scientific American,* February 1970.

Tobias, P. V. "The Taung Skull Revisited." *Natural History,* 83 (10):38–43 (1974).

Wade, Nicholas. "Voice From the Dead Names New Suspect for Piltdown Hoax." *Science,* 8 December 1978.

Walker, Alan, and Leakey, Richard E. F. "The Hominids of East Turkana." *Scientific American,* August 1978.

Weiner, J. S. *The Piltdown Forgery.* New York: Dover, 1980.

Zihlman, Adrienne L. "A Behavioral Reconstruction of *Australopithecus*." In *Hominid Origins,* Kathleen Reich, editor. Washington D.C.: University Press of America, 1983.

CHAPTER 4: INTERPRETING THE EVIDENCE

Binford, Lewis R. *Bones, Ancient Men and Modern Myths.* New York: Academic Press, 1981.

Brain, C. K. *The Hunters or the Hunted?* Chicago: University of Chicago Press, 1981.

Bunn, Henry, et al. "FxJj50: An Early Pleistocene Site in Northern Kenya." *World Archaeology,* October 1980.

———. "Archaeological Evidence for Meat-Eating by Plio-Pleistocene Hominids from Koobi Fora and Olduvai Gorge." *Nature,* 18 June 1981.

Connolly, Kevin, and Elliott, John. "The Evolution and Ontogeny of Hand Function." In *Ethological Studies of Child Behavior.* New York: Cambridge University Press, 1972.

Isaac, Glynn. "Early Stone Tools—an Adaptive Threshold?" In *Problems in Economic and Social Archaeology.* Edited by G. Sieveking et al. London: Duckworth, 1975.

Keeley, Lawrence H. *Experimental Determination of Stone Tool Uses.* Chicago: University of Chicago Press, 1979.

———, and Toth, N. "Microwear Polishes on Early Stone Tools from Koobi Fora, Kenya." *Nature,* 293:464–465 (1981).

Leakey L. S. B. "Olduvai Gorge." *Scientific American,* January 1954.

———. "Finding the World's Earliest Man." *National Geographic,* September 1960.

———. "Exploring 1,750,000 Years into Man's Past."*National Geographic,* October 1961.

Leakey, Mary D. "A Review of the Oldowan Culture from Olduvai Gorge, Tanzania." *Nature,* 30 April 1966.

Lewin, Roger. "Protohuman Activity Etched in Fossil Bones." *Science,* 3 July 1981.

Napier, John. "Studies of the Hands of Living Primates." *Proceedings of the Zoological Society of London,* September 1960.

———. "The Evolution of the Hand." *Scientific American,* December 1962.

———. "The Antiquity of Human Walking." *Scientific American,* April 1967.

Pfeiffer, John E. "Dr. Leakey and His Olduvai Digs." *Think Magazine,* September 1963.

Potts, Richard Bruce. "Lower Pleistocene Site Formation and Hominid Activities at Olduvai Gorge, Tanzania." Doctoral dissertation, Harvard University, 1982.

———, and Shipman, P. "Cutmarks Made by Stone Tools on Bones from Olduvai Gorge, Tanzania." *Nature,* 18 June 1981.

Shipman, Pat. *Life History of a Fossil: An Introduction to Taphonomy and Paleoecology.* Cambridge, Mass.: Harvard University Press, 1981.

———. "Taphonomy of *Ramapithecus Wickeri* at Fort Ternan, Kenya." Museum of Anthropology, University of Missouri, Museum Brief 26, 1982.

Toth, Nicholas. "The Stone Technologies of Early Hominids from Koobi Fora, Kenya: An Experimental Approach." Doctoral dissertation, University of California, Berkeley, 1982.

Zihlman, Adrienne L. "Interpretations of Early Hominid Locomotion." In *African Hominidae of the Plio-Pleistocene.* London: Duckworth, 1976.

CHAPTER 5: THE FOOD QUEST AND MEAT EATING

Ericson, Jonathan E.; Sullivan, Charles H.; and Boaz, N. T. "Diets of Pliocene Mammals from Omo, Ethiopia, Deduced from Carbon Isotopic Ratios in Tooth Apatite." In *Palaeogeography, Palaeoclimatology, Palaeoecology.* Amsterdam: Elsevier, 1981.

Gaulin, Steven J. C.; Kurland, Jeffrey A.; and Strum, S. C. "Primate Predation and Bioenergetics." *Science,* 23 January 1976.

Harding, Robert S. O., and Teleki, Geza. *Omnivorous Primates.* New York: Columbia University Press, 1981.

Hasagawa, Toshikazu, et al. "New Evidence on Scavenging Behavior in Wild Chimpanzees." *Current Anthropology,* April 1983.

Isaac, Glynn. "The Food-Sharing Behavior of Protohuman Hominids." *Scientific American,* April 1978.

Lewin, Roger. "Ethiopian Stone Tools Are the World's Oldest." *Science,* 20 February 1981.

Mitchell, Donald D. "Human Bipedal Locomotion: Speed and Endurance Variation and Its Implications for Early Hominid Evolution." Unpublished manuscript, State University of New York College at Buffalo.

Pennycuick, C. J. "The Soaring Flight of Vultures." *Scientific American,* December 1973.

Perper, Timothy, and Schrire, Carmel. "The Origin of Flesh-Eating." In *Second Conference of the Monell Center for the Chemical Senses and Nutrition.* New York: Academic Press, 1977.

Schoeninger, Margaret J. "Diet and Status at Chalcatzingo: Some Empirical and Technical Aspects of Strontium Analysis." *American Journal of Physical Anthropology,* January 1977.

Shipman, Pat, and Phillips-Conroy, Jane. "Hominid Tool-making versus Carnivore Scavenging." *American Journal of Physical Anthropology,* January 1977.

Spencer, Frank, and Boaz, Noel T. "Form and Particle Size as Determinants of Taxonomic Affinities in Plio-Pleistocene Mammalian Coprolites." Paper presented at annual meeting of American Association of Physical Anthropologists, Indianapolis, Indiana, April 1983.

Strum, Shirley C. "Life with the 'Pumphouse Gang.' " *National Geographic,* May 1975.

Walker, A. "Diet and Teeth." *Philosophical Transactions of the Royal Society of London* B, 292:57–64 (1981).

Washburn, S. L., and DeVore, Irven. "Social Behavior of Baboons and Early Man." In *Social Life of Early Man.* Chicago: Aldine, 1961.

Watanabe, Hitoshi. "Running, Creeping and Climbing: A New Ecological and Evolutionary Perspective on Human Locomotion." *Mankind,* June 1971.

CHAPTER 6: OUT OF AFRICA

Binford, Lewis R., and Ho, Chuan-kun. "Taphonomy at a Distance: Zhoukoudian—The Cave Home of Beijing Man?" In press.

Bordes, François. *The Old Stone Age.* New York: McGraw-Hill, 1968, chaps. 3 and 4.

Butzer, Karl W. "Environment and Archeology." 2nd ed. Chicago: Aldine, 1971, chap. 2.

———, and Isaac, Glynn, eds. *After the Australopithecines: Stratigraphy, Ecology and Culture Change in the Middle Pleistocene.* Chicago: Aldine, 1975.

Chard, Chester S. "Implications of Early Human Migrations from Africa to Europe." *Man,* August 1963.

Clark, J. Desmond. "A Comparison of the Late Acheulian Industries of Africa and the Middle East." In *After the Australopithecines: Stratigraphy, Ecology and Culture Change in the Middle Pleistocene.* Chicago: Aldine, 1975.

———. "Africa in Prehistory: Peripheral or Paramount?" *Man,* June 1975.

———, and Kurashina, Hiro. "An Analysis of Earlier Stone Age Bifaces from Gadeb, Northern Bale Highlands, Ethiopia." *South African Archeological Bulletin,* 34:93–109 (1979).

Freeman, L. G., and Howell, F. C. "Torralba: An Acheulian Butchering Site on the Spanish Meseta." New York: Academic Press, 1984.

Howell, F. Clark. "Observations on the Earlier Phases of the European Lower Paleolithic." In *"Recent Studies in Paleoanthropology," American Anthropologist* Special Publication, April 1966.

Isaac, Glynn. "The Diet of Early Man: Aspects of Archaeological Evidence from Lower and Middle Pleistocene Sites in Africa." *World Archaeology,* June 1969.

————. "Middle Pleistocene Stratigraphy and Cultural Patterns in East Africa." In *After the Australopithecines: Stratigraphy, Ecology and Culture Change in the Middle Pleistocene.* Chicago: Aldine, 1975.

Ju-kang, Woo. "The Skull of Lantian Man." *Current Anthropology,* February 1966.

Klein, Richard G. "An Overview of the Torralba Fauna." In *Torralba: An Acheulian Butchering Site on the Spanish Meseta.* New York: Academic Press, 1984.

Lumley, Henry de. "A Paleolithic Camp at Nice." *Scientific American,* May 1969.

Oakley, Kenneth P. *Man the Tool-Maker.* 6th ed. Chicago: University of Chicago Press, 1976, pp. 39–70.

————. *Frameworks for Dating Fossil Man.* Chicago: Aldine, 1964, pp. 217–240.

————, et al "A Reappraisal of the Clactonian Spearpoint." *Proceedings of the Prehistoric Society,* 43:13–30 (1977).

Pfeiffer, John E. "Man the Hunter." *Horizon,* Spring 1971.

Shipman, Pat, and Rose, Jennie. "Early Hominid Hunting, Butchering, and Carcass-Processing Behaviors." *Journal of Anthropological Archaeology,* 2:57–98 (1983).

————. Evidence of Butchering and Hominid Activities at Torralba and Ambrona: An Evaluation Using Microscopic Techniques." In press.

Shipman, Pat; Bosler, Wendy; and Davis, Karen Lee. "Butchering of Giant Geladas at an Acheulian Site." *Current Anthropology,* June 1981.

Solheim, Wilhelm G. "Southeast Asia and the West." *Science,* 25 August 1967.

Stiles, Daniel. "Early Acheulian and Developed Olduwan." *Current Anthropology,* March 1979.

Villa, Paola. "Conjoinable Pieces and Site Formation Processes." *American Antiquity,* April 1982.

Walker, Alan. "The Koobi Fora Hominids and Their Bearing on the Origins of the Genus *Homo.*" In *Homo erectus,* Toronto: University Toronto Press, 1981.

————; Zimmerman, M. R.; and Leakey, R. E. F. "A Possible Case of Hypervitaminosis A in *Homo erectus.*" *Nature,* 18 March 1982.

Yi, Seonbok, and Clark, G. A. "Observations of the Lower Palaeolithic of Northeast Asia." *Current Anthropology,* April 1983.

CHAPTER 7: ORGANIZING FOR SURVIVAL

Clark, J. Desmond, et al. "Palaeoanthropological Discoveries in the Middle Awash Valley, Ethiopia." *Nature,* 2 February 1983.

Craik, K. J. W. *The Nature of Explanation.* New York: Cambridge University Press, 1952.

Rightmire, G. Philip. "Patterns in the Evolution of *Homo erectus.*" *Paleobiology* 7 (2):241–246 (1981).

Rukang, Wu, and Shenlong, Lin, "Peking Man." *Scientific American,* June 1983.

Schaller, George B., and Lowther, Gordon R. "The Relevance of Carnivore Behavior to the Study of Early Hominids." *Southwestern Journal of Anthropology,* Winter 1969.

Shapiro, Harry. "The Strange Unfinished Saga of Peking Man." *Natural History,* November 1971.

Denham, Woodrow W. "Population Structure, Infant Transport, and Infanticide among Pleistocene and Modern Hunter-Gatherers." *Journal of Anthropological Research,* Autumn 1974.

Eiseley, Loren C. "Man the Fire-Maker." *Scientific American,* September 1954.

Fox, Robin. "The Evolution of Human Sexual Behavior." *New York Times Magazine*, 24 March 1968.

———. "Sexual Selection and the Evolution of Human Kinship Systems." In *Sexual Selection and the Descent of Man*. Chicago: Aldine, 1972.

———. "Primate Kin and Human Kinship." In *Biosocial Anthropology*. London: Malaby Press, 1975.

Harris, John W. K. "Cultural Beginnings; Plio-Pleistocene Archaeological Occurrences From the Afar, Ethiopia." *African Archaeological Review*, 1:3–31 (1983).

Holloway, Ralph L. *The Role of Human Social Behavior in the Evolution of the Brain*. New York: American Museum of Natural History, 1973.

Jelinek, Arthur J. "The Lower Paleolithic: Current Evidence and Interpretations." *Annual Review of Anthropology* 6:11–32 (1977).

Lashley, K. S. "Persistent Problems in the Evolution of Mind." *Quarterly Review of Biology*, March 1949.

Lawick-Goodall, Jane van. *In the Shadow of Man*. Boston: Houghton Mifflin, 1971.

Mann, Alan. "Australopithecine Demographic Patterns." In *African Hominidae of the Plio-Pleistocene*. London: Duckworth, 1976.

Oakley, Kenneth P. "Fire as Palaeolithic Tool and Weapon." *Proceedings of the Prehistoric Society* 21 (1955).

Pfeiffer, John E. *The Human Brain*. New York: Harper & Row, 1955, chaps. 2 and 3.

———. "When *Homo Erectus* Tamed Fire He Tamed Himself." *New York Times Magazine*, 11 December 1966.

Radinsky, Leonard. *The Fossil Record of Primate Brain Evolution*. New York: American Museum of Natural History, 1979.

———. "Brain Evolution in Extinct South American Ungulates." In *Brain, Behavior and Evolution*. Vol. 18, no. 4, 1981.

Silberbauer, George B. *Hunter and Habitat in the Central Kalahari Desert*. New York: Cambridge University Press, 1981.

Tanner, Nancy, and Zihlman, Adrienne. "Women in Evolution. Part I: Innovation and Selection in Human Origins." *Signs*, Spring 1976.

Thomas, Elizabeth Marshall. *The Harmless People*. New York: Knopf, 1959.

Tiger, Lionel. *Men in Groups*. New York: Random House, 1969.

———, and Fox, Robin. *The Imperial Animal*. New York: Holt, Rinehart and Winston, 1971.

Trivers, Robert L. "The Evolution of Reciprocal Altruism." *Quarterly Review of Biology*, March 1971.

Young, J. Z. "The Organization of a Memory System." *Proceedings of the Royal Society* 163B (23 November 1975).

CHAPTER 8: THE PACE QUICKENS

Auel, Jean M. *The Clan of the Cave Bear*. New York: Crown, 1980.

Howell, F. Clark. "The Evolutionary Significance of Variation and Varieties of 'Neanderthal' Man." *Quarterly Review of Biology*, December 1975.

Leroi-Gourhan, Arlette. "The Flowers Found with Shanidar IV, a Neanderthal Burial in Iraq." *Science*, 7 November 1975.

Pfeiffer, John E. *The Creative Explosion*. New York: Harper & Row, 1982.

Rightmire, G. Philip. "Patterns in the Evolution of *Homo erectus*." *Paleobiology* 7(2):241–246 (1981).

Ronen, Avraham, ed. "The Transition from Lower to Middle Palaeolithic and the Origin of Modern Man." *British Archaeological Reports*, International Series 151, 1982.

Smith, Fred H. *The Neanderthal Remains from Krapina.* University of Tennessee, Department of Anthropology, Reports of Investigation 15, 1976.

Solecki, Ralph S. *Shanidar: The First Flower People.* New York: Knopf, 1971.

———. "Shanidar IV, a Neanderthal Flower Burial in Northern Iraq." *Science,* 28 November 1975.

Straus, William L., and Cave, A. J. E. "Pathology and the Posture of Neanderthal Man." *Quarterly Review of Biology,* December 1957.

Stringer, B. C. "Towards a Solution to the Neanderthal Problem." *Journal of Human Evolution* 11:431–438 (1982).

Trinkaus, Erik. "The Shanidar Neanderthals." New York: Academic Press, 1983.

———. "Artificial Cranial Deformation of the Shanidar 1 and 5 Neanderthals." *Current Anthropology,* April 1982.

———, and Howells, William W. "The Neanderthals." *Scientific American,* December 1979.

———, and Smith, Fred H. "The Future of the Neanderthals: A Construction of Recent Human Evolution." In press.

White, J. Peter. "Pleistocene Fossilmanship." *Quarterly Review of Archaeology,* March 1982.

Wolpoff, Milford H. "Paleoanthropology." New York: Knopf, 1980, chap. 10.

CHAPTER 9: NEANDERTHAL STUDIES: THE BEGINNINGS OF DIVERSITY

ApSimon, A. M. "The Last Neanderthal in France?" *Nature,* 25 September 1980.

Banfield, A. W. F. "Migratory Caribou." *Natural History,* May 1961.

Binford, Lewis R. *An Archeological Perspective.* New York: Seminar Press, 1972, pp. 187–194.

———. *In Pursuit of the Past.* New York: Thames and Hudson, 1983. chap. 4.

———. *Working at Archeology.* New York: Academic Press, 1983, pt. II.

Boaz, N. T.; Ninkovich, D.; and Rossignol-Strick, M. "Paleoclimatic Setting for *Homo sapiens neanderthalensis.*" *Naturwissenschaften* 69:29–33 (1982).

Bordes, François. "Mousterian Cultures in Europe." *Science,* 22 September 1961.

———. "Physical Evolution and Technological Evolution in Man: A Parallelism." *World Archaeology,* June 1971.

———. "Time and Space Limits of the Mousterian." In *Stone Tools and Cultural Markers.* Edited by R. V. S. Wright. Canberra: Australian Institute of Aboriginal Studies, 1977.

———, and Sonneville-Bordes, Denise de. "The Significance of Variability in Palaeolithic Assemblages." *World Archaeology* 2:61–73 (1970).

Brace, C. Loring. "The Fate of the 'Classic' Neanderthals: A Consideration of Hominid Catastrophism." *Current Anthropology,* February 1964.

Frayer, David W. "Metric Dental Change in the European Upper Paleolithic and Mesolithic." *American Journal of Physical Anthropology,* January 1977.

Howell, F. Clark. "Isimila: A Paleolithic Site in Africa." *Scientific American,* October 1961.

Jelinek, Arthur J. "The Tabun Cave and Paleolithic Man in the Levant." *Science,* 25 June 1982.

Kelsall, J. P. *The Caribou.* Ottawa: Canadian Wildlife Service, 1968.

Klein, Richard G. "The Mousterian of European Russia." *Proceedings of the Prehistoric Society* 25 (1969).

Laville, Henri. "The Relative Position of Mousterian Industries in the Climatic Chronology of the Early Wurm in the Perigord." *World Archaeology,* February 1973.

Smith, Fred H. "Upper Pleistocene Hominid Evolution in South Central Europe." *Current Anthropology,* December 1982.

Trinkaus, Erik. *The Origin of Anatomically Modern Humans.* In press.

White, Randall. "Rethinking the Middle/Upper Paleolithic Transition." *Current Anthropology,* April 1982.

CHAPTER 10: AN EVOLUTIONARY EXPLOSION

Bahn, Paul. "Inter-Site and Inter-Regional Links During the Upper Paleolithic: The Pyrenean Evidence." *Oxford Journal of Archaeology,* November 1982.

Baker, John R. "Cro-Magnon Man, 1868–1968." *Endeavour,* May 1968.

Binford, Lewis R. *In Pursuit of the Past.* New York: Thames and Hudson, 1983, chap. 7.

Bricker, Harvey M. "Upper Palaeolithic Archaeology." *Annual Review of Anthropology* 5 (October 1976).

Collins, Desmond. *The Human Revolution.* Oxford: Phaidon Press, 1976.

Freeman, L. G., and Echegaray, J. Gonzales. "Aurignacian Structural Features and Burials at Cueva Morin (Santander, Spain)." *Nature,* 23 May 1970.

Frison, George C.; Wilson, Michael; and Wilson, Diane J. "Fossil Bison and Artifacts from an Early Altithermal Period Arroyo Trap in Wyoming." *American Antiquity,* January 1976.

Garrod, Dorothy A. E. "The Relations Between Southwest Asia and Europe in the Later Paleolithic Age." *Journal of World History,* July 1953.

Gladkih, M; Kornietz, N.; and Soffer, Olga. "Of Mammoths and Men: The Russian Plain Circa 15,000 Years Ago." *Scientific American,* in press.

Gould, Richard A. "Spears and Spear-Throwers of the Western Desert Aborigines of Australia." *American Museum Novitates,* 18 February 1970.

Klein, Richard G. "Ice-Age Hunters of the Ukraine." *Scientific American,* June 1974.

Larick, Roy Ralph III. "The Circulation of Solutrean Foliate Point Cherts: Residential Mobility in the Perigord." Doctoral dissertation, State University of New York at Binghamton, 1983.

Mongait, A. L. "Archaeology in the U.S.S.R." Baltimore: Penguin Books, 1961.

Newcomer, Mark. "Experiments in Upper Paleolithic Bone Work." In *Methodologie Appliquee à L'Industrie de L'Os Prehistorique, Colloques Internationeaux du Centre National de la Recherche Scientifique,* no. 568 (1976).

Pericot-Garcia, L. "A New Site with the Remarkable Parpallo-Type Solutrean Points." *Current Anthropology,* October 1961.

Pfeiffer, John E. *The Creative Explosion.* New York: Harper & Row, 1982, chaps. 3 and 4.

Rigaud, Jean-Philippe. "The Paleolithic in the Perigord: The Data from the Southwest of the Sarlat Area and Its Implications for Human Behavior." Doctoral dissertation, University of Bordeaux, 1982.

Sackett, James R. "Method and Theory of Upper Paleolithic Archeology in Southwestern France." In *New Perspectives in Archeology.* Chicago: Aldine, 1968.

Schild, Romuald. "The Final Paleolithic Settlements of the European Plain." *Scientific American,* January 1976.

Sheets, Payson D., and Muto, Guy R. "Pressure Blades and Total Cutting Edge: An Experiment in Lithic Technology." *Science,* 11 February 1972.

Smith, Fred H. "Upper Pleistocene Hominid Evolution in South-Central Europe: A Review of the Evidence and Analysis of Trends." *Current Anthropology,* December 1982.

Smith, Philip E. L. "The Solutrean Culture." *Scientific American,* August 1964.

Sonneville-Bordes, Denise de. "Upper Paleolithic Cultures in Western Europe." *Science,* 18 October 1963.

Speth, John D. *Bison Kills and Bone Counts.* Chicago: University of Chicago Press, 1983.

Straus, Lawrence Guy. "A New Interpretation of the Cantabrian Solutrean." *Current Anthropology,* June 1976.

Trinkaus, Erik. "The Origin of Anatomically Modern Men." In press.

Wheat, Joe Ben. "A Paleo-Indian Bison Kill." *Scientific American,* 216:44–52 (1967).

White, Randall. "Rethinking the Middle/Upper Paleolithic Transition." *Current Anthropology,* April 1982.

Whitmore, Frank C., et al. "Elephant Teeth from the Atlantic Continental Shelf." *Science,* 16 June 1967.

Wobst, H. Martin. "Boundary Conditions for Paleolithic Social Systems: A Simulation Approach." *American Antiquity,* April 1974.

CHAPTER 11: ART, SYMBOL, SOCIETY

Bauman, Hans. *The Caves of the Great Hunters.* New York: Pantheon Books, 1954.

Bender, Barbara. "Gatherer-Hunter to Farmer: A Social Perspective." *World Archaeology,* October 1978.

Breuil, Abbé H. *Four Hundred Centuries of Cave Art.* Montignac, 1952.

Brodrick, A. H. *Father of Prehistory.* New York: Morrow, 1963.

Cohen, Mark Nathan. *The Food Crisis in Prehistory.* New Haven: Yale University Press, 1977.

Collins, Desmond. "Prehistoric Art." *Discovery,* May 1965.

Conkey, Margaret W. *Art and Design in the Stone Age.* San Francisco: Freeman, 1983.

Couraud, C., and Bahn, P. G. "Azilian Pebbles in British Collections: A Re-examination." In press.

Dams, Lya and Marcel. "Prehistoric Rock Art of the Spanish Levant." *Illustrated London News,* March 1973.

———. "Prehistoric Rock Art Discoveries." *Illustrated London News,* November 1973.

———. "Cave Art of La Pileta." *Illustrated London News,* April 1976.

———. "Prehistoric Rock Art in Western Europe." *Illustrated London News,* March 1981.

———. "Cave Art Discoveries in Southern Spain." *Illustrated London News,* November 1982.

Flannery, Kent V. "The Origins of Agriculture." *Annual Review of Anthropology* 2 (1973).

Giedion, S. *The Beginnings of Art.* New York: Pantheon Books, 1962.

Graziosi, Paolo. *Palaeolithic Art.* New York: McGraw-Hill, 1960.

Hadingham, Evan. *Secrets of the Ice Age.* New York: Walker, 1979.

Harlan, Jack R., and Zohary, Daniel. "Distribution of Wild Wheats and Barley." *Science,* 2 September 1966.

Harris, David R. "New Light on Plant Domestication and the Origins of Agriculture." *Geographical Review,* January 1967.

Hole, Frank; Flannery, Kent V.; and Neely, James A. "Prehistory and Human Ecology of the Deh Luran Plain." *Memoirs of the Museum of Anthropology,* no. 1, University of Michigan, 1969.

Hope, Francis. "Cave." *New Statesman,* 27 October 1972.

Laming, Annette. *Lascaux.* Baltimore: Penguin Books, 1959.

Leroi-Gourhan, André. *Treasures of Prehistoric Art.* New York: Abrams, 1967.

———. "The Evolution of Paleolithic Art." *Scientific American,* February 1968.

Leroi-Gourhan, Arlette. "The Archaeology of Lascaux Cave." *Scientific American,* June 1982.

———, and Allain, Jacques. *Lascaux Inconnu.* Paris: Centre National de la Recherche Scientifique, 1979.

Marshack, Alexander. "Lunar Notation on Upper Paleolithic Remains." *Science,* 6 November 1964.

———. *Roots of Civilization.* New York: McGraw-Hill, 1972.

———. "Upper Paleolithic Notation and Symbol." *Science,* 24 November 1972.

———. "The Meander as a System: The Analysis and Recognition of Iconographic Units in Upper Paleolithic Compositions." In *Form in Indigenous Art.* Edited by Peter J. Ucko. Canberra: Australian Institute of Aboriginal Studies, 1977.

———. "The Art and Symbols of Ice Age Man." *Human Nature,* September 1978.

Pfeiffer, John E. *The Emergence of Society.* New York: McGraw-Hill, 1977.

———. *The Creative Explosion.* New York: Harper & Row, 1982.

———. "Was Europe's Fabulous Cave Art the Start of the Information Age?" *Smithsonian Magazine,* April 1983.

Sieveking, Ann. *The Cave Artists.* New York: Thames and Hudson, 1979.

———, and Sieveking, Gale. *The Caves of France and Northern Spain.* London: Longacre 1962.

Speth, John D., and Spielmann, Katherine A. "Energy Source, Protein Metabolism, and Hunter-Gatherer Subsistence Strategies." *Journal of Anthropological Archaeology,* 2:1–3 (1983).

Ucko, Peter, and Rosenfeld, Andrée. *Paleolithic Cave Art.* London: Weidenfeld and Nicolson, 1967.

Wobst, H. Martin. "Stylistic Behavior and Information Exchange." Museum of Anthropology, *Anthropological Papers,* no. 61, University of Michigan, 1976.

CHAPTER 12: LIVING PREHISTORY: PRIMATE STUDIES

Altmann, Jeanne. *Baboon Mothers and Infants.* Cambridge, Mass.: Harvard University Press, 1980.

Buirski, Peter, et al. "A Field Study of Emotion, Dominance, and Social Behavior in a Group of Baboons (*Papio anubis*)." *Primates,* March 1973.

Busse, Curt, and Hamilton, William J. III. "Infant Carrying by Male Chacma Baboons." *Science,* 12 June 1981.

Denham, Woodrow W. "Energy Relations and Some Basic Properties of Primate Social Organization." *American Anthropologist,* February 1971.

DeVore, Irven. "The Social Behavior and Organization of Baboon Troops." Doctoral dissertation, University of Chicago, March 1962.

———. "Mother-Infant Relations in Free-Ranging Baboons." In *Maternal Behavior in Mammals.* New York: Wiley, 1963.

Eisenberg, John F. "The Social Organization of Mammals." *Handbuch der Zoologie* 10, no. 7 (1965).

Hall, K. R. L., and DeVore, Irven. "Baboon Social Behavior." In *Primate Behavior.* New York: Holt, Rinehart and Winston, 1965.

Hrdy, Sarah Blaffer. "Infanticide as a Primate Reproduction Strategy." *American Scientist,* January–February 1977.

Lancaster, Jane Beckman. "In Praise of the Achieving Female Monkey." *Psychology Today,* September 1973.

Silk, Joan B. "Local Resource Competition and Facultative Adjustment of Sex Ratios in Relation to Competitive Abilities." *American Naturalist,* June 1982.

Smuts, Barbara. "Special Relationships Between Adult Male and Female Baboons (*Papio anubis*)." Doctoral dissertation, Stanford University, January 1982.

Wasser, Samuel K. "Reproductive Competition and Cooperation Among Female Yellow Baboons." In *Social Behavior of Female Vertebrates*. New York: Academic Press, 1983.

CHAPTER 13: CHIMPANZEES: OUR CLOSEST LIVING RELATIVES

Chance, M. R. A. "Köhler's Apes—How Did They Perform?" *Man,* September 1960.

Chisholm, James S. "On the Evolution of Rules." In *The Social Structure of Attention*. New York: Wiley, 1976.

Fagen, Robert. *Animal Play Behavior*. New York: Oxford University Press, 1981.

Fox, Robin. "Primate Kin and Human Kinship." In *Biosocial Anthropology*. London: Malaby Press, 1975.

Harding, Robert, and Strum, Shirley. "The Predatory Baboons of Kekapey." *Natural History,* 85:46–53 (1976).

Itani, Junichiro. "Twenty Years with Mount Takasaki Monkeys." In *Primate Organization and Conservation*. New York: Wiley, 1975.

———, and Suzuki, Akira. "The Social Unit of Chimpanzees." *Primates* 8:355–381 (1967).

Kortlandt, Adriaan. "Chimpanzees in the Wild." *Scientific American,* May 1962.

Lawick-Goodall, Jane van. "My Life Among Wild Chimpanzees." *National Geographic,* August 1963.

———. *My Friends the Wild Chimpanzees*. Washington, D.C.: National Geographic Society, 1967.

———. "Mother-Offspring Relationships in Free-Ranging Chimpanzees." In *Primate Ethology*. Chicago: Aldine, 1967.

———. "The Behavior of Free-Living Chimpanzees in the Gombe Stream Reserve." *Animal Behaviour Monographs* 1 (1968).

McGrew, W. C.; Tutin, C. E. G.; and Baldwin, P. J. "Chimpanzees, Tools, and Termites: Cross-Cultural Comparisons of Senegal, Tanzania, and Rio Muni." *Man* 14:185–214 (1979).

———. "New Data on Meat Eating by Wild Chimpanzees." *Current Anthropology,* March 1979.

———. "Chimpanzees in a Hot, Dry and Open Habitat: Mt. Assirik, Senegal, West Africa." *Journal of Human Evolution* 10:227–244 (1981).

Paterson, James D. "Ecologically Differentiated Patterns of Aggressive and Sexual Behavior in Two Troops of Ugandan Baboons, *Papio anubis*." *American Journal of Physical Anthropology,* March 1973.

Pfeiffer, John E. "The Apish Origins of Human Tension." *Harper's Magazine,* July 1963.

Reynolds, Vernon. "The 'Man of the Woods.' " *Natural History,* January 1964.

———. "Chimpanzees of the Budongo Forest." In *Primate Behavior*. New York: Holt, Rinehart and Winston, 1965.

———. "Kinship and the Family in Monkeys, Apes and Man." *Man,* June 1968.

Rowell, T. E. "Forest-Living Baboons in Uganda." *Journal of Zoology* (London) 149:344–364 (1966).

———. "A Quantitative Comparison of the Behavior of a Wild and a Caged Baboon Group." *Animal Behavior,* October 1967.

———. Variability in the Social Organization of Primates. In *Primate Ethology*. Chicago: Aldine, 1967.

Strum, S. C. "Primate Predation: Interim Report on the Development of a Tradition in a Troop of Olive Baboons." *Science,* 28 February 1975.

Teleki, Geza. "Chimpanzee Subsistence Technology: Materials and Skills." *Journal of Human Evolution* 3:575–594 (1974).

Waal, Frans de. *Chimpanzee Politics: Power and Sex Among Apes.* New York: Harper and Row, 1982.

Wrangham, Richard Walter. "The Behavioral Ecology of Chimpanzees in Gombe National Park, Tanzania." Doctoral dissertation, University of Cambridge, 1975.

CHAPTER 14: PRIMATES AND OTHER SPECIES

Bischof, Norbert. "Comparative Ethology of Incest Avoidance." In *Biosocial Anthropology.* London: Malaby Press, 1975.

Dawkins, Richard. *The Selfish Gene.* New York: Oxford University Press, 1976.

Estes, Richard D. "Predators and Scavengers." *Natural History,* February and March 1967.

———, and Goddard, John. "Prey Selection and Hunting Behavior of the African Wild Dog." *Journal of Wildlife Management,* January 1967.

Fox, M. W. "A Comparative Study of the Development of Facial Expression of Canids: Wolf, Coyote and Foxes." *Behaviour* 36:49–73 (1970).

———. "Socio-Ecological Implications of Individual Differences in Wolf Litters: A Developmental and Evolutionary Perspective." *Behaviour* 41:298–313 (1972).

Gallup, Gordon G., Jr. "Chimpanzees: Self-Recognition." *Science,* 2 January 1970.

———. "Chimps and Self-Concept." *Psychology Today,* March 1971.

———. "Towards an Operational Definition of Self-Awareness." In *Socio-ecology and Psychology of Primates.* Chicago: Aldine, 1975.

Harcourt, A. H., et al. "Testis Weight, Body Weight, and Breeding Systems in Primates." *Nature,* 3 September 1981.

Harlow, Harry F., and Margaret K. "Social Deprivation in Monkeys." *Scientific American,* November 1962.

———. "Affection in Primates." *Discovery,* January 1966.

———, and Suomi, Stephen J. "Social Recovery by Isolation-Reared Monkeys." *Proceedings of the National Academy of Sciences,* July 1971.

Hinde, R. A. "Rhesus Monkey Aunts." In *Determinants of Infant Behavior.* Vol. 3. New York: Wiley, 1965.

———. "The Study of Mother-Infant Interaction in Captive Group-Living Rhesus Monkeys." *Proceedings of the Royal Society,* B169 (1968).

———. "Effects of Brief Separation from Mothers on Rhesus Monkeys." *Science,* 9 July 1971.

———; Rowell, T. E.; and Spencer-Booth, Y. "Behaviour of Socially Living Rhesus Monkeys in their First Six Months." *Proceedings of the Zoological Society of London* 143, pt. 4 (1964).

Hrdy, Sarah Blaffer. *The Woman That Never Evolved.* Cambridge, Mass.: Harvard University Press, 1981.

Kühme, Wolfdietrich. "Communal Food Distribution and Division of Labor in African Hunting Dogs." *Nature,* 30 January 1965.

Lewin, Roger. "How Did Humans Evolve Big Brains?" *Science,* 21 May 1982.

Martin, R. D. "Relative Brain Size and Basal Metabolic Rate in Terrestrial Vertebrates." *Nature,* 3 September 1981.

Mason, William A., and Kenney, M. D. "Redirection of Filial Attachments in Rhesus Monkeys: Dogs as Surrogate Mothers." *Science,* 22 March 1974.

Missakian, Elizabeth A. "Genealogical Mating Activity in Free-Ranging Groups of Rhesus Monkeys (*Macaca mulatta*) on Cayo Santiago." Master's thesis, Rockefeller University, New York, 1971.

Pfeiffer, A. J., and Koebner, L. "The Resocialization of Single-Caged Chimpanzees and the Establishment of an Island Colony." *Journal of Medical Primatology* 7:70–81 (1978).

Schaller, George B. *Serengeti—A Kingdom of Predators.* New York: Knopf, 1972.

———. *The Serengeti Lion.* Chicago: University of Chicago Press, 1972.

Sherman, Paul W. "Nepotism and the Evolution of Alarm Calls." *Science,* 23 September 1977.

———. "The Limits of Ground Squirrel Nepotism." In *Sociobiology: Beyond Nature/Nurture?* Boulder, Colo.: Westview Press, 1980.

Simpson, M. J. A., et al. "Infant-Related Influences on Birth Intervals in Rhesus Monkeys." *Nature,* 5 March 1981.

Thompson, Philip R. "A Cross-Species Analysis of Carnivore, Primate, and Hominid Behavior." *Journal of Human Evolution* 4:113–124 (1975).

Trivers, Robert L. "The Evolution of Reciprocal Altruism." *Quarterly Review of Biology,* March 1971.

Uetz, George W.; Kane, Thomas C.; and Stratton, Gail E. "Variation in the Social Grouping Tendency of a Communal Web-Building Spider." *Science,* 6 August 1982.

Wilson, E. O. *Sociobiology: The New Synthesis.* Cambridge, Mass.: Harvard University Press, 1975.

Wrangham, Richard W. "On the Evolution of Ape Social Systems." *Social Science Information* 18:335–368 (1979).

———. "An Ecological Model of Female-Bonded Primate Groups." *Behaviour,* vol. 75, pts. 3–4 (1981).

Wright, R. V. S. "Imitative Learning of a Flaked Stone Technology—the Case of an Orangutan." *Mankind,* December 1972.

Zimen, Erik. "Social Dynamics of the Wolf Pack." In *Social Ecology of Canids.* New York: Van Nostrand, 1973.

CHAPTER 15: CONTEMPORARY HUNTER-GATHERERS

Elkin, A. D. *The Australian Aborigines.* New York: Doubleday, 1964.

Gould, R. A. "Notes on Hunting, Butchering, and Sharing of Game Among the Ngatatjara and Their Neighbors in the West Australian Desert." *Kroeber Anthropological Society Papers,* no. 36, Spring 1967.

———. "Chipping Stones in the Outback," *Natural History,* February 1968.

———. "Living Archeology: The Ngatatjara of Western Australia." *Southwestern Journal of Anthropology,* Summer 1968.

———. *Yiwara: Foragers of the Australian Desert.* New York: Scribner, 1969.

———. "The Archaeologist as Ethnographer: A Case from the Western Desert of Australia." *World Archaeology,* October 1971.

———. *Living Archaeology.* New York: Cambridge University Press, 1980.

Jones, Rhys. "The Demography of Hunters and Farmers in Tasmania." In *Aboriginal Man and Environment in Australia.* Canberra: Australian National University Press, 1971.

Mulvaney, D. J. "The Prehistory of the Australian Aborigine." *Scientific American,* March 1966.

Peterson, Nicolas. "Totemism Yesterday: Sentiment and Local Organisation Among the Australian Aborigines." *Man,* March 1972.

———. "Hunter-Gatherer Territoriality: The Perspective from Australia." *American Anthropologist,* March 1975.

Pfeiffer, John E. *The Creative Explosion.* New York: Harper & Row, 1982, chap. 10.

Strehlow, T. G. H. *Aranda Traditions.* Melbourne: Melbourne University Press, 1947.

———. "Culture, Social Structure, and Environment in Aboriginal Central Australia." In *Aboriginal Man in Australia.* Sydney: Angus and Robertson, 1965.

Tindale, Norman B. "The Pitjandjara." In *Hunters and Gatherers Today.* New York: Holt, Rinehart and Winston, 1972.

White, Carmel, and Peterson, Nicolas. "Ethnographic Interpretations of the Prehistory of Western Arnhem Land." *Southwestern Journal of Anthropology,* Spring 1969.

CHAPTER 16: THE BEHAVIOR OF HUNTER-GATHERERS

Binford, Lewis R. *Nunamiut Ethnoarchaeology.* New York: Academic Press, 1977.

———. *In Pursuit of the Past.* New York: Thames and Hudson, 1983, chap. 6.

Birdsell, Joseph B. "Some Environmental and Cultural Factors Influencing the Structuring of Australian Aboriginal Populations." *American Naturalist,* Supplement, May–June 1953.

———. "Some Population Problems Involving Pleistocene Man." *Cold Spring Harbor Symposium on Quantitative Biology* 22 (1957).

———. "On Population Structure in Generalized Hunting and Collecting Populations." *Evolution,* June 1958.

Cashdan, Elizabeth A. "Egalitarianism Among Hunters and Gatherers." *American Anthropologist,* March 1980.

———. "Territoriality Among Human Foragers: Ecological Models and an Application to Four Bushman Groups." *Current Anthropology,* February 1983.

Draper, Patricia. "Social and Economic Constraints on !Kung Childhood." In *Kalahari Hunter-Gatherers.* Cambridge, Mass.: Harvard University Press, 1976.

———. "!Kung Bushman Childhood." Doctoral dissertation, Harvard University, 1972.

Harris, David R., ed. *Human Ecology in Savanna Environments.* New York: Academic Press, 1980.

Hawkes, Kristen; Hill, Kim; and O'Connell, James F. "Why Hunters Gather: Optimal Foraging and the Ache of Eastern Paraguay." *American Ethologist,* May 1982.

Helm, June, and Leacock, Eleanor Burke. "The Hunting Tribes of Subarctic Canada." In *Northern American Indians in Historical Perspective.* New York: Random House, 1971.

Howell, N. *Demography of the Dobe Area !Kung.* New York: Academic Press, 1979.

Jochim, Michael A. *Hunter-Gatherer Subsistence and Settlement: A Predictive Model.* New York: Academic Press, 1976.

———. *Strategies for Survival.* New York: Academic Press, 1981.

Katz, Richard. *Boiling Energy: Community Healing Among the Kalahari !Kung.* Cambridge, Mass.: Harvard University Press, 1982.

Lee, Richard B. "Subsistence Ecology of !Kung Bushmen." Doctoral dissertation, University of California, Berkeley, 1965.

———. "Eating Christmas in the Kalahari." *Natural History,* December 1969.

———. *The !Kung San: Men, Women, and Work in a Foraging Society.* New York: Cambridge University Press, 1979.

————, and DeVore, Irven, eds. *Man the Hunter.* Chicago: Aldine, 1968.

————, and Devore, Irven. *Kalahari Hunter-Gatherers.* Cambridge, Mass.: Harvard University Press, 1976.

Shoumatoff, Alex. "The Ituri Forest." *New Yorker.* 6 February 1984.

Silberbauer, George B. *Hunter and Habitat in the Central Kalahari Desert.* New York: Cambridge University Press, 1981.

Thomas, Elizabeth Marshall. *The Harmless People.* New York: Knopf, 1959.

Wilmsen, Edwin. "Biological Variables in Forager Fertility Performance: A Critique of Bongaarts' Model." *Working Paper No. 60,* African Studies Center, Boston University 1982.

————. "Studies in Diet, Nutrition, and Fertility Among a Group of Kalahari Bushmen in Botswana." *Social Science Information* 21, 1:95–125 (1982).

Winterhalder, Bruce. "Stalking the Fundamental Theorem: Notes on a Nutritious If Dangerous Quarry." Paper delivered at the Symposium on Optimization in Anthropology and Ecology, University of Nebraska, Lincoln, 22–23 April 1982.

————. "Opportunity Cost-Foraging for Stationary and Mobile Predators." *American Naturalist,* July 1983.

————, and Smith, Eric Alden, eds. *Hunter-Gatherer Foraging Strategies.* Chicago: University of Chicago Press, 1981.

Wobst, H. Martin. "Boundary Conditions for Paleolithic Social Systems: A Simulation Approach." *American Antiquity,* April 1974.

Yellen, John. *Archeological Approaches to the Present: Models for Interpreting the Past.* New York: Academic Press, 1977.

CHAPTER 17: EXPERIMENTAL ARCHEOLOGY

Callahan, Errett. *The Pamunkey Project: An Overview.* Paper read at 41st annual meeting, Society for American Archeology, St. Louis, Missouri, 7 May 1976.

Chilcott, John H., and Deetz, James J. "The Construction and Uses of a Laboratory Archeological Site." *American Antiquity,* January 1964.

Crabtree, Don E. "A Stoneworker's Approach to Analyzing and Replicating the Lindenmeier Folsom. *Tebiwa* (journal of the Idaho State University Museum) 9, no.1 (1966).

————, and Butcher, B. Robert. "Notes on Experiments in Flint Knapping. I: Heat Treatment of Silica Materials." *Tebiwa* (journal of the Idaho State University Museum) 7, no. 1 (1964).

Flenniken, J. Jeffrey. "Reevaluation of the Lindenmeier Folsom: A Replication Experiment in Lithic Technology." *American Antiquity,* July 1978.

Harlan, Jack R. "A Wild Wheat Harvest in Turkey." *Archaeology,* June 1967.

Isaac, Glynn. "The Diet of Early Man: Aspects of Archaeological Evidence from Lower and Middle Pleistocene Sites in Africa." *World Archaeology,* February 1971.

Jewell, P. A. "An Experiment in Field Archaeology." *Advancement of Science,* May 1961.

Keeley, Lawrence H. *Experimental Determination of Stone Tool Uses.* Chicago: University of Chicago Press, 1979.

————, and Newcomer, M. H. "Microwear Analysis of Experimental Flint Tools: A Test Case." *Journal of Archaeological Science* 4:29–62 (1977).

Pfeiffer, John E. "Dr. Leakey and His Olduvai Digs." *Think Magazine,* September 1963.

Schindler, Debra L., et al. "Aboriginal Thermal Alteration of a Central Pennsylvania Jasper: Analytical and Behavioral Implications." *American Antiquity,* July 1982.

Toth, Nicholas. "The Stone Technologies of Early Hominids from Koobi Fora, Kenya: An Experimental Approach." Doctoral dissertation, University of California, Berkeley, 1982.

Turnbaugh, William A. "An On-Campus Alternative to the Archaeological Field School" *American Antiquity,* April 1976.

White, Randall. "The Manipulation and Use of Burins in Incision and Notation." *Canadian Journal of Anthropology,* Spring 1982.

Witthoft, John. "The Art of Flint Chipping." *Ohio Archeologist,* October 1956–July 1957.

CHAPTER 18: THE HUMAN INFANT: A STUDY IN LIVING PREHISTORY

Ainsworth, Mary D. Salter. *Infancy in Uganda.* Baltimore: Johns Hopkins Press, 1967.

———, et al. *Patterns of Attachment: A Psychological Study of the Strange Situation.* Hillsdale, N.J.: Lawrence Erlbaum Associates, 1978.

Ambrose, J. A. "The Smiling and Related Responses in Early Human Infancy: An Experimental and Theoretical Study of Their Course and Significance." Doctoral dissertation, University of London, 1960.

———. "The Development of the Smiling Response in Early Infancy." In *Determinants of Infant Behavior I.* Edited by B. M. Foss. New York: Wiley, 1961.

Andrew, R. J. "The Origin and Evolution of the Calls and Facial Expressions of the Primates." Behaviour 20 (1963).

Beach, Frank A., and Jaynes, Julian. "Effects of Early Experience upon the Behavior of Animals." *Psychological Bulletin,* May 1954.

Bowlby, John. "An Ethological Approach to Research in Child Development." *British Journal of Medical Psychology* 30, 4 (1957).

———. "The Nature of the Child's Tie to His Mother." *International Journal of Psychoanalysis* 39, pt. 5 (1958).

———. "Ethology and the Development of Object Relations." *International Journal of Psychoanalysis* 41, pts. 4 and 5 (1960).

Field, Tiffany M., et al. "Discrimination and Imitation of Facial Expressions by Neonates." *Science,* 8 October 1982.

Jones, N. G. Blurton. "Comparative Aspects of Mother-Child Contact." In *Ethological Studies of Child Behavior.* New York: Cambridge University Press, 1972.

———, and Leach, Gill M. "Behaviour of Children and their Mothers at Separation and Greeting." In *Ethological Studies of Child Behaviour.* New York: Cambridge University Press, 1972.

Kagan, Jerome. "Do Infants Think?" *Scientific American,* March 1972.

Lettvin, J.E., et al. "What the Frog's Eye Tells the Frog's Brain." *Proceedings of the Institute of Radio Engineers,* November 1959.

Meltzoff, Andrew N., and Moore, M. Keith. "Imitation of Facial and Manual Gestures by Human Neonates." *Science,* 7 October 1977.

Pfeiffer, John E. "Vision in Frogs." *Natural History,* November 1962.

Restak, Richard M. "Newborn Knowledge." *Science* 82, January/February.

Trivers, Robert L. "Parent-Offspring Conflict." *American Zoologist,* 14:249–264 (1974).

CHAPTER 19: THE EVOLUTION OF LANGUAGE

Andrew, R. J. "Evolution of Intelligence and Vocal Mimicking." *Science,* 24 August 1962.

Bickerton, Derek. *Roots of Language.* Ann Arbor, Mich.: Karoma Publishers, 1981.

Bordes, François. "Physical Evolution and Technological Evolution in Man: A Parallelism." *World Archaeology,* June 1971.

Brown, Roger. *A First Language: The Early Stages.* Cambridge, Mass.: Harvard University Press, 1973.

Cheney, Dorothy L., and Seyfarth, Robert M. "How Vervet Monkeys Perceive Their Grunts: Field Playback Experiments." *Animal Behaviour,* in press.

Chomsky, Noam. "The Formal Nature of Language." In Lenneberg, Eric H. *Biological Foundations of Language.* New York: Wiley, 1967.

———. *Reflections on Language.* New York: Pantheon, 1975.

Damasio, Antonio R., and Geschwind, Norman. "The Neural Basis of Language," *Annual Reviews of the Neurosciences,* 1984.

Foster, Mary Lecron. "The Symbolic Structure of Primordial Language." In *Perspectives in Human Evolution IV.* Staples Press 1976.

Fouts, Roger S. "Acquisition and Testing of Gestural Signs in Four Young Chimpanzees." *Science,* 1 June 1973.

Gardner, R. Allen, and Beatrice T. "Teaching Sign Language to Chimpanzee." *Science,* 15 August 1969.

———. "Early Signs of Language in Child and Chimpanzee." *Science,* 28 February 1975.

———. "Comparative Psychology and Language." *Annals of the New York Academy of Sciences* 309:37–76 (1978).

———. "Two Comparative Psychologists Look at Language Acquisition." In *Children's Language.* Vol. 2. Edited by K. E. Nelson. New York: Halsted Press, 1980.

———. "Early Signs of Reference in Children and Chimpanzees." In press.

Geschwind, Norman. "The Development of the Brain and the Evolution of Language." Monograph series of *Languages and Linguistics,* no. 17 (April 1964).

Glasersfeld, Ernst von. "Signs, Communication and Language." *Journal of Human Evolution* 3:465–474 (1974).

Greenberg, Joseph H. "Language Universals." In *Current Trends in Linguistics.* The Hague: Mouton, 1966.

Haldane, J. B. S. "Animal Communication and the Origin of Language." *Science Progress* 23 (1955).

Harnad, Steven; Steklis, Horst; and Lancaster, Jane, eds. "The Origins and Evolution of Language and Speech." *Annals of the New York Academy of Sciences* 280 (1976).

Hayes, C. *The Ape in Our House.* New York: Harper & Row, 1951.

Hewes, Gordon W. *Language Origins: A Bibliography.* Department of Anthropology, University of Colorado, 1971.

———. "Primate Communication and the Gestural Origin of Language." *Current Anthropology,* February–April 1973.

Hill, Jane H. "Language Contact Systems and Human Adaptations." *Journal of Anthropological Research,* Spring 1978.

Hockett, Charles F. "The Origin of Speech." *Scientific American,* September 1960.

———. "Comments on 'Current Trends in Linguistics.' " *Current Anthropology,* April–June 1968.

———, and Ascher, Robert. "The Human Revolution." *Current Anthropology,* June 1964.

Kellogg, Winthrop N. "Communication and Language in the Home-Raised Chimpanzee." *Science,* 25 October 1968.

Keyser, Samuel J. "Our Manner of Speaking." *Technology Review,* February 1964.

Laitman, Jeffrey T. "Tracing the Origins of Human Speech." *Mount Sinai Review,* Winter 1983.

Lancaster, Jane B. "Primate Communication Systems and the Emergence of Human Language." In *Primates: Studies in Adaptation and Variability.* New York: Holt, Rinehart and Winston, 1968.

Lemay, M., and Geschwind, N. "Hemispheric Differences in the Brains of Great Apes." *Brain, Behavior and Evolution* 11:48–52 (1975).

Lenneberg, Eric H. "Biological Foundations of Language." *Hospital Practice*, December 1967.

———. *Biological Foundations of Language*. New York: Wiley, 1967.

MacDonald, Critchley. "The Evolution of Man's Capacity for Language." In *Evolution After Darwin*. Vol. 2. Chicago: University of Chicago Press, 1960.

———. "The Nature of Animal Communication and Its Relation to Language in Man." *Journal of The Mount Sinai Hospital*, May–June 1961.

Miller, George A. "Some Psychological Studies of Grammar." *American Psychologist*, November 1962.

———. "The Psycholinguists." *Encounter*, July 1974.

———. "Communication and the Structure of Behavior." In *Disorders of Communication*. Vol. 42. Research Publications, Association for Research in Nervous and Mental Disease, 1964.

———. "Linguistic Communication as a Biological Process." In *Biology and the Human Sciences*. Oxford: Oxford University Press, 1972.

Moskowitz, Breyne Arlene. "The Acquisition of Language." *Scientific American*, November 1978.

Passingham, R. E. "Changes in the Size and Organization of the Brain in Man and His Ancestors." *Brain, Behavior and Evolution* 11:73–90 (1975).

Pfeiffer, John. "Early Man Stages a Summit Meeting in New York City." *Smithsonian*, August 1984.

Premack, David. "A Functional Analysis of Language." *Journal of the Experimental Analysis of Behavior*, July 1970.

———. *Intelligence in Ape and Man*. Hillsdale, N.J.: Lawrence Erlbaum Associates, 1976.

———, and Premack, Ann J. *The Mind of an Ape*. New York: Norton, 1983.

———, and Schwartz, Arthur. "Preparations for Discussing Behaviorism with Chimpanzee." In *The Genesis of Language*. Cambridge, Mass.; M.I.T. Press, 1966.

Rumbaugh, D. M., ed. *Language Learning by a Chimpanzee: The LANA Project*. New York: Academic Press, 1977.

———; Gill, Timothy V.; and Glasersfeld, E. C. von. "Reading and Sentence Completion by a Chimpanzee (*Pan*)." *Science*, 16 November 1973.

Savage-Rumbaugh, E. Sue, et al. "Reference: The Linguistic Essential." *Science*, 21 November 1980.

Seyfarth, Robert M., and Cheney, Dorothy L. "The Ontogeny of Vervet Monkey Alarm Calling Behavior: A Preliminary Report." *Zeitschrift für Tierpsychologie* 54:37–56 (1980).

Seyfarth, Robert M.; Cheney, Dorothy L.; and Marler, Peter. "Monkey Responses to Three Different Alarm Calls: Evidence of Predator Classification and Semantic Communication." *Science*, 14 November 1980.

Struhsaker, T. T. "Auditory Communication Among Vervet Monkeys." In *Social Communication Among Primates*. Edited by S. Altmann. Chicago: University of Chicago Press, 1967.

Tobias, Phillip V. "Recent Advances in the Evolution of the Hominids, with Special Reference to Brain and Speech." Pontifical Academy of Sciences, *Scripta Varia*, June 1983.

White, Randall, "Thoughts on Language and Social Interaction in the Stone Age." In press.

Yeni-Konshian, Grace H., and Benson, Dennis A. "Anatomical Study of Cerebral Asymmetry in the Temporal Lobe of Humans, Chimpanzees, and Rhesus Monkeys." *Science*, 23 April 1976.

CHAPTER 20: THE POWER OF THE PAST

Bekoff, Marc. "The Development of Social Interaction, Play, and Metacommunication in Mammals: An Ethological Perspective." *Quarterly Review of Biology,* December 1972.

Brannigan, Christopher R., and Humphries, David A. "Human Nonverbal Behavior, a Means of Communication." In *Ethological Studies of Child Behavior.* New York: Cambridge University Press, 1972.

Chance, M. R. A. "A Biological Perspective on Convulsions." *Colloques Internationaux du Centre National de la Recherche Scientifique,* no. 112 (1963).

Dissanayake, Ellen. "An Hypothesis of the Evolution of Art from Play." *Leonardo* 7 (3):211–218 (1974).

Fagen, Robert. "Play as Innovation: Models of the Origin, Transmission and Fixation or Loss of Novel Behaviors in Animal 'Cultures.' " Doctoral dissertation, Harvard University, 1974.

————. "Exercise, Play and Physical Training in Animals." In *Perspectives in Ethology,* vol. 2. New York: Plenum, 1976.

————. "Modelling How and Why Play Works." In *Play: Its Role in Evolution and Development*. New York: Viking, 1977.

Fox, Robin. "Human Mating Patterns in Ethological Perspective." *Animals,* July 1967.

————. "In the Beginning: Aspects of Hominid Behavioural Evolution." *Man,* September 1967.

Good, Robert A. "Disorders of the Immune System." *Hospital Practice,* January 1967.

Hartung, John. "On Natural Selection and the Inheritance of Wealth." *Current Anthropology,* December 1976.

Humphries, D. C.; Humphries, D. A.; and Driver, P. M. "Erratic Display as a Device Against Predators." *Science,* 30 June 1967.

Hutt, Corinne. "Exploration and Play in Children." *Symposia of the Zoological Society of London,* no. 18 (1966).

————. "Specific and Diversive Exploration." In *Advances in Child Development and Behavior.* Vol. 5. New York: Academic Press, 1970.

Jones, N. G. Blurton. "An Ethological Study of Some Aspects of Social Behaviour of Children in Nursery School." In *Primate Ethology.* Chicago: Aldine, 1967.

————. "An Ethologist Looks at Socialisation and Nursery School." In *The Integration of the Child into a Social World.* New York: Cambridge University Press, 1972.

Mackenzie, Norman. "Sweating It Out with B-P." *New Statesman,* 15 October 1965.

McGrew, W. C. "Aspects of Social Development in Nursery School Children, with Emphasis on Introduction to the Group." In *Ethological Studies of Child Behavior.* New York: Cambridge University Press, 1972.

McGuire, Michael T. "Social Dominance Relationships in Male Vervet Monkeys: A Possible Model for the Study of Dominance Relationships in Human Political Systems." *International Political Science Review* 3:11–32 (1982).

Omark, Donald R. "Peer Group Formation in Young Children. Action." Doctoral dissertation, University of Chicago, 1972.

————, and Edelman, Murray S. "A Developmental Study of Group Formation in Children." In *The Use of Direct Observation to Study Instructional-Learning Behavior in School Settings.* Learning Research and Development Center, University of Pittsburgh, 1974.

Pfeiffer, John E. *The Emergence of Society.* New York: McGraw-Hill, 1977, chap. 1.

Shweder, Richard A. "Likeness and Likelihood in Everyday Thought: Magical Thinking in Judgments about Personality." *Currrent Anthropology,* December 1977.

Southwick, Charles L. "Rhesus Monkeys in North India." In *Primate Behavior*. New York: Holt, Rinehart and Winston, 1965.

Tiger, Lionel. *Men in Groups*. New York: Random House, 1969.

———— and Fox, Robin. *The Imperial Animal*. New York: Holt, Rinehart and Winston, 1971.

————. "The Zoological Perspective in Social Science." *Man*, March 1966.

Tinbergen, N. "Aggression and Fear in the Normal Sexual Behavior of Some Animals." In *The Pathology and Treatment of Sexual Deviation*. New York: Oxford University Press, 1964.

———— "On War and Peace in Animals and Man." *Science,* 28 June 1968.

White, Robert W. "Motivation Reconsidered: The Concept of Competence." *Psychological Review,* September 1959.

EPILOGUE: THINGS TO COME—CAN WE MAKE IT?

Alexander, Christopher. *The City as a Mechanism for Sustaining Human Contact*. Institute of Urban and Regional Planning, University of California, Berkeley, Working Paper no. 5 (October 1966).

Albelson, Philip H. "Electronics and Scientific Communication." *Science,* 17 October 1980.

Ayres, Robert, and Miller, Steve. "Industrial Robots on the Line." *Technology Review,* May/June 1982.

Chen, Pichao, and Kols, Adrienne. "Population and Birth Planning in The People's Republic of China." *Population Reports,* Johns Hopkins University, January—February 1982.

Dillon, Wilton S. "Gifts and Nations." The Hague: Mouton, 1968.

Duda, Richard O., and Shortliffe, Edward H. "Expert Systems Research." *Science,* 15 April 1983.

Hartung, John. "Polygyny and Inheritance of Wealth." *Current Anthropology,* February 1982.

Hench, L. L. "Biomaterials." *Science,* 23 May 1980.

Kanter, Rosabeth Moss. *Men and Women of the Corporation*. New York: Basic Books, 1977.

Keller, Suzanne. "Does the Family Have a Future?" *Journal of Comparative Family Studies,* Spring 1971.

Mathews, Jay. "Breeding a New China." *Washington Post,* 21 July 1980.

Miller, George A. "Computerworld: A Non-Orwellian View." *National Elementary Principal,* January 1980.

Minsky, Marvin. "Why People Think Computers Can't." *AI (Artificial Intelligence) Magazine,* Fall 1982.

Parr, A. E. "Urbanity and the Urban Scene." *Landscape,* Spring 1967.

Pfeiffer, John. "The Tribe That Talks Peace and Makes War." *Horizon,* January 1977.

————. "Countdown to Habitat One." *Omni,* October 1980.

————. "Silliness and Survival." *Science* 81, November.

Robinson, Arthur L. "Computer Chess: Belle Sweeps the Board." *Science,* 17 October 1980.

Tiger, Lionel. *Optimism, the Biology of Hope*. New York: Simon and Schuster, 1979.

Ziporyn, Terra. "Computer-Assisted Medical Decision-Making: Interest Growing." *Journal of the American Medical Association,* 27 August 1983.

Index

Note: Page numbers in italics refer to illustrations.